Calvin's Crusaders in the Wars That Made America

Calvin's Crusaders in the Wars That Made America

The Story of Nathaniel and Isabella Scudder—
Princeton Patriots of the Revolutionary Era

DAVID T. FISHER

RESOURCE *Publications* · Eugene, Oregon

CALVIN'S CRUSADERS IN THE WARS THAT MADE AMERICA
The Story of Nathaniel and Isabella Scudder—Princeton Patriots of the Revolutionary Era

Resource Publications
An Imprint of Wipf and Stock Publishers
199 W. 8th Ave., Suite 3
Eugene, OR 97401

www.wipfandstock.com

PAPERBACK ISBN: 978-1-6667-3085-2
HARDCOVER ISBN: 978-1-6667-2285-7
EBOOK ISBN: 978-1-6667-2286-4

SEPTEMBER 24, 2021

This book is dedicated to my wife, Étel Rauhof-Fisher, whose assistance and encouragement were essential for the completion of the project.

CONTENTS

Preface and Acknowledgements

In 1996, Princeton celebrated its 250th anniversary, and the Princeton Alumni Weekly included a quotation from my earliest Princeton ancestor from the Class of 1751, Nathaniel Scudder. I was intrigued to discover that he had refused another term in the Continental Congress because he could no longer afford it, and he was unwilling to participate in the corrupt activities that many of his colleagues were engaged in. He was the only person to serve in the Continental Congress who was killed in action in the War of American Independence. Wanting to learn more, I embarked on an extensive research project which led to my discovery of vastly differing motivations that drove the rebels of 1776: Plantation owners worried that the British might free their slaves or limit their importation, Scotch-Irish immigrants detested policies that hindered them from settling areas promised to Native Americans, merchants resented the self-serving mercantilist trade policies of the mother country — but, for many graduates of Nassau Hall, it was all about religion. Like Nathaniel Scudder, the descendants of Calvinist Puritans feared the loss of the hard-won religious freedom that was their original and primary reason for immigration to North America. To prevent that, they were willing to defy the most formidable war machine of the age in a long and bitter asymmetric struggle for independence.

Decades of research uncovered many fascinating, surprising, and little-known aspects of that era. Rather than compiling yet another history book about the War of American Independence that would only be of interest to specialists, I decided instead to reach out to a broader audience by turning the results of my research into a historical novel designed to entertain but also to stimulate interest in the foundation era. Although the book is a novel, it follows the events very closely — all the major events described really happened, all the important characters really existed (see Dramatis Personae) but almost all the dialogues are completely fictional. Each of the main characters, whether fictional or historic, symbolizes a thread woven into the fabric that later became America, threads that are still much in evidence today.

The material for this novel was gleaned from hundreds of sources: history books, articles, archive materials, biographical sketches of Princeton alumni as well as local tales handed down by generations of New Jersey natives. Among the most useful sources are undoubtedly the archives of the Scudder Association Foundation and the book it published in 1976, *Scudders in the American Revolution* by Hamilton

Cochran. Several of the works of Michael Adelberg including *The American Revolution in Monmouth County* and *The Razing of Tinton Falls* provide extremely useful accounts of what was really happening on the ground in revolutionary New Jersey. His bibliography and amazing database of historical documents guided much of my research. The outstanding books of my fellow Princetonian, David Hackett Fischer (no relation), were a constant source of inspiration. In particular, *Washington's Crossing* and *Albion's Seed* are required reading for anyone seeking to understand the roots of early America. The same goes for *The War That Made America: A Short History of the French and Indian War* by Fred Anderson which convincingly describes how that earlier war set the stage for the War of American Independence. The pervasive ideological influence that the Scottish Enlightenment exerted on the founders of the College of New Jersey (later Princeton University) is well documented in *The Scottish Enlightenment: The Scots' Invention of the Modern World* by Arthur Herman. The intense Calvinist religiosity of Princeton's founders is clearly depicted in *The Journal of Esther Edwards Burr, 1754–1757* edited by Carol F. Karlsen and Laurie Crumpacker. Another rich source of insights is Sheila L. Skemp's biography of William Franklin, son of Benjamin Franklin, the last royal governor of New Jersey and leader of Loyalist resistance to the Revolution. Finally, a good appreciation for the "look and feel" of colonial New Jersey when much of it was still a wilderness inhabited by pirates and smugglers is provided by *Smugglers' Woods—Jaunts and Journeys in Colonial and Revolutionary New Jersey* by Arthur D. Pierce. In addition to these great books, I was much aided by the archives of the Monmouth County Historical Association and the friendly and helpful people there who volunteer so much of their time to keep history alive. The same should be said of Kathleen and Michael Pippen, new jersians born and bred, who helped me follow up on many of the leads I unearthed and chauffeured me to numerous historical sites during my visits to the state. I am also very grateful to my classmate, Paul Sittenfeld, for his encouragement as well as for the introduction to my editor, Shana Kelly, who offered useful feedback for the improvement of the manuscript. Last but certainly not least, I want to thank another fellow Princetonian, Professor Lewis Hinchman, for his meticulous final editing of the manuscript and his thoughtful and detailed suggestions.

Although I am much indebted to these and others for the help they offered and the many insights they have shared, I take full responsibility for any inaccuracies or possible misinterpretations of the historical record. The view of the characters and motives of the people involved as presented in the dialogues is entirely my own.

PROLOGUE: DARIEN PENINSULA – 1699

CAPTAIN JOHN ANDERSON AND his First Mate Andrew Ferguson ducked instinctively as the cannon ball from the Spanish galleon whooshed just a few feet over their heads.

"Hard to port, Ferguson, hard to port!" shouted Captain Anderson, "That Spanish bastard has our range, the next ball will rip our heads off. Get us before the wind. Our only hope is to outrun him."

"Aye Captain, course changed 90 degrees due south," answered Ferguson.

As the ship veered abruptly in the direction of the wind, all the sails on the three-mast barquentine billowed out, catching the wind full on causing the vessel to spurt forward. Another ball from the Spanish galleon landed in the water where the *Unicorn* had been just moments before. As the lightly loaded ship picked up speed, the distance to the heavily armed Spanish galleon slowly increased. Its cannon balls splashed into the sea further and further behind the *Unicorn*.

"That was a close call, Captain," said Ferguson with a sign of relief, "Maybe we should not have left half of the *Unicorn*'s cannon in Edinburgh."

"They wouldn't have been enough to help us against a heavily-armed galleon," explained Captain Anderson, "The only feasible strategy is to outrun our enemies with a fast ship. Besides, we need as much storage capacity as possible if we want to rescue many of those poor fools in Darien."

"How many do you think there will be, sir?" asked Ferguson.

"They started off with several thousand settlers, but the last report spoke of dozens of people dying every day," replied Captain Anderson, "That is why the Darien Company decided to send us to pull them out, so long as there are still people to rescue. We are probably lucky if we can get a few hundred out of there. I wonder if Paterson himself is still alive."

"Paterson, isn't he the one who came up that lunatic idea for a Scottish colony on the Darien Peninsula?" asked Ferguson.

"Indeed, the same," answered Captain Anderson, "He was convinced that that wretched mosquito-infested coastal area of Panama which we will soon have the pleasure to visit was 'the door of the seas and the key to the Universe' as he put it. He thought that a base there would allow Scotland to dominate both the Atlantic and the Pacific."

"Anyone who has sailed in this part of the world could have warned him of the dangers, the fevers, the wild savages, the Spanish warships," said Ferguson, "That stretch of coast has been Spanish for 150 years. They would never tolerate another nation trying to set up there."

"Unfortunately, William Paterson did not let facts intrude on his visions. He was a fast talker and had an extraordinary ability to infect people with such enthusiasm that few bothered to investigate the feasibility of his projects," explained Captain Anderson, "He presented it as a matter of national pride. England was developing faster than Scotland because of its colonial adventures. Scotland, therefore, needed to get into the game as well. Paterson was able to cast his plan as a patriotic necessity essential to the future well-being of the Scottish nation. He managed to collect 400,000 pounds for his hare-brained scheme. The entire upper class of Scotland put their savings at his disposal. God only knows what this debacle holds in store for the future of our poor country."

"Perhaps the survivors could start again somewhere else?" suggested Ferguson.

"Their 400,000 pounds have definitely gone up in smoke, but if those people can find a place that allows them to settle in peace, they might still have a chance," answered Captain Anderson, "They certainly are a tough lot and those that survive Darien will be tougher yet. They are convinced that their salvation lies somewhere in the New World and see themselves as being on a holy mission. I remember when they departed from Leith Harbor a few years ago amid the prayers, tears and well wishes of the entire population of Edinburgh. They had five thousand English-language Bibles on board to help them convert the heathen Indians. When they got to Darien, they realized that they had not packed enough food. They should have brought more supplies instead of Bibles."

Ferguson winced slightly at the captain's somewhat blasphemous disparagement of the Bible project. He was used to hearing the captain's cynical remarks whenever anything related to religious zealotry was discussed. Still, as a superstitious sailor, he would rather not offend the Creator unnecessarily, especially during a dangerous mission like this one.

The *Unicorn* continued south for half a day until the captain was confident that he had left the Spanish galleon far enough behind. He then changed course again toward the West in the direction of Darien. After another few days the verdant coastline of Central America came into view on the horizon.

"Land, ahoy," shouted the sailor in the crow's nest, "I think I see a Scottish flag in the distance to the northwest."

"That will be atop Fort St. Andrew," confirmed the captain, "That is the only thing the settlers actually managed to construct, and it was to become Scotland's impregnable base of operations in the New World. Now it is battered regularly by Spanish men-of-war. Let's hope its cannons can keep the enemy at bay long enough for us to load the survivors. Hoist our Scottish colors, lads, so they know not to fire in our direction!"

As the *Unicorn* approached the settlement the sight that greeted the sailors was enough to make even the most hardened Jack Tar gasp. The beach in front of the Fort was covered with several hundred men and women who looked as though they had endured the Final Judgement. Clad in rags with sunken faces, they were covered with festering insect bites. Many had that sickly yellow tint to their skin that indicated the dreadful fever endemic to these parts that had already claimed so many lives.

"We shouldn't touch them," blurted a nervous boatswain's mate, "They are all infected with the pest. They will spread it to us!"

A concerned murmur arose among the other crewmen.

Captain Anderson turned an angry face toward the seaman. Pulling a pistol out of his belt he marched over to the offending man and grabbed him by the neck.

"I am the only man giving orders on this ship," the captain said through clenched teeth pointing the barrel of his pistol into the man's mouth, "And anyone who doesn't understand that is going to be eating some lead very quickly now. And as for the rest of you," continued the captain turning toward the other members of the crew that had gathered, "You know that as your captain I would not send you on a suicide mission. I have been to these parts before, and I know what's ailing those people on shore. It is not the pest. It is a fever caused by the polluted night air of this place and it does not spread from person to person. You needn't worry about touching these people. Most of them will probably die but they won't infect you. We just need to look lively now and get our work finished here as quickly as possible. The sooner we are back out to sea, the safer we are."

Releasing the sailor, the captain glared with defiant self-confidence at the other crew members. Their subdued downcast glances satisfied him that he had restored his authority.

"Now then, ready the tender so that I can meet with their representatives," commanded the captain.

After the *Unicorn* anchored in the bay, the captain with the other ship's officers went to shore in the tender where they were greeted by none other than William Paterson, the originator of the doomed Darien project.

"Our prayers have been answered," William Paterson raised his arms toward the sky, "Our 300 brave settlers who have survived so many travails will yet be saved. Praise the Lord!"

"The *Unicorn* cannot possibly take on so many passengers," Captain Anderson stopped him short in order to quickly dampen any unrealistic expectations, "At the most 180 if they are willing to be stacked up like African slaves. The local authorities have to make a selection. Only those with the best chance of survival should be chosen. Three more ships left Scotland with us. They all took different routes to avoid interception by the Spanish or by pirates. Those that don't go with us can go with one of the other ships."

"It is clear that all the settlers cannot fit on one ship," Paterson quickly agreed, "I will organize the selection that you suggest. I, for one, must get back to Edinburgh as soon as possible to deal with the financial repercussions of this …uh. . . setback. Even though it pains me that I must leave my beloved wife of many years buried here on this beach."

Captain Anderson and First Mate Ferguson looked at each other and without exchanging a word immediately understood that Paterson's selection would somehow wind up benefiting Paterson.

It did not take long for Paterson and the surviving leaders of the Darien community to select about half of the survivors for embarkment on the *Unicorn*. There were protests from those who were told to wait for the next ships, but they were already in such a weakened condition that most of them quickly resigned themselves to their fate. Captain Anderson soothed them a bit by unloading some of the supplies that the *Unicorn* had on board to tide them over until the other ships arrived.

"We will head for Jamaica and resupply ourselves there for the journey over the Atlantic," Captain explained to First Mate Ferguson and the other senior crew members, "We need to make haste because we are heading into summer and the hurricane season. If we can streak through to Kingston without being caught by pirates or Spanish, we should be able to catch a good wind for a quick crossing to Scotland before the storms start in earnest."

The selected survivors with their meagre possessions were soon aboard the *Unicorn*. Most of them came with barely more than the shirts on their backs. Any bulky property had in any case to be left to the remaining settlers in order to maximize the number of passengers that could fit aboard the *Unicorn*. By the time the sun was setting over the isthmus, Captain Anderson was ready to set sail for the open seas. The crew worked especially quickly since no one wanted to experience the noxious night air of Darien and the fevers that lurked therein. With all sails set the *Unicorn* sailed off briskly into the darkening horizon on a northerly course. Captain Anderson wanted to get as far as he could the first night to avoid another encounter with Spanish warships. He knew that the *Unicorn* now heavily laden would have a harder time outrunning an attacking ship.

As the sun rose the next day, Captain Anderson was pleased to see that they had been lucky with the prevailing winds and appeared to be making good time. An astrolabe measurement at noon confirmed that the *Unicorn* was fast approaching the latitude of Jamaica. Unfortunately, several of the passengers had succumbed to their fevers during the night and had to be dumped overboard.

Just as Captain Anderson was beginning to feel confident that the Jamaica leg of the journey would soon be accomplished, the sailor in the crow's nest shouted, "Ship ahoy on starboard, Captain, she seems to be heading in the same direction we are."

Captain Anderson peering through his telescope soon confirmed that a well-armed ship was sailing in the same direction as the *Unicorn* but on a convergence course that would bring both ships within hailing distance of each other.

"It seems to be flying British colors," said Captain Anderson with some relief, "It's probably a British privateer heading to the same place we are. Kingston is the lair for privateers that prey on Spanish shipping. That's where Henry Morgan was based for years. A British privateer would not normally attack a Scottish ship, but you can never be too certain. Out here on the Spanish Main there is only a thin line between privateers and pirates."

"Shall we ready the gun crews, just in case?" asked the First Mate.

"That's a waste of time," said Captain Anderson, "We could not win a fight with that one with all these people on board. Best not to provoke them. Better to have the passengers with the yellow fever come out on board and stand clearly visible to the other ship. That will make them think twice about boarding us."

As the course of the two ships gradually converged, the tension rose among the crew members of the *Unicorn*. As they escorted the sick passengers to the railings, each sailor kept an anxious eye out for the places where the weapons were stowed. The *Unicorn* was soon within shouting distance of the heavily armed British privateer by the name of *Serpent*. Captain Anderson could see from their appearance that the sailors on the other ship were as dangerous a lot of cutthroats as could be found on the Spanish Main.

The captain of the *Serpent* hailed the *Unicorn*, "This is Her Majesty's ship, the *Serpent*, returning to our home port of Kingston from a mission against the Spanish. What business have you in this area?"

"We are a Scottish ship on a rescue mission to take these poor sick settlers back to their homeland," shouted Captain Anderson, "We are also headed toward Kingston to take on supplies. Can you tell us how far we are away?"

"If the wind holds, we should be arriving in Kingston within a day," answered the captain of the *Serpent*, "You can follow us there if you will, but keep your distance. I don't want any outbreaks of fever among my crew."

First Mate Ferguson smiled at Captain Anderson in admiration that his clever ruse had probably saved them from the depredations of what was obviously a pack of pirates. And he had provided them with a pilot into the port of Kingston which they might otherwise have spent days trying to find.

In the late afternoon, the Union Jack flying over the port of Kingston appeared on the horizon. The *Unicorn* followed the *Serpent* into the bay anchoring at a distance to shore sufficient to allay any anxieties about contact with the sick survivors. Captain Anderson, First Mate Ferguson and several other crew members set off in the tender to buy enough fresh supplies for the crossing. As they approached the shore, they saw the crew of the *Serpent* already busy unloading the booty from their privateering venture. By the light of a large bonfire, they were setting up a kind of open-air market for the stolen goods. They were greeted by a noisy crowd of rum-swilling Jack Tars offering toasts to the successes of their friends and colleagues. Women of the night were informing the sailors of the many delights that could be purchased with their ill-gotten gains. Someone started to sing a chanty accompanied by a squeeze box and many in the crowd started to dance in the street. The whole unloading procedure seemed to be turning into a raucous bacchanal.

"Our men would love to have shore leave for just one night before the crossing," suggested First Mate Ferguson.

"No shore leave for anyone tonight," replied Captain Anderson sternly, "We need to leave again quickly to make as much distance as possible under the cover of darkness. We will have to slip between Cuba and Hispaniola in order to get to the Bahamas. From there we will follow a northeasterly course out of the hurricane zone. Besides, this den of iniquity would be the ruin of our crew. After tonight they would be useless for days and we have no time to lose."

Captain Anderson arranged to have several dozen barrels each of salt pork, hard tack, and fresh water delivered to the ship within hours so that they were ready to sail before midnight. As the *Unicorn* sailed off into the night the crew gazed longingly at the wild party growing in intensity at the port.

The *Unicorn* made it past Cuba and Hispaniola in the dark without incident. As the sun rose, however, Captain Anderson was alarmed to see storm clouds gathering on the horizon.

"All hands report to their storm stations!" ordered Captain Anderson, "Strike the main-sail. Get the passengers below and batten the hatches. Those below take turns manning the bilge pumps. It looks like we will have to ride out a tropical storm."

As the crew rushed about fulfilling the captain's orders, the wind began to blow more intensely in a northeasterly direction.

"At least the wind is driving us in the direction we want to go," remarked First Mate Ferguson.

"That will do us no good if it gets too strong. There are dozens of reefs and sand-bars it could smash us on if we lose control of the ship," warned Captain Anderson.

The wind speed continued to increase and soon the *Unicorn* was surfing swells that resembled small mountains.

"Strike the rest of the sails, Ferguson!" shouted the captain, "And all hands lash themselves to their duty stations. This wind can sweep a man overboard in a twinkling and we will need every sailor we've got in order to survive this one."

As the wind approached hurricane velocity, the hollowing grew so loud that orders could no longer be heard. Captain Anderson had to rely on the experience and training of his crew to perform the functions necessary to keep the vessel afloat. The ship sped along at a frightening speed even though all sails had been struck. The First Mate and the Helmsman manned the wheel together to keep the rudder as stable as possible. Luckily, the storm had blown the ship so far out to sea that they were in little danger of striking reefs. Nonetheless the slightest mishap at this speed could cause them to break apart and founder. As the screeching of the wind reached an infernal intensity, the main mast snapped just above the deck with a report like a thunderclap. It fell forward dragging its rigging with it, striking the forward mast and smashing the yardarm. Immediately understanding the mortal danger that the broken debris posed for the stability of the ship, several sailors loosened their lashings enough to fight their way over to cut the rigging holding the mast and the spars on deck. After several tense moments of hacking away at the ropes, the whole entanglement was swept overboard along with two of the brave men whose actions saved the ship from capsizing.

"God have mercy on their souls," muttered Captain Anderson, determined now more than ever that they somehow had to come through all this so that the sacrifice of those fine sailors would not be in vain.

The storm continued unabated for the rest of the day. Without the two forward masts, the ship was actually a bit more stable and no longer reached the velocities it had before. Nevertheless, it was only the iron will to survive that allowed the crew to overcome their complete and utter exhaustion. As night fell, the storm gradually lessened. When it was clear that they had survived the worst of the hurricane, each crew member on deck sank down at his station whispering a prayer of thanks and falling into a deep sleep.

The next day was sunny and calm. The *Unicorn* bereft of her two forward masts sailed at a leisurely tempo powered only by an improvised sail on the aft mast. The survivors less two who had passed away during the storm were back on deck praising the Lord for their good fortune. William Paterson was wondering aloud what great mission He might have in store for them. What other reason could there be for their miraculous survival?

"The only reason you're alive is because my lads risked their lives to save you," thought Captain Anderson to himself as he took an astrolabe reading to determine their latitude.

"Our survival is far from certain," Captain Anderson said aloud, "Our ship is no longer seaworthy, and we are quickly running out of supplies. Our only hope to reach land soon before we sink. In any case we won't be getting back to Scotland on this ship."

"But I must get back to Scotland as quickly as possible to report to our investors, especially now that a company ship has been ruined." Paterson said with a pomposity totally at odds with his disastrous financial situation.

"Well, you can thank God that any of us are still alive because we might not be much longer," retorted Captain Anderson darkly as he wondered to himself if there was indeed any justifiable hope of survival. Just as he began to resign himself to a dismal fate an enormous flock of white birds appeared on the horizon. Although not a religious person, he could not help feeling that this was a sign from Providence that not all was lost.

"Ferguson!" he shouted, "Those birds yonder are surely proof that land is near. Steer us in the direction whence they came!"

Not long after a distant shore came into view. In addition to thousands of birds they could see a verdant coast lined with what appeared to be cedar swamps. As luck would have it, they were soon hailed by a local schooner.

The captain of the schooner introduced himself as Daniel Leeds who informed them that the land they saw was the colony of Nova Caesarea and that he was surveying it on behalf of the owners who were known as the Proprietors.

"Is there a place where one can safely land this ship," asked Captain Anderson, "I fear that we could sink at any moment."

"Not around here," replied Leeds, "This coast is treacherous with many reefs and sandbars. But I can tow you to the next decent harbor at Perth Amboy. There you will be able meet a representative of the Proprietors who might be able to help you."

Gratefully accepting Leeds' offer Captain Anderson ordered his crew to tether the wrecked ship to the schooner. Together they proceeded slowly within view of the coast but at a safe distance from the reefs and shoals. Arriving at the harbor town of Perth Amboy Captain Anderson cut the tether and ran the *Unicorn* onto the beach. He then ordered the evacuation of all its passengers and cargo. A crowd soon gathered to gawk at the ruined vessel and ask the crew what had befallen them.

"I am John Anderson, captain of this vessel," Captain Anderson addressed the crowd, "We are carrying survivors from Darien, and I need to speak to a representative of the Proprietors."

"That would be me," a man perhaps 10 years older than Captain Anderson with a thick Scottish accent stepped out from the crowd, "I am John Reid, the Surveyor-General of the province. I represent the Proprietors. What is it that you need to discuss?"

"I want to know how quickly we can get our brethren back to Scotland," William Paterson pushed himself into the conversation.

"It seems your brethren have had enough travel for a while," replied John Reid casting a critical eye at Paterson and his bedraggled passengers, "Captain Anderson, perhaps you would accompany me to my office where we can discuss how these poor people might best be helped."

Anderson followed Reid to his office a few streets away leaving Paterson, the crew, and the survivors standing on the beach trying to sort out what little cargo was still intact after the storm. Reid motioned to one of two comfortable leather chairs while he decanted a bottle of real Highland Single Malt. Anderson sank gratefully into the chair thinking how long it had been since he had felt such comfort. It was the first time he had sniffed the peaty aroma of a Highland Single Malt since he left Scotland.

As the two men savored the strong spirits, Anderson recounted the entire sad story of the Darien Debacle and the travails that they had endured in the last weeks. He emphasized the role that Paterson had played in the folly and made it clear to Reid that neither Paterson nor the survivors were in any position to drive hard bargains.

"Maybe Providence played a role in this after all," said Reid after listening to Anderson's story, "It so happens that we are in dire need of settlers here, especially ones who are more cooperative than the ones we have now. We have great tracts of land to lease but nobody to farm them, at least nobody who has a decent respect for property rights."

"What seems to be the problem?" asked Captain Anderson, "I would think there would be great interest in getting access to fertile virgin territory."

"Oh, there is plenty of interest alright, but you have to understand the background here," explained Reid, "The current Proprietors purchased the land from the original owner, Lord Carteret, who had been granted this place from the Duke of York after he threw out the Dutch. The Proprietors were generally the younger sons of Scottish aristocratic families limited in their enjoyment of the grand lifestyle of landed gentry by the principle of primogeniture. They dreamed of establishing a feudal paradise for themselves in the New World with all the privileges that their older brothers enjoyed in Scotland. They planned to distribute the land to docile peasants and live comfortably from the quitrents. What they did not realize was that there were people already living here and Carteret's people had experienced armed rebellion when they tried to impose the quitrent system on them. That was the reason they were able to buy the proprietorship so cheaply."

"But who are these people who were already here?" asked Captain Anderson.

"It's a motley lot," answered Reid, "They're Dutchman, Swedes, French Huguenots, and every sort of British religious group you can imagine, most of them dissident Calvinists. Right after the English conquered New Netherlands the new English military governor, Colonel Richard Nicolls, at the behest of the Duke of York, tried to populate the area as quickly as possible. He offered generous tracts of land to English yeomen from New England who were happy to move to the frontier. They purchased land from the Lenape Indians unaware that much of the property had been promised to the Proprietors who based their claims on the royal grants originally made to Berkeley and Carteret. The British immigrants have been filtering in for generations from New England through Long Island. They are accustomed to the freeholder system of New England and have no respect at all for the claims of Stuart courtiers. They are, after all, descendants of the kind of Puritans who have already beheaded one Stuart. They think that quitrents are an outrageous offense against their idea of covenant which in their view binds congregations and towns together in a special pact with God with no intermediaries."

"I can imagine how difficult it is to deal with these people," Captain Anderson said, "Religious fanatics can be very stubborn."

"Indeed, they can," agreed Reid, "These people simply don't acknowledge any overlord. They have been too much on their own for too long. And they are armed to the teeth. They have always organized their own militias to protect themselves and don't take orders from anyone except for their own leaders who are usually dissident preachers. Whenever anyone tries to impose the rule of law on them, they riot."

"I don't think you will have that problem with our Darien survivors," said Captain Anderson, "They will be thankful for any conditions you may care to offer them. They are Scotsmen who are used to the quitrent system at home. After Darien, they will be grateful for any way to rescue their dreams. And you needn't pay any mind to Paterson. He and the Darien Company are ruined, they are walking dead."

"Judging by the way you rescued the Darien survivors from utter disaster," said Reid, "I think you might be just the man to convince them to take up our offers. The Proprietors would be most grateful, and they tend to show their gratitude in generous ways."

"I would be pleased to help," answered Anderson, relieved that some new prospects were opening up for him as well, "I like projects that are a bit of a challenge."

Reid smiled thoughtfully nodding his head. He liked the young sea captain who seemed to have the same kind of bold self-confidence as himself. He was certain that this would be the beginning of a fruitful cooperation.

The two men soon became close allies. Anderson and Reid organized immediate relief for the survivors through Reid's connections in the Quaker community. Anderson then set about negotiating land tenure agreements with the survivors on behalf of the Proprietors. For each successful lease he was paid a commission and was soon on his way to a modest degree of prosperity. His work kept him busy for the next year. Both the Darien survivors and the Proprietors were delighted with the results of Anderson's efforts. The Proprietors, in fact, were so pleased that they encouraged Reid to entrust the young man with ever more managerial responsibilities. Reid was happy to oblige and began to treat Anderson like a member of his family. The relationship grew so felicitous that when Anderson asked for the hand of Reid's daughter, Anna, in marriage, he agreed without hesitation and promised the couple a generous estate in Manalapan as dowry.

BOOK 1

Isabella's First Sacrifice– 1737–1770

Chapter 1

THE NEW ARK OF THE COVENANT – 1749

BUT, JACOB, WHY IN the Lord's name would you want to move into the wilds of the Jerseys?" Abia Scudder wrung her hands in frustration at her husband's latest idea, "Here on Long Island we have everything we need, our mill is doing well, and our relatives live not far away."

"The place is filling up with unsavory characters, Abia," answered Jacob Scudder with a self-righteous scowl, "I am not sure if this is the best place to bring up pious children. Besides we can sell our mill and farm here for a good price and buy twice the amount of land in the virgin territory of Eastern Jersey. Several of my cousins have already moved there and been very successful. I am convinced that this is what the Lord meant for us. That is the new Canaan. Why, one of the towns there is even called the New Ark, a fitting place for God-fearing people to renew their covenant with the Almighty in the pristine wilderness."

Nathaniel listened nervously to his parents arguing. As a teenager he had no right to comment on the relative merits of each side of the argument, but he knew his father's enthusiasm would very likely overpower any objections his exhausted mother might be able to make. His father was a bundle of energy and had a way of bolstering his plans with religious arguments that made resistance from his mother seem almost impious. Helpless to counter such onslaughts, Abia would generally give in to whatever plans Jacob might be laying but at the same she would be unable to mask completely her feelings of resentment. Although Nathaniel relished his father's latest plan for new adventures on the frontier, he regretted the tension that always arose when Jacob ran roughshod over Abia's concerns. Each defeat seemed to make Abia a bit more exhausted and irritable.

"I think you will better see the wisdom in this after you have listened to Reverend Edwards this evening at the revival," said Jacob in his patronizing tone, "All over people are waking up to the possibilities that beckon if we just put our faith in the

Lord and organize our polities based on His principles. Reverend Edwards teaches us that we need to open our hearts to the Lord and let His Grace guide us."

That evening Nathaniel accompanied his parents to a large tent which had been set up to accommodate the crowds that Reverend Edwards often drew. People came from far and wide to listen to the famous New Light preacher who encouraged his listeners to seek a direct experience of the Divine. Some came just to witness the dramatic scenes which often seemed to result from the pastor's exhortations. An atmosphere of tense expectation developed as the crowd waited impatiently for the minister to begin.

Finally, a man with the white collar and black robe of a Calvinist preacher stepped up to the improvised pulpit.

"Good evening, Friends in Christ," he began in a strong, confident voice, "This evening I would like to speak to you about the just anger that God feels toward all who are out of Christ and the wretched tortures that are in store for them. The wrath of God burns against them, their damnation does not slumber; the pit is prepared, the fire is made ready, the furnace is now hot, ready to receive them; the flames do now rage and glow. The glittering sword is whet, and held over them, and the pit hath opened its mouth under them."

Edwards continued in this vein for a long time describing in almost sadistic detail what awaits the non-repentant sinner at the hands of an almighty and wrathful God. He noted that since everyone is born a sinner and seldom can resist the lures of Satan, all of us deserve this horrible fate. Nathaniel began to feel more and more depressed at the obvious hopelessness of the human situation. As he looked around the congregation, he noticed that many people, including his mother, had begun to weep softly.

"There is nothing that keeps wicked men at any one moment out of hell, but the mere pleasure of God," continued Edwards, his voice rising in a crescendo, "In His own good time all the wicked will meet their inevitable fates. It can happen at any moment, but God alone decides when that will be. And all your pitiable efforts to avoid that fate are useless. God alone decides who will be saved and who will suffer forever."

Signs of increasing anxiety were in evidence among the congregation. The weeping increased in intensity, and many looked downright distraught.

"You are asking yourself now, what can I do to be saved?" shouted Edwards, "The answer is nothing, absolutely nothing, you will be saved only if God wills it. All you can do is accept the will of God and accept it joyfully, because there is nothing that God wills that is not perfect."

At that point Abia Scudder was seized by an intense shudder and fell into the arms of her husband. With Nathaniel's help Jacob managed to drag the convulsing woman out of the tent and lay her down on the meadow in the fresh air. After a time, the shuddering eased, and Abia lay with her eyes closed softly moaning. As Jacob stroked her hair to calm her, Nathaniel ran to fetch the family's horse and wagon. Together they gently lifted her up and placed her in a lying position in the back of the wagon. Jacob sat next to her and drew her head into his lap while Nathaniel, fearing to put strain on her, drove the horse and wagon at a carefully measured pace back to their farm. Upon arrival Jacob and Nathaniel once again lifted Abia and carried her to her bed.

"Shall I fetch the doctor?" asked Nathaniel anxiously, "Perhaps she has had an attack of apoplexy."

"No, I think she will be alright," answered Jacob, "I think she has just had the conversion experience and was temporarily overwhelmed by the power of the Almighty. Now she just needs rest."

And rest she did. Abia remained in her bed for over a week. Nathaniel carefully attended to her each day and was relieved to note that after a few days the color seemed to be coming back to her cheeks. After a week she was able to sit up in her bed and eat normally again. To Nathaniel's great surprise, despite her illness, his mother was actually in a better mood than she had experienced for a long time. She was calm, relaxed and smiled frequently in an almost beatific manner.

"This is a result of having received God's grace," explained Jacob, "It can strike you like a thunderbolt. It is no wonder that she needs a few days to recuperate. But you will see, she will be much happier and healthier now because she has accepted the Lord's will."

And so it came to pass that Abia Scudder was indeed a changed woman. For her now everything was the Lord's will to be accepted joyously without complaint. Nathaniel was pleased to note that the frequent disagreements between Jacob and Abia which used to create so much tension seemed to be a thing of the past. She also no longer offered any resistance when Jacob discussed his plans for relocating the family to the New Jersey frontier.

Jacob paid several visits to his relatives in the Jerseys to scout for real estate. Returning from his third visit he burst into the house to proclaim his success.

"I have met a man named Dr. Daniel Brinton who has made me an outstanding offer," announced Jacob with ebullient enthusiasm, "Several large mills located on a 100-acre tract of the finest farming land for only 1400 pounds. We can sell our holdings here for much more and realize a handsome profit."

"It seems that the Lord has surely blessed your project, Jacob," responded Abia with calm equanimity. "Otherwise, you would not have found such a wonderful opportunity."

"Right you are, Abia," continued Jacob confidently, "And there are yet more signs of His Grace. Several pastors from the Presbyterian Synod of New York have convinced the royal governor of New Jersey to grant a charter for a new college to train pious young men. With the profit we earned from the sale of our lands here we will be able to pay for a fine education for Nathaniel."

This part of his father's plan was new to Nathaniel but came as a pleasant surprise.

"Why father, I am grateful for this unexpected honor," responded Nathaniel respectfully, "What kind of a college is this that you speak of?"

"Well, you might recall that several of our leading New Light Presbyterians have been trying to establish a college for some time to educate young men for responsible roles in the community, in particular to supply our growing congregations with pastors of the True Religion."

"Yes, I do recall your having mentioned that this has long been a major concern of pastors such as Reverend Edwards and Reverend Tennent," answered Nathaniel.

"But Lewis, the last Anglican governor of New Jersey, was always opposed because he hated the freedom of worship that our Presbyterian faith holds dear," continued Jacob, "He wanted to keep control of religion in the hands of Papist Anglican bishops who want to place themselves between us and our God. When Lewis died, however, the new acting governor, Hamilton, was a Scotsman who was more open-minded toward true religion; he finally granted the pastors their charter. The new royal governor who followed him, Belcher, confirmed it so now it is an established institution that is operating in the parsonage of Reverend Aaron Burr in the town called the New Ark. From here learned scholars will fan out to spread the Word in our new Canaan. And you, Nathaniel, will be one of them."

Nathaniel was excited by the prospect of getting the education of a learned gentleman and gratified that his father was willing and able to pay for such a privilege. He had, however, never considered that he might spend his life as a minister although serving the community in some way would certainly be desirable. He was much more interested in natural rather than moral philosophy but both subjects were part of every college curriculum and the choice of a career lay far in the future.

Chapter 2

MANALAPAN – 1756

NATHANIEL SCUDDER SAT IN the library of the parsonage of Reverend Aaron Burr on the corner of Broad and William Streets in Newark. He was there together with his friend and classmate, Benjamin Prime, both of whom were preparing themselves for a career as physicians. Nathaniel was trying to concentrate his thoughts on the volume of Galen's *De pulsibus* lying in front of him. Although the text was in Latin, a language he had thoroughly mastered, he kept reading the same few lines over and over. His inability to concentrate was very upsetting because he was preparing for an important examination at the College of New Jersey which he was scheduled to take before the imminent move of the college from Newark to the little town of Princeton. He had borrowed the book from a local scholar and wanted to return it before the move. He took a deep breath and began the page again.

Benjamin, sitting across from him, cast an annoyed look.

"Natty, you are huffing and puffing like an old bellows. What in the world is wrong with you?"

"Oh Benjie, I'm afraid I just can't concentrate. There is a fair maiden whose face I cannot banish from my thoughts," said Nathaniel by way of apology.

"Don't tell me you're in love!" responded Benjamin incredulously. "Let me guess; a verse comes to mind:

> Sukey smiled at Nat
> Smitten he doffed his hat
> Should his love he show
> From Esther he can expect a blow."

"You and your silly doggerel," Nathaniel shot back. "And keep your voice down, if Esther Burr hears you and thinks we are mocking her sister, we could both indeed be in real trouble. Besides, you are way off the mark. It is not Susanna Edwards. She is just a child. The very idea of it is just perverse!"

"Well, we are all born depraved as Reverend Burr never ceases to remind us. Why should you be any different? Come on now, you can share your secret with me. I might even be able to give you some good advice," Benjamin smiled archly.

Nathaniel thought that perhaps it might, in fact, ease his inner turmoil if he could discuss his secret obsession with someone.

"You must promise to say not a word to anyone!"

"I'd rather spend a week in the stocks," affirmed Benjamin solemnly.

"Ok, then, the lady's name is Isabella Anderson," confessed Nathaniel abjectly.

"Isabella Anderson?!? From the Andersons of Monmouth County, one of the wealthiest and most influential families in the colony?!?" Benjamin's voice rose in a crescendo of disbelief.

"I know, I know," Nathaniel answered with resignation, "There is no way a princess like that is going to be interested in a miller's son. In addition, she is part of that Scottish aristocracy that lays claim to most of the eastern Jerseys. I will never have occasion to meet her on a social level. I only ever catch a glimpse of her when I attend Sunday service at Reverend Tennent's meeting house down in Manalapan when I am working on my medical internship with Dr. Clark. And I certainly can't chat her up when we are in church."

"Ah, well, let me think," reflected Benjamin pensively, "If you attend the same church, that is already a good beginning. Perhaps you can strike up a conversation after services."

"Very unlikely," Nathaniel replied gloomily, "She is accompanied by her mother and a servant who drives their wagon and they do not tarry after the services."

"Not to despair, Natty," encouraged Benjamin, "There is a solution to everything. You must patiently wait every Sunday for an opportunity to make a gallant impression."

Nathaniel thought that his friend was overly optimistic, but he was so desperately in love that he was willing to try anything. He resolved to attend services regularly on every coming Sunday in the hope that he would somehow find a pretense to meet the girl without seeming impertinent.

On the next Sunday Nathaniel left early for Manalapan from his boarding room near Monmouth Courthouse to make certain that he was in time for the service. He had donned his best powdered wig, ruffled white shirt, cravat, and dark coat although the summer heat was bound to make him uncomfortable. He stood in the back of the meeting house and gazed at the beautiful Isabella dressed in a gorgeous grey gown and blue petticoat. He had never seen any of the women in his staid Puritan family looking like that. He could not take his eyes off the lovely girl sitting in the first pew except when his staring seemed to attract the disapproving glances of the good Presbyterian churchgoers. Reverend Tennent was expatiating about the wiles of Satan who never tired of luring young people into sinful debauchery and Nathaniel began to feel that the Puritan preacher was speaking directly to him.

The servant who had driven the wagon waited patiently outside while Isabella and her mother attended the service. Shortly after it was over and the congregation came out of the church. Isabella and her mother proceeded directly to their wagon and were helped inside by the servant. After sitting down Isabella remembered that she had forgotten her parasol in the church.

"Dunmore, could you please fetch my parasol. I am afraid I left it in our pew," Isabella asked.

After the servant had entered the church, as luck would have it a sharp noise caused the horses pulling the now driverless wagon to bolt and head off at a brisk trot.

At that moment Nathaniel realized he had a God-given opportunity for demonstrating his gallantry. He jumped on his horse and galloped off quickly in the direction of the departing wagon with the frightened ladies.

After about a mile he overtook the racing wagon and deftly managed to jump from his horse into the driver's seat of the wagon and grab the reins.

"Whoa, whoa," he shouted to the horses while pulling hard on the reins.

As the horses slowed to a walk, the two ladies breathed a collective sigh of relief.

"Well, young man, that was certainly a gallant act," Isabella's mother remarked, "On behalf of my daughter and myself let me thank you for your aid. I am Hannah Anderson, and this is my daughter, Isabella."

"I am honored to have been of service," he said, "Permit me to introduce myself. I am Nathaniel Scudder; I am a student at the College of New Jersey, and I am currently living in Manalapan to learn the physician's art from Dr. Clark."

Isabella regarded her young helper with interest. She had noticed the earnest but handsome young man already during several church services and wondered who he might be. Perhaps this was a good time to find out.

"That is an interesting coincidence," said Isabella, "Dr. Clark is our family doctor."

"Shall we return to the meeting house to fetch your servant?" Nathaniel inquired uncertainly, wondering how best to prolong the encounter, "If you are in a hurry, I will be happy to drive you to your estate."

"That actually would be very helpful," replied Hannah Anderson, "We are expecting guests this afternoon and Dunmore will find his way home. Anderson Manor is just a few miles down this road."

Nathaniel whispered a prayer of thanks for his great good fortune. Together they trotted off in the direction of the Anderson estate.

Nathaniel wracked his brains to figure out how to start a conversation with the object of his obsessions without seeming impertinent to her mother. They came from vastly different worlds, and he feared that they had little in common.

"Anderson is an interesting name," he blurted out finally, "Is it Danish?"

"Our family is originally Scottish," answered Isabella. "My grandfather was a sea captain from the area of the Moray Firth in Scotland. He came to the Jerseys on the way back from rescuing the poor settlers from Darien."

"Could that be the former royal governor, John Anderson?" asked Nathaniel knowing full well that the Anderson family was descended from that famous man who had served for decades on the royal council and was renowned for his efforts to promote harmony between the Anglican and dissident Calvinist factions in New Jersey.

"The same," answered Isabella, "But he was royal governor only for a short time before he died."

"His services to the province are well-known," said Nathaniel, eager for an opportunity to show his respect for Isabella's family.

"Unfortunately, his work remains unfinished," interjected Hannah Anderson, "There still is so much conflict among the various groups in this province. I wonder if we will ever be able to achieve a real sense of community here."

"For that we need leaders who can follow in Governor Anderson's footsteps," opined Nathaniel, grateful for an opportunity to introduce himself as a budding scholar, "I, for one, am optimistic for I think that Governor Belcher is such a person. He was, for example, instrumental in the establishment of my college and insisted that it educate leaders in all fields, not just in theology."

"How interesting," answered Isabella, "Is that why you came here? Is your family from here?"

"Well, we are originally from England, but my ancestors came to the Massachusetts Bay Colony several generations ago. My great-grandfather was a very devout man who thought that the freedom to pursue true religion could best be found in the wilderness of New England," Nathaniel explained hesitatingly, fearing that Isabella might jump to the conclusion that his family were religious fanatics.

"Oh, I have read about how the first King Charles foolishly persecuted certain kinds of Protestants which finally resulted in that dreadful civil war," interjected Isabella, "Your ancestors probably had good reasons to try their luck in the new world. Many of the Scotsmen that came with my grandfather had very similar motives."

Deeply relieved by Isabella's encouragement and impressed by her knowledge of history, Nathaniel continued, "Eventually, some of my family moved to Long Island as New England began to fill up with immigrants less interested in maintaining the religious ideals of the original settlers. New territories to the west seemed to offer not only new land but also a more wholesome environment. I, myself, was born in Huntington, Long Island, but my father decided to move to the Jerseys in the 1740's. Eventually he bought a mill and a hundred acres of farmland near Princeton in 1749."

"Was that for business reasons?" asked Isabella.

Isabella's encouraging manner relaxed Nathaniel and he decided to let her know the whole story. "Actually, he had a mill in Huntington and was doing quite well there as well. I think his main motivation was religious."

"Really?" remarked Hannah Anderson, "I would not think the Jerseys offer a more wholesome environment than Long Island."

"It had to do with an experience my parents had when I was young," explained Nathaniel, "At that time they heard a sermon by Reverend Jonathan Edwards that greatly impressed them."

"Ah yes, the famous evangelist," exclaimed Hannah, "Reverend Tennent has cited him on a number of occasions. Apparently, he is very eloquent."

"Indeed, he is," Nathaniel continued, "Attending one of his sermons was quite an experience."

"And what was so remarkable about what he had to say?" asked Isabella.

"It was not so much what he said but the way he said it," explained Nathaniel. "He had a way of eliciting strong emotional responses from his listeners and he encouraged people to seek God with the heart more than with the mind. He declared that to be saved it was necessary to have a real conversion experience that touched you to the depth of your soul."

"And did his sermon affect you in that way?" asked Isabella.

"No, as a boy I actually found his bombastic manner to be a bit frightening," answered Nathaniel, "But it had a strong effect on many of the participants, including my mother. She was one of the many people there who broke down in tears, in the end almost fainting. My father practically had to carry her home and she stayed in bed for almost a week with a strange sort of fever."

"That must have been frightening indeed!" exclaimed Isabella.

"I was afraid she was going to die," agreed Nathaniel, "but in the end she recovered completely and became convinced that she had been born again in the grace of God. The interesting thing was that before that experience she often seemed to be quite unhappy and quarreled often with my father, but after her recovery she was almost always in a good mood and never disagreed with my father again. She docilely went about her duties with never a word of complaint."

"That probably pleased your father," commented Hannah with a rueful smile but charmed by the naive boy's willingness to reveal family secrets.

"He was, of course, delighted and became an enthusiastic supporter of the revival project," continued Nathaniel, "He read every pamphlet he could get his hands on and became particularly devoted to the sermons of men like Jonathan Dickinson, Jonathan Edwards, Aaron Burr, John Pearson and William Tennent."

"Is that the same Reverend Tennent that we heard today?" asked Isabella.

"No, it was his father who was also the founder of the Log College in Pennsylvania, an institution devoted to training ministers with an emphasis on the theology of direct experience of God's grace." explained Nathaniel.

"Quite a few ministers apparently attended the Log College," commented Hannah, "But I don't think it exists anymore, does it?"

"That is correct," responded Nathaniel, "It operated from 1726 until 1746, but then Dickinson, Edwards, Burr, and several graduates of the Log College decided to try to establish a new institution which would maintain the so-called 'New Side' approach to theology but also expand its curriculum to include other subjects. That is what eventually became the College of New Jersey where I am just finishing my studies. When my father heard about the new institution, he immediately decided that I should study there. He assumed, of course, that I would become a minister in the footsteps of the divines he so admired."

"And so we will soon be hearing from you from the pulpit?" inquired Isabella with a hint of disappointment in her voice.

"I am afraid not," answered Nathaniel, "I have always been more interested in natural philosophy than in theology, although I consider myself to be a God-fearing man. I plan to become a physician which is why I am currently learning the practical details from Dr. William Clark here in this area."

"Working with Dr. Clark is quite fascinating," continued Nathaniel, immensely pleased to discover that yet another link might possibly be forged between himself, Isabella, and her family, "He has such vast practical experience. It is an excellent supplement to the theoretical knowledge I received in my master's studies. And it is so gratifying to learn to help sick people effectively."

"You seem quite idealistic, Nathaniel," remarked Hannah pensively, "Perhaps you should have become a theologian after all."

"You are certainly correct that I feel a strong desire to serve my fellow man," said Nathaniel, "That is a characteristic that the College of New Jersey tries hard to instill in its students. But I think I can offer more in the way of healing people's bodies. Healing souls is a business I often find quite baffling. In any case my college differs from the Log College in that it strives to produce scholars proficient in different areas. Reverend Burr always stresses that one can serve God in many ways, not only as a minister but also as a public servant, lawyer, farmer, businessman or, as in my case, as a doctor. The important thing is to cultivate a selfless desire to serve."

"Those are very noble goals," enthused Isabella, charmed by Nathaniel's earnest idealism.

"Unfortunately, not everyone sees it that way," continued Nathaniel, "Many are afraid that the college would become a hotbed of Calvinist radicalism, producing dozens of firebrand pastors who would rail against the Papist tendencies of the Anglican hierarchy," explained Nathaniel, "But that was not the intention of the founders at all. They wanted to establish a college of liberal arts and sciences that would educate not only pastors but also graduates proficient in other learned professions as well, people who would become 'ornaments of the state as well as the church' as they phrased it. They, therefore, proposed to make the plan of education as extensive as circumstances would permit. Furthermore, they did not want to limit enrollments to Presbyterians but sought to give access to people of all persuasions. In their view that it was the Anglicans who wanted to restrict religious freedom in the colonies. It was they, after all, who continuously endeavored to restrict the right to hold office to members of the Church of England. The opponents of the charter were not satisfied, however, and threatened to test the validity of the charter in court. Finally, the issue came before the new governor, Jonathan Belcher, who as a Congregationalist was not so vehemently opposed to the founders as the Anglicans were. He issued a second charter very similar to the first but with some modifications to ensure that the concerns of the state were given due expression."

"Governor Belcher is such a wise statesman," remarked Isabella, "My father admires him greatly for his efforts to make peace among the competing factions and religions in the colony. With this charter I assume the college could begin operations without opposition?"

"Actually, the college already began operations in the parsonage of Jonathan Dickinson in Elizabethtown in 1747 but he died a few months later," explained Nathaniel, "Then the college moved to the Newark parsonage of Reverend Burr which is where I received my education. The new charter was issued in 1748 but the college had already been in operation for over a year. I received my bachelor's degree in Newark in 1751. Since then, I have been working on a master's degree. The college will be moving soon to the town of Princeton, not far from my parents' home in a beautiful new building. That is where I will be finishing up my degree."

"I know about that building," said Isabella, "An acquaintance of mine, Annis Boudinot, has occasion to visit Princeton frequently and she told me that a most impressive stone edifice was being erected near the home of her future in-laws, the Stocktons. She is engaged to be married soon to Richard Stockton and then she will be a neighbor of your college. Do you know Richard?"

"It is a small world, indeed," replied Nathaniel, "Richard graduated from the College of New Jersey as well, but he was few years ahead of me. I believe he was among the first graduating classes to receive a degree. Then, if I remember correctly, he went on to study law with David Ogden."

"That is correct," confirmed Isabella, "Richard was admitted to the bar in 1754 and is apparently enjoying great successes. Annis talks constantly about what a brilliant career he has in front of him. I think she is greatly looking forward to becoming the mistress of Morven—that is the name of the Stockton estate in Princeton."

"I am sure she is," added Nathaniel, thoughtfully, wondering how he could possibly compete successfully for Isabella's affections in such exalted social circles, "The Stockton family is one of the most prominent in the colony."

"Yes, and Annis is quite the poet," added Isabella, "I can just picture Annis living in luxury at Morven leisurely composing odes reminiscent of the bards of antiquity and organizing salons for artists, musicians, and poets."

"I can imagine that very vividly as well," agreed Nathaniel, thinking ruefully to himself that this was just the sort of grand aristocratic lifestyle that his parents would regard as the ultimate decadence but also the lifestyle that Isabella was accustomed to and undoubtedly expected to maintain.

"I have just had a wonderful idea!" said Isabella suddenly interrupting Nathaniel's brooding, "Annis is planning an autumn ball in a few weeks at Morven which I was planning to attend. Perhaps you would like to come as well. Then you could show me the new building."

"But I am sure that I will not be receiving an invitation," stuttered Nathaniel, "I don't know Richard that well and Annis not at all." He could have added that he had never attended a ball in his life and would not know even how to begin a minuet.

"Oh, don't worry about that," reassured Isabella, "Annis is a good friend and, if I ask her, she will add your name to the list. And after all, you are almost a classmate of Richard's."

"Well, if you think. . ." Nathaniel hesitated, alarmed and excited at the same time.

"Good, then it is settled!" confirmed Isabella, "Where should Annis send the invitation?"

"I think the best would be to send it to the college addressed to me," answered Nathaniel whose first thought was to avoid his parents getting wind of it followed quickly by severe anxieties regarding his ability to cope with the completely unfamiliar challenges of an aristocratic social event.

"Well, now tell me more about your studies. What is it like to be a student at the College of New Jersey?" inquired Hannah Anderson.

"Fascinating, but very intense," replied Nathaniel, "In order to qualify for admission we had to be able to render Virgil and Tully's Orations into English, to translate English into good Latin and to know enough Greek to translate the four Evangelists into Latin or English."

Now it was Isabella's turn to be impressed. "Where did you learn all those skills?" she asked.

"Mostly from our pastor. He tutored me for several years," replied Nathaniel, "Once at the college the curriculum consisted in further study of the Latin and Greek languages, the elements of mathematics, natural philosophy, moral philosophy, rhetoric, and logic. And, of course, we were also well instructed in the doctrines and precepts of the Christian faith by none other than President Burr who, by the way, is married to Reverend Jonathan Edwards' daughter, Esther."

"It sounds like a lot of work but did all that knowledge turn out to be useful?" asked Isabella.

"It is certainly useful in training the mind to handle difficult problems and, of course, for developing self-discipline," answered Nathaniel somewhat defensively, "If one develops such learning skills, then one can apply them to any practical problems that might arise in life."

"What practical problems do you think you can solve with the knowledge you have acquired so far?" teased Isabella with a saucy smile.

"I am just at the point where I am learning to apply the theoretical knowledge about natural philosophy that I gained in my master's course to the problem of restoring sick people to good health," Nathanial explained in his defense. "For example, I have just finished Harvey's book 'De motu cordis' about the circulation of the blood and it helps to understand why some people become apoplectic. In addition, I have learned much about the various healing herbs and how to concoct potions to combat many ailments. Of course, I still have much to learn even though I have essentially finished my master's degree. That is why I am working as a medical intern for Dr. Clark. Reverend Tennent, who is also a trustee of the college, suggested that I do my practical internship with him. That is how I wound up coming to this area. Dr. Clark is said to know an effective cure for an amazing number of diseases."

"I can certainly confirm that," agreed Isabella, "He has been our family doctor for years. He always seems to have just the right potion or poultice for every ailment. And he has a very gentle and careful manner with his patients. Unlike some doctors one hears of, you don't have to worry that Dr. Clark is going to make you sicker than you already are. If you master his skills, then I would have no qualms about entrusting my health care to you someday."

The thought of the intimacy involved in being Isabella's physician was so stimulating that Nathaniel felt a rush of blood to his face. "I think I might have a bit more to learn before I can accept such an important challenge," stammered Nathaniel.

"Well, then, young man, now you have a strong motivation to concentrate on your internship," remarked Hannah, secretly amused by the ardor of the blushing young man.

"That I do, that I do," replied Nathaniel dreamily as Anderson Manor came into view.

"This has been a very enjoyable ride," Isabella thanked him again, "And remember, you will be getting an invitation from Annis Boudinot shortly and I am looking forward to seeing you at Morven."

As Nathaniel waved goodbye, he was almost dumbstruck by the events of the day. Everything had developed far better than he could possibly have imagined. Isabella did not seem to be put off by his parents' religiosity and even seemed to have a favorable view of the medical profession. Now his only serious problem was to find out how to dance the minuet in the few weeks remaining until the ball.

Chapter 3

Crossweeksung – 1756

After a night sweetened by dreams of Isabella, Nathaniel rose before first light and hurried to the stable of his medical mentor, Dr. William Clark. Parallel to his master's degree program at the College of New Jersey he had been apprenticed to Dr. Clark for the last several years to learn the practical aspects of being a physician. At CNJ he received a very intense theoretical education which involved studying all the medical classics, most of them in the original Latin or Greek. It was Dr. Clark, however, who taught him how to cure illnesses.

Today they were scheduled to visit a settlement of the Lenni Lenape Indians in Crossweeksung. During the long ride there and back Nathaniel hoped he might have a chance to interview Dr. Clark regarding his knowledge of the Anderson family and glean more information about the girl of his dreams. He would have to await exactly the right moment, however, and first concentrate on his duties.

The Indians of the Crossweeksung community had been converted to Christianity by the famous New Light pastor, David Brainerd, who was held in high esteem by the Presbyterian theologians associated with the College of New Jersey. Brainerd had been refused his degree by Yale College because of critical comments he had made concerning a Yale faculty member. This was widely regarded as outrageously unfair by his New Light brethren and one of the reasons they decided to found a new college. In fact, President Burr had once stated that without the Brainerd affair, the College of New Jersey might never have come into existence. Although David Brainerd had died an untimely death from tuberculosis in 1747, his missionary work was continued by his brother, John Brainerd, and was considered to be one of the signal achievements of the Great Awakening revival movement. Just before his death David Brainerd entrusted his diary to the Reverend Jonathan Edwards who published it with commentary as a guidebook for Christian missionaries. The story of David Brainerd's dedication, Christ-like self-sacrifice, and suffering became a major inspiration for many evangelists. Nathaniel had heard John Brainerd speak several times at the College of New

Jersey in Newark and was very impressed by his stories about the performance of God's work among the Indians. He was pleased to hear from Dr. Clark that a request for a visit by an English physician had been received by Reverend Tennent and passed on to Dr. Clark. At last he would have an opportunity to inspect the Brainerd project firsthand.

As he waited for Dr. Clark, he walked down the row of magnificent horses that were kept in the stable. He recalled again Dr. Clark's emphasis on horsemanship as an essential skill for a medical man. Dr. Clark had pointed out that speed in reaching a person in need of medical assistance often made the difference between life and death. It was essential, therefore, not only to be an excellent rider with great endurance but also to maintain a stable full of healthy mounts ready to ride at a moment's notice. Top grade horses were as important as medical instruments as the physician's tools of the trade. Dr. Clark also explained that physicians played a unique role in the communication essential for the maintenance of the community. Few other professionals had occasion to visit the many remote farms as frequently as physicians. The local physician was the one person whom everyone knew and the primary conveyor of regional news. He was the one who had firsthand knowledge of the real problems that ordinary citizens were confronting. This aspect of a physician's service also entailed many hours on horseback. Since he loved horses and felt completely at home in the saddle, this was a prospect of his future profession that Nathaniel found very pleasing.

As the late summer sun rose in the East, Dr. Clark walked briskly into the stable.

"Good morning, Nathaniel," he greeted, "glad to see that you are up and ready to go. We have a long ride ahead of us this morning."

"Good morning, sir," answered Nathaniel, "I have brought all the instruments from the office that you requested—screw tourniquet, tenaculum, scalpel, and amputation saw. Do you think we will actually need to perform an amputation?"

"I hope not, but fear that it will probably be necessary," replied Dr. Clark, "my old friend Okwes is both the sachem of the Lenape community in Crossweeksung and an accomplished nentpike or medicine man. Lenape nentpikes are outstanding herbalists who are very skilled in healing most types of wounds. Apparently, his son, Chinkwe, has been wounded while participating in a campaign with a New Jersey militia regiment in northern New York. Under normal circumstances a Lenape nentpike would have no problem curing almost any non-fatal wound. Their herbal remedies are at least a good as ours, sometimes better. The fact that Okwes has asked for our help means that he is confronted with something unusual. I assume Chinkwe's wound was not treated in a timely manner and became inflamed on his way back to New Jersey. Surgery is the only problem I can think of that might require our help."

Nathaniel felt a surge of anxiety at the prospect of participating in a major surgical operation for the first time. Under Dr. Clark's tutelage he had performed a few minor procedures already such as the removal of a musket ball from the buttocks of a trespasser on someone's farm and the lancing of several carbuncles. He had even delivered a baby once more or less on his own with Dr. Clark looking on. An amputation, however, was a much more serious and dangerous operation. He had heard stories about screaming patients and hemorrhaging limbs and was not looking forward to this bloody exercise. On the other hand, this skill was an essential part of his professional training and the sooner he mastered it, the better.

Nathaniel noted with interest that Chinkwe had been marching with the New Jersey militia against the French on the New York border. Like all men in the colony between the ages of 16 and 60 Nathaniel drilled regularly with a militia unit and was eager to prove his patriotism by taking up arms against the French Papists who continually threatened the northern and western borders of British North America. In his militia unit in Newark the New Jersey militiamen were renowned for having served bravely in every encounter with the enemy since the founding of the colony in the 17th Century. In each major conflict—King William's War, Queen Anne's War, and King George's War—the New Jersey militiamen played a significant role in keeping the French and their Indian allies at bay. None of the peace treaties that ended these conflicts, however, was comprehensive enough to avoid renewed conflict along the vast and amorphous boundary areas that divided British North America from the territories claimed by France. After the end of King George's War, renewed French incursions into the disputed Ohio territory eventually prompted the governor of Virginia, Robert Dinwiddie, to send a young major of the Virginia militia, George Washington, at the head of a company into the area to warn off the French. It came to a bloody confrontation when Major Washington successfully ambushed a French unit at the Battle of Jumonville Glen in May of 1754. Washington's daring attack fascinated Nathaniel at the time since he and Washington were about the same age and Nathaniel dreamed of the glory that such an adventure might entail. The conflict escalated from there, however, and Washington soon had to endure setbacks. The British Crown decided to send Major General Edward Braddock with 2000 men to take Fort Duquesne in June of 1755 and finally put an end to French aggression on the frontier. The expedition was a disaster, however, ending with a rout of the British troops and the death of General Braddock.

This defeat sent a shock wave through all of British North America and increased the feeling of hostile encirclement by New France. It was deemed particularly foreboding by Calvinist frontier settlers who were convinced that the French were engaged in a holy war designed to reverse the gains of the Reformation by inciting savages to butcher mercilessly all opponents of Rome. Esther Burr, the wife of the college president, Aaron Burr, had repeatedly expressed her belief that these reverses were a result of moral backsliding on the part of the inhabitants of the British colonies. In her view the population had become much too materialistic and consumed with greed for worldly pleasures. For this reason, God was punishing his children for forsaking the True Religion and nothing short of a sincere religious revival would save the day. Nathaniel became so concerned that she might be right that he considered dropping out of his master's program and following the example of Major Washington. Dr. Clark, however, pointed out to him that in every military conflict that he was familiar with, many more soldiers died from lack of proper medical care than from enemy fire. If Nathaniel really wanted to serve his country, therefore, the best course of action would be to concentrate on his medical studies. The inescapable logic of Dr. Clark's argument convinced Nathaniel and he decided to postpone any military adventures until after the completion of his medical training. Now he hoped that he and Dr. Clark would be able to save Chinkwe and thus render at least some small service to the cause of the New Jersey militia.

Dr. Clark and Nathaniel mounted up and rode off at a brisk trot. The settlement at Crossweeksung was about 25 miles southwest of Monmouth Court House. Much of the way was through densely forested area so even at a fast pace with good horses they would need the better part of a half a day to get there. In addition to the medical equipment and water they each had a loaded musket and several pistols. They would be skirting the upper boundary of the Pine Barrens, an area renowned for murderous highwaymen so they would have to be prepared to defend themselves if necessary.

During their ride Nathaniel was interested in finding out as much as he could about the people they would be visiting.

"How long have you known the Indians at Crossweeksung, Dr. Clark?" asked Nathaniel.

"I visited there the first time shortly before the death of David Brainerd, about ten years ago," responded Dr. Clark, "Reverend Brainerd had bought several Indian converts to the church in Manalapan to be baptized. That is where I met Okwes. After his baptism he received the Christian name of John Ockum but when I met him, he was called Okwes and that is what I still call him. It means fox in the Lenape language and that is an apt name for him, he is very clever and incredibly observant. Actually, his Indian name is much longer because it means something like 'fox who misses no details' but that is too difficult for a White man to pronounce. We agreed to shorten it to just fox. When he heard that I was a doctor, he was interested in learning about my methods because he was the village nentpike or medicine man. That was the beginning of a fruitful relationship in which I learned much about Indian methods of healing."

"Is it true that some of their methods are superior to ours?" asked Nathaniel.

"They are definitely very versed in the use of herbal remedies," replied Dr. Clark.

"But surely the plants they use are known to us as well?" queried Nathaniel.

"Some are, some are not," explained Dr. Clark, "Some of the plants grow around here such as willows and cattails and we use them as well. Others they get through trade with Indians further west and we are not sure of their composition. In addition, they have special procedures for harvesting the herbs which apparently increases their potency. But how and why that works is somewhat of mystery. In any case, whenever you need to heal a flesh wound, use Okwe's herbs if you have the opportunity."

"But he apparently is not able to cure Chinkwe's wound," objected Nathaniel.

"If the inflammation is too far advanced, not even the best herbs are effective. At that point only surgery can help and that is probably why we have been summoned. The Indians have less experience in those kinds of procedures and understand little about internal anatomy," explained Dr. Clark.

"In that case, perhaps we should have brought along some opium," said Nathaniel, "if our patient has to suffer much pain, that might aggravate his condition."

"That will not be necessary," continued Dr. Clark, "Indians have a remarkable capacity for enduring pain and the use of opium might even be considered an affront. That is one of the reasons I wanted you to come along today to learn about amputation techniques. If this were a White man, we would need several people to hold the patient down and all the screaming and shrieking would make it more difficult for you to concentrate on the lesson. As you will see, that will not be the case today."

Nathaniel was awed by this revelation. He knew that the Indians were fearless warriors who were much in demand for service with the colonial militias. This Spartan aspect of their culture was, however, new to him and he was deeply impressed.

As the sun reached its zenith overhead, Dr. Clark and Nathaniel emerged from the forest into an open area containing several dome-shaped structures. An elderly Indian emerged from one of the larger structures and greeted Dr. Clark gravely.

"Welcome, Doctor William," greeted the elderly Indian man, "I am very glad you could come so quickly."

"Good to see you again, Okwes. I have heard that Chinkwe is suffering from a festering wound he received while marching with the Jersey militia on the Canadian border," Dr. Clark responded.

"He was with the unit fortifying Fort Oswego when the French attacked. Shamefully the fort commander ordered surrender without putting up much of a fight." Okwes explained, "The French offered the fort's defenders safe passage to French custody in Montreal for later exchange. But after the gates were open, the French soldiers and their Indian allies drank the fort's supply of rum and went on a rampage. The Indians began to murder and scalp their prisoners while the French tried half-heartedly to restrain them. When Chinkwe saw that many of the French's Indian allies were Ottawas who are well known for ritual cannibalism, he realized he had to run for it. He managed to dive into the Oswego River and swim to a boat piloted by John Gull of the Jersey militia. Unfortunately, an arrow struck him in the foot just before he could dive into the river. The wound was a small one, but it took quite a while for Gull to get Chinkwe back to New Jersey. By then the small wound grew steadily worse and now none of my remedies seem to help."

Okwes lead Dr. Clark and Nathaniel into his dwelling. Somewhat longer than the others it was constructed from an oblong circle of poles that had been pushed into the ground and then bent over one another to make a domed frame which then had been covered with sheets of bark and skins. Inside the longhouse were platforms of poles on either side that were used as beds. In the center smoke rose from a fire and disappeared through an opening in the roof. Corn and herbs hung from the roof, and it smelled as though some pungent herb had been burned in the fire probably to ward off disease. There on one of the beds lay Chinkwe with his eyes closed. Dr. Clark gently lifted the blanket covering Chinkwe and examined his leg. The wound itself was indeed just a small puncture on the foot. But from the wound all the way up to the calf the leg the signs of necrosis were unmistakable.

"I am afraid the lower part of the leg must come off as quickly as possible," Dr. Clark announced solemnly, "Otherwise the necrosis will just continue spreading until it kills him."

Okwes nodded sadly, "I was afraid that might be necessary. Let us get it over with."

Dr. Clark with the help of Nathaniel and the Indians quickly constructed a make-shift operating table out of saplings lashed together and covered with blankets. Gently they picked up Chinkwe and moved him onto the table. Although conscious, Chinkwe uttered not a sound and seemed to be in a kind of trance.

"Now, Nathaniel, time is of the essence in every amputation," instructed Dr. Clark, "With or without opium, the pain is intense, and you want to minimize the time the patient has to endure it. The first step is to apply the screw tourniquet directly above the place where the amputation is to occur. In this case it will be in the middle of the upper leg because we will amputate just above the knee. The tourniquet will stop the bleeding long enough so that I can amputate without his hemorrhaging to death. After the tourniquet is tightened, I will cut through the flesh down to the bone with a scalpel. Then you will pull back the flesh back with a leather thong so I can saw off the leg in such a way as to avoid a pointed stump. After the leg is removed, I will use the tenaculum to pull out each artery which you will then tie off with a small length of fine rawhide. Once all arteries have been tied off, we apply herbs and bandage the stump."

Nathaniel nodded. They had already gone through the steps before, and Nathaniel had practiced both with the operation of the screw tourniquet and tying the knots in the rawhide strips. Dr. Clark, however, believed that repetition was the key to learning, so he always went through the steps of every procedure one more time before actually doing it. Nathaniel considered Dr. Clark's teaching methods to be helpful and reassuring.

Nathaniel carefully slipped the screw tourniquet over Chinkwe's leg and brought it up to the level suggested by Dr. Clark. He began slowly to tighten the screw and continued until Dr. Clark signaled that it was tight enough. The next steps went by in rapid succession. It seemed to take only seconds for Dr. Clark to make incisions around the leg down to the bone. He then fitted a leather strap on the flesh of the upper part of the leg and handed the ends to Nathaniel. Nathaniel used the strap to pull the flesh up out of the way of the amputation saw. Dr. Clark had the bone sawed through almost as fast as he had made the incisions. Then he pulled out each important blood vessel and held it extended while Nathaniel tied it off. All the time

Chinkwe lay rigid with his eyes closed. Nathaniel was not certain if he was in a coma or some kind of a trance. Fortunately, the entire operation was completed in a matter of minutes and Chinkwe seemed abruptly to relax his muscles.

Applying the bandages around the stump Dr. Clark said to Okwes, "He is going to sleep for days now but I think he will recover well. After the wound has healed for a few months, we can fit a wooden leg for him."

"You and your assistant have our sincere thanks," responded Okwes, "What would you have in return?"

"Oh, just the usual," answered Dr. Clark, "My supply of those wound-healing herbs of yours has run low. If you can replenish my store, that would be fair compensation for our efforts."

"We will be happy to oblige," agreed Okwes, "but we will need to deliver it in several parts because some of the herbs are not available right now."

"No problem at all," said Dr. Clark, "I still have some left and we will see each other again in a few months when we come by to check on Chinkwe's leg. By the way have your people had cases of the pox? I believe we inoculated most of them a few years ago."

"The older ones were inoculated but the younger people not yet," replied Okwes.

"Then we should plan on doing that soon as well," suggested Dr. Clark, "Especially if they are volunteering for military service. Army camps are crawling with disease."

"God's grace upon you for all your help and wisdom, Dr. William," Okwes said gratefully.

After a hearty meal of venison, corn, and squash, Dr. Clark and Nathaniel mounted up for the long ride back to Monmouth Courthouse. As they waved goodbye to the Lenape, Nathaniel felt tired but at the same time exhilarated. They had saved an otherwise doomed man and at the same time demonstrated Christian solidarity with Brainerd's Indian community. This gave Nathaniel a feeling of immense satisfaction. He felt grateful that his profession would afford him such opportunities to do God's work.

The beatific glow on Nathaniel's features did not go unnoticed by Dr. Clark.

"You are obviously made for this work, Nathaniel," Dr. Clark, "You assisted me very well today and handled the strain of a major operation with admirable calm. The challenge even seemed to heighten your concentration."

"It did, indeed, sir," answered Nathaniel, "I was greatly impressed by the skill and speed with which you handled the amputation. It was very fascinating. I only hope that I will master these techniques one day."

"Repetition is the mother of all science," assured Dr. Clark, "Now that you know how it is done, you just need to take every chance to hone your skills. You may in fact soon be getting those chances more often since King George finally declared war on the French last May. The only good thing about war is that young doctors get a lot of practice."

Nathaniel's mood of exhilaration quickly dissipated at the thought of a major war, of the many casualties like Chinkwe that would result and of the fate of his friends and relatives.

"What Okwes told us about Chinkwe's experiences in the north is not very encouraging," remarked Nathaniel, "it sounds as though the French are consolidating their position and winning many allies among the Indians."

"Many Indian tribes fear that the rising number of British settlers trying to expand westward are a threat to their way of life," explained Dr. Clark, "The French are mostly interested in the fur trade and less in farming. That makes the French useful partners and less of a threat for the Indians. If we are going to meet this challenge, the mother country will need to send over more regular troops. With local militias alone we are unlikely to prevail."

At the mention of the word "militia" Nathaniel saw an opportunity to shift the conversation to the subject of the Anderson family to find out what intelligence the good doctor might offer.

"I drilled regularly with the militia in Newark when I was studying full time at the college," Nathaniel mentioned, "Perhaps I should seek out the local militia in Manalapan. I assume that the owners of the major estates such as the Andersons take the initiative in organizing militia units in the area of Manalapan and Monmouth Courthouse."

"It is certainly true that all civic activities depend on support from the leading families," agreed Dr. Clark, "Nothing in Manalapan happens if Kenneth Anderson is against it. I can ask him what the status is of militia activities in Manalapan, if you like. He and his family have been patients of mine for years. "

"I would be pleased to have the honor of meeting Mr. Anderson," Nathaniel replied quickly, "It would be interesting to learn how the leading gentlemen of our area view the current crisis."

"Kenneth Anderson is an interesting man, very well read and a fervent Whig," continued Dr. Clark, "he is convinced that independent landed gentlemen like himself are the bedrock upon which British liberties rest. Although his father was a member of the royal council of New Jersey for years, he believes that state power concentrated in a centralized administration is a danger to the freedoms achieved by the Glorious Revolution of 1688. He is also a loyal member of Reverend Tennent's reformed church and, therefore, suspicious of efforts by the Anglican hierarchy to establish hegemony in the colonies."

Nathaniel was pleasantly surprised and pleased to hear that Kenneth Anderson's political orientation was not so very different from his own.

"I had imagined that such a prominent landowner would have tended more toward Tory views," mused Nathaniel, "Did he not receive his lands by the grace of the Proprietors who in turn based their claims on a royal grant?"

"I doubt that Kenneth Anderson sees his property rights as dependent on any-one other than God Almighty," replied Dr. Clark, "His father acquired vast amounts of property in exchange for services rendered to the Proprietors, but he insisted on receiving them as a freeholder without any further obligations. Kenneth Anderson inherited those contracts and manages his estate as its uncontested lawful owner. Nei-ther the Proprietors nor any others can lay claims on his lands. He has never been involved in any land disputes and does not take sides in those matters other than that he believes in the rule of law and the protection of property rights."

All this was very encouraging for Nathaniel to hear. Isabella's father sounded like a reasonable and fair-minded person. Nathaniel looked forward to meeting him now with much less apprehension than he had previously felt.

"He probably is not that involved in militia matters because he has no sons," continued Dr. Clark, "he has a lovely daughter, however, who is the apple of his eye. But perhaps because he has no male heirs, he is giving her a very unconventional upbringing. She has received an education more fit for a son and is disconcertingly self-confident. The young man who marries her will have his hands full."

Nathaniel smiled to himself at this revelation. It made perfect sense consider-ing the character traits Nathaniel had already experienced. Isabella had been raised a princess in an enlightened intellectual environment. Wooing her might turn out to be a challenge but the prize was all the more desirable.

Chapter 4

MORVEN – 1756

NATHANIEL SAT IN THE library of the College of New Jersey which was still located in the parsonage of Reverend Aaron Burr in Newark although it would soon be moved to the new building in Princeton. True to her promise Isabella had gotten Annis Boudinot to send him an invitation to a ball to be held at Morven, the estate of her future in-laws in Princeton. Nathaniel had just read the contents of the invitation to his friend, Benjamin Prime.

"Cheers, Natty, you are moving up in the world," quipped Benjamin, "that soiree will be attended by everyone of prominence both in New Jersey and from New York and Philadelphia as well. The Stockton family is one of the most influential in the middle colonies."

Benjamin's words elicited a numb feeling of inadequacy on the part of Nathaniel. He had never attended anything even remotely comparable and had no idea what was expected of him.

"I am afraid this could be a disaster, Benjie," Nathaniel gloomily predicted, "I would not even know how to begin the dances that are performed at balls. Dancing is considered to be a work of the Devil among my religious relatives."

"Luckily for you," smiled Benjamin, "your best friend is a poet and we poets know about such things. In addition, now that I am officially a tutor at the college, I will be able to get myself on the invitation list as well so you will not have to go there alone."

"Do you really know how to dance things as the gavotte and the minuet?" asked Nathaniel incredulously, "Where did you have occasion to learn such frivolity?"

"As I said," continued Benjamin airily, "poetry is about music and dancing is about moving in time with music, so all these things are closely related. We will concentrate on the minuet. That is danced the most frequently. If you can learn to do the basic steps, you can avoid seeming totally out of place at the ball. The first thing to know is that minuets are in three-quarters time. You simply walk through various patterns dipping your arms in time to the music."

At that point Benjamin began to chant in ¾ tact while moving in a circle and raising and lowering his arms to the beat. Nathaniel watched with awe as his friend moved around the library really looking as though he knew how to dance a minuet.

"The basic minuet step-combination consists of four steps," instructed Benjamin, "you begin with a plié on your left foot rising to the ball of your right foot on beat 1, then straighten both legs, heels close together. Then you do the same thing beginning with your right foot. Keep the legs straight, walk forward on the ball of your right foot and then your left foot on beats 4 and 5. On beat six, sink into plié with the left foot flat. Then you start again on beat one, rising to ball of right foot and everything is repeated."

Benjamin demonstrated the basic foot walk while Nathaniel watched with fascination.

"Once you have practiced the basic steps, you need to learn the most important patterns," Benjamin continued in his best didactic manner, "you will start off facing Isabella on the dance floor in a rectangular space in which you will dance the figures. Then you bow to her and turn and bow to the audience. The dance consists of a fixed set of figures: a lead-in figure, a Z figure, a right-hand turn, a left-hand turn and a two-hand turn with ending. You begin with the lead-in figure in which both dancers curve sideways to meet at the back of the space and then walk to the middle holding inside hands. You then whirl Isabella around three-quarters of a turn and then both of you dance sideways to the corner of the space. This is followed by a Z figure in which both of you dance sideways to the other corner and then cross diagonally through the middle of the space, changing corners and then sideways to each other's previous corner. Then comes the right-hand turn in which you dance sideways from one corner to the other and then diagonally to meet grasping each other with the right hands turning around and dancing back to the corner. This is followed by another Z figure, a left-hand turn like the right-hand turn, another Z figure and an ending with a two-hand turn. It is just those few basic figures that are always punctuated by one or more Z figures. It is all quite simple if you grasp the symmetry of it."

Nathaniel was furiously taking notes and wondering if there was any way he could master such complexity in time for the ball.

"It is all a matter of geometry," reassured Benjamin, "Just try to understand the basic principles and then let the music guide you. Actually, let Isabella guide you. If you just try smoothly to anticipate all her movements, it will look as though you know what you are doing. Here try to do one sequence of the basic figures."

Overcoming his shyness Nathaniel began to follow Benjamin's movements around the library. Just as he thought he was beginning to discern the patterns that Benjamin had explained, the door to the library opened abruptly and Esther Burr entered the room with a glowering look on her face.

"Whatever is this noise I hear," she demanded indignantly, "I thought someone had brought horses into the library. It has woken up my baby."

"Benjamin was just explaining to me the patterns of…" stammered Nathaniel.

"A dance, are you discussing a dance?" interrupted Esther Burr incredulously, "Is this what pious scholars are using their time for in the library these days? I am sure that Reverend Burr will be dismayed to hear what progress the Devil is making among the students of the College of New Jersey!"

After that abrupt outburst Esther Burr turned on her heel and stalked out of the library. Nathaniel glanced sheepishly at Benjamin stricken by the thought of the damage that this incident might do to his reputation at the college.

As Nathaniel looked questioningly at Benjamin, a smile began to form slowly on Benjamin's face.

"Not to worry, Natty," said Benjamin lightly, "Esther is just annoyed that you work up her noisy brat. Just be sure to take those notes and practice the figures before the ball. The people there are more likely to be impressed by your dancing abilities than by your piousness. And besides, I will be there to give you moral support."

The Harvest Moon Ball took place on a warm September evening. As Benjamin and Nathaniel, dressed in their best outfits, approached the Stockton residence they could see a gathering of people on the lawn in front of the large mansion. Black servants in elegant suits greeted the arriving guests, some helping them to dismount and taking their horses to the stables, others escorting the guests toward the house. Nathaniel said a silent prayer of thanks that Benjamin was there with him. Had he been alone, he was sure that he would have been seized by an urgent desire to bolt from the scene. He had never been to such an event before and he found it quite unnerving. Benjamin, however, acted as though he did this kind of thing on regular basis. Whether or not that was true, his display of nonchalant self-confidence soothed Nathaniel's nerves.

After they dismounted and the servants lead their horses away, an officious head servant asked for their invitations and scrutinized them carefully.

"Please follow me for your introduction to the hosts," he instructed Nathaniel and Benjamin in a haughty tone.

He then led them both toward the mansion where an elderly lady and gentleman were greeting a line of visitors lined up before the door. Nathaniel and Benjamin assumed that this couple was John and Abigail Stockton, the owners of Morven and parents of Richard Stockton. Taking their place in line Nathaniel and Benjamin watched as the head servant took their invitations to another servant standing next to Mr. and Mrs. Stockton whose apparent function was to announce each visitor.

When at last Nathaniel and Benjamin came to the front of the line, the servant read from the invitations, "Mr. Benjamin Prime, Tutor at the College of New Jersey, and Mr. Nathaniel Scudder, Student at the College of New Jersey."

Following the example of the people who had proceed them Nathaniel and Benjamin removed their hats and made a low bow to the hosts.

"Welcome to Morven, gentlemen," greeted John Stockton with a friendly smile, "We are pleased to have the pleasure of your company. We are always happy to meet people associated with our son's alma mater. "

"Mr. and Mrs. Stockton, it is an honor to be here and to make your acquaintance," responded Benjamin with practiced savoir faire.

"It is an honor for me as well," added Nathaniel quickly hoping that this was the appropriate thing for him to say.

"We hope you enjoy the evening," said Mrs. Stockton and gesturing to another servant behind her, "James here will introduce you to the other guests."

As the servant James led Nathaniel and Benjamin into the mansion, the first people they ran into were the young couple whose engagement was to be officially announced that evening, Annis Boudinot and Richard Stockton. Richard Stockton immediately recognized Nathaniel and Benjamin from his visits to the College of New Jersey although he had graduated three years earlier than they.

"A hearty welcome to my fellow alumni," greeted Richard pleasantly, "Let me introduce you to my fiancée, Miss Annis Boudinot. Annis, these are Mr. Benjamin Prime and Mr. Nathaniel Scudder, two graduates of my alma mater."

Again, Nathaniel and Benjamin made a low bow to the couple.

"As always, I am very pleased to meet scholars from my husband's college," smiled Annis prettily, carefully scrutinizing Nathaniel as the person she knew to be Isabella's ardent admirer.

"I was very gratified to receive the invitation," replied Nathaniel, charmed by the elegance of Isabella's girlfriend and hoping earnestly that he was passing muster.

"It is particularly delightful for me to meet a fellow poet," added Benjamin, "I hope I will have the opportunity to hear you recite your works at some point."

"A poet, as well as a scholar," replied Annis with a smile that seemed to reveal a secret agenda, "The College of New Jersey never ceases to impress. Perhaps we will have the opportunity to exchange ideas on the subject of versifying. But first I would like to take over from James and introduce both of you to some others I am sure you would like to meet."

At this point the servant James deferred to Annis with a polite nod as she led Benjamin and Nathaniel further into the mansion in the direction of an older couple standing in the corner of the drawing room. In the meantime, Richard Stockton was already in the process of greeting a different set of guests. The couple toward which Annis was heading was listening to a dapper-looking younger man accompanied by a very fashionably dressed young woman. Nathaniel was completely mesmerized both by the beautiful interior of Morven as well as by the elegance of the guests in attendance.

"The older couple over there is from your area of Monmouth County, Mr. Scudder. They are Kenneth and Hannah Anderson. Perhaps you know them?" asked Annis, smiling archly, "The two people they are listening to are William Franklin and his fiancée, Elizabeth Graeme. William is the son of the famous scientist and publisher, Benjamin Franklin. Elizabeth is the daughter of Dr. Graeme."

Lowering her voice Annis added in a conspiratorial tone, "William and Elizabeth would like to get married soon as well but their parents are discouraging it.".

Nathaniel felt a surge of excitement as he realized that Annis and Isabella had obviously colluded to set up an opportunity for him to meet her parents. As he and Benjamin followed Annis toward the area where they were standing, he could hear William Franklin holding forth on the challenges that the war with France would bring for the colonies.

"I see no alternative but a significant increase in the deployment of Regulars," Franklin was saying, "Obviously our militias are not up to the task of keeping the French in check. Our navy is doing a good job but there are limits to what a volunteer militia can accomplish."

"The Jersey militia have acquitted themselves quite well in past conflicts," replied Kenneth Anderson somewhat testily, "I am apprehensive what a standing army of Regulars might mean for our English freedoms. It will cost vast amounts of money and be outside the control of our local assemblies. In my opinion, one of the greatest guarantees of freedom offered by the Bill of Rights of 1688 was that a standing army cannot be established without parliamentary approval. There are good reasons to fear an army too far removed from the control of our institutions."

"But the Regulars would be stationed here only with the approval of Parliament," objected Franklin, "And besides, the provinces have been reluctant to muster the number of militiamen that would be needed to do the job."

"The recruitment problems have something to do with the royal proclamation of 1754 that made all provincial officers junior in rank to all regular officers. That means that a provincial colonel like me would have to take commands from some fuzz-faced redcoat ensign. That is hardly likely to encourage experienced militiamen to volunteer. In addition, if Parliament wants us to foot the bill, it would be appropriate to seek the approval of our local legislatures," responded Anderson, "British subjects must take responsibility for guaranteeing their own freedoms and people here are represented only in our assemblies and not in Parliament."

At that point Annis arrived with Nathaniel and Benjamin and waited politely for a break in the conversation. Anderson and Franklin paused and turned with a smile toward Annis.

"Please excuse the interruption, ladies and gentlemen," said Annis, "But I would like to introduce two of our latest arrivals. May I present Mr. Benjamin Prime, recently appointed tutor at the College of New Jersey and Mr. Nathaniel Scudder, Assistant to Dr. Clark of Monmouth County and a graduate of the same institution. Nathaniel,

Benjamin please meet Colonel and Mrs. Kenneth Anderson, Miss Elizabeth Graeme and Mr. William Franklin."

Bowing again Nathaniel and Benjamin said almost simultaneously, "A pleasure to make your acquaintance."

"I have already had the pleasure of meeting young Master Scudder," Hannah Anderson said. Turning to her husband she added, "This is the young man I told you about who rescued Isabella and me when our horses bolted in front of the meeting house."

Turning his attention to Nathaniel, Colonel Anderson said, "Well, let me express my gratitude for your gallant assistance of my wife and daughter. It is a pleasure to meet both of you, particularly William Clark's assistant. Dr. Clark has been our family doctor for years. How did you come to be his assistant, Nathaniel?"

"Reverend Tennent is a trustee of my college where I am finishing up my master's degree. When he heard that I planned to become a physician, he suggested that I seek an internship with Dr. Clark," answered Nathaniel, "Dr. Clark agreed to accept me as his assistant, so I took up temporary lodging near Monmouth Courthouse. I work with him most of the time and visit the college now and again to continue work on my master's degree. I hope to finish both courses of study within the next year or so."

"I am glad to hear that Dr. Clark is training a well-educated assistant," Colonel Anderson continued, "He is getting on in years and it is difficult to find a doctor you can trust. Perhaps you will be able to succeed him one day as Monmouth County's favorite physician."

"I still have so much to learn," replied Nathaniel with an abashed expression, "But Dr. Clark is a wonderful teacher, and I would be honored to be able someday to follow in his footsteps."

Smiling his approval of what he considered to be the appropriateness of Nathaniel's modesty, Colonel Anderson continued, "In fact, it seems to me that I have seen you at Reverend Tennent's meeting house on some occasion. Can that be?"

"Oh yes, indeed," answered Nathaniel, "If I am in Monmouth on a Sabbath, I always try to come and hear Reverend Tennent's sermon. He is held in great esteem by the president of my college, Reverend Burr, and we students are strongly encouraged to pay heed to his spiritual guidance."

"In that case, we will undoubtedly be seeing you more often," interjected Hannah Anderson, "We have also great supporters of Reverend Tennent's congregation."

Nathaniel smiled politely in agreement thinking to himself with immense pleasure that the introduction could not have gone better. He marveled at the efficiency with which the two young ladies, Isabella and Annis, had engineered this meeting. At the same time, he could sense some vague feeling of apprehension about having been a pawn, albeit a willing one, in someone's else's plan. That could, however, not diminish the exhilaration he felt due to the rapid progress of his relationship with Isabella.

Her obviously having taken the initiative in this project was proof of her genuine interest in him, a fact that he found almost overwhelming.

Quickly noticing the dazed and blissful look that was settling on Nathaniel's features Benjamin tried to keep the conversation clicking along before the other participants began to wonder what could be affecting young Master Scudder.

"I am also planning to become a physician, but I would prefer to go back to the mother country and find out what the state of medicine is there," Benjamin announced to the group in general.

"What a coincidence," said William Franklin, "I am planning the very same thing, but in the field of law, rather than medicine. When are you going?"

"I have not made concrete plans yet," answered Benjamin, "I have just taken a position as a tutor at the college. I would like to try this for a year or two before continuing my education in Britain."

"I want to leave as soon as possible," announced Franklin, and smiling in the direction of Elizabeth Graeme, "Just as soon as I can get this lovely lady to be my wife."

A cloud crossing the features of Elizabeth Graeme seemed to indicate that this topic was somehow fraught with tension. "Your father's critical articles about the Pennsylvania Proprietors are certainly not conducive to that end," Elizabeth remarked with a touch of bitterness in her voice, "Many of my father's business associates take them as a personal affront. Hardly a good basis for nuptial negotiations."

Quickly changing the topic of conversation, Franklin attempted to pick up where he had left off in his discussion with Colonel Anderson.

"Colonel Anderson, do you really think the New Jersey militia can rise to the challenge that Governor Belcher has posed with his offer of assistance against the French?" asked Franklin.

"If everyone is as conscious of his duties as young Shippen here," answered Anderson turning with a smile to the young man in the militia uniform who was approaching them. "Joseph Shippen has just been commissioned a captain in the Pennsylvania militia. If we can get more young men to follow his example, we should be able to handle the situation on our own."

Nathaniel feeling somewhat defensive, quickly informed the group, "All of us at the college of New Jersey drill regularly with the militia in Newark. Now that the college is moving to Princeton town, we will probably have to change units, but I am sure that all the students stand ready and willing to do their duty."

"In that case, you can continue right down in Monmouth. Our militia drills once a month and we look forward to having you in our unit. You are probably down there now most of the time with Dr. Clark?" asked Anderson.

"I would be honored," answered Nathaniel, delighted once again for an additional opportunity to build his relationship with the Andersons, "Dr. Clark and I just performed a leg amputation on a Lenape warrior who was with the Jersey militia in Oswego. It made me very aware of the dire dangers we face. I am ready to help wherever I can. Dr. Clark says, however, that more soldiers die of diseases than are shot in the field and I would, therefore, be able to make myself most useful by finishing my medical education."

"Dr. Clark is right, of course, but the one activity does not exclude the other," said Colonel Anderson, "I am sure he will have nothing against giving up your assistance for a day a month to drill with my militia. By the way, when you were treating the Lenape warrior, did you learn any details about the events in Oswego?"

"The warrior was suffering severely so he could not talk himself. But apparently, it was quite a disaster according to the warrior's father who said the garrison surrendered too quickly having been promised safe passage but then many were butchered by drunk Indians and French soldiers. The warrior was lucky he managed to escape," replied Nathaniel.

"This kind of news needs to be circulated more effectively to the inhabitants of this colony," Colonel Anderson said angrily, "Perhaps if they would understand what atrocities await them at the hands of the French Papists and their heathen allies, they might be keener to do their patriotic duties with the militia."

"Maybe they would also be less willing to trade with the enemy," added William Franklin, casting an accusing glance in the direction of William Livingston who was standing on the other side of the room with his wife, Susannah. "Now that we are officially at war with the French, perhaps Livingston Manor will put an end to its lucrative trade with the French. As a lawyer and colleague of Richard Stockton, I would think that Lawyer Livingston would not want to be in flagrant violation of British law."

"Quite so, quite so," agreed Colonel Anderson, "But with the French willing to pay much higher prices for farm produce, many will continue to be tempted."

"Another good argument for more Regulars," responded Franklin with a smile, "the better to enforce British law in the lawless parts of this continent."

At that point Nathaniel's heart skipped a beat because he saw Isabella accompanied by another young lady, a teenage boy, and a young man approaching the group.

"Here comes my little brother, Elias," announced Annis, "Of course, in the company of two lovely ladies, Isabella Anderson, and my future sister-in-law, Hannah Stockton. Elias has just begun his legal apprenticeship with Richard. The second young man is Josiah Ogden who has just finished his degree at the college and also plans to go into the law profession."

"Following in the footsteps of his father, David, no doubt," remarked William Franklin.

At the mention of the name Ogden Nathaniel felt a surge of misgiving. David Ogden was a wealthy lawyer of the upper-class Anglican faction in Newark and famous for his defense of the property rights of the Proprietors to the chagrin of all Presbyterian yeomen. His son was just the sort of wealthy young aristocrat that the Andersons probably hoped their daughter would marry one day. He wondered if young Ogden had designs on the girl of his dreams. His anxiety was quickly dissipated when Isabella arrived and flashed a refulgent smile in his direction. It was obvious, at least to the younger people present, that sparks were flying between the two.

Again seeking to distract the people from Nathaniel and Isabella before the mutual infatuation became too apparent, Benjamin quipped, "It seems that we have an abundance of lawyers here this evening. There must be a nest somewhere."

"Indeed, there is no shortage of lawyers in this province," agreed Colonel Anderson with a critical glance at William Franklin, "And it would be helpful if they all were more interested in promoting British rights than in finding ways to contest the propriety rights of honest yeomen on behalf of speculators."

"My father would certainly agree with you on that point," replied Franklin with a consensual smile.

Their conversation was interrupted by the ringing sound made by a slave tapping a glass with a silver spoon. The hosts having finished greeting the last arriving guests walked to the center of the room.

Smiling right and left to the assembled visitors John Stockton said, "Honored guests, Abigail and I are very pleased to welcome you all here at Morven. As you know, we have organized this Harvest Moon Ball to announce officially the upcoming marriage of our son, Richard Stockton, to the charming and talented Annis Boudinot."

Spontaneous applause erupted from the assemblage as all the guests nodded and smiled in the direction of the young couple. Servants circulated with trays of filled wine glasses which they distributed to the guests.

Taking one of the glasses John Stockton continued, "I would like you to join me now in raising your glasses to the health, happiness, and nuptial bliss of the betrothed."

"To the betrothed!" responded the crowd almost in unison.

"Regarding the evening's activities," continued Stockton, "You are first invited to enjoy the culinary delights our kitchen has prepared for you. Then we will proceed to the musical part of the evening. We have the good fortune to have with us this evening Mr. William Franklin, one of the organizers of the Philadelphia Dancing Assemblies to lead the way to the dance floor."

John Stockton taking the hand of his wife then led the group into a dining room with a long table. He and his wife took their seats at the head of the table and motioned to the guests to be seated on either side. Richard Stockton and Annis Boudinot sat down at the opposite end of the table. The servants had already placed numerous dishes with all kinds of delectable courses down the middle of the table. Nathaniel and Benjamin sat down on one side of the table. To Nathaniel's great delight Isabella seated herself next to him. The rest of the guests distributed themselves among the other open seats. Nathaniel was almost faint with pleasure. He could scarcely believe he was sitting here in this elegant ambiance next to the girl of his dreams together with some of the most influential people in the middle colonies.

"I had an interesting conversation with your father," he began, "he encouraged me to drill with the Monmouth militia now that I am spending more time in your area than at the college."

"Father never misses an opportunity to promote the militia," responded Isabella, "I will look out for you at the next drill which usually happens on or near our estate."

This explicit expression of interest encouraged Nathaniel to reveal his own feelings. Since the buzz of conversation of the many guests was now loud enough to prevent others from hearing his words, he lowered his voice and said earnestly to Isabella, "Nothing would delight me more than having the opportunity to see you very frequently."

Smiling with satisfaction at Nathaniel's obvious infatuation Isabella began to survey the many courses on the table. "The Stocktons are marvelous hosts, don't you think?" Isabella asked.

"Marvelous indeed," murmured Nathaniel distractedly, food being the very last thing on his mind.

The next hour went by in a flash. The guests made polite conversation as they sampled the various delicacies of the Stockton kitchen. Nathaniel could barely pay attention to what was being said as he savored the magical feeling of being close to Isabella. At length, the sound of a servant tapping a glass again brought Nathaniel out of his revery.

John Stockton rose again from his seat and addressed the guests, "As I noted earlier, we have the pleasure of the company of William Franklin this evening, one of the founders of the Philadelphia Dancing Assemblies. He is well-versed us the latest European dancing fashions so I will ask him to lead us all in the musical part of the evening. Ladies and Gentlemen, if you will all just follow him and Miss Graeme to the next room."

William Franklin stood up and bowed gallantly to Elizabeth Graeme and then taking her hand led her into the adjoining room where a small orchestra was set up to play. The other couples followed lining up on either side of the room with ladies and gentlemen facing each other. Nathaniel and Isabella followed third after Richard Stockton and Annis Boudinot. Facing Isabella across the room Nathaniel realized with trepidation that he would only have two examples to observe before he had to risk his newly acquired knowledge on the dance floor. As the orchestra began to play, William Franklin and Elizabeth Graeme bowed gracefully to each other and went smoothly through the figures that Benjamin had tried to explain to Nathaniel. To Nathaniel's relief it did not in fact look that difficult. After the first two dancers had finished their formations, the second couple, Richard Stockton and Annis Boudinot, bowed to each other and repeated the same patterns as the first couple. Nathaniel noted to his satisfaction that Richard Stockton was not quite as well-versed in the dancing art as William Franklin had been. Perfection was, therefore, mercifully, not expected. Nathaniel also recalled Benjamin's advice to try subtly to follow Isabella's lead. When their turn to bow to each other came, Nathaniel was beginning to warm to the challenge. His unbelievable good fortune to be here tonight with beautiful Isabella among some of the most influential people of the middle provinces he felt was a sure sign of benevolent Providence. As he faced Isabella, he felt a surge of energy arise in him imbuing him a self-confidence that he would not have expected. He smiled and bowed toward Isabella and let himself be transported by the gentle sounds of the orchestra. After what seemed to be a very short period, he found himself back at the end of the line facing Isabella. Judging by the approving smile on her face, the dance must have been a success. He glanced over to Benjamin on the sidelines who was smiling his satisfaction with his trainee's progress.

After the dance was over, the couples re-mingled with the other guests. Nathaniel flushed with his success at his first encounter with people of such high social standing became uncharacteristically extroverted. He, Isabella, Benjamin, Richard Stockton and Annis Boudinot became the center of a constantly shifting group of talkative guests. Nathaniel was introduced to William Alexander, the wealthy son of James Alexander, the head of the New Jersey Board of Proprietors. He met Richard's friend from Monmouth County, John Covenhoven. He had a long talk about the new building for the college with Peter Livingston, an undergraduate also from the wealthy Livingston clan of New York. Isabella proved very adept at promoting exchanges by introducing people, charmingly soliciting different opinions and interjecting a clever repartee now and again.

Everyone was having such a wonderful time that it was with great disappointment that Nathaniel noticed Colonel Anderson signaling to Isabella by pointing to his watch.

Turning to Nathaniel and smiling prettily Isabella said, "I am afraid it is time to go. I hope you had an interesting time at the ball."

"I have never had such a wonderful time in my life," answered Nathaniel enthusiastically, "Thank you so much for making this possible. I hope I will have the pleasure of your company again soon?"

"At the latest after Reverend Tennent's service next Sunday," proposed Isabella.

"I would not miss it for the world," Nathaniel called after her as she walked away in the direction of her parents.

Chapter 5

SCUDDER'S MILLS – 1756

AFTER THANKING THE STOCKTONS for their gracious hospitality, Nathaniel and Benjamin left Morven in the direction of Nassau Hall, the new building that was soon to house the College of New Jersey. Benjamin as a tutor had a room in the vicinity of the building. Nathaniel was planning to continue on to his parents' home just outside of Princeton to stay overnight before returning to Monmouth Courthouse the next day. Benjamin took the opportunity to begin a discussion of "lessons learned" with Nathaniel whom he now considered his apprentice in the skills of social climbing.

"I must say, Natty, you did very well tonight," commented Benjamin, "One would never have thought that that was the first time in your life you had ever seen a dance floor."

"It was Isabella's enchanting presence," answered Nathaniel dreamily, "It was the kind of evening when anything could be possible."

"It was my outstanding instruction," corrected Benjamin sternly, "And you will need more of it if you are going to follow up on the opportunities presented to you this evening. If you want to be successful in your courtship of Isabella, you will have to learn to feel at ease with people of this level of society. You do realize that some of the richest and most influential people in the middle provinces were there tonight, don't you?"

"Of course, I do," replied Nathaniel defensively, "I think I must have met almost everyone there this evening. They all seemed most charming."

"Well, you need to look behind the scenes and see how the various people fit into the power politics of these provinces. Take young Franklin, for instance—he is dying to marry the lovely Elizabeth, but her father won't have him because Franklin's father, Benjamin, keeps writing nasty articles about the Pennsylvania Proprietors of whom Elizabeth's father is a glowing supporter."

"Ah, now I understand what that tense exchange between William Franklin and Elizabeth Graeme before the dance was all about," said Nathaniel.

"Old Franklin is right about the Pennsylvania Proprietors, William Penn was a decent fellow, but his sons are scoundrels who stop at nothing to swindle the Indians out of their property rights. The so-called 'Walking Purchase' that they organized was probably the biggest land theft in the history of the colonies," explained Benjamin, "Unfortunately Elizabeth's father is one of their investors, so he does not want to see their dirty wash exposed in the press."

"So William has to choose between loyalty to his father and love for Elizabeth," concluded Nathaniel sadly, thinking how such a conflict of loyalties could well be part of his own future.

"The Franklins would like to see the Pennsylvania Proprietors replaced by a royal government, the same way it happened here in New Jersey at the beginning of this century," continued Benjamin.

"But that did not end the power of the New Jersey Proprietors here," countered Nathaniel, "They still try to claim the lands of farmers who have paid for their farms legitimately and work the soil with their own hands. My father even worries that someday some lawyer will show up at his door with a claim on his mills or his land although he bought both legally a few years ago."

"Yes," agreed Benjamin, "So much in this country revolves around greed for land. The proprietors swindle the yeomen, the yeomen swindle the Indians. Some swindle everyone they can. And everybody exploits the African slaves who are the ones who actually do most of the work. Take William Alexander, for instance, his father James Alexander was for years the biggest land speculator in the colony. That's how they got so rich. William now wants to live like a lord. He even claims title to the Earldom of Stirling. He is building a feudal manor at Basking Ridge complete with its own deer park. Or young Ogden whose father has the law firm where Richard Stockton works. That law firm is specialized in pursuing land claims litigation against Presbyterian yeomen. Or the Livingstons, two of whom were there tonight. That family owns a huge plantation in New York with dozens of slaves and makes a fortune out of selling contraband to the French in Canada."

"How is that possible?" asked Nathaniel indignantly, "That is treason, isn't it?"

"It is now that we are officially at war with the French," explained Benjamin, "But they don't actually sell directly to the French. They sell to the Iroquois who then sell to the French. The Iroquois love to play the British and the French off against each other. Of course, many merchants sell to the French because they pay the best prices, and it is easy to ship contraband from myriad small American harbors to French controlled areas. Our new British commander here, Lord Loudoun, would have to embargo all outgoing shipping if he wanted to put an end to that."

"I hope he does not decide to do that," said Nathaniel, "Dr. Clark gets much of his medical supplies from privateers along the coast. They are our main source of opium and of Peruvian bark, the best medicine against fevers. In fact, we are scheduled to make a foray there soon to resupply our medicine chest."

"And so you see, everyone has some reason for breaking the rules," noted Benjamin wryly, "At the end of the day, we are all sinners and can only hope that we will be saved by God's grace even though we don't deserve it."

"On that note I will say goodnight, Benjamin," said Nathaniel, "And many thanks for the background information you have provided me with. It will be a great help navigating the treacherous shoals of New Jersey society. But tomorrow I have an even more difficult mission—I have to explain to my parents that I love a young lady who is undoubtedly quite different from their expectations of the ideal daughter-in-law."

"Good luck with that, Natty," replied Benjamin smiling and doffing his hat as he turned his horse in the direction of his rooming house, "You will need all the rhetorical skills you learned at college for that task."

Smiling farewell to Benjamin, Nathaniel continued on his way to Scudder's Mill a few miles away from Princeton. He was looking forward to seeing his parents and brothers and sisters. They would be asleep at this time in the evening, but he would see them all early the next morning at breakfast. They knew that he had been invited to the home of a prominent family and would be very interested in what he had to report. He struggled to develop a strategy for explaining how he had come to be invited and for breaking the news of his love for Isabella.

As he approached the mill, he saw that a candle was still burning in his old room that he shared with his 17-year-old brother, William. Nathaniel quietly tethered his horse in the stable and proceeded as quietly as he could to his room where he found his brother wide awake.

"Tell me, how was it, Natty?" asked William in an excited whisper.

"It was magnificent, Will," answered Nathaniel, lying down on his bed and blowing out the candle, "But I will tell you all about it in the morning. We don't want to wake our parents. I want father to be well-rested and in a good mood tomorrow when I tell him about my future plans."

With a disappointed sigh William turned over and was soon snoring, while Nathaniel stayed awake for hours thinking about Isabella and how he would explain to his parents that he had found the love of his life.

As befitting hard-working Presbyterians, the Scudder family rose at first light and were already sitting around the kitchen table when Nathaniel and William came down from their room. Nathaniel was still a bit drowsy from having slept only a few hours and his father gave him a suspicious frown as he greeted the family. At age 49 his father, Jacob Scudder, was very much the stern patriarch who regarded late night revelry as the work of the Devil. Nathaniel quickly took his place at the table next to his brothers, William and Lemuel, and his sister, Ruth. As the kitchen servants prepared breakfast, the family sat in silence, heads bowed, waiting for Jacob to say morning prayers.

When the servants indicated that the food was ready, Jacob began, "Lord, accept our humble thanks for Thy bounteous gifts that Thee hath bestowed upon us undeserving sinners. Grant that Thy life be maintained in our lives today and every day and give us the strength to avoid the temptations of the Evil One." Casting a glance at Nathaniel he continued in a rising crescendo, "Let us not fall prey to the lure of material pleasures or to the illusions of grandeur that wealth and prestige engender. We are all just insignificant worms pitifully trying to subsist in this Valley of Tears. Our only hope to avoid that world of misery, that lake of burning brimstone, that dreadful pit of the glowing flames of Thy wrath, hell's wide open gaping mouth lies in humbly serving Thee as best we can."

Gesturing to the servants to bring the food, Jacob turned to Nathaniel, "Well son, what have you been doing lately to earn God's forgiveness?"

"I hope to serve God by helping to alleviate the misery of his suffering children," answered Nathaniel. This type of exchange was familiar ground ever since Nathaniel had first indicated to Jacob that he was planning to become a physician instead of a minister. Jacob had never been completely convinced by Nathaniel's arguments but had to admit that physicians were not completely useless, especially as many pastors were also practicing physicians. Jacob hoped that Nathaniel would also someday come to bridge the two professions. "It was Reverend Tennent after all who proposed I become Dr. Clark's apprentice."

Conceding the point with a less than convinced grunt Jacob continued, "And is attending late night affairs at the home of Lawyer Ogden's apprentice part of your apprenticeship?"

At the mention of the Ogdens, Nathaniel knew the direction that his father's arguments would take. David Ogden, who represented the interests of the New Jersey Proprietors and the Anglican hierarchy, was the bête noir for every self-respecting Presbyterian. Not only did he help the Proprietors to dispossess Presbyterian yeomen who had bought their land from the Indians but also aided the detested Anglican establishment in trying to increase its influence in the American colonies. For Jacob Scudder he was one of Satan's most dangerous imps.

"The occasion was the announcement of the betrothal of Richard Stockton and Annis Boudinot, both of whom are ardent supporters of the College of New Jersey and New Light evangelism. Richard's father was, in fact, one of the college's founders," explained Nathaniel, "Richard works closely with Governor Belcher to try to resolve the conflicts between the Proprietors and our brethren. It is a cause that President Burr considers to be very worthy."

"And how did you come to be invited to such an august occasion?" asked Jacob.

"It came through the Anderson family. I met them at Reverend Tennent's meeting house," answered Nathaniel, suppressing the fact that he had actually only met Isabella and her mother there.

"The Andersons!" exclaimed Jacob, "John Anderson was one of the Proprietors' favorite henchmen. By helping them he amassed a great fortune at the expense of many pious farmers."

"His son, Kenneth, is a loyal member of Reverend Tennent's flock and a most patriotic colonel in the Monmouth militia," answered Nathaniel, "I cannot imagine that he would be a part of anything that would be inimical to True Religion. And his daughter, Isabella, is a lady of exceptional virtue."

"A daughter, a daughter, you say?" retorted Jacob, "Don't tell me that some aristocratic Jezebel has turned your head?"

"Father! Isabella is no Jezebel," exclaimed Nathaniel hotly, "She is an extraordinarily intelligent and pious young lady. I am honored to have made her acquaintance."

The vehemence of Nathaniel's reaction spoke volumes to Jacob. He understood immediately that his son was hopelessly in love. Despite his reservations about upper class decadence his finely tuned mercantile instincts would not let him overlook the possibilities of what might turn into a very profitable alliance.

"Well, hopefully you have done nothing to compromise the lady's honor," queried Jacob.

"I would sooner perish, father." replied Nathaniel bowing his head in agonized earnestness.

"In that case it is imperative that you write to Colonel Anderson as soon as possible proposing a matrimonial alliance," declared Jacob.

Nathaniel looked up with an expression of surprised delight. He had not expected his father to agree so readily to what had seemed so recently to be an almost impossible dream.

"Nothing would please me more, father, but … but. I am not quite certain how. . ." stuttered Nathaniel.

"The details you can leave up to me. That is what fathers are for," assured Jacob benevolently, "After all, I have some experience with your two older sisters whom I managed to marry off very well. It is all a question of presenting the alliance as a matter of practical benefit to both families. At your age your thoughts are undoubtedly clouded by emotion, but fathers are only interested in what is good for their children. In your letter you need to make it clear what advantages will be forthcoming from the proposed union. The letters I received from the suitors of Phebe and Lucretia are a good place to start. The letter that your brother-in-law Joseph Cowart wrote to bid for the hand of Lucretia I found particularly convincing. It is important that you describe what an upright and successful family you come from and what outstanding prospects await you."

"But I am still just a student and an apprentice physician," objected Nathaniel, "What do I really have to offer such a well-situated landowner?"

"Don't sell yourself too short, son," encouraged Jacob, "You have an excellent education and I hear from Dr. Clark that you are making outstanding progress in your apprenticeship. Besides, it is not just you but your entire family that is making the proposal. We might not be as rich as the Andersons, but we are among the oldest and most honorable families in the colonies. It is people like us that turned a wilderness into this prosperous country."

Buoyed up by his father's confidence, Nathaniel began to hope that this might not be such a far-fetched project after all.

"And how do I deliver the letter?" he asked, "Can I just go hand it to him when I show up for militia drill?"

"That would be one way to do it, but it would be better if one of Colonel Anderson's own acquaintances could act as intermediary," advised Jacob.

"I have it!" exclaimed Nathaniel, "Dr. Clark has been the family doctor of the Andersons for years. Perhaps he would agree to be the intermediary."

"That would be an excellent strategy," agreed Jacob, "Son, I can see you are learning fast. But first let us go through the points that you should include in the letter."

Jacob and Nathaniel spent the next hour reading through the proposals that Jacob had received from the suitors of his daughters and making notes about the details Nathaniel should include in his letter. Finally, both were satisfied that they had developed a convincing set of arguments.

"Dear Father, I cannot thank you enough!" exclaimed Nathaniel rising, "I will ride back to Monmouth Courthouse immediately and work on the final copy."

"Keep me apprised of your progress, son," smiled Jacob, "And don't forget to pray to the Savior to bless this project."

Chapter 6

Tom's River – 1756

Nathaniel worked feverishly over the next few days writing and re-writing his marriage proposal. Following his father's advice and using as models the proposals that his father had received for his sisters, he tried to include everything he could think of that would convince Colonel Anderson that his union with Isabella would be beneficial to the Anderson family. He talked about his successes at the College of New Jersey, his fine prospects for a great career in medicine and his affinity for the Whig philosophy that clearly was so dear to Colonel Anderson. He wrote eloquently about his vision for founding a family that would be a credit to the Anderson family tradition of public service. After discarding many drafts, he finally had a letter that he thought might stand a chance of success. Now all he needed to do was to convince Dr. Clark to present the letter to Colonel Anderson.

An opportunity to broach the subject soon arose. Dr. Clark informed Nathaniel that they were to journey together again to Crossweeksung to administer the promised smallpox vaccinations to the Indians there and then to continue to Tom's River to procure some of the more exotic medicines that they needed. Tom's River was notorious as a haven for smugglers who dealt regularly if illegally with the Spanish and French entrepôts in the Caribbean. There practically anything could be procured and at rates much lower than available from the merchants in New York City or Philadelphia who had to import all articles indirectly by way of England subject to the exorbitant British tax duties. It was there that Dr. Clark purchased the Peruvian bark so effective in reducing fevers and the opium needed for pain relief. Dr. Clark like most of the population of New Jersey had no compunctions about circumventing the onerous trade restrictions that the British mercantile system sought to impose. He saw no reason why some greedy merchants in London should profit at the expense of the poor farmers on the frontier who desperately needed these medicines and could never afford them at the official prices. The village at Tom's River had no customs inspector. The many small coves and dangerous shoals made it practically inaccessible for seaborn inspectors. The local people, however, with decades of experience as whalers and privateers came and went as they pleased.

For the inoculation of the Indians at Crossweeksung against smallpox Nathaniel and Dr. Clark had carefully prepared threads that had been exposed to the disease. Dr. Clark was very proud of his use of this most modern of inoculation methods. The older method consisted of inserting purulent matter gathered from a pustule on a pox victim into a small scratch in the skin of the patient. If all went well, the patient would then develop a mild case of the pox which would then afford future immunity from the disease. Unfortunately, some would develop a full case of the sickness from which they often died. Although this happened to only about one in a hundred cases of inoculation, many people were still understandably reluctant to take the risk even though the chances of death when contracting smallpox naturally were one in five. Dr. Clark had learned a new method in which a piece of thread moistened in a pustule of a smallpox victim was dried by exposure to air and stored in a clean glass vial until use. It was advisable for this purpose to select a smallpox victim with a relatively light case who was already on the way to recovery. One of these threads would then be imbedded in an incision and secured by a bandage. The resultant fever was then much milder. Dr. Clark had never lost a single patient using this method. Dr. Clark and Nathaniel packed a half-dozen of the vials along with the money they would need to buy medicines at Tom's River. They also armed themselves well since they would be passing through some lawless territory on their way to Tom's River from Crossweeksung. In the Pine Barrens area there was no shortage of cutthroats who would murder them for a fraction of the value they were carrying.

Nathaniel and Dr. Clark mounted up early and rode off in the direction of Crossweeksung. It was a lovely fall day and the ride through the heavily wooded landscape of central New Jersey was quite pleasant. Around noon time they emerged into the familiar clearing with the domed dwellings that was the Indian camp. Okwes came out of his dwelling immediately to greet Dr. Clark and Nathaniel. Hopping out after him was Chinkwe supporting himself on a makeshift crutch.

"Welcome, my friends," greeted Okwes, "It is a great pleasure to see you again."

"Glad to see that Chinkwe is recovering well," responded Dr. Clark, "In a few months, we can fit him with an artificial leg that will make him much more mobile. As promised, I have bought along the pox medicine that will protect your people against that dreadful malady."

"May the Ruler of the Universe bless you for your efforts," smiled Okwes gratefully, "I have already explained to the six young people who still need to be inoculated how the procedure works. They are ready for the treatment. Afterwards, Reverend Brainerd asks that we join him for dinner."

"That will be a pleasure," agreed Dr. Clark, "I am interested in hearing about his missionary efforts among your kinfolk in the Ohio territory."

Dr. Clark was pleased and relieved to see that the six people to be inoculated were all strong, healthy children in early adolescence. These were the most unlikely to suffer unduly from the effects of the inoculation. Dr. Clark made the small incisions on the arms of each of the patients. Nathaniel implanted a thread into each of the incisions and bound them carefully. Dr. Clark then instructed Okwes that the children should be put to bed and covered warmly. To be on the safe side they should be isolated from any others who had not already been inoculated. They were to eat a vegetarian diet until completely recovered from the fever. After the onset of the fever, they were to receive a daily dose of Glauber's salts and water in order to purge their bodies of poisons. Okwes was familiar with these procedures from past inoculation He also knew that he needed to report to Dr. Clark if any of the patients did not develop a fever. In those cases, the inoculation would have to be repeated.

After the inoculations had been performed Dr. Clark and Nathaniel spent the rest of the afternoon examining other Indians with minor ailments that did not respond to Okwes' traditional methods. As the sun began to set, Dr. Clark, Nathaniel and Okwes rode the short distance to the log cabin where Reverend John Brainerd resided when he was staying at the Indian camp.

Dr. Clark, Reverend Brainerd and Nathaniel were well acquainted from previous visits as well as from Reverend Brainerd's sermons at the College of New Jersey and at Reverend Tennent's meeting house in Manalapan. They greeted each other cordially. Reverend Brainerd beckoned to a table where a large pot of venison soup stood next to several long loafs of cornbread.

"So happy to see you again, John," Dr. Clark addressed Reverend Brainerd familiarly as the men took their places at the table, "We are getting frightening reports from the Ohio country these days. Apparently, more and more Indians there are allying with the French and perpetrating unspeakable crimes against British settlers."

"I am afraid there is indeed a great deal of turmoil in the Ohio region, William," responded Reverend Brainerd, "The French are afraid that colonists from Pennsylvania and Virginia are planning to colonize the area. The French governor, Vaudreuil, is convinced that only by actively recruiting as many Indian warriors as possible can the French compensate for our much larger population. Unfortunately, the Indian way of warfare involves some embarrassing practices from the standpoint of European officer gentlemen. Since you are eating, I will refrain from too much detail."

"Embarrassing practices! That is putting it mildly!" exclaimed Dr. Clark, "I remember back in '52 when a French Indian raiding party decided to punish the Miami chieftain, Memeskia, for cooperating with British traders at Pickawillany. The Indian warriors ripped out the still beating hearts of Memeskia and one of the traders, boiled, and ate them while their French allies looked on. This was a lesson for the survivors among the traders who were then sent as prisoners to Montreal."

Nathaniel smiled grimly to himself. For Dr. Clark anatomical details were just clinical facts. It did not occur to him for a moment that such graphic descriptions might turn the stomachs of non-physicians.

"Most French officers are scandalized by that kind of behavior, but they probably could not stop their Indian allies in the frenzied aftermath of battle even if they wanted to," explained Reverend Brainerd, "And the French do have good reason to worry about the intentions of Virginian land speculators. Virginia's gentry has grown rich through tobacco cultivation. They have imported thousands of African slaves to do the work. Trouble is that tobacco exhausts the soil while the number of slaves continues to increase by natural proliferation. You have more and more slaves working less and less fertile land. Sooner or later, you must look for westward expansion or worry about a slave rebellion. That was why Governor Dinwiddie sent young George Washington on that Jumonville Glen business. The governor was working on behalf of a group of land speculators interested in developing the Ohio territory. The governor is even said to have a financial interest in this Ohio Company."

"That makes perfect sense," mused Dr. Clark, "It also explains why some of the Indians there are so susceptible to French blandishments."

"Yes and of course, it makes the work of a missionary much more difficult," continued Reverend Brainerd, "How can we get the Indians to accept Christ and abandon their sinful ways if our own people are so obviously driven by greed alone? Let me tell you about a visit I made to a mixed council of Indians on the Susquehanna River a few years ago. When I tried to spread the Word, they told me in no uncertain terms that I had it all wrong. They said that the Great Spirit had originally created three couples, an Indian, a Black, and a White couple and placed them on different continents so each could develop in its own way. The White couple was made last so that White man should understand that he is merely the younger brother with no reason to feel superior. The Great Spirit gave the White couple a book to live by, but this has no relevance for Indians and Blacks. It was time for them to go back to their traditional beliefs and reject everything about White civilization. Finally, they told me that the White people were surely contriving a conspiracy to deprive them of their land and make them slaves in the same way that it had happened to the coastal Indians and that I was probably just an agent of that conspiracy. They spoke of a new Prophet named Neolin who would lead all the Indians to forget their differences and unite in rejecting everything about White culture."

Nathaniel listened with fascination to Reverend Brainerd's explanation of events that Nathaniel had heard about but never really understood in detail. The potential conflict between the religious interests of men like Reverend Brainerd and the commercial interests of men like Governor Dinwiddie was an interesting aspect that he had not considered before.

"Good Lord!" exclaimed Dr. Clark, "A pan-Indian religious revival would be a very remarkable phenomenon. But it would certainly be as much of a problem for the French as for us. What do you think, Okwes?"

"Speaking for my kinsmen in the Ohio territory, it seems to me that the French are in a better position to appeal to the desire for freedom that many tribes there feel. The French only want to trade. They don't bring large numbers of settlers, so they are less threatening for us. The Whites don't understand what we have been through since they arrived. Before the Whites came, we were ten times as many as now. Our fathers had plenty of game and skins, our plains were full of deer, our woods full of turkeys, and our inlets full of fish and fowl. But then came the English who took more and more of our land, cut down the grass with scythes and felled the trees with axes. Their cows and horses ate the grass, their hogs spoiled our clam banks, and we all became afraid that we would starve. But it came even worse. Suddenly new diseases appeared among us that we had never seen before. Huge numbers were carried off in epidemics within weeks. Tribes were so reduced that they had to raid other tribes to steal women and children to repopulate their own areas. Our group decided to convert to the White Man's God because He had obviously given the Whites very strong medicine that we desperately needed. All the tribes were in fierce competition for the resources needed to trade successfully with the Whites for iron tools, muskets, gun powder, and whiskey. Finally in the Beaver Wars fought to control access to the hides needed for trading, the Iroquois got the upper hand. The Six Nations managed to organize a kind of empire where they dominate many different tribes including those in the Ohio valley. The French were happy to recognize Iroquois domination so long the English were kept out. Now that more and more British traders and land speculators are drawn to the Ohio territory, the French are beginning to think that the Iroquois are no longer powerful enough there to keep their end of the bargain. They are seeking new allies."

"That is a good explanation why the Ohio territory has become so unstable," commented Reverend Brainerd, "The French are worried about losing out there to the British. The Iroquois are worried that they will no longer be recognized as the legitimate suzerains by the French and the local tribes just want to be free of all outside interference."

"That is exactly right, my friend," continued Okwes, "The Six Nations used to play the British and the French off against each other but now events seem to be pushing them closer to an alliance with the British. The representative of the Six Nations in the Ohio territory is Tanaghrisson, called the Half-King because of his mixed blood ancestry. The Half-King is supposed to keep all the tribes under the influence of the Six Nations. Because of the influence of Neolin's revival movement but also because the Iroquois have helped Whites to steal their land, the local tribal chiefs in the Ohio country are getting less and less inclined to do his bidding. He needs ever more trade articles to use for diplomatic gifts to bolster his influence. A few years ago at a conference in Logstown he accepted 1000 pounds worth of wampum in return for his permission to the Ohio Company to build a strong house at The Forks. But his influence continues to diminish. That is why he accompanied Washington to Jumonville Glen and why he murdered a captive French officer even though that soldier had diplomatic status."

"I remember hearing about that," commented Dr. Clark, "Apparently it was another incident where Indian allies got out of the control of the White men they were accompanying. The French officers are not the only ones that have to deal with this problem; I understand that Washington was as surprised and shocked by the Indians' behavior as any European trained officer would be."

"Tanaghrisson was not out of control," corrected Okwes, "For the Half-King it was a good opportunity to force the issue. He seems to think that a war between the British and the French will enable him to reassert the power of the Six Nations over the tribes of the Ohio country. By murdering a diplomatic envoy, he made that war a lot more probable. Now the war has come. It will be the British together with the Six Nations against the French and all the western Indian tribes that the French are able to enlist. It is unclear how this will turn out, but it will have terrible consequences no matter which side is successful."

Nathaniel, Dr. Clark and Reverend Brainerd looked silently back and forth to one another slowly realizing the implications of Okwes' prophetic analysis. It was becoming clear to them that momentous events were unfolding. The current conflict was not going to be a repeat of past, more or less indecisive conflicts between the French and the British such as Queen Anne's War or King George's War. This time a major holocaust was in the making that could decisively change the character of North America.

As this grim and foreboding truth penetrated the consciousness of the four men, they fell silent in contemplation of what that could mean for each of them.

Finally, Dr. Clark summarized in his practical way, "Well Nathaniel, it looks as though we will be in greater need of those medicines than we thought. Let us bed down for the night and get an early start to Tom's River."

"May the Lord protect you on your missions of mercy," said Reverend Brainerd to the three men as they stood up to leave, "Nathaniel and William, you are, of course, welcome to spread your blankets in front of my humble hearth."

Nathaniel and Dr. Clark were awakened at first light by Reverend Brainerd stoking the fireplace to get ready for breakfast. After a lengthy prayer by Reverend Brainerd the three men sat down to a simple breakfast of corn meal bread and tea.

"Do you have a long distance ahead of you today, William?" inquired Reverend Brainerd, "Our modest breakfast offering might not be adequate for a long journey."

"No problem at all, John," replied Dr. Clark, "We are going to meet Sam Bigelow for lunch at Daniel Grigg's Tavern in Tom's River. We should be able to get there already in the late morning without hurrying."

"Daniel Grigg's Tavern! That den of iniquity!" exclaimed Reverend Brainerd sternly, "The people who frequent that place are no good company for your young apprentice, nor for you for that matter."

"We are on strictly medical business there, Reverend," soothed Dr. Clark, "It is the closest place for me to buy the Peruvian bark and the opium I need for my patients. The other wares on offer there are not our concern."

"Still, it is a place of many evils and dangers. Be aware that the Devil lurks there in every shadow," insisted Reverend Brainerd.

"That is why I am taking this well-armed, strapping young man along," reassured Dr. Clark, "We at least will not offer an easy target to any scoundrels."

"I will prayer for your safe return," promised Reverend Brainerd, "The Lord is our best Protector."

After saying farewell to Reverend Brainerd, the two men stopped by Okwes long house to leave him enough doses of Glauber's Salts for the inoculation patients and to pick up some of his remarkable healing herbs. They then continued due south at an easy trot to intercept the road that connected Tom's River with the larger towns in the north and west.

After a few miles they encountered the rough but well-travelled road that led through the dense forest and marsh land toward Tom's River. The forests were foreboding and mysterious with giant pines and oaks. In marshy areas huge cedars rose from the swamps encrusted at the bottom with exotic and colorful mosses. Together with other wild vegetation they formed almost impenetrable tangles closing off outside light and creating a strange sepulchral gloaming for large stretches of the way.

"It is easy to see why simple people believe that witches and warlocks inhabit this area," remarked Nathaniel.

"There may not be witches and warlocks here, but there are quite a few odd creatures none the less," said Dr. Clark, "Squatters have been moving here for decades to live off the land and steal resources. They are called Swamp Angels and some of them still even live in caves. The Proprietors officially own most of this area, but it is so inaccessible that the Swamp Angels have little to fear of eviction. They have lived here for generations, taking timber, making pitch, and turpentine and selling it to the traders passing back and forth to and from Egg Harbor or Tom's River."

"And perhaps waylaying the odd traveler now and again?" wondered Nathaniel.

"There are undoubtedly some cutthroats among them, but incidents seem to be relatively rare," answered Dr. Clark, "I think the lonely traveler is more endangered by the wolves, bears, and panthers that roam these forests. Plenty of villages still offer bounties for their heads. I would not want to make this journey at night. The real cutthroats, however, usually stay closer to the shore. There you have a hardy mixture of hunters, trappers, whalers, speculators, pirates, smugglers and privateers. Many of the people fit into more than one of those categories. These are men with few scruples and much experience of violence. And the rule of the King's Law is as absent there as it is in these forests."

At that moment they heard the rumble of a heavy wagon approaching from the southeast along the sandy road. Sitting on top were a White man with a musket and a Black slave driving a team of powerful horses. The wagon was loaded to capacity with huge barrels of molasses.

"Here is a good example of the trade that goes on here," instructed Dr. Clark, "That wagon has just taken delivery from a ship from the Caribbean and will bring the molasses to a rum distillery further north. In the Spanish and French islands such as Guadeloupe, Martinique or Santo Domingo the price of molasses is 25 to 40 percent less than that from the British plantation islands. The disadvantaged owners of the British plantations in London managed to get Parliament to pass the Molasses Act in 1733 which set a duty of six cents on the gallon. But all that did was create greater opportunities for smugglers to increase their profits. Instead of just smuggling they began to bribe officials as well. A lucrative side industry grew up specializing in forging clearance papers, mislabeling cargoes and masking illegal imports. At Tom's River and Egg Harbor they don't even have to bother with such complications because there aren't any customs inspectors there and if there were, they wouldn't last long."

"But now that we are war with France," asked Nathaniel, "Doesn't it make it more difficult to continue this business?"

"Quite the contrary," responded Dr. Clark, "The French are in dire need of North American provisions, so they are willing to pay even more for them than before. An investment of ten shillings brings a profit of between fifty shillings and three pounds. There is no shortage of people who are bold enough to confront danger for those odds. Now that the war is officially on, they can say they got their illicit goods through privateering. And you saw how dense the surrounding forest is and you know how treacherous the coast is. These people are protected on all sides. How could the king's forces of order ever run down the smugglers in such a difficult environment, particularly since the smugglers know every nook and cranny. You would need more soldiers than the king has to impose law and order on this area."

After several hours on the road having passed wagons laden with goods going in both directions, Dr. Clark and Nathaniel finally came to the outskirts of Tom's River. From a distance it seemed to be a pleasant little village on the northern shore of the river just before it widened out into a bay that eventually emptied into the Atlantic. Further out in the ocean the sand bars were visible that made the approach to the small harbor so treacherous for anyone who had not grown up there. As Dr. Clark and Nathaniel came closer, they could see that the little village was actually a bustling entrepôt with several different trading establishments where people were loading and unloading wagons. Facing the waterfront was Daniel's Griggs Tavern, apparently already enjoying a rollicking business even though it was not even noon yet. Assorted

Jack Tars were carousing loudly with some of the local swain and loose women in front of the entrance.

"The sailors waste no time getting drunk the minute they get into port," explained Dr. Clark, "They know their greedy captains will sell their cargo quickly so their ships can embark on the next voyage as soon as possible. They might have only a short time in port and want to make the most of it. If they get too drunk, they'll get shanghaied onto some vessel in short order in any case."

Nathaniel at first looked with fascination at this strange conglomeration of people and could not help thinking about the Biblical tales of Sodom and Gomorrah. He wondered how people could possibly want to live like this and recalled Reverend Brainerd's warnings. Then following Dr. Clark in the direction of the tavern and uttering a prayer under his breath, he avoided eye contact with the lascivious creatures leering at him from the crowd.

Sam Bigelow was already waiting for them inside the tavern. A large and imposing man who looked more than a match for any of the riffraff outside the tavern, he was seated at the most spacious table like some baron holding court. Seeing again his customer of many years Sam greeted Dr. Clark heartily.

"Very pleased to see you again, William, welcome to my humble emporium," said Bigelow standing up and bowing theatrically at the waist, "I have reserved some excellent medicines of the highest quality especially for you. And who is this strapping young lad you have with you. Hopefully not an imperial customs inspector?"

"Greetings, Sam. This is my apprentice, Nathaniel Scudder, whom I would like to introduce to you. He is a graduate of the College of New Jersey and already well-versed in the apothecary's skills. Now I am teaching him all my secrets. He will soon be a regular customer of yours as well."

"Welcome, Nathaniel," smiled Bigelow, "I look forward to the same mutually beneficial relationship with you as I have had with Dr. Clark for many years. In fact, when you are finished with your apprenticeship you might consider hiring on to one of my ships as a surgeon's mate for a voyage or two. A successful privateering venture can make a rich man out of you in a short time. I have had voyages that were so lucrative that the share of the booty for a common seaman was three hundred pounds."

Nathaniel gasped at this number. He knew that some of his fellow graduates who were schoolteachers were earning 60 pounds a year. This was five times as much in a single voyage! Before he could reply, Dr. Clark interrupted, "What Sam didn't tell you is that it is also very easy to get your throat slit on your first voyage and then your share of the booty is a warm corner of Hell."

"Don't exaggerate, William," countered Bigelow, "I almost never lose a sailor. It is all a matter of good organization and picking the right team. All my men are hand-picked with years of experience in the whaling trade. Men used to fighting giant creatures from small boats in stormy seas have no problem facing the relatively mild challenges of privateering. In any case, Nathaniel, if you ever have the need to make big money in a short time, I am the man to come to see."

"I will remember that, sir," replied Nathaniel thoughtfully.

"Before we get down to the commercial side of our meeting, I would like to invite both of you to a hearty lunch," announced Bigelow ebulliently.

Nathaniel and Dr. Clark smiled gratefully. They had travelled a long way on Reverend Brainerd's Puritan breakfast, and they were both ravenous. Bigelow had already ordered the specialty of the house: lamb shank with gravy, potatoes, and corn. He called to a girl waiting in the door of the kitchen to bring the food along with tankards of cider. The girl quickly disappeared into the kitchen and returned with a tray heavily laden with fragrant dishes. While serving the three men, she seemed to take an especial interest in Nathaniel smiling prettily whenever she made eye contact with him.

When she returned to the kitchen, Bigelow leered at Nathaniel uttering conspiratorially, "Nathaniel, it seems that Betsy has taken a shine to you. Maybe you ought to spend a few hours longer in Tom's River. There is much to amuse a young man of your age here."

Turning bright crimson, Nathaniel exclaimed, "Oh no, sir, that would be completely out of the question!"

Immensely enjoying Nathaniel's embarrassment, Bigelow continued to needle him, "What's wrong, isn't our Betsy pretty enough for you?"

"No, I mean yes, she is very attractive, but . . ." stammered Nathaniel, shaking his head and casting his eyes down to his plate, ". . . but my heart belongs to another."

"A young gentleman in love," laughed Bigelow, "in that case we would not want to lead you into temptation!"

"Let's move away from temptations and talk about business," said Dr. Clark putting an end to Bigelow's teasing game.

Bigelow and Dr. Clark then proceeded to discuss the state of the market for the kind of commodities that Dr. Clark was interested in. Bigelow pointed out that the Peruvian Bark was especially difficult to obtain this year and would cost a bit more than it did last year. Finding the quality of opium that Dr. Clark wanted required, according to Bigelow, nothing less than heroic and insanely dangerous missions to the lands of the Infidels. After a half hour of good-natured haggling Dr. Clark and Sam Bigelow agreed on a price for several saddle bags of Peruvian Bark and a small pouch of the finest Indian opium. After finishing their meal, the three men walked over to Bigelow's barn where they picked up their purchases, thanked Bigelow for the excellent lunch and went to fetch their horses.

It was mid-afternoon when they mounted their horses and rode out of Tom's River in the direction of Monmouth Courthouse. The weather was still fine and the forest not quite as dense as before. The more dangerous segment of their journey was now over. Both men were in a good mood satisfied that their journey had been a success. For Nathaniel it had been particularly interesting because he had learned so much about the roots of the current war that he hadn't known before, and he had got to experience the exotic atmosphere of an extralegal entrepôt. As he was wondering just how many sinful attractions might await one in such a place, Dr. Clark broke the silence:

"Nathaniel, I was pleased to see that you were not lured by that trollop at Daniel Grigg's Tavern," said Dr. Clark affably, "It did not surprise me that a student of Reverend Burr would have good resistance to temptations of the flesh, but I did wonder about this mention of your heart belonging to another. Do you want to tell me anything about this?"

Swallowing a large lump in his throat Nathaniel thought to himself that it is now or never.

"Indeed, sir, there is something I have been wanting to discuss with you for some time. I just could not seem to find the right moment," confessed Nathaniel.

"Affairs of the heart are often awkward to discuss, Nathaniel," Dr. Clark tried in his friendly manner to soothe Nathaniel's nervousness, "But you should know that you can trust me with any of your secrets. I was young once myself, you know."

Feeling a flood of relief Nathaniel blurted out to Dr. Clark everything about his love for Isabella and his earnest desire to marry her. He told him about his father's surprising and encouraging advice and that he had reason to believe that Isabella might not be averse to his proposal. He averred that his only problem was to convince Colonel Anderson of the desirability of the match. And that was what Nathaniel had wanted to talk to him about.

"I understand," said Dr. Clark smiling kindly, "You are worried that the Andersons might not think that a miller's son is an appropriate match for their princess, and you would like me as their family doctor of many years to say something on your behalf?"

"I have taken great pains to write a proposal letter describing what advantages would be forthcoming from such a union," explained Nathaniel, "But it could make all the difference in the world if you would agree to deliver it to Colonel Anderson."

"I will do more than deliver the letter, Nathaniel," agreed Dr. Clark, "I will tell Kenneth Anderson that he can be happy to have such a fine prospect for a son-in-law. A budding physician is not such a bad choice after all. At least he will have someone who can look after his gout."

Nathaniel laughed nervously but was so overjoyed he could have embraced the man. He felt as though he were floating in some enchanted dream on his way ever closer to Isabella.

Chapter 7

OH BLISSFUL DAY – 1757

"KENNETH, WE HAVE BEEN friends for decades and you know I would not have agreed to convey the letter, if I did not think Nathaniel would be an excellent match for Isabella," Dr. Clark presented his arguments on Nathaniel's behalf in his calm, logical manner, "Nathaniel will soon be one of the only college trained physicians in this area and I can personally vouch for his professional quality. He is also the oldest son of a prosperous miller with a 100-acre farm."

"I know, I know," Colonel Anderson said, shaking his head, "I have met the lad and he makes a good impression, but his family's situation is a bit meager. Also, I am not sure that a physician would be the right one to manage my estate efficiently. He will be attending to his patients rather than to business affairs. I only have my one daughter, you know, after the tragic death of her little sister, so I will have to rely on my son-in-law to guard my legacy properly."

"In that case, you need a very honest, God-fearing son-in-law that you can trust," countered Dr. Clark, "Nathaniel is a pious young man who would never cheat you."

"You certainly have a point there," replied Colonel Anderson, "But I have to discuss this with Isabella. She is quite head-strong, you know. I have already had to reject proposals from some very well-situated men because she would not hear of it. I don't think there is any point forcing her into a match in which she would not be happy."

"Yes, indeed," Dr. Clark smiled thoughtfully. He knew very well about Isabella's independent frame of mind and that this would certainly give pause to many young men seeking a more traditional sort of wife. Nathaniel was obviously so smitten, however, that every aspect of Isabella was a delight to him. Since it seemed that Colonel Anderson was planning to leave the decision up to her, Dr. Clark could safely assume that his mission had been accomplished.

✳ ✳ ✳

Nathaniel's heart was pounding like a drum when he opened the letter that Dr. Clark had brought back from Colonel Anderson in response to his proposal. To his immense delight Colonel Anderson wrote that both he and Isabella were in agreement.

"Praise be the Lord!" exclaimed Nathaniel, "They have accepted my proposal!"

"Well, congratulations, Nathaniel," said Dr. Clark smiling, "I told you, you should not sell yourself too cheap. I was sure it was going to work out. The girl apparently wants you and she is a young lady who is accustomed to getting what she wants."

"Oh I would give her anything that were in my power to give!" sighed Nathaniel, "I just hope that I will be successful enough not to disappoint her."

"Fortunately for you, she is the lone heiress to a vast estate," said Dr. Clark, "I am certain that Colonel Anderson will set you both up in fine fashion. In fact, the next step is for your father to meet with him and discuss the practical details."

"Yes, yes," agreed Nathaniel breathlessly, "I will ride to their estate immediately to find out when a visit from my father would be convenient. And thank you so much for your help, Dr. Clark, words cannot express my gratitude!"

"My pleasure, Nathaniel," replied Dr. Clark, "I have known Isabella since she was a child and am happy that she will be marrying a decent, God-fearing young man and not one of those supercilious fops from the proprietary elite."

Nathaniel galloped quickly to the Anderson estate and almost fainted with delight when a beaming Isabella greeted him at the door. Bowing deeply, he declared himself to be the happiest man alive and promised that his heart would belong to her for the rest of his days. Accepting his pledge with a self-assured and graceful nod of her head Isabella led him into the drawing room where her father was reading. Colonel Anderson greeted Nathaniel warmly congratulating him on the well-written proposal and telling them how pleased he was to have such a superbly educated future son-in-law.

"Well, Nathaniel, I can see that you are a young man of considerable learning," began Colonel Anderson, "Your vision for the future of our family was quite compelling. I was pleased by your optimistic enthusiasm for building a better world and your thoughts about the key moral role that educated leaders must play in this. I assume this reflects the teaching at the College of New Jersey these days. Are there particular philosophers who are emphasized there?"

"We begin, of course, studying the Latin and Greek classics," explained Nathaniel, "But, the most interesting for most of us are some of the more contemporary Scottish and English philosophers."

"Which ones, for example," queried Colonel Anderson further.

"John Locke holds a great fascination for me," answered Nathaniel, "He was not only a brilliant philosopher but a physician as well. He is a scholar that one can admire on many different levels. He has inspired my belief that there is no contradiction between moral and natural philosophy. Apparent contradictions are only due to our ignorance and will be resolved sooner or later through the ever-increasing body of knowledge. That is why I am so optimistic about the future. I am simply overwhelmed and delighted by the possibilities that the growth of scientific enquiry has unleashed since the beginning of the Reformation once the dead hand of a corrupt ideology was lifted from the people."

"Locke is an excellent choice," replied Colonel Anderson, "I share his views about natural law, the importance of freedom, and the consent of the governed as the source of the legitimacy of governments."

"Locke really does provide the best philosophical justification for our system of government and the principles of the Glorious Revolution," continued Nathaniel, "But I do differ about some details."

"And what might those be," asked Colonel Anderson.

"Locke rejects innate characteristics of the mind," explained Nathaniel, "He thought that the human mind was a tabula rasa, an empty slate, that was completely conditioned by an individual's experience."

"That seems as reasonable hypothesis as any," mused Colonel Anderson.

"But that makes it difficult to account for moral decisions," countered Nathaniel, "A later philosopher from the University of Glasgow, Francis Hutcheson, whose works are popular at my college, taught that humans are endowed with a moral sense that can distinguish between virtuous and vicious actions. This seems very plausible to me because people obviously get pleasure from performing virtuous acts and abhor cruelty. They don't have to be taught the difference. It is also a form of natural law. When I can help a patient back to health, I experience an immense feeling of satisfaction. Such a feeling is a spontaneous reaction to virtue which occurs naturally and would seem, therefore, to be an innate quality of the mind."

"Perhaps it is an innate quality of some minds," answered Colonel Anderson skeptically, "I am not sure it is a quality of all minds. The existence of evil and evil people cannot be denied."

Not wanting to dampen Nathaniel's youthful enthusiasm, he quickly added, "I am, nevertheless, very pleased to note that it is obviously a quality of your mind so I can be sure you will take good care of my Isabella."

"Of all things, that is my most cherished goal," pledged Nathaniel fervently.

"Good. I am happy to hear that we are in complete agreement regarding our main priority," continued Colonel Anderson with a smile of satisfaction, "Now we can get down to business. We need to arrange a meeting with your parents at their earliest convenience so we can plan the wedding and attend to the many details of setting up a new household. I would suggest that we arrange the meeting with Reverend Tennent since he knows both families and will be the one to make the official announcement at the meeting house."

"That is a very good idea," agreed Nathaniel, "I will inform my parents immediately. I am sure that they will be pleased to come to Manalapan whenever it is convenient for you and Reverend Tennent."

Two weeks later the families met at the home of Reverend Tennent. Jacob and Abia Scudder, Kenneth and Hannah Anderson, Nathaniel and Isabella, and Reverend Tennent sat together in the Tennent home after having attended the service in the meeting house.

"I think that spring is always a good time for weddings," said Reverend Tennent, paging through his appointment book, "The 23rd of next March would be nice. I will make the official announcement soon and request the members of the congregation to stand ready to help with the home building. When the house is about finished the local magistrate can then conclude the contract. Spring will just be starting—an auspicious time to begin a new family."

"But that is almost five months from now," blurted Nathaniel unable to conceal his impatience, glancing desperately in Isabella's direction, "Would it not be feasible to marry sooner?"

"Ah the impatience of youth," soothed Colonel Anderson, "There is so much to attend to before the wedding that those five months will slip by faster than you think. You have to live somewhere, for example, and getting that organized is a good deal of work. I can give you a nice plot of land near Monmouth Courthouse but erecting a house upon it will take some time."

"The colonel is absolutely right," agreed Jacob Scudder, "You also have to finish your studies at the college and your apprenticeship with Dr. Clark. I can raise your monthly stipend a bit but you will eventually have to earn your own living. A wife and family are a great deal of responsibility."

"You are both right, of course," answered Nathaniel, "It was childish of me to be so impatient especially since we will be completely dependent on our parents for another year or two before I can practice on my own. I did not want to appear ungrateful . . ."

"Father is certainly correct. There is so much to do. The time will fly," chimed in Isabella, "I am greatly looking forward to planning our new home. You can leave that up to me and concentrate on finishing your studies."

"I can provide the lumber for the new house," offered Jacob Scudder, "I am just now clearing a large, wooded area on our farm which has outstanding building material."

"Once the plans are set, erecting a house and barn will go quite quickly," added Reverend Tennent, "Our congregation has every sort of craftsman. After the harvest is in, they will be happy to volunteer to help. I have seen them raise a barn over the course of a weekend. That is an important part of our idea of community."

"Among my servants are several outstanding carpenters," volunteered Colonel Anderson, "They, of course, are at your disposal as well."

The next weeks flew by as the newly betrothed delighted in the performance of the many tasks needed to build their home and prepare for the wedding. Most of the planning was done by Isabella who turned out to have a real talent for project management as well as a fine aesthetic sense. Nathaniel quickly realized that he was well advised to defer to Isabella's judgement in most matters having to do with their new home. Her remarkable management abilities added a new dimension to his admiration for her.

Nathaniel for his part was busy with both his apprenticeship and his studies. As Dr. Clark had predicted, the escalating war generated much work for physicians. Gradually more and more wounded and dying militiamen returned from the front needing care. Nathaniel had the opportunity to treat many kinds of wounds and fevers, and became quite proficient in surgical procedures. Several prisoners of war brought back by the militia died in captivity. Their unclaimed corpses gave Nathaniel the important possibility of learning anatomy by dissection. Under Dr. Clark's direction he thus was able to gain knowledge that was in normal times only rarely obtainable; most apprentice physicians had to make do with the occasional condemned criminal. In addition, the British troop build-up brought with it an influx of military physicians from whom Nathaniel and Dr. Clark could learn the latest techniques being developed in Europe. Although the escalation of hostilities and the disturbing news of defeats of the British forces caused much anxiety, it was for Nathaniel nevertheless an extremely fascinating time. He was learning his craft at an incredibly fast pace and preparing to marry the most wonderful woman he had ever known. Despite a general sense of foreboding, therefore, he nevertheless felt that he was on the threshold of a new era that somehow held great promise for him and his new family.

That this new era would also present serious challenges became apparent one winter morning when the militia brought a wagon full of wounded from the front to Dr. Clark's house. The wounded were from a British settlement in western Pennsylvania that had been attacked by an Indian war party allied with the French. Nathaniel was shocked to see that some of the wounded had been scalped but had somehow survived the ordeal.

"For the Indians the scalp as a trophy is more important than killing the enemy," explained Dr. Clark, "It is proof of a warrior's bravery that he can show off to all his tribe members."

"Is there any hope that these poor people can be saved?" asked Nathaniel in a low voice while servants carefully unloaded the wounded and laid them on piles of straw in Dr. Clark's barn.

"If left untreated, the scalped ones will eventually die. The exposed skull is too smooth for scar tissue to form. After a time, the bone will turn black, the tissue will start to die and soon afterward the patient as well. The only hope is to pierce the diploe, the area between two layers of compact bone containing red bone marrow, at many different intervals. Once the diploe is pierced granulation occurs and fleshy projections will form on the surface. If one is lucky, these projections will eventually form scar tissue that can spread over the exposed cranium. Let's have a closer look at these people and see if we can save anyone."

As Nathaniel and Dr. Clark examined each of the half-dozen wounded more carefully, they were pleased to discover that many of the wounds were fairly superficial. The Indians obviously had not intended to kill their victims. They wanted them to escape to spread terror among the other British settlers to discourage them from moving into the Ohio country.

"Dr. Clark, does this not remind you of our conversation with Okwes?" asked Nathaniel, "It seems that his prophecy about French success in gaining the support of the Indians in the Ohio country is coming true."

"I fear you could be right," answered Dr. Clark, "It is certainly true that the Iroquois hold the key to the balance of power between the British and French empires in North America. If we want to win this struggle, our leaders will have to take that into account. From what I hear Lord Loudoun does not seem to understand these issues. Your future father-in-law has very definite views on that subject."

That evening after spending the day helping Dr. Clark attend to the wounds of the refugees Nathaniel again paid a visit to Anderson Manor. The Anderson family was fascinated to hear Nathaniel's news about the fate of the refugees from western Pennsylvania.

"Colonel Anderson, sir, Dr. Clark mentioned that you are skeptical about Lord Loudoun's strategy for overcoming the French," inquired Nathaniel, "And I must say that the torrent of bad news from the front is very worrisome. What in your opinion needs to be done?"

"Loudoun is a typical arrogant aristocrat with no appreciation of local conditions," answered Colonel Anderson vehemently, "He wants to mount a gigantic campaign and expects us to fund it without any say in how it is organized. He just demands money without any respect for our constitutional prerogatives. Regarding local volunteers, the lowest most inexperienced Regular outranks the highest colonial militiaman, so who would be daft enough to volunteer? Those who do like young George Washington are refused Regular commissions. We also need the support of the Iroquois in order to counter the many Indian allies that the French have organized, but here again his ignorant arrogance causes him to disregard this issue completely. If he continues like this, I see disaster on the horizon."

"The wife of our college president, Esther Burr, shares your pessimistic view," said Nathaniel, "She is convinced that the French victories are a result of our moral failings. In her opinion God is testing us and we will only succeed if we find our way back to righteousness."

"Well, to the extent that ignorant hubris is a moral failing, she is certainly correct," agreed Colonel Anderson.

"Speaking of Esther Burr, I recently visited Annis Boudinot in Princeton," interjected Isabella, "She has become quite a close friend of Mrs. Burr. According to Annis, Esther Burr is currently not pessimistic at all but actually quite optimistic that God will soon intervene on our behalf."

"And just how did she come to that conclusion?" asked Colonel Anderson, raising his eyebrow.

"Well, it seems that a number of the students at Nassau Hall have been seized by a great sense of urgency regarding the saving of their immortal souls," explained Isabella, "Esther Burr sees it as a sign that God is smiling on her husband's mission to lead pious young men to Jesus. Annis even composed a poem about it. I can only remember two of the lines, 'O Blissful day with what a sacred Light, Dost Thou appear to my Enraptured sight', very pretty, don't you think?"

"This sounds like the kind of revivalism that is not going to sit well with the families of some of those pious young men," responded Colonel Anderson with a frown, "Many Anglicans see these outbursts of religious emotion as a source of disorder in society. Reverend Burr hoped that the new college would help to reconcile the various religious and ethnic groups in New Jersey. I hope his conversion efforts don't turn out to be counterproductive."

"In fact, I heard that David Ogden upon hearing the news withdrew his three sons from the college," confirmed Isabella, "Esther is afraid that more of the students' families might follow suit but that that is just the Devil trying to undo the Lord's work and that one just has to have faith."

"Still the Burrs would be well-advised to proceed carefully in this," warned Colonel Anderson, "It would not be good for the college to alienate many of the leading families in this colony just to promote a vision of religion that not everyone shares. When Governor Belcher granted the charter, he explicitly prescribed liberal and inclusive policies regarding religious issues."

Nathaniel also was not certain if the events in Nassau Hall were to be welcomed or not. On the one hand he believed in the Scriptures and what they foretold, on the other hand he often felt that Esther Burr's millenarian views were excessively literal. The blissful day that he saw in his near future was not the Millennium but that day at the end of March when he would finally have Isabella to himself. The weeks were flying by, and the agreed date would soon be at hand. He had intended to invite many of the students from the college, and he hoped that their ecstatic conversion experiences would not detract from what the wonderful wedding that he and Isabella were planning.

"A good friend of mine, Benjamin Prime, is a tutor at the college," volunteered Nathaniel, "I will ask him what is really going on. Perhaps it is not as dramatic as we think."

"That is a good idea," agreed Colonel Anderson, "It would be interesting to hear from someone who has experienced these young gentlemen firsthand."

He had wanted to talk to Benjamin about the upcoming wedding in any case, and following up on his future stepfather's information request gave him an additional incentive to seek out his old friend in Princeton a few days later.

"What going on with our scholars, Benjie?" asked Nathaniel with a tone of mock reproach in his voice, "Have you tutors turned them into a bunch of fanatics?"

"I tutor my charges only in the rational approach to physick," replied Benjamin haughtily, "For tutoring in matters of Revelation others are in charge."

"Are things as dramatic as I have heard?" asked Nathaniel, "Allegedly some families are pulling their sons out of the college for fear of radical indoctrination."

"No, no, it is not all that bad," answered Benjamin, "Reverend Burr got very excited because it seemed that some students were finally taking his hell-fire-and-brimstone preaching seriously. I would say that some of the younger students were truly frightened by his dire predictions and others were reacting the way they thought that Reverend Burr wanted them to react. It will all calm down soon. I will give them all a good dose of difficult science problems so they will have something else to occupy their minds."

"You wouldn't be undermining the good Pasteur's efforts, would you now, Benjie?" asked Nathaniel with a smirk on his lips, "In any case, my future father-in-law will be relieved to hear that my fellow college students will be in a state to attend my wedding."

"Oh, you need not worry about that, Natty," answered Benjamin, "They will be in a state alright, a state to make your wedding night a torture."

"Nothing could make my wedding night a torture, Benjie," sighed Nathaniel, "I will be transported to the edge of paradise."

"There is a problem to be solved before your rapture, Natty," contradicted Benjamin, "Once you and Isabella have retired to your room, the party will continue and will become increasingly rowdy. Finally, the drunken swains will come and pound on your door. They won't let up until they've been able to steal one of the bride's stockings."

"Then we will just have to bar the door with heavy irons," responded Nathaniel with a determined frown.

"Consummating your marriage while your bedroom door is being broken down is not a rational approach," explained the college tutor, "I have a much better plan. Listen to this."

Nathaniel listened carefully and had to agree that Benjamin as so often had found a clever way to solve the problem.

The erection of a house and a barn proceeded as quickly as Reverend Tennent had predicted. By the middle of March, the members of the congregation aided by Colonel Anderson's slaves had built a very comfortable two-story house with a spacious barn next to it. The barn was large enough for the many horses that Nathaniel would need as a traveling physician. Isabella had planned everything lovingly in great detail including quarters for servants upstairs in the barn.

On the 23rd of March both families met at the new home accompanied by many friends from the congregation in Manalapan as well as from the college in Princeton. The official ceremony began as Nathaniel and Isabella stood in front of Judge Jonathan

Forman who solemnly read aloud the terms of the nuptial agreement. He asked each of them in turn if they agreed with the requirements of matrimony. As both quickly and breathlessly expressed their affirmation and turned to embrace, a great shout went up from the participants. Friends and family crowded around the couple congratulating them and wishing them a wonderful future. Glasses of cider were passed around to all.

Annis Boudinot tapped her glass with a spoon calling for silence.

"As many of you know," she began as the crowd quieted down, "Richard and I will soon be following in this couple's footsteps. For this reason, the deeper meaning of this wonderful day is very present for me so I would like to propose a toast to the newlyweds in the form of a verse:

> May Nathaniel and Isabella in joy and health,
> In their beautiful home reside,
> And be blessed with children, love and wealth,
> And be their parents' pride,
> Their mutual vows each year repeat,
> At friendship's sacred shrine,
> While heart meets heart,
> In rapture sweet,
> Resembling joys divine."

A burst of applause went up from the assembled guests as everyone lifted their glasses to Nathaniel and Isabella.

Again a clinking of a spoon against a glass. Considering himself quite the poet in his own right Benjamin was not about to miss the opportunity to demonstrate his versifying talents.

"That was very lovely, Annis, as always, your verses are an inspiration," Benjamin began gallantly bowing in Annis' direction, "since I have been Nathaniel's personal consultant from the very beginning of this courtship, it is with great satisfaction that I experience this day and would like to add a few lines of my own in honor of the couple."

A frisson of anxiety swept over Nathaniel as it occurred to him that Benjamin knew many things about this courtship that Nathaniel would prefer to remain confidential. He frowned a warning at Benjamin.

Raising his glass and smiling in the direction of Nathaniel and Isabella, Benjamin was not to be deterred.

> "Nathaniel and Isabella,
> Like music these names combine,
> It was clear to any poet,
> That their lives must soon entwine.
> So I encouraged my friend,

To pursue his end,
And to seek his goal divine,
And helped him often,
Wherever I could,
So his joy is also mine!
To the Newlyweds!"

Again applause erupted from the guests as everyone raised their glasses to the couple.

"Just how was it that Benjamin helped you?" asked Isabella in a whisper to Nathaniel slightly knitting her eyebrows.

"Oh, just general advice," answered Nathaniel with a sigh of relief that Benjamin had not gone into details, "At an early stage I confided in him about my feelings for you and he encouraged me not to give up until I had won your hand."

"I see," said Isabella smiling to herself recalling the plans she herself had made with Annis Boudinot.

At that point three fiddlers from the local militia struck up a lively tune and the party got into full swing. After an hour or so Nathaniel thought he had waited long enough for his prize. Taking Isabella's hand, he smiled and nodded toward the staircase. That immediately caused the assembled guests to become even more raucous.

"Natty, are you sure you know what you are doing?" shouted one of the college students, "Perhaps you need some more instruction!"

"As an apprentice physician I have no need of your assistance," answered Nathaniel, smiling while shaking his head and starting up the stairs, "I have been comprehensively schooled in all the relevant details."

Hoots of derision rose up from the young men present who vied with each other to be the first to follow the couple up the stairs. Nathaniel glanced over to Benjamin who with a wink of his eye disappeared out of the front door. Nathaniel and Isabella quickly hurried into their bedroom and barred the door.

"Good Lord," exclaimed Isabella as the guests started to pound on the bedroom door, "Have those boys taken leave of their senses? I thought your college taught them to be gentlemen."

"Not to fear," answered Nathaniel, "If you would but allow me to remove your stocking, I have a plan to end this disturbance quickly."

Isabella smiled quizzically but seemed pleased when Nathaniel knelt before her, lifted her dress and carefully rolled down the stocking on her left leg. Her pleasure turned to surprise when Nathaniel then stood up, walked to the window, and threw the stocking down to Benjamin who was waiting below.

"It is the stocking, you see," explained Nathaniel, "The swains won't stop their antics until they get hold of the bride's stocking. Benjamin was waiting below and will now take the trophy inside and show it to the crowd. At that point they are obliged to stop their nonsense and let us alone."

"Ah, now I understand what kinds of assistance your friend Benjamin provides," replied Isabella with an expression of mock annoyance, "Well if that what is necessary to get rid of those fools, so be it."

Her frown transformed itself into a smile as Nathaniel knelt again and rolled down the other stocking gently kissing her legs and savoring the scent of her body. As the noise outside the door gradually ceased, she helped Nathaniel remove the rest of her garments. Soon they both stood naked in the moonlit room and gazed in wonderment at each other's bodies. As they melted into each other's arms Nathaniel thought to himself that there could be no pleasure this side of Paradise that could possibly compare to what he felt now.

Chapter 8

BAD TIMES BECKON – 1757

FOR THE NEXT FEW days Nathaniel felt as though he were walking on air. The delight he experienced being able to live with Isabella increased day by day until it reached an almost frightening intensity. At work Dr. Clark immediately recognized the symptoms of his assistant's waning concentration and decided not to let him assist in any surgical procedures for a few days.

"When you come down from your cloud, Nathaniel," he said with a knowing smile, "We can continue with your medical training."

"Oh, please excuse me sir," replied Nathaniel, shocked to realize that his preoccupation was so obvious, "I realize that my attention wanders a bit lately but …but. . . life is so eventful of late."

"Don't worry, Nathaniel, the state you are in is perfectly predictable," explained Dr. Clark with a wry smile, "It will soon pass but until then I don't want you amputating the wrong leg of some poor patient."

Grateful for Dr. Clark's patience but embarrassed by his inability to concentrate on vital tasks, Nathaniel decided that this might be a good time to ride to Princeton to say farewell to Benjamin who was planning to depart for studies in England in the near future. He could stay overnight at his parents'. Perhaps a night away from Isabella might help him to calm down although just the thought of separation even for day was painful.

That evening Nathaniel brooded over how best to tell Isabella that he was planning a short excursion without her. He assumed that she would be just as reluctant to endure separation as he was.

"Darling, this week I must pay a short visit to the college," he began, "Do you think you can manage without me for a day or so?"

"Of course, my love," Isabella replied quickly to Nathaniel's surprise, "The servants that my father gave us are planning to move into the servants' quarters this week and I have much to do to get everything organized."

"When you are here," she continued with an erotically suggestive smile kissing him on the end of his nose, "We have a way of wasting so much time."

"Wasting, indeed!" exclaimed Nathaniel taken aback, "And here I was feeling great qualms about leaving my dearly beloved even for a day."

"Absence makes the heart grow fonder," Isabella countered while embracing Nathaniel and running her hands up his back, "Perhaps I have to send you off somewhere at regular intervals so that your love for me will continue to grow. Besides you are not leaving today, are you?"

Overwhelmed by desire Nathaniel picked up a laughing Isabella and carried upstairs to their bedroom. As they urgently took off each other's clothes, Nathaniel realized that it would take more than a trip to Princeton to overcome his sense of bewitchment.

A few days later Nathaniel was sitting in the Washington Arms tavern on Nassau Street in Princeton drinking a glass of cider with Benjamin.

"I thought you were planning to leave for England in the next few weeks," said Nathaniel after hearing that Benjamin's departure date had been postponed.

"I was but that scoundrel of a Loudoun has embargoed all shipping until he launches his big attack against the French," explained Benjamin, "He is convinced that the colonies are full of smugglers and traitors who would be happy to sell secrets to the enemy. By keeping all ships in port, he thinks he can prevent that from happening."

"What a disaster!" exclaimed Nathaniel, "Getting his invasion of New France organized could take months. He can't just stop all trade for all that time. The livelihoods of thousands of people depend on it."

"He can and he did," replied Benjamin, "Any American vessel caught on the high seas now will be considered a pirate. The ports will soon be overflowing with unemployed seamen and the traders are already pulling their hair out."

"My father-in-law thinks that Loudoun doesn't have a clue about how to win this war," said Nathaniel, "And when I see this madness, I think he is probably right."

"He is right, indeed," agreed Benjamin, "Loudoun thinks that both the colonists and the Indians are totally useless, and that he can win the war without their help. It is the epitome of hubris."

"Well, as Colonel Anderson points out, he does want our help, as least as far as financing his campaign is concerned," added Nathaniel, "He just doesn't want our advice."

"Speaking of Colonel Anderson how do you like being part of the Anderson estate now?" asked Benjamin with a mischievous grin.

"Just because my father-in-law gave us a plot of land as a wedding gift does not mean I am part of the Anderson estate," objected Nathaniel, "Although I must admit that I am overwhelmed by the generosity of my in-laws. They just gave Isabella two servants. One of them you have already met. He is the young man who was the driver of the Anderson's wagon in Manalapan. His name is Dunmore."

"That you owe for your opportunity for gallantry?" asked Benjamin.

"The same," confirmed Nathaniel, "He and his wife, Beth, have just moved into our servants' quarters. They have taken care of Isabella since she was a child, and it just seemed natural that they should continue with us."

"I seem to recall your having once expressed moral reservations about the institution of enforced servitude. Has your new status as a landed country gentleman caused you to revise your viewpoint?" teased Benjamin.

"I continue to believe that all men should be free," answered Nathaniel defensively, "But reforming established institutions is not something that can be done overnight. If all the slaves were suddenly freed, how would they support themselves? Do you realize if you want to free a slave in New Jersey you have to post a bond to cover any expenses that might result in case that person becomes a ward of the state? For example, it would cost Colonel Anderson a small fortune in bonds to free his slaves even he wanted to. And then there is the question of the shortage of the supply of free labor."

"If the slaves were freed, they could work for a wage, and then there would be no shortage of free labor," contradicted Benjamin.

"I think it will eventually come to that," agreed Nathaniel. "But it still needs to be a gradual process," he added loftily, "In the meantime, I think that the moral imperative is to treat servants fairly and help them to develop mentally and spiritually."

"Spoken like a true lord of the manor," said Benjamin, always pleased with himself whenever he could expose a trace of hypocrisy in his friend's moralistic arguments, "But however you chose to organize Dunmore's continuing development, you must remember that you owe him gratitude for the opportunity to become acquainted with Isabella."

A few days later during a visit to the Anderson estate, Nathaniel related Benjamin's story to Isabella and her father and mother.

"That is absolute madness," exploded Colonel Anderson, "Anyone with half an eye can see that Loudoun is heading for disaster. He completely misunderstands how things work in North America. He thinks he can just demand money from the colonial governments without any consent of the governed, billet troops wherever he pleases and impose ruinous trade restrictions at a whim. But worst of all he is completely oblivious of the fundamental importance of our relationship with the Iroquois Confederacy. Without their support we have no hope of defeating the French."

"But I thought they were already our allies—surely Loudoun would not be foolish enough to end that alliance?" asked Nathaniel.

"The Iroquois Confederacy is the third major power on this continent," explained Colonel Anderson, "And they hold the key to the overall balance of power. But they play each side off against the other. They have a great need for European products such as guns and metal tomahawks. In order to secure their trade, they have always sought to dominate the supply of furs that they need to trade for these things. That is what resulted in the Beaver Wars of the last century. The Dutch were willing to trade European weapons for furs and the Iroquois used them to push back the French and their Indian allies. After the British took over, they continued the same policy. Eventually the Iroquois came to dominate many of the tribes and territory from Canada down into the Ohio territory."

"Don't we have such common interests that an alliance makes sense for both sides?" asked Isabella.

"Yes, but the Iroquois don't want either side to get too powerful," answered the colonel, "That is why the last two wars against the French ended indecisively. Just when we were on the verge of victory our Iroquois allies would see to it that our offensives got bogged down in the wilderness. In order to insure effective military support, we need to convince them of the benefits of loyalty to the alliance. That means a steady flow of diplomatic gifts and repeated ceremonial acknowledgement of their hegemony in the areas they control. We have been quite successful in this area in the past, but Loudoun has discontinued all of that. He thinks we don't need the help of a bunch of savages."

"It is just a manner of ignorance," added Hannah Anderson, "Loudoun has no conception of the complexities of our situation. He told us at a reception at the governor's house that for him the Indians and the colonial militias are irrelevant in the current struggle. Success in his opinion depends solely on the successful deployment of well-trained regular troops. I am afraid he will meet the same fate as General Braddock."

Riding back to their new homestead from the Anderson Estate in their carriage driven by Dunmore, Nathaniel and Isabella continued to discuss the current depressing state of affairs.

"Your parents' opinion of Loudoun's chances of success is certainly worrisome," said Nathaniel, "I cannot understand why the authorities in London are so blind to the realities on this continent. Why won't they take the advice of people like your father who really understand the situation here?"

"Perhaps it will take another tragedy like the defeat in the campaign against Fort Duquesne to wake them up," ventured Isabella, "I wonder what the consequence of this for our plans will be. I was so looking forward to starting a family soon, but these uncertain times give me pause. Can we really bring children into such a dangerous world?"

Pulling Isabella close to him in the carriage Nathaniel tried manfully to reassure his young bride.

"It is indeed very worrisome," he began, "But I have faith in the Lord. Nothing happens without His consent. I continue to believe, as my ancestors did, that we have a holy mission on this continent. I cannot believe that He would permit the Papists and their savage allies to destroy our grand project for promoting True Religion. As John Winthrop said on his way to the Massachusetts Bay Colony, our community will be as a city on a hill acting as a shining example of righteousness to the peoples of the world. Perhaps this is all just a test to see if we are capable of maintaining our Covenant with God. We must strengthen our faith and prove that we are worthy. We cannot allow ourselves to despair. That would be an insult to the goodness of Providence. Of course, we must continue with our plans to found our family and do good in this world."

Snuggling into Nathaniel's shoulder Isabella felt comforted by Nathaniel's faith in their future and the strength of his convictions.

"I am so happy I married you," she whispered gazing lovingly into his eyes, "You give me confidence to face the challenges that we must deal with."

"Speaking of challenges," Nathaniel continued, "When I was in Princeton, Esther Burr asked if we would like to pay her a visit."

"That would be quite an honor," answered Isabella, "Why do you call it a challenge? Mrs. Burr seemed like a decent person when I met her, and Annis Boudinot has apparently developed a close relationship with her."

"Mrs. Burr is indeed an outstanding person, but she can be—how shall I say—a bit intense. She is also somewhat old-fashioned as regards things that our generation might consider to be just harmlessly amusing."

Nathaniel then told her about the incident with his dancing lesson in the college library. Isabella nodded thoughtfully musing to herself that the meeting with Reverend Burr's wife could turn out to be a challenge indeed.

A few weeks later Nathaniel and Isabella were driven by Dunmore in their carriage to Princeton to the new home of the Burr family. Isabella made certain that she was not dressed too flamboyantly in order not to offend Puritan sensibilities. President Burr, as usual, was off somewhere on official duties, probably fundraising for the college. Esther Burr was home alone with her two children, her sister, Sukie, and her Black maidservant.

Esther answered the door personally smiling at the visitors and bidding them enter. Nathaniel taking off his hat bowed low to Esther and rising up began, "Many thanks for this gracious invitation, Mrs. Burr, I believe you have already made the acquaintance of my wife?"

"Indeed, I have had the pleasure," replied Esther, "I welcome both of you to our home. President Burr is off on urgent business, but he sends you his regards."

"We are honored to be your guests, Ms. Burr," added Isabella, "This is the first time that Nathaniel and I have attended a social function as a couple—except for our wedding, of course."

"Yes, well I can see that both of you still have the warm glow of the newly wed, but that will soon pass as all things do," said Esther with that air of theological certainty peculiar to preachers' daughters, "It is important that young couples starting out quickly develop a realistic attitude about the inevitable suffering that they will be facing."

Isabella was spared having to voice her objection to this in her opinion overly pessimistic view of the future by the maidservant's announcing that tea and biscuits were to be served immediately in the dining room.

As they took their places around the table, Nathaniel tried to head off what he feared might develop into an argument between Esther and Isabella by giving a general affirmation of Esther's gloomy Calvinist world view.

"Suffering is something I experience every day," affirmed Nathaniel, "Every day wounded militia men return from the front. Dr. Clark and I have our hands full. One cannot help but reflect on the meaning of it all."

"Exactly! One should never stop reflecting on the meaning of it and what it means for our salvation. We are in the middle of a grand confrontation between good and evil, and most people choose to ignore its meaning and carry on as though nothing were happening. It is a test for all of us." Esther shook her head with a determined frown.

"It is above all a test for Lord Loudoun's strategy," commented Isabella with a wry smile, "With competent leadership a victory over the French should be feasible. After all, the population of British North America is many times that of New France. It is not clear, however, that Loudoun's strategy is the right one."

Taken aback by Isabella's self-confident pronouncement, Esther fixed a critical eye on this young lady who dared to express such a controversial view.

"I don't think any of us are experts in military strategy," replied Esther coldly, "But I know decadence when I see it, and decadence is everywhere on the increase. Everywhere you turn you see people more interested in material acquisition than in striving toward the Kingdom of God. It is a wonder that He has not already crushed us underfoot like the wretched worms that we are. We can only hope that through His grace alone we undeserving sinners might be saved."

"Surely it is only through God's grace that we can hope to prevail," affirmed Nathaniel quickly, trying again to steer away from a confrontation between his worldly rational wife and this resolute Calvinist New Light ideologue, "But I am confident that most people in the colony are willing to do their duty and given adequate leadership will be able to fight off the Papists and their savage allies."

"We can only pray that this will be the case but everywhere one sees greed, debauchery, and disrespect for the True Religion. My dear husband has worked himself into a state of exhaustion to try to save the souls of the college students but just as he is now making progress he is being attacked from all sides. When I witness this, I can only believe that things will have to get much worse before they can get better. People will have to suffer still more before they come to their senses."

Nathaniel understood how distraught the Burrs must be. The move to Princeton was a mammoth undertaking and President Burr had made superhuman efforts to find funds for the project and bring it to a successful conclusion. The scandal about the withdrawal of the students had also created a huge additional emotional burden. The students who had been withdrawn were the sons of wealthy and influential people, the kind of people that the Burrs had long sought to win over to the cause of promoting the college. And to top it all off her father was the pastor in Stockbridge, a settlement not very far from the border that was periodically threatened by Indians loyal to the French.

"The great work of your husband is widely known and appreciated," said Nathaniel attempting to mitigate Esther's dire view of the current situation, "Governor Belcher himself is said to be an ardent supporter of both President Burr and the college."

"But Governor Belcher is not a well man," countered Esther, "Lord knows who will replace him. It could be another one like Governor Morris who tried to prevent the college's foundation."

"The college exists now for almost ten years and thanks to President Burr is well established," re-assured Nathaniel, "It has produced quite a few successful graduates. I cannot imagine that anything could endanger it now."

"The Devil is a wily adversary," insisted Esther, "We dare not lower our defenses even for a moment und must devote all of our strength to the Lord's work."

"That we must, that we must," agreed Nathaniel, "And to that end we must be getting back to Manalapan. Loudoun's troop build-up has put enormous strain on the facilities in Monmouth County. Overcrowding is resulting in the spread of the typical diseases. Dr. Clark told me that more soldiers die from camp fever than from enemy bullets. Much work awaits me."

"May God bless your efforts with much success," responded Esther gravely, "I shall pray fervently that we prevail in this test of our virtue."

"Your prayers are much appreciated," said Nathaniel rising together with Isabella and both bowing in Esther's direction, "Please give our respectful greetings and good wishes to President Burr."

Leaving the Burr residence Nathaniel and Isabella returned to their carriage and bade Dunmore drive them back to Manalapan.

"Well, she certainly is a dreary sort," commented Isabella, "If I had to be around her all the time, I think I should suffer a chronic case of melancholia."

"I warned you, she is a bit intense," responded Nathaniel, "But she and her husband have worked incredibly hard to make the college a success. She is not normally quite so depressed as we experienced her today. I think the strain has gotten to be too much for both of them."

"Let's hope her pessimism does not turn out to be accurate, but my father is also none too optimistic, albeit for different reasons."

The next weeks continued to be very busy for Nathaniel and Isabella. Isabella sought to fight off her growing feelings of foreboding by immersing herself in the business of furbishing and running their new home. Since Loudoun's embargo made the procurement of anything problematical that could not be found locally, she had plenty to do. Dr. Clark and Nathaniel had to deal with a continuous flow of refugees from the western territories who had been terrorized by France's Indian allies. In addition, more and more British troops arrived at New York and were billeted in the surrounding areas. While supplying the soldiers generated quite a bit of business for local merchants, the officers' tendency to seize whatever they needed caused much resentment. After many delays, Loudoun was finally ready to move and to the great relief of the local population the British army started to head north. The embargo was lifted at last.

One day in early September Nathaniel and Isabella were summoned by Colonel Anderson to come to the estate as quickly as possible. When they arrived there, they found Kenneth and Hannah Anderson in a state of great turmoil.

"Whatever is wrong," Isabella asked anxiously, alarmed to see her normally so calm parents so distraught, "Has someone died in the family?"

"Not in the family," answered her father grimly, "Governor Belcher passed away on the 31st of August. I just received word from friends on the Royal Council. It is a dark day for New Jersey and that in the middle of a war."

"Do you know how it happened," asked Nathaniel, "I know he had health problems, but they did not seem to be the kind of illnesses that would cause death."

"I am certain that it had something to do with the dreadful news from the front that has been arriving lately," answered Colonel Anderson, "He probably got so upset that he suffered a stroke."

"What kind of bad news?" asked Nathaniel, "Has Loudoun's invasion of Canada not been successful?"

"It has been a complete and utter disaster," replied Colonel Anderson angrily, "Just as I predicted it would be. The fool was planning to attack Quebec and conquer New France once and for all. But first he tried to take the French base at Louisbourg. When he got there, he found more French ships than he expected, so he turned around and headed home. In the meantime, a large French and Indian force overwhelmed the troops he had left at Fort William Henry and, by all accounts, committed an abominable massacre of the soldiers and civilians after they surrendered!"

"Oh my God, how dreadful!" exclaimed Nathaniel, "No wonder the governor was so upset. He was one of the few provincial governors who answered Loudoun's call for troops. I am sure that many New Jersey militiamen were involved. This is indeed a dark day for New Jersey."

"Yes, many of my finest militiamen were in that expedition," continued Colonel Anderson, "I sent them at Governor Belcher's behest. Now I have no idea if any of them will return home. This is all a result of Loudoun's incompetence. When I heard this summer that William Pitt had agreed to form a coalition with Lord Newcastle, I had hoped that a new energetic leader like Pitt could turn things around. But as long as he leaves that fool of a Loudoun in charge over here, things will only get worse. In any case, we must make haste to attend Governor Belcher's funeral. It will be held this coming Sabbath in Elizabethtown. Reverend Burr will deliver the sermon."

Nathaniel, Isabella and Isabella's parents left early in the morning the following Sunday in order to get to Elizabethtown in time for the funeral ceremony. As they entered the meeting house, they saw the coffin with the body of Governor Belcher lying in state in the front. After they took their seats among many of the colony's most distinguished figures, their sense of devastation was heightened by the appearance of a haggard and exhausted President Burr who entered the meeting house and walked slowly to the pulpit with his head bowed.

"To pass over in silence, true merit, when rendered conspicuous by the honors and dignities of this world," began Reverend Burr, "would be injustice to the living, as such characters, when set in a fair light, attract the esteem and engage the imitation of others."

Burr continued with a biography of the deceased recounting all the services that he had rendered to his country and especially to New Jersey after he became the royal governor. He particularly emphasized Belcher's contribution to the damping down what had almost escalated to a civil war between the Proprietor class and the Calvinist yeomen.

"When he first arrived, he found the province thrown into the utmost confusion by tumults and riotous disorders, which had for some time prevailed; these he labored with his whole power to prevent and suppress. The above confusions, joined to the unhappy controversy between the two branches of the legislature, rendered the first part of his administration peculiarly difficult. But by his steady, wise, and prudent measures, these difficulties have been happily removed."

And, Burr, of course, could not fail to mention the thing for which he and his fellow Presbyterians were particularly grateful.

"Nor should I pass over in silence what will distinguish Governor Belcher's administration, not only in the present, but I trust, in all succeeding ages. I mean his being the Founder and Promoter, the chief Patron and Benefactor of the College of New Jersey—an estimation calculated to promote the important interests of religion, liberty, and learning."

Burr summed up by pointing out that all Belcher's achievements had to do with his being a True Christian and only such true Christians can lead us to success out of the terrible situation in which we now found ourselves.

"Consider, my friends, how loudly we are called upon for activity and diligence in this day," continued Burr, his voice rising and taking on the hortatory certainty of the convinced Calvinist, "It is a time of great public calamity and distress; the cloud gathers thick and darkens over us. The news of our misfortunes, like Job's messengers, follow at the heels of each other, and what is yet to come, I am sure we have reason to be greatly afraid. Alas! How is our nation and land filled with sin! Our abounding iniquities and heaven-daring abominations do, as it were, challenge the Almighty to vindicate the honor of his affronted Majesty. We are engaged in a war with a politic, bold, and enterprising enemy, who have found means to frustrate our high-raised expectations and to baffle us in our most important undertakings. Our counsels and schemes Heaven seems to have turned into foolishness; our vain boasts have been repeatedly blasted; all our designs against the enemy strangely dashed; shame and confusion have been thrown upon us. We may therefore tremble at what is like to be the final issue of so many disastrous events, especially if matters proceed with us as they have done ever since the commencement of the present war."

Despite his state of exhaustion Burr was an extraordinarily gifted preacher, able to connect with his listeners and amplify their feelings of anxiety and sense of impending doom if they did not mend their ways. He skillfully harangued his audience with the necessity of being ready to sacrifice for the common good. By the end of his sermon Nathaniel, like most of the men in the meeting house, was ready to grab a musket and march off to the front.

Instead, he continued to pursue his duty by assisting Dr. Clark. Reverend Burr had also indicated that this was the best course. In fact, one of the last agreements Burr had forged with Governor Belcher was that students at the college would not have to interrupt their studies with militia duty since they would be more useful to their communities as graduates. Within two weeks of Belcher's funeral Reverend Burr himself died, again sending a shock wave through the colony's elite. For Nathaniel the double deaths, the dreadful news from Fort William Henry, and the steady stream of diseased and wounded militiamen returning from the front produced the conviction that he was in the midst of an epochal struggle between good and evil. With grim determination he worked long hours with Dr. Clark, but no matter how many hours he worked, there was no end to the number of mutilated patients who needed attention.

During the fall several militiamen returned who had been taken prisoner by the Indians after the surrender of Fort William McHenry but had managed somehow to escape. One such person was a Jersey militiaman who had made it all the way back through Indian country with a musket ball in his shoulder. He was being debriefed at a British Army camp near Sandy Hook. Since he was a New Jersey militiaman and the British were short of surgeon's mates, the British commander suggested to Colonel Anderson that the New Jersey militia take care of its own. At Colonel Anderson's request, therefore, Nathaniel and Dr. Clark rode to the British camp to have a look at the wounded man, one Jedediah Hall from Perth Amboy.

They found him at a campfire surrounded by three young British regulars that he was entertaining with lurid tales of his experiences.

"If it wasn't for God's good grace, I might in the belly of one of them Ottawas," Hall announced gravely.

"Do they actually eat prisoners?" asked the youngest recruit incredulously, staring wide-eyed at Hall.

"You betcha," answered Hall, "Them savages are imps of the Devil. Five of us, three militiamen and two women camp followers, were taken prisoner by the heathens after the cowardly Frenchmen did not protect us as they promised. They dragged us off deep into Indian country and then proceeded to have their fun with us. They grabbed one of the men, tore off his clothes, and tied him to a stake in front of a big fire. We were forced to sit in a circle around him. Then one of the savages cut a strip of skin off his bare chest about an inch wide and eight inches long. He tore it off, put it on a stick and roasted it over the fire, while our poor comrade writhed and screamed in pain at the stake. Afterwards he ate a piece of it and forced some of the prisoners to do the same."

The young recruit who had asked the question first turned white and then a light shade of green. It looked as though he was about to lose the contents of his stomach any minute.

"The imp out of hell then continued flaying the poor bastard until he bled to death. That night I decided to run for it. Getting shot down on the fly would be better than being the next one at the stake. I took a ball in the shoulder but managed to disappear into the dark. The Indians were headed in the opposite direction and didn't want to spend too much time following me. In any case they were more interested to get the two women prisoners back to their home camp to adopt into their tribe. I don't want to think what happened to the other male prisoner. After a day or so heading south, I ran into some friendly Indians, and they put some kind of paste onto the wound, I think they made it out of cattail roots. The wound didn't give me no trouble after that, and I was able to hitch a ride with a boat headed down the Hudson. That was how I got here."

"You were very lucky to run into that second group of Indians," said Dr. Clark after examining the militiaman's shoulder, "There are no signs of inflammation. The wound is almost completely healed. We should cut it open, however, and remove the ball, otherwise you might have permanent pain. You obviously have good blood so the wound will heal quickly. We'll use the same potion that the Indians used to keep away the inflammation."

Under the watchful eyes of Dr. Clark, Nathaniel quickly performed the simple operation, applied a poultice of the herbs that they had obtained in Crossweeksung and bandaged the wound.

"We will be back in a few days to check up on it," promised Dr. Clark, "And don't put the fear of the Devil into those young recruits. They will be marching north soon, and they need to be fearless."

Several days later Nathaniel and Dr. Clark visited the camp again to check up on the militiaman's convalescence. When they approached the camp, they were surprised to see that some kind of official ceremony was in progress. The troops were lined up in formation in front of a stake driven into the ground to which a young man was bound. He was naked down to the waste. Behind him stood a burly sergeant major with a cat-o-nine-tails in his hand. Looking closer they saw to their alarm that it was the young recruit who had been listening to Hall's tales at the campfire just a few days ago. The drums rolled as an officer marched up to the lad with a piece of paper in his hand. When the drum roll stopped, the officer read aloud from the paper.

"Private Jenkins, you were apprehended in a cowardly attempt to desert from your unit yesterday. This kind of behavior is completely unacceptable for a British soldier. As a lesson to you and any others who might contemplate such shameful behavior, you are hereby sentenced to 500 lashes. Sergeant Major—please proceed."

"He won't survive that!" Nathaniel turned to Dr. Clark with a shocked expression on his face, "Look at him, he's just a skinny little lad, probably tubercular. He will be dead before they are finished carrying out the sentence."

"Indeed, he probably will be," responded Dr. Clark sadly, "This is unfortunately the way the Regulars enforce discipline in His Majesty's army. The boy's life counts for nothing. What counts is the effect on the other recruits."

Nathaniel winced each time the whip came down on the boy's back. Within minutes the skin had been flayed off and the bones became visible. Mercifully, the lad quickly lost consciousness. Nathaniel wanted to rush forward and plead for the boy's life, but Dr. Clark held him back.

"There is no point, Nathaniel," explained Dr. Clark, "There is no way to save that boy. They will carry out the sentence to the end, even if it means killing him. This is another aspect of the tragedy of war that you will have to get used to."

Nathaniel and Dr. Clark could not bear to listen to the sickening sound of the crack of the whip on mutilated meat. They walked over to the area where they had last seen Jedediah Hall and found him again at the campfire.

"I hope you realize what your tall tales have accomplished!" blurted Nathaniel hotly when he saw Hall.

"Those wasn't no tall tales, those was the truth," answered Hall defensively, "I didn't tell that young fellow to desert. I just wanted him to know what was in store for him in Injun country if he gets taken prisoner."

"Well, he doesn't need to worry about getting flayed by Indians, he is getting flayed by his own comrades," Nathaniel countered in disgust.

"That's why ain't no militiaman goin' to volunteer as a Redcoat, they're almost as cruel as the Injuns."

Exasperated, Nathaniel took a threatening step toward Hall, but Dr. Clark moved in front of him.

"Nathaniel, we are here to attend to Mr. Hall's wound, he is not responsible for the policies of the British Army," Dr. Clark warned raising his hand.

Nathaniel immediately regretted losing his temper and nodded his head quickly trying to recover his professional demeanor. Dr. Clark then calmly examined Hall's wound and pronounced him well on his way to complete recovery.

In the months following the incident with Hall Nathaniel underwent an abrupt descent from the euphoria he had experienced after marrying Isabella. He was burdened, of course, by the misery he had to contend with daily but that was not the main source of his depression. He was deeply troubled by his own irrational reaction to Hall's comment about the cruelty of the British Army. After careful consideration he realized that his anger resulted from Hall's having struck a nerve. On the one hand, he had a deep patriotic desire for the British to triumph over the French; on the other hand, the brutality of war in general and of the British officers clouded the moral issues in confusing ways. The impression of incompetence generated by Loudoun's military setbacks as well as by his petulant hectoring of the colonial authorities added to Nathaniel's growing feeling of foreboding that had begun with the deaths of Governor Belcher and President Burr. Nathaniel could not dispel the impression that his country was on the road to disaster and prayed fervently that God would lead them out of this Valley of Tears.

Nathaniel's downward spiral reached its nadir in February. After a particularly trying day attending to wounded soldiers and refugees, Nathaniel dropped by the Anderson Manor to discuss with Colonel Anderson arrangements for some of the wounded from his militia unit. His father-in-law had just returned from a governor's meeting and was livid with rage.

"You would not believe the cheek of that scoundrel, Loudoun!" fumed Colonel Anderson, "After organizing nothing but defeats for the past year, he had the nerve to accuse us all of a lack of patriotism. He wants us to pour even more money into his lap so he can just continue to sit here and waste money by building up a gigantic force instead of taking the war to the enemy. He is either too cowardly or too incompetent to organize a bold stroke against the French. If that man continues to lead us, we are surely doomed!"

Chapter 9

THE TIDE TURNS – 1758–1759

FOR WEEKS AFTER LISTENING to Colonel Anderson's outburst about Loudoun Nathaniel was preoccupied with worries about the fate of British North America in the face of such obvious incompetence. He also fretted that the emotional strain would take a toll on his father-in-law who was on the verge of apoplexy every time Loudoun's name was mentioned. A message from Anderson Manor requesting Nathaniel and Isabella to come immediately to hear important news filled them both, therefore, with great trepidation.

Nathaniel and Isabella remained silent, exchanging worried looks as Dunmore hurried them over to Anderson Manor in the carriage. They had heard to their shock that the newly appointed president of the College of New Jersey and father of Esther Burr, Reverend Jonathan Edwards, had succumbed to the effects of a botched small-pox vaccination. His daughter Esther, who had been going downhill since the death of her husband, was reported to be herself in very weak condition. The college, a bulwark of the True Religion, was now leaderless and at a time when it was rumored that an avowed enemy of Puritan ideals, Thomas Seeker, would become Archbishop of Canterbury. Nathaniel worried that between the Jesuits in the North and the Papists in the Anglican Church their beloved community and its sacred Covenant were mortally threatened on two fronts.

As they passed through the main gate, they were relieved to see Isabella's parents smiling at them from the porte-cochere.

"I have wonderful news!" beamed Colonel Anderson, "Pitt has sent two letters to Governor Pownall of Massachusetts. In the first he announced that Loudoun is being recalled. In the second, that the objections of provincial governments will be addressed in full. Finally, our prayers have been answered."

"That's wonderful news," beamed Nathaniel, as he jumped from the carriage and turned to help Isabella step down, "At last, the Lord is taking pity on us wretches. Perhaps now it will be possible to turn the tide."

"For the first time in years I feel that that might be a real prospect," agreed Colonel Anderson, "I have instructions to expand the Monmouth militia to the extent possible. Minister Pitt has agreed to reimburse the colonial governments for all expenses they incur in the war effort. Militia officers will be on an equal par with Regulars. Finally, we have a government that sees the necessity of listening to people who understand the situation in North America."

"And who is to be the new commander?" asked Isabella, "Is it someone who is likely to listen to good advice?"

"It is to be Loudoun's assistant, James Abercrombie," answered Colonel Anderson, "Not perhaps the ideal choice but, in any case, after Loudoun any change is welcome. Abercrombie is apparently a very good organizer, and he is being granted vast resources, so some improvement is inevitable."

"Let us hope so," Hannah Anderson joined the conversation, "But come children, let's not stand here at the porte-cochere. Come inside. Betsy has baked a cake to celebrate this auspicious turn of events."

Nathaniel and Isabella followed Colonel Anderson and Mrs. Anderson into the drawing room where the servants had laid out a sumptuous high tea. A smiling, ebullient Colonel Anderson gestured for all to take a seat while he readied himself to hold forth on the exciting turn of events. Nathaniel, Isabella as well as Hannah Anderson, pleased to see the colonel in such an optimistic mood, dutifully took their seats and waited in excited anticipation of the details he would soon relate.

"As you know, many of us in the political leadership of this colony have long had our doubts about Loudoun's strategy for winning this war," he began, "One of these is Thomas Pownall who was Lieutenant Governor under Governor Belcher for a time. He later became a close adviser to William Pitt and so impressed him that he was eventually appointed governor of Massachusetts to replace that bungler, Shirley. In January of this year Governor Pownall wrote to Pitt giving him an unvarnished account of the disaster we are facing and making practical suggestions how this challenge could be met. To the immense delight of everyone who understands the colonies, Pitt has written back, completely accepting all of Governor Pownall's suggestions."

"Praise the Lord!" exclaimed Nathaniel, "He has not forsaken us after all. Now we must prove ourselves worthy by doing our utmost to insure victory."

"That we must," agreed Colonel Anderson enthusiastically, "This will be a logistical challenge of the first magnitude. All the plantations must increase production in order to ensure that our vast army of the righteous will be properly supplied. I am thinking of buying more slaves and putting fallow land into production."

Nathaniel was a bit taken aback by the colonel's obvious preoccupation with the commercial opportunities of the military build-up. Hitherto he had seen these issues purely in terms of a great struggle between good and evil. Now he began to understand that the war against the French had many dimensions that he had not considered.

"Surely we must be willing to accept any sacrifice that will help us prevail," he ventured hesitatingly.

"Indeed," agreed the colonel, "But our sacrifices will be in terms of the blood and bravery of our militia. Pitt has absolved us of the necessity of financing this struggle, a project which would have ruined us. Money will now pour into the colonies from the mother country so that we can develop the true potential of this vast land."

"But won't that money have to be paid back eventually?" asked Isabella with a quizzical smile.

"Once we have driven the French Papists out of North America, we will be able to exploit the immense resources of this great continent without having to worry about their depredations," assured the colonel, "The debts are merely an investment which will be well worth it. But first we must insure victory. To do this we must expand and equip the militia with all deliberate haste. We will need to order uniforms, guns, powder, horses, carriages, and other supplies—everything that is needed for a huge build-up of our fighting capacity."

Nathaniel understood immediately that procurement on such a level would amount to a gigantic stimulation of economic activity in the local economy. The many tradesmen that had been idled by Loudoun's embargo would now have more to do than they could have imagined. Production of all kinds would have to expand to an unprecedented degree. There would be no more sailors loitering around the ports, no more blacksmiths without sufficient work to do, no farmers with time on their hands—everyone would be caught up in the swell of activity that Pitt's generous financing would make possible.

"And you, Nathaniel, and Dr. Clark will have plenty of work as well," continued Colonel Anderson, "On the basis of Pitt's generous offer of financing, the Assembly has authorized the re-mustering of the militia. We will be able to bring our troop strength back up again to 500 replacing those killed and missing after the battles at Fort Oswego and Fort William Henry. The troops will be furnished with new uniforms and weapons. In the next weeks we will outfit and drill them thoroughly. Then they will join the Regulars for an assault on Fort Carillon on Lake Champlain. You and Dr. Clark are to check out all the new recruits and make certain that they are in good fighting condition."

Nathaniel nodded enthusiastically, recalling Dr. Clark's oft-repeated statement that more soldiers died of camp fever than of bullet wounds on the battlefield. If sickly recruits could be filtered out at the beginning, a much healthier militia would be the result. Nathaniel would thus be able to make a concrete contribution to the war effort without having to leave his beloved Isabella. The Andersons and the Scudders spent the rest of the afternoon in excited discussions about the concrete steps necessary to insure victory.

In the following days and weeks Nathaniel threw himself with great dedication into the task of helping to re-muster the militia. While doing his rounds to outlying farms with Dr. Clark he encouraged healthy young men to consider volunteering. Those that did he then thoroughly examined when they reported to Colonel Anderson's militia headquarters. In this way he met many young men around his age. He noted with satisfaction that he was making many new friends and that this was perhaps his reward for doing the Lord's work.

One such new friend was John Burnes, a farmer's son from Manalapan who was the same age as Nathaniel, and also just recently married to his childhood sweetheart, Agatha. Not only had John volunteered, but Agatha as well had agreed to join the militia camp followers who provided the logistical support for the militia when they were deployed away from home. Such sturdy peasant girls were an essential element of a traveling army for cooking, cleaning, and boosting the moral of the troops. A simple but devout couple, John and Agatha had been impressed by Nathaniel's learned arguments about the necessity of confronting the French before their Jesuit propaganda turned all the Indians of North America into enemies of the True Religion. For their part, Nathaniel and Isabella were flattered by the obvious deference that the young couple accorded them as representatives of Anderson Manor.

On the day of John's muster Nathaniel and Isabella came to Anderson Manor to inspect the troops at the side of Colonel Anderson. Nathaniel was moved by the sight of the serried ranks of fresh militia units replete in the smart new blue uniforms that the Assembly had provided. He knew many of the young men personally who were standing there proudly in their blue coats and breeches augmented with red lapels and red waistcoats. This was a far cry from the crude buckskin outfits that most militiamen wore. The new uniforms had somehow transformed a bunch of farmers' sons into something that actually looked like an army!

Walking down the first row of troops Colonel Anderson and Nathaniel stopped in front of John Burnes who presented his musket in his best imitation of a British regular.

"You are cutting a gallant figure, Private Burnes, Nathaniel here informed me that you and your wife are marching off to war together."

"That is correct, Colonel, sir. Dr. Scudder convinced me that I owed it to my country to volunteer. And my wife wouldn't hear of staying home alone without me. We are both looking forward to driving the Papists out of North America and subduing their savage allies!"

"Well said, Private, well said. With such brave patriots on our side, I am confident that the Lord will lead us to victory."

Nathaniel smiled at John as the inspection team moved on down the rows noting proudly that for the first time someone had referred to him as "Dr. Scudder," although strictly speaking his internship was not yet completed. He was also proud of the role he had played in convincing so many of the volunteers of the dire necessity of defeating the French for the sake of the True Religion. In so doing he had discovered that he had a gift for exhortation that was almost as good as that of a preacher. Perhaps his father had been right, and he should have become a minister. On the other hand, he knew that his hortatory abilities only extended to things he really believed in deeply. And not all aspects of a parson's job could evoke the intensity of feeling that he felt for this great struggle between Good and Evil.

After Colonel Anderson had completed his inspection of the troops, he together with Nathaniel and Isabella proceeded back in the direction of the main mansion. As they approached the house, they noticed that a courier's horse was tethered next to the porte-cochere. Thinking that some important news regarding the disposition of the new troops might have arrived from the royal governor they hurriedly entered the building and found the courier handing over a letter to Hannah Anderson.

"It seems that Reverend Jacob Green from the college in Princeton has sent you a message," Hannah explained to her husband holding the letter out to him.

"I wonder what message Reverend Green could have for me," Colonel Anderson said aloud, ripping open the seal on the letter.

"Jacob Green is the acting president of the college since Reverend Edwards died," Nathaniel hastened to explain, "The trustees wanted to elect Samuel Davies, but he is reluctant to abandon his pastoral work in Virginia."

"Oh Lord," Colonel Anderson exclaimed after quickly reading through the short message, "Another tragic event. Esther Burr has expired! What a dreadful series of events for the college. First, her husband last year, then her father and now her!"

"Oh, how terrible," cried Isabella, "Three such good people all dying within the course of a year. I recall how Esther at our last visit was so vehement about the urgency of doing the Lord's work and confronting the French. Now that that seems finally about to happen, she will not get to experience it."

"I am not really surprised," commented Nathaniel, "When I saw her at her father's funeral in Princeton last month, she looked terrible. She muttered something about hoping that the Lord would soon relieve her of her worldly burdens."

"Let us pray for the repose of the soul of a devout woman," added Colonel Anderson piously nodding his head, "The Lord in His inscrutable wisdom often demands sacrifices from us which we must accept joyously, confident in the knowledge that His Divine Plan is the only road to salvation. Let us renew our devotion to the cause that Esther Burr so earnestly espoused."

"Amen!" exclaimed Hannah, Nathaniel, and Isabella simultaneously.

Nathaniel resolved to view the deaths in the leadership of his beloved college as further reasons to redouble his efforts to help prepare the militia. The deceased had labored hard to instill a sense of duty in the college's students, and now he felt even more motivated to act in a manner that they would approve of. For this reason, he spent many unpaid hours providing health care to the new recruits and assisting his father-in-law in organizing their drill. In this he was greatly encouraged by Isabella who was proud of the approbation that Nathaniel's work was earning him with her father. As spring turned into summer the re-mustered militia now dubbed the "Jersey

Blues" was deemed ready to face the enemy. Amid great fanfare the troops departed for Sandy Hook where they would board British navy vessels. They then would be transported up the Hudson to join the formidable army that General Abercrombie was organizing to overwhelm Fort Carillon on Lake Champlain.

As Nathaniel watched the troops march off, he felt a surge of pride for his efforts and growing confidence of success. It was rumored that Abercrombie had carefully organized the logistics for the largest troop concentration yet seen in North America, as many as 16,000 soldiers. Surely, Nathaniel thought, this army would be able to march through to Montreal sweeping away all resistance before it.

It was, therefore, a tremendous shock when a few weeks later the first news began to filter back to New Jersey that Abercrombie's invincible force had met with humiliating defeat at the hands of the French General Montcalm. It reached Nathaniel and Isabella in the form of an urgent message from Colonel Anderson to come to Anderson Manor immediately.

As they approached the mansion, they were again met by Colonel Anderson in front of the porte-cochere. This time, however, he was not smiling.

"I thought it might have been a mistake to let Loudoun's assistant replace him. They should have brought in fresh blood at the top," Colonel Anderson exclaimed bitterly, "That fool of an Abercrombie is as oblivious to the realities of North America as Loudoun was!"

Stepping down from the carriage, Isabella cast a worried look at Nathaniel. The apoplectic appearance of her father caused her to fear for his health as much as for the whatever dreadful news he might be bearing.

"Despite an overwhelming superiority in men and equipment, Abercrombie has managed to hand the enemy a great victory. The first remnants of our Jersey militia have returned, and the survivors tell a very depressing story. Apparently, hundreds if not thousands from our side are dead, wounded or missing. But come and see for yourselves. Let us go over to the bivouac area."

Colonel Anderson, Nathaniel and Isabella hurried over to bivouac area where bedraggled militiamen were unloading wagons containing the dead and the wounded. Nathaniel was startled to see that the young man he had especially mentored, John Burnes, was sitting in one of the wagons clutching a bloodied rag to what was left of his left arm.

"John, John, whatever has happened to you," Nathaniel cried out.

"They made us charge through a bati without cannon support," he answered through clenched teeth, "I made it to the wall but then a cutlass stroke to my arm ended my attack."

"And Agatha, what has become of Agatha?" asked Isabella anxiously.

"She is one of the many missing. Probably kidnapped by Indians," answered John before slumping back into the wagon fainting from the loss of blood.

"We must attend to him immediately before he bleeds to death!" shouted Nathaniel rushing over to haul John off the wagon with the help of a few militiamen. The men carried John over to a bench while Isabella ran back to the carriage to fetch Nathaniel's physician's bag. When she returned, Nathaniel applied a tourniquet to John's upper arm before carefully removing the bloody rag and cutting away the remnants of the sleeve.

"The saber blow cut right down to the bone severing an artery and some tendons," Nathaniel diagnosed as he inspected the wound, "He has lost much blood, but we can probably save the arm, although it might not be much use to him in the future. The wound fever does not seem to have set in yet so if we sew up the severed blood vessels to stop the bleeding, he might have a chance."

Colonel Anderson had also sent for Dr. Clark and Nathaniel would have preferred to assist him in this operation but there was no time to wait for him to arrive. It was a wonder that John had survived this long, so Nathaniel knew he had no time to waste. He began immediately to apply sutures to all the severed blood vessels. Afterward he closed the wound and fitted it with a poultice of the Lenape healing herbs. Then he carefully bandaged the arm and prayed that John would survive.

At that point Dr. Clark thundered into sight astride one of his fastest stallions. He rode up to the group of people and dismounted.

"I came as fast as I could after getting your message, Colonel," said Dr. Clark breathing heavily from his long gallop, "From the tone I surmised that there would be work here for me and Nathaniel."

"As well there is, Doctor," answered Colonel Anderson, "Dozens of our boys have been killed and wounded at Fort Carillon. What you see here is what is left of our proud troop. Nathaniel has already begun with this poor boy here but there are many more who need your attention."

Dr. Clark quickly inspected the work Nathaniel had done on John and indicated that he was pleased with its quality.

"I can see I have taught you well," said Dr. Clark with an approving smile, "Now let's get over to those other poor fellows and see how many we can save."

Isabella and Colonel Anderson decided to leave the physicians to their task. Nathaniel and Dr. Clark worked the rest of the day and long into the night ministering to the wounded who had survived the long journey from Fort Carillon. Utterly exhausted and depressed by the tragic failure of the mission Nathaniel finally returned home late to find Isabella waiting up for him.

"Poor Nathaniel," soothed Isabella, "You look so tired. You have really exerted yourself beyond the call of duty."

Sinking down to his knees, wrapping his arms around Isabella and putting his head against her stomach, Nathaniel let his anguish pour forth.

"No matter how hard I work I can't undo the damage that my advice has caused to so many families," he moaned, "So many of those young men volunteered because I encouraged them to do so. I feel a great burden of guilt. In the future I cannot encourage young men to go to war unless I go with them myself."

"I can understand you feel somehow responsible for these people, darling," said Isabella, stroking Nathaniel's hair, "But soon you will have other responsibilities that you may consider even more important. You are going to be a father."

Nathaniel fell back on his haunches and gazed up at Isabella with a dazed expression on his face which quickly turned into a smile of wonder.

"Are you sure," he stuttered, "That . . . that is magnificent!"

"Yes, I am quite certain. My monthly bleeding is already several weeks overdue, and I am beginning to feel that nausea in the morning that the midwives talk about. I was going to tell you this morning but then the message came from my father, so I decided to postpone the news."

"Oh, my darling, I can't tell you how delighted I am," Nathaniel's burden of fatigue seemed to be lifted off his shoulders as if by magic. He jumped to his feet and embraced Isabella, "The Lord certainly works His wonders in mysterious ways. Just a few minutes ago I was in the depths of depression but now life has a whole new meaning for me. This must be a sign that the Lord means well with us. But now we should get some sleep. This day has been exhausting for you as well and now, in your delicate condition . . . "

Nathaniel awoke the next morning to the sound of Isabella retching into the night basin. He immediately jumped up and held her head. After she had recovered her composure, he suggested that she go back to bed and rest. He would have the servants fix breakfast and bring it to her.

"The very thought of food disgusts me!" exclaimed Isabella, "Don't worry about me. I will be alright. The midwife told me that this is completely natural."

"The midwife is right, but you still need to eat," explained Nathaniel smiling, "After all you have two you need to nourish now. I will have Beth bring you some light fruit perhaps with a spot of peppermint tea to ease the nausea."

Pleased by Nathaniel's solicitous attitude Isabella agreed to go back to bed and wait for Beth to bring her breakfast. Nathaniel then took off again to Anderson Manor to tell his in-laws the good news and check up on the patients that he and Dr. Clark had treated the day before.

"That's wonderful news!" thundered Colonel Anderson when Nathaniel told him a grandchild was on the way. Hannah Anderson was also almost moved to tears when she heard it.

"Just think, Kenneth, we are about to become grandparents!"

"All the more reason to redouble our efforts to make certain our grandchildren grow up in environment purged of Jesuit influence."

Nodding enthusiastically in agreement, Nathaniel set off together with Colonel Anderson to check on the patients he had treated yesterday, and to find out more about how this disaster could have happened.

Nathaniel's first stop was to see John Burnes. Nathaniel was relieved to see that John's wound was beginning to heal and that he was able to carry on a conversation.

"Tell me, John, how could this have happened? I thought we had the French vastly outnumbered."

"Indeed, we did but that Montcalm is a wily bastard and Abercrombie played into his hands."

"Now how could that be?" asked Colonel Anderson with exasperation, "I thought the British army leadership had learned from their mistakes."

"Well, they still have much to learn if you ask me, sir," explained John, "First of all they wanted us to march in formation like on a parade field in Europe. But the New York frontier is not a parade field, it is a dense forest where one has to move like an Indian. The result was that our neat formations dispersed in a chaotic way, the cannon wagons could not keep up with the advancing soldiers. We also had no idea what was awaiting us. Abercrombie did not see fit to use our Indian guides to gather proper intelligence. He was so certain of victory that he ordered our units to attack as soon as possible without reconnoitering the area or waiting for the artillery to get in position. But Montcalm had constructed a bati of sharpened saplings pointing out from the wall of the fort. If the cannons had been in place, they could have blasted the bati into splinters. As it was, our units were ordered to attack head on. Wave after wave were cut down as they tried to climb through the bati. I was in one of the later waves and almost made it before a French officer lowered his cutlass on me."

"Oh my God, I don't believe it!" shouted Colonel Anderson, "When will they learn they are not fighting a classical engagement on the plains of Europe! This is really outrageous. I am going to go to the highest levels to protest it. If the high command does not realize the importance of utilizing our Indian allies, we could still lose this war despite our enormous efforts!"

Colonel Anderson stomped off with determined mien and Nathaniel hoped that his father-in-law would indeed be able to influence the course of future events. For his part Nathaniel had plenty to do over the next weeks. There were many wounded to be nursed back to health and, of course, there was Isabella's pregnancy which Nathaniel was determined to micromanage. His daily examinations and lengthy recommendations about optimal health management became so tedious that Isabella had to ask him to stop.

"You need not worry me continuously with your prescriptions," she said irritably, "I know you mean well but I am doing just fine. Beth is taking great care of me. She just gave birth herself last year to a strapping young boy, so she knows what she's about."

"Indeed, indeed," admitted Nathaniel, sensing that he really had been making a nuisance of himself, "I know I can be obsessive sometimes, but you and our child are the most important things in my life."

Over the next days and weeks Nathaniel managed to rein in his urge to keep Isabella under his constant surveillance. In any case he had more than enough to do tending the wounded militiamen. He was also buoyed by more exciting news from the front. Apparently, the British fleet had achieved a great victory at Fort Louisbourg which guarded the entrance to the St. Lawrence. This could turn out to be a decisive turn of events. The French garrison near the Gulf of St. Lawrence guarded the approaches to the major French cities of Quebec and Montreal. Its loss would be a devastating blow to the French war effort.

As summer turned into fall the news from the front continued to improve. Not only did the details about the capture of Fort Louisbourg confirm the remarkable British victory, but news also arrived about another great British victory at Fort Frontenac in which units of the Jersey Blues had participated. The French surrender of this fort on the eastern end of Lake Ontario where it empties into the St. Lawrence effectively destroyed the ability of the French army command in Montreal and Quebec to communicate with its troops in the Ohio Valley. Nathaniel and Colonel Anderson learned of this fortunate turn of events from one of the returning militiamen, Samuel Covenhoven, who had been at the scene.

"It was actually dead easy, Colonel Anderson sir," explained Covenhoven, "There were only about a hundred Frenchies there even counting the women and children. Colonel Bradstreet had over a hundred regulars and thousands of us militiamen. They quickly understood they didn't have a chance and surrendered."

"Just as I have been preaching for years!" exclaimed Colonel Anderson triumphantly, "Bradstreet obviously realized the value of using North Americans to fight in North America. Now if we can strike an agreement with the Iroquois Confederacy, we can drive the French out of North America for good. I am going to do my best to achieve exactly that. I have been appointed to a delegation from New Jersey to negotiate with the Indians."

"How exciting! Congratulations!" Nathaniel beamed with admiration at his father-in-law, "When and where is this going to happen?"

"Delegations from New Jersey and Pennsylvania are due to meet in Easton, Pennsylvania with representatives of 13 Indian nations including the Iroquois. We have explicit orders from our governors that we are to do what is necessary to get the Indians on our side. It is supposed to start in the middle of October so I will be leaving soon."

After the colonel's departure Nathaniel, Isabella, and Hannah Anderson spent the next weeks alternating between excitement about the colonel's crucial mission and anxiety about the dangers he might be facing. Easton, close to the western frontier where settlers were slaughtered by Indians on a regular basis, was not considered a safe area. Although Indians generally respected the right of safe passage to and from such councils, it was impossible to know what could happen should the negotiations break down.

More than a month later the colonel finally returned with the small group of militia guards and servants who had accompanied him on the trip. In anticipation of his arrival Nathaniel, Isabella and Hannah Anderson had gathered at Anderson Manor. When the colonel came into view, they could immediately sense the air of the successful statesman.

"It is done!" announced the colonel with a confident smile, "We have signed an agreement with all the Indian nations that were present. They will no longer fight against the British. The French are finished."

"Oh what wonderful news," cried Hannah Anderson clasping her hands together in a gesture of thanks, "Praise be to the Almighty."

"Father, you must tell us all the details! What an exciting adventure! Tell us exactly how it was to deal with the savages." Isabella could barely contain her curiosity.

"Well, it was quite fascinating," began Colonel Anderson, "There were about 500 representatives of the various tribes including the Iroquois Confederacy, the Lenape and the Shawnee. The conference began, of course, by our presenting the Indians with many gifts and wampum. Our spokesman was the Attorney General of Pennsylvania, Benjamin Chew, a most impressive lawyer. There were many issues to be resolved beginning with that outrageous swindle, the so-called Walking Purchase of 1737. Our side agreed to revise the results of that agreement and to respect the Indians' hunting rights in the Ohio Valley. The Lenape agreed to cede all remaining claims within the province of New Jersey in exchange for the sum of one thousand Spanish dollars. All the tribes present agreed not to fight against the British and to discourage any other Indians from doing so as well."

Thinking about his Lenape friends in the settlement of Crossweeksung Nathaniel asked, "Does that mean the Lenape here will have to leave?"

"Not really," replied the colonel, "Those few Lenape who still live here will be able to stay but they will have no land claims beyond the immediate area where they live. In any case the French are finished. General Forbes and Colonel Bouquet are advancing now on Fort Duquesne with an overwhelming force. They will surely finish the job that they began in September. Now that Frontenac and Louisbourg have fallen and most of the Indians are on our side, the French will not be able to resupply their forces there. It is only a matter of time until they are driven out."

The colonel's words proved to be prophetic. By the end of November, the French had realized the hopelessness of their situation in the Ohio country. They burned the fort and withdrew. When Forbes army arrived, all they found were the charred ruins and the grisly remains of the British victims of the first assault in September, the heads of highlanders impaled on stakes with their kilts wrapped around the bottom. The British rebuilt the fort and named it Fort Pitt in honor of the minister who helped turn the tide.

In December Reverend Tennent held a special prayer meeting at Manalapan to commemorate the great victories that had been achieved that year. Specifically citing the contribution made by the New Jersey Blues he praised the bravery and willingness to sacrifice that the militiamen had exhibited.

"The sons of our American soil have proved that they are capable of expunging the Papist scourge that has threatened us. Those who doubted our fortitude have been proven wrong. Our initial defeats were the result of hubris on the part of arrogant aristocrats who have no understanding of the special nature of our society. We shall adhere to our sacred covenant with the Almighty to protect and develop His New Kingdom here in North America. Despite what Archbishop Seeker may think, we do not need bishops here to accomplish our goals. We need no one to mediate between ourselves and our God. All we need is unflinching adherence to the True Religion."

Chapter 10

ANNUS MIRABILIS – 1759–1760

AFTER THE END OF the special prayer meeting Isabella and Nathaniel proceeded to Anderson Manor to have Sunday dinner with the Anderson family.

"Why do you suppose Reverend Tennent is so exercised by the new archbishop?" asked Isabella.

"Thomas Seeker is known to be an enemy of reformed Christian congregations," answered Nathaniel, "He is one of those who would like to make the Church of England as papist as possible. It is feared that he would like to impose a bishop on North America who would limit the freedom of practitioners of the True Religion. If the Church of England were to try to re-impose the strictures that led to the Civil War in Britain in the last century, it would be fiercely resisted in North America. So many of our ancestors came here to escape the tyranny of Charles I—it is unthinkable that we would submit to any kind of counter reformation."

"Do you really think that is possible?" asked Isabella, "No one could be foolish enough to jeopardize the current feeling of national unity at a time when that sentiment is taking us from success to success."

"It would be madness," agreed Nathaniel, "But, unfortunately not unthinkable. The Church of England is the bulwark of royalist privilege that can always become a threat whenever pampered courtiers are favored over honest, hardworking Christians. Many recall receiving notices from absentee landlords to pay quitrents for land they had legitimately bought and farmed for generations. We still have land riots to this day because of such usurpation of private property."

"You are right, of course, darling," conceded Isabella, "We must indeed do everything to make certain that the True Religion remains strong and unassailable in our country."

Arriving at Anderson Manor Isabella and Nathaniel noticed the signs of vastly increased activity. Colonel Anderson had indeed embarked on a significant expansion of the productive capacity of the estate. He had bought about a dozen additional slaves in order to clear more land for planting in the spring. The rest of the staff was busy turning this year's harvest into usable products to be sold to the burgeoning military. The manor veritably hummed with activity. Pigs, cows, and geese were being slaughtered, salted, and smoked; wheat, potatoes, and onions sorted into great sacks cucumbers cured in brine; ears of corn hung up to dry. Everything to help a hungry army get through the winter was being prepared as hastily as possible.

"Prices are already up by 10 percent in the last month," shouted an ebullient Colonel Anderson in greeting his daughter and son-in-law, "We could easily sell twice the amount we were able to produce this year. At this rate we will have to triple the capacity of this estate next year to keep up with demand."

"My father reports the same thing," replied Nathaniel, "Both his grist mill and his lumber mill are working around the clock to keep up with farmers' demand for his services. He doesn't know where to get the workers to keep going like this with so many of the able-bodied men signing up for militia duty. I am also affected by the boom. Everywhere people are working their fingers to the bone which, of course, results in more accidents and sickness. Dr. Clark has asked me to take over many of his patients because he does not have the time to visit them. He is also getting on in years and likes to leave the long rides to outlying farms to me. Everywhere I go, it is the same thing. This province has turned into a beehive of activity."

At dinner the conversation centered on the vast opportunities that were opening up as a result of the massive mobilization that Pitt's policies had made possible. The opportunities as it turned out were benefitting not just honest and patriotic landowners like the Andersons.

"All of the farms that I visit on my medical rounds are expanding production as fast as they can," remarked Nathaniel, "But apparently not all of it is destined for the British army or the militia. Some of the farmers have admitted to me that they can sell their wares in the direction of Tom's River much more profitably then to the local military procurement agents."

"That is certainly true," agreed Colonel Anderson, "The French in the Caribbean islands are willing to pay 20 or 30 percent more for farm produce than is obtainable in this province. That is treasonous, of course, but many are willing to do it. They can also trade their products for sugar and rum on very favorable terms because they avoid having to pay the British duties. Thomas Penn told me not long ago that the port of Philadelphia is swarming with shallops from French ports unloading illegal cargoes."

"That is outrageous!" exclaimed Isabella, "Don't they have any qualms about aiding the enemy?"

"Well, as Esther Burr often said, greed might yet be the undoing of this province," pontificated Nathaniel, "The lure of mammon is Satan's most potent weapon."

Annoyed by Nathaniel's pompous manner Isabella retorted irritably, "I seem to recall that you and Dr. Clark don't mind dealing with the smugglers at Tom's River."

"Now, now," soothed Colonel Anderson, "Don't be so hard on your poor husband. The trade that Dr. Clark and Nathaniel engage in is not for personal gain."

Nathaniel was relieved that his father-in-law tried to mollify Isabella who was becoming increasingly prone to bouts of irritability as her pregnancy progressed to an uncomfortable stage. She sometimes seemed to blame Nathaniel for the discomfort she had to endure.

"I know, I know, I apologize. But I just can't understand why something can't be done about this."

"Because there *is* nothing to be done about it," explained Colonel Anderson, "First of all, not all of the trade in French goods is illegal. Some of it results from privateering which is not only legal but desirable since it weakens the French. Secondly, His Majesty's government is partly to blame because the Navigation Acts restrict trade in stupid ways. Why should some monopolist in London take a cut of trade that he has nothing to do with? And finally, there is really no feasible way to combat it effectively. The Jersey shore in the area of Tom's River and Little Egg Harbor with its many inlets and treacherous shoals is practically beyond the control of any government. Only locals can navigate that area successfully. The entire Royal Navy would not be able to patrol there effectively. Also, the overland trade routes from there to Philadelphia and other cities run through the Pine Barrens, another area which is essentially impenetrable for the forces of law and order."

"Whatever the details of the trading, we need to be thankful for the Lord's good will," Hannah Anderson added, seeking to guide the conversation in a more harmonious direction, "We are blessed as never before with the bounty of this land. Some of the British regulars that I talked to are amazed at the wealth and prosperity they see here. They say that ordinary farmers here live as well as wealthy gentry in the mother country."

"We surely have much to be thankful for," agreed Nathaniel smiling at his mother-in-law, "I am particularly grateful that Isabella remains healthy, that her pregnancy appears to be going well and that we can live so comfortably from the provisions we receive from Anderson Manor thanks to your generosity."

"It is our pleasure," said the colonel, "After all, we also have an intense interest in the production of healthy heirs to Anderson Manor."

This shared interest was Nathaniel's central focus for the rest of the winter. He did everything he could to make Isabella comfortable as her midriff continued to expand to remarkable proportions and he only smiled benignly at the occasional outburst of hostility. Their servant, Beth, was a great help since she had recently gone through the same ordeal and could, therefore, soothe Isabella's fears. Nathaniel had already delivered several babies but, of course, could not really understand Isabella's anxieties the way another woman could.

"Judging by the size of that belly, Miss Isabella, I guess it is going to be a big, strapping boy that is going to pop out of you soon," predicted Beth.

"God help me!" groaned Isabella, "Will I ever be pretty again after this?"

"You don't worry 'bout nothing," assured Beth, "Everything is going to be just fine."

And fine it was. Beth's predictions turned out to be perfectly accurate. Thanks to the intensive good care Isabella got through the winter without catching any illnesses and after a relatively short labor, she gave birth to John Anderson Scudder on the 22nd of March, 1759. Nathaniel and the Andersons were beside themselves with joy.

"Do you realize that it is almost exactly two years to the day since we were married?" asked Nathaniel standing with his parents-in-law in front of the bed where an exhausted but contented Isabella lay with the baby in her arms, "What a magnificent anniversary present!"

The joy of the new arrival energized both the Scudder and Anderson families. The colonel went about the expansion of the estate with renewed enthusiasm now that he had been blessed with a healthy heir. Nathaniel was in such a state of happy delirium that he was not bothered at all by the increasing number of tasks that Dr. Clark delegated to him. On the contrary he was flattered that Dr. Clark seemed to regard him more and more as a colleague rather than an apprentice. Isabella was completely absorbed by the fascination of watching her infant develop. Jacob and Abia Scudder were equally intrigued and even took time off from the booming mill business to visit the baby frequently. The positive mood in both families was further enhanced by the rapidly improving political climate in the colony. The British forces were chalking up success after success both in Canada and in the Caribbean. The wave of optimism generated by the good news from the front was amplified by the stimulating effects of a burgeoning war economy. For Nathaniel the time seemed to fly by at an ever-increasing rate. In a very short time, he would both finish his apprenticeship and receive his master's degree from the college. The rapidity of the transition from student apprenticeship to adult fatherhood was almost dizzying although he was thrilled at the prospects of taking responsibility for a family.

On one of his visits to Nassau Hall to finish up the last requirements for his master's, Nathaniel had the pleasure of meeting the new president, Samuel Davies. Davies had long been held in highest esteem since he and Gilbert Tennent had successfully raised the funds in Great Britain to build Nassau Hall. The trustees had wanted to appoint Davies as the new president right after the death of Jonathan Edwards. Davies, however, being a modest man, initially refused saying that another trustee, Samuel Finley, was more qualified. He also was reluctant to give up what he considered to be his vital mission in Virginia. As the first non-Anglican, dissident preacher licensed there he had been the first to promote the literacy of the slave population. In a colony where slaves could have fingers hacked off for having the audacity to learn to write, Davies had courageously insisted that no one, regardless of race or social status, can have True Religion without *both* hearing and reading the Word of God. Eventually the trustees to their great joy were able to convince him that the mission of the college was as important as the mission he was giving up.

The day Nathaniel met Reverend Davies he had an appointment with the senior tutor, Mr. Jeremiah Halsey. Nathaniel had essentially finished all his course work as well as his apprenticeship and planned, therefore, to make his formal application for the granting of his master's degree. He proceeded to Nassau Hall to make his case to Halsey.

"Well, Mr. Scudder," Halsey began, leafing through Nathaniel's file, "It looks as though we will soon have to call you Dr. Scudder. The reports from the tutors are outstanding and Dr. Clark has certified in writing that you have mastered all the practical skills of a physician."

"I am grateful that everyone is satisfied with my work," replied Nathaniel trying to sound as modest as possible.

"There is just one more hurdle you need to take," added Halsey, closing the file and looking up at Nathaniel, "You need to convince our new president that you are fit to join that august community of scholars that this college strives to produce. He has decided to personally verify the qualifications of every degree recipient."

A bit taken aback, not having expected new challenges to arise at this stage, Nathaniel nevertheless expressed his willingness to meet whatever requirements were necessary.

"It will be a great honor to meet the esteemed reverend and seek his approbation for my advancement."

"You can do that right now. He is currently upstairs in the library. He has great plans for this college and wants to enlist the community of scholars who are graduates to assist him in this. Go and convince him that you are suitable for this project."

Nathaniel took his leave from Mr. Halsey and hastened up the stairs. He knocked and, when he heard a voice say, "Come in," he stepped through the door making a low bow to the clergyman seated at a table.

"Come in, come in," repeated the surprisingly young man seated at the table, "You must be young Mr. Scudder. Mr. Halsey told me that you are about to receive your master's degree."

"If you deem me worthy, Reverend Davies," replied Nathaniel, "With the college's permission I would like to devote my life to the service of our community as a physician."

"A laudable aim, Mr. Scudder. By the way I have been admiring the college's book collection here. A large and well-sorted collection of books is the most ornamental and useful furniture of a college, don't you think?"

"Indeed, I do," replied Nathaniel, "I am awed by the knowledge contained in those books and grateful that I have had the opportunity to absorb some small part of it."

"What portion of that knowledge do you think you have absorbed?" asked Reverend Davies.

Somewhat shaken by the reverend's abrupt transition to examination mode, Nathaniel was unsure how to respond, "Reverend Davies, sir, I have read many of those books but . . . but . . . it is impossible to say what portion of that immense knowledge I have mastered. I would humbly submit that in any case it is only a beginning and that a lifetime would not suffice to master it all."

"That is exactly the right answer, Mr. Scudder," said Reverend Davies much to Nathaniel's relief, "Learning is indeed the task of a lifetime and receiving your master's degree is only a station along the way. The important thing is that you have learned how to learn. And this library will be available to you even after commencement. I plan to organize our assets more systematically. I have counted over 1200 volumes but there is no overview. I would like to compile a catalogue of all the books so that scholars can find the information they need more quickly."

"That is a splendid idea, sir," said Nathaniel with genuine enthusiasm, "That would have been such a help during my studies and will surely be a great help in my profession. If I can assist in any way, please just let me know."

"I would be interested in any comments you may have on the books in the natural philosophy area so I can include them in the catalogue, but I dare say you will probably be more useful to the college as a physician. Perhaps you could drop by now and again, and make certain our young scholars are not wanting for medical attention?"

"I would be honored, sir," answered Nathaniel, immensely pleased to be able to demonstrate in this way his commitment to community service and enormously relieved that he had apparently passed Reverend Davies' final examination. Riding up to Princeton from Monmouth a few times a month would not be a great burden. It would give him the opportunity to visit his parents frequently and to continue his relationship with the college. He really was interested in reading many of those books he had not read yet.

The weeks between Nathaniel's meeting with President Davies and the commencement in September flew by. Just before the commencement was about to happen news reached the colony that the British had won a great victory at Quebec after a month's long siege of the city. Although the British General Wolfe had unfortunately suffered a hero's death, the French army had met with a disastrous defeat. General Montcalm, the best French general, had also been killed, so it seemed only a matter of time before the French war effort in North America would collapse completely. The expanded militia worked smoothly with the Regulars. The Iroquois remained on the side of the British. The colonists felt they were partners in empire with their kinsmen from the mother country. The mood at the commencement was, therefore, one of exuberance. People began to talk of this being the *annus mirabilis*, the year of miracles in which the True Religion would triumph over the Papists and their savage allies.

At the commencement ceremony, 18 pious young men were to receive their bachelor's degree and eight their master's; all were convinced that great things lie ahead.

"Whatever be your place," President Davies told them in his address, "imbibe and cherish a public spirit. Serve your generation."

This they were more than prepared to do. There was an empire to build, and they were all eager to play their parts.

The granting of Nathaniel's master's degree also marked the formal end of his internship with Dr. Clark who was more than pleased to accept Nathaniel as a colleague on an equal basis.

"There is more work than 10 doctors could do in our area alone," explained Dr. Clark while congratulating Nathaniel on the conclusion of his studies, "We should continue our collaboration. Besides, I am getting too old to gallop all over the country. That's a job for a younger man."

"I am flattered by your offer, Dr. Clark, I welcome the opportunity to continue learning from you. You will always be my esteemed mentor."

And so Nathaniel's medical career got off to a very good start. He took over many of Dr. Clark's patients and through his connection to Nassau Hall was able to extend his practice to the Princeton area as well. He also was keen to repay Colonel Anderson's generosity by tending to the servant population of Anderson Manor. As one of the few university-trained physicians in the colony he soon became one of the most sought-after healers despite his young age. Nathaniel was grateful for his success which he attributed to his vow to devote his life to community service. Every Sabbath, therefore, he attended Reverend Tennent's meeting house to give thanks to God for showing him the way to Grace.

On one such occasion in the late fall, he was intrigued by a sermon that was inspired by discourses written by one Reverend Jonathan Mayhew of Boston. Reverend Tennent was convinced that Mayhew's ideas best summarized the meaning of the war for North Americans.

"Reverend Mayhew advises us to understand that we are all partners in a great transatlantic political community based on common allegiance, shared religious convictions and devotion to English laws and liberties," explained Reverend Tennent, "There is a direct connection between the impending defeat of the French and the events prophesied in the Revelation of Saint John 'that would consume and destroy the beast and the false prophet with their adherents.'"

"Reverend Mayhew predicts that this land will know great happiness," continued Reverend Tennent, "Religion will soon be professed and practiced in far greater purity and perfection than since the times of the apostles. We are approaching nothing less than the face of a dawning millennium!"

Nathaniel was extremely moved by this sermon. For him it explained why he had been blessed with such great good fortune in recent years. His winning Isabella as his bride, his successful education, his growing prosperity, the gift of a healthy son—perhaps these things were God's way of showing Nathaniel that his decision to devote his life to the service of humanity was favorably acknowledged. The idea of a dawning millennium greatly inspired him. The course of current events was certainly remarkable, and he felt himself to be a man with a mission in the unfolding drama. He plunged into his work with eager anticipation of the wonderful future awaiting him and his family.

His rapidly expanding practice involved many hours on horseback visiting farms all over Monmouth County and even riding up to Princeton several times a month. The constant traveling was time-consuming, but he was aided by access to the finest horses that Anderson Manor had to offer. He had always loved to ride like the wind, and it was a real pleasure to put these fine beasts through their paces. Using his best horses, he could gallop to Princeton in less than half a day. If he left his horse at Scudder's Mills and picked up a fresh mount, he could get back and forth to Princeton in one working day.

Through his many travels he also had occasion to meet a wide variety of people throughout the colony. He was gratified that his services were in such high demand and exhilarated by the varied and beautiful countryside that the colony had to offer. His only regret was not being able to spend more time with his beloved wife and son, but he consoled himself with the belief that everything he was doing he was doing for them.

Throughout the winter he made many trips to the college in Princeton to check out the students and make certain that they were in good health. He timed his first visit to coincide with a visit to Princeton by his old friend, Benjamin Prime. Benjamin had resigned from his job as tutor shortly after President Burr died and moved back to Long Island. His plans to go to Europe having been temporarily thwarted by Loudoun's embargo and the continuing danger of travel during war time, Benjamin had decided instead to try his hand at practicing medicine for a while in his home territory before again making the attempt to study abroad. He came back to Princeton now and again to use the library and had sent a letter to Nathaniel announcing his next visit.

On the appointed day Nathaniel rode to Princeton early enough to meet the "Flying Wagon" from New York which Benjamin had said he would be traveling with. While awaiting Benjamin's arrival on Nassau Street Nathaniel was amused to see several dapper-looking, bewigged and beruffled students loitering around the station where the Flying Wagon would stop. At length, a cloud of dust and the pounding of hooves announced the arrival of the great coach.

As Benjamin descended from the coach with sour mien holding a handkerchief over his mouth to ward off the dust Nathaniel greeted him enthusiastically.

"Benjie, it's so good to see you. I can't believe that years have rushed by since we were here together the last time. How have you been?"

"Life rolls tediously on," replied Benjamin wryly, "I suspect that you have the better lot. I spend most of my time arguing with my father, the old miser, and trying to convince the local swains of the superiority of my medical skills. They are a superstitious lot, however, and prefer the advice of the local quacks over my scientific methods. My only consolation is writing poetry about the glorious exploits of our fighting men. When the war is over, I plan to make another attempt at studying abroad."

As the pair walked from the coach station in the direction of Nassau Hall, Nathaniel trying to be upbeat said, "Did you notice all those fine young gentlemen at the stagecoach station? I wonder what they are waiting for. They seem to be much more stylish than in our day."

"Indeed," replied Benjamin, "They love to come out to meet the flying wagon during their recesses. I suspect they hope to catch a glimpse of some strumpet on her way from New York to Philadelphia. President Burr moved the college out to this remote location to remove the young scholars from the temptations of New York City, but the Devil is not deterred by geographical barriers."

"Come, come, Benjie, don't be so cynical, they are a fine-looking bunch of young men. I am greatly looking forward to attending to their health care needs."

"Well, you had better cover your nose when you do," said Benjamin, "They might appear neater than we did due to the new president's dress code but unlike in our student days all the students now live together in Nassau Hall. I had the misfortune of walking past their quarters the last time I visited. Most barns smell better."

Nathaniel and Benjamin parted company in Nassau Hall with Benjamin proceeding to the library and Nathaniel to the students' quarters. They resolved to meet again later after each had accomplished the tasks they had come to do. It turned out that Benjamin's warning, if anything, was understated. A sickening miasma met Nathaniel at the entrance to the students' quarters. Closer investigation revealed that the young scholars had no conception of personal hygiene. For most of them it was their first time living on their own without parental discipline. The result was living quarters more akin to a pigsty than to a dormitory fit for human habitation. His first action, therefore, was to give all the students a stern lecture on the subject of cleanliness being next to Godliness and important for their health as well.

"Very good, Dr. Scudder, very good," commented President Davies later after hearing Nathaniel's first report, "When I walked past the dormitory, I thought that some small animal had crawled under the floorboards, died and putrefied. I am pleased to hear that the dreadful funk has a simple explanation."

"Yes, hopefully the young gentlemen will take my suggestions to heart," said Nathaniel.

"Oh, I will make certain they are reminded regularly. I see it as one of my primary duties to instill greater discipline in the student body. I have formulated a set of rules for proper conduct that each new student is required to copy and copy again if any violations occur."

"That is an interesting approach," replied Nathaniel, "In my day President Burr was also concerned about good deportment but we learned his expectations mostly through exhortations delivered during his sermons."

"I don't believe in leaving anything up to chance," continued President Davies, "For example, I have formulated a specific dress code that students are now required to adhere to. I have also explicitly ruled that no student is permitted to keep his head covered within ten rods of the president and five rods of the tutors."

"I can appreciate that with a growing number of students, a more systematic way of inculcating self-discipline is necessary," agreed Nathaniel, "After all, we all want our graduates to become ornaments of society. Knowledge alone would be insufficient preparation for a life of service to God and country."

"Well said, Dr. Scudder, but let us get back to the physical well-being of our charges. Do you have any further suggestions for keeping the student body in an optimal state of health?"

"As a matter of fact, I do, sir," replied Nathaniel, "As part of my duties as a physician I have occasion to travel far and wide across this colony, and visit many outlying farms and towns. In recent months the pox has been taking an increasingly dreadful toll. I would suggest we inoculate the students."

"Inoculation!" the blood drained from President Davies' face as he uttered the word, "Isn't that the procedure that cost my predecessor his life?"

"Yes, it is, sir," answered Nathaniel, "But I fear that the inoculation of President Edwards was not done properly. There are risks involved but these can be minimized if the proper procedure is followed. As you said, one should not leave anything up to chance. If the pox takes hold here on its own, the entire student body could be wiped out. That is a much more dangerous proposition than the risk imposed by inoculation. For this reason, I have inoculated everyone in my family."

Nathaniel then explained at length the advantages of the method that he had learned from Dr. Clark.

"Not one of the patients that Dr. Clark and I have inoculated has ever died," assured Nathaniel, "And these are all healthy young men. The probability of a mishap is very low."

After several moments of intense consideration, President Davies reluctantly gave Nathaniel permission to carry out the inoculations during his next visit. Back in Manalapan Nathaniel consulted with Dr. Clark. Together they selected a set of inoculation threads that had been prepared in the optimal manner. Returning to Princeton Nathaniel used these threads to inoculate every student in Nassau Hall and instructed President Davies and the tutors on how to care for the students when the fever broke out. Then the waiting began. It was clear to Nathaniel that if any of the students would die, the repercussions for him and his career not to mention for the college would be devastating. His anxiety was exacerbated by the fact that some of the students he inoculated had relatives in Monmouth County. One of them, young Thomas Henderson, was the son of John Henderson, an elder in Reverend Tennent's church.

Although he was confident that Dr. Clark's method would achieve the usual positive results, Nathaniel nevertheless prayed fervently to the Almighty that nothing would go wrong. Attending church services on the Sabbath after the inoculation Nathaniel had to endure the anxious scrutiny of some of the relatives.

"I hope you know what you're doing," John Henderson said to him grimly at the conclusion of services, "The boy is the apple of my eye. I could not bear it if anything were to happen to him."

"It's in the Lord's hands now, Mr. Henderson," answered Nathaniel piously and then, trying to display more confidence than he felt, added, "But I have no qualms about putting the fate of our scholars at his mercy—fiat voluntas suas."

On the way back from the church services Isabella asked nervously, "Nathaniel, are you certain that the inoculation was such a good idea? After all, if you had done nothing, nobody would have blamed you if the pox had struck any of the students. Now it will be your responsibility if anything bad happens."

Sighing heavily Nathaniel answered, "Yes, everyone would then say the young doctor took a foolish risk in recommending the inoculation. But I really have no choice but to minister to my patients to the best of my knowledge and God help me if I get it wrong. A physician's work always carries great risks. It is so often a matter of life and death, but I can only pray for the Lord's help in carrying this heavy burden of responsibility."

Isabella gazed at him thoughtfully for a moment and then suddenly feeling an enhanced understanding of his immense dedication to his calling, took his hand in hers and whispered, "Don't worry, Nathaniel, I have complete confidence in your abilities. Everything will be alright."

And indeed, everything turned out very well. The next day Nathaniel galloped up to Princeton to find his charges all in quite good condition. They all had come down with a mild fever, but no one had a full-blown case of the pox. The inoculation had been a complete success. Breathing a sigh of relief Nathaniel could report to President Davies that his scholars would soon return to perfect health and henceforth be immune to the dreaded disease. The success of the procedure greatly enhanced Nathaniel's standing in the Princeton community. Two of the inoculated students, Thomas Henderson and Benjamin Rush, were so impressed that they announced their intention to become physicians themselves. Thomas Henderson even asked Nathaniel if he might intern with him since he was from Nathaniel's own neighborhood. Nathaniel agreed at once to take the young man on as an apprentice as soon as he graduated. It was already clear that Nathaniel's practice was on such a growth trajectory that he would soon need all the help he could get.

A few weeks after the successful conclusion of the inoculation project Nathaniel decided to visit the eminent silver smith Elias Boudinot who had his business on

Nassau Street. To celebrate the upcoming first anniversary of the birth of their son, Nathaniel planned to give Isabella a special present. Since Boudinot's daughter was Isabella's special friend of long standing, Nathaniel thought Isabella would be particularly pleased to have something wrought by the renowned craftsman. It would be expensive, but he felt that he could easily afford it since he had been able to earn a remarkable amount of money in the short time he had been practicing independently.

As he entered the shop, the elder Boudinot greeted him with a smile, "Ah, young Dr. Scudder, welcome. Come in, come in. I have heard great things about your medical successes. If I have need of a physician, I will certainly be happy to make use of your services. What can I do for you this fine day?"

"Good afternoon, sir. Today I am not on a medical mission. I would like to purchase a gift for my wife to celebrate our son's first birthday," replied Nathaniel.

"For Annis's favorite friend, is it? Well, I have just the thing for such a lovely lady."

Boudinot brought out an exquisitely designed silver tea pot the likes of which Nathaniel had never seen before. His Puritan parents would probably have been scandalized by such opulence, but Nathaniel was certain that Isabella would be delighted. He quickly reached an agreement on the price with Boudinot who offered Nathaniel a significant discount because it was for one of his daughter's best friends.

Nathaniel's instincts proved correct. On the day John Anderson Scudder turned one year old, he presented Isabella with the gift, and she was as surprised as she was pleased.

"Nathaniel, this is wonderful! Where did you find such a beautiful thing?"

"It was made by Annis' father, and it is to celebrate the finest mother in the world, darling," answered Nathaniel, "When I look at our beautiful, healthy son who is already beginning to walk and talk, I feel the necessity of rewarding his lovely mother. I know that my work and frequent absences are a burden for you, but I want you to know that you are always on my mind. And although community service is my main motivation, my work is not without its material benefits—it makes it possible to afford gifts like this."

"I am glad you think I am doing such a good job raising your son," replied Isabella, "Your parents seem to think that I am not strict enough, and worry that in your absence I might spoil our child."

"My parents are old-fashioned Puritans who believe that children must be harshly disciplined because of the burden of original sin. I am convinced, however, that as regards child-rearing, Locke was right, and one should rely on developing a child's rationality rather than meting out punishments. I would even go further and say that Hutcheson's theory of innate goodness applies to children as well. You are doing a fine job of rearing our boy, and I am endlessly grateful to you for it."

As the months flew by, Nathaniel and Isabella were fascinated to observe the rapid development of their son. Baby John grew quickly and seemed to learn new things much faster than other children. Both parents were convinced that he was destined for great things. Isabella's parents were of the same opinion and insisted on frequent visits of the young family to Anderson Manor. The delight they all shared about John's progress was further enhanced by the continuous flow of good news from the front.

"New York and New Jersey together have raised over 17,000 militia men," recounted Colonel Anderson on one such occasion, "They support over 20,000 Regulars. This is almost as much as the entire population of New France. It can only be a matter of months until they collapse."

Colonel Anderson's prediction had already come true in September. The British took Quebec forcing the French governor Vaudreuil to surrender. Soon the British flag was waving over Detroit and the war was effectively over in North America. On his frequent visits to Princeton Nathaniel discussed the significance of these developments with President Davies.

"The world is well-rid of that imp out of hell, Vaudreuil," Davies announced, "He was one of the main proponents of encouraging savages to murder our settlers. It was even too much for the French generals who had at least some honor left in them."

"What do you think will become of all the Indians who have been converted to Papism?" asked Nathaniel, "Do you think they will continue to be a problem?"

"We must renew our efforts to spread the True Religion," answered President Davies, "It is now more important than ever. It is altogether a time of renewal. We now have a new king and stand at the threshold of a new era—great and important challenges await us."

President Davies' energy and enthusiasm were inspirational for Nathaniel. Davies' combination of religious fervor and intellectual discipline convinced Nathaniel that the college had a patriotic as well as a pious mission. In fact, he was certain that the two could not be separated and gratified that he had the opportunity to work with President Davies to contribute to the noble project. President Davies apparently had a similar effect on the students in Nassau Hall—out of the 16 recent graduates of the Class of 1760 ten had indicated their desire to preach the Gospel. Davies's sermons were not only intellectually stimulating but also aesthetically pleasing. He augmented his preaching with many poems and hymns that he composed himself. He was consistently able to convince his audiences that any seeming contradictions between theology, scientific inquiry and aesthetics were merely the result of ignorance and could be dispelled by earnest self-discipline.

On the 1st of January of the new year President Davies delivered a sermon in Nassau Hall which deeply affected Nathaniel as well as the students he was preaching to. He began by quoting from Jeremiah 28:16 "Thus says the Lord—I am about to remove you from the face of the earth. *This very year you are going to die!*"

With this shocking introduction Davies endeavored to give the students a sense of urgency regarding the necessity of embarking without delay on a life of pious devotion to duty, "While we are entering upon the threshold of a new year, it may be proper for us to stand, and pause, and take a serious view of the occurrences that *may* happen to us this year—that we may be prepared to meet them."

All who heard the sermon were stirred with emotion and charged with enthusiasm to serve God and country. It was, therefore, a dreadful shock when just a few weeks later President Davies himself suddenly died from an attack of pneumonia. It was as though his address on New Year's Day had been prophetic and Nathaniel felt once again the fateful and heavy hand of urgent duty.

Chapter 11

Victory and Vengeance – 1761–1763

In the weeks following the death of President Davies Nathaniel could not stop thinking of the meaning of Davies' New Year's sermon. Its apocalyptical urgency weighed on his soul. This feeling was intensified by the ongoing series of dramatic events continuously reminding him of the critical importance of the vast and fateful struggle currently unfolding in North America. Although most fighting between British and French regulars ended after the surrender of Vaudreuil, the war was far from officially over. Many French outposts across the gigantic area of New France continued to be garrisoned by hostile forces. The Indian allies of the French apparently believed that King Louis was planning to send a huge relief force to turn the tide again in favor of the French. The border areas between New France and the British colonies remained, therefore, a dangerous place, especially for traders and farmers in remote areas. General Amherst was determined to pacify the entire region with as much brute force as necessary. Since most of the violence seemed to come from the Indian allies of the French, he forbade the sale of gunpowder and weapons to the Indians in general. Although this policy seemed to hasten the collapse of a bloody uprising of the Cherokee for want of gunpowder, it alienated not only the Indians who had been allied with the French but those who had been allied with the British as well. The natives began to suspect that the British would not honor the agreements they had made in Easton once they had conquered the French. Against the advice from people more experienced in Indian affairs, Amherst also discontinued the practice of diplomatic gift giving. For these reasons the war rumbled on and the optimistic vision of Reverend Mayhew that had so inspired Nathaniel a few months ago seemed still very far off. Nathaniel wondered how much more sacrifice would be necessary until the construction of the "City on the Hill" could be continued without impediments.

These issues were a frequent subject of conversation whenever Nathaniel and Isabella visited Anderson Manor. Colonel Anderson, having played a role in the negotiations at Easton, was doubtful about Amherst's policies.

"This will turn out to be another disaster," predicted Colonel Anderson grimly, "Amherst is making the same mistakes as his predecessors. Why are the British generals such blockheads? Don't they realize that our success so far was contingent on our agreements with the Iroquois Confederacy? Easton has to be the model for our relationships with the Indians. That is our only hope for weaning their loyalties away from the French."

"I remember meeting General Amherst at a reception not long ago," said Hannah Anderson, "He did indeed make a somewhat arrogant impression. He seemed to think that now that the French have been decisively defeated in North America, nothing can stop British Regulars from pacifying the newly won territory and that allies are no longer needed."

"He is in for a big surprise," replied Colonel Anderson, "His views are based entirely on ignorance. Why does he not listen to Sir William Johnson? He is after all the official Superintendent of Indian Affairs, and one of the few British generals who really understands the Indians and is respected by them. In some recent correspondence he informed me that he was concerned about rumors he had heard to the effect that war belts are beginning to circulate among many of the tribes in the West. And not only among Indian allies of the French. He is planning to organize another council with the Indians to try and defuse the hostility."

"But surely the Indians without the aid of the French could not seriously threaten us here?" asked Isabella with a shudder of trepidation.

"Not here perhaps," answered Nathaniel, "But in western Pennsylvania and the Ohio Country there are plenty of settlers who are exposed to Indian raids, and it will be very difficult for regular troops to protect them. The Indians don't confront our army units. They attack remote farmsteads, murder the men and carry off the women and children. We are already experiencing a flow of refugees from the West bearing tales of unbelievable savagery."

"Well I am only slightly relieved," continued Isabella, "Because I have an important announcement to make. I am again with child, and I don't fancy the idea of seeing Nathaniel scalped and myself and my children carried off into the wilds."

The surprise announcement instantly turned the atmosphere in the room from solemnity to joyousness. Nathaniel jumped up and embraced Isabella passionately.

"Every time I feel overwhelmed by the burdens of destiny, you give me new reason to persevere. For me you are the Lord's messenger of hope. There is no sacrifice I would not bear to protect you and our children. May God bless you and protect you."

Moved by the spontaneous sincerity of Nathaniel's outburst Hannah Anderson added, "We are truly blessed with so much good fortune, we must give constant thanks to the Lord and seek to fulfill His expectations of us."

"As it turns out, Reverend Tennent has some concrete suggestions how we might do the Lord's work," said Colonel Anderson, "The refugee stream seems likely to increase given Amherst's stubbornness and we will have our hands full coping with it. Reverend Tennent suggests that we make refugee relief the focus of the work of our congregation."

"That is an excellent idea!" agreed Nathaniel enthusiastically, "I feel an intense need to compensate for all of our good fortune and would be only too happy to assist in this mission."

"Be careful what you commit to," cautioned Isabella, "You are already working night and day, and now you will soon have a second child who will require your attention. Your son John is already getting to the age where he needs more of your time."

"You are right, of course, darling," conceded Nathaniel, "I have not been the perfect father in the last two years, but I pray to the Lord for guidance. After the upcoming graduation at the college, I will have Thomas Henderson as an apprentice. I am hoping that he can take over some of my tasks, so I have more time for my family."

"I also plan to give you two more servants to celebrate the blessed event," announced Colonel Anderson, "That should make life easier for the both of you."

Buoyed by the Anderson's generosity and grateful for the eagerly awaited expansion of their family Nathaniel and Isabella were pleased to immerse themselves in their church's refugee relief project. This included not only finding places for the refugees to live but also counseling distraught people who had witnessed more than the eye could bear. The mere sight of an Indian, even of the peaceful and pious native residents of New Jersey, was enough to provoke some of them into a homicidal rage. The potential for escalating violence became clear to Nathaniel during an effort to find temporary accommodations for a farmer from western Pennsylvania who had lost his entire family in an Indian raid. Nathaniel had the idea to ask John Burnes to let the refugee, Caleb Johnson, stay at his farm. He reasoned that John with his handicapped arm from the Battle of Fort Carillon could use some temporary help and that, after all, the two men had in their respective tragedies something in common. The fallacy in his reasoning soon became apparent.

"John, John, Nat Scudder here," Nathaniel called out as he approached the Burnes farm on horseback followed closely by Caleb Johnson on a borrowed mount, "I am here on a mission from Reverend Tennent. We have a refugee here who is also a victim of Indian violence, and I am here to ask your help. This is Caleb Johnson whose family has suffered a terrible calamity."

"Welcome, Dr. Scudder," answered John Burnes coming out of his log cabin, "And welcome to you Caleb Johnson. I will be happy to help in any way I can. I know what these savages are capable of."

The two men dismounted and shook hands with John Burnes who invited them into his modest cabin to sit at the dinner table.

"Caleb here came with his family from Northern Ireland a few years ago and set out to build a new life for his family in the virgin territory of western Pennsylvania. Unfortunately, although the French seem to be defeated, their savage allies continue to perpetrate violent crimes among the settlers. I will let Caleb tell you the story in his own words."

"The savages brutally murdered my whole family," Caleb began, but then broke into sobs as he was forced to relive in his mind the atrocity that he had witnessed. For a long time, he could not continue but at length recovered his composure.

"I had gone off fishing on that day and left my wife, Sue, and our two teenage sons, Bill and Tom, at our homestead. I was gone several hours and when I returned, I was alarmed at the smell of smoke as I approached our clearing. Afraid that something terrible had happened, I crept up as quietly as I could. Then I saw that a bunch of about ten painted savages had set our cabin alight, and were dancing and yelping in front of the bonfire. My wife and the two boys lay dead in the yard. I could barely resist the temptation to empty my musket at the devils, but I knew it was hopeless. I decided to wait to fight another day."

"May God give us the opportunity!" shouted John Burnes, "I stand ready to wipe those bastards off the face of the Earth. They kidnapped my beloved Agatha at Fort Carillon and ruined my life forever."

"After exhausting themselves for another hour with dancing and yelping the savage beasts finally left our yard," Caleb continued, "I waited until I was sure they were gone before going over to my loved ones. They had been brutally tortured. Apparently, the savages had taken various metal tools, pots, and the like and heated them in the fire. Then, judging by the burns on their hands, they forced my family to pick up the red-hot objects with their bare hands. The boys had awls stuck through their eyes. Finally, they hacked them to pieces with tomahawks and scalped them. They were so brutally mutilated that they were hardly recognizable anymore."

Caleb was again overcome with emotion and covered his face with his hands.

"My God, what beasts from hell!" exclaimed John, "It makes me sick to think that my dearly beloved wife is among them. I can only pray that a similar fate has not befallen her. Something must be done about these animals. We cannot suffer them to live among us anymore."

"Something is being done, John," Nathaniel, alarmed by the escalating vehemence, endeavored to calm his friend, "Amherst has authorized several large contingents of Regulars who will occupy all the French outposts and bring everyone to justice who has blood on their hands."

"They all have blood on their hands!" exclaimed Caleb, "They can never be trusted. We will only be safe when they are all dead!"

"That is not a Christian attitude," admonished Nathaniel, "There are plenty of Indians who have converted to the True Religion and should not be put in the same category as the murderers you have spoken of."

Nathaniel's pious injunctions fell on deaf ears with both Caleb and John. Their eyes continued to burn with hatred. Leaving Caleb to stay at John's farm Nathaniel rode back home wondering whether it had been such a good idea to bring the two men together.

A few weeks later he had occasion to discuss this disturbing incident with Reverend Samuel Finley, the newly appointed president of the College of New Jersey. Nathaniel had come to Nassau Hall at the invitation of the acting president, Mr. Halsey, to meet the man who would be taking over officially in the coming autumn. Since the new president up until now presided over the school he had founded on the Pennsylvania border, Nathaniel was anxious for possible insights he might have concerning the frightening escalation of hostilities in western Pennsylvania.

"It was depressing to see John and Caleb, two Christian men, descend into such a murderous rage," Nathaniel recounted his experience at John's farm, "I had thought they could have given solace to each other, but instead they just want to join a crusade to cleanse North America of its native people."

"Atrocities breed atrocities," Reverend Finley remarked gravely, "The settlers in the west have already suffered much at the hands of France's savage allies. The desire for revenge is understandable but unacceptable and un-Christian. We must redouble our efforts to bring the True Religion to the native people and free them from Papist influences. And we must see to it that our Christian brethren accept and protect those who see the Light."

"I am afraid that might be quite a challenge," said Nathaniel ruefully, "If the violence continues to escalate on the frontier, there will be more and more victims who want revenge."

"Part of the problem is that the province of Pennsylvania does not provide adequate security," explained Reverend Finley, "The government is dominated by Quaker pacifists who want to have peaceful dealings with the Indians. But if there is no protection for western settlers, they will take matters into their own hands sooner or later."

"One can only hope that General Amherst will be successful in pacifying our western borders," replied Nathaniel, "But some people think he will only make matters worse."

"They might be right. Violence begets violence." concurred Reverend Finley, "In the long term we have no choice but to bring the Word to the benighted savages. That is why our college has such an important mission. We need to produce even more scholars who can evangelize for the True Religion."

"I am certain that you are completely correct, Reverend," answered Nathaniel, "I have been long convinced that our college has a holy mission. That is why I stand ready to assist in any way I can."

"Thank you, Nathaniel. I am pleased to see that you are meeting the expectations that we trustees originally intended when we started this institution."

Riding back to Manalapan Nathaniel reflected on the inspirational effect that the college presidents always had on him. Whenever one felt almost overwhelmed by the challenges of life, these men were able to point clearly the way to salvation. He felt a surge of energizing optimism and confidence that he was doing what God intended.

As he delved into his work and his church projects with renewed enthusiasm, the months flew by with seemingly increasing speed. The commencement in September with the official installation of President Finley came and went, followed by a new challenge—training his recently graduated intern, Thomas Henderson. The young man was bright and hard-working. Training him turned out to be a surprisingly enjoyable experience. It also enabled Nathaniel both to indulge his pedagogical instincts as well as to expand both his medical practice and his community service activities for the church. But his heightened level of activity seemed to make time pass even more quickly. Isabella's second pregnancy seemed somehow much shorter than the first one, even though it was exactly the same number of months. In no time at all it was February and their second son, Joseph, came into the world.

"Congratulations, my dear daughter and son-in-law," Colonel Anderson lifted his glass in the direction of his wife and son-in-law gathered around Isabella's bed, "Another healthy boy! Let me propose a toast to the health and happiness of our growing family."

"God be praised for our great good fortune," said Hannah Anderson raising her glass as well.

"And to the most wonderful wife imaginable," added Nathaniel raising his glass to Isabella.

"Let us hope that these two boys can grow up in peaceful circumstances," said Isabella wearily holding her newborn son to her breast, "Hardly have we finished the war with the French, now we are at war with Spain, and we still have no peace with the Indians."

"That is certainly something we need all pray for," agreed Colonel Anderson, "I received some correspondence from Sir William Johnson recently. He told me that, although he worked hard to organize a peace council with the Indians, war belts continue to circulate. I am not worried about the Spanish and the French are finished but establishing peace with their former Indian allies will remain a challenge for some time."

"President Finley holds that the only Christian solution is more evangelizing of the Indians," ventured Nathaniel, "He thinks the college has a divine mission to produce missionaries of the True Religion to accomplish that goal."

"I think we will need more than just missionaries," replied Colonel Anderson, „We will need a political solution—thousands of Ulster immigrants are pouring into western Pennsylvania and the Ohio Country, into lands the Indians consider their own. We will have to restrain these newcomers to the terms of the Treaty of Easton, or the Indians are never going to make peace. That won't be easy because the Ulstermen think they have a right to their Promised Land. And as far as the Indians are concerned, they think that they themselves are the Israelites against the Canaanites."

Nathaniel shuddered to think that his Presbyterian co-religionists could fall into such a misinterpretation of the Holy Scriptures. He had discussed this at length with

President Finley who was unshakable in his conviction that genocidal attitudes towards Indians were un-Christian and that every soul deserved to have the chance of salvation. He speculated that greed for land might have something to do with the appeal of this heresy. Over the course of the following months, however, his church work showed him that this heretical form of Presbyterianism had increasing appeal to the steady stream of refugees from the west.

The joy Nathaniel had felt at the birth of his second son was soon almost eclipsed by his mounting anxiety that the violence of the frontier might find its way to New Jersey and impinge on the relatively peaceful lives of his family. By the time summer came, his worries were exacerbated by troubling news from Anderson Manor. Returning home after a busy day treating refugees and listening to their harrowing tales, he was startled to see a distraught Isabella waiting for him in the yard.

"Nathaniel, Nathaniel," cried Isabella, "A servant just came to tell me that my mother has been taken by a dreadful fever. She is apparently almost delirious!"

"Have Dunmore drive you there in the wagon!" ordered Nathaniel, "I will fly there immediately and meet you there."

Arriving at Anderson Manor Nathaniel leaped from his horse and grabbing his medical bag handed the reins over to a waiting servant. Colonel Anderson waving frantically from the door urged Nathaniel to follow him quickly. As they both raced breathlessly up the stairs in the direction of Hannah Anderson's bedroom, Colonel Anderson explained what had transpired.

"Up until yesterday we thought she was just feeling a bit under the weather. She complained of pains in her joints. She has been feeling quite exhausted since our trip to Philadelphia a few weeks ago and I thought that the discomfort came from the long rough ride in the coach. But then in the night she suddenly developed a high fever and started to vomit. I tried to reach you this morning, but you had already departed on your rounds."

"She might have contracted the disease in Philadelphia," explained Nathaniel, "At this time of year the swampy marshes around the city are known to cause serious fevers."

As they entered Hannah's bedroom, Nathaniel's worst fears were confirmed when he saw the yellowish pallor in Hannah's face.

"I am afraid she does have the swamp fever," Nathaniel announced, "I hope we are not too late. Fortunately, I have some of the Peruvian bark with me. She needs to drink an incoction made from this. If the disease has not progressed too far, it will cure her. In the meantime, we have to keep her cool with wet compresses and pray that our medicine works."

The incoction was hastily made by the servants according to Nathaniel's instructions. He repeatedly attempted to get her to drink it but between the weakness and vomiting he could not be sure that the medicine was getting into her stomach. In the meantime, Isabella had also arrived, and they took turns applying cold compresses to her mother's forehead. Unfortunately, as the hours passed there was little sign of improvement. Having also been informed about the seriousness of Hannah's situation Colonel Anderson's brother, John, arrived bringing along Reverend Tennent. In an attempt to console Colonel Anderson, Reverend Tennent reminded him that the only consolation in times like this is to rely on the justice of the Living God.

"Brother, Kenneth," Reverend Tennent began, "Do not fear. Our sister, Hannah, has always been a faithful Christian. She will either recover or she will have eternal bliss, as the Lord decides."

"Of course, of course," stammered Colonel Anderson, barely restraining a sob, "But she is still such a young and beautiful woman, she is only 44 years old this year. I know we must accept God's will joyously, but I just cannot imagine life without her."

The family together with Reverend Tennent held vigil over Hannah late into the night. In the wee hours of the morning Isabella cried out, "She is getting cooler, perhaps the fever has broken!"

Nathaniel held a mirror up to her nose and seeing no vapor turned sadly to the assembled, "I am afraid she has left us."

Isabella burst into tears and rushed to embrace her father who manfully fought the urge to dissolve into tears himself. Instead, he took a deep breath and attempted to comfort his daughter.

"Reverend Tennent is right, my darling daughter, nothing happens but that God wills it. We must accept what He decrees. Your mother will always be with us in our hearts."

The sudden and unexpected death of Hannah Anderson reinforced all the dread and sense of foreboding that had been building up in Nathaniel during his months of ministering to the refugees. The firsthand reports of the atrocities that the refugees had suffered as well as their frequently expressed desire on for violent revenge were profoundly depressing for Nathaniel. He was at a loss to think how this vicious circle of increasing hatred could ever be broken.

This became depressingly clear to him on the occasion of a love feast that Reverend Tennent organized in the fall. Traditionally the congregation welcomed all who came in peace to proclaim the greatness of God and the brotherhood of man. Love feasts were one of the few occasions where Whites, Indians and Blacks participated in one communal ceremony. On this occasion, however, a considerable number of refugees from the west attended. They did not seem to be moved by Reverend Tennent's admonitions to brotherly love but hung back and glared sullenly at the few Indians in attendance.

"Our Reverend John Elder has a different take on these Injuns," muttered Caleb Johnson to John Burnes. "He says we should be like Joshua when the Lord ordered the Israelites into Canaan. The Lord told him to kill the Canaanites and take the Promised Land. That is exactly what we have to do if we are to fulfill our destiny!"

Nathaniel standing together with several Christianized Indians overhearing these heretical opinions turned to see some of the other refugees nodding in agreement.

"My granddaddy was with Cromwell at Drogheda," continued Caleb, "We need to do the same to them Injuns as Cromwell did with them Irish Papists."

"I remember another thing that Reverend Elder was always telling us," continued another tall, black-bearded refugee who looked himself like a figure out of the Old Testament, "he said the fact that so many Injuns died of the pox was proof that the Lord was not ready to save them. The Lord is clearing out the back country to make room for us."

"That is utter nonsense," exclaimed Nathaniel, no longer able to listen to such foolishness, "I have inoculated dozens of Indians and those inoculated do not die of the pox, just like inoculated Whites do not."

"Inoculating Injuns is getting in the way of the Lord's work!" exclaimed the black-bearded refugee, and all at once several of the rougher looking refugees began to move threateningly in the direction of Nathaniel and the Indians.

"That will be quite enough!" shouted Reverend Tennent who had observed the exchanges, "This is a feast of love in honor of the Lord, shame on any of you who desecrate this holy occasion. Repent for your own sins before you punish the sins of others!"

Reverend Tennent's spirited warning galvanized the rest of the congregation who came to stand around Nathaniel and the small group of Indians and join hands defiantly staring at the refugees.

"And think of the Christian charity that you have received here with us," continued Reverend Tennent eloquently, "And resolve to return that charity to everyone you encounter who is in need. Otherwise, you are not a true Christian, and you are sure to burn in Hell for all Eternity!"

Reverend Tennent's rebuke had the desired effect. The aggressive refugees uncertain of their theological justification in the face of the preacher's self-confident scolding retreated reluctantly muttering to themselves and eventually slinking away. As always Nathaniel was deeply impressed by the power of the Word but also very concerned that the refugees had not seen the Light at all and were still in thrall to the powers of Evil.

Nathaniel had little time to brood long over the forces of good and evil. Not long after the love feast Isabella announced that she was pregnant again.

"So soon! Joseph is barely 8 months old!" exclaimed Nathaniel, delighted and concerned at the same time, concerned that three pregnancies in such short order might be too much of a burden for his frail wife.

"I must say, I would have preferred to wait with this one," replied Isabella wearily, "Thank God for the servants, I couldn't possibly cope with the work of three children on my own without them. And thank God that Beth is also producing one child after another herself so that she can always help nurse my babies as well."

"I have some news also," announced Nathaniel, hoping to take Isabella's mind off the drudgery of child rearing and the lingering sadness of her mother's early demise, "President Finley told me that William Franklin has been appointed royal governor of New Jersey."

"William Franklin, how interesting," Isabella brightened up at the recollection of the social event where she had met Franklin, "I heard that his plans to marry Elizabeth Graeme went awry."

"It turns out that he wound up marrying a different Elizabeth when he was in London. Then his father managed to get him appointed royal governor. He will be coming to take up office here in a few months. President Finley has sent him an invitation to visit the college. We might even get an opportunity to meet him."

"That would be interesting," mused Isabella, "I remember a very agitated conversation between my father and William Franklin. At the time young Master Franklin seemed to think that the solution to the colony's problems was stationing more Regulars here. I wonder if he still believes in such simple solutions."

"He and his father have been saying for years that Pennsylvania would be better off with the enlightened rule of a royal governor rather than being run by proprietors. Now William will have the opportunity to demonstrate how enlightened a royal governor can be. Let us give him a chance—it will be interesting to see what an energetic, ambitious young man can accomplish."

"I just hope I am not as big as a house when I get to meet him," added Isabella ruefully, "He probably won't even recognize me from the time we last met."

"He cannot help but be dazzled by your beauty as every man is who comes into your presence," assured Nathaniel gallantly kissing the hand of his beloved wife, "And when you are pregnant, you exude an inner glow that makes you even more beautiful."

What with an expanding practice, two small children, a pregnant wife, new servants and a new intern to train Nathaniel was caught up in a flurry of activity that made the days fly by. There never seemed to be enough time to deal with all the tasks at hand. Autumn quickly turned into winter. President Finley announced to Nathaniel that William Franklin would be visiting Princeton in March and that he and Isabella would be welcome to attend the event.

"We are invited to come to hear the new governor address the students and faculty at the college in Princeton," Nathaniel informed Isabella, "It should not be a problem for you. You are barely showing at four months."

"Thank God for that," replied Isabella with relief, "And this is the season for heavy clothing under which I can hide my bulges."

"Omnia vanitas!" Nathaniel raised a finger in mock reproach, "Praise the Lord that you are so beautiful with and without bulges."

A few weeks before the scheduled visit of the new governor Nathaniel received a letter from Benjamin informing him that he as a former tutor was also planning to attend the event in Princeton. He went on to tell Nathaniel that his long-delayed trip to Europe was finally going to happen in a few months and he wanted to hear what William Franklin had to say about his sojourn in England. He recalled the conversation they had had years ago at Morven when both were planning to leave for England in a short time. Franklin had actually left and obviously had made a success of his time abroad. Benjamin hoped that he would be similarly successful.

When the appointed day arrived Nathaniel and Isabella rode in the carriage to Princeton accompanied by Colonel Anderson. They were happy that they had been able to talk him into accompanying them and hoped that it might end months of his solitary brooding. It was the first time since Hannah's death that he had consented to participate in a social event.

When they finally arrived in Princeton, they saw that a substantial crowd was already gathered in front of Nassau Hall although the governor's entourage had not yet arrived. Students, tutors, and townspeople were milling about awaiting a glimpse of the young new royal governor.

At length the governor's entourage swept into town—the official carriage of the royal governor accompanied by an honor guard of militiamen, on its way from Perth Amboy, the capital of eastern New Jersey to Burlington, the capital of western New Jersey. The governor had taken the oath of office in Perth Amboy and would take it a second time in Burlington. This was his first official tour of his province and the college deemed it an honor that he included Nassau Hall among his stops. As his carriage stopped in front of Nassau Hall President Finley went out to greet him.

"Welcome to Nassau Hall, Your Excellency," began President Finley, "It is a great pleasure to greet a governor whose education under the influence and direction of the very eminent Dr. Franklin makes him an outstanding advocate for institutions of learning."

President Finley accompanied the governor to a raised platform where he could address the crowd.

"I am very pleased to be here," began Franklin graciously, "And indeed my father inculcated in me a great respect for learning. I, therefore, praise the mission of this college—the careful instruction of youth in the principles of religion, loyalty, and sound learning is of the greatest utility to society."

Franklin then went on to explain his vision for the future of the province. He spoke of the great opportunities that were beckoning now that the French were defeated, and the whole area of the continent from the coast to the Mississippi river was under British control. He described what he considered to be a harmony of interests between an enlightened government in Britain and loyal colonists in North America to make the best use of the resources of the vast land now at their disposal.

The governor's speech was optimistic and stimulating and was greeted by nods of approval from most of those present. After the speech the governor was pleased to explain his vision in more detail to some of the prominent attendees.

"I agree that there need be no inherent conflict of interest between the provinces and the mother country." began Colonel Anderson, "But I am not certain that the ruling groups in London are always as informed as they should be about conditions here in the provinces."

"I see it as my job to make certain that our government is well supplied with all the information they need to make rational decisions about all important colonial issues," replied Franklin, "As an American who has experienced and greatly respects England, I think I can appreciate both sides of any argument in order to find appropriate compromises. I have great faith that a rational solution can always be found for any issue which maximizes benefits for both the colony and the mother country."

"Not all policies of the Board of Trade can be considered the epitome of rationality," objected Colonel Anderson, "They are criticized even by leading scholars in Britain. I can only hope that you will be able to convince them that many of the restrictions on our economic development are ill-advised."

"I will certainly try my best, Colonel," responded Franklin, "I am a firm believer in the great economic potential of this giant country. I want to do everything I can to foster its development. I am convinced, however, that our Lords and Masters in London have the best interests of the empire at heart and besides, as you already pointed out, a lively and critical debate is taking place in enlightened circles which will undoubtedly eventually result in improved policies."

"Could you tell us more about the enlightened circles in London, Your Excellency," Benjamin Prime asked with excited anticipation of his own upcoming departure.

"London is in many ways the capital of the world," Franklin began with genuine enthusiasm, "It hums with intellectual activity—scholars, artists, scientists, statesmen, and tradesmen come from far and wide to develop new ideas and enrich each other. It is probably the most interesting place in the world to live."

"It must be quite a sacrifice for you then, Your Excellency," remarked Isabella somewhat coquettishly, "to be banished to the wilds of New Jersey."

"Not at all, not at all," the governor hastened to reply, "It is an honor to take up the challenge of bringing the benefits of the metropolitan center to our outlying territories."

On the way back to Manalapan in the carriage Colonel Anderson agreed with Nathaniel and Isabella that the handsome young governor had acquitted himself quite well at the event.

"I liked his emphasis on rational policy development," ventured Nathaniel, "Maybe the son of a scientist will be able to guide the province in an enlightened direction."

"They certainly are an elegant couple," added Isabella, "Perhaps they will add some style to the somewhat rustic social life in this province."

"We will see how long his enthusiastic optimism holds out," said Colonel Anderson, "His first confrontation with the Assembly might blunt it a bit—they are also not always amenable to rational compromises. If the rumors I hear are correct, his first challenge might be coming soon. War belt circulation among the western tribes is reported to have reached a frenzied level. Without an agreement with the Indians, many regulars will have to be deployed and paid for. We will see if Governor Franklin can pry money out of the Assembly for that."

Colonel Anderson's fears turned out to be justified. Only a few weeks after the reception in Princeton word came through that a large force of Indians had laid siege to Detroit. In addition, Indian attacks all over the western frontier suddenly increased in intensity. The flow of refugees to New Jersey increased dramatically and with it the anxiety of the general populace. Reverend Tennent's refugee relief program was almost overwhelmed by frightened people traumatized by what they had experienced. General Amherst put an urgent call out to all colonial governments to provide militia units as well as supplies and accommodations for the Regulars.

At their regular after-service Sunday dinners at Anderson Manor the rising anxiety level was the prime topic of conversation.

"Now he asks for help," muttered Colonel Anderson, "Amherst is a fool. He should have listened to our advice. We have been warning him for years that he has to reach an accommodation with the Indians. Instead, he has pursued such ham-fisted policies in the occupation of the French territories that he was bound to rile the savages. Now Franklin is telling the Assembly we have no choice but to pay for Amherst's mistakes."

"He is probably correct that Amherst's forces are in desperate need of relief," said Nathaniel and, gazing anxiously at his very pregnant wife, added "Whatever mistakes have been made, the savages still must be stopped."

"And they will be stopped," replied Colonel Anderson, "Despite my annoyance over Amherst's foolish policies, I will try to convince the Assembly to support another militia call-up. I have no doubt that we will prevail militarily—the question remains what the political solution will look like at the end."

True to his word Colonel Anderson presided over a very successful new mustering of militia. He was aided in this effort by a continuous flow of frightening news being brought from the front by the ever-increasing numbers of refugees. The word was that many different Indian tribes had combined under the leadership of an Ottawa war chief named Pontiac. For the first time many of the Indian tribes had overcome their mutual hostility and united in a holy war against the Europeans. Pontiac's forces were able not only to seal off Fort Detroit but also to destroy several other British forts. A large force was reportedly on its way to besiege Fort Pitt. The possible fall of Fort Pitt was such a frightening prospect that volunteers came in droves to sign up for militia duty.

Nathaniel again agreed to vet the volunteers to make certain that they were fit for military duty. Among them he was not surprised to see John Burnes and Caleb Johnson.

"John, are you certain you want to take part in this campaign?" Nathaniel asked, "Your lame arm is going to make it difficult for you to take part in any skirmishes."

"I still have one fighting arm," answered Burnes defiantly, "Besides we are joining Colonel Henry Bouquet's force which has the vital mission to relieve the besieged forts and to force the Indians to return all hostages. There might be some slight chance that I will find my Agatha again."

Nathaniel nodded thoughtfully not wanting to ruin John Burnes' slim hopes, although the probability of success seemed minuscule.

"All I want to do is just kill ten Injuns for each one they murdered in my family," commented Caleb Johnson darkly.

Nathaniel was again struck by the depth of hatred and the bloodlust that Caleb's words revealed, although his hostility toward the Indians was perfectly understandable under the circumstances. In a few days a good number of volunteers were ready to march off in the direction of Pennsylvania to join Bouquet's relief force. As Nathaniel watched the men departing with grim looks of determination on their faces, he could not dispel a strange feeling of foreboding that much evil would soon ensue. The feeling of foreboding increased a few weeks later when news arrived that Fort Pitt was indeed under attack.

The Scudders spent much of the month of July praying fervently with Reverend Tennent's congregation for the success of Bouquet's relief mission and the safety of the volunteers from Monmouth County. Adding to the anxiety, Isabella was approaching the end of her third pregnancy in a very uncomfortable state, the muggy New Jersey weather adding to her discomfort.

In August just as the continuing uncertainty was causing new lows in the general mood a note arrived from Anderson Manor requesting that they come immediately to hear some very good news. Isabella's dark frame of mind brightened instantly.

"My father has just returned from Philadelphia," said Isabella excitedly, "Any good news he has must have to do with success at the front."

"Right you are, darling, let us get to Anderson Manor right away. You are due at any minute, but Dunmore will drive us carefully in the coach to guard your tender state."

Arriving at Anderson Manor Nathaniel and Isabella were greeted by an ecstatic Colonel Anderson at the porte-cochere.

"I just got back from Philadelphia with some wonderful news!" he shouted, "Bouquet has won a great victory at a place called Bushy Run. The Indian uprising has been dealt a fatal blow. The bells tolled all night in Philadelphia."

"Praise be to the Lord!" exclaimed Nathaniel, helping Isabella down from the coach, "At last the tide has turned. It can now only a matter of time until the new territories are pacified."

"That is likely but still only if a rational policy toward the Indians is followed," said Colonel Anderson, "It looks now, however, that Amherst is going to be replaced by Gates. Perhaps he will have the sense to defer to Sir William Johnson's judgement in this matter."

As the four walked into the salon, Nathaniel noticed a look of desperation on the face of his wife.

"Is something wrong, my dear?" he queried.

Isabella said nothing but looked down in shocked disbelief at the spreading wetness on her dress.

"Her water has broken," exclaimed Nathaniel quickly scooping Isabella up in his arms, "We must get her to bed immediately."

Nathaniel carried Isabella up to her old bedroom and laid her gently on the bed.

"Don't worry, darling, everything will be just fine," Nathaniel sought to calm Isabella who continued to have a perplexed look on her face, "The trip in the coach was too much after all at this late stage but it is about time in any case. It looks like our next child will be born in your girlhood bed."

Isabella went almost immediately into labor and after a mercifully short time their first daughter was born. Nathaniel and his father-in-law were ecstatic.

"Praise the Lord," shouted Colonel Anderson, "He has not only given us victory in the field but also a beautiful baby girl. Exactly a year ago he took my Hannah from us but has now blessed us with new life!"

Everyone agreed immediately that the new addition to the family was to be named Hannah.

The colonel sank to his knees at the edge of Isabella's bed and with hands clasped in prayer gazed with wonder at the little present from heaven. In his mind's eye he could envision Hannah Anderson's beautiful countenance superimposed on the face of the lovely infant. He thought to himself how essential it was to have faith in the wisdom and generosity of God.

Nathaniel was dazed by their good fortune. He had been worried that there might be complications with Isabella's third pregnancy so soon after the second. But it had turned out to be the easiest birth of all. Nathaniel felt overwhelmed by the bounties of Providence and resolved to show himself worthy to the Lord in every possible way.

There was no shortage of opportunities to serve the Lord by serving the community. As summer turned into fall the results of British victories were evident in the diminishing flow of refugees. Instead, demobilized militiamen were beginning to return in increasing numbers, many of whom needed medical attention. They brought with them lurid tales about how the campaigns had been conducted.

One day Nathaniel had occasion to treat a festering wound suffered by a young militiaman who had endured the entire two-month siege of Fort Pitt.

"That must have been quite an ordeal," Nathaniel sought to praise the militiaman's contribution to the victory, "You and your comrades were very brave."

"Well, it was on again, off again," said the militiaman, "The Indians surrounded the fort and attacked people who left the stockade. But then they would send chiefs to negotiate. At one of these negotiations the commander gave them smallpox-infected blankets as gifts. That might have been what finally finished them off."

Nathaniel could not believe his ears.

"Do you mean to tell me that our British officers would stoop to such an abominable tactic? It could result in thousands of innocent people being infected!"

"You can believe it," answered the militiaman, "Amherst personally suggested that to both Ecuyer and Bouquet. That's war. What do you think those Injuns would have done to us if they had breached our defenses?"

Nathaniel was shocked. His enthusiasm for the British campaign was anchored in his belief that they were on a mission for the Lord, eliminating Papist rule and bringing the True Religion to the native peoples. That his side in the conflict could have perpetrated such a reckless, genocidal act was almost more than he could believe. Later, when discussing it with his father-in-law, he came to understand more of the complexity of the issues involved.

"This is an abominable act," agreed Colonel Anderson, "It does not surprise me, however. It is just another proof of Amherst's incompetence. Thank God, he has been replaced by Gage. Apparently, people in London have finally realized that we must seek accommodation with the Indians if we want to quiet down this revolt. The king has issued a proclamation which essentially enshrines the agreement we reached in Easton as the law of the land."

"Do you think that this will finally end the conflict?" asked Nathaniel.

"I think that the armed uprising will come to an end within weeks," replied the colonel, "The hard part will be enforcing the agreement among our own people. The proclamation promises to reserve territory west of the Appalachians for Indians and to prohibit advancement of White settlers into the area. There are many of our settlers, however, who covet those lands and applaud the attempt to wipe out as many Indians as possible with smallpox or other means."

"Yes, I remember the un-Christian views expressed by some of the refugees at last year's love feast."

"Well, I am afraid we haven't seen the last of that," predicted the colonel gloomily.

Pontiac capitulated at Detroit and Indian power in the Ohio valley was broken. The Indians were even forced to return many of the captives that they had kidnapped over the last few years. Reverend Tennent's love feast that year was particularly joyous because several of the people from Manalapan who had been missing for years turned up among the returned prisoners. Nathaniel and Isabella were especially pleased to see John Burnes and his wife, Agatha, who was holding the hand of a small boy. Both Agatha and the boy looked more like Indians than White settlers.

"They may look like Injuns, but it is Agatha and my son," explained John Burnes, "It turns out that Agatha was already pregnant when she was captured. The Injuns adopted them and gave them both Injun names, but we renamed the boy 'Nat' in your honor. You told me never to give up hope and you were right."

"That must have a harrowing experience!" exclaimed Isabella, turning to Agatha, „One hears the most frightening stories about the fate of people captured by the Indians."

"I was petrified at the beginning," admitted Agatha, "I thought I would certainly be ravished and brutally murdered by our captors, but that did not come to pass. Pleading for mercy I managed to make clear to the leader of the band with sign language that I was with child. He then placed me under his personal protection. After a long march through the forest, we arrived at an Indian settlement. To my surprise the Indian women there were very kind to me. They washed me, anointed me with fragrant herbs and painted my face with bright colors. I did not understand at first but later I realized that they were preparing me for adoption into their tribe."

"How amazing," replied Isabella, "How incredibly fortunate you were."

"I later came to understand that my fate was not at all unusual," explained Agatha, "The Indian communities all suffer the loss of many of their number through disease and warfare. Their greatest fear is the extinction of their tribes, so they try to solve the problem by capturing women and small children in order to adopt them."

"Praised be the Lord," cried Nathaniel, deeply moved by this most improbable reunion, "Perhaps there is yet hope of redemption, even for people as full of hatred as Caleb Johnson."

John's face darkened at the mention of the name Caleb Johnson.

"That's a man I no longer want anything to do with," he muttered, "He has turned into a murderer. He said that Agatha and Nat had been converted into savages through black magic and could never be trusted again. He advised me to slit their throats before they committed some treachery. He then left to join a group in Paxton who want to make a holy war on the Injuns. He wants to kill them all, even those who are peaceful and have converted to the True Religion."

Nathaniel's feelings of joyous ecstasy at the miraculous reunion of the Burnes family quickly dissipated as he realized that the second part of Colonel Anderson's prophecy would also undoubtedly come to pass.

Chapter 12

Sugar and Stamps – 1764–1766

THE CONESTOGA INDIANS WAITED nervously in the workhouse in Lancaster, Pennsylvania for the workhouse keeper, Felix Donnally, to return and unlock the door. These seven adults and seven children were all that remained of the Christianized Indians who had lived peacefully for generations at Indian Town under the direct protection of the government of Pennsylvania. They were the lucky ones, most of whom had not been present at dawn on the 14th of December when a hoard of White vigilantes had raided their village and brutally murdered and scalped seven people who had been asleep in their lodges. The survivors had been visiting White farm communities in the area in order to sell the baskets and brooms with which they maintained their livelihood. They heard about the massacre from the only Indian who managed to escape, a young boy named Tongquas whose Christian name was Chrisly. Chrisly had managed to slip off into the woods and elude the killers. He had run quickly to inform Captain Thomas McKee, the local official in charge of keeping order in the area. McKee in turn had reported the incident to the chief judge in Lancaster County, Edward Shippen. Shippen, fearing that the vigilantes would return to finish the job, ordered the surviving Conestogas to be brought to the workhouse jail in Lancaster for their own protection. The Indians were now upset because the jailor, Felix Donnally, had ordered them inside, locked the door and disappeared hours ago. The day before Donnally, who lived in the workhouse with his family, had sent his wife and children away to stay with relatives.

"What's happening," Chrisly asked Tenseedaagua, also known as Will Sock, the de-facto head of the Conestoga Indian community since the previous chief, Old Sheehays, had been murdered two weeks before, "Are the White men getting ready to kill us too?"

"Don't worry," replied Tenseedaagua trying to display more conviction than he felt in order to calm the distraught members of his tribe, "We are here by order of Judge Shippen who re-affirmed that we are under the express protection of the governor of Pennsylvania. This is a large town with many people who know that we are

Christians and have always been loyal to the British. It will not be possible for evil men to sneak in here and harm us. Sheriff Hay and his men have been ordered to guard us."

"How can you be so confident?" objected Kyunqueagoah also known as Captain John, "We thought we were under the governor's protection at Indian Town. When I warned Old Sheehays that we should move further north to a place where our people are more numerous, he just laughed and said that the English would wrap him in their matchcoats and secure him from all dangers. Now he, my son, Tee-kau-ley, and all the others who stayed at Indian Town have been brutally murdered and scalped. I say you cannot trust the White devils. Even if some of them promise honestly to protect us, there are too many who hate us and covet our land. These evil ones seem to be getting more and more numerous."

"It is too late now," said Kanianguas, wife of Tenseedaagua, known to the Whites as Molly, shaking her head in sad resignation, "My father, Old Sheehays, was perhaps too trusting but now we have no choice but to hope that the Whites here will do their Christian duty. Let us get down on our knees and pray to the Savior to soften their hearts."

All fourteen Indians in the workhouse reluctantly followed her advice, knelt on the brick floor and bowed their heads in prayer.

In the early afternoon of that day over sixty Paxton Rangers rode into Lancaster scowling in grim determination. These were many of the same men who had murdered the Conestogas at Indian Town. They were armed with muskets, tomahawks and knives. Riding at the head of the group were Matthias Smith, James Gibson and Caleb Johnson.

"Are you sure this is such a good idea," asked Smith, "I don't like the idea that there are so many witnesses here. What if some of the locals try to protect those bastards? I don't want to have to kill any White men. We'd surely get murder charges hung on us in that case."

"Don't worry," replied Gibson, "I have it on good authority that almost everyone will be attending a late Christmas service being held in St. James Episcopal Church this afternoon. Nobody will try to stop us. Anybody protecting the workhouse will only often token resistance. All they want is an alibi to give to those weak-willed Quakers back in Philadelphia in case they make a fuss."

"Exactly," agreed Caleb Johnson, "It is just like Reverend Elder said, we ain't supposed to kill any God-fearing Christians but everyone knows the Injuns ain't real Christians. They just make believe so they can stay among us and spy for the murderous savages who have killed my family. Besides most of the people here will be happy once we have rid this place of these bloodthirsty savages."

Approaching the workhouse, the Paxton Rangers saw two men with raised muskets standing in front of the door, the county sheriff, John Hay, and the county coroner, Matthias Slough. James Gibson rode up to them raising his hand to signal to his Paxton Rangers to line up in front of the entrance.

"The people in this building are under the protection of Governor Penn," announced Hay with a tremor in his voice as he eyed the large number of determined vigilantes, "You people are to stand down!"

"We ain't standing down for nobody," answered Gibson, "We're here to arrest Pontiac's spies who are responsible for the brutal murders of hundreds of White settlers. We don't mean you White men no harm as long as you don't try to prevent us from doing justice."

A tense moment ensured as Hay and Slough scanned the imposing number of armed ruffians. At length, both lowered their weapons and stood aside. Several of the Paxton Rangers then jumped from their horses and together picking up a large log proceeded to ram the door off its hinges. Led by James Gibson they pushed into the workhouse. Tenseedaagua ran toward them with arms spread apart.

"Stop, stop," he cried, "We are Christians, we have always been on your side. You have no reason to hate us."

"You lying bastard, we know you are just a spy for Pontiac but now you are going to get what you deserve," shouted Gibson, then thrusted his musket right into the mouth of Tenseedaagua and pulled the trigger.

As Tenseedaagua's brains spattered in a wide arc over the Indians in the room, the women and children began to scream. The Indian men rushed forward in a vain attempt to defend themselves as dozens of vigilantes poured into the room firing their weapons. In a frenzy of murderous exuberance Caleb Johnson swung his tomahawk right and left, first into the temple of the boy, Exundas, then into the throat of his brother, Shae-e-koh.

"That is for Bill and that is for Tom," he screamed.

The killing exhilarated him, and he searched wild-eyed around the room for his next victim. Seeing the woman, Kanianguas, still kneeling on the floor and praying, he rushed over to her and buried his tomahawk deep in the middle of her skull cleaving it almost in half.

"And that is for Sue," he shouted, thrilled by the almost orgasmic pleasure that the atrocity gave him.

Within minutes all the Indians were dead or severely wounded. The workhouse was covered in blood. The vigilantes dragged the dead and dying out into the yard and proceeded to scalp every one of them. Since there were so many vigilantes and so few Indians many of the men were frustrated that there was no one left to kill. They vented their frustration by hacking off hands, feet, noses and ears. Soon no Indians were left alive, and all had been brutally mutilated. The vigilantes then remounted, taking the scalps and other macabre trophies and hooting triumphantly, rode proudly out of town.

By that time the commotion had alerted the good citizens of Lancaster who ran out of St. James church and rushed to the workhouse with Judge Shippen in the lead.

When they got to the workhouse, they saw Sheriff Hays and Coroner Slough leaning on their muskets surveying the carnage.

"This is outrageous," shouted Judge Shippen, "Who did this dreadful atrocity? Did you recognize anyone?"

"They weren't from here," answered Hays shaking his head and shrugging his shoulders, "I didn't know any of them."

* * *

In January Nathaniel rode with Thomas Henderson up to Princeton to see how the young scholars were faring in what turned out to be a very cold winter. After attending to several students who were suffering from severe colds, he and Thomas dropped by President Finley's office to pay their respects.

"I am very glad to see you, Dr. Scudder, and young Master Henderson as well," President Finley greeted them cordially, "I have some important news for you that I gleaned in a recent meeting with Governor Franklin. But first, how are our students faring? I trust that their illnesses are nothing serious?"

"We are pleased to report that the afflictions that several boys are suffering are simply common colds," answered Nathaniel as he and Thomas bowed politely to the president, "If they keep warm and take the teas we have prescribed, they should be fit again very soon. Pray tell what important news you have from Governor Franklin."

"I visited him a few days ago in Burlington and he told me about a dreadful tragedy that has befallen a group of Christian Indians in Lancaster," began President Finley with grave demeanor, "Apparently, a group of vigilantes massacred an entire tribe of Conestoga Indians including women and children. These people were peaceful Christians who were under the direct protection of Governor Penn and one of our trustees, Judge Edward Shippen. The men called themselves the Paxton Rangers and they conducted themselves in the most brutal fashion. They weren't satisfied with just killing their victims but scalped and mutilated the bodies as well. It belies the imagination that Christian Englishmen could conduct themselves in such an abominable fashion."

At the mention of the word "Paxton," Nathaniel's mouth dropped open, "Oh my God," he exclaimed, "I have heard tell of that group. One of the refugees who was sheltered with us in Monmouth allegedly joined up with them after serving in the militia that helped raise the siege at Fort Pitt. He and his friends are a brutal lot. He and his family suffered greatly at the hands of the savages and now their hearts are full of hatred and lust for revenge. When he was here, he spoke of one Reverend Elder who preaches against reconciliation with the Indians, saying that they are like the Canaanites and must be destroyed."

"I know this Reverend Elder," answered President Finley, "I am ashamed to say that he calls himself a Presbyterian, but he preaches a gospel of hatred designed to appeal to his Ulstermen who are blinded by greed and can think of nothing but killing the Indians and stealing their land. What is worse, Governor William Franklin learned from his father, Benjamin Franklin, that these murderers are threatening to march on Philadelphia and eliminate the peaceful Lenni Lenape who are sheltered there. Governor Penn fears a general uprising in western Pennsylvania of frontiersmen stirred up by these rabble rousers. Benjamin Franklin has organized additional militia units to defend the city but it may be necessary to evacuate the poor Indians to here or to New York. You might be called upon to help attend to these poor souls, Nathaniel. Let us pray that these people are not successful in sullying the True Religion with their un-Christian heresies."

"We stand ready to help in any way we can," said Nathaniel earnestly while Thomas nodded his head vigorously.

Nathaniel and Thomas bowed their heads as President Finley invoked a prayer beseeching the Lord to enlighten their Presbyterian brethren in western Pennsylvania and make them see the error of their ways.

After leaving Nassau Hall Nathaniel decided to stop off at his parents' home before heading back to Monmouth. Thomas, already well acquainted with Nathaniel's family, was pleased to come along and say hello again. He was particularly interested in seeing how Nathaniel's younger sister Ruth was developing. The last time he had seen her, Ruth was just beginning to blossom into young womanhood.

As Nathaniel and Thomas approached Scudder's Mills they saw Nathaniel's two brothers, William and Lemuel, standing at the loading ramp of the grist mill.

"What are you two strapping young swains doing standing around idly?" called Nathaniel in jest, "Start swinging those bags of grist."

"We wish we had some bags to swing," answered William somberly, "We are waiting for farmers to bring us their grain, but lean times have arrived. They tell us that they can't sell as much flour as they used to the sugar islands, so they just store their grain hoping for better times."

Normally when Nathaniel visited Scudder's Mills the farmers were lined up waiting to have their turns at the mill. Now it seemed that both the grist mill and the lumber mill were idle. Nathaniel and Thomas dismounted and climbed up on the loading ramp to query the two brothers in more detail.

"Now that you mention it," began Nathaniel, "This place has an eerie stillness about it. Where is father and where are all the workers?"

"Father is out visiting farmers to collect some of the fees for turning their logs into lumber," answered William, "But most of them don't have any cash to pay their bills with. They are also having trouble selling their stuff now that the army stopped ordering so much."

"Now that the war is over," continued Lemuel, "The Royal Navy has more time to prevent colonial merchants from selling to the French and Spanish sugar islands. But the British sugar islands currently have a glut of everything we produce."

"To make matters worse," added William, "Lots of militiamen are returning from the front and want to restart their farms but they can't get credit to buy seeds or new livestock. So they won't be customers of ours anytime soon either."

Nathaniel was devastated to learn the extent of the ill effects that the end of the war was causing for his parents and siblings. He knew his father had invested heavily to expand his business during the war in order to meet increased demand. He wondered to what extent Jacob Scudder had gone into debt for his expansion. He experienced a flash of anxiety when he realized that Anderson Manor probably had similar problems but on an even larger scale. Since a large part of the prosperity that he and Isabella had been enjoying was due to the generosity of his father-in-law, he knew that the war's end would bring new challenges for his immediate family as well. After learning that his mother and sister were also not at home, Nathaniel and Thomas decided to head back to Monmouth without further ado—Nathaniel was anxious to discuss these matters with his father-in-law to hear how he sized up the situation.

The next day Nathaniel and Isabella hurried to Anderson Manor to share the disturbing news items that Nathaniel had brought back from Princeton with Isabella's father.

"I am not surprised about the fate of the Indians," said Kenneth Anderson after hearing Nathaniel's account of the Conestoga massacre, "Those Ulstermen who are pouring into the frontier country think that, now the French are defeated, they can just murder the Indians and steal their land. But the British government has promised the Indians that no permanent White settlers will be allowed to settle west of the Proclamation Line. If we don't respect our agreements, there will be no end to the troubles on the frontier. And, worst of all, it will give the officials in London a good excuse to station regular army troops here in perpetuity. That would be the beginning of the end of our English liberties."

"If the troops are needed to keep the Indians and settlers from killing each other, how would that affect our English liberties?" asked Isabella.

"Because, unlike the militias, the Regulars are not answerable to the colonial assemblies," answered Colonel Anderson, "A standing army that is not controlled by the people's representatives is the first step to tyranny. That is why it was agreed in the Bill of Rights of 1689 that there would be no standing armies in peacetime without the consent of the people's representatives. Moreover, the troops will have to be paid for and that money will come out of our pockets without our having any say about how it is used. The best is to keep the frontier as peaceful as possible and send the Regulars back home. Any changes in the Proclamation Line need to be carefully negotiated with the Indians by people who understand local conditions."

"Supplying the king's troops was, however, very good for business," added Nathaniel and went on to explain the negative effect that the end of the war was having for Scudder's Mills.

"Indeed, it was," agreed Colonel Anderson, "And everyone profited while the good times lasted, but too many financed their business with loans from British merchant houses and now they will struggle to pay it all back. Fortunately, Anderson Manor is less indebted than most so we can survive a lean period, but there are lots of yeomen farmers who stand to lose everything if they can't sell their produce. And now that the British government is cracking down hard on smugglers, it is getting harder to find buyers."

"You once told me that the whole Royal Navy could not shut down the smuggling that goes on along our New Jersey coast. Has that changed?" asked Isabella.

"I doubt that it will ever be possible to shut it down completely as long as the incentives remain," explained Colonel Anderson, "But it used to be much easier. Most of the customs officials did not even live here but relied on corrupt local deputies. The easiest way to make a fortune used to be to get a job as a customs collector and take bribes from merchants instead of enforcing the law. Since the Revenue Act of 1762 that is changing. Now London is sending its own officials who can serve search warrants on merchants suspected of having contraband goods. And the Royal Navy is encouraged to apprehend and detain smugglers. The British government ran up huge debts to defeat the French and now they want the colonies to help pay it off."

"On the face of it, that seems reasonable enough," mused Nathaniel.

"It won't help anyone to stifle the colonies' economies," continued Colonel Anderson, "New Jersey has prospered primarily due to a century of benign neglect. Settlers were able to develop their lands as best suited local conditions without interference from officials on the other side of the ocean. If the British government impoverishes its entrepreneurial class in North America there won't be any surplus to share. We have all we can do to take care of the debts that we ourselves all incurred during the war without having to be bled dry by London officials."

"Now I understand the conflict better," said Nathaniel, "It is a question of fairness regarding who gets to pay how much for the war."

"It is, indeed," agreed the colonel, "And New Jersey has always paid its fair share. The New Jersey Blues have fought bravely on all fronts. The colony has incurred debts of over 200,000 pounds that it must cope with. The standing army we don't need, and we don't want to pay for it. Parliament wants to get the money from us, so they don't have to raise land taxes in England. This proves that Parliament does not adequately represent the people in the colonies, and we need, therefore, to guard the prerogatives of our assemblies."

As always, his father-in-law's explanations brought the issues into sharp perspective for Nathaniel. He now felt that he understood much better what was at stake but still wondered what could be done about it.

"I am beginning to understand how misguided policies can really hurt people, even if unintentionally," said Nathaniel, "But surely Governor Franklin will be able to influence the Board of Trade to discontinue policies that are clearly destructive."

"We will see how well young Franklin is able to find compromises," said Colonel Anderson, "He apparently believes that the only cause of bad colonial policy is misinformation but, in many cases, there are clear-cut conflicts of interest and he will have to take sides. If he sides with London bureaucrats against our elected Assembly, he can expect resistance."

"What form could this resistance take?" asked Isabella.

"In some places a royal customs collector is already taking his life in his hands if he tries to hinder a smuggler from pursuing his business," answered the colonel, "Tarring and feathering happens quite frequently, and reactions will get more violent as the situation of the yeomen farmers deteriorates. The government would be wise not to fan the flames. You saw how quickly the vigilantes in western Pennsylvania got organized. The frontiersmen are all well-armed and are unaccustomed to taking orders. There is a great potential for more violence. Fortunately, for now, our courts still afford some protection for colonials, so they are not forced to take matters into their own hands. But if all of London's rules were enforced to the letter, this country would become a tinderbox."

"It is becoming clear to me just how precarious the situation is," commented Nathaniel thoughtfully, "Let's hope that the governor is able to present our side of the argument convincingly."

"The important thing that the Board of Trade has to understand is that it is not in their interest to ruin our economy. We can only afford to buy British goods when our businesses can grow unrestricted by short-sighted regulations that benefit only a minority on the other side of the ocean," continued the colonel, "Free trade is the road to prosperity for all. The two things that Franklin must do are to promote free trade and to get a paper currency emission approved so farms and businesses can finance their investments. That is how he could pull this colony out of the downward spiral we seem to be heading toward. But I am not confident that he will be able to convince those blockheads on the Board of Trade."

In the days following the conversation with his father-in-law Nathaniel thought long and hard about how the tightening of the rules by the Board of Trade might wind up affecting him personally. He quickly realized that his greatest vulnerability was his supply of exotic medicines. Continuing in Doctor Clark's tradition Nathaniel had maintained his connections for opium and Peruvian bark in the smuggler's paradise of Tom's River. These essential medications were only available through Spanish and French traders with whom the colonists were not allowed to trade. If the British authorities were successful in closing those trade routes, it would have a devastating impact on Nathaniel's ability to reduce suffering. For him the moral question was clear—his duty to alleviate human misery far outweighed any obligation to customs officers. He, therefore, decided that at the very least he should attempt to stock up as quickly as possible on whatever was still available from the traders at Tom's River. He was anxious to find out just how badly the traders were being affected by the new policies. It was also time for his assistant, Thomas Henderson, to meet the people that he would need to deal with in the future, assuming this type of trade really had a future.

Nathaniel had to wait a few weeks before undertaking his journey. The rough road heading in the direction of Tom's River was a muddy morass in the early spring and Nathaniel wanted to wait until it was dry enough to prevent their horses from getting bogged down. When he felt he could risk it, he instructed Thomas Henderson about how they should prepare their journey.

"We will be heading to a pretty lawless part of the country," warned Nathaniel, "We need to be well-armed and riding good fast horses. We will be carrying a good deal of money to buy medicines and there is no shortage of cutthroats who would slit our throats and dump us into the swamp for a fraction of the money we will be carrying."

"I will take my best musket and two pistols, Dr. Scudder," assured Thomas with youthful bravado, "You can count on me if any rascals try to make trouble."

"The two of us would be no match for a determined band of outlaws," warned Nathaniel, "But most thieves on the road will be wary of starting anything with two obviously well-armed riders on fast horses. There are easier targets for those kinds of scoundrels. And remember, when we get to Tom's River there will be all kinds of rogues carousing and fighting amongst themselves, but we will avoid having anything to do with them. We are going to meet the main trader there, Sam Bigelow, who is the boss of that place. As long as we are customers of his no one will dare bother us."

The next morning rose at dawn and set off at a brisk pace. The further they proceeded to the southwest, the denser the forest became and the fewer farmhouses they passed. Nevertheless, they were surprised to note that there was a considerable amount of traffic in the other direction. Ox carts hauling casks of molasses to destinations to the north and east rumbled by.

"Those are contraband from French and Spanish sugar islands," remarked Nathaniel, "They will be distilled into rum at some stills out in the swamps and then sold in the cities. I saw them the last time I made this journey, but I am surprised to see that there seem to be even more than before. I would have thought that the smuggling trade would have suffered more from the increased customs inspections. I will have to ask Sam Bigelow about this."

After several hours of hard riding Nathaniel and Thomas reached the little settlement at Tom's River. The initial scene was much as Nathaniel had described to Thomas. Two ships were being unloaded at the dock and some of the crew members were debarking on shore leave. Some loose-looking women were waiting for them at the end of the dock. One of the prettier ones smiled lasciviously at a young sailor coming her way who immediately threw his arm around her and headed toward Sam Bigelow's tavern. On the way there they passed by a pockmarked rogue with a peg leg sitting on a tree stump. Just as the couple passed the rogue stuck out his peg leg and tripped the sailor.

"Not so fast, little fella," growled the pockmarked rogue, "If you wants to fuck our girls, you has to pay a fee up front!"

The sailor smarting from his fall and disgusted by the appearance of the peg leg pimp jumped up red-faced and pulled a dagger out of his belt.

"I will pay you a fee alright," shouted the sailor, "How about six inches of cold steel?"

As the sailor advanced toward the pimp, a shot rang out. As the youth sank to the ground looking down bewilderedly at the spreading red stain in the middle of his chest, Nathaniel and Thomas could see another shifty looking character behind him holding a smoking pistol. Thomas was aghast at this cold-blooded attack and instinctively started to head toward the stricken sailor.

"Stay where you are," warned Nathaniel, "We don't want to have anything to do with those scoundrels. It is too late for that sailor. There is nothing you can do to help him now."

"But they just murdered that man in cold blood!" exclaimed Thomas.

"Yes, but he pulled a knife on the one with the peg leg," explained Nathaniel, "The rogues are obviously in cahoots and will say that it was all a matter of self-defense."

Thomas reluctantly let himself be led away in the direction of Sam Bigelow's tavern. Pushing through the motley crowd that had gathered at the sound of the shot, Nathaniel and Thomas entered the tavern.

Seeing them Sam Bigelow enthroned at his usual table called out, "Ah, young Dr. Scudder, welcome to my humble emporium. I hope the rabble outside did not cause any problems for you."

"Not for us, but for a young sailor who has just been murdered before our eyes!" Thomas blurted out indignantly.

"Excuse us, Sam," Nathaniel hastened to add, "I would like you to meet my new assistant, Thomas Henderson. Thomas is not accustomed to the rough life out here on the frontier. Our visit today is part of his education in more ways than one."

"And an important part, I might add," Sam laughed, "Not only for the trade connections but also for what you learn about the depths of human nature. This is where you find out what Hobbes meant by the bellum omnium contra omnes."

Surprised and impressed that this rustic frontiersman could quote Hobbes, Thomas continued in a more subdued tone, "But sir, surely such violence cannot go unpunished. Is there no constable here who would enforce the law?"

"What laws we respect, we enforce on our own," answered Sam, "The king's constables and customs inspectors steer clear of this place if they know what's good for them. The sailors who visit here must adhere to our terms of trade. And that includes paying for their entertainment as we see fit."

"That reminds me of something I wanted to ask," Nathaniel interjected, "On the way down here we saw more carts loaded with molasses than the last time I visited. I would have thought that the new measures to curtail smuggling would have reduced the trade."

"Not at all, quite the contrary," answered Sam jovially, "The more the Board of Trade tries to restrict trade with the French and Spanish sugar islands, the more lucrative that trade becomes. Any success that the authorities can achieve in Philadelphia, Burlington or Perth Amboy results in more business for us. The population wants lots of cheap rum which requires lots of cheap molasses. Plenty of people are willing to taking considerable risks to provide that supply."

"But what about the Royal Navy?" asked Thomas, "I heard that they now are commissioned to arrest all smugglers and put them on trial in vice-admiralty courts instead of provincial courts. Does that not raise the risks to unacceptable levels?"

"The higher the risks, the greater the profits," explained Sam with a cynical smile, "By raising the costs and risks the Board of Trade drives new customers into our arms. And to stop us, they have to catch us first. The coastline between here and Egg Harbor is so full of hazards that only experienced locals can navigate it. And in addition to the natural hazards there are man-made ones. I trade with a man named Zephaniah Steelman who does a profitable business down near Absecon Beach salvaging merchandise from wrecks. Some people say that these wrecks have something to do with lanterns that Zephaniah ties to the backs of his cows that he lets wander on the beach. At night those flashing lights look like a lighthouse but if you follow those lights your ship winds up on the shoals and your cargo with Zephaniah."

"I assume that the ships that bring the opium and Peruvian bark that we need are piloted by experienced hands?" asked Nathaniel.

"I trained them all myself," answered Sam exuding self-confidence, "You can depend on Sam Bigelow to procure what you need in the future as in the past. By the way, speaking of opium I recently surprised a ship's surgeon who didn't think he would be able to find such merchandise in these parts."

"What was he looking to buy?" asked Nathaniel.

"Oh, at first he wasn't looking to buy anything," answered Sam, "He was just in the bar getting drunk and bragging about what miracles he could perform. He announced that he had transformed old men who couldn't get it up anymore into insatiable roosters. This was, of course, a subject that interested the depraved perverts who hang around here and they immediately wanted to know how he did it."

"I'd like to know that myself," remarked Nathaniel, "Did he offer some kind of aphrodisiac?"

"No, he said you needed an operation where he replaced your own tired balls with those of a billy goat. He said he had done it many times and it always worked."

"That is outrageous!" exclaimed Nathaniel, "Any qualified physician knows that you can't graft animal parts onto humans. The man must be a quack!"

"I think he didn't reckon that anyone would take him up on it," continued Sam, "But then old George Gallagher piped up and said he would try anything that would restore his youthful randiness. The surgeon looked worried and said, no, that operation is painful and cannot be performed without opium."

"Uh oh," said Nathaniel ruefully, "I think I know what happens next."

"Right you are!" exclaimed Sam, "I said 'gentlemen, look no further, Sam Bigelow can sell you everything you need from opium to billy goats.' The surgeon looked even more worried, but he couldn't turn back now without admitting that his tall tales were all lies. So, George had his balls replaced and the surgeon disappeared early the next morning."

"Did George survive the operation?" asked Thomas.

"He is still alive but is not doing well. The wound from the operation refuses to heal." answered Sam.

"And it won't heal so long as the foreign parts are in him," explained Nathaniel, "It might already be too late for him. We need to see him immediately."

Sam led Nathaniel and Thomas to the small cabin where George Gallagher lived. Upon entering the cabin, they were struck by the stench of gangrenous flesh. Sam explained to George that Nathaniel and Thomas were physicians who might be able to help him.

A quick examination of the area of the wound revealed that the tell-tale black signs of necrosis had already spread throughout the scrotum and penis.

"The only thing we can do is to remove all the poisoned flesh and hope the disease has not already entered your body," Nathaniel said gently, "It is your only hope of recovery, and it must be done immediately if you are to survive."

"No, never!" screamed George Gallagher, "I would rather die with my dick intact than spend the rest of my life as a eunuch!"

After several more unsuccessful attempts to convince George Gallagher of the necessity of the procedure the three men left and headed back to Sam Bigelow's tavern.

"How long has he got?" asked Sam.

"Not long I'm afraid," answered Nathaniel, "The poison is already entering his body. He will die of sepsis within days."

"I don't understand how a surgeon could have performed such an irresponsible act," said Thomas indignantly, "Even a rank beginner would know that such a procedure is impossible."

"There are a lot of quacks among those ship surgeons," explained Sam, "All they know how to do is to bandage wounds and to hack off mangled limbs and dip the stump in tar. I am sure that he had never before performed the operation that he did on poor George. He just got carried away bragging to his drunken mates and then didn't want to admit it."

"Unfortunately, the quacks are not limited to ships' surgeons," added Nathaniel, "Thomas, you will have to get used to the fact that there are more mountebanks around than qualified physicians. And it is often difficult to convince sick people not to take their nostrums. They tell patients what they want to hear and often promise the impossible. Some of the physician's primary duties are, therefore, to promote understanding of natural philosophy and to combat superstition and irrationality. This is the only way to make people immune to the blandishments of dishonest charlatans."

"Well, good luck with that!" said Sam with a sardonic grimace, "You will have quite a task enlightening the brutes that come through this place. Maybe the government should spend more effort arresting murderous quacks than trying to disrupt the sugar trade. Rum would be cheaper, and we'd have less deaths at the hands of scoundrels."

Back at Sam's tavern Nathaniel and Thomas concluded their transactions for Peruvian bark and opium. Nathaniel had to pay for these things with Spanish coins because Sam could not purchase anything from the smugglers with proclamation money. The paper money issued by the colony of New Jersey was worthless in the Spanish and French sugar islands. Nathaniel had had to obtain the pieces of eight at great expense because his patients usually paid in proclamation money. Recently many had begun to pay with barter goods because even the proclamation money was getting scarce as the economy slowed down from its wartime pace. Nathaniel wondered to himself how long he would be able to afford to buy the imported medicines he needed.

On the way back to Manalapan Nathaniel and Thomas rode in silence both thinking about the suffering and the inevitable but completely unnecessary death of George Gallagher. Nathaniel brooded very intensively about the problem of quackery and the difficulty of enlightening the masses. Sam's suggestion that such scoundrels should be arrested as criminals was appealing but given how unsuccessful the government was enforcing the trade laws, it seemed unlikely that this could solve the problem.

As the pair reached their destination a plan began to form in Nathaniel's mind.

"The longer I think about the problem of quackery, the more I come to the conclusion, that we honest physicians will have to offer the solution," Nathaniel announced, "The problem is that anyone can claim to be a physician on the flimsiest basis. The qualified physicians must band together, set standards and organize the certification of properly trained persons. Then, perhaps, it will be possible to discourage the public from using the services of disreputable quacks."

"That seems like a practical approach," agreed Thomas, "If such an organization existed, I would be pleased to become a member."

Arriving back at his home near Monmouth Courthouse Nathaniel bid a hasty farewell to Thomas and rushed in to tell Isabella about his brilliant new idea. Baby Hannah was lying, screaming in her crib, while the servant Beth tried unsuccessfully to comfort her. Two-year Joseph was crawling around the floor babbling loudly while his older brother, John, tried to keep him from getting into things where he might hurt himself. Isabella sat exhausted in her chair and looked up at Nathaniel with an air of barely concealed irritation.

"I expected you hours ago," she said with a frown, "The baby has a colic and has been screaming all day. I was beginning to think I had to call a different doctor."

"Sorry to hear that you have been having a tough day, darling," Nathaniel answered brightly, "I will have Hannah calmed in no time. Just a pin drop of this opium with a bit of milk and honey, and she will be sound asleep in no time."

While preparing the medication for Hannah, Nathaniel explained the reason for his delay, the dreadful effects of quackery and his plan to unite the honest physicians of New Jersey to combat this evil.

Listening to Nathaniel's enthusiastic plans Isabella's irritation faded into resignation. She had always admired Nathaniel's spontaneous idealism and his desire to save the world. She was, however, increasingly aware of the burden that this put on their personal situation and the limits of her own energy.

After a deep sigh, she responded, "Nathaniel, your idea is, of course, laudable, and I agree with you that quackery is a terrible thing, but you do not have the time to solve all the problems of this world. You are already attending to the Indian refugees from Pennsylvania, the students in Princeton and a vast number of other people. You need to spend more time with your family. John is learning all his lessons very quickly and will soon need much more of your attention."

"I see your point," answered Nathaniel thoughtfully, "I really don't have time for another major project right now and my family has priority. I will spend much more time with John from now on. In fact, I will take him with me on my next trip. I have to visit Crossweeksung to buy more Indian medicine and to attend to the Lenape refugees there."

"You want to take the boy out into the wilderness?" exclaimed Isabella, "That is not what I had in mind about spending more time with your son. He is just a little boy!"

"Dunmore tells me that he is already excellent on horseback," countered Nathaniel, "And he is always saying how he would like to become a physician someday. This way I can spend many hours with him teaching him all the things he needs to know to qualify for college."

"Nathaniel! That is way too dangerous for such a child. What if something happens to him out in the wilderness?" objected Isabella vehemently.

All this time John had been listening with rapt attention to his parents' conversation. Finally, he could not restrain himself any longer.

"Please, Mama, let me go with Father. I am not a little boy anymore and I am not afraid of the wilderness. I would love to meet the Indians at Crossweeksung and see how father heals them."

Isabella, realizing that it would be hopeless to resist such a determined male coalition, again breathed a deep sigh of resignation and turned to Nathaniel, "I don't think it is a good idea but if both of you are convinced that it is, then so be it."

"Don't worry, darling," reassured Nathaniel, "Thomas will be accompanying me as well. We will take good care of Johnny. We will take our time and stay overnight again at Reverend Brainerd's house. It will be interesting for Johnny to meet him as well."

A few weeks later, Nathaniel, Thomas, and John saddled up for the long ride to Crossweeksung. John was extremely proud to be included in such an important mission. It was almost like being treated as a grown-up. As the three horses trotted off at a brisk pace, John resolved to conduct himself in such a way that his father would be proud of him. After they had travelled for a few hours, they found themselves in a densely forested area with few farms. John had heard stories of the wild beasts and men who roamed this area, but he refused to show any signs of the rising trepidation that he felt. He assured himself that his father would master any dangerous situation that might arise.

At length, the smell of woodsmoke alerted Nathaniel and Thomas to the presence of a large human settlement in the vicinity. Not long after they espied the long huts of the Leni Lenape settlement at Crossweeksung. As they approached, Nathaniel noticed that there were many more Indians there than at his last visit. Riding into the village they saw the familiar face of Okwes, the sachem of the tribe.

"Welcome, Dr. Nathaniel," greeted Okwes, "We are very glad to see you. There are many refugees here from our kinsmen in Pennsylvania. Although they are all Christians, they have been driven out by murderous Whites who want to steal their land."

"I know, Okwes," replied Nathaniel, "I have heard about these tragedies. That is why I have come. Both Governor Penn and Governor Franklin abhor this un-Christian behavior and want to redress these grievances. President Finley in Princeton has conveyed their desire to me that we are to alleviate their suffering as best we can."

"God bless you for that," answered Okwes, "Reverend Brainerd told us that we could expect help from our Christian brethren here in New Jersey and we are very grateful."

Nathaniel and Thomas spent the next few hours inspecting the refugees, treating their illnesses and inoculating some of them against the pox. John watched with wide-eyed fascination. He was especially moved by plight of some of the children who looked totally exhausted and under-nourished. Nathaniel for his part could not stop thinking about the pervasiveness of evil in the world. He recalled how a relatively short time ago he was treating White refugees from Indian massacres and how the roles had now been reversed. He thought of President Finley's words— "atrocities breed atrocities"—and wondered why people could not just heed Jesus' injunction to turn the other cheek. That evening after having treated all the refugees and received supplies of Indian medicines in return Nathaniel, Thomas, and John retired to Reverend Brainerd's cabin where the three men mused about the significance of the latest developments.

"This is an unmitigated disaster," asserted Reverend Brainerd, "Attacks on Indians who have converted to the True Religion destroy our credibility completely. Decades of missionary work are being undone before our eyes."

"I find it particularly troubling that many of the perpetrators seem to be our fellow Presbyterians," added Nathaniel, "It is incomprehensible to me that a Presbyterian pastor could have encouraged these dreadful acts."

"I think this has less to do with religion than with greed," opined Thomas Henderson, "Many people I have talked to are upset about the restriction of settlements beyond the Proclamation Line. They see all that empty land in the West and wonder why they cannot just settle there. Their greed for land colors their theology. That is why they like to think of the Indians as the Canaanites. It gives them an excuse to steal their land."

"I am afraid you are right," agreed Reverend Brainerd, "It is indeed frightening to see how the Evil One can use even the Scriptures to delude people into sin. We can only pray that through the Lord's grace we will find our way out of this confusion."

Exhausted from the busy day of treating the refugees, Nathaniel, Thomas, and John lay down early to sleep on the hard floor of Reverend Brainerd's cabin. They rose early the next morning to get an early start for the long ride back to Monmouth.

As they retraced their route through the forest, Nathaniel was pleased to note that his young son had held up very well during the trip.

"Well, John," he asked, "This is your first experience with a physician's mission. Do you still think you want to be a doctor?"

"Now, more than ever, Father," John answered, "I want to do the Lord's work just the way you are doing. The sight of those suffering Indian children made me so sad that the only thing I could think of is how we might help them."

"That is exactly the right attitude," beamed Nathaniel proudly, "Taking you along was the right decision. From now on you will accompany me more often on my visits."

And so it came to pass that Nathaniel, Thomas, and John spent the next months riding together about the countryside, visiting farms and taking care of sick people. Nathaniel used the long rides to teach John everything from Latin grammar to the basic principles of natural philosophy. Thomas, having recently graduated from the college at Princeton, also contributed much to their conversations by describing to John the intellectual atmosphere that awaited him there. Nathaniel greatly enjoyed the role of teacher and mentor not only to Thomas but to his young son as well. John's intelligence, energy, and enthusiasm were a constant source of delight to Nathaniel. Nathaniel was able, therefore, to maintain a positive and optimistic attitude toward life despite the ominous political and economic developments that were casting their shadow over the colony.

Nathaniel could not ignore, however, that many of the farms that he visited were doing noticeably less well than they had in the past. His patients often had to pay in produce since even proclamation money was getting so scarce. As fall approached, the level of anxiety continued to rise as farmers wondered where they would be able to sell their grain. Army procurement was dwindling down and there seemed to be a grain glut in the sugar islands. To make matters worse the restrictions of the Sugar Act started to be felt in the colonies as the price of rum began to rise. The level of trade between the colony and the Caribbean islands decreased dramatically. Honest yeomen suffered while rogues were able to profit by ignoring the rules. Nathaniel was amazed by the increasing anger he encountered among his patients. The government's attempts to crack down on smuggling only increased this tension. Respect for the government and its laws declined precipitously as honest, hardworking people began to see themselves as the victims of callous and illogical policies and smugglers as heroic saviors of the common folk.

Instead of adjusting their policies to relieve the hard-pressed colonists, the British government stubbornly continued to try to squeeze revenue out of them. Despite the efforts of Governor Franklin to convince the Board of Trade that a currency emission was urgently needed, the British Parliament passed a bill to end the use of paper money in the colonies. When this became known in New Jersey, people of all classes were shocked.

"How could they enact such a stupid policy against the explicit recommendations of their own royal governor?" asked Nathaniel at one of the family get-togethers at Anderson Manor.

"From their standpoint it does not appear to be stupid," explained Colonel Anderson, "The Board of Trade is satisfying the complaints of British merchants who are afraid that proclamation money issued by colonial assemblies could one day turn out to be worthless. They want to be paid in sterling."

"But if they drain all the sterling out of the colonies, what can we pay them with. They surely want us to keep buying their wares."

"That is exactly right," agreed the colonel, "They are not currently buying enough of what we produce, but tax and restrict our trade in so many ways, and then wonder why we can't pay sterling. But there is also an issue of power. What they especially don't like is seeing colonial assemblies influencing monetary policy. They want to wrest control of that away from us but then don't provide us with an adequate medium of exchange. It's as outrageous as it is incompetent!"

As fall turned into winter Nathaniel's mood started to darken as he brooded over the implications of what he was seeing around him and his father-in-law's explanation of it. Just a short time earlier everyone he knew had rejoiced in being partners in empire with the victorious British war machine. Now everyone was dismayed that the mother country to whom they had been patriotically devoted could treat them in such a despicable manner. The victorious British army now felt like an instrument of repression, the cost of which could ruin the fragile colonial economies. The British authorities were treating the colonists hardly better than slaves.

As so often in the past when Nathaniel had reached a nadir of downhearted-ness, Isabella came to his rescue. As he and John returned from a long ride on a cold December day, Isabella was waiting in the doorway and greeted them with a beaming smile.

"Welcome home, my two busy men," she called to them, "I have surprises for you. Not just one but two."

"Oh, we love surprises, don't we John," Nathaniel answered as he and the boy dismounted handing the reins of both horses to Dunmore."

"Well, I will save the better one for last. The first is this letter from your old friend, Benjamin Prime. It seems he will soon be returning from his trip abroad," announced Isabella.

"How wonderful it will be to see that old curmudgeon again," exclaimed Nathaniel, "If that is only the second-best surprise, I can't wait to hear the next one."

"You are about to become a father again, and John will have a new baby brother or sister."

Nathaniel rushed to embrace Isabella, followed closely by Johnny who threw his arms around his mother's knees.

"Take it easy boys," laughed Isabella, "You are going to knock me over in my delicate condition."

"I would never let you fall, my precious darling," answered Nathaniel gallantly, "Not the most wonderful spouse that a man could imagine. If it's a boy this time, I think we ought to name it after your father."

"That would certainly please him," agreed Isabella, "But let's just wait and see what the Lord has in store for us."

As always, the news that a new addition to the family was on the way shook Nathaniel out of the doldrums. Even though the economic situation in the colony was clearly deteriorating, Nathaniel felt confident that he could always provide for his household. It was not a great imposition to accept barter goods from his less affluent customers. Anderson Manor was also not as pressed as many estates because Colonel Anderson had resisted the temptation to overinvest so the generosity from that quarter continued unabated. Instead of gloom Nathaniel began to feel annoyance at the obtuseness of British policy.

This feeling escalated to outrage when he heard the news that Colonel Anderson had to offer during a visit to Anderson Manor to celebrate the upcoming blessed event.

"I just heard from our Attorney General, Cortlandt Skinner, that Governor Franklin has received a letter from the Earl of Halifax asking for a list of public documents that might be the object of a stamp tax," announced the colonel.

"What kind of a tax?" asked Nathaniel incredulously.

"A stamp tax, every legal document such as a deed, a contract, etc. would need a government stamp which would require a fee," answered the colonel, his voice rising in indignation, "It would be an unprecedented attempt to extort money from the colonies without the approval of the assemblies. Up until now, the excuse has always been that the levies were necessary to regulate trade. But this has nothing to do with trade regulation. It is just a bald-faced attempt to suck money out of our economy!"

"That is outrageous!" agreed Nathaniel, "I see so much agony during my visits to patients. So many people are just barely surviving. Where are they supposed to get the money to pay for stamps?"

"They won't be able to," answered the colonel, "If Parliament is so foolish as to enact such a law, they can expect violent resistance. They have no right to impose that kind of a tax without the approval of the assemblies."

"But surely Governor Franklin will be able to convince the Board of Trade that such a law would have devastating consequences for our economy," said Nathaniel hopefully, "he often talks about how important it is to promote the local economy."

"Apparently he complied immediately with the request. He seems oblivious to the trouble that awaits him if such a law would be implemented. Moreover, his influence over the Board of Trade is obviously limited. He was not able to convince them of the necessity of a paper currency emission even though it would have been in his own personal interests."

As winter turned into spring ominous straws were in the wind. By May it became known that Parliament had indeed passed the outrageous law and rumor had it that a royal stamp distributor had be appointed in each colony. During a visit to Princeton Nathaniel asked President Finley if he had heard about such an appointment.

"Indeed, I have," answered Finley, "I am told that it is a merchant named William Coxe."

"I would not like to be in his shoes," said Nathaniel, "There is so much anger in the populace. If they have someone to direct their ire toward, it could get very dangerous. I don't think the governor understands just how precarious the current situation is."

"Perhaps you will have the opportunity to tell him yourself," continued President Finley, "The governor plans to hold a large celebration next month in honor of the king's birthday. We have been asked to name representatives of the college who might like to attend. I will see to it that you and your wife are invited. I assume that your father-in-law will be getting an invitation in any case."

Back in Monmouth Nathaniel hastened to inform Isabella about the coming invitation. He suspected that Isabella sometimes missed the elegant social life that she had enjoyed before becoming a wife and mother. He hoped that the news would give her something to look forward to.

"And just like the last time I met him, I will be as big as a house," remarked Isabella testily, "The governor will think that I am continuously pregnant."

"He will be as charmed as he was every time he has met you," replied Nathaniel defensively, "And besides, it is a sign of God's grace that we are to be blessed with a fourth child. The governor has only managed to produce one illegitimate son. His wife will probably be envious of you."

"The legitimacy issue seems to run in that family," added Isabella," Annis told me that no one seems to know who the governor's mother is."

Despite her misgivings Isabella did, in fact, greatly look forward to what her friend, Annis Boudinot Stockton, assured her would be the social event of the year. She sent to Philadelphia for the best silks and satins, and enlisted the help of a female servant from Anderson Manor who was a skilled seamstress. She had the seamstress produce a gown to her exact specifications carefully designed to conceal her swelling midriff.

On the appointed day Nathaniel and Isabella together with Colonel Anderson departed early in the big coach for the long journey to the governor's mansion in Burlington. When they arrived in Burlington, they fell in with many other carriages carrying the prominence of New Jersey and Pennsylvania to the governor's celebration. After the carriages had been parked, the celebrants marched to the governor's house where they toasted the king's health to the sound of brass cannons firing salutes from the lawn. Governor Franklin and his elegant wife, Elizabeth, greeted the guests with smiles and polite social banter that immediately charmed one and all. After the initial round of toasts Governor Franklin bid the guests attention for the main event of the celebration. Stepping up to a large portrait covered with a linen curtain the governor pulled a string to reveal full-length portraits of the king and queen. The audience applauded enthusiastically as the governor raised his glass for yet one more toast.

The formal part of the celebration being complete the guests were free to mingle as an orchestra began to play Vivaldi in the background. Nathaniel recognized many of the same people that he had seen at his very first social event years ago at Morven. Even his old friend Benjamin Prime had managed to wangle an invitation and had come all the way from New York to attend. He knew that a large section of the elite of New Jersey and Pennsylvania were present, and it would be interesting to hear how these people were reacting to the tumult unleashed by the recent acts of Parliament. Not only had the dreaded Stamp Act been implemented but also a Quartering Act forcing colonies to provide accommodations for British troops even though the war was over. When Nathaniel saw his father-in-law conversing with the governor, he knew what the topic would be.

"Mark my words, your honor, this Stamp Act will be a disaster," asserted Colonel Anderson darkly, "You will have all the colonies up in arms about it."

"I am quite confident that the citizens of New Jersey are on the whole law-abiding citizens and will submit to the will of Parliament," countered the governor, "Did the Assembly not reject the invitation of Massachusetts to send delegates to a Stamp Act Congress this fall?"

"That they did," conceded Colonel Anderson, "But Speaker Ogden brought up the issue right at the end of the session after many delegates had already gone home.

He also dismissed its significance for New Jersey's trade. But he is wrong, this law is very bad for trade. As the meaning of the act begins to sink in, you will see more and more resistance."

"I will not tolerate lawlessness in this colony," retorted the governor stridently, "One can be of different opinions regarding the desirability of this measure, but the law is the law! I have appointed a capable Stamp Distributor, William Coxe, who I am certain will see to it that the king's revenue is collected."

As the governor moved on to hobnob with the other guests, Nathaniel and Colonel Anderson exchanged looks of grim frustration and foreboding. He was abundantly clear that the governor had no inkling of the depths of the anti-British sentiment that was rapidly spreading in the colonies and the tumult that was about to ensue. The decision of the Assembly not to send delegates to the Stamp Act Congress had lulled him into complacency.

Benjamin Prime who had been standing within hearing distance approached Nathaniel and Colonel Anderson.

"He seems to be living in his own little world, doesn't he?" remarked Benjamin with a wry smile.

"A world, I'm afraid, which might soon have to endure some very unpleasant surprises," replied Colonel Anderson shaking his head in dismay.

For Nathaniel the atmosphere of organized gaiety at the reception took on an air of unreality in the face of the serious threats to peace in the current situation. Isabella standing nearby with Annis Stockton and Elizabeth Franklin was listening to Elizabeth going on about her travails adjusting to the rustic conditions in the colony and how much more pleasant life in London had been. Nathaniel could not help thinking that if this were the Franklin's greatest problem, the governor would be lucky indeed.

Although the Franklins had managed to charm most of the attendees at their grand event and to convince themselves that the elite of New Jersey would offer no serious resistance to the new laws, anxiety about the impact on the fragile economy continued to grow in the weeks that followed. As Isabella went into the final weeks of her pregnancy, reports began to reach Monmouth of demonstrations in other colonies against the Stamp Act that were turning into riots. Nathaniel hoped for Isabella's sake that no such violence would come to Monmouth Courthouse because it was right around the corner from their home. Fortunately, things stayed relatively calm and at the end of August Isabella delivered a healthy baby boy.

The reception of the newborn at Anderson Manor a few weeks later was marked by prayer and rejoicing. Isabella's father was overwhelmed by feelings of gratitude to Nathaniel and Isabella for having already provided four healthy heirs. Colonel Anderson was particularly pleased that the new baby was to have his name. Amid all the good cheer, however, the deteriorating political situation was never far from anyone's mind and the conversation soon drifted in that direction.

"Father, is it true that mobs have threatened the Stamp Distributor in Boston?" asked Isabella, "Do you think violence could come to New Jersey as well?"

"Mobs calling themselves the Sons of Liberty have indeed attacked the homes of both the Stamp Distributor and the Chief Justice. Regarding the possibility of violence coming to New Jersey it can and it has. After receiving some thinly veiled threats and hearing about the attacks in Boston, William Coxe has resigned from his position of Stamp Distributor before he even got to distribute any stamps. That would have been problematical in any case because a ship called the *Faithful Steward* that was bringing the stamps and stamp tax paper just got wrecked off Absecon Beach. Now New Jersey has no Stamp Distributor, no stamps and no stamp tax paper. The governor's plans are as wrecked as the *Faithful Steward.*"

The mention of Absecon Beach reminded Nathaniel of Sam Bigelow's tale about Zephaniah Steel's cows, and he wondered if the wreck of the *Faithful Steward* was really an accident. In any case he could imagine what would happen to any Stamp Distributor who would try to collect taxes in Tom's River or Egg Harbor.

"But the real blow to Franklin is coming soon," continued Colonel Anderson, "Robert Ogden has come under such massive public pressure that he is planning to convene a rump session of the Assembly on his own authority and nominate himself and two others to go to the Stamp Act Congress after all. The governor will be severely embarrassed when he has to explain that to the Board of Trade after telling them that New Jersey would offer no resistance."

Soon thereafter Nathaniel had occasion to see just how quickly hostility toward the Stamp Act was growing in the populace. Accompanied by Benjamin Prime he attended the college commencement in Princeton. Since Governor Franklin and his wife were also in attendance, Nathaniel was amazed to hear not less than three young scholars who had the temerity to deliver lengthy diatribes about this violation of colonial rights. The governor listened with a look of increasing petulance on his face and lost no time departing as soon as the formalities came to an end.

After the ceremony Benjamin insisted that he and Nathaniel accompany the graduates to the new tavern, Hudibras Inn, which was rapidly becoming the favorite haunt of the students. As a former tutor Benjamin was delighted to be back in his element exchanging quips with the students and holding forth on his own views on the current situation. Refusing to be outdone by the increasingly raucous Whiggery of the young men, Benjamin proposed "an excellent new song for the Sons of Liberty in America." He had spontaneously jotted down two verses which he now bid the students to sing with him:

"In Story we're told, How our Fathers of old,
Brav'd the Rage of the Winds and the Waves,
And cross'd the Deep o'er, To this desolate Shore,
All because they were loth to be SLAVES, *Brave Boys,*
All because they were loth to be SLAVES.

Yet a strange Scheme of late, Has been form'd in the State,
By a Knot of political Knaves,
Who in secret rejoice. That the Parliament's Voice,
Has condemn'd us by Law to be SLAVES, *Brave Boys*,
Has condemn'd us by Law to be SLAVES."

After a few tries the students had the song down pat and to Benjamin's great pleasure repeatedly thundered the verses out with rugged abandon. After each performance Benjamin bought the boys another round of New Jersey Lightning to toast the upcoming Stamp Act Congress. Each toast led to but another round of increasingly slurred singing. Fearing for the health of the students Nathaniel decided it was time to put an end to Benjamin's little party.

"Benjie, if we are going to stay over at my parents', we must not come too late," warned Nathaniel, "You know they are early to bed, early to rise."

"Ah, yes," muttered Benjamin, reluctantly standing up to leave, "Your God-fearing Puritan parents would not approve of our staying too long in this den of iniquity."

Riding to Scudder's Mills in the cool autumn evening seemed to clear Benjamin's head a bit and he began to enthuse about the students and the possibilities for using taverns to organize resistance to tyranny.

"Weren't they a great lot, Natty? I am gratified to see that our young scholars are such convinced Whigs. Why I think if we went from tavern to tavern teaching my song, we would generate an irrepressible movement."

"You also might also get yourself arrested for sedition if you incite people to violence," warned Nathaniel.

The possibilities for violence generated by hatred of the Stamp Act became very apparent in the following weeks. The Stamp Act Congress met and agreed to organize resistance against the law. This was quickly followed by highly effective boycotts throughout the colonies against British merchants. The refusal of speaker of the New Jersey Assembly, Robert Ogden, to sign the petition of the Stamp Act Congress sparked riots all over the colony at which Ogden was burnt in effigy. At a hostile session of the Assembly at the end of November Ogden was forced to resign and was replaced by Cortlandt Skinner. To Governor Franklin's great annoyance, the Assembly then voted approval of the Stamp Act Congress petition and went on to enact a separate petition of its own. Although he had tried desperately to do the bidding of his lords and masters in London, it became increasingly clear to him that the law was unenforceable, and he did his best to convince the Board of Trade of that fact. Franklin was appalled by the obvious propensity of the populace to resort to extralegal action but also unwilling to risk physical harm by tilting at windmills for a hopeless cause. As the winter progressed, the situation became more and more untenable. Franklin was unable to convince the Board of Trade to appoint a replacement for William Coxe and did not want to rile up the population by appointing one himself. By February New

Jersey courts could no longer function, debtors were refusing to pay creditors and the business slump caused by the end of the war deepened dramatically.

When it looked as though the political and economic system was about to collapse, relief came with word that Parliament under pressure from British merchants squeezed by colonial non-importation agreements had nullified the Stamp Act while at the same time affirming its basic prerogative to tax the colonies. Governor Franklin was delighted that his faith in the rationality of British government had been vindicated. The Assembly, however, reacted sullenly, concerned that the Declaratory Act passed at the same time as the repeal of the Stamp Act was a license for the disenfranchisement of colonial assemblies. Franklin was surprised and offended that the gracious act of Parliament was not received more gratefully, and that the Assembly continued to maintain an attitude of hostility toward him just because he had tried to uphold the law.

"All these people rattling on about the Declaration Act are pretended patriots," he opined publicly after a particularly rancorous session, "They are just using this law as a pretext to launch further protests where unprincipled demagogues actuated by a mere propensity to mischief can stir up the population."

It was clear that the gulf that the Stamp Act had opened between the royal government and the colonists was not going to be bridged so easily.

Chapter 13

WITHERSPOON – 1766–1768

DESPITE THE STAMP ACT'S repeal, the emotional turmoil that the struggle against it had unleashed continued to roil the political waters. For the first time the colonies had formally banded together and forced the Board of Trade to back down. For British public officials this bordered dangerously on sedition; an illegitimate body had defied British law and gotten away with it. For most of the colonists, however, it was an example of courageous and effective defense of British rights and liberties, reaffirming the principles of the Glorious Revolution.

"The right of resistance is a fundamental Calvinist principle," explained President Finley to Nathaniel during a visit to Nassau Hall, "Since Adam's fall all humans are depraved so the possibility always exists that human rulers can err. God's grace is our only hope to avoid the error that we are all prone to. In this case the Board of Trade was attempting to limit our liberties in a significant manner. If ever they are successful in such limitation of liberty, there is no telling where it will stop. The next step could be the establishment of a false religion that suppresses the True Religion and makes achieving a state of grace that much more unlikely."

"Thank God that the Society for the Propagation of the Gospel in Foreign Parts has not been successful in establishing an Anglican hierarchy in New Jersey," responded Nathaniel, "Reverend Tennent insists that their secret aim is to set up a diocesan court system of the kind that used to torture dissident parsons who dared preach against papist idolatry."

"And right he is," agreed President Finley, "The Anglican hierarchy is a willing tool of those greedy landowners who are wont to use false religion to justify and maintain their ill-gotten gains. But their authority is illegitimate, the only true authority is Scripture, and we must never allow rapacious men to come between us and the Word. Political freedom and religious freedom are inseparable. That is why the victory over the Stamp Act is so significant. Come with me out into the garden. I want to show you something."

Nathaniel followed President Finley out of Nassau Hall into the garden of his residence next door.

"Look at these two young sycamores, Dr. Scudder," said President Finley, "I have just had them planted to commemorate this remarkable victory for freedom. I will call them the Stamp Act Sycamores. This type of tree gets very old so I hope they will remind people long after my death of the significance of this moment in history."

At the mention of the word, death, Nathaniel could not help noticing that in the bright light of the garden the president looked distinctly unhealthy. His skin had a yellow pallor that Nathaniel knew to be a harbinger of serious illnesses.

"Excuse me, sir," Nathaniel began, "I am not your physician, but I noticed that your complexion has signs of a possible malady. Have you discussed this with your physicians?"

"I just came back from visiting them in Philadelphia," answered President Finley calmly, "They agree that my liver is failing and that there is nothing to be done about it."

"Oh my God, I am so sorry to hear that," exclaimed Nathaniel, "You have done so much for the college. The thought of losing you fills me with fear and trepidation for its future!"

"It is God's will," Finley replied with a beatific smile, "I have no wish to live even one hour longer than what the Lord has allotted me. I submit joyously to His judgement."

"But surely the continuity of the great project of developing this institution must be pleasing to the Almighty!" objected Nathaniel.

"That I firmly believe," responded Finley, "And I am grateful that the Lord in His beneficence has allowed me to serve this noble purpose for a time. But all things on this earth are finite, the project will continue without me. Perhaps the Lord will grace us with a new leader who will take the college to even greater heights. In any case, I have already informed the trustees that they should begin the search for a new president."

Nathaniel was devastated. In sharp contrast to the equanimity that President Finley exhibited, Nathaniel felt overwhelmed by a sense of impending doom. So convinced was he of the holy mission of the college that the demise of its leadership always filled him with anxiety for the future. In just a few years he had experienced the sudden deaths of Aaron Burr, Jonathan Edwards and Samuel Davies, and each time he feared that the great experiment of the college in Princeton might not survive the loss of its leadership. Now Samuel Finley was to die, and the old anxieties rushed back like some recurring nightmare.

In his distraught state Nathaniel was unable to continue the conversation with President Finley. The finality of Finley's revelation made all further remarks appear trivial. In any case he was due to pick up Isabella soon who was visiting Annis

Boudinot Stockton at Morven. He bid solemn farewell to President Finley and summoned the carriage waiting for him on Nassau Street.

Arriving at Morven a few minutes later Nathaniel was greeted by Annis and Richard Stockton who stood together with Isabella in the beautiful garden in front of the main villa. The downcast looks on their faces indicated that they also were aware of the depressing news. Richard Stockton, as a trustee of the college, would have been among those that President Finley briefed about his impending demise. Stepping down from the carriage Nathaniel bowed to the Stocktons and briefly embraced Isabella.

"I can see by the looks in your faces that you already know of the sad fate of President Finley," ventured Nathaniel.

"Indeed, we do," answered Richard Stockton, "The trustees have begun to deliberate how we can best meet this challenge. In order to maintain the momentum of the college's development we will need to find a very remarkable candidate to replace Samuel Finley."

"I can imagine that that will not be a simple task," agreed Nathaniel, "By all accounts he was a very gifted teacher."

"He certainly was. I experienced him myself at the Nottingham Academy," Stockton continued, "And his scholarship was recognized as far away as Scotland; he was one of very few Americans to receive an honorary degree from the University of Glasgow. I know of no available scholar in this country who could replace him. The trustees have decided to concentrate their search on Scotland."

"Why just on Scotland?" asked Annis Boudinot, "Why not broaden the search to other countries as well? There must be good Reformed divines in other places such as the Netherlands or Switzerland, as well."

"Right now, no place in the world compares to Scotland in the quality of university education." explained Stockton, "The universities there are hotbeds of intellectual ferment. For years, the Presbyterian Kirk has systematically promoted literacy in order that everyone might read the Scriptures. This has resulted in a much higher literacy rate than anywhere else in Europe which in turn has produced many scholars seeking university education. The Kirk's position that there is no inherent contradiction between science and Scripture has generated a very fruitful flowering of scholarship in many subjects. Nowhere is there such broad tolerance of intellectual discourse."

"I have heard that this tolerance on occasion goes too far," interjected Isabella, "Does not an infidel like David Hume endanger the True Religion?"

"It is true that David Hume and others from the so-called Moderate Party present a challenge to some of the doctrines of the Kirk," answered Stockton, "But fortunately there are scholars who effectively expose the shortcomings of excessively radical views. All in all, the controversies have produced a wealth of new scholarship, and we would be very fortunate if we could transplant some of that intellectual fervor to this country."

"Do the trustees have any particular scholar in mind?" asked Nathaniel.

"In fact, there is overall agreement that if we could convince the Reverend John Witherspoon to take the appointment, it would be the optimal outcome for our college. He is the most eloquent of those in the Evangelical Party who resist the atheistic elements within the Moderate Party. He is an outstanding pastor, author, and scholar and he is even reputed to be a direct descendent of John Knox. The Presbyterian cause in North America could not have a better advocate. He might also be able to help resolve the split between Old Side and New Light Presbyterians. As it happens, Annis and I will be leaving for an extended visit to Great Britain in the next few weeks and the trustees have asked me to broach the subject with him."

"Isn't that exciting, Nathaniel," exclaimed Isabella, "Annis has told me that Richard might even get to meet King George."

"The trustees have also asked me to convey their gratitude to the government for the repeal of the Stamp Act and to present our views about how the North American colonies could best continue to develop," continued Stockton, "I will, of course, also solicit financial support for our college emphasizing the key role it plays in the production of competent leadership."

"God be pleased to bless your mission with success," Nathaniel said with relief, "Isabella and I will pray for you and eagerly await reports of your progress."

"Another friend of the college will be traveling to the mother country at the same time. Do you know Benjamin Rush?"

"Yes, indeed, I think he graduated in 1760 and went on to intern with Dr. Redman in Philadelphia," answered Nathaniel, "I counseled him when he was an undergraduate—a fine young man."

"Well, he is just finishing his internship and Dr. Redman has convinced him that he should continue his study of medicine at the University of Edinburgh. Perhaps he can help convince Reverend Witherspoon to accept our offer."

On the way back to Monmouth in the carriage Isabella was positively giddy about the prospect of her girlfriend embarking on such a great adventure in the mother country.

"Oh, Nathaniel, wouldn't that be wonderful to travel to Great Britain and meet all those interesting and powerful people?"

"It certainly would," agreed Nathaniel, "But to receive such honors requires much duty to public service. Richard has selflessly served as a trustee of the college for years devoting great time and effort to making it a success."

"You also devote much of your time to helping others without pay," remarked Isabella, "Perhaps you will rise to such honors yourself one day."

"Yes, but I recall your warning me about overcommitting myself," said Nathaniel slyly.

"I did, indeed," admitted Isabella, "But, of course, if such activity should lead to your being recognized as a leader of our society, then some sacrifices might be worthwhile."

Nathaniel at last had an opening to discuss a sensitive subject that he had wanted to bring up for a few days now.

"Isabella, do you remember what I told you about the necessity of physicians uniting against quackery?"

"Yes," replied Isabella warily.

"Well, look at this issue of the New York Mercury that Thomas Henderson gave me the other day."

Taking the newspaper being proffered to her by Nathaniel, Isabella read the following advertisement:

> A considerable number of the Practitioners of Physic and Surgery, in East New Jersey, having agreed to form a Society for their mutual improvement, the advancement of the profession and promotion of the public good, and desirous of extending as much as possible the usefulness of their scheme, and of cultivating the utmost harmony and friendship with their brethren, hereby request and invite every gentleman of the profession in the province, that may approve of their design, to attend their first meeting, which will be held at Mr. Duff's, in the city of New Brunswick, on Wednesday, the 23d of July, at which time and place the Constitution and Regulations of the Society are to be settled and subscribed. East New Jersey, June 27th, 1766.

"I think that this will become an important organization," explained Nathaniel, "I have heard that many of the prominent physicians plan to join. If I want to make a name for myself in the public eye, I should really be a part of this."

Isabella had to agree with Nathaniel's logic even though she still worried about Nathaniel's tendency to overextend himself in idealistic projects. In this case, however, she could hope that the self-interestedness of the other doctors might imbue him with some practical sense.

"Perhaps the good physicians will agree on a standard list of prices for various procedures and medications," she suggested archly raising an eyebrow, "Then at least we would know the value of the free care you continuously bestow on people who cannot pay. That might make people appreciate it more."

"I am certain that that will be one of the first topics to be discussed," assured Nathaniel, "After all, overcharging for worthless cures is one of the typical evils of quackery."

After a few hours in the carriage the familiar landscapes of Manalapan and Freehold came into view. As they approached their home Nathaniel and Isabella were surprised and alarmed to see several people milling around near their house. When they got closer, they realized that it was Agatha Burnes with her son, Nat, with distraught expressions on their faces.

"Dr. Scudder, Dr. Scudder, you must come quickly," cried Agatha, "Something terrible has happened to John. He attempted to stop a fox hunt from trampling our wheat field, but the hunters just ran him down with their horses. Now he is lying unconscious and bleeding in the field and I fear for his life."

Without further ado, Nathaniel bid Agatha and little John to climb into the carriage and told Dunmore the driver to head to the Burnes farm at top speed. Fortunately, he had, as always, his physician's kit with him. Despite being exhausted by the ride from Princeton Isabella insisted on going with them to comfort Agatha.

"There, there, Agatha," she said as the carriage sped off in the direction of the Burnes farm, "Not to worry. I am sure that Nathaniel will have John back in shape in no time. How did this accident happen?"

"It was no accident. It was that vicious rogue, Cornelius Skinner," replied Agatha bitterly, "This is not the first time he has trampled our land with his arrogant friends. The first time he did it, John went to his estate to complain. The overseer on Skinner's estate told him that Skinner had rights to all the land in our area through the Proprietors. When John told him that he had bought his farm free and clear from the previous owner, he was told that the previous owner did not have a legal claim, that the land belonged to Skinner and that John would have to pay a quitrent if he wanted to continue to farm it."

"That is outrageous!" exclaimed Isabella and turning to Nathaniel asked "Nathaniel, how can this be?"

"It is unfortunately quite common," explained Nathaniel with an angry frown, "Many honest yeomen who have bought their lands from the Indians find their claims disputed by the Proprietors and their clients. Most of the farmers can't afford a lawyer so they have a hard time getting legal redress. In the meantime, the would-be lords and masters act like the pretentious British aristocrats they aspire to emulate and take all manner of liberties with the lands they claim to own. A favorite gesture is to charge through farms on foxhunts ruining whatever is in their way. In this way they think they can show the peasants who is boss."

Nathaniel's recounting of the escapades of New Jersey's pseudo aristocrats brought tears of anger and frustration to Agatha's eyes. "Dr. Scudder, can they throw us off our land? John has worked so hard with his disabled arm, and we are just at the point where the hay must be harvested, or it will rot in the fields."

Flushing red with anger Isabella cried, "Agatha, I know what a God-fearing and hard-working family you are. You and John have suffered much on behalf of this colony, and I will not countenance this outrage. Nathaniel and I will do what we can to help you. Don't worry about the hay harvest. We will send some of our servants to help you."

"I only want John to get well," wailed Agatha, "God bless you both for your Christian charity."

After an anxious half hour of driving the carriage at full speed, they arrived at the Burnes farm and rushed out to the section of the wheat field that Agatha indicated was the scene of the incident. Next to a long swath of flattened wheat they saw a crumpled and bloody figure lying. Anger welled up in Nathaniel as he saw the wanton destruction and the pitiful sight of the injured farmer.

Jumping down from the carriage he rushed over to John Burnes and placed a finger on his neck to feel the pulse. He breathed a sigh of relief as he detected a strong and steady beat. The blood turned out to be from superficial wounds and no broken bones were apparent.

Turning smiling to Isabella, Agatha and Nat, he said, "Don't worry. He is going to make it. Dunmore, come help me get him out of the sun."

Back at the Burnes cabin Nathaniel and Dunmore carried John into the bedroom and laid him gently on the bed. As Nathaniel wiped John's forehead with a cold wet towel, he began to move and groan slightly. After a few minutes he was awake but still dazed and shook his head in frustration unable to marshal his thoughts clearly.

"Just try to relax, John," cautioned Nathaniel, "You probably have a concussion, but I don't think you have any fatal injuries. You need to stay calm and rest for the next few days."

"But, but . . . the hay harvest," stammered John.

"We will help you with that," promised Nathaniel, "Dunmore will come over tomorrow with a few experienced field hands and will have your hay cut and stacked in no time. And I am sure you can expect additional assistance from our other brethren in Reverend Tennent's congregation. Trust in the Lord and everything will turn out fine."

"God bless you, God bless you," repeated John and Agatha almost simultaneously.

On the way back to the Scudder farm in the carriage Nathaniel and Isabella had an animated discussion about the situation they had just witnessed.

"I was so outraged," exclaimed Isabella, "I had no idea that the Proprietor landowners were acting in such a predatory fashion. I knew, of course, that there are often land disputes. But they should be settled in the courts, not by trampling down a poor farmer's hay harvest."

"The greed of these people is incomprehensible," agreed Nathaniel, "They want to recreate the backward feudal society that our ancestors came here to escape. But I don't think they will be successful. The True Religion is well entrenched here and teaches people the importance of defending liberty. Such people won't tolerate the imposition of a foreign nobility on a freeholding yeoman citizenry."

"Yes, but theoretically, if they have a good legal case, the Skinner clan could just have John Burnes arrested for trespassing and throw him into jail," objected Isabella.

"The problem that the Proprietors have is that the forces of order here are the local militias which include almost all able-bodied men between the ages of 16 and 60," explained Nathaniel, "So even if they are able to get a sheriff to arrest a yeoman who considers himself a freeholder, the local militia—of which he will certainly be a member—will probably come and bust him out of jail."

"Ah, now I understand why so many in the Proprietary party are keen to have additional Regulars stationed here. It would help them impose their will on the farmers when the militia is not cooperative."

"Exactly," agreed Nathaniel, "It is exactly as your father always says—standing armies are the enemies of liberty."

A few weeks later the time came for the first meeting of the physicians of New Jersey to form a society for the advancement of the profession. Nathaniel decided to go there together with Thomas Henderson and see what goals the new organization was to have before deciding if he should join. Nathaniel and Thomas agreed that they only wanted to be part of the initiative if it pursued the high-minded principles they had in mind. Arriving at Duff's Tavern in Newark they met a group of about a dozen physicians who were discussing the constitution of the new organization. Among the men Nathaniel spotted someone he knew.

Leaning over to Thomas he whispered, "See that handsome gentleman over there? I know him. His name is William Burnett. He graduated from the college a few years before me while it was still in Newark. He was the best in his class. He is also a prominent member of the Presbyterian church in Newark. If he is typical of the men starting this society, I think we can be happy to join."

Several of the physicians present had apparently already drawn up a draft constitution for the organization and it was decided that Dr. Burnett should read it aloud so that all present could have the opportunity to discuss its provisions.

"Firstly, that we will never enter any house in quality of our profession, nor undertake any case, either in physic or surgery, but with the purest intention of giving the utmost relief and assistance that our art shall enable us, which we will diligently and faithfully exert for that purpose," began Burnett.

He went on to describe the ways the members of the society would work together, help each other, learn from each other and charitably attend to the indigent who could not afford to pay for their medical care. They agreed to meet at least twice a year and share information to the benefit of the profession. As he went through the various articles Nathaniel became more and more convinced that this society was exactly what he and Thomas had had in mind. When Burnett finally read out the last article, Nathaniel was certain that this was an initiative that he could wholeheartedly support.

"Lastly, this Society will do all in their power to discourage and discountenance all quacks, mountebanks, imposters, or other ignorant pretenders to medicine; and will on no account support or patronize any but those who have been regularly initiated into medicine, either at some university, or under the direction of some able master or masters, or who by the study of the theory and of the practice of the art, have otherwise qualified themselves to the satisfaction of this Society for the exercise of the profession," concluded Burnett.

"God be praised!" said Nathaniel turning to Thomas, "This is exactly what our profession needs so desperately. Let us proceed immediately to Dr. Burnett and apply for admission at the next meeting."

As the physicians in attendance lined up to sign the constitution, Nathaniel and Thomas moved through the crowd toward Dr. Burnett.

"Dr. Burnett, I don't know if you remember me from President Burr's college, but I am Nathaniel Scudder. After graduating from the college, I apprenticed under Dr. William Clark and this is my apprentice Thomas Henderson, also a graduate of the College of New Jersey in Princeton. We were both very impressed by the society's constitution and would like to join at our next opportunity."

"Dr. Scudder, I do remember you and have heard through Reverend Tennent that you are a credit to our profession. I will be happy to propose both of you for membership at our next meeting. It will, in fact, be held in Princeton. As acting president, Reverend Tennent has suggested that we conduct the next meeting there because he feels that the college will be producing many candidates for our profession."

After the meeting Thomas and Nathaniel mounted their horses and headed back in the direction of Freehold talking animatedly about the prospects of the new organization.

"Thomas, I am convinced that this New Jersey Medical Society could make a dramatic difference in the quality of care available in this province. If that indeed comes to pass, it might become a model for other provinces. The need is so obvious."

"I hope you are correct, Dr. Scudder," responded Thomas, "In any case I am quite looking forward to learning about the techniques and experiences that other physicians have to report."

After they had ridden about five miles storm clouds swept in from the sea and it looked as though a summer cloud burst was imminent.

"I say, Thomas, we had best take cover. I know of a tavern called the Sign of the Hogshead right up ahead in Elizabethtown. We can stop there for dinner. It is owned by the Widow Chetwood who is renowned for the quality of her pork roasts. She is also an inexhaustible source of news about everything that is happening in eastern New Jersey. Let's stop there and fortify ourselves for the long ride home. Perhaps the storm will blow over in a few hours."

As thunder started to rumble the two urged their mounts to a gallop in order to get to the inn before the rain began. In just a few minutes the sign with the picture of the boar came into sight. They quickly tethered their horses and hurried into the tavern.

"Ah, it's Dr. Scudder, is it?" greeted the Widow Chetwood as they entered, "And who is this handsome young swain with him?"

"That is my apprentice, Mrs. Chetwood," answered Nathaniel, "His name is Thomas Henderson, and he will soon be a physician himself. We were just attending the founding meeting of the New Jersey Medical Society in Newark."

"A medical society? Is that an organization to sell medicines?" asked the widow.

"No, it's a society of physicians dedicated to improving the art and discouraging quackery." Thomas enthusiastically explained.

"Well, that sounds like a noble plan," replied the widow, "A lot better plan than our lords and masters in the British military have for us."

"What might that be?" queried Nathaniel.

"I have just been informed that the 28th Regiment of British Regulars is going to be quartered in Elizabethtown, and that anyone owning a house here might be obliged to offer accommodation to soldiers."

"But wouldn't that mean extra business for the inn," asked Thomas ingenuously.

"It's the kind of business I can do without! In my experience soldiers are a rowdy lot. They pester our servant girls and start fights. The streets won't be safe at night as long as they're here."

"Why are they stationing Regulars in Elizabethtown?" asked Nathaniel, "There are no dangerous Indians anywhere near here, and the local militia has no problem maintaining the public order."

"That's just the point," answered the widow, "We don't need them or want them. They don't maintain order, they create disorder. But many people say the Proprietors want them here to enforce eviction orders that the militia refuses to serve. Others think it has to do with the cracking down on smugglers. Since local juries often acquit people accused of smuggling, the Board of Trade wants to set up vice-admiralty courts without juries and use Regulars to enforce their rulings."

"That is outrageous. Trial by jury is a sacred English right!" Thomas Henderson was indignant.

"You are surely correct, Thomas," agreed Nathaniel, "One can really not escape the impression that there are people in the government who would enslave us. Whatever the purpose of those Regulars is, it surely does not bode well for the residents of this province. Whether they help the Proprietors to force honest yeomen off their land or enforce ridiculous restrictions on trade, either way it is bad news for us."

By the time Nathaniel and Thomas had finished a hearty dinner of roast pork, corn bread and cider the storm began to abate, and they decided they could head on in the direction of Freehold. They thanked the Widow Chetwood for her outstanding hospitality and her interesting news items and promised to make her inn a regular stop whenever they had occasion to travel in her area.

"Just make certain to keep me informed of any news from down your way," said the widow smiling and waving good-bye, "I have a responsibility to keep our citizens informed about matters of importance in this province."

"That is a noble calling which we will certainly support," answered Nathaniel and he and Thomas mounted their horses and trotted off in the direction of Freehold.

Over the next weeks and months Nathaniel had more than one occasion to brood over the significance of the quartering of Regulars in the province. Many of his yeomen patients were coming under increasing pressures, from the economic downturn, from the increased suppression of smugglers who were among their best customers and from frequent legal challenges by the Proprietors to their freeholder status. Everywhere Nathaniel went, the growing anger of the province's farmers and merchants was palpable.

On New Year's Day on a visit to Anderson Manor Nathaniel had occasion to discuss these developments with his father-in-law. Colonel Anderson was not surprised at Nathaniel's description of the hardships that people all over the countryside were having to endure.

"Now that Rockingham's government has fallen, it can only get worse," prophesized Colonel Anderson, "He had at least the sense to recognize that the Stamp Act had to be repealed. But now he has been replaced by William Pitt who has picked Charles Townshend as Chancellor of the Exchequer. Townshend thinks he can squeeze even more money out of the colonies. I shudder to think what foolishness we will have to put up with on his account."

"When I hear you talking like that, father," said Isabella, "I feel rising anxieties and that at a time when I have another important announcement to make."

Seeing the surprised look on his father-in-law's face Nathaniel explained smiling, "Isabella is with child again. I just examined her this morning. Every time she enlarges our family, she worries about the world she is bringing our progeny into."

"You needn't worry, my darling daughter," reassured the Colonel grasping his daughter's hands with a grateful smile, "We have the means to protect you and the rest of our family. You shall not want for anything. I am so proud of you and Nathaniel. After losing my beloved Hannah, you are all I have. Aside from that, I am confident that we will weather the coming trials better than most. We have not gone into debt like so many others and can survive a long downturn in our markets. The only thing that concerns me is the potential for violence and turmoil I see. If Townshend squeezes the people here too hard, they are not just going to accept it. They are going to resist and if the Regulars are used to quell the resistance, there could be bloodshed."

The image of British Regulars forcing people like John Burnes off their homesteads at bayonet point was shocking for Nathaniel. The rumor that these people would soon not be protected by juries of their peers heightened his anxiety. He could clearly see how quickly constitutional rights could melt away if they were not fiercely protected.

"You are absolutely right, father," agreed Nathaniel, "I cannot imagine that the farmers and merchants who are my patients will stand idly by and let their rights and their means of livelihood be taken away from them. They will, indeed, resist."

Over the course of the next months, it became increasingly clear that their fears about Townshend's plans were more than justified. He turned out to be dead serious about extracting the maximum revenue from the colonies in order to give land tax breaks to his supporters in Britain. This was also the subject of numerous discussions with Reverend Tennent whom Nathaniel came to see even more often now that the pastor had been named president pro tempore in Princeton awaiting the decision of Reverend Witherspoon.

"I don't know where all this will lead. So many of my patients are already suffering, Reverend Tennent," complained Nathaniel, "There are so many in need that there are not enough hours in the day to help everyone. Sometimes I feel dismally unequal to the task the Lord has given me."

"Quite the contrary, Nathaniel, I know that your engagement is exemplary," said Reverend Tennent, "I also know that you don't charge the poor ones. That is exactly the right attitude that all of our congregation must adopt. That is what the idea of Covenant is all about. I am also pleased that you have volunteered to help develop the Medical Society. I would, therefore, like to suggest that you become an elder of our church."

"I am surely not worthy of that honor!" Nathaniel exclaimed, genuinely shocked at the suggestion, "My expertise is medicine not theology."

"You are living the righteous life of a true Christian and that is what is important," contradicted the pastor, "As an elder, you will set an example for the other members of our congregation."

And so it came to pass that Nathaniel became an extremely influential member of Reverend Tennent's congregation. His elevation to the status of elder made him an object of deference to many Presbyterians in Monmouth County and beyond. Even Isabella became less critical of all the time he spent away from the family helping others. She understood that this was part of the leadership role that Nathaniel was coming to play in their community, and that it was a moral imperative to accept this burden graciously, if not joyously.

For Nathaniel, the closer relationship with Reverend Tennent afforded the opportunity to have an insider view of the political anxieties currently besetting the trustees of the college.

"We are all concerned that Reverend Witherspoon has not accepted our offer as yet," Reverend Tennent confided one day in a conversation with Nathaniel, "It is imperative that our college be seen to have determined and capable leadership. We suspect Governor Franklin might have designs to intervene in the selection procedure to favor an Anglican divine. That would be a great setback for the True Religion in this colony."

"I can well imagine that strengthening Anglican influence here would please the governor's lords and masters in London," agreed Nathaniel, "It would be one step closer to the formal establishment of an Anglican hierarchy here."

"An Anglican president of our college would certainly have a very negative effect on religious freedom and inquiry. It is already clear that the governor is not comfortable with our college's having a monopoly on education in this colony, even though we cater to all Reformed denominations. A few months ago, he approved a charter approving a new college to be called Queen's College in honor of Her Majesty, Queen Charlotte."

"Do you think he might try to promote that as an Anglican rival to our college?" asked Nathaniel.

"I have no doubt that he would if he could," replied Reverend Tennent, "But the intellectual stimulus for the new college comes apparently from the Dutch Reformed community so I am still optimistic that it will not become a hotbed of Papist propaganda. Still, it is competition at a time when our finances are in a rather precarious state. It is difficult to maintain the momentum for a college project especially when we ourselves are in dire need of strong leadership. I wish I knew more about the Queen's College plan."

"I now have occasion to visit Newark fairly frequently to attend meetings of the Medical Society. The doctors I see come from all over eastern New Jersey. Perhaps I can glean some information from my Dutch Reformed colleagues about the state of their project."

"That would certainly be helpful, Nathaniel, God bless you," agreed Reverend Tennent gratefully.

The next meeting of the Medical Society was scheduled for the end of July. Isabella decided that she would like to come along and meet some of the colleagues that Nathaniel had told her about. They decided to make an outing of it with an overnight stay in Elizabethtown at Widow Chetwood's inn.

After a leisurely ride in the carriage Nathaniel and Isabella arrived in Elizabethtown in the early evening. On their way through town to the Sign of the Hogshead they were surprised to see British Regulars in full uniform with fixed bayonets standing around in small groups in the streets. Arriving at the tavern they quickly parked the carriage and hurried inside to find out what the cause of the military turnout was.

"Dr. Scudder, you always arrive in such attractive company," greeted Widow Chetwood cordially, "The last time with a handsome young man and now with a beautiful lady."

"I would like you to meet my wife, Isabella, Mrs. Chetwood," answered Nathaniel, "She is accompanying me this time to my meeting with the Medical Society. But when I see all those armed people outside, I wonder if this might have been the wrong time to bring her along."

"Those ruffians are about to clear out of town," explained the widow, "And none too soon, I tell you. We have had a terrible year with them just as I had predicted. Finally, our complaints have been acknowledged and the 28th will be shipped back to the mother country. They are all done up in their battle gear because they are going to be marched off to their ships this evening. But they are all already half-drunk so we will breathe a sigh of relief when they're finally out of here."

As though to confirm the widow's anxieties at that moment three troglodytic Regulars barged rudely into the tavern. White wigs askew and wine spots on their uniforms, they drunkenly surveyed the interior of the inn.

Stamping the floor with his musket to command attention their apparent ringleader, a bullet-headed sergeant with a face pockmarked and blemished by years of dissolute living, snarled, "What ya got to drink?"

"Nothing for the likes of you," answered the widow resolutely, "We don't serve drunks and we don't serve armed men, so you lose out on both counts."

Just as the drunken sergeant was about to reply to the widow, he caught sight of Isabella.

"And what do we have here, a little princess of the colony? Just the kind of pretty morsel we'd like to sample before leaving this God-forsaken backwater," sneered the sergeant slurring his speech and leering at Isabella.

"Keep a civil tongue in your head, you rogue!" shouted Nathaniel, taking a step toward the sergeant, "That is my wife. Either you apologize or I will have you flogged."

With surprising speed given their state of inebriation the sergeant's two comrades fell upon Nathaniel pinning his arms behind him.

"We'll see who does the flogging here," said the sergeant with a sinister smile as he began to unbuckle his trousers, "But first you can watch while I show your wife what a real cock is like."

At that moment, a deafening blast caused everyone to duck involuntarily. Recovering from their shock they saw the widow with two pistols, the one just fired pointed at the ceiling, the other at the sergeant's head.

"It would be a shame, sergeant, if you had to be shipped back to your unit in a box," announced the widow calmly and added with steely determination, "I can't miss at this range, and you wouldn't be the first scoundrel that I have rid the world of."

There was something in the widow's voice that confirmed to the experienced soldier that she was indeed capable of following through on her threat. After pondering the situation for a long minute, the sergeant finally laughed and said, "Come on, lads, let go of him and let's begone. We still have a lot of drinking and whoring to do before our ship leaves."

With that the rowdy lot left the tavern and Isabella swooned into Nathaniel's arms. Nathaniel eased Isabella onto a bench as the Widow Chetwood barred the door to the tavern.

"There are probably more of those louts prowling the streets so I think we had best close for the evening," announced the widow, "You and your lovely wife should stay here at the inn and keep off the streets until those rascals are gone."

"We were planning to stay overnight with you in any case. I can't thank you enough for your courageous intervention, Mrs. Chetwood. Isabella is six months pregnant with our fifth child. The thought of the harm they could have done to her and the baby is unbearable."

"I keep two loaded pistols behind the bar for just such occasions," the widow answered with a smile, "I don't tolerate any ruffians molesting my guests. Since that regiment has been stationed here, I have had to brandish them more than once."

After a few minutes Isabella began to recover and sat up on the bench. Her feelings of faintness quickly changed to anger as she recalled what had just transpired.

"I can't believe that representatives of his Majesty's army could act in such vile fashion", exclaimed Isabella, "This is incredibly outrageous!"

At that moment they began to hear loud voices, gun shots, and the breaking of glass. When they looked out the window, they saw groups of drunken Regulars with fixed bayonets marauding through the streets shouting and yelling, shooting their muskets in the air, randomly breaking windows, overturning wagons and threatening any of the town's residents who dared to protest. The unruly mob carried on like this for several hours until the officers finally succeeded in getting their regiment aboard the troop ships.

When Isabella and Nathaniel came down to breakfast the next morning the town was quiet again but looked as though it had been the scene of a battle.

"Their ships finally sailed off around four this morning," the widow greeted them with a relieved smile, "It is a wonder, but no one seems to have been killed. The mess they made will take a while to get cleaned up, however."

"The town should send an invoice to General Gage for the damages," exclaimed Isabella angrily.

"That would be an utter waste of time," explained the widow resignedly, "He would just say that that is the cost of quartering troops here for our own protection. We can just be happy that for some reason he has decided to station those brutes somewhere else. But we should all spread the word about what happens to communities who are afflicted with the Quartering Act."

"That we will," promised Nathaniel, "That we will."

Later that day Nathaniel kept his promise straight away by recounting his and Isabella's experiences in Elizabethtown to the doctors gathered for the meeting of the New Jersey Medical Society in Newark. Many were indignant but few were surprised. Several had tales of their own of abuses by Regulars in other communities including molesting of the womanhood, general harassment of civilians as well as the occasional impressment of young men into military service. It became apparent during the conversations that many of the doctors shared Nathaniel's anxieties about the government's true intentions. Few believed that the Regulars were there to protect them. Most suspected that the real purpose was to establish options for coercing the populace in ways that the local militia never would. All agreed that their newly formed doctors' network might be useful for keeping the people informed about what was really going on. After all, few people spent so much time on horseback as the doctors, visiting remote farms and listening to the troubles that their patients had to relate. Together with the churches they were well suited to promote communications in the widely dispersed population of the province.

Over the next weeks and months Nathaniel had many occasions to discuss these issues with his patients, his relatives, his friends, and his neighbors. It became increasingly apparent that the Board of Trade was determined to extort money systematically from the colonies and to use force to accomplish this end, if necessary. The Board felt that the failure of the Stamp Act had to do with its being an "internal" tax and that an "external" tax, such as a tax on imports, would be more acceptable to the colonists. No one, they reasoned, could take issue with the right of the Board of Trade to regulate trade. With this in mind, the new Chancellor of the Exchequer, Charles Townshend, decided to impose import duties on paper, paint, lead, glass, and tea. These were items that the colonies were not allowed to manufacture themselves and could only be legally imported from Great Britain. This was accompanied by a crackdown on smuggling and the establishment of vice admiralty courts which took over the prosecution of anyone accused of violating the new rules. Using so-called writs of assistance, they could confiscate any shipment they suspected of being in violation of the law.

"This is not just about revenue to finance the army in North America," opined Colonel Anderson when discussing this with Nathaniel and Reverend Tennent, "Their true goal is to collect sufficient revenue to be able to pay the salaries of governors and judges here in the colonies. That will make them independent of our assemblies and our juries and willing enforcers of unconstitutional, repressive measures. They want us to finance our own enslavement!"

"You are absolutely correct, Colonel," agreed Reverend Tennent, "Times are grim, indeed, and if the Papist elements in Great Britain have their way, the True Religion could come under serious threat. We must diligently warn our co-religionists to be prepared to resist any encroachments on our traditional freedoms."

"The leading role of the college in Princeton was never more important," added Nathaniel, "Our pious graduates have a holy mission to educate the people about these dangers."

"Unfortunately, our beloved college is in a desperate state," continued Reverend Tennent, "Richard Stockton, recently returned from England, has informed the trustees that Reverend Witherspoon has refused our appointment to the presidency. Apparently, his wife has reservations about moving to what she thinks is a wild and dangerous place. We have appointed Reverend Samuel Blair as an interim solution but, although exceedingly pious, he is still a young man and does not yet have the stature to mobilize the financial resources that the college so desperately needs."

"That is terrible news!" exclaimed Nathaniel, "We were all counting on Reverend Witherspoon to provide new impulses for the college and to unite us Presbyterians in the struggle to spread the True Faith."

"We have written to Benjamin Rush who has been befriended by the Witherspoon family," said Reverend Tennent, "We hope that he can make it clear to the reverend and his wife how important his mission would be in North America. Young Rush is also a fine example of the product that our college produces. He is our last hope that he may be able to change the Witherspoons' minds."

"We will pray for his success," replied Nathaniel fervently.

As summer turned into autumn Nathaniel's level of anxiety continued to increase. Isabella's fifth pregnancy was nearing its end and she seemed to be having a more difficult time than with her previous pregnancies. Unlike so many of the families they knew, they had been lucky that her first four births had gone so well, both for Isabella and the babies. Nathaniel was well aware of how unusual this was. In addition, everywhere Nathaniel went, he heard stories of the hardships that British policies were inflicting on the farmers and merchants of the colony. The leadership crisis of his beloved college also only added to his feelings of impending doom. He and the other elders of Reverend Tennent's congregation spent many hours praying intensely that God would deliver them from the many threats they perceived to their community's welfare.

By the end of the year, however, their prayers seemed to be answered. In October Isabella gave birth to a healthy baby girl that they named Lydia. A few weeks later Reverend Tennent informed the congregation that Benjamin Rush had been successful in convincing the Witherspoons to accept the college's offer. As the new year began, Nathaniel was overwhelmed by feelings of redemption. The Lord had blessed him and Isabella with another beautiful child and had somehow moved the Witherspoons to come to the aid of the distressed college. Nathaniel was convinced that all this was not coincidental, that it was all part of the mission that Divine Providence had in store for him and his community.

"Everything that is happening now was preordained before the beginning of time," stated Reverend Tennent firmly during one of their many conversations at Anderson Manor, "Reverend Witherspoon apparently shares our belief that Second Coming will happen here in the New World, far away from the corruption and iniquity of Europe. He is willing to give up a comfortable life in Scotland to become part of this Divine Mission. The Lord be praised!"

"He comes at a time when we are desperately in need of firm leadership," agreed Colonel Anderson, "I have just received a letter from a farmer in Pennsylvania who clearly points out the dangers we are currently facing. He shows convincingly that the New York Restraining Act passed last year is a dire threat to our colonial liberties. Although he thinks that the New York Assembly acted somewhat imprudently in resisting the Quartering Act, he nonetheless makes clear that the punishment meted out is an imminent danger to all of us."

"How is a dispute between the New York Assembly and Parliament an imminent danger for us in New Jersey?" asked Isabella.

"The farmer argues that the New York Assembly was constitutionally resisting a form of taxation, and that punishment by stripping it of all legislative power by force of arms is a threat to liberty everywhere," explained the Colonel.

"I can certainly sympathize with New York in their opposition to the Quartering Act," added Nathaniel, "In Elizabethtown we experienced the violence that Regulars are capable of. I think that the Pennsylvania farmer is right in calling this matter to the attention of all of us."

"We must show solidarity with all lovers of liberty," agreed Reverend Tennent emphatically and, raising his finger and his voice, held forth on the biblical significance of the current events, "There are many perpetrators of evil who would curtail our hard-won freedoms and introduce the same sort of corruption and venality that prevails in the Old World. It is our duty before God to do whatever is necessary to prevent this from happening. We must recognize who is on the side of the Beast and who is on the side of the Lord of Hosts when the seven trumpets sound. As it says in Revelation 13:16,17 'He causes all, both small and great, rich and poor, free and slave, to receive a mark on their right hand or on their foreheads, and that no one may buy or sell except one who has the mark or the name of the beast, or the number of his name.' We can see from this passage that we can recognize the Evil One by the kinds of restrictions he tries to place on us. The Stamp Act was such a restriction. Even though it was repealed, Satan has obviously not given up yet. We must, therefore, remain steadfast in our will to resist the Evil One."

"Amen!" exclaimed Nathaniel and Colonel Anderson almost simultaneously, while Isabella shuddered at the thought of the violence that could soon engulf their lives. The memory of the incident with the thuggish Regulars in Elizabethtown continued to cause her great anxiety. Seeing how upset she was, Nathaniel tried to assure her that despite the escalating rhetoric, they were in no immediate danger.

"Let us pray that the government will realize the errors of its ways and not provoke the colonists unnecessarily," Nathaniel said, "I recall Governor Franklin's saying that he is confident that he will be able to present the case of the colonists of New Jersey so convincingly to the Board of Trade that compromises will be found."

"He doesn't seem to have been so successful with the Board of Trade up until now," objected Colonel Anderson, "He has not gotten anywhere with his proposal for a currency emission although that it is so obviously needed to relieve the dreadful economic situation we have. The Board of Trade thinks Franklin does not have sufficient control over the Assembly while most people in the Assembly thinks he a lackey of the Crown. This unfortunately is what can happen to someone who is trying to forge a compromise between two incompatible viewpoints."

Isabella's premonition of imminent turbulence was confirmed just a few weeks later when her father spoke about a conversation he had had with the Speaker of the Assembly.

"Cortlandt Skinner told me today that he has received a Circular Letter from the Massachusetts Assembly suggesting united action among the colonies to resist the Townshend Acts. Apparently, Samuel Adams thinks what worked against the Stamp Act will work again against the Townshend Acts," Isabella's father reported, "Sam Adams is a bit of a hothead, but he is certainly correct when he talks about how outrageous the high-handed policies of the Board of Trade are."

"I wonder how Governor Franklin will handle this," mused Nathaniel, "Did Skinner give any indication of how the governor will react?"

"The Assembly was meeting in Amboy and the governor is in Burlington," replied the colonel, "I don't think the governor has been informed yet, and I suspect that Skinner might try to craft his own response without consulting him."

"This could lead to quite a crisis," remarked Nathaniel, "I can't imagine that the governor as the king's representative here could countenance organized resistance against acts of Parliament, but I also can't imagine that the Assembly can afford to ignore a legitimate petition of the Assembly of Massachusetts."

"Precisely," agreed the colonel, "This is bound to lead to confrontation. Governor Franklin will have to convince Lord Hillsborough, the new Secretary of State for the colonies, that he can enforce the law and that he has the New Jersey Assembly under control, However, he can't really stop it from communicating with the assembly of another colony. And when this happens as it probably will, Lord Hillsborough will be angry, and it will be interesting to see how he reacts."

Within just a few months it became evident how Hillsborough was going to react. He sent an order to all royal governors to dissolve any colonial legislature that responded to the Massachusetts Circular Letter. After Governor Franklin read the letter, he hastened to reassure Hillsborough that he was confident that the Assembly of New Jersey would not cooperate in any illegal initiatives. Unfortunately for him, the Speaker of the New Jersey Assembly had, in fact, already responded to Massachusetts without revealing this to the governor. When Hillsborough found out, he was predictably outraged and issued a stinging rebuke to Governor Franklin pronouncing him derelict in his duties. A mortified William Franklin responded to the criticism with a lengthy letter defending his own actions, castigating his enemies and vowing with iron determination to enforce royal prerogatives in New Jersey with a vengeance. The crisis came at a bad time for him just when he was trying to engineer several real estate deals west of the Proclamation Line for which he needed the approval of the Board of Trade. He needed to get back in their graces with all deliberate haste by vigorously enforcing the laws of the realm. In New Jersey as in most other colonies royal customs agents issued even more writs of assistance and eagerly confiscated any goods they claimed were contraband. The powers these offices enjoyed attracted opportunists who were as corrupt as the pirates and smugglers they were supposed to apprehend. Honest merchants as well as criminals were swept up in Townshend's dragnet. Royal revenues from the colonies began to increase significantly. Merchants and yeomen groaned under the knout of the taxman as the economy continued to contract.

Throughout the spring tension continued to increase all over the colonies finally bursting into a full-blown crisis in June. News about dramatic events in Boston spread quickly and within weeks became the topic of animated conversations at Anderson Manor.

"I have just received a letter from a business associate in Boston," Colonel Anderson informed Nathaniel and Isabella during one of their Sunday visits, "I think the greedy tax collectors have finally gone too far. They are trying to bring charges against John Hancock, one of Boston's richest and most influential merchants. They confiscated one of his ships even though it had been properly inspected and cleared just a month earlier. It is clearly a case of thievery by scheming bureaucrats. Wherever they see wealth they go after it. No honest merchant is safe from their corrupt depredations."

"Surely, they can't get away with that!" exclaimed Isabella, "A man as influential as Mr. Hancock will certainly be able to get that reversed in court."

"We will see," answered the Colonel, "Hancock will fight it in court, of course, but the interesting thing about this incident is that the people of Boston reacted violently when they saw Hancock's ship being impounded. At the behest of the Sons of Liberty a crowd attacked the customs house, threatened the inspectors and burned one of their boats. The inspectors had to flee to Fort Williams to seek protection by Regular troops. The Sons of Liberty then organized a public meeting which called for a boycott of British goods. This is going to turn into a *cause célèbre*. I am sure the boycott will be approved and that other colonies will follow. The question is how the British authorities will react."

"Judging by what we hear from Governor Franklin it looks like military repression is in the offing," said Nathaniel. "He says again and again that he will not permit mob rule in New Jersey. If a similar incident here occurs with similar resistance by the people, he will have no choice but to use violence."

"God preserve us!" exclaimed Isabella, "I have five small children, the eldest is just nine years old. How can I bring them up in such lawless times? Are all our leaders mad?"

"Don't you worry, my darling," assured Nathaniel, displaying more courage than he felt, "As long as the good people of these colonies show solidarity with each other, we will be able to protect our families and our liberties. If our current leaders are unable to fulfill their duties in this, God will send us new leaders to show us the way."

Despite Nathaniel's soothing words the general atmosphere of crisis continued to worsen as spring turned into summer. Confidence in the leadership of Governor Franklin deteriorated sharply after it became known that without his prior approval the Assembly had sent a petition to the king asking for repeal of the Townshend duties. Seeking to reassure Hillsborough that he had everything under control in New

Jersey, Franklin quickly dispatched a letter insisting that the legislators had not answered the Massachusetts letter and that there was no disposition in the people of his colony to enter into any unwarrantable combination with the Bay Colony. He became panic-stricken in July, however, when he found out that Cortlandt Skinner had indeed sent a letter to Massachusetts expressing approval of the Bay Colony's initiative. He had barely time to recover from the shock of Skinner's duplicity, when the colony was rocked again by the news that the house of Stephen Skinner, treasurer of East Jersey, had been burglarized with the loss of 6000 pounds from the colony's treasury. Although the burglary had nothing to with Franklin, it created new financial strains and mistrust; the governor would now struggle to convince Hillsborough, the New Jersey Assembly and the people of the colony that he would be able to provide the leadership necessary to halt the slide toward fateful confrontation.

"I would be surprised if Franklin recovers from this debacle," opined Colonel Anderson during a discussion in August with Reverend Tennent, Nathaniel, and Isabella, "Hillsborough undoubtedly thinks he's an idiot who doesn't even know what the Assembly is up to, and the Assembly thinks he is a lackey of Hillsborough. The ship New Jersey seems to be adrift without a captain at the helm. Lord protect us!"

"And protect us He will," assured Reverend Tennent, "This week I witnessed what might be a sign of His deliverance. After a harrowing 11 week trip the Reverend Witherspoon and his wife have finally arrived here safe and sound. We met them in Philadelphia and accompanied them to Princeton. All along the way the entourage was greeted by crowds of people expressing joy and hopefulness. When we finally arrived at the college, the students had brilliantly illuminated Nassau Hall by putting candles in every window. The effect was overwhelming."

"I am sure that Reverend Witherspoon is a fine man, and that the college is fortunate to have him. But what can one pastor do to alleviate the current dreadful situation?" asked Isabella.

"He can provide the leadership we need to resist the encroachments of greedy and corrupt individuals," answered Reverend Tennent, "What we need is steadfast moral leadership to help produce more ministers of the True Religion who then can educate the people to resist evil. God has sent us Witherspoon to provide that leadership."

Chapter 14

Turbulence and Tragedy – 1768–1770

Nathaniel was so impressed by Reverend Tennent's fervor, that he decided to travel to Princeton the following week to hear the famous divine's inauguration address. He took his son Johnny along so that the boy could get a taste of what a college education would be like. Although not yet 10, young John was growing up to be a serious lad who took great interest in all the things his father taught him. He had already memorized the important Latin declensions and conjugations convincing his father that he had that sort of prodigious memory that is so essential for a physician. He also seemed to have a natural talent for empathizing with the sick people that he met when Nathaniel took him along on the trips to patients. Nathaniel was certain that he would grow up to be an outstanding physician.

When father and son arrived in Princeton, they saw a large gathering of people in front of Nassau Hall. Not only the college students, the trustees and the tutors but also numerous people from the town and surrounding countryside and many who had, like Nathaniel and John, come from afar to welcome the new president. After tethering their horses on Nassau Street, they walked quickly toward the front steps of Nassau Hall anticipating that the official inauguration was soon to begin. Just as they arrived, Reverend Tennent walked up the steps, turned to face the crowd and raised his arms asking for its attention.

"Thank you all for coming here today to welcome our new president," Reverend Tennent's voice boomed out over the audience, "We give thanks to the Almighty that our prayers have been answered, that He has seen fit to send us a pious leader who is qualified like no other to guide our college on its sacred mission. We welcome Dr. Witherspoon and his wife to our institution and pledge our utmost support for the great things we are confident he will accomplish. Dr. Witherspoon will now enlighten us regarding his vision for our beloved college."

As the crowd applauded, Dr. Witherspoon mounted the steps, took his place beside Reverend Tennent and began to read an address in Latin.

Nathaniel found that Witherspoon's strong Scottish accent and trilled r's actually made his Latin easier to understand but he knew that John would struggle to understand with his only basic knowledge of Latin vocabulary.

"Don't worry, Johnny," he whispered, "Just try to understand as much as you can, and I will explain it to you on our ride back home. It's about the connections and mutual influences of learning and piety—a very fascinating subject."

After Witherspoon had delivered his speech, Reverend Tennent solemnly administered the oath of office at the conclusion of which the crowd enthusiastically applauded as the college officials retired into Nassau Hall for Witherspoon's first meeting of the board. Nathaniel had hoped to have the opportunity to exchange a few words with the new president but, since there would be no opportunity for that today, he decided to head straight back to Monmouth.

"Now tell me, Johnny," asked Nathaniel once they were back on the road to Monmouth, "Did you understand anything that President Witherspoon had to say?"

John shook his head, "I could get quite a few vocabulary words, but I would have to see it all written down in order to get the sense of what he was saying."

"In order to understand what he was getting at," explained Nathaniel, "You must understand that many people think that scientific knowledge undermines faith in the Scriptures, and try, therefore, to suppress scientific enquiry. The Papists, for example, used to burn people at the stake for suggesting the world is round. But we Presbyterians have always believed that all apparent contradictions result from the incompleteness of our knowledge and will eventually be resolved. It is, therefore, a sacred duty to seek as much knowledge as possible. President Witherspoon argued that there is a basic interdependence and unity between science and piety, and that the most important role of the college is to make that clear to young minds."

As they rode past Hightstown on their way back to Monmouth Courthouse, Nathaniel was jolted by loud cries coming from the center of town. An angry crowd of people had encircled an individual who, wide-eyed with fear, desperately looked around for some escape route.

"That's him, I tell you," shouted one of the crowd poking his finger into the chest of the cowering captive, "He's the one who ratted on me to the Custom's Board. They then sent a platoon of Regulars over who seized all the molasses I had stored in my barn. They're probably going to sell it themselves on the black market and split the profits. I say, he's a common thief and ought to be strung up on the next tree."

Nathaniel rode quickly up to the assembled group and announced firmly, "But that would be murder, gentlemen, even if the man is guilty, the punishment should fit the crime."

"Who are you to butt in on our business?" shouted the accuser threateningly, "Are you a friend of the customs agents and their crooked accomplices who want to steal our property?"

"Most certainly not, sir," answered Nathaniel calmly, "I am no friend of the current tax policies which I view as unconstitutional. I am a mere physician whose destiny is to save lives. In this case yours if I can prevent you from foolishly committing a capital crime. The proper response to this kind of tyranny is collective action such as our compatriots in Boston have recently agreed on."

"A boycott of British wares is not going to bring back my molasses! This man needs to be punished!" cried the accuser trying to stir up the ire of the others in the crowd.

Nathaniel's cool demeanor and rational arguments had, however, succeeded in calming the crowd somewhat. It no longer looked as though the prisoner had to fear for his life. Still, some sanction was thought to be appropriate, and the snitch was taken into custody pending discussion of the most appropriate punishment. The threat of precipitous violence having passed, Nathaniel decided that he and John could continue to Monmouth.

"I was so proud of you, father," exclaimed John after they had ridden out of Hightstown, "The way you faced down the crowd!"

"I was just doing my Christian duty, Johnny" Nathaniel explained, "A good Christian cannot sit idly by when evil is being perpetrated."

"But the man had himself done something evil, hadn't he? Did he not deserve to be punished?"

"Perhaps he did, Johnny, but perhaps the confiscated molasses was indeed contraband, and the government was within its rights to seize it."

"What do you think will happen to him?"

"He will probably be lowered into a barrel of hot pine pitch, then rolled in goose feathers and run out of town on a rail. It is very unpleasant but not fatal. The purpose is to make a spectacle of him to discourage others from cooperating with the Custom's Board. I think that we at least saved his wretched life. Whether or not the punishment is just is difficult to say. I think that non-violent means of protest such as the Boston boycott are more appropriate and effective. But the forceful imposition of unjust policies will inevitably provoke violence as we have seen today."

Violent opposition by the Sons of Liberty to the imposition of Townshend Act taxes in Boston indeed soon did reach such proportions that British troops were stationed there in October to protect royal officials and quell the resistance. The presence of the troops only served to fuel the fury of the colonists. Throughout the colonies acts of passive and active resistance became more and more frequent and violent. It became increasingly clear that the main goal of the Townshend Acts was to extract enough revenue from the colonies to pay governors and judges thus making them independent of elected colonial assemblies. No one doubted that the purpose of this was to coerce the colonies into submitting to an unconstitutional diminution of their freedoms. The gulf between the colonists and their British rulers widened as attitudes hardened.

People throughout the colonies became obsessed with these issues, especially in dissident congregations where preachers regularly warned their flocks about the dire consequences of a loss of freedom. President Witherspoon took the lead in this effort. Immediately after his inauguration he began visiting Presbyterian congregations far and wide to solicit donations for the support of the cash-strapped college. In his appeals he stressed the urgency of the need to spread the True Religion by training young leaders who would ably defend the freedoms won in the Glorious Revolution. He linked the current hardships everyone was facing to insidious efforts from afar to weaken local government. During a guest sermon at Reverend Tennent's congregation in Manalapan he explained his view of the current turmoil.

"Dunna be deceived," he thundered in his deep Scottish brogue, "The occupation of Boston is only the first step in an attempt to subvert what our fathers and grandfathers died to protect—our God-given right to control our own destiny. It is not for ignorant and corrupt officials on the other side of the Atlantic to decide how we order our lives. Only our elected assemblies have the legitimacy and the local knowledge to do that. If royal officials are not under their control, and they will not be if they are paid through taxes not approved by our assemblies, all manner of mischief will occur. For the sake of our immortal souls, therefore, we must resist outside efforts to interfere with the governance of this colony!"

Nathaniel listened with fascination to Witherspoon's arguments. Although it was essentially the same line taken by most of Nathaniel's Whig friends and associates, Witherspoon delivered it with a clarity and an emotional intensity that made his listeners want to jump up and join the Sons of Liberty.

"We are currently blessed by a huge influx of our fellow religionists from Ulster and the Border Lands," continued Witherspoon, "They are spreading rapidly throughout this giant land and taming the wilderness. They have great potential for turning the country into the place that the Almighty intended."

Nathaniel found this part of the argument less convincing, having been appalled at the violence perpetrated by some of his Presbyterian co-religionists in Pennsylvania. But then Witherspoon went on to make even that proposition plausible.

"Our brethren are not ready yet for their historical mission," he conceded, "But it is our duty to make them ready. We need to educate pious young men who will go out into the wilderness and preach the True Religion to these roughhewn pioneers, to make them worthy of governing themselves and controlling their own destinies. If we can do that, we can build a new and better world but to do that we need your help."

Nathaniel smiled to himself as he realized how cleverly Witherspoon had segued from the global struggle of good versus evil to the financial needs of the college. He made a mental note to increase his own donation this year.

To Nathaniel's great satisfaction Witherspoon's seeds seem to fall on fertile ground in Reverend Tennent's congregation. The brethren became more convinced than ever of the urgent need to defend the True Religion by protecting their constitutional rights, specifically by resisting the Townshend duties. They came to understand that it was not just a matter of money but of fundamental liberties. As this message was repeated again and again at other dissident congregations, more and more people became conscious of themselves as being part of a burgeoning movement with a high moral purpose. Many joined the growing number of colonists demanding that the Assembly petition the king to recognize its sovereignty in matters concerning the colony. A letter to this effect from the Assembly caused great consternation among British government officials, many of whom saw it as a treasonous attack on the authority of the king in Parliament. An embarrassed but resigned Governor Franklin tried to explain to Lord Hillsborough the mood of the colonists in New Jersey: "Men's minds are sour'd, a sullen discontent prevails and, in my opinion, no force on earth is sufficient to make the Assemblies acknowledge by any act of theirs, that the Parliament has a right to impose taxes on America."

As the year drew to a close, tensions continued to rise. Ever larger numbers of merchants, craftsmen and traders encouraged, and sometimes intimidated, by the Sons of Liberty participated in the increasingly effective boycott of British goods. If rational arguments did not suffice to convince a merchant of the desirability of participation, the Sons of Liberty did not hesitate to set fire to the recalcitrant merchant's storehouse or to tar and feather anyone thought to be a spy for the government. Increasing violence contributed to the already desolate mood that prevailed throughout the colony. Times were hard and getting harder straining the bonds of community among the colony's residents. Although Nathaniel and his family were somewhat shielded from the worst of this through the wealth of Anderson Manor, he experienced through his patients and his parents the frustration that many people were enduring.

"The farmers have no money to pay for my milling," complained Jacob Scudder to Nathaniel during a New Year's visit to Scudder's Mills, "But I just can't turn away customers that I have been dealing with for years, particularly if they are members of our congregation. That would be a clear violation of our Covenant."

"Perhaps they will be able to pay at some point," suggested Nathaniel, trying to sound optimistic.

"Perhaps," agreed Jacob, "But if they don't, there is not much I can do about it. Taking a debtor to court usually costs more than the amount of the debt. But if someone can't pay, the costs of the lawyer and the court get piled on top of what he already owes. If he then must go to debtor's prison, there is no hope that the debt will ever be serviced. The only ones who win in the end are the lawyers, especially if they get to foreclose on the debtor's farm."

"Ah, yes, the lawyers," said Nathaniel, "How often have I heard this complaint? Down Monmouth way so many of my patients are plagued by lawsuits brought by persons contesting the legality of land purchases made under the Monmouth Patent. Speculators claiming rights through the Proprietors sue honest yeomen who have been tilling the land for generations. Then the poor devils have the choice of either paying the quitrents or bankrupting themselves by engaging in expensive lawsuits and winding up in debtors' prison. Given the current disastrous economic situation both options threaten their livelihoods. They are peaceful, pious men but they are at their wits' end. The debtors' prisons are full to overflowing. I fear there might soon be an explosion."

"And the worst part of it is," agreed Jacob, "That many lawyers encourage speculators to bring frivolous lawsuits knowing full well that the yeomen cannot afford to defend themselves. It is outrageous. I don't understand why our government permits this."

"My father-in-law thinks it is because the governor himself is mainly interested in land speculation and does not want to offend the speculators. Franklin thinks the Assembly does not pay him enough, so he plans to enrich himself by joining various projects that involve obtaining land west of the Proclamation Line. That means working with the same sort of scoundrels who are constantly trying to dispossess our pious yeomen."

"But speculating in land west of the Proclamation Line will only rile the Indians necessitating the stationing of more troops and the levying of more taxes to pay for them," objected Jacob.

"Franklin is treading quite carefully on this issue. In order to curry favor with the Indians he has executed several people accused of murdering Indians. You might remember he hanged the men who murdered those Oneida refugees awhile back. That seems to have had the desired effect. At a recent gathering of three thousand Indians organized by William Johnson in Fort Stanwix, New York, he was even awarded the title of 'Dispenser of Justice' and they agreed to the westward movement of the border that his speculators wanted. Apparently, he greatly profited from the acquisition of new lands. Now he needs to mollify the Board of Trade so they will not cancel his gains. That means he will do everything in his power to enforce the laws as they are; we cannot expect great reform efforts from him."

"Greed, greed, greed! Wherever you look!" exclaimed Jacob, "Instead of being thankful to the Lord for this bounteous land He has offered us, people can't resist the corrupt pursuit of Mammon. It's time to throw the moneylenders out of the temple!"

Despite Jacob's diatribe against the commercial class the influence of anyone in a position to lend money could only grow at this time in the colony. Import taxes on paper, paint, lead, glass, and tea drove up costs for these items at a time when many people were struggling to cope with rising debt and the currency shortage. To make matters worse increasing pressure from the Sons of Liberty to adhere to the boycott created a fraught situation for any merchants dependent on trade in the taxed items. Not only were they forced to raise prices in a weakening market, but they also ran the risk of violence from vigilantes bent on enforcing the non-importation agreement. To top it all off a customs inspector might self-servingly accuse them of dealing in smuggled goods and simply confiscate their inventories. Any attempt to seek redress through the courts could easily subject the aggrieved to exorbitant fees, long delays and further frustration. Many felt threatened by existential dangers no matter which way they turned.

Over the next months the level of frustration spiraled upward as uncertainty about the future generated ever deeper anxieties. Violent encounters became more and more common as the various contending groups came to feel morally justified in resorting to extra-legal actions. Society seemed to be fraying before the horrified eyes of peace-loving colonists.

In the course of the spring, it became clear to Nathaniel just how deeply the current malaise was going to affect everyone's lives, and not only those who were directly involved. As was usual at this time of year, Isabella wanted to redecorate their home by having a fresh coat of paint applied.

"I hope that the paint merchant in Perth Amboy is still in business," she said to Nathaniel one afternoon, "I have heard that paint is getting harder and harder to find."

"That is true, love," replied Nathaniel, "It is one of the items being taxed and is also, therefore, covered by the non-importation agreement. But I have heard that the merchants in Perth Amboy are not as strict in adhering to non-importation as the Sons of Liberty would like."

"While I am in general sympathetic to the boycott, we have to get the paint from somewhere and I don't recall your having mentioned that your smuggler friends from Tom's River had any on offer," said Isabella archly raising an eyebrow.

"Yes," agreed Nathaniel with a rueful smile, "I suspect that they continue to concentrate on more lucrative traffic. But if you want to try to find some at Perth Amboy, I will accompany you. Traders in boycotted goods are living dangerously these days, and I don't want you to wind up in the middle of a riot."

A few days later Nathaniel and Isabella set off for Perth Amboy in a wagon driven by a well-armed Dunmore. When they reached the town, they headed down to the waterfront where numerous international traders had their shops. Isabella always was pleased to visit this area, not only because the commercial bustle offered a taste of European sophistication, but also because it was where her grandfather had landed so many years ago with the refugees from the Darien Debacle and begun the saga of the Anderson family in the New World. Many of the sturdy Scots he had rescued had stayed in the area and developed lucrative trading businesses importing manufactured goods from Great Britain and exporting food stuffs to Caribbean sugar islands controlled by the British. One such man was Ebenezer Morrison whose grandfather claimed to have sailed with Captain John Anderson on that fateful voyage. Morrison had specialized in the importation of the finest paints from Great Britain. Like most merchants in Perth Amboy, he was opposed to the non-importation agreement even though the import tax on paint hurt his business. It was instructive for Nathaniel to probe the reasoning behind this seeming contradiction.

"I don't like the taxes any more than anyone else," explained Morrison, "But what am I to do? I support my family with this business, and I have no other source of high-quality paints. Business is difficult enough since the end of the war and I must contend with dozens of farmers who can't pay their debts. Then, to add insult to injury, the Sons of Liberty threaten continually to burn my stocks if I don't quit trading. They have no respect for private property!"

"But perhaps if they are successful in their boycott, this weight will be lifted from us," objected Nathaniel.

"Perhaps," continued Morrison, "And it is certainly their right to boycott my business if they so choose but not to burn my paints!"

"You are quite right about that!" agreed Isabella, her voice rising in indignation, "Nobody has the right to threaten you with violence just for doing what you have always done, even if they don't agree with you politically."

"They don't just threaten with violence, they actually carry it out. You might recall Ben McIntyre who used to deal in glass and lead for windows?"

"Indeed, I do," replied Isabella, "He supplied us with the glass and lead we needed when we built our house. Is he still in business?"

"Well, he met a very bad end just a few weeks ago. He was delivering his wares to some farms in western Monmouth when he was attacked by a group of men. They stole everything he had including the wagon and his horse and left him with a slit throat on the side of the road. By the time he was found, he had bled to death. His attackers had scratched a grisly message on his chest with the point of a knife—'Boycott.'"

"I can't believe that the Sons of Liberty would stoop to such a vile act!" exclaimed Nathaniel. "That sounds more like the work of Pine Robbers who were trying to disguise their robbery as a politically motivated action."

"Could be, could be," mused Morrison, "He was, in fact, found not far from the Pine Barrens, but there is no doubt that the threats of the Sons of Liberty provide cover for much unlawful violence."

Shaken by the images of brutality that Morrison described, Isabella was barely able to concentrate on the selection of the paints she needed.

"Do you think we could be attacked on our way home?" she asked Nathaniel in a quivering voice, "The memory of that horrible incident in Elizabethtown continues to haunt me."

"That is very unlikely," Nathaniel attempted to soothe her nerves, "Dunmore and I are both well-armed and we won't be going anywhere near the Pine Barrens, so I am not fearing a robbery. The Sons of Liberty are not likely to accost us in or around Perth Amboy because most of the people here are on firmly on the side of the Board of Trade. The customs inspectors will leave us alone because we can prove purchase from a reputable dealer."

Somewhat comforted by Nathaniel's reassurances, Isabella finally chose several barrels of paint which Dunmore then loaded onto the wagon. They then headed through the center of town to get back on the road to Monmouth Courthouse. Passing the elegant Proprietor House reminded Isabella once again of the many conflicts roiling the waters of the province.

"Isn't that the building that the Proprietors had erected as a residence for the governor?" she asked.

"Yes, indeed," answered Nathaniel, "But William Franklin has not yet taken up residence there because he did not want to seem to be a tool of the East Jersey Proprietors. For now, he spends most of his time in Burlington so he can play the neutral arbitrator between the Proprietors and their many enemies."

"So much turmoil," lamented Isabella, "Wherever I look I see increasing hatred and division. Why does it have to be like that? This province could be a paradise on earth. It seems such a short time ago we all were rejoicing in the defeat of the French and considered ourselves fortunate partners in empire with the mother country. Why can't people just settle their differences with compromises and get on with it?"

"That is a good question, dearest," replied Nathaniel, "But man is basically corrupt and only a few seek the redemption that our Lord offers us by renouncing greed. The economic downturn since the end of the war and the incessant attempts by the Board of Trade to milk the colonies have combined with older conflicts to bring out the worst in people here. Everyone is feeling increasingly frustrated for one reason or another and that frustration fuels the growing hostility between the different groups in our communities. Sometimes I have the feeling that our society is fragmenting before our very eyes."

Nathaniel and Isabella made it back to Monmouth Courthouse without incident but the anxieties they felt only increased over the following months and became the general topic of conversation among the people they associated with.

Just how serious the situation soon became abundantly clear. Only a few weeks later Nathaniel and Isabella had the pleasure of a visit from Richard Stockton who was scheduled to appear at a hearing in Monmouth Courthouse when it opened the next morning. Stockton often visited the Scudders when he had business at the courthouse since the Scudder's home was within easy walking distance. He could stay over at the Scudders and appear fresh and rested at the morning session of the court. They woke up on this morning and were amazed to see a crowd of several hundred yeomen milling around in front of the courthouse. The throng was so large that it filled the entire street that ran in front of the courthouse and the Scudder residence. The crowd was chanting loudly, "We will not be slaves! We will not be slaves!" over and over again. Several in the middle of the mob were busy erecting a long pole in front of the courthouse.

"Whatever are those people up to?" exclaimed Isabella anxiously, "That is a very unruly looking mob out there. Hopefully, they are not going to ransack our property."

"That's not likely," assured Nathaniel, "This looks like a political demonstration. That pole they are erecting over there is a so-called 'Liberty Pole'. That is a favorite gesture of the Sons of Liberty when they organize a protest. It is a custom from ancient Rome. The assassins of Caesar used such poles with a cap or pileus on top to symbolize liberation from the dictator."

"They still look like a bunch of ruffians to me," replied Isabella, her irritation unassuaged by Nathaniel's reassurances and learned explanation, "Sons of Liberty, indeed, what about our liberty and the liberty of our guest to move freely on the street in front of our house?"

"If it is a political demonstration, there is a political solution," ventured Richard Stockton, "I will go and talk to them and see what they want."

Clad in his lawyer's attire Stockton walked over to the nearest protestor and inquired what matter might have brought him here this day.

"We are here to shut down this criminal operation!" shouted the man, angrily shaking his fist in Stockton's face, "We are not allowing any of you serpents into the courthouse until we get a guarantee that only the king's business will be conducted there. No more sucking the blood out of innocent farmers!"

The man's vehemence and the hostile stares of the other demonstrators convinced Stockton that there was no point in trying to gain access to the courthouse just then, so he walked back to the Scudder house. In the course of the day other lawyers who had been barred from entering the courthouse gathered at the Scudder residence to discuss possible strategies with Richard Stockton.

"This is quite outrageous!" fretted Isabella, "These people are taking the law into their own hands. They can't just shut down the court. Why doesn't someone send for the militia?"

"We don't have enough militia in the whole county to take on a mob this size," countered Stockton, "Besides many of our militiamen are probably part of that crowd. I think the best strategy is to wait a bit and then try to reason with them. They do, after all, have some legitimate grievances that should be addressed by the Assembly."

"My father-in-law has expressed the same opinion," agreed Nathaniel, "I think your strategy might be able to defuse this crisis and prevent bloodshed."

All present agreed with Stockton's plan. He was nominated to represent the lawyers as a "gentleman of the court" and offer compromise. It was decided to wait until the next day in the hope that the vehemence of the demonstrators would wane somewhat with time.

Early the next day Richard Stockton mounted his beautiful white charger and rode boldly into the midst of the crowd of demonstrators.

"Hear me, yeomen of Monmouth!" his stentorian voice trained in years of courtroom pleas boomed out over the assembled farmers, "I am here as a gentleman of the court to tell you that we have heard your complaints and agree that you have legitimate grievances which must be addressed."

The assembled farmers looked at each other with surprised smiles. Could it be that their demonstration had actually resulted in at least a partial victory? The hostility that had characterized the crowd on the first day began to transform into expectant curiosity as all heads turned in the direction of Richard Stockton to hear what compromises might be offered.

"I have been authorized by the court to note carefully exactly what complaints you have," continued Stockton, "This information will be used to formulate specific reforms which will be taken up by the Assembly. I can promise you that all legitimate grievances will be redressed so that the blessed liberty that is so near and dear to all of us will be preserved. My clerks stand ready to document your concerns."

Stockton's aura of confidence and authority had the desired effect. As Stockton's clerks began to circulate through the crowd, many of the farmers were pleased to recount their personal difficulties with the legal system. The fact that someone was willing to listen to their complaints did much to soothe their hostility. Several of them helped take down the liberty pole and it looked as though order would soon be completely restored.

Stockton returned to the Scudder residence and was greeted like a conquering hero by the Scudders and the lawyers and clerks assembled there.

"That was a marvelous performance, Richard," Isabella said greatly relieved to see the crowd beginning to disperse, "Wait until I tell Annis. She will want to write a poem about you."

"That might be a bit premature," replied Stockton, "We have calmed them down for now, but they won't stay calm for long if some of their just complaints are not redressed."

Nathaniel was also duly impressed by the leadership qualities that Stockton had displayed.

"I think it was brilliant to record their difficulties as a basis for new legislation," Nathaniel added, "It was amazing how quickly the atmosphere of rebelliousness was transformed."

"It could just as quickly deteriorate again," warned Stockton, "The court should stay closed today to let them savor what they consider to be a victory. But it will have to re-open tomorrow and that could lead to a new riot. I will ride to Burlington immediately and inform the governor that he might have to deal with violence."

Stockton's prediction nearly came true the next day when many lawyers returned to the courthouse preparing to carry on business as usual. Word spread quickly throughout the countryside that the court was again in session and many of the participants in the demonstration the day before felt they had been deceived.

Nathaniel and Isabella were unpleasantly surprised when they looked out of their window and saw several dozen farmers converging on the courthouse.

"Oh no!" cried Isabella, "It is going to start all over again."

A cloud of dust announced the arrival of several dozen horsemen galloping into town. At first Nathaniel thought they were farmers coming back to renew the demonstration. But then it became apparent that these were sheriffs armed with muskets, pistols, and swords.

"Apparently the governor has decided to deal with this with violence instead of negotiation," Nathaniel said in a foreboding tone, "Hopefully this will not get out of hand."

As Nathaniel and Isabella watched from their home, the sheriffs attacked the demonstrators beating them with the flat side of their swords. Since there were many fewer demonstrators than on the first day, they were no match for the well-armed, mounted law enforcers and quickly withdrew. The sheriffs took up positions surrounding the courthouse and prevented anyone from approaching that did not have official business with the court. Again calm seem to be restored.

"Thank God!" cried Isabella, "I was afraid we were going to be in the middle of another riot. The governor has saved us."

"Beating those farmers does not solve the problem," contradicted Nathaniel, "It would have been better to continue the negotiations. This is just storing up tinder for a bigger fire later."

Although the government appeared to have scored a victory over the rioters, the problems were far from solved and tension continued to grow over the ensuing months. By October it was clear to the elite of Monmouth County that something had to be done if the rule of law was to prevail.

"I was frightened to death when that mob was outside our doors in July," said Isabella, her voice quavering with trepidation, "They, they … could have done anything on that first day when so many of them were here. If Richard Stockton had not talked them into dispersing, no one could have stopped them. Now I fear I am with child again. In the past I always rejoiced to accept God's gift of a new life but now I fear it because I don't know what kind of a world I am bringing this baby into."

"Mob rule is, of course, dreadful and we cannot let it come to that," Nathaniel tried to assuage Isabella's anxieties, "But, praise the Lord, this time violence was largely avoided. However, Richard got the crowd to disperse by promising compromise. If we don't deliver on those compromises, we will not solve the problem."

In early January Nathaniel and Isabella were again unpleasantly surprised when they looked out their window to see a large crowd gathering again in front of Monmouth Courthouse. This time hundreds of farmers armed with clubs were shouting their defiance at the sheriffs who, astonished by the size and vehemence of the demonstration, made no attempt to drive them off. Nathaniel was amazed to see that even his friend, John Burnes, was among the participants.

"Is that John I see over there?" asked Isabella incredulously, "I always considered him to be a pious and law-abiding citizen. What is he doing making common cause with that rabble?"

"Most of those men are pious and law-abiding citizens," explained Nathaniel, "But they are at their wits' end. When someone like John feels he has no choice but to revolt, you can see just how far things have come."

"God preserve us!" cried Isabella, "I am so distraught that I cannot sleep at night. And now this!"

"Try to calm yourself, dear," Nathaniel attempted to soothe his wife's nerves, "Those people are not here to harm us. I suspect they just want to prevent the court from proceeding with lawsuits that they regard as unfair. As long as the government does not try to disperse them with force, I don't think this will degenerate into violence."

Fortunately, the High Sheriff did not attempt to call out the militia, recognizing that such a large and determined mob would not be subdued without a bloodbath. Aside from resolutely blocking the entry of lawyers into the court, the crowd did not engage in any other forms of extra-legal activity. Finally, a representative of the Grand Jury reached out to the mob leaders admitting that mistakes had been made and that reforms were in the offing. Although many in the crowd were skeptical having once before been duped, the people listened when Reverend Tennent appeared to inform them of the progress being made on their behalf in the Assembly.

"Yeomen of Monmouth," began Tennent, "As all of you know, I have long opposed the legal chicanery that has plagued so many of our pious fellow Christians for decades now and have been subjected to such myself."

Many in the crowd nodded as they remembered how the good pastor had once been arrested himself for the crime of a charlatan who resembled him.

"I understand your frustration and impatience," continued Tennent, "I know that imps of Satan such as Bernardus LeGrange have ruined honest farmers with his vicious and devious lawsuits. But I assure you on my honor as a Christian, that I am convinced that real progress is imminent. The Assembly is considering two measures which I am sure are going to make your lot more bearable. The Act for the Relief of Insolvent Debtors will enable many to avoid debtors' prison by restructuring their debts. Another is titled 'Act to erect Courts for the Trial of Causes 10 pounds and under.' At these courts, claims can be decided by a justice of the peace without lawyers, juries and other court expenses. Honest men will be able to settle their differences among themselves without being bled dry by the greedy serpents of the Evil One!"

The crowd roared its approval but still maintained its determined and confrontational attitude.

"Just let LeGrange dare come to this county," shouted one of the demonstrators, "We will string him up right in front of this courthouse!"

"Mob violence is not the answer!" admonished Tennent, "Up until now there have been no serious injuries and it should stay like that. You have right on your side, but you must not sully your moral position but committing grievous crimes."

The preacher's exhortations seemed to give pause to many of the demonstrators, but the ringleaders remained defiant.

"We will believe that the government is treating us fairly if and when concrete changes are enacted," cried one well-armed, big-boned farmer. "Until then we stand ready to mobilize on short notice. Should the government seek to punish any one of our colleagues, all of us will react. If the justice system remains unjust, we will shut it down!"

And so the atmosphere in Monmouth remained tense despite Reverend Tennent's attempt to defuse the situation. Reports arriving from a similar confrontation in Newark added fuel to the flames which in turn greatly heightened Isabella's anxieties.

"You said the mob meant us no harm," she lamented, "Did you hear that the mob in Newark burned down David Ogden's barn? What is to prevent them from burning down our barn or our house even?"

"David Ogden was directly involved in the issues that the crowd was protesting against," Nathaniel tried to calm his distraught wife. "They hold him responsible for the arbitration which resulted in the Indian Purchasers' loss of property rights. We are not a party to anything that could give the people here cause to want to harm us or our property."

"You never know what madness a mob might get into their heads," protested Isabella, "Annis' brother, Elias, is being viciously maligned in the press right now although I am sure he did his best to help the farmers with their property claims. A mob often focuses its anger on the wrong people and then God help them!"

"You are right, of course," soothed Nathaniel, "Mob violence is a thing to be feared, but I know that Elias has been rebutting these allegations in letters to newspapers quite effectively. He explained that William Crane's unwillingness to compromise in the land dispute was a big factor in the unfavorable ruling. Eventually as the truth becomes known, his reputation will be restored. It is important to try to calm tempers with rational arguments that lead to a just solution."

Calming tempers turned out, however, to be easier said than done. During the following weeks, the yeomen of Monmouth remained adamant and continued to disrupt the operation of the court. Governor Franklin was appalled at the open defiance of the law and vowed to restore the Crown's authority. Tensions continued to increase so that when in March Colonel Anderson invited Nathaniel and Isabella to Anderson Manor to hear news recently arrived from Boston, they feared the worst.

"It has come to bloodshed," announced Colonel Anderson darkly, "British Regulars have opened fire on unarmed civilians in Boston. Several men are reported dead and a number wounded. The Sons of Liberty are calling for the arrest of the soldiers responsible."

"Oh, my God," cried Isabella, "The situation is getting completely out of hand. The same tragedy could easily repeat itself right outside our house. The farmers vow to fight. The governor threatens to send in the Regulars. How is this all going to end!"

"The only way to end the standoff is through compromise," answered Nathaniel, "The legitimate claims of the farmers have to be addressed by the Assembly and I am confident that they will be."

"The laws under consideration are quite reasonable," added Colonel Anderson, "But Governor Franklin's vow to punish the Monmouth protestors only exacerbates the situation. He should support the new laws and not seek to increase the anger. Instead, he has asked the council and courts to bring rioters to speedy justice and wants to appoint 'gentlemen of rank and character' to assist the Supreme Court judges in obtaining indictments and securing justice."

"That will completely undo whatever good the new laws could achieve," remarked Nathaniel.

"Of course, it will," agreed Colonel Anderson, "But Franklin is being obstinate. He thinks the reason the farmers are being so aggressive is the leniency with which they were treated last July. Now he wants to show the Board of Trade that he has everything under control in New Jersey by enacting swift and harsh punishment. This also, of course, has to do with his desire to get the Board of Trade to sign off on his land development schemes. If he can cast himself as the protector of the Crown's prerogatives here, they are more likely to acquiesce to his plans."

"What if he orders the Regulars into Monmouth?" asked Isabella in a tone of rising desperation, "There could be bullets flying in front of our house! They could hit our children!"

"If that looked imminent, you would all simply come and stay at the manor," Colonel Anderson assured her, "You should not work yourself into a hysterical state of mind. You will all be taken care of. Don't worry about Franklin. He may want swift and harsh punishment but when it comes to Monmouth citizens, we can get the Monmouth County Grand Jury to delay the indictments until things get calmer. We are going to get this situation under control."

Although Isabella had great confidence in her father's ability and influence, the unending threat of violent confrontations continued to unnerve her. She would toss and turn every night frequently dreaming of bloody encounters between Regulars and civilians or the tarring and feathering of customs officials. Finally in the late spring just weeks before the baby was due, Nathaniel was awoken by a loud scream.

"No, not this one," cried Isabella, "Please!"

"Wake up, darling," soothed Nathaniel, "You are just having another bad dream. It will pass."

Isabella sat straight upright in bed, her eyes wide open and a look of terror on her face.

"Nathaniel, this was not a dream! The Lord is going to take our baby!" she cried, "He said He has given me five beautiful children, but this one is going to Him!"

Unsettled by the vehemence of Isabella's revelation, Nathaniel began to stroke his wife's forehead in an effort to calm her down. Then he looked down and saw that her nightgown was drenched.

"Oh my God," Nathaniel cried, "I think your water has broken."

Nathaniel knew from many deliveries that when the water broke prematurely, it was never a good sign. He and Isabella stared at each other wide-eyed for a moment in disbelief.

"It might still go well," blurted Nathaniel trying anxiously to dispel the sense of impending tragedy, "Sometimes premature births survive."

Isabella slowly shook her head.

"No, Nathaniel, not this time," she uttered resignedly, "It is the Lord's will."

When the little boy came into the world, it was immediately apparent that he would soon be leaving it. After four days he passed away. Nathaniel and Isabella decided not to give him a name.

"He belongs to the Lord now," explained Isabella, "Jesus will give him his name."

BOOK 2

ISABELLA'S SECOND SACRIFICE – 1770–1782

Chapter 15

Jacob's Testament – 1770–1772

During the summer of 1770 the famous New Light theologian, George Whitefield, was conducting a revival tour through Pennsylvania, New Jersey and New York during which Dr. Witherspoon was able to persuade him to preach to the students at Nassau Hall. Whitefield had the same mesmerizing effect on the students and trustees that he was renowned for throughout the colonies. Reverend Tennent was so affected by his sermon that he prevailed upon Whitefield to bring his revival message to the congregation at Manalapan. Although Nathaniel was somewhat reluctant to expose Isabella to yet more emotional upheaval, he decided in the end that she might derive some comfort if Whitefield could bolster her faith in the justice of Providence. The loss of the little boy had cast her into a deep depression and nothing Nathaniel could say seemed to alleviate her suffering. Nathaniel remembered how his mother had been comforted by the revival sermon of Jonathan Edwards so many years ago and hoped that Whitefield could have a similar effect on Isabella.

While arranging for Whitefield's appearance in Manalapan, Reverend Tennent briefed him on the tragedy that Nathaniel, an elder of the congregation, and his wife had suffered. Whitefield always tried to make his sermons as relevant for his listeners as he could and constructed his message accordingly.

"Sacrifice is the path to redemption," he began, "When the Lord offers us an opportunity to sacrifice on His behalf, it is our sacred duty, not only to comply, but to comply joyously."

Nathaniel held Isabella's hand as she struggled to fight back the tears as Whitefield proceeded to read from Genesis 22.

"The Lord called to Abraham and said 'Take your son, your only son whom you love so much and go to the land of Moriah. There on a mountain that I will show you, offer him as a sacrifice to me.'"

Isabella shuddered as she realized the application of the ancient story to her own situation. Whitefield described Abraham's submission to God's will and the redemption resulting from his obedient reverence for God from not having kept back his only son.

"And the angel of the Lord called to Abraham from heaven a second time, 'I make a vow by my own name—the Lord is speaking—that I will richly bless you. Because you did this and did not keep back your only son from me, I promise that I will give you as many descendants as there are stars in the sky or grains of sand along the seashore. Your descendants will conquer their enemies. All the nations will ask me to bless them as I have blessed your descendants—all because you obeyed my command.'"

Whitefield went on to explain how important it is to understand that nothing occurs, but that God wills it and even though we may not understand it at the time, it is a sure sign of grace to be able to accept without hesitation the will of Providence.

As Whitefield explained these matters, Isabella began to relax. Her tears dried and her face began slowly to glow with a beatific expression as she raised her eyes to heaven. Nathaniel realized to his great relief that that the sermon had had the therapeutic effect that he had hoped for, and Isabella's depressions would now cease.

In the days following the service Isabella seemed to have overcome not only her depression but also the anxiety that she had been exhibiting over the last months, the anxiety that Nathaniel suspected to have been a factor in the failure of her pregnancy.

"I understand now that we have trials to face and that we must face them with equanimity and trust in the Lord," she confided in Nathaniel.

"You are absolutely right, my dear," replied Nathaniel, "I agree with you completely. I sincerely believe that all the turbulence of recent months is a sign that we are on the threshold of a new era. We need to devote ourselves steadfastly to the struggle for the New Jerusalem."

"But it is not quite clear to me just what our personal roles are in this struggle. Do you feel that you know what the Lord expects of us?" asked Isabella.

"No one can claim to know exactly what the Lord wants," answered Nathaniel, "But as I pray for guidance, I am inspired by the example of other pious people who are seeking to do the Lord's will. I have heard from Reverend Tennent, for example, that the entire student population of Nassau Hall was smitten by Reverend Whitefield's sermon there recently."

"What does that have to do with guidance for doing the Lord's will?"

"Well, apparently the students were inspired to make sacrifices of their own to show their devotion to the cause of our Whig liberties. Following Dr. Witherspoon's teachings, they are convinced that the emasculation of the rights of our local assemblies is a first step toward limiting our freedom to practice the True Religion. They are determined to resist in the name of the Lord."

"And what form does this resistance take?"

"You might recall that your father told us that the merchants in New York recently sent a letter to the Committee of Merchants in Philadelphia informing them that they did not intend to adhere to the Non-Importation Agreement but planned to order goods from the mother country."

"Yes, I remember father having mentioned that. And what can a bunch of students do against the actions of New York merchants?"

"They can and did mobilize opinion by a public spectacle. At the tolling of the college bell, they went in procession to a place fronting the college and burnt a copy of the letter by the hands of a hangman hired for the purpose with hearty wishes that the names of all promoters of such a daring breach of faith may be blasted in the eyes of every lover of liberty and their names handed down to posterity as betrayers of their country."

"Do you think that will have any real effect?" asked Isabella skeptically.

"Oh, I am sure it will," answered Nathaniel, "The students' action has been reported in several newspapers and might well give pause to some of the merchants resisting the Non-Importation Agreement. In addition, quite a few of these pious youths will soon be pastors and will carry their message to many different congregations. In this way Dr. Witherspoon's doctrines will reach an even wider audience."

"That could well be, but where is the personal sacrifice of these boys?"

"It is important that they are girding their loins for a struggle that could very well become violent and encouraging others to do so. On the personal level they have all signed an agreement that they will attend commencement services in September in home-spun clothing and spurn fashionable dress imported from England. That will have a palpable effect on some of the uncooperative merchants and also be a boon to shepherds in this colony, not to mention the operators of fulling mills and other merchants."

A few weeks later Nathaniel and Isabella decided to attend the commencement exercises in Nassau Hall to see just how faithful the 22 graduating students would adhere to the brave promises of their summer protest, particularly since it was known that Governor Franklin, a vehement opponent of any measures against the policies of the royal government, would be in attendance. The Scudders were not disappointed. The students were all attired in American cloth, some of them casting defiant glances in the direction of the governor. A feeling of nervous anticipation rippled through the audience as people began to sense a feeling of approaching confrontation. Not far from Nathaniel and Isabella, Governor Franklin sitting stiffly nodded politely in the direction of Isabella with a rather artificial smile set on his lips.

A physician from New Brunswick whom Nathaniel knew from the Medical Association turned to Nathaniel and Isabella to whisper just loud enough for the governor to hear it, "How happy, ought we to esteem ourselves, when we see some of our youth, who will probably fill some of the highest stations in their country, when their fathers have fallen asleep, so early declaring their love to their country; and we hope this will meet with that esteem which is their due and that many at this critical juncture will follow their laudable example in encouraging our own manufactures."

The smile disappeared from the governor's face as he cast a disdainful glance in the direction of the New Brunswick physician.

First to speak was John Cosins Ogden who delivered a moving defense of the proposition "The Non-Importation Agreement reflects a Glory on the American Merchants and was a noble exertion of self-denial and public spirit." As young Ogden proceeded through his arguments, the governor's face became set in stone with deep furrows of disapproval creasing his forehead.

The next to speak was Samuel Baldwin who reminded the audience that "National characters depend upon moral, not physical causes" further developing Ogden's thesis that support of the Non-Importation Agreement was a moral necessity. Franklin's expression of disapproval transformed itself into one of indignation.

The final address was given by Frederick Frelinghuysen who spoke on the "The Utility of American Manufactures." For the governor this was not quite as provocative as the first two but nevertheless contained sentiments that Franklin regarded as borderline subversive.

After the ceremony the audience, graduates and staff were invited to a reception in honor of the new degree holders. Nathaniel and Isabella sought out President Witherspoon in order to congratulate him on the graduation of his son, James, who by all accounts was a young man of great promise. They found him in a heated discussion with Governor Franklin.

"Dr. Witherspoon, I must say I was appalled at the partisan ramblings of your students!" exclaimed Franklin angrily, "I thought the purpose of this institution was to educate young men to be ornaments of society!"

"Indeed, it is," replied Witherspoon confidently, "And part of that is to teach them how to make a critical analysis of the burning issues of the day. Whether or not you agree with the particular views presented, did you not find the logical arguments of my students compelling?"

Witherspoon trilled the r in the "burning issues" for emphasis while glaring at Franklin with all the self-assuredness of the rock-ribbed Presbyterian that he was.

"Not in the least," answered Franklin, "I found much of it downright subversive. They are after all counseling resistance to policies of the king in Parliament."

"That is your interpretation, sir," countered Witherspoon, "One could as easily argue that they are merely arguing for the preservation of basic British rights as guaranteed in the Proclamation of 1689. As you know, the blessed William's legacy is very important to us at Nassau Hall."

"Nobody is arguing against the Bill of Rights," Franklin retorted, adding ominously, "But these young men have no experience in the ways of the world and are not qualified to pass judgement on royal policies. I rather doubt that the distinguished gentlemen serving as your trustees will be pleased to hear that this academy is fostering ideas that are potentially subversive to royal authority."

With that scarcely veiled threat Governor Franklin angrily departed from Nassau Hall. Nathaniel watched him go and then turned to President Witherspoon.

"Dr. Witherspoon, permit me to say that in my opinion Governor Franklin is completely wrong in the assessment of our graduates. The conduct and expressions of the collegians show that the truly noble and patriotic spirit which inflames the breasts of the those who are real lovers of their country, is already implanted in theirs. What too sanguine hopes can we have of those gentlemen and such principles so early instilled in them."

"Thank you, Dr. Scudder," Witherspoon replied gratefully, "The governor, of course, has to defend royal authority but, as Calvin taught us, even royal authority has its limits. I am curious if Governor Franklin's conception of royal authority will result in the limitation of freedom of inquiry at out academy."

"That is something we cannot ever permit to happen!" exclaimed Nathaniel vehemently.

"I am confident that we are remaining true to our founding principles," continued Witherspoon calmly, "The governor suspects that the college is a hotbed of Presbyterian radicalism but young Ogden, who delivered the most controversial address, is, in fact, an Anglican. Franklin may think that freedom of inquiry leads to potentially subversive debates, but he is wrong to suppose that suppressing such discussions will solve his problems. Suppression would only increase the intensity of the controversies. He already has his hands full dealing with the rampant smuggling in this colony which is itself a result of the failed policies of the Board of Trade. The governor would do well to inquire himself into what some eminent Scottish scholars such as Adam Smith have to say about the follies that are being perpetrated just now."

Nathaniel got a further sense of the challenges facing Franklin later that fall when he, as secretary of the Medical Society, convened a meeting at the house of Brook Farmer in New Brunswick. Physicians from all over the colony were in attendance and many reported having had to bandage the wounds of people involved in violent skirmishes with customs inspectors. As often as not, the customs inspectors and their helpers were on the losing side of such skirmishes. One such incident was recounted by Dr. Robert Harris of Cape May.

"It looks as though there will be plenty of work for physicians in our area if present government policies continue," ventured Harris.

"How do the royal government's policies affect the work of a physician?" asked Nathaniel.

"Well, a new customs collector named John Hatton has recently been assigned to our area," answered Harris, "He is petty, overbearing, and insolent and has quickly made enemies of practically everyone in the vicinity of Cape May. One of his first acts was to declare that our Common Pleas Justices, Thomas Leaming, John Leonard, and James Whilden, were in league with the smugglers."

"That does not seem like a very diplomatic way to win the cooperation of the populace," remarked Nathaniel.

"That was only the beginning," continued Harris, "Hatton proceeds from the assumption that all merchants are transporting smuggled goods and attempts to seize them without due process. Our merchants are not used to such high-handed behavior and naturally tend to resist."

Nathaniel knew very well, of course, from his dealings with the merchants of Tom's River, what extreme forms such resistance could take.

"I can see that this story is not going to end well," remarked Nathaniel wryly.

"No, indeed," agreed Harris, "Although I am pleased to say there was no loss of life on this occasion. Shortly after Hatton arrived at Cape May a ship, the Prince of Wales, came into the bay where it was met by several pilot boats who immediately set to unload her. Hatton, his son, and a Black aide rowed out to the boats and loudly announced their intention to impound what Hatton said was contraband. They were met by a volley of fire from the boats and were soon captured and disarmed. The sailors gave them all a good beating, but then set them free with a warning to mind their own business."

"I suppose they were lucky this time around," said Nathaniel, "They might have met with an altogether more unpleasant fate."

"Yes, of course," exclaimed Harris, "But that is the problem with this pig-headed Hatton. He doesn't know when to let well enough alone. Instead, he then sends his son to follow the supposed contraband to Philadelphia. The boy locates one of the boats but then runs into a mob of sailors armed with clubs who tear the dressing from his wounds on his head and arms, dump a pot of tar on him and cover him with feathers. They then dragged him through the streets, put him in the pillory and ducked him in the river. After they tired of tormenting him, they rowed him over to the Jersey side and dumped him on the shore. By the time Hatton brought him to me, he was more dead than alive, but I managed to bind him up well enough."

"Perhaps that will be a lesson to Hatton to be more careful about riling the locals," suggested Nathaniel.

"Don't bet on that!" countered Harris, "When I suggested that it was perhaps not a good idea to try to impose his will on a whole community with just three men, he shouted that he represented His Majesty's government and that he would see to it that Governor Franklin punishes each and every one of the outlaws who had abused him and his son."

A few weeks later Nathaniel and Isabella had occasion to consider the mounting difficulties faced by the royal governor in a conversation with Colonel Anderson at Anderson Manor. Recounting the episode, he had heard at the meeting of the Medical Society, Nathaniel wondered aloud if the repression envisaged by Hatton was even feasible.

"Quite unlikely," opined Colonel Anderson, "Even if Franklin could get the Board of Trade to support the massive troop build-up of Regulars that such repression would require, it would only exacerbate his conflicts with the Assembly. People are already annoyed that he has appointed Stephen Skinner to the New Jersey Council even though 6000 pounds from the New Jersey treasury disappeared during his tenure as treasurer. And then there is the question of Franklin's interest in land speculation west of the Proclamation Line. I'd say he has enough to worry about without wasting his time trying to support a slightly deranged customs collector."

The growing tensions between the royal governor and the Assembly and people of New Jersey were also a frequent topic in the church services of Reverend Tennent's congregation. While the good pastor always preached that Jesus expected his flock to seek peaceful solutions to problems, his continuous emphasis on the general corruption of man served to confirm his congregants' belief in the necessity of resistance. This general feeling was enhanced by visits from Reverend Witherspoon who exhorted the congregants to understand that they were part of a holy mission for the advancement of knowledge, and that they should not countenance any interference from outsiders who were obviously unqualified to judge what was good for the people of this colony. He pointed out what fine progress his college was making in educating young men who would soon be able to do a much better job at leading the colony than ignorant outsiders and their local lackeys. As an example, he cited the new emphasis he was placing on natural philosophy to train leaders competent in the practical arts necessary to build a new country. He mentioned in this regard the Rittenhouse Orrery that he had purchased for the college and that would soon be installed in Nassau Hall. He contended that this device for understanding the heavens was superior to anything available as yet in the Old World and that it proved what potential this country had.

His mention of natural philosophy as the key to the country's future electrified Nathaniel. He too believed that the most damning aspect of Papist doctrine was the resistance to scientific progress it had so often exhibited in the past. He was convinced that this was the most important reason to defend the independence of the dissident congregations so that the dead hand of superstition could never again thwart the progress of knowledge. Upon hearing Witherspoon's sermon, he resolved immediately to seek a demonstration of the remarkable new device for Johnny and Isabella. As soon as the sermon was finished, Nathaniel conveyed his enthusiasm to Witherspoon who in turn promised to invite the Scudders to Nassau Hall as soon as the orrery could be demonstrated.

A few months later an invitation arrived from Nassau Hall to witness a demonstration of the remarkable new piece of scientific equipment. On the appointed day Nathaniel, Isabella, and Johnny full of anticipation set off for Princeton in their carriage.

In the library of Nassau Hall a device had been set up which resembled a rather complicated clock with a crank in the middle of a field of stars. The hand of the clock held what looked like several discs of various sizes. Superimposed on the main face was a smaller circular field which showed dates and times. On the right side was another contraption that contained additional discs. It was not immediately obvious why this was such an important scientific achievement but then Dr. Witherspoon began to explain.

"Orreries are mechanical models of the solar system that illustrate or predict the relative positions and motions of the planets and moons according to the heliocentric model," began Witherspoon, "Such devices have been constructed since antiquity, but the first modern version was developed for Charles Boyle, 4th Earl of Orrery, in 1704, hence the name."

Noticing the intense interest with which young Johnny Scudder was peering at the mechanism, Witherspoon turned to the boy and asked, "Well, young man, can you imagine what heavenly bodies this device might be representing?"

"I am only guessing, sir, but I think the big circle in the center is probably the sun and the six discs on the hands of the clock are probably the six planets, Mercury, Venus, Earth, Mars, Jupiter and Saturn."

"Excellent, excellent!" congratulated Witherspoon, "I can see we have someone here who has a talent for natural philosophy."

"Johnny has already begun to read Newton's Principia," Nathaniel added proudly, "He has been looking forward to this visit for weeks now."

"As I turn the crank," Witherspoon continued, "You can see that the discs representing the planets move. They are aligned accurately with the names of the major star constellations on the outer rim. The inner clock face shows the time and date. One turn of the crank represents one day. By turning the crank one can determine the exact position of each planet at any time and date. In a similar fashion the lunarium here on the right represents the positions of the earth, the sun and the moon. It can be used to predict the timing of eclipses of the sun and the moon."

"We had a similar device when I was an undergraduate when the college was still in Newark," interjected Nathaniel, "Lewis Evans used it in his lectures on natural philosophy. It was somewhat simpler, however, and, as I recall its prediction of the positions of the planets was not completely accurate. Mr. Evans said it needed to be recalibrated through telescope observation every few cycles."

"That is exactly right," replied Witherspoon, "What makes this device so unique is that it remains accurate over long periods of time."

"How is that possible?" asked Isabella, "Both devices work on the same principles, don't they? What does this device do that the earlier models did not?"

"Both are mechanical models of the solar system, but this one more accurately represents the actual movements of the heavenly bodies," explained Witherspoon, "The problem is that earlier models represented the movements of the planets as though the orbits were concentric circles on the same plane."

"Now, I understand!" exclaimed Johnny, "The true orbits are ellipses, and they are on different planes!"

"Exactly!" Witherspoon confirmed, "The genius of this device is that Rittenhouse figured out a way to arrange the gear wheels to represent the elliptical orbits and their different planes. Take a look at the back and you can see how he did this. Observe how some of the gear wheels are off center and others are tilted slightly. By carefully constructing their relationships he managed to model the movements of the heavenly bodies with remarkable precision. To my knowledge there is no other device in the world at the present time that is as accurate as this one."

Isabella, Nathaniel and Johnny stared at the delicate cog wheels with rapt fascination understanding now why the device was such a unique achievement.

"This man, Rittenhouse, must be quite a genius," remarked Nathaniel.

"The most remarkable thing about him is that he had no formal training in natural philosophy," added Witherspoon, "He is actually a watch maker who has autodidactically taught himself everything that is known about the solar system. That makes his achievement even more impressive. I am going to recommend to the trustees that we confer an honorary degree on him at the next commencement in September."

"I think that is an excellent idea," agreed Nathaniel, "As a student I enjoyed my natural philosophy courses the most, which, of course, is why I became a physician. I am gratified to see that the college is putting additional emphasis on that part of the curriculum. For students like my son, Johnny, here it will offer tremendous motivation."

"Indeed," said Witherspoon, "If we want to build a new country and a better world, we need to produce more than just clergymen and lawyers. By the way, I have the impression that your son would be ready to start his freshman year in the fall."

"But he is only 12 years old," objected Isabella, "He is too young to be leaving home so soon."

"Yes, he is a bit young still," agreed Nathaniel, "But he has already imbibed more knowledge of natural philosophy at my side than many who are twice his age. Besides his grandparents live only a few miles away so he will not be totally separated from his family."

Isabella cast skeptical glances in the direction of Nathaniel, Dr. Witherspoon and Johnny.

"Mother, it would be so wonderful to stay in Nassau Hall and learn more about these fascinating subjects," pleaded Johnny, "There is so much more to learn, and I can't wait to get started."

It became obvious to Isabella that further resistance against the expressed wishes of Nathaniel, Dr. Witherspoon and Johnny was hopeless, and she reluctantly began to nod her head.

"Very well, it is hard for a mother to see her firstborn leave the nest so soon but sooner or later it is inevitable. I think, however, we ought to talk it over with grandfather and grandmother. After all, they will have added responsibility and they are not getting any younger."

"I was planning to stop by and see my parents on the way home in any case," replied Nathaniel, "I am sure mother and father will be delighted to hear that Johnny will be near them in the fall."

After thanking Dr. Witherspoon profusely for the fascinating demonstration, Nathaniel, Isabella and Johnny set off in the direction of Scudder's Mills. When they got there, they were surprised to find Jacob Scudder confined to his bed.

"I have been trying to get him to send for you for weeks now," Nathaniel's mother, Abia, complained, wringing her hands, "But you know how stubborn he can be, he contends that all he needs is a little rest and there is no reason for you to come all the way from Freehold just for his sake. His legs are very swollen, and he does not have the energy he used to have."

"The truth is he has been working much too hard for a man his age," added Nathaniel's brother, William, "He thinks that the only way to cope with hard times is to work harder himself. I try to get him to leave more up to me but, as you know, he is a very determined man."

"Yes, indeed, I know how determined our father is, but I will give him a thorough examination and perhaps he will take a doctor's advice."

Nathaniel went to his father's bedroom and knocked gently on the door. When he entered, Jacob looked up with an expression of annoyance.

"Did your mother send for you after all?" he asked irritably, "I told her she should not make such a fuss about a little shortness of breath."

"She did not send for me, Father," replied Nathaniel, "I happened to be visiting Nassau Hall to show Isabella and Johnny the Rittenhouse Orrery. President Wither-spoon was so impressed with Johnny's knowledge of natural philosophy that he suggested he start in the freshman class in the fall. I wanted to let you know that you will be seeing more of your grandson come September."

"That is indeed good news!" Jacob exclaimed, "I regret not having more time to spend with my grandchildren, but life has become a struggle of late and one is duty-bound to accept the trials that the Lord has decided to test us with."

"Well, let me see if I can help you stay fit for dealing with these challenges," said Nathaniel, "Let me have a look at those swollen legs."

"I am sure it is nothing important," answered Jacob, reluctantly pulling the covers from his lower body, "And even if it is, I am ready to accept joyously whatever fate the Lord has in store for me."

An examination of Jacob's legs and feet quickly confirmed Nathaniel's suspicions that his father did indeed suffer from a serious malady.

"Father, I am afraid you have the dropsy," began Nathaniel, "The shortness of breath, lack of energy and the swelling in the legs and feet are all typical symptoms of the kind of dropsy that results from a weakening heart. As the heart grows weaker, it can no longer pump blood efficiently enough through your body, so fluids start to build up in your extremities. That is what causes the swelling."

"We all have to go sometime," replied Jacob with perfect equanimity, "I am old and have enjoyed a blessed life. I am ready to go whenever the Lord sees fit to call me."

"This does not necessarily mean that you are going to drop dead soon, father, there are a number of things I can do to relieve your discomfort. I will bleed you a bit to relieve the fluid buildup and prescribe some diuretic herbs which should also help. And we should prop up your legs as long as you are bedridden."

"I am gratified to see that you have become such a competent physician, Nathaniel, but it is clear that I am entering the final chapter of my life in this world, and I look forward to reaping the rewards that all faithful Christians hope for. I will follow your advice, but what is more important for me, however, is to explain to you how I intend to settle my affairs before I go."

"Father, whatever you decide is fine with me as I am sure it is with mother and my siblings. Right now, you need to rest. You should be feeling better in a few days and then you will have plenty of time to make whatever arrangements you feel necessary."

"No, Nathaniel, I have already given this matter a lot of thought and I want you to understand the reasoning behind my decisions and most of all, what I expect of you. I have decided to leave the mills to your brother, William, because he is the most likely to maintain the business, although I have stipulated that he reimburse you and your siblings with cash to a modest degree. I have spent a good deal of money on your education, and I did that, because I always felt that you were destined for a higher purpose than running a milling business."

"Father, I completely support your decision. I am eternally grateful to you for making it possible for me to study and to learn the practice of medicine. I have no need of compensation from Will, and I will continue to help him anyway that I can."

"He might indeed need your help, Nathaniel, and I know he will always be able to count on you. I think, however, that my distribution of our modest wealth is equitable. The important thing in my mind is that you live up to my expectations by serving the Lord through service to our community. I am greatly pleased to see how far you have progressed in this regard. I truly believe, however, that we are entering a phase in the development of this country that will try men's souls. It will be a time when steadfast leadership is necessary. You must never forget that your great-grandfather, Thomas, came to Salem in 1632 in order to help found the New Jerusalem. This is the sacred mission that the Lord has foreseen for us. If, as I believe, the decisive struggle is soon at hand, you must promise me that you will never shirk from your responsibilities."

Emotionally smitten by his father's entreaty Nathaniel grasped his father's hand fighting back the tears, "Father, I solemnly swear that I will face any challenge to see to it that your will is fulfilled."

After recovering his composure Nathaniel proceeded to bleed Jacob with the assistance of Johnny who had become quite proficient at holding the cup for this procedure.

"As you can see, father, your grandson has already learned a great deal about the healing arts. He has been helping me now for several years. His studies at Nassau Hall will complement the practical part of his education so that I expect that he will be a qualified physician by the time he graduates. He has already mastered a great deal of herbal lore. When he moves to Nassau Hall in September, he will be available to you at short notice, to care for you until I can get up here from Freehold."

"I am grateful to both of you for your concern," replied Jacob smiling, "But do not fret too much, the Lord's will shall prevail. I will, of course, be pleased to see both of you more frequently and it is a delight to see my grandson following your example in the path of community service. I am also pleased that, as long as I am around, I will have the opportunity to remind Johnny now and again of his duty to God and country."

"Grandfather, it is an honor to be at your service," said Johnny and, eager to demonstrate his newly acquired knowledge, added, "Some of our patients get a bit light-headed after this procedure but if we prop up your feet, it should pass soon enough."

"Quite correct," agreed Nathaniel, "And I will leave a small bag of herbs. You should drink an infusion of this each morning before breakfast and that will help you to pass off your excessive fluids. Before I leave today, I will instruct mother just exactly how this infusion is to be brewed. Oh, and try to avoid eating salty foods. They tend to increase fluid retention."

After administering to Jacob and instructing the rest of the family in the proper care of him in his condition, Nathaniel, Isabella, and Johnny set off for Freehold in their wagon. On their way home the conversation revolved around the new challenges facing the family—caring for Jacob and preparing Johnny for entering Nassau Hall in the fall.

"Given your father's sickly condition, do you really think it is a good idea to burden your parents with the responsibility of looking after Johnny in the fall?" ventured Isabella.

"They are delighted that they will be seeing more of us in the future," reassured Nathaniel, "I think that Johnny will be more of an asset for them than a burden. Besides I will be coming up here much more frequently now to check on my father so I will have a chance to monitor Johnny's progress as well."

"I am also looking forward to taking responsibility for grandfather's care," Johnny resolutely assured them, "I will not be a burden on anyone."

"I am sure you won't, son," agreed Nathaniel, "And it will be a good experience for you to care for your grandfather and learn something from his pious ways. He probably will not be with us that much longer so this might be a God-given opportunity to learn some important lessons about life."

Nathaniel's schedule became even more hectic than usual over the ensuing months. Visiting his father every week and putting the finishing touches on Johnny's preparation for college eliminated what little free time he had had up until then. The months flew by and soon it was time for Johnny to move to Nassau Hall. Nathaniel, Isabella, and Johnny decided to mark the occasion by attending together the commencement in Princeton that September. They were joined by their friends, Richard and Annis Stockton. Listening to the patriotic speeches of the students they were gratified to see that the students continued to be as committed as ever to the concept of liberty. One of the students, Hugh Henry Brackenridge, presented a poem written by another underclassman, Philip Freneau:

> This is a land of ev'ry joyous fount
> Of liberty and life; sweet liberty
> Without whose aid the noblest genius fails,
> And Science irretrievably must die. . .

> I see a train, a glorious train appear
> Of Patriots plac'd in equal fame with those
> Who nobly fell for Athens or for Rome.
> The Sons of Boston resolute and brave
> The firm supporters of our injur'd right,
> Shall lose their splendours in the brighter beams
> Of patriots fam'd and heroes yet unborn.

Animated by the political ferment that was so obviously gripping the students, Johnny enthused, "Father, mother is that not wonderful? A glorious train of patriots. . . I can hardly wait to be part of this."

"Hopefully none of them will have 'to nobly fall' for their beliefs", remarked Isabella ruefully.

"Ah, but their desire to emulate the heroes of Athens and Rome, is that not very touching," Annis Stockton countered, closing her eyes and smiling beatifically, "Those are sentiments that appeal to the heart of a poet."

Always the consummate realist Richard Stockton added, "Yes, yes those are noble aspirations but there are plenty of people in this province who will think that students should concentrate on academics and not on politics. Dr. Witherspoon will probably reap some criticism for this."

"Although I am sure that Dr. Witherspoon is in agreement with the sentiments the students have expressed," said Nathaniel, "I rather suspect that it is the times more than anything else that agitates the students. My father-in-law recently told me that Governor Franklin has received word from the Board of Trade that the judicial reforms the Assembly passed in response to the riots of last year have been cancelled. That will surely agitate many in this colony, not just the students."

"Right you are, Nathaniel," agreed Stockton, "I hope it does not pose problems for our project to establish a foundation to support the widows and children of deceased Presbyterian clergy. The governor must agree to that and get the Board of Trade to agree as well."

"I can't imagine that the governor would oppose it," said Nathaniel, "After all, he set up a similar foundation two years ago to support the widows and children of Anglican clergy. It would be grossly unfair if the same rights were not granted to our Presbyterian congregations. In any case it has such broad support it would be foolish for the Board of Trade to block it. I will be signing the petition for Monmouth County along with Charles McKnight and William Tennent."

"I am signing it as well," said Stockton, "All together about 24 prominent men of the colony are on board. It would be foolish indeed, if the Board of Trade continues to promote confrontation, but it is altogether possible that they don't realize how much potential there is for resistance here."

In the event both the governor and the Board of Trade approved the foundation which duly came into being. For a time it looked as though it might be possible to edge away from the atmosphere of confrontation that had so long agitated the colony. The signers from Monmouth County were so encouraged by the success that they decided to embark immediately on another project, the refurbishment of the Mattisonia Grammer School.

Isabella was perplexed that Nathaniel was embarking on yet another project for which he really had no time.

"Actually, this will save me time," Nathaniel argued, "Our son, Joseph, has been inspired by Johnny's success and now also dreams of going to Nassau Hall. The trouble is I don't have the time to devote to his education the effort I expended on Johnny. In addition, Joseph is not interested in natural philosophy. The sight of blood makes him feel faint. It is much better that a quality school is available for him and other local children to attend. Young Moses Allen will come from Nassau Hall to instruct the children. Our boys will be in excellent hands. Joseph will get good instruction in Latin and Greek and be ready to enter Nassau Hall as well when the time comes."

The school project was also a success, and the first students took up their studies in January. The hoped-for relaxation of tensions, however, did not develop. Although riots on the scale of those that had occurred twice in front of Monmouth Courthouse did not recur, the yeomen of New Jersey had by no means resigned themselves to the rejection of the Assembly's acts for debtors' relief and the simplified procedures for the resolution of debts. Demonstrations continued sporadically and tensions between debtors and creditors continued to mount.

Those who took a prominent position on the Whig side could expect to be attacked by ardent supporters of Crown privilege and not only verbally. Nathaniel was shocked to hear in February that a farm belonging to Dr. Witherspoon had burned to the ground. He wondered if that might have something to do with Witherspoon's well-publicized promotion of Whig ideology among the students of Nassau Hall. This supposition became even more compelling in March when anonymous letters under the pseudonym "Causidicus" began appearing in certain newspapers. Ostensibly replying to a fundraising letter that Witherspoon had sent to parishioners in the sugar islands. Causdicus attacked Witherspoon bitterly for sowing seeds of sedition among his students. It became clear to Nathaniel that a dangerous polarization of opinion was in the offing and that a confrontation with the enemies of the True Religion might be unavoidable.

His ominous premonitions of impending crisis reached new levels one morning in May when Johnny galloped into Freehold exhausted from several hours of hard riding.

"Father, father, come quickly," yelled Johnny, "Will summoned me very early this morning to tell me that Grandfather is in a very bad way. I rushed over to look at him and he was barely breathing. If you want to see him alive once more, you must ride immediately to Scudder's Mills."

Nathaniel quickly grabbed his medical bag and saddled his fastest horse.

"Johnny, you did very well to alert me but now you must stay here and rest," ordered Nathaniel, "That was an amazing feat of endurance, and I don't want you to fall ill. I will rush as fast as I can to try to save my father."

"But Father . . . " began Johnny.

"No," said Nathaniel, "You will only slow me down. Get some rest, inform your mother and both of you can come in the wagon after you have recovered your strength."

Nathaniel galloped off in the direction of Scudder's Mills as though the devil himself was pursuing him, all the time praying that his father would live long enough to benefit from his ministrations.

When he arrived several hours later, Will was waiting in the yard.

"I think his time has come, Nathaniel," Will said, "He is still alive, but barely breathing. I don't think there is much you can do."

Rushing up to his father's bedroom, Nathaniel saw quickly that Will was probably right. Bending over his father he whispered in his ear, "Father, it is Nathaniel, I am going to try to give you some relief."

Jacob opened his eyes and smiled exhaustedly at Nathaniel, shaking his head ever so slightly, "Don't bother, my son, I am about to get my reward. Just promise . . ."

Nathaniel knelt of the floor grasping his father's hand, holding back the sobs and repeating over and over, "I promise, Father, I promise." as he felt the pulse in his father's wrist became fainter and fainter until finally it stopped.

Chapter 16

Tea Party – 1772–1773

Despite the mounting tensions, or perhaps because of them, young John Scudder had a fascinating first year in Nassau Hall. The student body was aflame with Whig zeal and John was thrilled to take part in the endless discussions. The students felt that they were on the threshold of a new era, poised to play vital roles in the unfolding of a great drama. They idolized Witherspoon for his courageous defense of liberty and open discourse. They also became increasingly convinced that a Tory conspiracy was afoot to harm the Whig cause. When a farm belonging to Witherspoon burned down in February, many were certain that it was arson. The students declared their resolve to defend liberty at all costs and pledged to each other that they would sooner take up arms than submit to tyranny.

It was against this background that John Scudder had the most exciting experience of his first year at Nassau Hall. The sun had just set one early summer evening and John was gazing dreamingly at the night sky from his room in Nassau Hall waiting for the moon to rise at the time the Rittenhouse Orrery predicted. He was jolted out of his reverie by the flash of a fireball striking the outside of the president's house. John screamed at the top of his lungs, "The president's house is on fire! Quickly lads, we must rush to his aid!"

One student ran to start ringing the bell while the rest led by the older undergraduates hurried out of Nassau Hall and quickly formed a bucket brigade to douse the flames, as they had learned to do through numerous drills. Upon hearing the commotion Witherspoon came out of his house and was shocked to see that someone had apparently thrown a firebomb at one corner of the building and the flames were threatening to spread to the roof.

"Very good, lads, very good," Witherspoon shouted encouragement to the students, "But we need to get the ladder and get some of that water up on the roof before it burns through to the rafters."

Under the guidance of Witherspoon, the tutors and the older undergraduates the students formed a remarkably efficient fire brigade and within an hour, it was clear that the house would be saved. When all danger was past, Witherspoon gathered his doughty charges on the lawn in front of Nassau Hall to thank them.

"You have shown both courage and ingenuity," Witherspoon praised the boys, "Without your vigilance and rapid reaction I might not be here speaking to you now, and I am very proud of you. I am confident that the cause of liberty will be well served with such young men as yourselves to defend it."

The boys' chests swelled with pride as they turned to congratulate each other on a job well done. The older boy who had been next to John in the bucket brigade nodded at John with a friendly smile, "Good job, Scudder, I can see you are going to be one we can count on."

"I am grateful that we had the chance to help the president," replied John, "This was so incredible. Do you think that someone was actually trying to kill him?"

"Maybe so, maybe not," answered the older boy, "Maybe some of the Tories are just trying to scare him so he will stop preaching liberty to us students. But we have shown them tonight that we will stand up to them."

At that point another shout went up from a boy who had returned to his room in Nassau Hall.

"Thieves! Thieves! Someone has broken into all our rooms and stolen our things while we were fighting the fire!"

And so it turned out that the arson attack on the president's home was just a diversion to draw everyone out of Nassau Hall in order to burgle the students' rooms. The premeditated evil of it convinced the students that they were under attack from dark forces, insidious enemies of their Whig beliefs. They were more than ever certain that confrontation would eventually become inevitable, and the only moral course of action would be to face it bravely.

Upon hearing of the burglary of Nassau Hall Nathaniel immediately rushed to Princeton to find out which of John's possessions had been stolen and needed to be replaced. He listened intently to John's recounting of the incident.

"This is a heinous and criminal act," Nathaniel said finally, shaking his head gravely, "But some good might come of it. I am sure the students now fully realize the dimension of the struggle lovers of liberty are going to face."

"You can be sure of that, Father—the students were already strongly affected by political issues but now their ardor will know no bounds. Wait until you hear the addresses that students are preparing for the next commencement ceremony."

The news of the arson and the political agitation of the students spread quickly throughout the colony. When September came around, many were eager to attend the commencement ceremony to witness the students' reaction to the events of the summer. Nathaniel and Isabella again attended with their friends, the Stocktons, eagerly anticipating a lively event. They were not disappointed. Along with the other Whigs in the audience they were thrilled to hear orations such as "Passive Obedience and Non-Resistance", "Independence of Spirit" and "The Advantages of political Liberty."

Others were not so thrilled. Nathaniel noticed that several attendees including Governor Franklin were casting dark looks at each after each oration and not applauding at the end. Nathaniel worried that the students' exhilaration might frighten some conservative members of the colony's elite which might in turn stimulate a backlash against Witherspoon's encouragement of open debate. That his fears would soon be realized became clear during a conversation at Anderson Manor a few weeks later with Isabella, Colonel Anderson and Reverend Tennent.

"Well, it looks like the trustees are going to clip the boys' wings at Nassau Hall," Colonel Anderson teased the trustee Tennent with a wry smile, "I would have thought that those orations would have warmed the cockles of Presbyterian hearts."

"Indeed, they did," agreed Reverend Tennent, "But it is not only Presbyterians we have to please, and we were bombarded with criticism in the press. We do not want to dampen the boys' enthusiasm for Whig liberties, but we are just requiring them to submit their orations for correction before the ceremony. We must be certain that they are not too provocative."

"That sounds like censorship to me," objected Nathaniel, "I am surprised that Dr. Witherspoon would agree to that."

"He and we had no choice," explained Tennent, "Apparently a widely-expressed feeling among some of the people in attendance was indignation over what they consider were improprieties at the ceremony. Some at the ceremony reported feeling and, I quote, 'more in the company of a circle of vociferous politicians at a coffee house than the meek disciples of wisdom in the calm shades of academic retirement.'"

Siding instinctively with their beloved son, John, Isabella tried to defend the views of the students.

"I thought that the orations were excellent and well-reasoned," Isabella argued, "Comparing them to vociferous politicians is outrageous."

"Nevertheless, some expressing this view are students' parents who are appalled at what they consider the indoctrination of their children with radical Whig ideology," continued Tennent, "Others are donors or potential donors that the college needs. And, of course, Governor Franklin is an ex officio trustee whose views we cannot simply ignore."

"Oh, yes, the honorable Governor Franklin," Colonel Anderson observed with a cynical smile, "Of course, now that the Privy Council has approved his Vandalia scheme, he cannot afford to be seen to be tolerating subversive ideologies."

"At the end of the day, it is all quite counterproductive," opined Nathaniel, "If they suppress the students' options for open debate, the resentment will only fester like a sore until the wound becomes intolerable."

"Franklin is in desperate need of some small victories," added Colonel Anderson, "The Assembly has refused to raise his salary and views his attempts to get himself on the Civil List as an attempt to escape their influence. They are about to try to force him to sue Skinner for reimbursement of the stolen treasury money. His suppression of open debate at Nassau Hall will only increase their hostility."

"And what is this Vandalia project all about," asked Isabella.

"It's all about land speculation," explained her father, "Ever since the Proclamation Line of 1763 was declared barring White settlers west of the Appalachians, there have been countless schemes to circumvent the agreement and get access to Indian lands after all. One of them is the Vandalia plan to colonize parts of the Ohio country. Franklin along with George Croghan and the Wharton clan have cooked up a scheme where the Indians agree to give up some lands as reparation for some of their depredations during the Pontiac uprising. Franklin's father, Ben, is involved as well and has been lobbying London for years to approve it. Hillsborough was always against it but the Privy Council just approved it. If they get it organized, they all might get rich. This is how William Franklin hopes to free himself from dependence on our Assembly."

"It will probably stimulate a land rush among the thousands of frontiersmen who are already seeping into Indian territory," added Nathaniel, "The Vandalia project will open the flood gates. Once part of the Ohio country is colonized, others will rush to do the same."

"And that will necessitate expanding the garrisons we already keep on the Proclamation Line," continued the colonel, "So we get back to the question who is going to pay for that. If Franklin thinks that the Assembly is going to raise taxes so he and his friends can get rich, he needs to have his head examined."

"Greed and corruption are roads that lead straight to hell!" Reverend Tennent sermonized, "The governor is appointed to guard the common weal not to enrich his business associates. His efforts to escape the influence of the Assembly do not bode well for our precious liberties."

"I heard from Annis Stockton that Ben Franklin actually tried to dissuade his son from trying to get himself on the Civil List because it would embroil him with his people," added Isabella.

"William should listen to his father who has a lot more political sense than his son," said the colonel. "The man seems to have no idea of how much his actions provoke the assemblymen. But that attitude is unfortunately typical among the Crown's servants not only in this country but in the mother country as well. They have a talent for doing things that are going to provoke their subjects in North America."

"What kinds of provocations are you thinking of specifically?" asked Isabella.

"Well, for instance, I just heard that Britain's highest judge, the Earl of Mansfield, made a ruling that any slave who sets his foot on English soil is to be set free. The colonies and slave transports are explicitly excluded, but still many people stand to lose a lot of their property."

"I am glad that does not apply here," said Isabella, "I don't know how I would cope with five children without our kitchen family."

"The problem is that if the government thinks they can divest people of their property with the stroke of a pen in England," cautioned the colonel, "Than what is to prevent them doing the same elsewhere? It is something we could probably deal with at Anderson Manor but for the southern colonies it would be completely unacceptable. In many places there are many more Black Africans than there are Whites. If the Negroes were all freed, they would overwhelm the White population."

"Perhaps this shows that the institution of slavery is not a good thing for all of us in the long term," opined Reverend Tennent, "Many of our Quaker neighbors are freeing their slaves and encouraging the rest of us to follow suit."

"That might work in the northern colonies," replied the colonel, "But the southern colonies will see no choice but to resist."

"If our servants were freed, they would probably just continue to work for us," speculated Nathaniel, "They are really like family, and we try to take care of them as best we can. It is difficult to imagine life without them. I am sure it must be different in the South where plantations have hundreds of slaves so that a familial relationship with their owners does not develop. I will have to remember to ask John what his fellow students from there think about these issues. A number of the boys now at Nassau Hall come from some of the largest plantations."

The next time Nathaniel visited Princeton he discussed the issue of liberty and slavery with John, a topic that John had repeatedly brought up himself in past conversations.

"Yes, I remember we talked about this before," said John, "I wanted to know how our kitchen family came to lose their freedom."

"Right," agreed Nathaniel, "And I pointed out that in this instance, they were all born into that situation. None of them ever had the status of a free person. I also explained that this involves a special responsibility to care for them. In a recent conversation with your grandfather, your mother and Reverend Tennent we were discussing the issue of emancipation."

"You are not planning to emancipate our kitchen family, are you?" asked John incredulously.

"No, I am afraid your mother would have a heart attack if she thought she had to do without them," replied Nathaniel, "But there is growing pressure for emancipation in some quarters. Recently in England the highest court has . . ."

"Oh yes, I know about that," interrupted John, "The judgement is known as *in parte Somersett*, and it is being hotly discussed among some of the students."

"Well then, you can imagine how slave owners might feel if they thought they could be deprived of their property by a court order."

"Indeed, it causes particular anxiety among our students from the South," continued John, "Although it does not affect them here, yet they would have to worry if they visited England and took their personal valets along, they would come back without them."

"I would be interested to know how this issue is being discussed at Nassau Hall, in particular what position do our Southern students take," asked Nathaniel, "And what guidance does President Witherspoon offer? I understand his farm employs slaves."

"I know just the person to ask about this," replied John, "James Madison is from one of the wealthiest families in Virginia. He recently graduated but stayed on to be tutored by President Witherspoon in Hebrew. He is very pious and has spent much time discussing moral issues with the president. I will ask him about his views on the subject and how it fits into the subject of liberty which Dr. Witherspoon is very keen on. I will let you know what I find out."

A few weeks later John was sitting in Hudibras tavern with his friend, Ichabod Burnet. John had known Ichabod long before coming to Nassau Hall because he was the son of Dr. William Burnet, one of the founders of the New Jersey Medical Association, and a friend of John's father. As usual they were animatedly discussing the burning issues of the day, in this case the moral conflicts that could arise through enforcement of the trade embargo.

"I am a firm supporter of embargos to resist unfair taxation," ventured Ichabod, "But refusing to purchase some merchant's goods is one thing and setting fire to his storeroom is something completely different. This is a clear violation of property rights and cannot be morally justified as some members of the Sons of Liberty seem to think."

"I don't think that the Sons of Liberty explicitly advocate the destruction of property," argued John, "Property obviously does get destroyed from time to time but it is often hard to know who is behind it. It could be a competitor of the merchant in question."

At that point John noticed that James Madison had just entered Hudibras and decided to take the opportunity to query him as he had promised his father.

"Ah, Mr. Madison," John addressed him with the deference due to someone who had already graduated and, therefore, had to be treated almost like a tutor, "Ichabod Burnet and I are just discussing the moral dimensions of property rights, and we would be flattered if you would share your thoughts on these matters with us."

"Well, gentlemen," replied Madison, "I will be happy to join in your discussion. The issues of freedom and property rights are at the center of all philosophical discourse."

"Indeed," agreed John, "Ichabod and I are convinced that our rights as free Englishmen are threatened by any arbitrary acts of Parliament that tax us without the approval of our assemblies and that we should, therefore, support embargos as a legitimate act of resistance."

"I agree with that position entirely," said Madison, "Taxes imposed without representation are clearly a threat to our liberties and must be resisted."

"And what about the question of slavery?" asked John, "If we regard liberty as a paramount moral issue, must we not also be for the emancipation of the slaves?"

"What does Dr. Witherspoon think about these issues?" added Ichabod, "He is always talking about liberty but is himself the owner of slaves."

"Dr. Witherspoon's philosophy is always imminently practical," answered Madison, "He thinks that slavery will in time disappear as servants become more educated and capable of rationally ordering their lives but that it would be vastly impractical in North America to emancipate the lower orders precipitously."

"But if the institution is fundamentally evil," countered Ichabod vehemently, "What do practicalities matter?"

"On a theoretical level one can argue that we are morally obliged to end every sort of evil immediately," replied Madison, "But that would fly in the face of Dr. Witherspoon's common-sense philosophy. He is wary of purely theoretical arguments, comparing such discourse to the medieval penchant for pointlessly debating how many angels would fit on the head of a pin. We are imperfect creatures born into an imperfect world and must carefully consider what the practical consequences of our efforts to improve society might be or risk that even the best of intentions might lead to undesirable results."

"That sounds suspiciously like a strategy for avoiding confronting evil if it involves hardship for oneself," said John.

"In the case of Witherspoon, I do not believe this applies," answered Madison, "Since my father has well over a hundred slaves, I have discussed the moral dimension of this with Dr. Witherspoon on a number of occasions and I am convinced that his advocacy of gradualism is a sincere belief and not some sort of hypocrisy."

"What did he say that makes you so sure?" asked Ichabod.

"Once when we were discussing the issue of emancipation of slaves, he told me a story from his time in his first ministry in Beith, Ayrshire in Scotland. He was approached by a young heathen African slave who was the property of a local joiner. The slave, whose name was Jamie, asked to be instructed in Christianity. Dr. Witherspoon was pleased to do this but when it came time to baptize him, Jamie's owner opposed the baptism fearing that it might instill fancies of freedom into his slave. Witherspoon baptized him anyway but at the same time warned Jamie that baptism by no means freed him from his servitude. Jamie then assumed the Scottish name Montgomery in honor of Witherspoon's wife and received from him a certificate of good Christian conduct which would enable him to worship and, when traveling, to take communion in other churches. Shortly thereafter Jamie ran away from his master and settled in Edinburgh. He worked there as a joiner until he was captured and imprisoned where he died."

"Well that certainly is a tragic story," said John, "But what is the moral of it all?"

"The moral is that morality is a complex and ambiguous issue," replied Madison, "Dr. Witherspoon helped save Jamie's immortal soul but caused him, at least indirectly, to lose such freedom as he possessed. The good doctor struggles to this day with the moral responsibility for his actions. Saving Jamie's soul was certainly worthwhile but in some sense was the cause of his untimely death."

"We have only a few servants," remarked John, "So it would not pose insurmountable problems to emancipate them if *in parte Somersett* were to be applied here. They would probably just keep working for us on a different basis. But in the case of your father, I can imagine things would get more complicated."

"Complicated is not the word," emphasized Madison, "If hundreds of slaves were to be emancipated from one day to the next, it would cause absolute chaos. There is also the question of the destruction of property. Our slaves represent a huge investment. If we had to free them without compensation, we would be financially ruined. A flourishing plantation would cease to function. And think what that would mean across the whole South. Thousands of propertyless people unaccustomed to caring for themselves would be suddenly cast adrift. It would result in a Hobbesian nightmare, the bellum omnium contra omnes! That would not be in the interest of anyone, least of all the Africans who would probably be slaughtered en masse by frightened Whites."

"Good Lord!", exclaimed Ichabod, "I can see that this is a problem not easily solved. I wonder if the day will ever come when the freedoms enjoyed by us Englishmen can be extended to all who live here."

As the boys were sitting there mulling over this complicated issue a young Negro girl came running down the staircase that led to the garret. Close behind her ran the owner of Hudibras, Jacob Hyer, clad only in a nightshirt.

"Fire, fire," she screamed, "The whole garret is on fire! Run for your lives!"

"Quickly gentlemen!" shouted Madison, "Let us fetch our new fire engine and perhaps we can save this place."

Following Madison's instructions, the students rushed over to Nassau Hall and hauled the newly acquired pump wagon out of its shed. As quickly as they could, they pulled the device over to Hudibras tavern, placed a long hose into a well, and began to pump water onto the roof of the tavern. By this time, however, the entire garret was a mass of flames and the roof looked about to collapse. Despite the valiant attempts of the students, it became quickly apparent that the main portion of the house was doomed. They were able to prevent the kitchen from catching fire by pulling down an entry which led from the kitchen into the house. The house itself, however, developed inexorably into a huge bonfire. The best the students could do was to save the neighboring house of the Paterson family by spraying water on it throughout the night. The boys worked through the night, and by 7 the next morning it appeared that the fire was finally extinguished. Exhausted and covered with soot the boys were relieved that at least the Paterson house had been saved.

"This is the third fire in the course of a year!" exclaimed John, "One could be forgiven for thinking that evil forces are plotting to intimidate Nassau Hall."

"That would not surprise me," agreed Ichabod, "I have heard that great pressure has been put on Dr. Witherspoon to restrict Whig activities among the students."

"Yes, that could be," replied Madison, "But let's not jump to conclusions. It could also be that the Negro wench in whose room the fire started simply forgot to put out her candle. Or that she deliberately set the fire in order to avoid being molested by Hyer."

"Molested by Hyer!?" blurted Ichabod, "Do you really think that old Hyer is shagging his Negro servants?"

"In the South it happens all the time," replied Madison, smiling at the young man's naiveté, "It is the dreadful sin of miscegenation, but many cannot avoid the temptation. When we catch one of our overseers indulging in such vile practices, he is lucky if to get off with just a flogging."

Madison's words reminded John of the dire warnings that his father had given him about entertaining carnal thoughts concerning any of the Scudder's female servants. In fact, he suspected that his father experienced a certain sense of relief after he was able to install his pubescent son in the all-male environment of Nassau Hall.

Despite James Madison's efforts to allay their fears, the news of a third fire affecting, if only indirectly, the students of Nassau Hall caused great consternation among them. Conspiracy theories sprung up like mushrooms after a rain. Many were convinced that the events were all part of an insidious plot to quell resistance to the growing threats against their liberties as Englishmen. It was not just the fires and the pressure put on trustees to limit students' commencement speeches but the general trend of increasing repression of the colonist's rights to self-government. The news that Governor Thomas Hutchinson of Massachusetts had been put on the Civil List was a case in point. This freed the governor from his financial dependence on the Assembly and was widely seen as an attempt to insulate the executive authority from the will of the people. Hutchinson was known for his obsequious obedience to the wishes of the Board of Trade even when these went against the interests of the colony. Hutchinson's success encouraged Governor Franklin to make his own attempt to get appointed to the Civil List stimulating suspicions in New Jersey that Franklin too wanted to free himself from the necessity of compromising with the Assembly. All good Whigs were convinced that such trends threatened arbitrary government unconstrained by the guarantes of the Glorious Revolution. Growing suspicion caused informed people to view all unfolding events in terms of possible plots to threaten their liberties.

Such was the case a few months later when news of a new Tea Act passed by Parliament reached the colonies. Since a tax on tea was the only tax officially retained when the Townshend Acts were repealed in 1770, the colonists were intensely interested in what new machinations the government might be up to. The tea tax that was retained after the repeal of the Townshend Acts was largely ceremonial to demonstrate Parliament's belief in its right to tax the colonies. It did not generate the same emotion as the original Townshend Act taxes because hardly anyone paid the tax. Colonists preferred to consume smuggled Dutch tea bypassing British providers. It thus came as a surprise that the new Tea Act allegedly would actually result in the availability of cheaper tea.

"Can it be that Parliament is really going to provide us with cheaper tea?" Nathaniel asked his father-in-law during a discussion at Anderson Manor.

"Don't be fooled," replied the colonel, "This is all just a deceptive scheme to help the East India Company while at the same time luring the North American colonies into buying taxed tea. The Company is on the verge of financial collapse and sitting on huge stores of unsold tea. In order to rescue the company Parliament has virtually eliminated the duty on tea exported from England. This makes the East India Company´s tea competitive with the smuggled Dutch variety."

"Well, what does it matter?" asked Isabella, "The important thing is that we get affordable tea. Why do you call the plan deceptive?"

"It is deceptive because it would establish the principle that Parliament has the right to tax us directly without the approval of our assemblies," explained the colonel, "That is exactly what we were trying to prevent with the non-importation agreement. Once the unfair advantage that Parliament has granted to the East India company results in the elimination of the competition, you can be sure that prices will go up again. In the meantime, some very wealthy and influential people here who are involved in the Dutch tea trade stand to lose a fortune."

"Another trap, in other words," Nathaniel concluded, "And an insidious one at that, if the price of tea is actually lower, many people won't realize that they are being duped into sacrificing their liberties as Englishmen."

"Exactly," agreed the colonel, "I think the Sons of Liberty have a job to do educating the people. Ever since Parliament eliminated most of the Townshend duties, one does not hear much from them. Maybe this will get them active again. And I would think that it would be in the interests of certain wealthy gentlemen in these colonies to promote those efforts as best they can."

"Organizing an effective boycott of tea that is cheaper than Dutch tea won't be easy," mused Isabella, "How should wealthy gentlemen promote those efforts?"

"The people must be made to realize that this is all part of a pattern to strip us of our liberties," answered the colonel, "And I have heard some interesting news from friends in Boston that might serve to wake people up to what is actually going on."

"What kind of news?" asked Nathaniel, "Does it confirm any of the conspiracy theories that are currently floating around?"

"It surely does," answered the colonel, "Not only that, but it will likely cause a lot of grief for Governor Hutchinson and for William Franklin as well."

"Pray, don't keep us in suspense any longer, Father!" exclaimed Isabella, always keen on any exciting gossip she could share with the local ladies, "What news could possibly embarrass two royal governors?"

"Apparently copies of letters written over the course of several years by Hutchinson and his assistant, Andrew Oliver, to the Board of Trade have found their way to

Boston. In these letters they viciously attacked the opponents of the Townshend Acts and advocated the use of force to subdue resistance to them."

"Well, it doesn't really come as a surprise that Hutchinson and Oliver are lackeys of the British government," commented Nathaniel.

"Yes, but advocating the use of force against duly elected members of the Massachusetts Assembly who are merely defending English liberties is clearly scandalous," explained the colonel, "This will completely destroy any credibility that Hutchinson might have had with the Assembly. The Sons of Liberty will have a heyday with this. This could be the beginning of the end for him even though he managed to get himself on the Civil List."

"How did such incendiary information come to light?" asked Isabella.

"That is the most interesting part of it," continued the colonel, "The copies were sent to Boston by none other than Benjamin Franklin, who would not say where he got them and asked that they not be published. But as you can imagine, such news could not long be kept secret and is now spreading like wildfire."

"This is bound to be a great embarrassment for William Franklin!" exclaimed Nathaniel, "His own father provides information to Whig sympathizers in Boston that completely discredits a royal governor. I wonder how that will affect their relationship."

"Even more interesting is how it will affect Ben Franklin's position in London," said the colonel, "I can't imagine that the gentlemen on the Board of Trade will be amused by this. And, as far as William Franklin's hopes for getting on the Civil List himself are concerned, I think he can forget about that."

"I also wonder how it will affect the relationship between a father and a son," added Isabella, "They seem to be on a collision course."

"They are, indeed," agreed the colonel, "William Franklin is hoping that the Vandalia project will go forward, and he will get rich. The last thing he wants is that his father upsets the Board of Trade so that they reconsider the permission they granted. Ben Franklin on the other hand sits in London and confronts the stupidity and venality of the British administration every day. His attempts to harmonize American and British interests are very often frustrated by greedy and power-hungry officials. No wonder he seems to be moving in a more radical direction. His sending those letters is dramatic proof of overwhelming frustration. His son, as royal governor, however, must disavow his father's actions if he wants to be considered a loyal servant of the Crown."

"What a dreadful position to be in," said Isabella, "I almost feel sorry for William. I heard, however, that he might have some relief in the Skinner affair because law enforcement officials have apparently arrested the person who absconded with the colony's treasury."

"That's true," agreed the colonel, "They arrested the head of a gang of counterfeiters named Samuel Ford, but he escaped jail and is said to have fled to New Orleans. Unless Franklin can re-arrest him and prove he was really the perpetrator it won't take much pressure off Stephen Skinner. But in order to accomplish that he would have to get the Assembly to allocate money for the manhunt. Given the doubts all of them are about William's motives, there is little chance they will agree to that."

The drama of the unfolding conflict between father and son was a microcosm of the larger conflict between the colonists and the mother country. It was with intense interest, therefore, that everyone awaited the commencement ceremony in Nassau Hall in September. As always, the royal governor would be in attendance. As always, the students were likely to favor the radical Whig positions that Benjamin Franklin had now apparently adopted. Although the speeches were now to be pre-vetted by the trustees, it was still possible that the controversies would break out into the open. In any case, Nathaniel and Isabella looked forward to the event with excited anticipation.

The speeches turned out, however, to be very uncontroversial. They were dominated by such esoteric topics as "Ambition", "Eloquence", "True Honor", "The Excellence and Benefit of Laws" and "Matter is not in any sense infinitely divisible."

"Well, I have experienced more entertaining commencement exercises," whispered Isabella to Nathaniel and John between addresses barely stifling a yawn.

"Yes, Mother, that is no wonder," explained John, "The trustees recently increased the penalty for not adhering to the guidelines. Now, whoever does not limit himself to exactly the approved version of his address will not receive his degree."

After the formal part of commencement was over, the participants, disappointed by the bland nature of the proceedings, gathered for the reception in the hopes that some interesting news might yet be gleaned. A smiling Governor Franklin obviously pleased that there were no provocative speeches this time, stayed to congratulate Dr. Witherspoon on the reinstatement of what he considered to be proper behavior among the students.

"Well, Dr. Witherspoon, I must say that this year's crop of graduates does not seem to have fallen prey to radical ideologies as was occasionally the case in the past."

"Our students today are as devoted to the preservation of our liberties as any in previous years." replied Dr. Witherspoon, "At our request they have merely agreed to refrain from including the discussion of controversial topics in their presentations. If you ask any one of them in private what they think of that provision of the Tea Act that imposes taxes here without the approval of our assemblies, you will find that everyone regards it as a violation of our basic British liberties."

"But that is nonsense," countered Franklin irritably, "Parliament must have the ability to finance the expenses of empire. Should British taxpayers alone carry the burden of paying for troops that we need here to keep law and order and to enforce the Proclamation Line? Do you realize that the citizens of the mother country pay over twenty times more taxes than we do here?"

"That may be the case," answered Witherspoon coolly, "It may very well be true that there are legitimate arguments for raising more revenue for governance, but it is all a matter of how the decisions are arrived at. Without the advice and consent of colonial assemblies, such decisions are illegitimate even if some of the goals are reasonable. We have, after all, no representatives in Parliament."

"The members of Parliament represent the empire as a whole, not just the boroughs they formally stand for," argued Franklin, his face reddening with frustration, "And it has been my experience that Parliament usually takes this responsibility more seriously than do many colonial assemblies. Many of the gentlemen in the assemblies seem to be only interested in their own self-aggrandizement and spare no thoughts for the good of the empire!"

"That is no doubt the reasoning behind Governor Hutchinson's evident desire to crack down on the rights of the members of his assembly." replied Witherspoon in a sly reference to the letters that Ben Franklin had sent to Boston, "But with all due respect, Governor, I believe that such disregard for the rights of the people can only lead to a constitutional crisis. I dare say, your much respected father might be expected to agree."

Stunned by what he recognized to be Witherspoon's allusion to his father's increasingly radical Whig position, Franklin sought to minimize the difference between his own and his father's politics.

"My father and I are in broad agreement that the elites in British North America and the elites of the mother country must find better ways to work together for the good of the empire. What differences of opinion might exist between us have to do with the fact that my father has spent years abroad and has not recently had to deal directly with some of the greedy and confrontational politicians in the colonial assemblies that make life so difficult for His Majesty's loyal servants on this side of the ocean."

"Yes, indeed," interjected Nathaniel with a wry smile, "Instead your father has to deal with the greedy and confrontational politicians on the Board of Trade. I can well imagine that representing legitimate colonial interests in London these days is a daunting task."

"Especially if certain gentlemen in the British government do not understand the growing importance of the British provinces in North American," added Dr. Witherspoon, "I believe it was your father who predicted some years ago that the differing population growth rates will rather soon result in there being a larger population of British citizens in North American than in England, Scotland, Wales, and Ireland combined. And a larger portion of the population has voting rights. Surely, the politicians in London cannot expect that we will accept the status of second-class citizens. That would be tantamount to enslavement!"

"No one in His Majesty's government wants to enslave free British citizens," protested Franklin, "But if the assemblies want full authority to govern, they must also accept the responsibilities of empire. Why, last year we had to abandon 22 forts in the backcountry because colonial assemblies would not agree to provide more revenue for the maintenance of our military. Poor General Gage is expected to police the vast area covered by the Proclamation Line Agreement with just 7,000 soldiers. I can tell you as a former army officer that that is a completely impossible task, but try to explain that to a typical colonial assemblyman."

"But are not standing armies a danger to liberty?" asked Nathaniel, "Why can't these tasks be left up to colonial militias? "

"Because those militias contain many people whose main design is to sabotage precisely those agreements with the Indians that our Regulars are charged to enforce," replied Franklin, "I can cite many instances where our troops who were protecting Indians from being driven from their lands were attacked by vigilantes. These outlaws are illegally moving onto Indian land and want nothing more than to murder the Indians and steal their land. Unfortunately, these outlaws seem to be well represented in colonial assemblies."

"Ah yes, the land issue," said Witherspoon archly, "I dare say that the greed for western lands is not limited to vigilantes. I also doubt that the gentlemen in the assemblies want to protect those lawless frontiersmen who are killing Indians, they are simply worried that those unauthorized settlers will get to the best parcels of land before they do."

Franklin blushed again as he realized that Witherspoon was making an oblique reference to the Vandalia scheme.

"The final disposition of the western lands is, of course, a key issue for the empire," continued Franklin somewhat less confrontationally, "It must be regulated and that means law and order must prevail in order to ensure that all legitimate interests are given due account. This will involve sober and fair negotiations between us in the colonies and His Majesty's government. Petulant protests on the part of our assemblies will not bring us closer to a solution."

"Let us hope that you and your father will in the end be able to work out an amicable solution to these problems that will convince both sides," said Nathaniel brightly, "I agree that an escalation of the conflict is in nobody's interest."

Just how difficult it would become to bridge the opinion gap between Crown officials and colonial elites became clearly apparent just a few months later. In November William Franklin was again reminded of the New Jersey Assembly's capacity for recalcitrance when he asked for money to go after the fugitive Ford and was refused. Compounding his irritation Franklin had to endure the public reading by the Speaker of letters from Virginia, Massachusetts, Connecticut, and Rhode Island calling upon the legislators to form permanent committees of correspondence to coordinate colonial protests against the Tea Act. Still Franklin remained convinced that a reasonable solution to the conflicts was still possible, especially as his father had expressed in recent letters his acceptance of the differences of opinion between them and his continued hope that a mutually beneficial accommodation could be found. William Franklin hoped that the vaguely subversive suggestions for committees of correspondence would soon be forgotten.

These optimistic hopes were to be dashed within the month. On December 16th about 50 radical Whigs disguised as Indians boarded three British ships in Boston harbor and dumped 342 crates of East India tea into the harbor. This wanton destruction of property was an intentional provocation that the British government could not possibly ignore. Hopes for an amicable solution to the differences dividing the colonists from the mother country sank along with the tea.

Chapter 17

ROAD TO REBELLION – 1774–1775

THE NEWS OF THE dramatic events in Boston spread like wildfire throughout the colonies. By the beginning of the new year students at Nassau Hall could talk about nothing else.

"I just received a letter from Thomas Melville from the Class of 1769!" announced Charles Beatty one day in late January to the students gathered in the library of Nassau Hall, "He actually participated in the heroic events in Boston Harbor last month!"

A great cheer went up from the assembled students who were delighted to hear that one of their brethren had had the courage to stand up for the rights of free Britons.

"He writes that the only tea remaining from the East India Company's cursed shipment are a few leaves that his wife found in his shoes the next morning!" continued Beatty laughing.

"We need to emulate his heroism!" shouted John Scudder, "Tea is the symbol of British suppression of colonial rights. Let us pledge to give up the evil brew to show our solidarity with the Boston patriots!"

"Let us go a step further," added Ichabod Burnet, "Let's gather all the tea we have here and put it to the torch!"

The plan was adopted by acclamation, and the students rushed to the steward's storeroom and confiscated the college's winter store of tea. This was dumped on the lawn in front of Nassau Hall. Each student then threw his personal store of tea on top of the pile until about a dozen pounds lay on the ground. Then the students hastily constructed a puppet out of straw, tied a tea cannister around its neck and labeled it "Thomas Hutchinson." They then threw the effigy onto the pile of tea and set it on fire as one of the students rang the bell of Nassau Hall. As President Witherspoon and the tutors looked on approvingly the tea went up in flames to the wild cheers of the assembled students. While the tea and straw turned into ashes, the students and officers of Nassau Hall solemnly pledged to abstain from the beverage until such time as the British government agreed to restore their rights and liberties.

In the same way that the destruction of the tea in Boston energized the students at Nassau Hall it also polarized opinion throughout the colonies. People who were suspicious of the motives of the British government became ever more convinced that they needed to take matters into their own hands. When the British military, complaining of a lack of funds, decided to abandon Fort Pitt, the Virginia militia immediately moved in and took it over. People like William Franklin and his supporters who wanted to safeguard Crown prerogatives in the colonies were appalled at such initiatives fearing the undermining of royal authority. Nowhere were the controversies more bitter than in Monmouth County. The Scudders and the Andersons along with most of the other members of Reverend Tennent's congregation were firmly on the side of the Whigs. These conflicts were often the subject of conversations at Anderson Manor following Sunday services at Reverend Tennent's meeting house.

"I am very confused," complained Isabella, "On the one hand Governor Franklin always talks about the necessity of safeguarding Crown authority and providing funds to support British troops so they can keep order in North America. On the other hand, I have heard that Governor Dunmore in Virginia is encouraging the Virginia militia to murder Indians and help people steal their land. Both Franklin and Dunmore represent the Crown, but their policies are hardly consistent."

"Right you are, my dear," explained Colonel Anderson, "Crown policies are indeed very contradictory. To understand these contradictions, you have to realize that it is all about greed for the land west of the Proclamation Line."

"Ah, yes," exclaimed Reverend Tennent, "When will people realize you cannot serve God and Mammon at the same time!"

"In this particular case," continued the colonel, "Both governors have contradictory goals regarding the Ohio territory. Franklin hopes that the Vandalia project will make him rich, but Dunmore tries to curry favor with his Assembly but laying claim to all the Ohio territory for Virginia. He would like to extend the boundaries of Virginia all the way to the Mississippi!"

"And both have to deal with the fact of tens of thousands of settlers who have already illegally moved into the territory west of the Proclamation Line just in the last few years," added Nathaniel, "The land speculators in the assemblies have to worry that even if they ever get to lay their hands on these lands, they will find squatters already in possession of the best lots."

Even as this discussion was taking place at Anderson Manor the British Parliament was passing the Boston Port Act to shut down the port of Boston until such time as the colonists would compensate the East India Company for the destroyed tea. With that law the British government crossed a critical line; it became clear that henceforth military coercion rather than persuasion was to be used to enforce government policies. The British government had fallen into the trap set for them by the Sons of Liberty. An entire city was to be held ransom for a dispute that had previously only involved one company and a minority of the citizenry. Businesses would fail and people would go hungry as trade between the city and the outside world was choked off by the blockade. The government apparently hoped that such a show of resolve would cow the colonies and dissuade them from further resistance to government orders. But when the news of the Boston Port Act reached the colonies, the reaction was completely different. Almost everyone was enraged and dismayed. Even people who were steadfastly loyal to the Crown disapproved of the arbitrariness of the decision. Throughout the colonies people rose up to declare their solidarity with the citizens of Boston.

Over the ensuing weeks the situation became bleaker and bleaker as it became clear that the British government had decided on a course of confrontation. The leading advocate of reconciliation between the elites of North America and Great Britain, Benjamin Franklin, had been publicly humiliated and dismissed from all his official posts. Everyone now realized that the only hope was organized resistance to the tyrannical measures of the British government. Isabella's uncle, Judge John Anderson, together with other leading citizens of Lower Freehold Township took the initiative and called for a public meeting to be held on June 6th at Monmouth Courthouse.

On the morning of the appointed day Isabella and Nathaniel were thrilled when they looked out of their window to see a large crowd of people gathering in front of the courthouse. Hurrying over to get a closer look at the arrivals they were pleased to see that all the leading families of the area were represented: the Andersons, the Smocks, the Formans, the Covenhovens, and the Holmes. Reverend Tennent was there as well along with many from his congregation: the Wikoffs, the Hendersons, the Gordons, the Hankinsons and most of the other elders of the church. In addition to the town gentry, there were also many local yeomen who had taken time off at a busy time of the year to participate in what they were certain was going to be an important event. The atmosphere was charged with a grim sense of determination.

When Judge Anderson called the meeting to order in the courthouse, the crowd was so large that it spilled out onto the lawn in front.

"People of Freehold," Judge Anderson began, "We have asked you to come here today because the fundamental liberties of free-born Americans are in danger of subversion!"

The crowd roared its agreement.

"The cause in which the inhabitants of Boston are now suffering is the common cause of the whole continent of North America and unless some general spirited measures for the public safety be speedily entered into there is just reason to fear that every province may in turn share the same fate with them. It is highly incumbent on us, therefore, to unite in some effectual means to obtain a repeal of the Boston Port Bill and any other that may follow it which shall be deemed subversive of the rights and privileges of free born Americans!"

"Let us march on the governor's mansion!" shouted one young hot-head, "We will show him what we think of his government. We will not be enslaved!"

"That will not achieve anything!" countered Nathaniel, fearing that the crowd might be goaded into actions that would only make matters worse, "Let us instead resolve to stop all importation and exportation from and to Great Britain and the West Indies until the Port Bill and any similar acts be repealed. That strategy has worked before and will work again."

"Dr. Scudder is absolutely correct," added Captain John Covenhoven, a highly regarded militia officer, "The last thing we want is a military confrontation where our boys would not stand a chance against the Regulars. The important thing is to show resolve by uniting with many other communities to show the government that we will never submit to tyranny!"

"An excellent suggestion," agreed Asher Holmes, another pillar of the community, "We must seek to form the broadest possible front with as many communities as we can organize in our county."

"And such an association can expand to include other counties all the way up to the provincial level," continued Peter Forman enthusiastically, "If every province acts accordingly, the government will have no recourse but to submit to our demands. They will be forced to by the very merchants they are trying to favor with their tax policies. When the merchants of London can no longer sell us their wares, they will soon apply pressure on Parliament to seek compromises."

"Exactly," agreed Nathaniel, "We need to form an association that is not subject to the constraints of the Assembly and cannot be disbanded at the behest of a royal governor, an association that represents a broad cross-section of the populace to insure the most effective boycott possible. Since Judge Anderson has taken the initiative with this meeting, I suggest we elect him to lead this effort."

"Thank you for your confidence, Dr. Scudder," replied Judge Anderson, "But I cannot do this alone, I need the assistance of a committee which represents the will of this township. I think that you, for example, would be an excellent person to serve on this committee. You are well known in our community and as a physician have frequent contacts with a large number of people. You can help spread the word throughout the county and beyond."

"I would be flattered to serve our community in this fashion," said Nathaniel, "And let us open the floor to more nominations so that our committee will be seen as being truly representative."

The meeting quickly agreed on the appointment of a committee of seven members. In addition to Nathaniel and Judge Anderson the nominees included Hendrick Smock, Asher Holmes, Peter Forman, John Forman, and Captain John Covenhoven. The committee was specifically charged with entering into correspondence with similar committees across the province to coordinate efforts to resist all tyrannical attempts to undermine the rights of free-born Americans.

Walking back to their home from the courthouse, Nathaniel and Isabella talked excitedly about Nathaniel's new political commitments.

"You seem to have made quite an impression on that meeting," remarked Isabella admiringly.

"It is certainly a heady feeling to have the trust of such a large number of people," said Nathaniel, "I hope I can live up to their expectations."

"Those who expect you to work for a peaceful resolution of the crisis will certainly not be disappointed. But there are also some who would rather resort to violence, and you will probably have to deal with provocations on their part."

"Yes, indeed," agreed Nathaniel, "That is why it is important that we organize a very broad-based and effective boycott before the hotheads of the world take matters into their own hands. I was planning in any case to visit Johnny in Princeton soon. Maybe I will get a chance to talk to President Witherspoon about how best to proceed."

When Nathaniel visited Princeton a few days later, he was surprised and a bit unsettled to see just how far the martial spirit had infected the students. The students had formed their own militia company distinct from that of the community and many students including his son, John, were strutting about in their green, yellow, and white uniforms.

"What is the meaning of this, young man," Nathaniel asked sternly, "Don't you think you should have first consulted me and your mother before donning the colors of war?"

"All of us want to show our solidarity with the noble patriots of Boston," John explained, "We are not really prepared for war. Unfortunately, we have not even half enough weapons to arm our unit. But Uncle Will said he could lend me a musket if things escalate."

Making a mental note to admonish his brother not to encourage violence, Nathaniel was torn between a grudging admiration for his son's courage and his fears for the boy's safety. He decided that the best way to influence his son would be to convince him of the efficacy of non-violent protest.

"War is a terrible thing, and we should avoid it if at all possible," began Nathaniel, "The best course of action is always peaceful negotiation and as good Christians we should avoid any provocations to violence."

He went on to explain the work of the committee he had been appointed to and how important it was to organize an effective but peaceful boycott to force Britain to respect the rights of free-born Americans. Although impressed that his father had acquired an official public role to play in the unfolding drama, John was still not quite convinced that peaceful protest alone would suffice to guarantee freedom.

"Of course, you are right to prefer peaceful solutions, father, but is it not also important to demonstrate publicly that we will not compromise on the issue of basic freedoms?"

"It certainly is, my son, but one must avoid provoking violence unnecessarily."

"Well, let's take a case in point," suggested John, "Last week a bunch of us decided to impress on the townspeople that they ought to adhere to the tea boycott as everyone here on campus is doing. About 40 of us marched to the house of someone we knew to be an avid tea consumer and demanded that he surrender his supply of tea. He did exactly that and we committed the tea to a bonfire amid the cheers of everyone in attendance. We then marched to the home of a well-known Tory to demand the same thing, but he fled before we got there. Our demands were peaceful, but they showed everyone where we stand and will make people think twice before defying the embargo."

Nathaniel had to suppress a smile at the thought of the 40 plucky lads forcing outraged adults to adhere to the boycott but still felt the need to caution his overzealous son.

"You are lucky that your demonstration remained peaceful, but the behavior of crowds can often be unpredictable. What would have happened, for example, if the person whose tea you expropriated had defended his property with a weapon? One of you could have been shot and the rest would probably then have attacked the shooter and done him grievous harm. So quickly can things get out of control!"

John nodded thoughtfully as the wisdom of his father's words sunk in. He began to realize that what started out as a fine frolic could easily have ended in tragedy.

"John, I am very proud of your defense of Whig liberties, but you must promise me that you will not take part in any actions that have a potential for violence. The success of our boycott depends in no small measure on our avoiding provocations that would give the enemies of freedom an excuse for violent confrontation. I will keep you informed about the progress that our committees of correspondence make and ask you and your fellow students to help us get the word out to as many people as possible."

Proud to become a trusted partner in his father's project John nodded vigorously, "You can count on me, father. We will coordinate all actions with your committee. Just let us know what you expect of us!"

Somewhat later in the day, Nathaniel had the opportunity to discuss these matters with President Witherspoon and expressed his concern that the young and impressionable students of Nassau Hall might be goaded into acts that would be dangerous for them and for the institution.

"We are aware of the dangers of overzealous behavior on the part of our students," Witherspoon conceded, "But we cannot deny the righteousness of their motivation. In my view it is better to let them publicly proclaim their beliefs than to try to suppress them as Governor Franklin seems to prefer. We had, for example, named a senior, Samuel Leake, to give the salutatory address at the next commencement. Because Leake had been an active organizer of the tea boycott, however, the Board at the behest of Franklin and his Tory friends forced me to withdraw Leake's name from consideration. It is incidents like this that convince young people that they must be prepared to go beyond peaceful discussions in the defense of liberty."

Nathaniel nodded in agreement. That was indeed the question. When is it necessary to go beyond peaceful discussions when liberty is at threat? The British government clearly was ready to use harmful force against the inhabitants of Boston to enforce the port closure. How long could one just turn the other cheek? These issues were bound to become the focus of intense discussions in the following weeks as the committees of correspondence from the various towns planned to meet at the county level to elect delegates to a Provincial Congress which in turn would send delegates to a Continental Congress. Nathaniel was aware that the creation of such a hierarchy of representative bodies might well be seen by some as a subversive attempt to undermine royal authority. He decided to ask Witherspoon's opinion about what the legitimate role of such bodies should be.

"In the end we are just reacting to the government's cruel and arbitrary treatment of the people of Boston," explained Nathaniel, "We don't mean to question royal authority, but we are convinced that Parliament is trampling on British liberties."

"And right you are, Dr. Scudder, and it will continue if it does not meet with determined resistance. There are obviously people in the government who would like to treat the colonists no better than slaves depriving them of the rights of free-born British subjects. The organization that you are forging right now might be able to make George III come to his senses and reign in some of his corrupt and scheming minions."

"I sincerely hope that we can convince him of the justness of our mission."

"Yes, but I think you have to be prepared for a struggle. Don't think that this will be an easy task. In my view the continental congress that results from all this organizing will have the primary duty of uniting the colonies for self-defense if all else fails."

Nathaniel was taken aback by Witherspoon's apparent readiness for escalation of the conflict.

"I still hope that an effectively organized trade boycott will force the government to reconsider as they did during the Stamp crisis."

"We all hope that but there are ominous signs that point toward more confrontation," replied Witherspoon, "I have recently been informed about an act of Parliament pertaining to Quebec province that is utterly outrageous."

"I know that Reverend Tennent has been concerned that the incorporation of Quebec into the Empire might increase the influence of Papism."

"There is no doubt about that," said Witherspoon, "Parliament has now officially guaranteed free practice of the Catholic faith and restored the right of the Catholic Church to impose tithes."

"Oh my God!" exclaimed Nathaniel, "Reverend Tennent was right. The gains of the Glorious Revolution are indeed endangered. What is to become of the True Religion?"

"That is only the beginning," continued Witherspoon, "Not only have they enabled a Papist entity on our northern borders, but they have also expanded its jurisdiction to include the entire back country. You have to wonder why we fought the French for so many years if we are just going to give the territory we were fighting for back to the French settlers."

"But that is madness! Why in heaven's name would Parliament follow such a daft policy? Are they trying to provoke a civil war?"

"It is partly to punish those colonies where the assemblies are making a nuisance of themselves from the government's point of view. Quebec does not have an elected assembly, so the government finds it easier to do whatever it wants. They can rule through the land-owning seigneurs and the Catholic ecclesiastics without bothering to consult the people. Any claims that English settlers think they might have in the Ohio country, they can probably forget."

"But that is unbelievable!" Nathaniel protested, "They are essentially imposing the same kind of absolutist tyranny that we fought so hard to defeat. If we countenance that, then it is only a matter of time until we are all enslaved."

"Now, Dr. Scudder, you see why I believe the new congress will have to be ready to defend our rights, if need be, with force of arms. You probably thought I was being overly confrontational, but you see that we are indeed already under attack. Everything we hold near and dear is in serious danger: our liberties including the right to practice the True Religion and to elect our own representatives, but also our rights to develop this country as we see fit. Now that the entire western frontier is under control of the province of Quebec it is the people in London who will decide who gets to settle new lands. If they think the Quebecois are more pliant politically, it could be Catholic Frenchmen instead of Presbyterian yeomen who fill up this giant country."

Nathaniel was shocked by this revelation. Up until that point he had wanted to believe that compromise was probable because it was the only thing that made sense for both the mother country and the colonies. But now he understood that the desire for power among unscrupulous politicians could indeed lead to a situation where violence became inevitable. Witherspoon was absolutely correct that the basic liberties of the Glorious Revolution were at stake and that one had to be prepared for what could turn out to be a life-or-death struggle. This grim realization preoccupied Nathaniel over the next few weeks as he helped organize the next phase of resistance: a meeting of all the town committees of correspondence in Monmouth County to elect representatives for a provincial congress which in turn would elect delegates for a Continental Congress which could represent all 13 colonies. It was clear to Nathaniel now that it was essential that this new Continental Congress be endowed with a powerful legitimacy sufficient to unite the colonies for whatever self-defense measures might become necessary.

The committee of correspondence of lower Freehold decided to invite the other townships of Monmouth County to a meeting to be held at Monmouth Courthouse on July 19th. Nathaniel was pleased to hear from his committee chair, Judge Anderson, that a majority of townships were planning to send delegations.

On the appointed day an impressive number of representatives from various townships arrived at Monmouth Courthouse where they were greeted by Judge Anderson and the rest of the committee of Lower Freehold. Nathaniel was relieved to see that enough towns were represented that the proceedings could be said to have a clear democratic legitimacy.

"Welcome, gentlemen, welcome to this important meeting," began Judge Anderson, "As you know, we are gathered here today to discuss how best we can defend our liberties that are so clearly threatened by the government's actions in Boston. Many of us feel that our best hope is to organize as broad a coalition as possible to enforce a boycott that will force the government to repeal some of its unjust legislation. The floor is now open to hear suggestions about how best to proceed."

John Taylor, a delegate from Shrewsbury and former sheriff took the floor.

"While I agree that the events in Boston are a grave threat to our liberties, we must be careful not to give the impression that we are challenging royal authority. It is important to emphasize that we are firm supporters of law and order and do not intend to set up a rival government."

"It is precisely because we respect British law and our glorious constitution, that we are forced to act," countered Nathaniel, "It is the Board of Trade who is trampling on British rights that have been sacred since the time of the Magna Carta. It is our duty as loyal Britons to make sure that that does not succeed. That is our patriotic duty to God, king, and country and to our posterity."

"Well said, Dr. Scudder," agreed Captain John Covenhoven, "We are loyal to the system established by the Glorious Revolution, and it is our fervent desire that in a Protestant succession the descendants of the illustrious House of Hanover may continue to sway the British scepter to the latest posterity. This should be included in any resolutions that this meeting formulates."

"Agreed but we also should make clear to the Board of Trade that economic cooperation is as at least as important to them as it is to us," added Peter Forman, one of the delegates from Lower Freehold, "We have economic power that we can organize so they should not think that they can coerce us into accepting any new form of slavery such as they are trying to impose on the people of Boston!"

"I agree entirely with Peter Forman," said Nathaniel, "We have power, and we will have to use it. But we should not have any illusions about the possible consequences. Everything depends on our ability to present a united front. A few days ago, I had the opportunity to discuss this with President Witherspoon in Princeton. In his view the Continental Congress that we are building from the ground up has the primary goal to unite the colonies and make them as one body, in any measure of self-defense, to assure the people of Great Britain that we will not submit voluntarily and convince them that it would be either impossible or unprofitable for them to compel us by open violence. He is convinced that Americans do deliberately prefer war with all its horrors and even extermination itself to slavery, riveted on us and our posterity."

The room fell silent, and Nathaniel realized that many delegates were as taken aback as he had been when he first heard Witherspoon utter these opinions. But in the meantime, he had realized that Witherspoon had already understood what many were still repressing, that they had to be prepared to counter violence with violence if need be or otherwise submit to slavery.

"Well, let's hope that it does not come to that," Edward Taylor, a delegate from Middletown, finally broke the silence, "I, for one, am confident that reason will prevail, and that when the government in London sees how determined we are, they will reconsider some of their more foolish legislation. In the meantime, we can best encourage people to unite for an effective boycott by showing our solidarity with the suffering people of Boston through concrete measures. I say let's collect what provisions we can and ship them to our friends in Boston to help alleviate the effects of the port closing. That will also show the government that coercive measures on their part will be met with solidarity on our part."

Murmurs of approval resonated through the meeting with people smiling and nodding to each other, relieved to hear a proposal for positive action short of taking to arms. It was quickly decided to canvass the farms of Monmouth County to hear what they could spare for the suffering inhabitants of Boston.

"An excellent proposal, Mr. Taylor," said Nathaniel, "During my physician's rounds I have occasion to visit many farms. I will be happy to solicit contributions. I am also sure that many in Reverend Tennent's congregation will be more than happy to fulfill their Christian duty."

Taylor's proposal galvanized the meeting and a consensus emerged for a list of nine resolutions to be published as the result of the deliberations. While proclaiming loyalty to George III and to the British constitution, the document promised spirited resistance to the repression of basic British liberties and pledged support for the new Continental Congress to coordinate that resistance. It also offered every assistance and alleviation to the people of Boston. The meeting appointed a committee of 11 delegates to the Provincial Congress to be chaired by Edward Taylor and including John Anderson, Nathaniel Scudder, and John Covenhoven from Lower Freehold. Just a few weeks later they all travelled to New Brunswick to nominate New Jersey's five delegates to the upcoming Continental Congress which was scheduled to meet for the first time in Philadelphia on the 5th of September.

Nathaniel's role in this remarkable process was the topic of excited conversations at Anderson Manor between Nathaniel, Isabella, Colonel Anderson, and Reverend Tennent.

"Well, tell me, Nathaniel," asked Colonel Anderson, "Do you think that the people representing New Jersey are going to stand up to the Board of Trade? I was pleased to hear that three of the five are from Elizabethtown so East Jersey will be strongly represented."

"Some are more likely than others to favor rigorous measures," replied Nathaniel, "I think there is broad agreement that an effective boycott has to be implemented but it is difficult to say just how far people will be willing to go. The two from West Jersey, Richard Smith and James Kinsey, are both Quakers so they cannot be expected to take up arms if it comes to that. Of the three from Elizabethtown, John De Hart, Stephen Crane, and William Livingston, only Livingston seems to be really aggressive in his defense of liberty."

"That does not surprise me," remarked Colonel Anderson with a smirk, "The Livingston clan has been making a fortune for years in the smuggling business and is probably feeling the pinch of the Crown's anti-smuggling initiatives."

"Now, now, Kenneth, you should not be so cynical," reproved Reverend Tennent, "The important thing is to keep a united front, and we can be happy that we have such an energetic advocate in the person of William Livingston, even if he is an Anglican."

"We all hope that reconciliation will still be possible," said Nathaniel, "But as President Witherspoon has convinced me, we must be prepared for the eventuality that the British government will continue to try to use force to make us accept the curtailment of our liberties. Our only hope of success is to make them believe that we are prepared to go to any lengths to prevent our reduction to slavery."

"Men always think that only the threat of violence can be effective," objected Isabella, "In my view sincere demonstrations of solidarity can be just as effective. How is it going anyway with our campaign to solicit aid for the suffering inhabitants of Boston?"

"In fact, it is going very well," answered Nathaniel brightly, "Everyone I talked to on my rounds has indicated a willingness to contribute at harvest time. The rye harvest seems to be particularly good this year so I think we will be able to offer significant assistance in a few weeks."

"That is my impression as well," agreed Reverend Tennent, "People in our congregation have already asked me where they could store their contributions for Boston. Based on the amounts already offered I think we are talking about hundreds of bushels of rye and rye meal."

"I will be happy to let them store it all at Anderson Manor," offered Colonel Anderson enthusiastically, "We can store it in our barns until we can organize transportation to Boston. If every county can help in this way, the government will at least not be able to starve the people of Boston into submission."

The level of excitement increased by the day as everyone awaited the convening of the First Continental Congress, the first officially elected body that could represent all the colonies. It was thus with particular anticipation that the Scudder family prepared to attend the commencement exercises at Nassau Hall that September. They not only wanted to enroll their son Joseph in his first semester of studies but also wanted to hear how people in the Princeton community were reacting to the unfolding drama. They also knew that in addition to staunch Whig Presbyterians there would also be a contingent of Tories including Governor Franklin in attendance. It promised to be a stimulating exchange of ideas.

The tameness of the commencement addresses belied an undercurrent of barely suppressed rebelliousness among the students.

"Don't be deceived by the peaceful facade," John Scudder whispered to his parents, "The students who wanted to express their outrage at the intolerable acts of Parliament have been forbidden to speak by the Trustees. All the students hope that the new congress will unite us for determined resistance to this tyranny."

After the formal parts of the ceremony were concluded many of the participants remained to discuss the prospects for political change in the coming months.

"I, for one, am cautiously optimistic," opined Governor Franklin, "I think that we have an opportunity for positive movement here. I have suggested that Crown representatives attend this congress as well and work with the delegates to forge a compromise that will benefit all. There are people in attendance such as Joseph Galloway that have proposed some very creative solutions and the Crown would do well to seize the opportunity for realistic negotiation."

"I fear it is the Crown's ministers who need a dose of realism," contradicted President Witherspoon, "To my knowledge, the Crown has not sent any representatives nor are they likely to. Your father seems to be of the opinion that only determined resistance can sway the people in charge right now."

"My father is getting old and is worn down by the difficult tasks that have confronted him in recent years," explained Franklin, "It is understandable that he is frustrated by the intransigence of some of the people he has had to deal with. But I have assured him that if he were here instead of in London, he would experience the same sort of skullduggery and venality that he complains about over there. In fact, I have urged him to move back here to get a more balanced perspective. I am sure that if he would come back, he would understand that peaceful reconciliation is the only viable alternative."

"But a good compromise will only be forthcoming if we negotiate from a position of strength," objected Nathaniel, "Right now the king's ministers seem to think that we can be bullied into submission by military force. We must, therefore, also employ force, in this case economic force, to show them that we have the means to resist effectively."

"And we must also demonstrate our solidarity with the suffering inhabitants of Boston," added Isabella, "We will not permit our brethren to be starved into submission!"

Taken aback by such defiant words, especially coming from such an elegant lady as Isabella, Governor Franklin was for the moment almost at a loss for words.

"But, but…" he stammered, "The Crown cannot just sit idly by and watch a bunch of rowdies break the law by destroying private property. At the very least, the town of

Boston should offer to compensate the East India Company for the loss of the tea. If they did that, I am certain that the port closure would be quickly reversed."

"If they did that, they would be sanctioning unconstitutional measures that fly in the face of our basic liberties," argued Witherspoon, "But it is not only the port closure that is at issue. For me personally the Quebec Act is at least as heinous. Why this empowers Papists more than anything that has happened since before the Glorious Revolution! And giving the Ohio Country back to the French is just as scandalous. Don't you realize that this also puts an end to your own Vandalia project?"

Franklin face reddened with anger as Witherspoon touched on an issue which was indeed an extremely sore subject for him. For years he had been dreaming of the independence that a successful Vandalia project would have afforded him but for the thuggish actions of some fanatics in Boston.

"All this would not have happened!" exclaimed Franklin, "Not the port closure, not the Quebec Act nor the other acts that so rile the inhabitants of these colonies, had not some reckless extremists taken the law into their own hands. It is of the utmost importance for the good of the empire that such mob rule be crushed. I am for compromise but as a loyal servant of the Crown, I will not conscience such flagrant violation of law and order."

Franklin stamped angrily out of Nassau Hall followed by some of his Tory associates.

"It seems the governor is trying to defend the use of violence against citizens who are only trying to protect basic British liberties," remarked Witherspoon.

"Indeed," agreed Nathaniel, "Up until now we colonists have proposed nothing more than peaceful boycotts."

"To the extent that the boycotts are effective the temptation to use force will surely increase," said Isabella forebodingly, "I fear this is all going to end in violent confrontation."

"It doesn't have to come to that," Nathaniel tried to assuage Isabella's anxieties, "If the Continental Congress demonstrates a convincing show of unity of purpose, perhaps the government will come to its senses."

"In any case we will soon see whether the thesis of Franklin son or Franklin father is the more realistic, will it be reconciliation or resistance?" mused Witherspoon.

This dichotomy reflected exactly the two sides that met for seven weeks in September and October. A conservative faction led by Joseph Galloway favored the former course, while a more radical faction led by Patrick Henry strived for a more decisive statement of the rights and liberties of the colonies. Although Galloway's favored "Plan of Union" was not passed, the forces of reconciliation dominated the final outcome of Congress's deliberations. It was agreed to send a formal petition to the king for repeal of the "Intolerable Acts" and to begin to boycott British goods from the 1st of December 1774. The West Indies were threatened with a boycott if they did not join in the non-importation of British goods. Committees of observation and inspection were to be set up in every colony to enforce the boycott. Should the "Intolerable Acts" not be repealed, the colonies would cease all exports to Britain after the 10th of September 1775. In addition to the details of the embargo, the Congress also provided for a Second Continental Congress to meet the following May.

Despite the relatively conciliatory tone of Congress's petition the threat of a boycott beginning already in a few weeks raised the anxiety level throughout the colonies. It also provoked a desire for action especially among the younger men. John, visiting his parents in the late fall, described the mood of students and recent graduates of Nassau Hall.

"I think that most of us are ready to take up arms if our liberties are at stake," he informed his parents, "The British government should not deceive itself into thinking that we will just accede to tyranny."

"Now listen to me, young man," admonished Isabella irritably, "There is no point in rushing to arms. Right now we are still hoping that peaceful measures will be enough to convince the government to relent. And some of our peaceful initiatives have already born fruit. Haven't they, Nathaniel?"

"Yes, indeed, my dear," replied Nathaniel, "Our committee of correspondence just received a very gracious letter from the Bostonians in which they thank us for having sent eleven hundred and forty bushels of rye and fifty barrels of rye meal for the suffering poor of the town. It is this kind of solidarity that will convince the British that we have formed a solid front to defend our liberties."

"I think more than charity will be necessary to convince the British," argued John, "And many people I know feel the same. Two students from the Class of 1772, Philip Fithian and Andrew Hunter, recently lead a group of about 40 patriots to a re-enactment of the Boston Tea Party but this time at Cohausey Creek."

"That is quite irresponsible!" scolded Isabella, "The more private property is wantonly destroyed, the more difficult it will be for the British to accept a compromise!"

"Your mother is quite right, John," agreed Nathaniel, "The tea party at Cohausey Creek is a direct challenge to the authority of Governor Franklin. He is a stickler for law and order, and he cannot just ignore such provocations. It will give him a good excuse to organize measures that undermine our boycott."

"He would have done that anyhow," replied John, "The boycott will cause pain for merchants who import goods from Great Britain, and the governor was always likely to side with them."

"I am afraid you are right on that count, son," continued Nathaniel, "In fact Franklin's recent move to Amboy would seem to indicate that the governor is bolstering his support by appeal to the proprietary and merchant elite."

"So how are you going to stop the merchants of Amboy from buying whatever they want in Britain and importing it to America?" asked John.

"There is no point in their importing goods if they can't sell them here, and that is how we propose to interrupt their commerce," explained Nathaniel, "We will keep an eye on which merchants are importing from Britain and then encourage our people to boycott them. In fact, at the next meeting of the Committee of Correspondence we are planning to implement one of the decisions of the Continental Congress and organize a Committee of Observation and Inspection to accomplish exactly that."

A few weeks later the Freehold Township Committee of Correspondence again chaired by Judge Anderson met to decide how the boycott could be effectively enforced. In response to Judge Anderson's call for suggestions a young man who had not been in attendance at previous meetings boldly took the floor.

"Some of you don't know me yet because I have spent the last few years in Maryland, but my name is David Forman, and I would like to offer my services to help force all the merchants in this colony to adhere strictly to the boycott that the Continental Congress has decreed. In my opinion we have to deal very severely with anyone who chooses not to cooperate."

Nathaniel was impressed by the determination that the young man exhibited although somewhat concerned about the aggressiveness of his tone. He knew many members of the Forman clan, but he was not quite sure where this one fit in. He remembered vaguely hearing from Reverend Tennent about a brash young Forman cousin who had attended the college in Princeton for a time but then had to drop out because of an affair with a young lady whom he eventually married. That story was certainly in keeping with the energetic but impulsive demeanor that seemed to characterize David Forman.

"I think we all agree that pressure will have to be applied to enforce maximum compliance with the resolutions of the Continental Congress," replied Judge Anderson, "But exactly to what extent that is necessary remains to be seen. It is to be hoped that the great majority of our fellow citizens will voluntarily adhere to the measures necessary to protect our liberties."

"The first thing we need to do," added Nathaniel, "is to organize a committee to gather all the information necessary to monitor the compliance with the boycott. The boycott of imports from England began officially just ten days ago. We first need to ascertain just how much is still being imported and by whom. Then we can propose measures to convince those who are still importing goods that such behavior is inimical to our liberties."

Nathaniel's reasoned and systematic approach met with the approval of most of the gentlemen in attendance but elicited an expression of slight annoyance from David Forman.

"Of course, we need to gather accurate information," conceded Forman with a note of impatience in his voice, "But I can tell you right now there are many enemies of liberty that are not particularly difficult to identify. I recently overheard a conversation among a group of merchants from Shrewsbury, and they are planning to ignore Congress's request to form a Committee of Observation and Inspection. They are getting fat through the importation and sale of British goods, and they have no intention of cooperating with anything that could reduce their prosperity."

"That may well be," agreed Judge Anderson, "And they are certainly not the only ones. That is the reason we need to appoint the committee right away and let them get to work. I would nominate all of the current members of the committee of correspondence and, in addition, David Forman whose zeal for rooting out the enemies of liberty will stand us in good stead."

Anderson's suggestions were adopted unanimously. As the Committee of Observation and Inspection took up its work over the next few weeks it became quickly clear that David Forman had been correct in identifying the merchants of Shrewsbury as harboring Tory sentiments. Moreover, it began to appear that the merchants of Shrewsbury were not alone and that there were plenty more Americans who would resist the boycott if it created financial hardship for them. The hope that most colonists would support the boycott out of a patriotic desire to protect liberty turned out to be somewhat naive. Clearly those who would not cooperate would have to be forced in some way but the question confronting the committee was what means would lead to the desired end? If exhortation and shaming were not effective, would violence be necessary? And if the number of resisters turned out to be significant, would the resources available to the Committee be sufficient?

The impression that resistance to Congress's resolutions might indeed turn out to be more widespread than the Whigs had hoped was enhanced by the determined campaign of Governor Franklin to undermine the legitimacy of both Congress and the committees that were everywhere being formed. The governor convened the Assembly in January for the first time in nine months and made a valiant attempt to portray the developing events as a danger to the esteemed British constitution that was the source of the Assembly's own legitimacy. While avoiding commenting on the substantive issues that divided America and England, he sought to caution them about the dangers that could result from mob rule by a bunch of self-selected zealots.

"If you give these misguided malcontents your approbation," he warned slyly, "you will do as much as lies in your power to destroy that form of government of which you are an important part. You cannot without a manifest breach of your trust suffer any body of men in this or any of the other provinces to usurp and exercise any of the powers vested in you by the constitution."

Feeling encouraged by murmurs of approval from some of the Assemblymen Franklin continued, "You have now pointed out to you, gentlemen, two roads—one evidently leading to peace, happiness, and a restoration of the public tranquility—the other inevitably conducting you to anarchy, misery, and all the horrors of a civil war."

Franklin felt encouraged by the Assembly's apparent acceptance of his argument about the importance of their legitimacy, but most Assemblymen saw no great contradiction between their goals and the goals of the committees. They were also quite prepared to support the convening of a 2nd Continental Congress. Although Franklin

knew that the Board of Trade would want all royal governors to discourage the sending of delegates to the 2nd Continental Congress, he also realized that this was already
a hopeless cause. He did not have the military resources in New Jersey to forcibly
suppress the activities of the committees. In fact, the only guarantee of his personal
safety was the fact that he now lived in Proprietary House in Amboy amidst many
Crown sympathizers. The only thing he could do to shore up the eroding power of the
Crown was to try and restrict the flow of munitions into the colony. Other than that,
he could only helplessly watch how the Committees of Observation and Inspection
pursed their goals in an increasingly aggressive fashion and report the details back to
Lord Dartmouth.

Franklin's efforts to encourage the publication of pamphlets critical of Congress
and supportive of the Crown's position also met with determined resistance. In March
the Freehold Committee of Observation and Inspection met to discuss a Tory pamphlet that had been passed to them for their opinion. It was entitled "Free Thoughts
on the Resolves of Congress" by one A.W. Farmer.

"This is the most pernicious and malignant piece of garbage I have ever read,"
raged David Forman, "It is clearly calculated to sap the foundations of American
liberty!"

"I quite agree," concurred Nathaniel, "It tries to weaken the very institution that
has the broadest support among the people."

"You are both correct, but the question is what are we going to do about it?"
asked Judge Anderson, "It is already in circulation so we cannot prevent people from
reading it, and the author does not live in our area so we cannot call him into account."

"But we can inform the public what we think about it," argued David Forman, "I
say we give it coat of tar and turkey buzzard feathers and nail it to the pillory post. The
feathers plucked from the most stinking of fowls will show everyone how odious we
consider these words from the enemies of liberty to be and what we will do to anyone
we can catch who dares to express such opinions."

The committee agreed unanimously to deal with that and similar pamphlets in
such manner and moved on to the next topics on the agenda, the refusal of Shrewsbury to meet the request of the Continental Congress to form a Committee of Observation and Inspection.

"I have said from the beginning that most of the Shrewsbury merchants are Tory
sympathizers," declared David Forman, "I say, if they refuse to appoint a committee,
we appoint one for them. I am sure we can find enough loyal patriots in that town to
take up our cause."

"Not a bad idea, David," remarked Nathaniel, "But we need to seek some sort
of democratic legitimacy. We cannot just arbitrarily say that we speak for the good
citizens of Shrewsbury."

"Nathaniel has a point," agreed Judge Anderson, "Let's take it up with the Provincial Congress when it meets. We can signal that we are willing to step in if Shrewsbury

shirks its responsibilities and if that body authorizes us to proceed, we can claim democratic legitimacy."

"This is just going to waste more time," retorted David Forman impatiently, "It is precisely in places like Shrewsbury where the boycott will be ignored. That is where we need to get started right away exposing the enemies of liberty!"

Although the older men in the committee could not help but admire Forman's zeal, they nevertheless agreed that democratic authorization was worth a certain time delay and resolved to wait for a decision of the Provincial Congress.

Later relating the incident to Isabella, Nathaniel explained his misgivings about David Forman's aggressive attitude.

"He is an admirable patriot," began Nathaniel, "But he is young and hot-headed. Sometimes I think he sees us already at war with Great Britain, although what we are trying to achieve is a compromise."

"It would be a shame if one young man's overzealous behavior would undermine the solidarity of our society," said Isabella, "There are plenty of people who are enraged at the high-handedness of the Board of Trade but would not go as far as to condone armed resistance to Crown authority."

"That is exactly our dilemma right now," continued Nathaniel, "In order to force a compromise we must present as broad a front as possible but also convince the authorities that we are resolved to go to any lengths to preserve our liberties. On the other hand, it would be a catastrophe if it would actually come to bloodshed, and many who now support us would abandon the cause."

"Particularly now when we have reason to believe that the threat of a success-ful boycott might be achieving its goal. My father told me that acquaintances of his close to Governor Franklin have indicated that the North Ministry is preparing just such a compromise proposal which could really achieve reconciliation between the colonies and the mother country. Apparently, they are even willing to retreat on their insistence on Parliament's right to tax the colonies."

"God knows I hope that that this rumor is true," answered Nathaniel, "But if it is, then why is it that the royal governors are doing their best to restrict the shipment of powder and ball to our militias? Given the dangers we constantly face from Indians and slave revolts, they must realize that effectively disarming our militias is something we could never tolerate."

"Perhaps they are trying a dual policy, the cudgel in one hand and an olive branch in the other," suggested Isabella, "The cudgel is probably directed at Massachusetts which the British government alleges is in open rebellion."

"Yes, indeed," agreed Nathaniel, "Our committee has received delegates from Boston who warned us that General Gage plans to disarm the local militias and seize their munitions. They propose that other colonies call up their militias and prepare for common defense."

"In that case let's hope that the olive branch that Governor Franklin wants to present is credible enough to stop this slide toward violence," concluded Isabella with trepidation.

The hopes of Nathaniel and Isabella for a peaceful reconciliation turned out to be doomed to disappointment. Unbeknownst to them at that time Secretary of State William Legge, Earl of Dartmouth, had already sent secret orders to Gage to disarm the rebels and to imprison their leaders. Gage decided to act on the 18th of April sending out a detachment of soldiers to seize the militia's military supplies at Concord and arrest their leaders. Warned by spies, the local militias turned out to defy them. The first confrontation at Lexington resulted in deaths on both sides. The situation quickly escalated as more and more militia units highly motivated by the exhortations of their Calvinist preachers joined the rebel ranks. The outnumbered Regulars were forced to retreat under constant and costly harassment to Boston where they were effectively cut off from the rest of the colony. The catastrophe that Nathaniel had feared had come to pass.

Chapter 18

The Midnight Ride – 1775–1776

A FEW DAYS AFTER receiving the news about Lexington and Concord Nathaniel and Isabella were awakened by a loud knocking on their front door. Nathaniel opened the door to see David Forman decked out in a militia officer's uniform.

"Nat, it is time to act, you need to put on your militia uniform and get ready to march," David Forman said excitedly, "There is a British man-of-war at Sandy Hook, and we suspect that Franklin will try to abscond with the colony's treasury and escape to that ship. We must stop him."

"But David, why would he abscond right now?" asked Isabella, "He has just called a meeting of the Assembly to present the British government's latest proposal for reconciliation. He obviously still hopes that he can still save the situation."

"It all could just be a bluff," retorted David Forman, "He knows that blood has been spilled and he also knows that he does not have enough military resources here to protect him if it comes to bloodshed here. He is probably just biding his time waiting for a chance to slip away taking our tax money with him. Some Whig patriots have already begun taking control of New York City so he can reckon that he does not have much time if he wants to get away."

"David, I think perhaps you are jumping to conclusions," Nathaniel attempted to calm the conversation down, "Have you any concrete indication that the governor is preparing to flee?"

"The treasury has been stolen once before," answered Forman hotly, "Many of us suspect that Franklin had something to do with that then, so it does not require a great stretch of the imagination to believe he is planning something similar again. We also know that he is a hide-bound Tory in his heart of hearts and that he is a spy for those who would oppress us!"

"My father and his associates firmly believe that the governor is really planning to present the government plan on the 16th of May, and I think it is important to hear him out," argued Isabella, "He is after all still the governor until competent authority declares otherwise."

"Don't you understand?" cried Forman, "He has already chosen sides. He has chosen to be our enemy! And he can do untold harm to the cause of liberty if we let him escape! He is already attempting to emasculate our militia by making it more difficult for us to procure munitions. The only question right now is who has the courage of his convictions to fight for liberty while we still can! Nat, are you marching with us or not?"

Nathaniel and Isabella looked at each other dumbfounded by Forman's ultimatum. Both suspected that Forman was exaggerating the situation, but, on the other hand, the events in Massachusetts made anything possible. After a few minutes of deliberation Nathaniel turned to David Forman and replied, "David, I will come with you, but primarily in my capacity as a physician. I believe that any military action against the governor is premature and must be authorized by the Provincial Congress, but I am willing to do my part and bind the wounds of our Whig patriots if it should actually come to violence."

Turning to an anxious Isabella he murmured in a lowered voice, "I will also try to see to it that our young bucks don't do anything rash."

Nathaniel had a servant saddle up one his best horses and taking his physician's bag rode off to join the 30 odd Monmouth militia men headed for Sandy Hook. Eventually they arrived at a bluff overlooking Sandy Hook where one of David Forman's lookouts was posted peering through a telescope at a mid-size British man-of-war anchored a short distance in front ot the Hook.

"Anything new, Sam?" David Forman queried the look-out, "Do they look like they're fixing to come our way?"

"Don't seem so, sir," answered the look-out, "Seems like there just here to pick up Tories fleeing New York City."

"That would make sense since our patriots seem to be taking control of the city," said Forman, "I would not mind giving those Tories a fiery sendoff."

"Tell me, Sam," asked Nathaniel, "How many cannons do you count on the side of the ship you can see?"

"About 30, Dr. Scudder," answered Sam.

"And how many seamen?

"There must be hundreds."

Turning to David Forman, Nathaniel asked, "And David how many cannons do we have up here on the bluff?"

"I can have a few swivel guns up here within a half hour," answered Forman defensively.

"David, that ship is not going to be within range of swivels from up here. Firing at that ship would be like poking your finger into a hornets' nest," counseled Nathaniel, "Those cannons on the ship would sweep our 30 men off this bluff in a matter of minutes. Then a swarm of armed seamen would race up here and finish the job. Governor Franklin's entourage is nowhere to be seen. The ship is obviously here for other reasons, and there is no reason for us to provoke an armed confrontation."

The militiamen within hearing range all nodded their heads in agreement with Nathaniel. David Forman had to accept that he would not be able to reach a consensus among the men to attack the ship.

"All right," agreed Forman reluctantly, "We certainly don't want to waste our powder until we have a better tactical advantage. But I don't trust Franklin. I say we march back through Amboy past his house to discourage any ideas he might have of absconding. But, Sam, you stay here and keep your eye on that ship. If there is any movement in our direction, send a rider immediately."

Thus the raggedy little band of militia men marched off in the direction of Amboy. Reaching Proprietary House, they marched defiantly by as a perplexed William Franklin peered out of his window wondering if he could really count on the Assembly's assurance that Crown officials would be protected from mob actions.

Arriving back in Freehold, Forman sought to impress on the militiamen that the emergency was not over.

"The governor apparently has not yet chosen to flee but we still need to keep an eye on him," Forman warned. "He is undoubtedly scheming with his fellow Tories on how best to rob us of our liberties."

"Well, we will have a good opportunity to keep an eye on him because he is scheduled to address the Assembly in a few days to present the latest proposals from our British lords and masters," Nathaniel reminded the men, "In the meantime we need to get the process of militia formation under control. It was clear at the Hook that we would not have stood a chance against the armed seamen from that man-of-war. We would need to recruit and arm a lot more men. Militias are springing up everywhere, but they need to be coordinated under the control of the Provincial Congress."

"Some of those militias are Tory formations that want to help Britain enslave us," Forman asserted, "We need to smoke them out and confront them for the traitors that they are!"

"I am afraid there might be some truth to what you are saying," conceded Nathaniel, "We were not able to convince the merchants of Shrewsbury to appoint a committee of observation and inspection, so we had to accept an alternative committee. It is not clear how much more resistance we can expect."

"Expect a lot more resistance," assured Forman, "And soon of the armed variety. My spies inform me that a certain Captain Henry Waddell is forming a grenadier company to protect the rights of merchants who want to continue trading with the mother country."

"That is outrageous!" exclaimed Nathaniel, "We can't permit the formation of militias that are not under the authority of the Provincial Congress. That is a recipe for civil war!"

"Then civil war it must be," concluded Forman, "And the governor is surreptitiously pulling the strings of his Tory puppets. The sooner we end his treachery, the better."

"I will try to reason with this Waddell," suggested Nathaniel, "I will outline the principles of legal militia formation as we see it. Perhaps we can convince them to accept the authority of the Provincial Congress."

"I think you are wasting your time," argued Forman, "But go right ahead. They will undoubtedly refuse but that will give us clear proof of their treachery. Mark my words, Nathaniel, we will be fighting these people one day."

Nathaniel still hoped that Forman was wrong but could not ignore a growing feeling of foreboding that he might not be. A few weeks later he had the opportunity to sound out his father-in-law on the subject.

"We are encountering quite a lack of cooperation from the merchants of Shrewsbury in implementing Congress's decisions," explained Nathaniel to Colonel Anderson, "Some of my militia colleagues suspect that Governor Franklin might be secretly organizing armed resistance to the decrees of Congress. Publicly he presents suggestions for reconciliation. What do you think, sir, is he seriously interested in peaceful solutions or is he treacherous?"

"It is clear that he is a loyal servant of the Crown and regards Congress as an illegitimate usurper of authority. He has openly warned the Assembly not to concede its constitutional powers to it. But when he presented North's latest plan to the Assembly, they decided to his chagrin to defer to Congress. His situation was not helped by an embarrassing letter revealed by Samuel Tucker in which Franklin rudely criticized Congress. And now his father is back and is rumored to have become an ardent supporter of the radical Whig position. Apparently, a meeting organized by Joseph Galloway for them to iron out their differences did not turn out to the younger Franklin's liking because his father openly revealed his preference for a full break with Britain."

"Good Lord!" exclaimed Nathaniel, "That must have been a shock for the governor. First the Assembly refuses to heed him, and then his own father goes over to the opposition."

"Indeed," agreed Colonel Anderson, "One could almost feel sorry for him because he really believes that the latest North plan is a basis for reconciliation. But his father only scoffed at it. And all that coming on top of the disaster for the British at Ticonderoga. One can imagine the kind of anxiety he is feeling right now. I am sure he is keeping Lord North well supplied with any information he might be able to garner but I don't think that he is actively organizing armed opposition to Congress just yet. I have no doubt, however, that he might do that if the situation from his standpoint continues to deteriorate. Right now, however, I think he still hopes that he might be able to salvage some of his authority and help engineer a peace agreement."

Militias loyal to the Crown such as Waddell's grenadier corps flatly refused to allow themselves to be integrated into a command structure loyal to the Provincial

Congress. By the end of the summer the king had declared the colonies to be in "open and avowed rebellion" and encouraged all loyal subjects "to use their utmost endeavors to withstand and suppress such rebellion." He also demanded that anyone carrying on "traitorous correspondence" be reported and punished. George III had obviously opted for a military solution to the problem.

The intransigent stance of the British government had the effect of hardening positions among the colonists as well. As the level of violence increased people felt pressured to clarify their positions. Many who would have preferred a negotiated solution were suddenly in danger of being labeled criminal by the Crown and disloyal by the Whigs. People who would never have dreamt of leaving the empire, now had to think hard about which side they were really on if they were forced to choose.

The clarification process was particularly dramatic regarding militia units. Nathaniel and the Committee of Observation and Inspection never doubted that the Provincial Congress had the ultimate authority over militia activities. They soon had to acknowledge, however, that units existed whose primary loyalty was to the Crown. Nathaniel was very pleased, therefore, when the Township Assessor in Middletown, George Taylor, called for a meeting to organize a Whig militia which was to be explicitly loyal to the Provincial Congress. After all the altercation with the Tory sympathizers of Shrewsbury it was a relief to hear of someone from that general area who seemed to be willing to defend the Whig cause. Nathaniel did not know much about him other than that he was the son of Edward Taylor, a prominent member of the New Jersey Assembly, who as a member of the Monmouth Committee of Correspondence had played a leading role in organizing aid for the struggling citizens of Boston. Some suspected that the Taylors as wealthy, landowning Anglicans might harbor Tory sympathies. Although they were on record as advocates of equal rights for colonists regarding taxation and representation, they were known to be firmly opposed to any notion of independence. George Taylor had also publicly opposed efforts lead by some Quakers last year to make it easier to manumit slaves in New Jersey. Nathaniel assumed, therefore, that he was basically a conservative, probably close to Proprietor circles, who was interested in maintaining the status quo as much as possible. Nathaniel was intrigued by the prospect of winning such a person over to the Whig cause. Someone like George Taylor could be a bridge between the Presbyterian Whigs in the Freehold area and the more Tory-prone Anglicans of the coast. In July Taylor had organized 48 Monmouthers into a local militia loyal to the Provincial Congress. The newly formed militia then elected him as their first captain. Now Taylor was calling for a meeting to expand the militia to include all of Monmouth County. Nathaniel decided that he definitely had to attend.

The meeting took place at Monmouth Courthouse in September. The leading citizens of most of the towns of Monmouth County were in attendance. As the organizer of the meeting George Taylor was the first to speak.

"Dear friends," he began, "Thank you all for answering my call to stand up for British liberties. You all know that my family are steadfast believers in the importance of maintaining both the liberties of the Glorious Revolution and our loyalty to George III."

Sitting next to Nathaniel, David Forman muttered in a low voice, "Good luck on squaring that circle. George III just declared all of us to be in open rebellion. He has ordered his lackeys to lock us up at the first opportunity."

Despite the murmurs emanating from attendees like David Forman, Taylor continued undeterred, "If we present a united front, it is still possible that we can bring the king's ministers who have so egregiously misinformed our Sovereign to their senses. For this reason, it is essential that we have a unitary command structure for our militias. We all need to march by the beat of the same drum and that drum shall be the Provincial Congress."

At that last sentence the crowd broke out into spontaneous applause. Even the more radical Whigs in the audience could agree on the importance of clearly establishing the authority of the Provincial Congress. Nathaniel was convinced that here was a man who could forge unity among the disparate factions of Monmouth County.

"I for one support George Taylor's initiative and would happily volunteer to serve in this militia." Nathaniel announced enthusiastically, "I propose that we elect him to be our colonel."

"I am pleased to sign up as well," David Forman joined in, "And I propose we elect Nathaniel Scudder as Lieutenant Colonel."

Most of the able-bodied men at the meeting quickly volunteered. A roster of additional officers was proposed and elected by acclamation. The militia of Monmouth County was now under a unified command loyal to the Provincial Congress. Militia units not integrated into the unified command were to be considered illegitimate and to be regarded as potential enemies.

In order to demonstrate his solidarity with the Whig movement Nathaniel decided to attend the commencement at Nassau Hall later that month in his militia uniform. His oldest son, John, would be receiving his degree at that ceremony and his second son, Joseph, having just finished his first year at Nassau Hall, would also be in attendance. In front of the boys Nathaniel wanted to make a public statement about where he stood regarding the burning issues of the day. He was pleased to see that many of the students including his sons were also decked out in military attire. The pall of war hung over the campus and there was much talk about girding one's loins for possible bloodshed. Gone were the restrictions on students' orations which now included such topics as "The Pernicious Effects of Arbitrary Power" and "The Growth and Decline of Empires."

After the ceremony a slightly distraught Isabella asked President Witherspoon where he thought all this would lead.

"I must say, President Witherspoon, I am a bit shocked at the martial tone of some of the students' addresses," began Isabella, "Would it not be better to encourage them to help find peaceful solutions to our problems?"

"I am afraid that the British Parliament is not interested in peaceful solutions," explained Witherspoon, "The corrupt people currently in control in London obviously want to frighten us out of standing up for our Whig liberties. We cannot let that happen. We should be proud of our young men's willingness to shed blood for the cause of freedom, and I am pleased that our Presbyterian brethren everywhere seem to be taking the lead in this movement. If separation from Britain is the only way we can guarantee our freedom to practice the True Religion, then that is God's will, and we must accept the challenge."

"I am afraid that some of our Presbyterian brethren on the frontier, especially those recently arrived from the Borderlands, are more interested in murdering the Indians and stealing their land than in defending the True Religion," remarked Isabella, "I am not sure we should make common cause with such ruffians."

"You are correct, Mrs. Scudder, that not all have laudable motives," conceded Witherspoon, "But at the end of the day, they are mostly Presbyterians who accept the authority of the True Religion. The influx of settlers into the western lands is a flood that cannot be stopped, so it is our responsibility, albeit a heavy one, to assume the leadership. I believe that our college has a holy mission to produce people who can guide those settlers back to the path of righteousness."

"President Witherspoon is quite right, mother," opined John who together with Joseph had been listening to the conversation, "Everyone would prefer a peaceful solution but not at the price of slavery! The British are clearly trying to annul the gains of the Glorious Revolution which was fought to prevent the Papists from regaining control of our religion. If we let outrages like the Quebec Act stand, then it is only a matter of time until our freedoms are completely extinguished."

"It has already come to bloodshed," said Nathaniel gravely, "As true Christians we must always prefer the peaceful solution, but we must also be ready to fight a holy war for the sake of our religion if that is the will of Providence." Turning to John he asked, "And now, my boy, you have your degree, and you have your medical training, how do you propose to serve God now?"

"I have been told that the militia of Bucks County is looking for a Surgeon's Mate," answered John, "They are on record as being ardent supporters of Congress. With your permission I will volunteer. That way I will get military training and more medical experience."

John's proposal as well as the dramatic militarization of society were the subjects of excited conversations at Anderson Manor over the ensuing weeks.

"I am just as nervous about John's future as you are, Isabella," said Nathaniel, "But I don't see how we can in good conscious discourage John from doing his part to support the militia."

"What about your militia unit, father?" asked Isabella, "Is it also gearing up for war?"

"Most of the men in my unit have signed up for the new formation," answered Colonel Anderson, "And they do that with my blessing. I have recognized George Taylor as the newly elected colonel. I am getting too old for active duty now so I will just participate in an advisory capacity." Smiling at Nathaniel he continued, "Besides I will be well-represented by my son-in-law who, I am proud to say, will take a leading role in this. I am sure that he will maintain the family honor if it should really come to blows. And I am proud that my grandson is answering the call of duty."

Isabella blanched at the thought of Nathaniel and John having to participate in violent actions.

"I still hope that my husband and my son can continue saving lives instead of taking them," said Isabella ruefully, "I understand that we all must show solidarity with the Whig cause, but I can't help hoping that Governor Franklin will be successful in forging some kind of compromise to avoid bloodshed."

"I am afraid that prospect is getting dimmer by the day," replied Nathaniel, "The governor's authority is melting away. Even his old friend, William Alexander, has accepted a commission in Washington's army. He will soon be welcoming General Washington and his wife to a visit in Newark, and there is nothing Governor Franklin can do to stop him. And Alexander is not the only one in the governor's circle to abandon him. He must be feeling very lonely right now."

"That was indeed very surprising to hear that William Alexander has decided to throw in his lot with Washington," remarked Isabella, "Why he was always the epitome of the Proprietor class. I never would have thought that he would make such a daring move."

"It is not as surprising as you might think," explained the colonel, "Alexander has long felt keen resentment because the Crown has refused to recognize his title as Lord Stirling. It is rather like the resentment that Washington felt when the British denied him a commission in the regular army. Besides, Alexander has been living beyond his means for years now, and he probably hopes that he can escape some of the huge debts he has to British merchants. Never forget, my dear, that most men do things for selfish reasons. Washington probably would not have accepted the command of the American army had not Governor Dunmore cancelled the claims to land in the Ohio country of all Virginians who dared to participate in the Continental Congress. Not everyone is as idealistic as your husband and your son."

"Governor Dunmore also provoked Virginia plantation owners by offering freedom to any slaves who were willing to fight for the British cause," added Nathaniel, "Imagine how landowners in New Jersey would react if Governor Franklin attempted to free their servants. Even those who do not share our concern for threats to religious liberty would turn against him. I dare say Franklin would be forced to seek refuge with the Royal Navy just as quickly as Dunmore was."

"I think Nathaniel is right on that score," agreed the Colonel, "I am certain that the fear of emancipation of slaves plays a significant role in the enthusiasm for the Whig cause of people like the Taylor family. Remember that George Taylor vehemently opposed the Quaker initiative last year to make voluntary emancipation of slaves easier in New Jersey. I am sure that as an Anglican he does not care a whit about our freedom to pursue the True Religion. Also he is probably not particularly concerned about the Papist resurgence in Quebec."

"I suppose that depends on whether or not the Taylors have designs on land grants in the Ohio country," continued Nathaniel, "Then, of course, they would also not be pleased that the Catholics of Quebec province have access to that land."

"Greed for land seems to be the defining sentiment on all sides," Isabella noted disgustedly, "Reverend Tennent has warned us many times where this will lead."

"Yes, my dear, but many of the concerns still have some legitimacy," countered Nathaniel, "How would you feel if Governor Franklin promised freedom to our kitchen family if they would volunteer to fight against our militia? And would you rather see the Ohio country settled by Catholic Frenchmen from Quebec province or Presbyterian yeomen?"

"I can't believe that any of our servants would take up arms against us," argued Isabella, "And I can't imagine Governor Franklin would ever propose such a measure."

"Let's hope you are correct on both accounts," said the colonel, "But it is highly uncertain how things will play out as tensions rise. Governor Dunmore at first tried to placate land-hungry Virginians by leading militia raids on the Shawnee. Only when the House of Burgesses became increasingly confrontational on the tax issue, did things escalate. Then he really angered people by having the British army confiscate supplies of powder and ball. This was also the way the conflict developed in Lexington and Concord, and the same thing could happen here. Franklin also tried to restrict our access to military supplies, but he is treading very carefully right now because he does not have the military resources that were available to the governors in Massachusetts or Virginia. In fact, he fears for his life, and has annoyed the Assembly repeatedly with pleas for guarantees of his personal safety."

Over the next few weeks, it became increasingly clear that Franklin had good reason to worry about his personal safety. In the beginning of January Congress issued orders that all "unworthy Americans" be disarmed and, if necessary, incarcerated unless they would swear to abstain from active resistance against the Whig authorities. These orders were interpreted by the Monmouth Committee of Observation and Inspection as a call to proceed aggressively against anyone perceived to be dangerous to the Whig cause.

"As I have said before, it is high time we put an end to the treachery being perpetrated by William Franklin!" David Forman proclaimed to the assembled committee members, "Colonel Lord Stirling has intercepted a bundle of letters from Franklin to Lord Dartmouth marked 'secret and confidential' as well as a letter from Cortlandt

Skinner to his brother. These letters prove beyond doubt that they are both up to no good. He has sent those letters to the Continental Congress in Philadelphia with the recommendation to take action against these Tories."

"Just what is in those letters that could serve as proof of criminal activity?" asked Nathaniel.

"Skinner wrote to his brother who is a British army officer informing him of so-called seditious activities among the colonists and urging military action against us!" replied Forman, "But apparently Franklin was able to warn Skinner in time that Lord Stirling was on his trail so that he was able to escape in a rowboat to a British man-of-war. If he is not guilty, why did he find it necessary to run away? The bloody coward even abandoned his wife and thirteen children in order to save his own hide."

"But Franklin has not attempted to run away, has he?" asked John Covenhoven.

"Not yet," answered Forman, "But that does not prove his innocence. Lord Stirling sent one of his subordinates, Lieutenant Colonel William Winds, with a contingent of militia men to Proprietary House to arrest Franklin to prevent him escaping as well."

"And so is the governor now in custody?" queried John Anderson.

"Unfortunately not," replied Forman with a frustrated sigh, "Franklin defiantly claimed that he had no intention of leaving the colony and threatened Winds with prosecution for treason for attempting to place an officer of the Crown under house arrest. Then the Chief Justice Frederick Smyth galloped up to Proprietary House with a warning that some of the British ships stationed at New York would surely demand the release of the royal governor. Winds was so unnerved that he let Smyth go to see Lord Stirling in order to plead Franklin's case. For reasons that no one can comprehend, Lord Stirling decided to let Franklin stay in Proprietary House."

"Perhaps Lord Stirling did not feel prepared to face military intervention from a British man-of-war just yet," ventured Asher Holmes.

"That could be," agreed Nathaniel, "But maybe the content of Franklin's letters was not subversive enough to establish his guilt. After all, as a royal governor it is his duty to keep Lord Dartmouth informed about events in this colony. He has never made a secret of his belief that the Provincial Congress does not have legitimate political authority and that the Assembly is the only legal legislature."

"We should not be naive," countered Forman hotly, "He is providing information to the British that is militarily relevant and encouraging Tories to aid our enemies. In my view he is no better than a spy and should be treated as such. Remember just last month we confiscated that sloop *Polly & Anne* that was stranded on Squan beach with a cargo of beef, pork, and other provisions. Its captain Haines claimed that the cargo was for sale to colonists but when we tore the labels off the casks and barrels, we found other labels directed to General Howe in Boston. That is a blatant violation of the embargo. Haines intended to put food in the bellies of soldiers who are killing our compatriots! Haines' guilt became even more clear when he subsequently broke jail and fled. Fortunately, we still have the rest of the crew in custody. These are the kinds of rogues that Franklin is aiding and abetting."

"You may be right," conceded John Anderson, "But we still have no concrete proof that Franklin is actively engaged in illegal activities. I suggest that at this point we should simply ask Nathaniel Scudder to draft a request to the New Jersey Council of Safety requesting permission to sell the vessel and its contents and to turn the prisoners over to the Provincial Congress. We will continue to keep an eye on Franklin and the minute we catch him actually committing a crime, we can act."

In keeping with the committee's recommendation Nathaniel with the assistance of his friend and former assistant, Thomas Henderson, formulated a petition to the New Jersey Council of Safety which quickly granted permission to auction off the contents of the *Polly & Anne* and keep its crew members in custody. To the great chagrin of David Forman, however, no immediate action was taken against Governor Franklin. Franklin continued to maintain the appearance of being the legitimate representative of Crown authority in the colony even while administrative structures completely beyond his control grew up around him. Keenly aware of his lack of military assets, however, he avoided any actions that might provoke the Whig authorities. These, for their part, were reluctant to prosecute the son of a leading member of the Whig leadership without clear evidence of treasonous behavior. They also did want to have to deal militarily just yet with a possible rescue attempt from the British man-of-war anchored just off Sandy Hook. Both sides spent the winter in anxious anticipation of what was going to happen next. Whigs dreaded a possible British invasion of New York while Governor Franklin and his allies secretly hoped that a decisive display of military superiority would restore Crown authority in the province. Tension mounted as winter turned into spring and everyone was certain that a decisive move by the British could not be long in coming.

Reverend Tennent informed his congregation that his fellow pastors had been discussing the situation and had concluded that the time had come to take a clear stand to guide their congregations to righteousness. He informed them that President Witherspoon had summarized this consensus very well and planned to deliver an important sermon in the following week to clarify the position. He suggested that anyone who could, should attend.

Nathaniel was always pleased to have a reason to visit Princeton to see his son, Joseph, as well as his relatives at the mill. Isabella welcomed every opportunity to be with her old friend, Annis Stockton. Both hoped that President Witherspoon would offer good moral guidance for dealing with these troubled times. Together with most of the Whig elite of Monmouth County they travelled to Princeton to hear Witherspoon's advice. As they took their places in the chapel, they were intrigued to see how many prominent citizens were in attendance. Apparently Presbyterian pastors around the colony had done a good job generating interest for what President Witherspoon would have to say.

President Witherspoon ascending the pulpit in a quietly dignified manner gazed for a few minutes in silence at the assembled congregation. Then he began to speak slowly in his deep Scottish brogue.

"Dear Friends in Christ," he began, "Today on this day of a general fast appointed by Congress throughout the United Colonies I want to speak to you of the dominion of Providence over the passions of men."

Witherspoon went on to argue that much more was currently at stake than the mere question of taxation. His reasoning centered on the importance of preserving religious liberty.

"There is not a single instance in history in which civil liberty was lost, and religious liberty preserved entire," he argued, "If, therefore, we yield up our temporal property, we at the same time deliver the conscience into bondage."

The congregation was shocked by the implication of Witherspoon's unambiguous support for the cause of independence.

Witherspoon concluded his sermon with what sounded to many like a call to arms.

"From all these circumstances I conclude favorably of the principles of the friends of liberty and do earnestly exhort you to adopt and act upon those which have been described, and resist the influence of every other."

After the sermon, aroused and anxious congregants moved to the lawn in front of Nassau Hall to discuss the dramatic implications of Witherspoon's exhortations.

"It is clear that President Witherspoon sees the current struggle as a latter-day Christian crusade," remarked Richard Stockton.

"I believe you are correct," agreed Nathaniel gravely, "And when I consider the issues from his perspective, I don't see how we can avoid becoming his crusaders. The fate of the True Religion is clearly at stake."

Isabella and Annis did not comment but merely exchanged worried glances.

"Yes, and it is high time we move decisively against the enemies of liberty," added David Forman darkly as he stepped up to include himself in the conversation.

"I assume by that you mean against Governor Franklin?" asked Nathaniel.

"Against Tories in general," replied Forman, "But against Franklin in particular because he is the one inspiring all manner of sedition. Did you hear about his latest ploy?"

"I know that he still considers the Provincial Congress to be illegitimate," ventured Nathaniel.

"Not only that, but he has had the audacity to command the Assembly to convene in Perth Amboy on June 20 to discuss 'matters of great importance' even though the Continental Congress called for the formation of new governments in all the colonies, governments that do not swear allegiance to the Crown of Great Britain," Forman explained angrily, "The governor has just proved himself to be in contempt of Congress!"

"I dare say the governor is losing touch with reality," remarked Richard Stockton, "Most of the Assembly members already defer to the Provincial Congress, and now we are having new elections which will increase both the legitimacy of the Provincial Congress and the number of delegates favorable to independence. By ignoring the democratic legitimacy of the new Provincial Congress Franklin could well provoke his own demise."

Over the next few weeks, new elections returned a Provincial Congress with no qualms about facing the governor's challenge head-on. The delegates called upon all New Jersey legislators to boycott the Assembly, and at the same time ordered an end to the payment of Governor Franklin's salary effectively terminating Crown authority in New Jersey. After obtaining the approval of the Continental Congress in Philadelphia, the Provincial Congress ordered Colonel Heard to proceed against the governor. Franklin was to be presented with a parole in which he promised to remain in Princeton, Bordentown or on his own farm at Rancocas Creek. If he refused this generous offer, he was to be taken into custody. Heard was admonished to carry out his orders with the utmost delicacy. Many were still reluctant to incarcerate a Crown official. "We are crossing a Rubicon," Jonathan Sergeant, one of the delegates was heard to say.

Unfortunately for Colonel Heard, Governor Franklin had no intention of letting his dismissal proceed in a delicate fashion. He was outraged and defiant after he read the parole that Heard offered him, and asked indignantly with what authority such an impertinent order had been issued. Handing it back with an air of contempt he made it clear that he would never consider submitting to what he considered to be illegitimate authority. Colonel Heard then sent to the Provincial Congress describing Franklin's recalcitrance and asking for further instructions. The Provincial Congress saw no alternative but to request permission from the Continental Congress to remove Franklin from the colony. The Continental Congress was prepared to grant the request but stipulated that Franklin first be granted a hearing before the Provincial Congress. When Heard informed Franklin that he would now be taken under guard to Burlington to face an inquiry by the Provincial Congress, Franklin warned Heard haughtily that he would one day be held personably accountable for his treason.

Franklin had decided not to cooperate in any way so that his guards were obliged to shove Franklin into his coach and forcibly transport him to Burlington accompanied by eighteen armed men. Even the long, exhausting, and humiliating journey did not succeed in softening Franklin's determination. Arriving in Burlington he glared with undisguised contempt at the delegates. The hearing was chaired by Samuel Tucker, the president of the Provincial Congress, sitting in the seat formally belonging to the chief justice. Seated to his left was President Witherspoon who returned Franklin's glare with equal animosity.

"Is it true, Mr. Franklin," began Tucker, "That you tried to convene the New Jersey Assembly on the twentieth of June against the orders of the Continental Congress?"

Franklin refused to legitimize the procedures of what he considered to be an "illegal assembly," instead reiterated his position that he had been falsely accused of being an enemy to his country, unfairly deprived of his salary and outrageously taken into custody by armed men lacking any legal authority.

"Do as you please," he told his captors scornfully, "And make the best of it."

From then on he fell completely silent.

Tucker tried to continue with the interrogation asking one question after another that even after a brief pause went unanswered, "Did you know of the Congressional Resolves of May 15? ... Did you issue the call for the assembly? ... What 'important business' did you plan to discuss with the New Jersey legislature? . . . Have you ever recommended the use of force against the colonies?"

Franklin remained obstinately silent until Tucker accused him of threatening Colonel Heard. At that point Franklin angrily shouted that this was the most outrageous accusation he had ever heard and demanded that Heard be brought before him to repeat the charge.

This created an uproar among the delegates who were becoming more and more incensed by Franklin's arrogant and condescending behavior.

Summing up what many of the delegates were thinking John Witherspoon lashed out at the now former governor.

"Mr. Franklin," Witherspoon thundered in his best hellfire and brimstone fashion "It is not for you to give orders to this democratically constituted body! You speak of legitimacy, but for all your fine airs and claims of gentility, everyone knows that you are nothing but a base-born bastard. I hereby move that the guards remove you to your quarters while the representatives of the people decide your fate!"

After Franklin's removal from the room the delegates quickly agreed to declare William Franklin "a virulent enemy to this country and a person who may prove dangerous to its cause." They immediately sent a courier to Philadelphia to report to the Continental Congress and ask it to designate a place for the former governor's confinement.

The unfolding of these dramatic events in Burlington occurred against the backdrop of increasing British naval presence off Sandy Hook. To the great alarm of the Monmouth militia several dozen additional men-of-war had appeared at the beginning of the month. The militia officers observing the ship movements from the heights on the New Jersey shore were uncertain if this had something to do with the arrest of the royal governor or if it was part of some larger invasion plan.

"I hope that the new Provincial Congress does not go overboard and provoke an invasion that we are not prepared to deal with," Colonel Taylor confided in his follow officers, "I for my part have signed a petition urging them not to opt for independence which would certainly result in all-out war with Great Britain."

"We are already at war," countered David Forman, "It is only a matter of time until the British attempt to force us into submission. During that time we need to deal with as many Tory collaborators as possible before they can aid the enemy. I hope the Provincial Congress finally puts an end to the activities of that collaborator-in-chief, William Franklin."

"I have heard from Doctor Witherspoon that Franklin will be interned outside the colony," Nathaniel informed his fellow officers, "I am afraid that David is correct and that we are effectively already at war. Franklin was the only Crown representative who still held out hopes for a negotiated settlement. All the others seem bent on a military solution."

"And how are we to deal with that?" asked Taylor exasperatedly, "Look at the forces that the empire is assembling. How long do you think we can hold out if the marines on those ships decide to march into New Jersey?"

"We will fade into the forest and shoot at them from behind the trees," answered David Forman, "Just like the brave minutemen did at Lexington and Concord. They will soon regret the moment they stepped onto New Jersey soil."

"In any case we need to monitor the ship movements carefully so we can inform the Provincial Congress immediately if it looks as though an invasion is imminent," advised Nathaniel, "Dr. Witherspoon has informed me that the Provincial Congress will decide very soon if our delegates to the Continental Congress should vote for independence or not. If it becomes clear that the British are about to exercise brutal force against us, that could very well tip the balance in favor of independence."

"It's precisely the decision for independence that could provoke an invasion," argued Taylor, "If that happens, the Provincial Congress should tell us who is going to help protect our farms and families here!"

"The Brits are going to use force no matter what the Provincial Congress decides or does not decide," said Forman, "We need to gird our loins for an invasion as well as a possible uprising by Tories here who are just waiting for the British forces to arrive. My spies also tell me that we will also have to contend with bands of Pine Robbers who are planning to use the bogus claim of loyalism to justify their vicious raids on patriotic Monmouth yeomen. We need to start hanging these rascals before they can do any harm."

Nathaniel listened to Forman's dire predictions with trepidation. The thought of his beloved family being threatened by murderous criminals swarming out of the Pine Barren cedar swamps from the west and lethal hordes of Regulars invading from the east made his blood run cold. On the one hand he had to agree with George Taylor about the precarious state of Monmouth's defenses; on the other hand David Forman was certainly correct in foreseeing the inevitability of armed conflict. Moreover, Dr. Witherspoon had convinced Nathaniel about the desirability of independence and that goal was certainly not attainable without armed struggle. Nathaniel remembered his father's admonition to be on the side of True Religion when the time of reckoning would arrive and decided that that time was now.

The anxiety level of the militiamen observing the British fleet jumped to a new level on the afternoon of July 1. The ships already anchored off the Hook began to move making way for new ships arriving from the sea. To the horror of the militia officers more and more ships began to appear. It soon began to seem as if the entire British fleet were descending on New York. Over the next few hours, the men observed over one hundred ships sail into the channel. Finally, around eleven in the evening Colonel Taylor decided it was time to inform the Provincial Congress.

"Colonel Scudder, you have the fastest steed, so I want to dispatch you immediately to bring this incredible news to Burlington," Taylor ordered, "And take this letter to John Covenhoven who is now vice president of the Provincial Congress. He knows our situation in Monmouth and will be able to advise the Provincial Congress and the Continental Congress appropriately."

Glad to be assigned a task to relieve his incessantly building tension, Nathaniel took the letter, mounted his horse and galloped off. It would be a long ride to Burlington, and he was not sure the mare he was riding would be able to hold the pace. He decided, therefore, to pass through Freehold on his way and exchange the mare for his best horse, Blackjack, the giant black stallion named for Oliver Cromwell's indefatigable war horse. This would also give him the opportunity to alert his family and instruct them to flee to Anderson Manor if an invasion should actually occur.

After an hour of hard riding Nathaniel burst into his stable waking the stable boy, Adam, asleep in the hay.

"Quickly, Adam," exclaimed Nathaniel, "Saddle up Blackjack. I must ride to Burlington this night!"

As Adam set to work, Isabella, woken up by the noise of Nathaniel's arrival, appeared in her night gown at the entrance to the stable.

"Nathaniel, whatever . . ." she began.

"The British are about to invade!" he shouted, "Dozens of ships have appeared off the Hook. It looks as though the entire British navy is about to descend on us. I have to get the news to Burlington as quickly as possible!"

"But, but . . . what about us?" asked Isabella, shocked and dismayed by the turn of events, "Is the British army on its way here? Who is going to protect us if you leave?"

"The immediate goal of any invasion would certainly be New York City," reassured Nathaniel, "Washington has set up many fortifications there so that will keep the British busy for at least awhile. In the meantime, our Monmouth militia should be able to protect our community. That is also one of the reasons I must get to Burlington immediately. I need to convince them not to withdraw any more of our Monmouth militia for service elsewhere. We need them to protect our families and farms right here. In any case we have organized a network of dispatchers who will spread any important news quickly throughout the colony. If an alert comes, you should take the children and the servants to Anderson Manor. Your father is not an official of the new government, so you should be safe there."

"And when will you be back?" asked Isabella, her tremulous voice betraying her growing anxiety.

Nathaniel suddenly realized the devastating effects that the situation was having on his frail wife and paused for a moment thoughtfully before taking Isabella gently into his arms.

"Darling," he began softly, "There is nothing more important to me than the safety of you and our children. I would gladly barricade myself in our house and fight off any invaders until my dying breath. But that would not be the most effective thing I could do right now. Far better to mobilize our patriotic forces to stop the British already in New York before they can reach us here. That is why it is so important that I leave for Burlington immediately."

Isabella was nodding her head in resigned agreement when suddenly distant sounds of explosions startled both of them.

"Was that cannon fire, Nathaniel?" asked Isabella wide-eyed.

"It indeed might have been," answered Nathaniel nervously, "But it might also have been thunder from a summer storm. In any case, I must be off!"

With that Nathaniel kissed Isabella passionately, jumped on his horse and was gone.

He galloped throughout the entire night past sleepy settlements that might soon be called to arms. He did not feel the slightest fatigue—his apprehension concerning the possible fate of his family kept him wide awake. He became increasingly obsessed with anxiety concerning the safety of his vulnerable loved ones. Images of his beautiful wife and the three children still at home, Hannah, Kenneth, and Lydia, and what might befall them at the hands of an invasion army circled incessantly in his mind causing him to drive himself and Blackjack to the limits of their endurance. He stopped only occasionally to allow his horse to drink a few draughts of water before hurrying on.

Finally in the early morning he arrived in Burlington and burst in on a sleepy John Covenhoven who was just about to have his breakfast. After hearing what Nathaniel had to say, Covenhoven abruptly stopped his breakfast preparations and immediately dispatched a courier with the following message to the Continental Congress in Philadelphia,

"We have this moment undoubted information, by Lieutenant Colonel Nathaniel Scudder, from Monmouth County, that about four o' clock yesterday afternoon, he observed nearly the whole of the enemy's fleet in motion, and at half past six in the afternoon, saw about one hundred and thirty sail in the channel from the Hook to New York . . . that he left Middleton at eleven o' clock last evening; and about four this morning, being at the highland, between Upper and Lower Freehold, heard heavy cannon fire. We also received, by Colonel Scudder, a letter from Colonel George Taylor, of Monmouth, dated yesterday, informing us of that county being so exposed to the enemy without, and the Tories among themselves, that he apprehends the militia will not be prevailed on to march to New York, and leave their wives and children to fall either a prey to the enemy, if they should be repulsed at New York, or be murdered by the Tories in their absence, who are imbodying themselves, and a considerable number already encamped at the Cedar Swamps."

On the same day the Continental Congress unanimously declared the independence of the United States of America. All the delegates from New Jersey signed the official text which was approved two days later.

Chapter 19

Invasion – 1776–1777

After John Covenhoven had gotten his message off to the Continental Congress, he and Nathaniel conferred about the next steps necessary to deal with the heightened threat of invasion.

"I think that the information you just delivered will convince the last doubters that we have no choice but to go for independence," asserted Covenhoven.

"I certainly hope you are correct, but it could also have the opposite effect," warned Nathaniel, "Our Colonel Taylor, for example, seems to think that the British force is so overwhelming that it is folly to try to seek a military solution."

"We are not the ones seeking a military solution!" exclaimed an exasperated Covenhoven, "But if we are attacked, we have to protect ourselves. I know that the Taylor clan like many others oppose independence, but it is the Brits who are refusing a negotiated settlement. You need to get some rest now, but I suggest you return as soon as possible to East Jersey and make the case for a spirited defense of our farms and families. General William Livingston will be conferring in Elizabethtown with General Hugh Mercer in a few days to organize the Flying Camp that General Washington has ordered. The Flying Camp will include militia forces from Pennsylvania, Maryland, Delaware and New Jersey who will cooperate to defend New Jersey. You need to participate in that meeting to insure them that the Monmouth militia will do its duty even if George Taylor is losing his nerve."

Nathaniel and Blackjack retired to a local inn to get some much-needed rest. Nathaniel only intended to sleep a few hours, but he was so exhausted that when he lay down, he immediately fell into a deep dreamless sleep. When he awoke, it was already in the middle of the night so he decided his best strategy would be to get up at dawn and embark on the day-long ride to Elizabethtown.

Arriving in Elizabethtown in the late afternoon he proceeded immediately to Liberty Hall, the palatial residence of the Livingston family. He was met at the entrance by a Black servant who informed him that the general was in a conference with several military men. Nathaniel asked the servant to tell General Livingston that Lieutenant Colonel Nathaniel Scudder of the Monmouth militia had arrived bearing news from the New Jersey Provincial Congress. The servant disappeared for a few minutes, then returned and politely ushered Nathaniel into a elegantly appointed library where several men were seated about a large table. Nathaniel recognized several leaders of county militias as well as William Livingston, George Taylor, and David Forman.

"Come in, come in, Dr. Scudder," Livingston greeted Nathaniel cordially, "Colonel Taylor has told me that he dispatched you two days ago to inform the Provincial Congress of a possible pending invasion. We are eager to hear what the reaction was."

"John Covenhoven was as shocked as we all were," answered Nathaniel, "He immediately forwarded the news to the Continental Congress in Philadelphia. He felt certain that it would galvanize opinion in favor of independence."

"That would be exactly the wrong thing to do!" exclaimed Taylor, "Let me bring you up to date on what has transpired since you left for Burlington. You saw all those ships arriving just before your departure. Well, shortly thereafter signal flags appeared on the halyards of those men-of-war and the entire armada began moving slowly in the direction of Long Island. Our troops in New York City, of course, raced to Brooklyn to meet the invasion force head on. But just as our defenders were in place, different signal flags appeared and the whole flotilla turned, sailed quickly to Staten Island and there disgorged thousands of British Regulars. They occupied every corner of the island with barely a shot being fired. It was the most amazing logistical feat I have ever witnessed. Since then, troop transports have been arriving there continuously. We are now facing thousands of highly professional troops, and the number is growing every day. How on earth does the Provincial Congress think we can defeat such a force? Our only hope is not to provoke them and try to reach some kind of compromise."

"The Brits are clearly not interested in compromise," contradicted Governor Livingston, "Like it or not, we are going to have to defend ourselves. That is why I would like you all to meet General Hugh Mercer here who has been appointed by General Washington to organize a Flying Camp for the defense of New Jersey. I am requesting all militia leaders to cooperate with General Mercer who will now outline his plans and talk about some of the problems he thinks we are facing."

"Thank you, General Livingston, and thanks to all representatives of militia units who have come here today," began General Mercer in a strong Scottish accent that reminded Nathaniel of John Witherspoon. Nathaniel had heard that the Scotsman was also a physician but that he had had extensive military experience in the war against the French. He was also rumored to have fought for Scotland during the Jacobite uprising. Nathaniel thought that he made an unusually calm and professional impression.

"I am not as pessimistic as Colonel Taylor," continued General Mercer, "I think that if the militias turn out as requested, we can organize an effective defense of the colony. My problem right now is that I never know just how many militiamen are likely to turn out and how long they will remain under my command. Recently whole units from the Monmouth militia just decided abruptly to return home."

"I think I can explain that, sir," offered Nathaniel, "I know a number of the men who recently went back to their farms, but it is not the case that they are deserting the cause. These are farmers who must take in their hay right now or risk the starvation of their livestock in the winter. They will return as soon as they have done what they have to do to insure the welfare of their families."

"I might add that many are also concerned about who is going to guard their families in their absence," said George Taylor, "I have petitioned the Provincial Congress many times for reinforcements to replace militia units who have been sent to the front, but none have been forthcoming. Militiamen find it difficult to understand why they should be removed to New York leaving no one at home to enforce law and order. And the promised pay for militia duty is always months in arrears if it gets paid at all. It is a wonder that anyone turns out under the circumstances."

"We will win this war together or we will lose it together," General Livingston sought to forestall any development of a defeatist attitude, "It is up to us to organize what resources we have effectively. There are undoubtedly many possible improvements to the way we handle militias which we should consider, but in the meantime we have an urgent need to attend to our defenses."

"Part of our defenses in Monmouth County must include cracking down on Tory spies and sympathizers," added David Forman, "Many a yeoman would gladly go off to war if he didn't have to worry about cutthroats menacing his family in his absence."

"The point is well taken that we also face threats from behind our own lines," agreed Mercer, "That means we not also have to keep a sharp eye on what the British military is doing in New York but also have to prevent Tory sympathizers from New Jersey from communicating with the British high command. For this reason, I am suggesting that we set up armed posts at Paulus Hook, Bergen, Elizabethtown, and Woodbridge. I will establish my headquarters at Perth Amboy where I can keep continuous watch on what is happening on Staten Island. That way we can intercept communications in either direction."

"But where are you going to get the men?" blurted a frustrated George Taylor, "Many of our Monmouth militia have already been assigned to help build fortifications in New York leaving their farms and families virtually defenseless. If the few left guarding the home front are sent to man the new armed posts, our men in New York will feel they have no choice but to return to defend their homes."

"The Flying Camp is designed to be composed of militia from all over the colonies rotating their deployments such that we can muster suitable numbers where they are needed most," explained Mercer, "We need to reassure your Monmouth men now in New York that we are not neglecting the defense of their homeland. Dr. Scudder, I am told that you are well known and trusted among the men of Monmouth. Perhaps you could visit the Monmouth units in New York City and convince them they need to stay on the job? I hope to be able to replace them eventually with militia units from New England but right now we urgently need to prepare for an attack which is certain to come very soon."

"An excellent suggestion, General Mercer," affirmed General Livingston, "I will also advise General Washington to release some of the New Jersey militia units so they can be stationed opposite Staten Island. That way the good citizens of New Jersey will not feel so directly exposed to the enemy. I will also circulate an order that all cattle, sheep, and horses near the shore be driven further into the New Jersey interior to keep them safe from foraging parties. Feeding the number of troops they already have on Staten Island will undoubtedly necessitate plundering on a grand scale."

"We also need to prosecute any New Jersey Tories we catch voluntarily selling their produce to the enemy," added David Forman, "The lure of being paid in sterling rather than in proclamation money will surely induce some people to betray their country."

The meeting concluded with a general consensus that General Mercer's plan was essentially sound but that everything depended on the ability of state legislatures to call up the requisite number of fighting men. General Livingston pledged to do his utmost to get the New Jersey Provincial Congress to set a good example by allocating sufficient militia forces to the Flying Camp. Nathaniel resolved to do his best to boost the morale of his Monmouth militia colleagues beginning with an immediate trip to New York City to inspect the troops and determine how many were in fighting condition.

The next day Nathaniel continued to New York City to visit the Monmouth militia units there. He was shocked by what he saw. As he approached the fortifications where the Monmouth militiamen were working, the putrid stench made him almost vomit. Holding a handkerchief over his face he approached the first man he recognized, the chaplain of the New Jersey militia, Philip Fithian. Nathaniel knew him from the time of his graduation from Nassau Hall in 1772. He was well known as an ardent Whig having achieved some notoriety in 1774 by helping to stage an imitation of the Boston Tea Party in New Jersey.

"Philip, I am appalled by the state of our troops here!" exclaimed Nathaniel, "Do our officers not understand the most basic rules of hygiene?"

"The officers are aware that field sanitation is important," explained Fithian, "But they have not the experience in organizing a deployment like this. The troops ease themselves in the ditches of the fortifications and foul their own drinking water. It is no surprise, therefore, that putrid fevers are becoming widespread among our troops."

"I came here to boost the morale of our men so they would hold the line here," said Nathaniel, "We were afraid that many would abandon the front, but it seems that illness is an even bigger threat to our combat readiness."

"It certainly is, Dr. Scudder, the vile water here sickens us all," agreed Fithian, "I feel sicker and weaker each day and many of our men are in the same condition or worse. Those who stay to fight might in the end be too weak to do so."

"Philip, you must avoid drinking that foul water!" warned Nathaniel, "If your illness develops into a full-fledged flux, you can easily die. I will try to impress on the officers here that it is vital to organize a supply of unpolluted water."

Nathaniel spent the next days warning and advising the junior officers about the importance of good hygiene. He explained what medications were useful for the flux and the putrid fevers, but he had no supply available in New York. In any case the three regimental hospitals were so filled with sick men that even his complete inventory at home would not have sufficed. He made a mental note to inform General Mercer, himself a physician, that medical supplies or the lack thereof could become a deciding factor in the upcoming struggle.

In addition to lecturing the junior officers on the basics of sanitation Nathaniel also sought to reassure them that the High Command had not forgotten them or the security of their families back home. He explained the concept of the Flying Camp and Mercer's plans to rotate militia duty among various state militias so that everyone would eventually have an opportunity to attend to domestic concerns. And most importantly, he conveyed the news that the Continental Congress had formally declared the independency of the United States of America, and that the time had come for momentous change. With all the missionary intensity of the convinced Presbyterian elder that he was, he impressed upon them the immense world-historical significance of this development and the importance of the role that each of them would play in standing up before God for liberty. He told them that General Washington himself would soon be coming to greet them and preside over a reading of the Declaration of Independence, and that everyone who could, had a duty to attend the ceremony.

Probably due to Nathaniel's exhortations the Monmouth militia turned out in force to hear the declaration, even though many could hardly stand. As the words rang out, however, a wave of energy seemed to pass through the crowd. Even the sickly seemed to be revived by the spirit of liberty expressed so elegantly. At the conclusion of the reading round after round of huzzahs spontaneously erupted from the multitude. As General Washington and his guard marched off the field ground in a dignified manner, an enthusiastic crowd of soldiers, sailors, and civilians danced and cheered to the music of fife and drum. Nathaniel was amazed to see militiamen who were only hours before sullen and depressed now rejoicing with abandon. After a wagon arrived with casks of rum donated by some ardent Whig, the mood swiftly escalated to such a level of ecstasy that Nathaniel began to worry that the troops would render themselves unfit to face the enemy.

While Nathaniel was still getting used to this miraculous transformation, a captain from Washington's artillery, who Nathaniel later found out to be one Oliver

Brown, rode up and shouted to the masses, "Patriots, follow me, we have unfinished business with George III!"

Since several Monmouth units followed the summons of the artillery captain, Nathaniel decided to accompany them as well to restrain his militiamen in case things got completely out of hand. As night was falling, the crowd marched down to the Bowling Green on the southern tip of the island where an equestrian statue of George III adorned in the fashion of a Roman emperor stood.

"There he is!" shouted Oliver Brown, "The tyrant who would make slaves of all of us. Let us tear him down and turn the lead of that statue into bullets for the defense of our country!"

"Down with the tyrant! Down with the tyrant!" chanted the crowd as someone fastened a lasso around the neck of George III. Many enthusiastically joined in pulling on the rope until the statue finally tipped off its base and crashed on the ground with the head breaking off on impact. This symbolic beheading of the king caused the crowd to erupt again in huzzas. Nathaniel for his part watched the proceedings with some misgiving. The crowd seemed to have more in common with a riotous mob rather than with disciplined soldiers. Nathaniel wondered to himself if enthusiasm alone would be enough to withstand the crack troops that George III had arrayed against the sick and undisciplined militiamen currently manning the barricades.

Nathaniel decided to ride to Princeton the next day to brief President Witherspoon on the state of defensive preparations in New York. As a member of both the Provincial Congress and the Continental Congress Witherspoon was enormously influential, and in Nathaniel's opinion could best convey a description of the problems facing the militia to those who might be able to do something about them. Arriving in Princeton in the early evening he was surprised to see Nassau Hall grandly illuminated and a large crowd of people gathered in front. Coming closer he could see that a celebration of American independence was in progress. The students were lined up in their militia uniforms in front of President Witherspoon and the faculty. President Witherspoon had apparently just read the Declaration of Independence to the assemblage. Having finished, he turned to the captain of the student guard and nodded.

"First platoon forward and raise arms!" cried the captain.

At that a third of the student militia stepped forward and raised their muskets.

"Long live the independent United States of America!" shouted Witherspoon.

A volley of shots rang out as the crowd cheered. The procedure was repeated two more times accompanied by ever wilder applause until a smiling President Witherspoon indicated that the formal part of the celebration was now concluded.

"God bless you all!" he shouted, "Now gird your loins for the defense of our sacred liberties!"

As the militia unit dismissed from formal duty began to mingle with the crowd Nathaniel was pleased to see that one of the young men was his son, Joseph, who greeted his father enthusiastically.

"It is a fine day to be alive!" shouted Joseph, "Long live the independent United States of America!"

"It is, indeed, an exciting time, son," agreed Nathaniel, "But also one fraught with mighty challenges. I have come to bring news about preparations for the defense of New York to President Witherspoon. Come with me and listen to the urgent tasks that await us."

Nathaniel and Joseph went over to greet President Witherspoon who was discussing with Reverend Tennent what independency would mean for the church.

"Make no mistake, William," said Witherspoon, "Since I was the only churchman to sign the Declaration, the British government now considers all of us Presbyterian pastors to be fomenters of rebellion. We must warn all our brethren that it would be dangerous to fall into their hands."

"It is an honorable burden that we bear, John," replied Tennent, "To be called a rebel right now is to bear witness for the True Religion!"

"Excuse me, gentlemen," interrupted Nathaniel, "I bring you tidings from New York City where I have just inspected some of our militia units. I am afraid that falling into enemy hands is a real and present danger for all of us if our new government cannot solve some of the problems we are facing."

"Dr. Scudder, I am grateful to you for coming here and anxious to hear what you experienced on the front," said Witherspoon his brow furrowed with concern.

Nathaniel then recounted the details of his visit and his conversations with Philip Fithian. He described the ghastly sanitation, the putrid fevers affecting large numbers of militiamen, the lack of planning, organization, and proper training.

"If we cannot organize our defenses better, we will need a miracle to survive the advance of the British Regulars," concluded Nathaniel.

"Only God can make miracles," said Witherspoon gravely, "We certainly should pray for one but in the meantime our government has approved some concrete measures that can help. The New Jersey Provincial Congress has renamed itself the Convention of the State of New Jersey. Our new government will now consist of a governor, a general assembly, and a council. The governor will now be commander-in-chief of the New Jersey militia and thus able to implement reforms directly."

"General Livingston will be delighted to hear that," said Nathaniel approvingly, "He has a number of outstanding ideas for reorganizing the militia."

"And the Convention has authorized a New Jersey contingent for the Flying Camp," continued Witherspoon, "That should go some way in helping Livingston and Mercer. I will do everything I can to convince the Convention to call out as many militiamen as possible. "

Encouraged by Witherspoon's news Nathaniel hastened to return to Monmouth County to reassure his militia colleagues that help was on the way. Witherspoon was as good as his word. Within a few weeks the Convention had called out one half of the militia to be part of the Flying Camp to be relieved by the other half after a month. The two halves would then do alternate months on duty. It seemed to Nathaniel that this was a feasible strategy, and he sought to convince his fellow officers in the Monmouth militia of the worthiness of the idea. Not all of his colleagues were in agreement

"It is about time that the New Jersey government is finally beginning to understand the direness of our situation," George Taylor complained, "I have only been warning them for months what would happen if we provoked the empire. And now they respond with too little too late!"

"But it is at least a beginning," argued Nathaniel, "I know we still have many problems to solve but the enthusiasm that our men display despite their hardships. . .."

"Enthusiasm is a wonderful thing but wait until they see the serried ranks of some of the world's most highly trained soldiers bearing down on them inexorably," interrupted Taylor, "They will drop their muskets and run all the way home. Do you realize that 8,000 Hessian mercenaries just arrived on Staten Island to add to the thousands of British troops already there? There must be over 40,000 in the British force altogether! And how many can we muster to stop them? To my knowledge General Greene has less than a tenth of that number and half of them are the New Jersey five-month levies whose term of enlistment is about to run out."

"I know that things do not look good," agreed Nathaniel reluctantly, "But what choice to we have at this point? The British refuse to negotiate in good faith."

"The British intended all along to enslave us," asserted David Forman, "Negotiations are a waste of time. They may attempt to deploy overwhelming force to subdue us quickly, but this is a vast country, too vast to be dominated even by the giant force they have amassed on Staten Island. If they break through into New Jersey, there will be yeomen firing at them from behind every tree and fencepost. They will get another taste of what it was like at Bunker Hill. Sooner or later they will give up and go home. Our task is to make sure that they are not able to install their Tory lackeys in positions of control before they leave."

"David, for you anyone favoring a peaceful solution is a Tory lackey!" responded George Taylor heatedly, "But picking a fight with the world's leading military power is madness, and I am having no part of it."

With that Taylor stormed out of the meeting leaving the remaining officers to wonder if the colonel was really giving up his command or just venting his anger and frustration. Within a few days it became apparent that his skepticism regarding the ability of the militia to stand up to British Regulars was more than justified. The British invasion of Long Island began with an amphibious force of 32,000 soldiers, the largest ever assembled by a European power. 3,500 poorly trained American soldiers under Major General Nathanael Greene, half of them short-term militiamen, gaped in awe as the British forces stormed ashore. As George Taylor had predicted, the Americans were no match for the overwhelming power of the invasion force. As General Mercer later reported, many of the militiamen ran from their posts on the first cannonade from the ships of the enemy. To make matters worse General Greene like so many of the other American soldiers fell extremely ill and had to be replaced. General Washington rushed to Long Island and appointed General Sullivan to take over. It quickly became apparent that Sullivan lacked the experience to cope with the deteriorating situation, and Washington replaced him with General Putnam. Three commanders in five days only compounded the confusion as the American lines of defense melted away. Washington had all he could do to evacuate what was left of his army to Manhattan. General Sullivan and General Lord Stirling wound up as prisoners of war.

Nathaniel received the terrible news about the collapse of the American defense of Long Island while attending a briefing at Elizabethtown with General Livingston and General Mercer. General Livingston had just been elected the first governor of the state of New Jersey and as such was now also commander of the entire New Jersey militia with the heavy responsibility of trying to rally his disheartened troops.

"Lt. Colonel Scudder," began Livingston, "Are you now the sole representative of the Monmouth militia? Where is your commanding officer, Colonel George Taylor when we need him the most?"

"I am afraid Colonel Taylor has decided to abandon the cause," explained Nathaniel, "He blames the current disaster on false decisions by New Jersey's government, and says he no longer wants to be a part of this project which in his opinion is doomed to failure."

"How do you see the situation?" inquired Livingston, "Do you think we are doomed to failure or are there still men in Monmouth who are willing to fight for liberty?"

"I think we have no moral alternative but to fight for our liberties," replied Nathaniel stoically, "Whether we win or lose is ultimately in God's hands, but one has to stand up for what is right regardless of the consequences. Sola gratia! At the end of the day only the Grace of God can save us. That being said, I was appalled by what I observed while visiting our militia in New York. There is much we need to do if we are to cope with this crisis."

"That's the spirit!" exclaimed Governor Livingston, "Instead of whining about the sad state of things we need to improve it. I will begin by promoting you to colonel to replace George Taylor. I have drawn up a list of reforms for the militia that I intend to promulgate as soon as possible. I would like to hear any suggestions you might have for improvements, especially since you are a physician. You see, General Mercer tells me that many of the men who leave his units are sent home for reasons of sickness. Henceforth I want sick soldiers to report instead to a field hospital. Getting sick should not be a way to get sent home."

"That is certainly a desirable change," agreed Nathaniel, "But what I have seen in New York are field hospitals that were completely overwhelmed by the number of sick soldiers. Much of the sickness had to do with the dreadful sanitary conditions in their camps. If the new policy is to work, it will be necessary to address the roots of the problem. My old mentor, Dr. Clark, once told me that more soldiers died of camp fever than from French bullets in the last war."

"As a physician who also fought in that war, I can tell you that your mentor was completely correct," agreed General Mercer, "If we don't want to send sick soldiers home, then we must make certain that the field hospitals are capable of handling the workload."

"And they need to be provisioned with adequate remedies for fevers and the flux. The ones I visited had run out of everything. I for my part will continue preaching to our junior officers that good sanitation will reduce the number of soldiers needing to go to the field hospitals in the first place," added Nathaniel.

"Now we are getting somewhere!" enthused General Livingston, "Supplying our field hospitals with medicines is one logistical problem. Another is supplying our soldiers with clean clothes and the other things that they need. That is another reason why soldiers apply for permission to return home. If we want our men to stay at the front, then we have to see that they have everything that they need."

"That is certainly the case," agreed General Mercer, "But the service duration of only one month before rotation will remain a nuisance. Is there no way we can convince the Assembly to increase that to six months?"

"I will surely try," promised Governor Livingston, "But it will be difficult because six months is a long time to neglect a farm."

Nathaniel headed back to Freehold to convey the wishes of Livingston and Mercer to the other officers of the Monmouth militia. He sought to impress on his men how crucial the participation of the Monmouth units in the Flying Camp would be. Despite his efforts, however, he received just a few days later an urgent message from General Mercer reporting that several Monmouth units had not shown up on schedule to take over their duties. Mercer confided that General Washington had requested that the militia stage a raid on Staten Island to throw the British off balance but that the Flying Camp was at present too weak to undertake even a token commando operation. Nathaniel immediately queried his fellow officers to ascertain the problem.

"It is not that our men are unwilling to fight," explained Asher Holmes who had recently returned from a one-month stint in the Flying Camp, "It is that they want to do the fighting right here where they can defend their farms and family. That sentiment is re-enforced by the tales they hear from returning militiamen about the disease and disorganization at the front."

"Also, many of them realize that they don't have to go to New York to find the enemy," added David Forman, "There are plenty of the enemy right here. And judging by the performance of Washington's army on Long Island they will soon be joined by British Regulars. Our best strategy is to concentrate our forces here where we know the lay of the land and have a tactical advantage."

"There is no way we can be successful if every local militia does only what they feel like doing," objected Nathaniel vehemently, "Washington is our commander-in-chief and Livingston is now governor and formal head of the militia. They were appointed by the governing bodies that we ourselves elected. We owe them our allegiance. Besides our only hope is a coordinated effort to confront the enemy. If we do not stand united behind our cause, the British will be able to divide and conquer us. It is in every farmer's interest to prevent that because, if the British break through, the pillaging will know no boundaries!"

Nathaniel's eloquent plea succeeded somewhat in mollifying the militia leaders but within a few days more bad news again generated anxious uncertainty. Word came that British forces had driven Washington out of New York City and the city itself was in flames. Several American attempts to damage the British fleet with fireships had miscarried due to a combination of British maneuverability and American incompetence. General Mercer wrote letters complaining about the scandalous behavior of the Pennsylvania and New Jersey militias in the face of the enemy. The only bright spot was that the deteriorating situation had at least inspired the Continental Congress to authorize the enlistment of 60,000 men into 88 new Continental regiments. Nathaniel prayed that the reform of the militia and the deployment of the new regiments could both happen quickly enough to withstand the coming storm.

The officers of the Monmouth militia worked frantically to try to turn their yeomen volunteers into competent soldiers. Recruiting new men was complicated, however, by the fact that many residents of Monmouth County were ambivalent in their attitudes toward the Whig cause. The issue of who could be trusted was a frequent subject of their deliberations.

"Have you heard about the latest blunder our lords and masters have made?" asked David Forman indignantly at one of their meetings, "It seems that a merchant ship named *Betsy* carrying contraband for the British ran aground near Shrewsbury and was impounded by our militia. Some fool then authorized that the ship and its contents to be turned over to none other than our traitorous former commander, George Taylor!"

"Apparently, some feel that Taylor has not really abandoned our cause and might still be won back to our cause," reasoned Nathaniel.

"That is absolute nonsense!" thundered Forman, "He and his whole family have obviously gone over to the Tory cause. Already in the summer he was issuing passes to well-known Shrewsbury Loyalists to visit the British army on Staten Island. He will probably sell the contents of the ship and use the proceeds to finance forays against us. I have it on good authority that that scoundrel of a Cortlandt Skinner has set up on Staten Island and begun organizing a network of traitors in our midst. As soon as the British army moves against us, these creatures will rise up and attack us from behind."

"It is very difficult to know what's in a man's heart," replied Nathaniel, "I have always known George Taylor as an honorable man although he has never made a secret of his distaste for independency. For quite a while he paid the militia out of his own pocket, and had to wait months for the Assembly to reimburse him. But whether or not Taylor is actively working against us, the secret organization of Tory militias in Monmouth is undoubtedly happening and we should try to disrupt it any way we can."

"During my last tour of duty with the Flying Camp, General Mercer spoke of Washington's desire to stage a raid on Staten Island," said Asher Holmes, "If we could get enough volunteers, we could make a lightning strike there and perhaps capture Cortlandt Skinner and put an end to his mischief."

"I say we make the rounds of the various militia units and see who would be willing to participate," suggested David Forman.

The officers proceeded to do exactly that and were pleasantly surprised that militiamen from many different counties were ready to join in order to catch such a prize as Skinner. They then sought out General Mercer who was delighted to hear that he would be able finally to carry out Washington's request. He had intelligence that a unit of Hessian soldiers was guarding Skinner and a group of other disaffected persons in a small village on the island. It was clear that the militia would be no match for the Hessians in a pitched battle so it was decided that a surprise night raid would have the greatest chance of success. The Americans would strike in the early morning under the cover of darkness, seize the Loyalists, and return with them to New Jersey. Two groups of militia units, one under General Mercer und one under Asher Holmes, were to cross over to Staten Island at two different points. The element of surprise was of the utmost importance so General Mercer cautioned all unit commanders to hold their fire until a signal from him.

Fortunately for the militia the night of the raid turned out to be pitch black so that both groups guided by locals were able to cross to Staten Island without detection by the Hessians. The advantage of darkness soon became a hindrance, however, as the various militia units struggled to keep contact with each other. Finally, one of the foremost militia units bumped into the first line of Hessian sentinels and began firing their muskets in panic. At the sound of the musket fire the Hessians guarding Skinner and his associates reacted quickly and spirited their charges away in the direction of the main Hessian garrison. In the meantime, the other militia units commenced firing, killing and wounding about twenty men. Since it was clear that the alerted Hessians would soon be sending reinforcements, Mercer decided to take what prisoners he could and retreat to New Jersey. He had only lost two men and captured eight Hessians and nine British soldiers. Due to the poor coordination and the inexperience of the militia units, however, he had not succeeded in the primary goal of capturing Cortlandt Skinner and the other members of his Loyalist cabal.

A few days later Nathaniel and his fellow militia officers went to Perth Amboy to review with General Mercer the performance of the militia units during the raid.

"Well, first let me thank you gentlemen that you were able to organize such a number of volunteers that the raid was even possible," began General Mercer, "I will be pleased to inform General Washington that the raid resulted in some success, but quite frankly, gentlemen, it could have been much better. Well-disciplined troops would have taken the whole group without the loss of a man. As it is, we lost two soldiers and the main prize was able to escape. Nevertheless, we were able to discover some interesting facts about the Hessian garrison which will be useful to Washington. Our lads fought bravely but are obviously very inexperienced. The question for us to discuss today is how we can improve the coordination of the militia units."

"Turning farmers into disciplined soldiers is a process that takes time," explained Nathaniel, "I detect no lack of enthusiasm among our volunteers, but they still need to be properly trained. As they acquire more combat experience they will surely improve."

"I am sure they will," agreed General Mercer, "But until that can happen, we have to hold the line against some of the best trained troops in the world. Some of the militia units have more battlefield experience than others. Any suggestions how we might bring a few more experienced units to the front lines?"

"Our most experienced militia units joined the expedition to invade Canada," said Nathaniel, "But we are getting reports that that project is not going well."

"Not going well? The Canada campaign is a bloody disaster!" exclaimed General Mercer, "Horatio Gates was given command of our northern forces in July in order to reverse the string of defeats we have been suffering, but he has not been able to stop the British from driving us out of Canada. The last I heard he was concentrating most of his forces at Fort Ticonderoga in hopes of preventing the British from occupying the Hudson Valley. One can only hope that he is successful. If not, we risk being cut off from our allies in New England."

"As a matter of fact, I have just received a report from John Cunningham, the commander of the Monmouth militia units in Ticonderoga," continued Nathaniel, "He actually sounded fairly optimistic. He said our regiment is esteemed by local commanders and been given command of an important redoubt called the Jersey battery. The redoubt is well equipped with eight heavy guns which have an excellent view over the lake. Near this redoubt are four others each mounting four or five guns. On Mount Independence there is a twenty-gun battery and above this a half-moon mounting four guns. The out lines are strong. Cunningham is confident that they will be able to hold the line against any British advance from the north."

"I wish I could say the same thing about our lines of defense," replied Mercer, "But we are lacking both men and equipment. Of course, it does no good to recall the experienced New Jersey militia units from Ticonderoga since their mission there is equally important. But, somehow, we need to strengthen this front. If the British start to move into New Jersey, I frankly have no idea how we long we can hold the line."

"We clearly have to find more volunteers," opined Asher Holmes, "We have shown with the raid on Staten Island that this is possible, but if we expect people to leave their home areas for extended periods, we must be able to supply them properly."

"There is no doubt about that," agreed General Mercer, "But that is one of our many unsolved problems. Let me give you an example. I recently sent a request to Governor Livingston for a large supply of shoes because I noticed that many of our militiamen were walking around almost barefoot although winter will soon be upon us. He entrusted the procurement to a talented young man named William Paterson."

"Oh, I know Paterson," interjected Nathaniel, "He graduated from Nassau Hall back in the 60's. He then went on to work for Richard Stockton. A fine young man indeed."

"Well, then you probably know that he a member of the Provincial Congress and is now the State Treasurer," continued Mercer, "He did a very systematic job of surveying the possible suppliers of shoes but in the end, could not acquire the goods because so many of New Jersey's cobblers are on militia duty!"

"Clearly calling out more militiamen may solve one problem but wind up creating others," observed Nathaniel.

"Nonetheless, we have no choice but to buttress Fort Washington as best we can," continued Mercer, "If Fort Washington falls, it will be only a matter of weeks before the British will invade New Jersey. Every New Jersey yeoman must be aware that there could soon be British foraging parties pillaging their farms and raping their women. It is in everyone's vital interests that the British be stopped in New York!"

"Many of our best militiamen are already at Fort Washington," objected David Forman, "And if it falls with heavy losses of men, who is going to protect their families and farms then? I can tell you that the Tories in Monmouth County are just awaiting their chance to fall on our backs."

"There is much truth in what David is saying," agreed Nathaniel, "We certainly have reason to doubt the loyalty of some of the armed formations that exist among us. I suggest we require every one of any standing to take a loyalty oath to the Provincial Congress. Those who refuse will have to be regarded as having gone over to the enemy. At least then we will know exactly where we stand and how many militiamen we will need to provide security at home."

"An excellent suggestion, Colonel Scudder," agreed Mercer, "Which I will pass on to Governor Livingston. In the meantime, any efforts you can make to see that the Monmouth militia at least meets its responsibilities for manning the Flying Camp would be greatly appreciated."

Convinced by Mercer's case for the importance of strengthening the Flying Camp, Nathaniel, Asher Holmes, and David Forman hurried back to Freehold determined to rally support for militia duty. A few days later a letter from Governor Livingston arrived announcing that Nathaniel's suggestion for extracting pledges of loyalty from militia officers was to be implemented as quickly as possible and suggesting that Nathaniel himself serve a one-year term in the New Jersey Legislative Council advising the governor.

As Nathaniel sought to convince other militia officers of the necessity of openly declaring loyalty to the New Jersey Convention he was surprised and dismayed to discover that many were reluctant to take an unambiguous stand. Apparently quite a few militia officers were trying to keep their options open pending the outcome of the defense of New York City. In the midst of his efforts to recruit more men for the Flying Camp Nathaniel's mission suddenly became immeasurably more difficult when news arrived that Fort Washington had indeed fallen to the British with the capture of over 2,800 men, many of them from the Monmouth militia. The militia officers who had pledged allegiance to the New Jersey Convention hastily met for a meeting at Monmouth Courthouse to deliberate how best to deal with the devastating turn of events.

"How do we stand with the loyalty oaths?" David Forman asked Nathaniel who had been leading the effort to promote the Whig position among the militia officers.

"The gentlemen you see here are the ones we can count on," answered Nathaniel, "Unfortunately quite a few are reluctant to commit to the cause. George Taylor has even written a letter to the Convention refusing to take any oaths because he considers the military situation hopeless. He claims that the militia is dissolving around him."

"I have said all along that he is a scoundrel!" exclaimed Forman, "He is not just taking a passive uncommitting role. In secret he is actively supporting people like Samuel Wright who is organizing a Tory militia called the New Jersey Volunteers. He has helped the notorious Middletown Tory, Daniel van Mater, collect horses to be used for a Tory cavalry. My cousin, Sam, told me that his duplicity is so obvious that none of the officers in his unit want to serve under him anymore. In fact, they want to elect Sam as his replacement. I tell you the whole Taylor clan are traitors who are just waiting to betray their countrymen to the British. We need to arrest them and put an end to their treachery as quickly as possible."

Although David Forman was famous for his uncompromising attitude toward anyone he considered to have Tory sympathies, it was clear to all who supported the Whig government that it was now time to act against the enemy in their midst.

"You are right, David," Nathaniel reluctantly agreed, "We need to replace those we suspect of disaffection from the Whig cause and promote those we can trust, like Asher Holmes here, whom I would recommend promoting to captain. I think we should also petition General Washington to open up a front here in Monmouth County. Since you have been warning us about the enemy within from the very beginning, I think you would be the best one to present the case to Washington."

"I will be happy to do exactly that," exclaimed Forman, "Now that the raw violence of the British military appears imminent, it should become quickly obvious to everyone who really supports the cause and who does not. In any case, I already have a long list of people to arrest if Washington provides me with men and authority."

A few days later Nathaniel met with his family and Reverend Tennent at Anderson Manor to discuss the deteriorating situation and contingency plans in case the British should get as far as Freehold.

"I have just received word that about 6,000 British troops have crossed into New Jersey," Nathaniel reported gravely, "We have to be prepared for the worst."

"How did they manage that?" exclaimed Colonel Anderson, "I thought we had numerous militia posts along the Hudson to prevent the Brits from getting across the river. Were our men asleep?"

"Apparently, they crossed above Fort Lee at the Palisades which were unguarded because nobody thought the British would want to cope with such a formidable natural barrier. But some Tories from the area guided them to the paths that lead to the top. The British were able to transfer many men completely unopposed. Now Hessian mercenaries are camped on the village green of Hackensack. The Tories greeted them as liberators but then were shocked when they were plundered by them and the British. It serves them right, but it shows you what is in store for us if we can't stop them somehow. Washington wants us all to deploy to Newark and join his troops but unfortunately the Flying Camp seems to have ceased to exist."

"What are we to do? asked Isabella frantically, "We have a nine-year-old daughter. I can't bear the thought that she could fall into the hands of some Hessian brute!"

"If Washington cannot stop the enemy at Newark, he will probably retreat in the direction of Pennsylvania, first to Brunswick, then to Princeton, Maidenhead, and finally cross over the Delaware into Pennsylvania. The bulk of the British force will follow him as closely as they can so that most of Monmouth would be a diversion for them."

"We have to think about this strategically," opined Colonel Anderson, "The British would be foolish to drive more people to the Whig cause. Unless one is publicly associated with the current government, I doubt that one will come to harm. That means that our militia officers, like you Nathaniel, must stay out of the way of the advancing troops. But Isabella and the children can simply come and stay at Anderson Manor. For all the British know I am just a respectable country squire loyal to George III."

"That strategy will certainly work for Isabella but not for me," said Reverend Tennent, "According to President Witherspoon the British regard the rebellion as a Presbyterian project. They will probably string me up on the first tree."

"That is certainly a danger to be considered," agreed Nathaniel, "But again, if you keep a low profile, you are probably safe in Monmouth County. Princeton, on the other hand, is right on the track that the British will take in pursuing Washington. I wonder what people there are planning to do."

"Both Richard Stockton and Reverend Witherspoon as signatories of the Declaration are marked men," interjected Isabella anxiously, "They will definitely have to flee the area. Annis mentioned the last time I saw her that Richard might come to our area to escape the British. She thought Reverend Witherspoon was thinking more in terms of Pennsylvania. But what about the students in Nassau Hall? What will become of Joseph?"

"I will ride to Nassau Hall and discuss this with Witherspoon," responded Nathaniel, "As far as the students are concerned, some will leave and join militia units. Others will stay at the farms of friends and relatives. I will suggest exactly that to Joseph. If it looks as though the British are going to occupy Princeton, he should just go and stay with Will's family at the mills. He would probably prefer to join a militia unit himself, but I will discourage that. Instead, I will encourage him to gather as much useful information as possible which he can share with the militia later."

"If they think he is a spy, they just might shoot him!" exclaimed Isabella, "Why can't we just go and bring him home?"

"Even if we brought him home, that would not lessen the danger," explained Nathaniel, "I know my son and he is determined to do his part for the cause. But if I can convince him that he is doing more for the cause with clandestine activity, that will keep him out of the active skirmishes, at least for now."

"I think Nathaniel has a point," agreed Colonel Anderson, "Joseph is still very young and British officers would probably not suspect him of being a militiaman. The strategy of keeping a low profile should work in most cases. What we have to be concerned about is the fact that we probably have many Tory sympathizers in Monmouth County who would betray Whig sympathizers at their first opportunity."

"Very true," agreed Nathaniel, "But I am happy to report that David Forman was able to convince General Washington of the importance of opening an anti-Tory front in Monmouth County. Forman's troops will soon be arresting quite a number of people here that he suspects of being disaffected from the Whig cause. I also heard from Governor Livingston that he intends to call out the entire New Jersey militia and dispatch it to Newark to support Washington."

A few days later Nathaniel rode up to Princeton to consult with President Witherspoon and to instruct Joseph about how best to cope with the situation.

"Reverend, I am afraid I must bring disturbing news," Nathaniel warned Witherspoon, "The enemy forces that have established a bridgehead in New Jersey are very strong. It is unlikely that Washington will be able to block their advance toward Philadelphia. Governor Livingston has called up the entire militia, but they will only be able to harass the enemy, not stop it. As a signer of the Declaration, you are in grave danger."

"As well I know," replied Witherspoon, "Not only as a signer of the Declaration but also as a Presbyterian clergyman I am surely at the top of the enemy's wanted list. I have already decided to close the college and to retreat to Pennsylvania. I am advising all my associates to do the same."

"A very wise decision, sir," agreed Nathaniel, "I hope the Stocktons are doing something similar."

"Richard told me he was planning to go to Monmouth and stay with John Covenhoven in order to keep out of the path of the British forces," explained Witherspoon, "I hope that is a wise thing to do. I think it better to put as much distance between myself and the British army as possible. I will be happy to take your son, Joseph, along with us if you so wish."

"That is extremely generous of you, Dr. Witherspoon," replied Nathaniel, "But I am making other arrangements with the family of my brother not far from here."

After the meeting with Witherspoon Nathaniel and Joseph rode over to the mills to confer with William and his family. On the way there Nathaniel explained to his son what he considered to be his patriotic duties.

"I have a very important mission for you, son," began Nathaniel, "It is likely that the British will soon come to occupy Nassau Hall. They regard it as a hotbed of rebel ideology. We cannot hope to block their path, but we can make life very difficult for them. Despite the overwhelming size of their army, they will have to stretch their lines very thin in order to occupy all of New Jersey. Our militias will harass them at every opportunity but avoid head-on confrontations where the enemy would surely win. In order to do this, we need to gather intelligence about their movements and troop strengths. That way we can strike unexpectedly and melt back into the countryside before they can marshal their forces. If we can keep them bogged down in New Jersey, they might not be able to get across the Delaware and attack Philadelphia. That is where you come in. I want you to play the role of a young student who is staying with his aunt and uncle until the college reopens. Do not admit to being a supporter of the Whig cause. Instead, discreetly gather what information you can and pass it on at your first opportunity to our militia. It is of the utmost importance that the British do not detect that you are a secret agent working for the cause."

Joseph's breast swelled with pride and his eyes glistened as he cast himself in the role of a secret agent in the service of liberty.

"I will do my very best," averred Joseph enthusiastically, "I am sure you are right that this is the best way I can serve my country."

When they arrived at the mills, they were met by William's wife, Mary, and Nathaniel's widowed mother, Abia. They were especially delighted to see Nathaniel and Joseph because William had been called out to the militia, and they were home alone with the children. Nathaniel's suggestion that Joseph stay with them while the college was closed was greeted with joy and relief.

"I am so happy to have a man about the house," exclaimed Mary, "One hears the wildest rumors about the advancing enemy troops. Will thought they would not molest women and children as long as they found no armed rebels, but I am not so sure. It will be reassuring to have Joseph here."

"The important thing is to avoid any connection with the Whig movement," advised Nathaniel, "You should just present yourselves as loyal subjects of George III. If they want to purchase supplies, by all means take their money, otherwise they will just confiscate whatever they want. If marauding bands of soldiers appear, then try to find an officer. In most cases he will keep his charges in line. And, Joseph, don't allow yourself to be provoked into an armed confrontation. There is no way that a lone militiaman can prevail over a group of well-trained Regulars. You must resist the temptation to show your bravery because the information you will gather is more valuable than one sacrificed life."

"I understand completely, father," Joseph agreed solemnly, "I must stay alive so I can pass the intelligence I gather to our troops."

Convinced that he had done all he could to minimize the danger to his son, Nathaniel hurried back to Freehold to reassure Isabella. When he arrived, he was confronted with yet another crisis.

"Nathaniel, I just heard that something terrible has befallen the Stocktons," exclaimed Isabella, "They had come to Monmouth to stay at the estate of John Covenhoven, thinking themselves under the protection of the loyal Monmouth militia. But then a group of Tory thugs appeared at the Covenhovens and kidnapped Richard! Annis does not know where they are taking him but is beside herself with anxiety."

"Oh my God!" exclaimed Nathaniel, "I had hoped that David Forman's campaign would suffice to force our Tories here at least to keep a low profile. But apparently they are emboldened by the approach of the British forces."

"David is, in fact, arresting everyone he thinks might be a Tory sympathizer," continued Isabella, "but it is not only real Tories we have to contend with. My father tells me that groups of Pine Robbers are also getting into the act. Pretending to be Loyalists they kidnap patriots and then sell them to the British. We not only have to fear traitors in our midst but criminals as well!"

"The situation is indeed dire," agreed Nathaniel, "I will advise David to remove his prisoners as quickly as possible to Philadelphia before they can be freed by the advancing British forces."

Nathaniel quickly called a meeting with David Forman who immediately agreed that they would have to evacuate his prisoners from New Jersey or risk having them freed by British troops. Sixteen suspected Tories were in custody so that it was necessary to organize a formidable guard to get the prisoners safely to the jail in Pennsylvania. As Washington's troops fell back in the face of the British advance, more and more people seemed to be heading in the direction of the Delaware. It was also rumored that Washington had ordered every boat within 40 miles north and 40 miles south of Trenton to be commandeered for his forces. Getting across the Delaware with such a large group was not going to be easy. At Nathaniel's suggestion they headed to a farm near the Delaware belonging to Nathaniel's cousins. Nathaniel hoped that they could give them advice on how best to get their charges to Philadelphia.

On their way to the Delaware Nathaniel's group passed through Princeton and were shocked to see how many people had already fled. Nassau Hall was empty. Many shops had been hastily shuddered. Morven had been left in the care of servants. Nathaniel hoped that Joseph had gotten himself safely to the mills. As they headed west in the direction of Maidenhead the road became more and more crowded with carriages carrying whole families with as many of their belongings as they could carry.

Shortly after leaving Maidenhead, they ran into none other than Dr. Witherspoon who was also fleeing west with his family.

"President Witherspoon!" Nathaniel called out, "It's me, Nathaniel Scudder, with the Monmouth militia. David Forman and I are escorting prisoners to safe keeping in Philadelphia."

"I am on my way to Pequea," answered Witherspoon, "That is, if I ever get across the Delaware. Everyone seems to have the same goal. I just ran into Reverend Spencer from Trenton. He was going in the other direction to Princeton to fetch his daughter, Margaret. But Margaret has also already fled so I told him to hasten back to Trenton, gather his goods and family and flee as well. It is open season on Presbyterian preachers these days!"

"Not only on them, unfortunately," said Nathaniel, "Richard Stockton was just abducted from John Covenhoven's estate by a Tory gang and delivered to the British."

"God help him!" exclaimed Witherspoon, "I shudder to think what that poor man will have to endure now. And his beloved Morven is sure to be plundered by the British army. I only hope the officers in charge will show some respect for our library in Nassau Hall."

"Perhaps Richard will be exchanged at some point," said Nathaniel, "One can only hope. But in any case, we have arrested a bunch of Monmouth Tories and want to see that they won't be kidnapping anyone else in the future. We are headed to my cousins, Amos and Jedediah Scudder, up near the falls, they know this area and can advise us how and where to do a crossing."

"The names sound familiar," replied Witherspoon, "I believe they are active in the Hunterdon County militia. In any case I wish you well with your mission. And remember, Colonel Scudder, no matter how bleak the outlook is, we can rest assured that we are doing God's work."

The closer Nathaniel's group got to the Delaware the more clogged the roads became. Night was falling and as they approached the river the shores were lit up with great bonfires. All manner of watercraft were continually passing and repassing back and forth across the river full of men, horses, weaponry, and baggage. The crush of fleeing people, the flickering of the fires and the bellowing of hundreds of men and animals struggling in and out of the boats created a hellish scene that reminded Nathaniel of visions of the Final Days. He imagined the frightened refugees to be the people of God fleeing the Beast and about to cross the Jordan. Since it was clear that all the ferry facilities near Trenton were completely overwhelmed, they proceeded north to the farm of Nathaniel's cousins.

Amos and Jedediah greeted Nathaniel and David warmly.

"It's a pleasure to help see these Tory rascals put out of business," remarked Amos, "You are right to get them to Pennsylvania before they can perpetrate any mischief. You can count on the Hunterdon militia to give you any support you need."

"The best thing for us would be to hand over the prisoners to a Pennsylvania militia who could then take them to jail in Philadelphia," said David Forman, "Then we could return quickly to Monmouth County and arrest more of the rascals."

"My son, John, is a surgeon's mate with the Bucks County militia," added Nathaniel, "Perhaps we could make contact with a militia unit through him."

"As a matter of fact, I know where cousin John is camped," said Jedediah, "I can ride north to Coryell's Ferry, cross over and bring him a message."

All agreed that this would be the quickest option. Coryell's Ferry would be less crowded than those closer to Trenton and Jedediah, riding alone would be able to make quick progress. In a few hours he returned with the good news that the Bucks County militia was sending over a guard to pick up the prisoners.

Nathaniel's group hurried to Coryell's Ferry to turn over their charges. Nathaniel had high hopes that his son might be part of the Bucks County guard and was overjoyed that this turned out to be the case. Approaching the ferry landing he saw his son waving from the boat.

"Praise the Lord that I get to see you in these tumultuous times!" shouted Nathaniel.

"Praise God indeed," answered John, rushing to embrace his father, "But tell me what has become of my brother? I have seen refugees coming from Princeton. Is he among them?"

"No, I am afraid not," answered Nathaniel, "I advised him to go and stay at the mills if the British approach and disguise himself as just a law-abiding young scholar. I hope that he was able to do that. On my way back to Monmouth I will pass by there to see if everything is all right."

"Be very careful, father," cautioned John, "According to the information we get, the British are hot on the heels of Washington's troops. As soon as he gets the bulk of his forces over the river, he will take with him everything that floats so that the British cannot easily follow him across. After that it will be very hard to escape to New Jersey."

"We know that, son," said Nathaniel, "But the British troops will be concentrated along the road from Brunswick through Princeton to Trenton. I will travel back alone north of the main route. David Forman will return to Monmouth with our militia unit south of the British line."

"The enemy will be sorely overstretched over the length of New Jersey," added David Forman, "If they try to widen the line of their occupation, they will be stretched even thinner, and our militiamen can pick them off before they even know we are there."

Nathaniel bid farewell to his son and David Forman and galloped off in the direction of Scudder's Mills but far enough to the north to avoid running into the main British force. On several occasions he had to change his route in order to avoid British foraging parties that he espied in the distance. As he passed by farms that had been brutally pillaged by British and Hessian soldiers, his anxiety about the safety of Joseph,

Mary, and his mother escalated to a fever pitch. He asked himself over and over why he had been so foolish as to leave them unguarded. After several hours of hard riding, he arrived in the neighborhood of the mills and was shocked to see a column of smoke rising over the treetops. Shouting his son's name, he burst onto the Scudder property and was appalled to see that both the grist mill and the fuller mill were consumed in flames. Circling around the burning mills he came to the barn which was still intact. Lying in the hay was his mother and Abia, but no sign of Joseph. Jumping off his horse he ran over to them and was relieved to see that they were both still alive although their clothing was torn and covered with filth.

"Oh my God, whatever has happened to you!" cried Nathaniel, kneeling beside them and quickly checking them for serious wounds. Both women were barely conscious and could not respond initially. Nathaniel propped them up and made each of them sip some water from his canteen. Eventually his mother came to enough to relate what had happened.

"Two British dragoons arrived and told us that they were looking for rebels," his mother began, "Since it was obvious that only Mary and I and Joseph were here, they asked Mary to let them inspect possible hiding places in the barn. After they went into the barn with Mary, I heard screams, and Joseph and I ran to the barn to see what was going on. The brutes were in the process of ravishing Mary. When Joseph tried to throw himself at them, one of them struck him so hard in the head that he passed out. The scoundrel then proceeded to ravish me as well. Can you imagine? An old woman like me!"

Abia shook her head and began to cry softly.

"Thank God you are both alive, mother, and you seem to have no serious injuries," Nathaniel attempted to comfort her, "But what became of Joseph?"

"They took Joseph with them when they rode off," answered his mother, "But I think he was still alive. They threw him into a wagon they had with them for foraging, and I think I saw him moving as they rode off."

Nathaniel murmured a short prayer of thanks that his family had apparently survived the outrageous attack but then began to plot his revenge. He vowed that in the future he would give no quarter, neither to enemy soldiers nor to the Tories who supported them.

Mary began to revive slowly and seemed crushed by the shame of what had happened.

"What is Will going to think of me?" she cried, "Now that I have been defiled by other men. How will I ever live down this shame?"

Nathaniel knew that victims of rape often had to contend with the additional burden of ostracism within their communities.

"Mary, and mother, listen to me," he commanded, "What happened is not your fault and you both have been victims of evil men. We will not compound this evil by subjecting you to further embarrassment. The abduction of my son and the destruction of your property are bad enough. What happened to both of you will remain our secret."

Chapter 20

Washington's Crossing – 1776–1777

When Joseph awoke, it took a while before his eyes adjusted to the gloom of the place where he was being kept. The musty smell made him think that he must be in a cellar somewhere. His head hurt and he groaned a bit as he tried to sit up.

"Glad to see you coming to, lad," said someone not far away, "We were afraid that that blow on the head might have done you in."

As Joseph's eyes came into focus, he could see that there were perhaps a dozen men in the room with him."

"Where. . .where am I," stammered Joseph.

"You, like us, are a prisoner of His Majesty's army. We are now being kept in the basement of Nassau Hall which has become a barracks and storage area for the British army," answered the man who had spoken first, "I don't know why you are here, but we are all suspected of being part of the rebel militia."

"But . . . but . . . I am just a student here," Joseph protested remembering his father's advice to stay undercover and pretend that he was a loyal subject of George III.

"The British are not particular about whom they arrest but maybe you can convince some officer of your innocence," continued the other prisoner, "They are all in a fluster right now because Washington has apparently re-crossed the Delaware, surprised a Hessian regiment in Trenton and taken many captives. They are gathering a massive force here and plan to crush Washington once and for all. We heard that Cornwallis has arrived with reinforcements and will lead the campaign himself."

The news shocked Joseph into a new sense of urgency. He was amazed to hear that Washington had dared to wage a successful attack on a Hessian regiment, but it was clear that retaliation would be swift and brutal. He needed to find out as much as he could about the gathering forces in Princeton and get word to the Americans as quickly as possible. He decided his best strategy would be to act the offended young gentleman who had been the victim of a mistake but could possibly offer information that would be useful to the British. He went to the cellar door and began pounding it with his fist.

"I must see General Cornwallis!" shouted Joseph, "I have important information for him."

At length a Hessian sentry opened the door and threatened Joseph with his bayonet.

"Don't shoot, sir," pleaded Joseph, "I am unjustly imprisoned. I must see General Cornwallis because I have important information for him!"

The Hessian soldier did not understand a word of English but understood that the young boy kept repeating the name, Cornwallis. He was not sure what the boy was getting at but he certainly did not look like the other scruffy rebels that they had been arresting lately. He decided to be on the safe side and take the boy to the commander who had made his headquarters in a villa not far from Nassau Hall.

As Joseph left Nassau Hall, he was appalled to see how it had been devastated. President Witherspoon's wonderful library and much of the scientific equipment had been destroyed. The same scene repeated itself when he arrived at Morven, the Stockton estate that Cornwallis had appropriated for his command post. Everything of value had been looted, the library burned, and the furniture ruined. The elegant villa that he had visited many times with his parents was almost unrecognizable. He was brought into what used to be the opulent dining room where General Cornwallis was seated behind a makeshift desk. Several Hessian officers were standing next to him.

"Why is your sentry bringing this young man to me?" asked Cornwallis.

After a brief conversation in German, the Hessian colonel answered, "The guard says this prisoner kept shouting the words 'Cornwallis' and 'information' so he thought he might know something useful."

"Well, young man, why were you imprisoned in Nassau Hall with the rest of that rebel pack?" asked Cornwallis, "Are you planning to fight against king and country?"

"No, sir," Joseph quickly answered, "I am a student here in Nassau Hall and a loyal subject of George III. I was staying with my relatives while the college is closed. Although we were harboring no rebels, two British hussars tried to molest my aunt. When I attempted to stop them, they knocked me out, and I woke up in the basement of Nassau Hall."

"If that is true, I will see that those men get flogged," promised Cornwallis, "But, tell me what do you know about the rebel militias?"

"At the farm where I was staying, I saw many militia units fleeing west before the advancing British forces," Joseph answered obediently.

"About how many militiamen would you estimate were on their way west?" asked Cornwallis.

"It seemed like a very great number," Joseph lied, "Although we only saw a part of the force, I would estimate that many thousands were involved."

Turning to the Hessian colonel Carl von Donop, Cornwallis said, "You see, Colonel von Donop, the rebels are indeed gathered in strength, we need to concentrate our 8,000 troops, and attack them with overwhelming force. Your idea to advance on Trenton in two columns would only weaken us."

Turning back to Joseph, he said, "Your information was very useful. General Howe has generously offered his protection to every loyal colonist who affirms his loyalty to the Crown. Since you have amply demonstrated your loyalty, I will give you a pass which you can show to any British soldiers who may question you."

Joseph thanked the general for his kindness and quickly departed, anxious to leave Morven and continue on his mission. He walked around Princeton carefully noting the deployment of men and artillery. As soon as he was confident that he had a good overview, he hastened to leave the British occupied area and find his way to the American forces. Now that he knew that the British were concentrating their forces on the Post Road to Trenton, he decided to try to head west by first going south until he hit the Sawmill Road which led to the Quaker Meeting House near Crossweeksung.

After walking a few miles down the road he was overtaken by a militia unit on horseback. To his delight he recognized that it was the Monmouth militia led by his father's subordinate, Asher Holmes.

"Ah, young Scudder!" shouted Holmes, "Your father will be relieved to hear that you are not in the hands of the enemy."

"I was, but I was able to talk my out," explained Joseph, "Now I have important intelligence for the American army about the disposition of enemy troops in Princeton."

"Then you can come with us," replied Holmes, "We are headed to Crosswicksung to report to the American commander there about the situation in Monmouth. We are being hard-pressed by the Tories who are now emboldened by the British advance. We will need the help of the Continental Army if we are to dislodge them."

Joseph jumped up onto a horse behind one of the militiamen, and the group continued in the direction of Crosswicksung.

"Do you have news of my father or the rest of my family?" asked Joseph anxiously.

"Your father and David Forman are leading the effort to put an end to the Tory uprising," answered Holmes, "But he told me if I see you, to tell you that your aunt and grandmother are safe."

"Praised be the Lord," exclaimed Joseph, "There are indeed signs and wonders that the righteous will prevail at the end! Dei sub numine viget!"

Arriving in Crosswicksung they were escorted into the presence of the American commander there, Colonel John Cadwalader, who was intensely interested to hear what they knew about the deployment of the British forces. Asher Holmes quickly briefed him on the situation in Monmouth County.

"There are few British troops there yet, but the Tories are openly defying the Convention and trying to set up a Loyalist government," explained Holmes, "Our militia forces are not strong enough to route them. We need reinforcements."

"I will pass that request to General Washington but right now our main concern is the British army. Have you information about that?" asked Cadwalader.

"I have just come from Princeton," Joseph piped up, "I can tell you everything about the British and Hessian forces there."

Joseph quickly related to an astounded Cadwalader how he had fallen into the hands of the British and then managed to escape.

"They are turning Princeton into an armed camp," Joseph continued, "I think there must be at least five thousand British and Hessian soldiers there. Eight cannons, all six-pounders are lined up across the west end of Nassau Street. Two other guns face north. Four guns are placed in the direction of Kingston Road to the east of the Hudibras Tavern. Breast works are being built on either side of the Post Road to Trenton. The town is fortified on every side except one. There are no sentries on the south side of town behind the college. That is the route I took when I left Princeton."

Amazed by the details that the young man was able to provide, Cadwalader continued his interrogation.

"Were you able to hear any details about what the British commander is planning?" he asked.

"Indeed, when I was being interviewed by General Cornwallis, he mentioned to one of the Hessian officers that he planned to send an overwhelming force down the Post Road and crush the rebels once and for all. The Hessian officer had advised a two-prong attack on Trenton, but Cornwallis thinks that one massive column will be the more effective."

The more Cadwalader heard from Joseph, the more excited he became. With Joseph's help he sketched a map of Princeton and the vicinity.

"And so, we could re-trace the route you just took, march up Sawmill Road, and attack the enemy from behind?" asked Cadwalader one more time just to be sure.

"Exactly," confirmed Joseph, "Right now no one in Princeton seems to be expecting that. The main force will shortly depart in the direction of Trenton along the Post Road."

Cadwalader ended the interview and rushed off to give Washington the important news. It would provide the basis for one of the boldest and most successful operations of the war. During the interview Joseph discovered that Cadwalader's unit was part of the Pennsylvania Associators. He decided to ask some of the militiamen in the camp if they had heard anything about his brother, John, who was serving with the Pennsylvania militia. The first few he spoke to could not remember someone named John Scudder but could recall one Amos Scudder from the Hunterdon militia who had guided them to Trenton after they crossed the Delaware.

"That is a cousin of mine, not my brother," remarked Joseph disappointedly but continued to ask more men. Finally, he ran across an older militiaman who had been treated in a field hospital for a minor wound shortly after crossing the Delaware.

"Yes, I do recall a young surgeon's mate named Scudder who was serving in a Pennsylvania militia unit," recalled the soldier, "He was assisting Dr. Benjamin Rush. They had set up a field hospital in the farm owned by the family of Amos Scudder up near the falls."

Joseph was ecstatic to hear that his brother was already on this side of the river not many miles away.

"And do you know if that militia unit will be joining us here?" cried Joseph.

"Nobody knows exactly what Washington has up his sleeve," replied the old soldier, "But it does seem that we are being joined by more and more men. One of the recent arrivals told me that the Hessians were poised to attack Trenton, and the Americans were dug in on the south side of Assunpink Creek. I suspect that your brother's militia unit is there in the meantime or that it is on its way here. All the men headed in our direction have been told to keep very quiet. The Old Fox has undoubtedly cooked up another surprise for those British bastards and their accursed allies. God grant him success!"

After listening to the old man Joseph began to pay more attention to the constant arrival of militiamen. At length he saw men arriving in the uniform of the Bucks County militia.

Rushing up to the first one he saw, he exclaimed, "My brother, John Scudder, is a surgeon's mate in your unit. Do you happen to know him?"

"Yes, of course," answered the militiaman, "He has been very busy these last few days binding our wounds. He should be arriving shortly. He is with the wagons carrying the wounded."

As the slowly moving heavy wagons with the militia's wounded rumbled into view Joseph espied his brother atop one of them tending to a soldier who had an arm amputated by a cannon ball. He raced toward the wagon, shouting, "John, John, is that you!"

"Joseph!" exclaimed John, "The Lord be praised. But keep your voice down. We have been ordered to travel as silently as possible."

After finishing the dressing on the wounded man John jumped down from the wagon and embraced his brother heartily.

"Do you know what is happening?" Joseph asked his brother, "Everyone here thinks that something is afoot, but no one knows exactly what."

Joseph quickly explained to his brother what he had experienced in the last few weeks and the intelligence about troop deployments in Princeton that he had delivered to Colonel Cadwalader.

"It all fits together," John mused, "I happened to talk to someone who turned out also to have studied at Nassau Hall, one Joseph Reed. Washington sent him out to gather information about the state of the roads south of the Post Road. I'll wager that he is planning to swoop around the British forces and attack Princeton from the south."

"But if the Hessians are about to attack Trenton, won't we need all the force we can muster to stop them?" asked Joseph.

"The Hessians already have the town. We were ordered to abandon Trenton and make a stand on the south side of Assunpink Creek," confided John, "We just made it out in time. In fact, our poor Presbyterian chaplain, John Rosbrugh, was not so lucky. In the confusion he lost his horse and was overtaken by a band of Hessians. They didn't even try to take him prisoner, but instead brutally murdered him with bayonets right there in the street even though he was unarmed. The Brits call our pastors the 'Black Regiment' and order that they be given no quarter."

"God have mercy on his immortal soul!" exclaimed Joseph.

"He died on his knees praying for our cause," continued John, "For the cause of liberty for the True Religion. Fortunately, the line held at the bridge over Assunpink Creek. Our cannons sent many Hessians to the hell fire that they deserve. But I conclude, nevertheless, that this is only a delaying action. Our men were instructed to make a lot of noise and to build big bonfires at night to convince the Hessians that our main force was preparing for a stand south of the bridge. Most of us, however, received whispered orders to continue east and fall in with Colonel Cadwalader's regiment."

"Then we are probably going to attack and liberate Princeton!" exclaimed Joseph, his eyes burning with missionary zeal, "How blessed are we to have this opportunity to serve the Lord!"

It turned out that Joseph's guess was very accurate. Washington had indeed decided to send his troops to attack the overextended British forces in Princeton and, if possible, in Brunswick, While the bulk of Cornwallis's army was barreling westward down the Post Road from Princeton to Trenton, Washington's soldiers would advance eastward on a parallel course south of the Post Road. Washington was fortunate that the advance of the British army was hindered by a thaw that turned the Post Road into a muddy morass. He divided his forces into two columns, a smaller one headed by General Nathanael Greene and the main force commanded by General Sullivan. Both columns would initially proceed up the Quaker Bridge Road. After the Quaker Meeting House the smaller column would wheel left, head toward the Post Road and block it in order to prevent the main British force from returning to Princeton. The main force would continue on to Princeton and attack it from the south.

John and Joseph sat in one of the wagons carrying the wounded of the Pennsylvania militias. They waited for a long time as units of Continentals marched past to take up positions in the van of the force. They were led by a elegantly dressed general.

"Could that be General Washington?" Joseph whispered.

"No, that is General Hugh Mercer," answered John, "He is also a gentleman from Virginia and dresses the part."

"Father has spoken of him in the highest terms," said Joseph, "But I never had the occasion to meet him."

It was well after midnight when Cadwalader's unit finally started to move. None too soon as far as John was concerned. The temperature had dropped precipitously in the night, and he feared that his patients might succumb faster from the cold than from their wounds. Finally the wagons with the wounded together with baggage wagons and two large guns rumbled off following the Pennsylvania militia as it marched off. The road surface crackled underneath the heavy wagons as the mud quickly froze solid.

"This is actually a blessing," remarked John, "We could not possibly make the progress we are if the road was still a morass, and we have some very marshy ground to cover."

"A blessing indeed," exclaimed Joseph, "It means the Lord is on our side! Yesterday the thaw to slow down the advancing British troops and today the freeze to expedite our progress!"

Despite the Lord's intervention the column soon came to a halt again. There was no gunfire to be heard so the reason could not be contact with the enemy. Partly out of curiosity, partly to keep warm Joseph jogged up to the front of Cadwalader's unit to try to find out what the delay was. It turned out that the old Quaker Bridge was not strong enough to handle the heavy wagons and the artillery. The Americans were thus forced to build a second, stronger bridge in order to move on. This took most of the rest of the night so that the column was not able to advance again until almost dawn.

The sun rose on a beautiful ice-cold winter morning. As the wagon with the wounded passed the Quaker meeting house John and Joseph could behold rolling hills and meadows covered with frost. Looking down on the frozen white path along which the column was advancing they could see the bloody footprints of some of the militiamen who only had rags for shoes.

Off in the distance they could see Mercer's troops in the van heading into the deep ravine of Stony Brook. Suddenly atop the ravine they could see soldiers in red uniforms. An officer on horseback was cantering along the edge with two spaniels gamboling before him.

"They are riding straight into a British unit!" shouted Joseph, "They don't seem to be aware of that."

"It seems that each group of soldiers cannot see the other group," ventured John, "But wait, someone has dispatched an express rider to warn them!"

Cadwalader's unit came to a halt to await orders on how to deal with the new situation. In the distance one could see the rider arriving at the van. After a brief exchange with the rider General Mercer led about 120 soldiers up the banks of the ravine to attack the British. As soon as the British saw the Americans advancing, they quickly formed into battle order and prepared to meet the American attack. The two sides clashed in a nearby orchard, and the din of volley after volley of musket fire could be heard all the way back to the wagons.

"I suspect we will be getting more passengers soon," remarked John ruefully, "Hopefully our boys are aiming better than the Brits."

"I am surprised that the Brits are putting up such a fight," said Joseph, "I thought that most of their forces were in Trenton, and we would run into only token resistance."

"The Brits and the Hessians are extraordinarily well-disciplined," explained John, "Even a token force can be expected to extract a heavy price before it retreats."

As if to confirm John's foreboding they could see a mob of militiamen fleeing out of the cloud of gun smoke lying over the orchard having been routed by a British bayonet charge.

"Oh my God!" shouted Joseph, "The Brits are not retreating, they are chasing our men off the field!"

At that moment Cadwalader ordered his unit to deploy from a marching column to a fighting line. As the line attempted to move forward, the militiamen fleeing from the bayonet charge ran into them and momentarily caused great confusion. Some began to flee as well but most held. The battery of Philadelphia artillery brought two long-barreled four-pounders into play. Firing deadly rounds of grape and canister into the enemy lines they managed to bring the advance of the British infantry to a halt. At that moment General Washington mounted upon a splendid white stallion galloped boldly into the ranks of the Philadelphia Associators and shouted encouragement:

"Parade with us, my brave fellows! There is but a handful of the enemy and we will have them directly."

Washington's daring example plunging into the center of the battle not thirty paces from the British line had an electrifying effect on his men. More and more American units came into the fight and the vastly outnumbered British soon had no choice but to retreat. As the British line broke some fled south in the direction of the main force in Trenton but others retreated toward Princeton to help the defenders there. The American columns continued their advance. As the wagons carrying the wounded reached the scene of the heaviest fighting, John and Joseph were shocked to see how many dead bodies were strewn across the meadows now stained bright red by the blood that could not sink into the frozen ground. Joseph struggled with the nausea that almost overwhelmed him when witnessing the gory scene while John jumped down from the wagon to see if any militiamen were among the groaning wounded lying in the field. Most of the dead and dying were British soldiers, however. The few wounded militiamen with a chance of survival were quickly loaded into the wagons, and they continued in the direction of Princeton. One of the wounded informed them that the gallant General Mercer had fallen in the melee because he refused to surrender when surrounded by British soldiers.

The sound of cannon and musket fire resumed in the distance indicating that the main American force had now reached Princeton. Again the British resistance was brisk and disciplined, but again they were no match for the concentrated American forces. They were, however, able to delay the Americans long enough so that most of the British garrison together with a large baggage train could escape in the direction of Brunswick. After a brief cannonade the token British force defending Nassau Hall surrendered, and the American forces took over the town. Since it was clear that Cornwallis would soon be hurrying back from Trenton with the main force, Washington ordered his army to march east toward Kingston. There he would have to decide whether or not to stick with his original plan to attack the huge British supply depot at Brunswick. As the wagon train with the dead and wounded of the Pennsylvania militia passed Nassau Hall, John and Joseph jumped down and ran over to see what was left of their beloved college. All the windows had been knocked out and the walls were scarred by the impact of bullets and cannon balls. The interior was completely devastated. In one of the rooms what had been a portrait of George II now had a gaping hole instead of a head. Deeply moved by the symbolism of that ruined picture and speechless at the sight of all the devastation, John and Joseph hurried back to their wagon to continue to follow Washington's forces.

Cadwalader's unit bivouacked in Rocky Hill a few miles outside of Kingston and awaited Washington's decision. After a few hours Cadwalader came with the news.

"As many of you know, we had hoped to be able to attack the lightly defended British supply depot in Brunswick," began Cadwalader, "But General Washington notes that all of you have been subjected to several days of severe stress without rest or sleep. He has decided in his wisdom not to risk an attack on Brunswick with such exhausted troops. Instead, we will retreat north in the direction of Morristown to an area the British will find hard to attack. In the meantime, our militias all over the state of New Jersey will relentlessly attack the enemy wherever and whenever feasible."

"But, Colonel Cadwalader, sir," Captain Asher Holmes raised his hand, "You will recall that I came to you with a request from the Monmouth militia for help from the Continental army to deal with the Tory insurgency in that county. If we go north with you, who will come to the aid of our compatriots facing the bulk of the enemy in Monmouth County?"

"I have not forgotten your request," replied Cadwalader, "In fact, I discussed this issue with General Washington and General Putnam at length. General Putnam has sent a force of Pennsylvania Continentals commanded by Lieutenant Colonel Francis Gurney as well as Major John Davis with a contingent of Cumberland militia to help our patriots in Monmouth County. You and the others here from the Monmouth militia are authorized to proceed immediately to Monmouth and to report to Colonel Nathaniel Scudder for further orders."

At the mention of their father's name John and Joseph could not resist crying out for joy. John's term of duty for the Bucks County militia had run out at the end of the year so he was free to apply to the Monmouth militia for a position of surgeon's mate. Joseph was also eager to take up arms against an enemy that he now had every reason to detest.

"Well boys," said Captain Holmes, smiling broadly "Let's hurry back home and see what tasks your father has in store for us."

Even though no one had slept for days, the prospect of returning home energized the Monmouth militiamen. They also knew that Cornwallis' vast force was in hot pursuit of the Continental army, outraged and seeking vengeance for the humiliation inflicted by Washington's daring campaign. The destroyed bridges and other barriers erected by the Americans would slow them down but eventually they would be arriving in overwhelming force. It was important for them to get as far to the southeast as possible before the British and Hessians arrived. They, therefore, mounted their horses and took off in the direction of Monmouth County without further ado.

The group headed toward the Scudder residence near Monmouth Courthouse in hopes of finding Nathaniel and whatever remained of the Monmouth militia. After riding throughout the night sleeping at times in their saddles, they arrived in the early morning in the vicinity of the Scudder home. They were shocked to see many soldiers milling about Monmouth Courthouse and were at first afraid that it might be the Tory militia. But then John and Joseph espied their father sitting on his great horse conversing with some of the other officers.

"Father, father!" shouted John, "We have come to help fight the Tories!"

Overjoyed to see his two sons unharmed in the company of friendly militiamen, Nathaniel rushed over to embrace them.

"Praised be the Lord!" cried Nathaniel, "I was sick with worry about the two of you. Surely your safe arrival here is a sign from Providence."

"We have just come from Princeton where Washington has achieved a great victory," explained John, "We heard that he has sent reinforcements to Monmouth to help end the Tory insurgency here. We want to join the struggle."

"I also have good tidings," replied Nathaniel, "Colonel Gurney of the Pennsylvania Continentals arrived yesterday with 200 soldiers just in the nick of time. As you probably have heard, the Loyalists here were greatly emboldened by the British invasion. They were successful in intimidating many of our militiamen, some of whom shamefully laid down their arms. Quite a number were coerced into signing pledges of loyalty to the Crown. Two of our leading Whigs, Richard Stockton and John Covenhoven were taken captive. I, myself, had to go into hiding to avoid capture. Two turncoats, Elisha Lawrence and John Morris, posted broadsides all over the county requiring all fit men to appear at Monmouth Courthouse on New Year's Day to join a new Loyalist militia. Over 70 people answered the call. Then Colonel Gurney and his men arrived, and we prepared to counter-attack. We intended to attack them in town about a half hour before night. Colonel Morris it seems got account of our arrival and had his men and baggage drawn toward Middletown. They set off from town and got about a mile and half. We immediately pushed after them; when they made a halt, we came up. About a quarter of an hour before night, we engaged them, and they stood us about eight minutes, a very heavy fire was kept up between us during that time. The enemy at last gave way and retreated very precipitously."

John and Joseph listened with rapt attention to what had transpired just outside their home.

"What is going to happen next?" asked Joseph, "Are we going to chase them out of the county?"

That is exactly what we are planning," replied Nathaniel, "This morning we are marching to Middletown and hope to finish them off once and for all."

At that moment David Forman galloped up to Nathaniel.

"Colonel Gurney has asked us to guide his troops to the route that the Tories are most likely to have taken," he said breathlessly, his eyes glowing with almost manic fervor, "Let us be off and put an end to that scum!"

The prospect of the chase made John and Joseph forget their fatigue. Along with Nathaniel and Forman they galloped off in the direction of Middletown. After about an hour they espied a group of about 30 tattered militiamen in the distance.

"There they are!" shouted Forman, "Forward boys, it is the time of reckoning. Let's send them all to stoke the Devil's fires!"

Raising his sword and emitting a blood-curdling battle cry, Forman raced off in the direction of the enemy. Nathaniel, his sons, Colonel Gurney and the militia hurried after him. The startled Loyalists noting the large number of militiamen bearing down on them made no attempt to form a battle line but instead threw down their weapons. Some raised their hands in surrender while others tried to run off into the nearby forest. Forman reaching the first man ignored his obvious efforts at capitulation and swung his saber viciously, loping off the man's head. The severed head arced up into the air landing near Joseph's horse. As Joseph struggled to avoid retching, Forman continued his frenzied hacking swiftly killing three more of the unarmed men.

"Stop, David, stop," shouted Nathaniel trying desperately to rein in his friend, "Don't you see that they are giving up?"

"I give no quarter to such treacherous scoundrels!" shouted Forman, "They were part of our militia but then they signed loyalty oaths to the Crown. The only way to treat such poisonous snakes is to lop off their heads."

"There will be no more killing!" shouted Colonel Gurney riding up to assist Nathaniel, "These men are now my prisoners. As General Washington has ordered, I will take them back to Philadelphia where they will have to answer for their duplicity. Our cause will not be served by the senseless murder of unarmed prisoners. That will only serve to justify British propaganda that claims that we are nothing but a bunch of barbarous rebels. Besides some of them might be useful for exchanging for some of our people captured by the British."

The logic of Gurney's argument caused Forman to pause for a moment, however reluctantly. Gurney's men quickly took control of the situation, arrested the remaining twenty odd Loyalists and led them away. Nathaniel and his sons recognized a few of them as former neighbors that Nathaniel had treated for various illnesses in the past. For Nathaniel and John it was shocking to think that they now had to fight against people that they had previously sought to heal.

"Mark my words," snarled a bitter Forman, "Every one of those bastards you leave alive will one day return and try to kill us!"

"We have a more important mission right now," countered Nathaniel, "Before Colonel Gurney arrived, Morris had already sent off a large baggage train along with many of his men to Middletown. Those are supplies we need to rebuild our militia after last month's debacle. Let us hurry on to Middletown before they can escape to New York where they will be protected by the bulk of the British army."

"Lead the way, Colonel Scudder," said Colonel Gurney, "Swiftness is of the utmost importance. We must get to Middletown before they get wind of the size of the force pursuing them."

Turning to David Forman, Colonel Gurney admonished him, "Colonel Forman, I have been charged with this mission by General Washington. When we get to Middletown, it is I who will be determining the order of battle. For the safety of our men and the success of our mission I expect everyone to follow my orders explicitly! Anyone who cannot accept that should fall out right now."

Nodding his head in reluctant compliance, Forman muttered, "As you say, Colonel Gurney, I am at your disposal."

Gurney's troops were soon joined by another smaller group of Delaware Continentals and Cumberland County militia lead by Major John Davis. This force had successfully vanquished a Tory force in upper Freehold and taken several prisoners.

"Colonel Scudder how far are we from Middletown?" queried Colonel Gurney.

"I estimate only about ten miles," replied Nathaniel, "We can be there in an hour or so."

"Excellent," said Gurney, "Let us be off right away. We do not know if any of the Tories we have so far encountered might have escaped to warn them so we must proceed carefully. We should try to envelope them as completely as possible before attacking to prevent them from absconding with the supplies."

The group proceeded rapidly in the direction of Middletown with Nathaniel in the lead. When they were about a mile from Middletown, Nathaniel signaled to the others that they would shortly be arriving. The soldiers were ordered to keep quiet as Nathaniel, Gurney, Davis, and Forman continued stealthily on foot. Luckily the Tories in their haste had not posted any pickets on the road leading to the town. The four men were able to sneak closer until they had a good view of what was left of the Loyalist force. A few dozen men were in the process of loading barrels onto some wagons.

"It looks like they have large supplies of powder and ball," whispered Gurney, "We have to organize a lightning strike so that they have no opportunity to escape or to destroy the munitions."

The four men returned quickly and quietly to their troops. Gurney summoned his platoon leaders and explained how he wanted the attack to unfold.

"We could just ride in there and overwhelm them by force of numbers," began Gurney, "But they have a huge supply of powder and ball which we want to confiscate. If we start firing like mad, we might just blow up the supplies that we need. So here is what I want you to do."

Gurney went on to explain that he wanted his men to sneak up very furtively and surround the Tory militia from three sides with several sharpshooters drawing a bead on some of the men working there. At his sign they would all stand up while he shouted to them to surrender. If they did not surrender immediately, the sharpshooters would pick off a few of them. Only if Gurney gave the command was heavy firing to commence.

After his men were all in place, Gurney stood up and shouted, "Men of New Jersey, freeze and you will be spared!"

At that signal over a hundred Pennsylvania continentals stood up from their hiding places with their muskets aimed at the Tories. One of the Tory officers started to run and was immediately shot through the head by a sharpshooter. The others, seeing that they were hopelessly outnumbered and that their officer was dead, threw down their weapons and raised their hands. Gurney and his men proceeded to arrest the prisoners and take stock of the supplies. It turned out to be much more than would fit on the wagons the Tories had available. That was probably the reason that they had not yet been able to remove it all.

"I will hasten back to Freehold and get more wagons," offered Nathaniel excitedly, "We can really use all these supplies to rebuild our militia."

"Very good," agreed Gurney, "But hurry, the British are not far away. We will stay here and guard the supplies and the prisoners until you return but we should not tarry any longer than necessary."

Nathaniel, John, and Joseph ran back to fetch their horses and galloped off in the direction of Freehold. Arriving after about an hour in Freehold they proceeded to Anderson Manor where they quickly explained the situation to Colonel Anderson. He immediately agreed to provide a half dozen large wagons and slaves to drive them. Before leaving to return to Middletown Nathaniel instructed his exhausted sons to inform their mother that they were back home safe and sound.

While Colonel Anderson sent a wagon to fetch his daughter to Anderson Manor, John and Joseph collapsed in the chairs in the living room and gratefully accepted the refreshments proffered by Colonel Anderson's servants. A short time later an excited Isabella accompanied by Hannah, Kenneth and Lydia arrived. Isabella was beside herself with delight that her boys had returned without any apparent harm, and that the family after weeks of fear and uncertainty was united again. The younger Scudder children all began to talk at once until Colonel Anderson raised his hand.

"Quiet now, children," he began, "I know you all can hardly wait to hear about the adventures that your brothers have had, but first let us give thanks to the Lord that they have survived this tumultuous period."

The children obediently quieted down. Everyone then stood up with their heads bowed in prayer.

"Almighty God," intoned Colonel Anderson, "We give thanks to Thee for sparing your humble servants, John and Joseph, and ask Thee to guide us in our quest to protect the True Religion from its enemies."

"Amen!" exclaimed all present in unison. Then the younger children resumed bombarding John and Joseph with questions.

"Wait, wait!" shouted John, "It is a long and dramatic story. Let us begin with Joseph's capture by the British."

The children as well as Isabella and her father listened with wide-eyed fascination to Joseph's recounting of the last few weeks. He told them how he had been taken prisoner and then released, how he had then had the good fortune to meet up with Monmouth militiamen who took him to Cadwalader's Pennsylvania unit where he eventually was able to find his brother. Then he and John took turns describing the momentous events in Trenton and Princeton ending finally with their reunion with their father and the victorious campaign to capture the Tories and their supplies in Middletown.

"Well, it seems as though the Pennsylvania militiamen are a cut above our Monmouth boys," snorted Colonel Anderson, "Half of the men here threw down their weapons as soon as the Tory militia appeared. Many of them immediately signed oaths of loyalty to the Crown. I must say I am ashamed of them."

"The Pennsylvania militiamen are indeed highly motivated," explained John thoughtfully, "I have now spent almost a year in their service, and I think I understand what propels them. Their enthusiasm for fighting the British is, however, not based entirely on idealism."

"What is it then?" asked Isabella, "How do they differ from our people here?"

"It is all about land," answered John, "They detest the British primarily because they tried to enforce the Proclamation Line Agreement and defend the rights of the Indians. They have all been promised tracts of land in the west if we are able to establish our independence."

"That makes perfect sense," agreed Colonel Anderson, "Our yeomen don't have as much to gain as they do. Our people already have their farms even if they occasionally have to deal with title disputes."

"They are also tough fighters with lots of combat experience," added John, "Out in the wilderness they were essentially on their own fighting the Indians. They are quite a brutal lot. Killing for them is second-nature."

"That sounds dreadful!" exclaimed Isabella, "I thought they were Presbyterians like us whose main interest is the defense of the True Religion!"

"They are indeed Presbyterians," explained Colonel Anderson, "But religion is not their foremost concern. Most of them are poor people from the border lands between Scotland and England, or from Ulster. Whereas Nathaniel's ancestors came to this country in the last century to escape religious persecution, they have come to escape poverty. It is not surprising that they are utterly rapacious."

"President Witherspoon says that the graduates from our college have a duty to civilize these people and lead them on to the path of righteousness," Joseph said.

"Well, I wish him good luck with that," replied the colonel cynically, "But that is certainly not going to happen overnight. In the meantime, we have the urgent task of rebuilding our shattered militia and imbuing them with the same fighting spirit that those wild frontiersmen have."

Just how difficult this task would be became ever clearer over the next few weeks as Nathaniel and the other militia leaders took stock of the effects of the British occupation on morale. Many friends and neighbors had succumbed to British pressure and signed loyalty oaths to the British Crown. Nathaniel, Isabella, David Forman, Thomas Henderson, Colonel Anderson, and Reverend Tennent spent many hours discussing ways to reconstitute the Monmouth militia as an effective force loyal to the new government.

"The problem is we just don't know whom we can trust anymore," fumed David Forman, "Even Richard Stockton, a signer of the Declaration of Independence, has betrayed us."

"I think 'betrayed' is too strong a word," countered Isabella angrily, "I saw Richard and Annis the other day shortly after he was released by the British. Richard looked dreadful. He had been brutally mishandled. Whatever he signed, he did so under extreme duress. He is lucky to have gotten out alive! Then he had to come home to find his home nearly destroyed by the British occupation. He and his family have sacrificed much for our country."

"He signed a parole pledging to have nothing to do with politics for the duration of the war," argued Forman, "If that is not traitorous, I don't know what is."

"He will be judged by his future actions," said Nathaniel, "If we condemn everyone who was forced to sign a loyalty oath during the Tory Ascendancy, we will not be able to field a militia at all. I think we should give Richard a chance to recover his health after all he has been through."

"That is certainly true," agreed Reverend Tennent, "But we still have the problem of figuring out who is really on our side. Most men are weak and corrupt and will switch loyalties for the sake of lucre. Faith in the True Religion is the best test for whom we can trust. The Anglicans, after all, must pledge allegiance to the British monarch, and the Quakers do not want to fight anyone. I think that only ones we can depend on are those who are steadfast members of reformed churches and, of those people, our Presbyterians are unquestionably the most reliable."

"You are surely correct," agreed Nathaniel, "Perhaps the best strategy might be that you and I embark on a recruitment drive, you as a Presbyterian clergyman and I as an elder in your church and colonel in the militia. Together we might be able to convince our brethren of the urgent necessity of joining the crusade to protect the True Religion."

"So be it!" agreed Reverend Tennent, his eyes gleaming with religious fervor, "Onward Christian soldiers!"

"As an elder in Reverend Tennent's congregation and an officer of the militia, I want to be part of this as well," Thomas Henderson joined in.

Everyone agreed that Nathaniel's idea was the best way forward so he, Reverend Tennent, and Thomas Henderson spent the next weeks visiting many villages and farms in Monmouth County, preaching the Calvinist message and exhorting people to join the rebellion for the sake of their immortal souls. They were aided in their efforts by the animosity that British and Hessian foraging parties were generating among the yeomen. It also helped that news of Washington's clever victories in Trenton and Princeton spread throughout the colony. People were encouraged by the fact that Washington's army was now safely holed up in Morristown where the British were unable to dislodge them. Guerilla attacks on British units became so frequent and successful that the enemy could only venture out into the wilds of New Jersey in heavily armed bands. It started to dawn on many people who were initially skeptical that the British army was not invincible after all. Winter was also a good time for recruiting because farmers had more free time on their hands.

The trio of William Tennent, Nathaniel Scudder, and Thomas Henderson proved to be very effective. Being physicians as well as militia officers and elders of the church Scudder and Henderson were known and respected by many people. Despite his advanced age Reverend Tennent rose to the occasion with an energy that belied his years. Wherever a larger group gathered Reverend Tennent would begin by recounting the mystical experience he had had as a young man when he had lain in a death-like state for several days. Just as plans for his funeral were being finalized, he had suddenly woken up and astounded everyone with the description of what he had experienced.

"While I was conversing with my brother on the state of my soul, and the fears I had entertained for my future welfare, I found myself, in an instant, in another state of existence, under the direction of a superior being, who ordered me to follow him. I was accordingly wafted along, I know not how, till I beheld at a distance an ineffable glory, the impression of which on my mind it is impossible to communicate to mortal man. I immediately reflected on my happy change, and thought, — Well, blessed be God! I am safe at last, notwithstanding all my fears. I saw an innumerable host of happy beings surrounding the inexpressible glory, in acts of adoration and joyous worship; but I did not see any bodily shape or representation in the glorious appearance. I heard things unutterable. I heard their songs and hallelujahs of thanksgiving and praise with unspeakable rapture. I felt joy unutterable and full of glory. I then applied to my conductor and requested leave to join the happy throng; on which he tapped me on the shoulder, and said, 'You must return to the earth.' "

Tennent went on to express his profound belief that he had been sent back from death with a mission to proclaim the imminent coming of the Lord, and that the current struggle was part of the Divine Plan. Each audience invariably listened with rapt fascination to Tennent's sermon which he delivered with such a convincing intensity that it surprised even Nathaniel, although he had heard the story many times before. After Tennent's introduction Nathaniel and Thomas took turns explaining the significance of recent victories, and how the tide could be turned decisively if only people were willing to do God's work.

The crowds experiencing these exhortations were often propelled into a state of religious ecstasy—crying, falling to their knees, and begging for the chance to serve the Lord. Men of all ages flocked around the two officers wanting to know how and where they could join militia units. Within a few weeks several hundred new recruits had volunteered to serve in the Monmouth militia. The immediate challenge to the Monmouth Whig leaders was now to train and equip the new soldiers, the vast majority of which were farmers with absolutely no military training. Although the level of enthusiasm was high, training sessions were hindered by severe snowstorms and heavy gales that swept the area in the beginning of February.

Late one stormy evening Nathaniel and Isabella were woken up by someone pounding on their door who turned out to be David Forman.

"Nat, we must muster our new militia units and march quickly to reinforce our men stationed in the cedars at the Navesink highlands," announced Forman excitedly, "I have just gotten word that this storm has caused an English victualing ship to run aground on Sandy Hook near Black Point. A small group of our men seized the vessel and placed a guard. But it won't be long until the British forces at the lighthouse realize what has happened and march down the peninsula and take back the ship. We must get there first and recover the prize!"

"Good Lord, David," exclaimed Nathaniel, "Our men have barely been trained yet. They would not be a match for British Regulars if they had to confront them right now."

"The British apparently don't know about the ship yet." replied Forman, "The only danger is that foraging parties might inadvertently stumble upon our men guarding the ship. Our militia should be strong enough to turn back something like that. If we act quickly while the weather is so bad, we can spirit away the cargo right from under the Brits' noses. I have dispatched messengers calling everyone in our area to proceed to the home of our quartermaster, Richard Hartshorn, who lives near Black Point and to get ready to unload the ship."

As so often Nathaniel was skeptical about David Forman's reckless plans, and slightly annoyed that he was presenting his fellow officers with a fait accompli without consulting them first. Nevertheless, he felt that he had no choice but to join his new recruits in what could turn out to be their first military confrontation.

"There are many Tories living up in that area," remarked Nathaniel, "Hopefully they don't get wind of our designs and betray them to the British."

"We'll draw and quarter any of the bastards who try to do that!" shouted Forman belligerently, "As I have often said, the only good Tory is a dead Tory!"

Nathaniel was filled with anxiety at the prospect of exposing his green recruits to the possibility of a pitched battle with British and Hessian professionals, but he decided that the only way he could help them now was to get to Hartshorn's house as quickly as possible and make sure that no unnecessary risks were taken. Nathaniel reluctantly donned his militia uniform while Isabella woke the servants and bid them saddle up Blackjack. Soon Nathaniel and David Forman were galloping off into the stormy night in the direction of the Navesink highlands.

After an hour or so of hard riding they came in sight of Richard Hartshorn's house. Nathaniel was impressed to see that quite a few other militiamen were already beginning to arrive. David Forman had set up a system whereby riders would fan out to carry messages and summon minutemen throughout the county. He could also always get any important intelligence to Washington's headquarter within a day. Clearly the system worked very well. Nathaniel and Forman quickly proceeded to the farmhouse where some of the local officers had already gathered.

"Welcome, gentlemen, welcome," Hartshorn greeted them cordially, "Glad to see that you made it through this terrible weather to join our action. The stranded ship is only a few miles away, but we have to wait until the storm abates a bit before it will be feasible to unload her."

"Haven't the British noticed the ship?" asked Nathaniel, "They are also just a few miles away."

"We keep a close watch on the units at the lighthouse and, of course, on the men of war anchored in the bay," answered Hartshorn, "But there does not seem to be any unusual activity there. I think they don't know yet about the stranded ship."

"Good, then we can set up camp in the cedars, wait for the rest of our men to arrive and get ready to move as soon as the weather breaks," suggested David Forman.

Unbeknownst to the Monmouth militia officers they had, in fact, already been betrayed. Peter McClees, a neighbor who had signed Howe's oath of loyalty, had heard about the militia's project and, together with other Tory sympathizers, had stolen off to the British unit stationed at the blockhouse on Sandy Hook and informed them about the militia's plan. The British immediately commissioned 170 men from their 26th Regiment on Staten Island as well as a Tory militia from New York to prepare for an attack. They were supported by the warship *Syren* with a large contingent of marines. As the Monmouth militia officers were discussing plans for recovering the cargo of the stranded ship, the superior British force was also just waiting for the weather to break.

✱ ✱ ✱

Jim Crawford and Matty Rue struggled to find moderately dry spots under the cedars where they could lay down their blankets for the night. It had been three days since they had answered the call to assemble at the Navesink highlands and the weather had been rotten the whole time.

"Good Lord, I hope that something happens soon," complained Jim Crawford, "This is the third night we have had to sleep out here in this miserable rain and snow. Reverend Tennent convinced me that it is my Christian duty to support this mission, but I would much rather be home with my Margaret and my seven children."

"I heard from Captain Hankinson that as soon as the weather lets up, we will hike down to the shore and unload the ship," said the much younger Matty Rue, struggling to sound optimistic, "Then it's back to the farm. I have just found out that I am soon to be a father, and I hate to leave my young wife alone."

"I have the feeling that the weather will soon be turning," replied Crawford, "We had better try to get some sleep because we will probably be heading out at the break of dawn."

The weather did, in fact, take a turn for the better and just before dawn Matty was awoken by a strange sound.

Thwack! Thwack! Thwack!

Matty sat up gazing around him to find out what was making the unusual noise. As his eyes came into focus, he saw a British soldier plunge his bayonet into the chest of Jim Crawford.

Thwack!

Matty quickly realized that the source of the noise was the sound of bayonets being thrust into the chests of the sleeping militiamen. Looking down the hill he saw a large line of British soldiers silently advancing and methodically murdering his compatriots without firing a shot. The snow was stained bright red with the blood of at least twenty dying militiamen. He jumped up looking around frantically for his weapon, but a British sergeant pointed his musket directly into his face.

"Not a sound, you rebel dog," the sergeant whispered, "Or you will join your fellows on the road to hell."

Seeing the overwhelming numbers of the enemy Matty threw up his hands in surrender as did most of the others who had not yet been dispatched.

✱ ✱ ✱

Nathaniel and the other officers staying at the home of Richard Hartshorn were awoken by the sound of musket fire. Looking out the window they were shocked to see many Redcoats attacking the unit guarding the house. It was immediately obvious that they were hopelessly outnumbered. The enemy soldiers were advancing relentlessly across an open field in front of the house. Behind the house was a thick forest. Fortunately, there appeared to be no enemy soldiers coming from that direction.

"Sound the retreat!" Nathaniel shouted to a drummer boy, "Into the forest, it is our only chance to escape!"

As the drummer boy beat the signal for retreat, Nathaniel and the other officers jumped onto their horses and led the surviving militia men into the woods. The thick vegetation provided cover for the survivors. Sharpshooters were able to make it too dangerous for the British Regulars to follow. Nathaniel was able to gather about 40 survivors and lead them through the forest to safety.

Back in Manalapan Nathaniel together with Thomas Henderson and David Forman met at Anderson Manor to inform Reverend Tennent, Colonel Anderson and the rest of the family about the disaster.

"We were betrayed, pure and simple!" fulminated David Forman heatedly, "I have said time and again, the Tories we don't kill today will come back to kill us tomorrow."

"Killing Tories alone is not the answer," countered Nathaniel solemnly, "I am afraid we have to examine our own mistakes critically if we want to avoid repeating them in the future. We took a large risk to retrieve the cargo of that boat and paid a heavy price. Over twenty men were killed and at least seventy taken prisoner including two captains and four lieutenants. We also lost several barrels of powder, hundreds of ball cartridges, and quite a few provisions. It is the biggest disaster that our militia has had to endure up until now. I doubt the cargo of that ship was worth all that, especially the lives of all those young volunteers."

"War is never without risks!" fumed David Forman, "We will never defeat the enemy without taking risks."

"That is certainly true," agreed Thomas Henderson, "But Nathaniel is also surely correct to point out that we have to make a careful assessment of the risks and rewards of our actions. Clearly we should avoid confrontations between an untrained yeomen militia and British professionals. We can be much more effective with insurgent tactics, but in pitched battles we cannot prevail without the help of the Continental Army. Our first task now is to rebuild the militia units we have just lost."

"I am more than ready to resume that holy effort!" exclaimed Reverend Tennent, "I will begin by visiting the families of those boys killed or captured and assuring them that their sacrifices will not go unrewarded. I will preach that rather than cowering down before the Beast, we must have the courage to stand with the Divine Hosts, for our eventual victory over the forces of evil can never be in doubt. For the sake of their immortal souls, they must have faith!"

As physicians, Nathaniel and Thomas Henderson, exchanged worried glances. They too were anxious to resume their recruiting efforts which had been so successful and were greatly moved by Reverend Tennent's passionate eloquence. They could not help but notice, however, what a toll the previous recruitment campaign had taken on the old man. His spirit was still indomitable, but his body looked to be on the verge of collapse. Both physicians worried that the good reverend would soon work himself up into a state of apoplexy.

Unburdened by such considerations David Forman encouraged the aging parson in his exhortations, "You are absolutely correct, Reverend Tennent, what we are facing is in fact a Holy War. It is our sacred duty to confront the Beast with all the violence we can muster. If you can motivate the faithful, I will be happy to lead them to avenge our martyrs by driving the Forces of Evil off Sandy Hook!"

And motivate them he did. With the reluctant support of Nathaniel and Thomas Henderson, the old preacher rose once more to the occasion and harangued the faithful about the urgent necessity of lining up on the side of the Lord in the Battle of all Battles. Sensing his own approaching demise, he was grateful to be able to spend the final chapter of his life as a soldier for Jesus. His absolute conviction that he was about to return to the blessed place that he had briefly experienced in his youth infused his sermons with a charismatic power that never failed to move his audiences. Dozens more volunteered to serve in the militia. But not all appreciated the effectiveness of his recruiting efforts. In towns with significant numbers of Tory sympathizers Tennent's sermons were considered seditious. Angry grumblings about the "Black Regiment" could be heard in some audiences. Notes with death threats were slid under his church's door.

"The Beast will not intimidate me!" exclaimed Tennent, "Crede Deo! It only motivates me more to join the battle."

Unfortunately, his physical condition was furthered weakened by the intense emotional state that he was experiencing. In the beginning of March the two physicians finally managed to convince him that he must take to his bed for a few days to regain his strength.

"In any case," argued Nathaniel, "You have accomplished your mission. Our militia has many new recruits to help us drive the British out of New Jersey. The Lord will surely not begrudge you a little rest."

"Nathaniel is right," added David Forman, "I now have a force of about 250 men and two six-pounders that I will use to attack the lighthouse and regain what has been stolen from us."

"Praised be the Lord!" shouted Reverend Tennent, "My spirit will be marching with you even as I lie here. How I long to see the walls of Jericho crumble before the Lord of Hosts!"

"We will have someone bring you news as soon as we have reached our goal," promised Thomas Henderson, "Now you need to rest and pray for our success."

The militia officers left the reverend to regain his strength and began gathering the militia for the attack on the lighthouse. After several hundred men had answered the call, David Forman led them with his two cannons to try to force the British garrison to surrender. Unfortunately the six-pounders were not powerful enough to breach the thick walls of the lighthouse and the block house. Musket volleys from the militiamen were equally ineffective. The garrison within sent off signal flares to call the British man-of-war, *Syren*, at anchor in the bay. When it became apparent, that the powerful ship was on its way to relieve the garrison. Forman ordered his men to retreat. This time there were at least few casualties on the American side although the goal had not been accomplished.

Back in Manalapan they were saddened to hear that Reverend Tennent had passed away in his sleep.

"At least we don't have to burden him with the depressing result of our latest exploit," remarked Thomas Henderson grimly.

"Yes, he has peace at last," agreed Nathaniel, "And he doesn't have to read the latest hate mail delivered to his church."

"Are those Tory bastards still trying to intimidate him?" asked David Forman.

"Are they ever," answered Nathaniel, "And they are getting more and more violent. Listen to the one I just found this morning. 'The punishment for sedition is death. Hanging is too good for rebel swine. You should be hung up in public to rot so that your stinking flesh will deter the fools in your congregation from rising against a legitimate sovereign.' "

"Well, they can't touch him now," said Thomas Henderson, "He has gone to his just reward."

"Actually, they could touch him," countered David Forman, "I wouldn't put it past those bastards to dig up his corpse and defile it in public."

"You know, David could be right," Nathaniel concurred, "Reverend Tennent has become a symbol of the struggle for protection of the True Religion. I could well imagine that those in thrall to the Evil One would want to desecrate that symbol in any vicious way possible."

"As elders of the church we cannot let that happen," agreed Thomas Henderson, "Until this great struggle is won, I say we bury the good pastor in a secret place that we only reveal to our most trusted comrades in arms."

"An excellent plan," enthused David Forman, "But just remember from our recent experience just how few people we can really trust."

"I have an idea," suggested Nathanial, "Where the reverend will be close to his flock but where his mortal remains will remain undisturbed."

Following Nathaniel's suggestion, they removed some of the floorboards from the church and dug a grave for the pastor. After a brief ceremony they closed the grave and replaced the boards. On the following Sunday the congregation was informed by the elders that Reverend Tennent was resting in a safe place that would be revealed at the appropriate time.

Returning home Nathaniel was anxious to see how his dear and somewhat vulnerable wife was coping with the stresses and uncertainties of the current situation. Since losing her last child her health never quite regained its former vigor, and Nathaniel sometimes felt guilty that he could not spend more time with her.

"Oh, Nathaniel," she greeted him wearily, "I am so glad that nothing has happened to my three men at war. I pray constantly the Lord will spare our family more sacrifices."

"We have indeed been lucky so far, especially when I think of some of our neighbors and my poor brother, Will, and his family," agreed Nathaniel, "Through the grace of God we have indeed been spared the worst until now but, come what may, we must simply put our fates confidently in His hand."

"How much longer do you think this is going to last?" asked Isabella plaintively, "I know it is God's will, but the task seems so . . . so overwhelming."

"It is impossible to say," answered Nathaniel, "That also is in God's hand. We have no choice but to play the role that the Almighty has deemed appropriate for us."

"You are right, of course," sighed Isabella, "But sometimes I don't know where to get the strength."

"Faith, my darling, sola fides," assured Nathaniel taking Isabella gently into his arms, "Faith is the only real source of strength."

"And if we keep the faith, I am confident that we will prevail in the end," he continued in an upbeat tone, "I am greatly encouraged by our recent successes. I think we have a good chance of driving the Brits and their Tory servants out of New Jersey in a few months. Our militia is making life hell for their forage parties. The Continental Army arrested hundreds of Tories when they swept through here so the enemy has far fewer traitors that they can rely on."

"Who are those arrested?" asked Isabella, "Are they people we know?"

"Yes, of course," answered Nathaniel, "Some were friends and neighbors. The whole Taylor family, for example. You would recognize most of the family names. In fact, I will soon be getting a list of all the captured Tories from Monmouth County who are currently awaiting trial in Philadelphia. Governor Livingston has asked me to look through the list and report back to him about the trustworthiness of the various individuals. Some apparently are ready to abjure their oaths of loyalty to the Crown and join our side in order to escape punishment. Others claim that they were never involved in loyalist activity. I am asked to make a judgement in each case. And, in the meantime, David Forman has been appointed Brigadier General of the New Jersey militia so we can expect many more arrests."

"What a dreadful responsibility!" exclaimed Isabella, "You will have to decide the fate of people who were our friends. I am glad I don't have to make such decisions."

"I will simply gather the facts and present them to the Committee of Safety. The Committee of Safety then decides based on the evidence if a certain person is to be summoned, further questioned and, perhaps, punished."

"Still dreadful, to think how our society is being wrenched apart!"

"I am afraid there is no alternative," explained Nathaniel grimly, "You have to understand that some of these people are exceedingly dangerous. Think about how that scoundrel McCrees betrayed us at Navesink, and how many of our poor boys are now rotting on prison ships in New York!"

"I know, I know," conceded Isabella shaking her head sadly, "Do you have any word about their fates? Is there any chance that they might come free one day? What Annis has told me about Richard's captivity was gruesome."

"Conditions there now are even more gruesome than what Richard experienced," confirmed Nathaniel, "What information seeps out describes a hell hole that defies the imagination. Dr. Witherspoon, in fact, has been assigned to an investigative committee to document the details so that General Washington can register a protest with General Howe. The wretched state of the prisoners is illegal even by British standards."

"Speaking of Dr. Witherspoon, do you know when classes might resume at Nassau Hall? Joseph needs to get back to his studies before he is tempted to join a militia and go off to war."

"Oh, by the way, John has volunteered to serve as a surgeon's mate in Asher Holmes' regiment now that his term of service in the Pennsylvania militia is over. At least he will be closer to home. Regarding Joseph's studies, right now Nassau Hall is being used as a barracks by the Continental Army. The board of trustees plans to meet at Cooper's Ferry in May to discuss how to repair the damage and get the college functioning again. I will ride up there since I must share some information with Dr. Witherspoon about our militiamen who were captured at Navesink. I will find out what plans are being made to get things going again. It will also be interesting to hear the information concerning the prison ships that Witherspoon has been able to gather so far."

A few weeks later Nathaniel departed for Cooper's Ferry. He took Joseph along so he could hear firsthand how the trustees were planning to get the studies going again. Nathaniel feared that he had been forced in the last months to neglect his fatherly duties due to the pressure of events, and he was pleased to have the opportunity to discuss Joseph's future with him on the long ride to the Delaware.

"If Nassau Hall is back in American hands, why doesn't Dr. Witherspoon just return and resume classes?" asked Joseph.

"As you could see for yourself, Nassau Hall has been badly damaged and would first have to be repaired," answered Nathaniel, "But that is not the main reason, it is still a bit early for Witherspoon to dare to come so close to British forces. He is considered by the Brits to be a ringleader of what they call the 'Presbyterian Rebellion.' If he were in Princeton, they might well be tempted to mount a lightning raid to seize him. For the time being he is safer if he can escape across the Delaware at short notice."

"Why is he so important to the British to arrest this one man?" Joseph wondered.

"Because the British realize that he is the spiritual leader for many who have joined the movement to resist tyranny. He was the only man of the cloth to sign the Declaration of Independence, and he is an inspiration to the many Presbyterian frontiersmen who are joining Washington's army in droves. Without the exhortations of our Presbyterian pastors, we would never have been able to recruit so many willing to risk their lives for freedom, for freedom from absolute monarchies and Papist domination! This was very evident in the success that Reverend Tennent had in his last weeks in helping us to refill the ranks of the Monmouth militia. Many of our Southern allies are in this in order to save their plantations and slaves, we are in this to save our souls!"

"John told me that many of the Presbyterian frontiersmen he met are in this to steal Indian land," countered Joseph mischievously.

Nathaniel smiled at his son's precocious appraisal of the political situation.

"Yes, Joseph," agreed Nathaniel, "There is that element as well. Dr. Witherspoon recognizes the basic corruption of all men but feels that people who have at least in theory embraced the doctrines of John Calvin might be able to be led to a higher purpose. In fact, he sees that goal as the primary mission of Nassau Hall. It is your generation that will be called upon to civilize those doughty frontiersmen and mitigate their greed."

"I think that it will take more than one generation to accomplish that," opined Joseph, "In the meantime Nassau Hall is not in operation so I might as well join a militia and advance the cause."

"All in good time," said Nathaniel, "I would be surprised if the trustees do not have a plan to reopen as soon as possible. And you will be much more valuable to the cause if you have finished your education."

Arriving in Cooper's Ferry Nathaniel and Joseph proceeded to the local meeting house where Dr. Witherspoon and the trustees of the college were holding their board meeting. Entering the building Nathaniel was pleased to see that in addition to Dr. Witherspoon and Governor Livingston eleven other trustees, including his old friend, Richard Stockton, were present. Clearly, despite the depredations of war, the leadership of the college was determined to renew its operation as quickly as possible.

"I would like to propose the following for consideration," Dr. Witherspoon stood to address the other board members, "As soon as the enemy is removed out of this state, I would like to call our students together at Princeton and proceed with their education as best we can. But for that I would like to request Governor Livingston to put an end to the quartering of troops in our building so that the necessary repairs can be carried out."

"I will order militia troops to refrain from using the building as soon as possible," responded Livingston, "And I will send a request to General Washington to instruct his troops accordingly as well. But, as you said yourself, the enemy must first be removed from the state, and for that we need our troops. I see that Colonel Scudder has just arrived. Perhaps he has some news about developments on the front. Colonel Scudder, how long do you think it will be before we have removed the enemy from our state?"

Nathaniel rose and bowed to the assembled dignitaries.

"I am actually quite confident that we can effectively prevent the enemy from occupying our state again as they did last year," answered Nathaniel, "Our militia is making life hell for the foraging units that dare to venture into our territory. General Foreman has arrested everyone in eastern New Jersey whom he suspects of harboring Tory sympathies. Washington will soon march part of his army out of Morristown to positions in Middlebrook to block any British advance toward Philadelphia. But Monmouth County is and will remain the skirmish line. Tories that David Forman has uprooted often escape to British lines and then organize raiding parties to kidnap our citizens or harass our leaders. This brings me to the main reason for my coming here. I bring news of the death of Reverend William Tennent of natural causes. Because of his valiant efforts to recruit for our cause, he was frequently the target of Tory harassment. For that reason he has been buried at a secret place to stymie any attempt to desecrate his mortal remains."

"A great leader has gone from us!" exclaimed Dr. Witherspoon, "But let us take his example as an inspiration for all of us. He fought to protect the freedom to practice the True Religion until his dying breath. And that is what we all must do as well for the sake of our immortal souls! As many of you know, I was appointed to a committee to investigate reports of ill treatment of our compatriots who have wound up in British prisons in New York. I swear to you that there has never been clearer evidence of the depravity of the enemy than the conditions they have created there. They refuse to treat our soldiers as prisoners of war saying they are merely lawless rebels who deserve the noose. They are packed together in putrid conditions on ships and in the Old Sugar House and fed garbage if anything at all. They are already dying like flies."

"I had a taste of that myself," remarked Richard Stockton, "Anything more than a few weeks there can be a death sentence. We must do whatever we can to convince General Howe that this is a severe blemish on his reputation as a gentleman, and that he must allow our representatives humanitarian access to the prisoners. General Washington has appointed Lewis Pintard to be resident agent to the prisoners. I am happy to report that my brother-in-law Elias Boudinot after some initial reluctance agreed to discharge the duties of commissary general of prisoners. He will endeavor to get food, clothing, money, and other essentials to our Americans held by the enemy. I ask all of you to give him whatever assistance you can."

"Elias is an excellent choice," said Nathaniel, "And his tasks could not be more urgent. I will spread the word to the farmers in Monmouth County that helping Elias is helping their friends, relatives, and neighbors who are winding up in the Sugar House in increasing numbers and facing starvation. The commissary general of prisoners is also responsible for the treatment of enemy prisoners in our hands. As General David Forman has pointed out on many occasions, those prisoners are our bargaining tokens, so we need to capture as many Brits and Tory sympathizers as possible. General Howe needs to be gently reminded that the treatment of these prisoners will be affected by his treatment of our people, and if he wants to free any of them, it will be in exchange for an equivalent number of our people."

"A very good point, Colonel Scudder," agreed Dr. Witherspoon, "For my part, I will write my report in great detail including all the grisly stories that our committee has been able to gather. Readers will shudder to find out to what depth the enemy has sunken and will see clearly that we are truly confronting the Beast."

"We should see to it that the report is widely distributed," suggested Nathaniel, "I can't imagine anything more effective in mobilizing sentiment for our cause. Anyone still harboring illusions about the benign nature of British rule will be shocked by the reality revealed in your report."

"My understanding is that General Washington plans to do exactly that," confirmed Witherspoon, "I will endeavor to make the report a clarion call to Christian soldiers!"

"That is precisely the strategy that Reverend Tennent used so successfully," added Nathaniel enthusiastically, "As an elder in Reverend Tennent's congregation I will see that the word goes out to all the reformed churches to urge their flocks to contribute to our crusade either by joining the militia or by supporting Elias' mission."

"I knew we could count on you, Colonel Scudder," said Governor Livingston with a smile, "That is why I suggested that you serve in my Privy Council as chair of the committee to recruit and provision the continental line. So many of our soldiers and militiamen are falling into British hands, however, that I suspect that recruitment of replacements for the captured will be our major challenge. Your strategy of motivating through the pulpit could well be our most promising strategy."

"I am confident that our exhortations will prompt many volunteers," replied Nathaniel, "But absorbing so large a number of new recruits presents problems that urgently need to be solved. General Forman reports from the front that the depredations of the enemy have resulted in many willing to fight for us but the Assembly refuses to pay them until they have signed the oath of loyalty to the State of New Jersey."

"But that is a reasonable requirement," objected Governor Livingston.

"Of course, it is," agreed Nathaniel, "But it all takes time, and many are destitute and in urgent need of assistance. They cannot wait until all formalities have been completed. The locals whose property has been spared destruction contribute whatever meager amount they can, but much property has been destroyed or stolen during the Tory uprising. The proceeds from the sale of the cargo of the impounded sloop, *Polly & Anne*, for example, were to be used to buy clothing for the continental troops in New Brunswick. Part of that money was stolen, however, and the clothing we were able to send was lost when the enemy drove our troops out of that town. The Monmouth militia has received no allotment for medical supplies, so I allowed my son who is a surgeon's mate to distribute my personal supply. I need those supplies for my patients, however, and I will have to replace them with my own money. Prices have risen of late, and my suppliers only accept British or Spanish currency. Although I give gladly, I am nearly at the limit of my philanthropic possibilities."

"That is completely clear, Colonel Scudder," assured Governor Livingston, "No one can expect the local population to bear the costs of war alone. I would ask you to submit a report detailing the amount of compensation that would be appropriate for people like yourself who are gallantly supporting our cause with their personal fortunes. I will then apply to the Assembly to grant appropriate compensation."

"Make no mistake, Colonel Scudder," added Dr. Witherspoon, "We understand and appreciate the sacrifices that people like you are making for the cause. It is well-documented in the report I will soon present. But I am convinced that our sacrifices are not in vain. We are witnessing a great and growing uprising of militia units all over the state. I think it is only a matter of weeks before we have driven the Brits out of this province. I intend to restart classes immediately and gather the students in Princeton as soon as the building is repaired. In fact, you are welcome to leave your son, Joseph, with me now in Pennsylvania to continue his education there until we can move back to Nassau Hall."

"That is very generous of you, sir," replied Nathaniel, greatly relieved that he would not have to talk Joseph out of risking his life in a militia unit.

"And please keep me up to date regarding your recruitment efforts," said Governor Livingston, "I greatly appreciate the information I get from you and General Forman and will always try to address the problems you identify, although I can't promise that I will always be successful. The challenges we face are daunting, but the enthusiasm of men like you and Forman gives me hope that we will prevail."

After bidding farewell to his son and the board Nathaniel headed immediately back in the direction of Monmouth County anxious to share the good news with Isabella that Joseph would now for a time at least be at a safe distance from the war zone and be able to continue his studies.

After a few hours of hard riding Nathaniel arrived at the Scudder residence in the early evening and rushed inside to tell Isabella how the meeting had gone. Entering the kitchen, he was surprised to see three of his Black servants, Beth, Pegg and Ellice alone in the kitchen cutting beans, and Isabella nowhere in sight, although at this time of day she would normally be supervising the preparation of the evening meal.

"Good evening, ladies," Nathaniel greeted them, "Do any of you know where my wife is off to?"

"One of the merchants came here for money and Miss Isabella didn't have it, so she said she was going to see her father," answered Beth.

Nathaniel felt a wave of irritation flow over him. At first, he was annoyed at the thought that Isabella would be borrowing money from his father-in-law. On second thought, however, he realized that she probably had no choice. Between his duties for the militia and the governor's Privy Council he hardly had time to practice his profession. The compensation for his public activities was meager, and usually in provincial currency that not everyone was willing to take as payment. His anger gave way to embarrassment over his inability to provide adequately for his family. By the time Isabella returned home an hour later, he was feeling quite contrite.

"I heard from the servants that you had to visit your father because you did not have enough money to pay a merchant," began Nathaniel, "I feel I must apologize for the stress I have had to subject you to lately."

"It is a hard time for everyone right now," Isabella replied with a weary smile, "You need not apologize. You are only doing your duty but some of the merchants are reluctant to accept provincial currency, so I had to borrow a few pounds from my father."

"I wish some of those fellows would also think about doing their duty to God and country," remarked Nathaniel angrily, "The governor has put me in charge of a committee to find ways to supply and provision the continental line, but I don't know how we can accomplish that if farmers and merchants will not accept the legal tender of our state."

"Well, many farmers in our area know that they can sell all they can produce to the British in New York for sterling," explained Isabella, "They ask themselves why should they sell for paper money from the state of New Jersey that might become worthless if our government fails."

"Our government is not going to fail!" exclaimed Nathaniel, "And those who persist in the so-called London trade will have cause to regret it sooner or later. David Forman has vowed to arrest everyone he believes to be sabotaging our cause in this way and their property will be confiscated."

"What happens to the confiscated property?" asked Isabella, "Does David get to keep it for himself?"

"Of course, not," replied Nathaniel indignantly, "All confiscated property must be disposed of as the Assembly sees fit. By the way, we might benefit from some of that. Governor Livingston has informed me that he will ask the Assembly to reimburse us for some of the money and medicine that we lost during the Tory insurrection. I am to make a report detailing what the Tory depredations have cost us and others in this area, and he will try to get us some compensation from the Assembly."

"I hope he is successful with that," said Isabella, "But make sure you include all the expenses that you have paid out of your own pocket. Our son, John, for example, has been using your medicines to treat the sick militiamen. I don't believe he has received any compensation for that, so you need to include that in your list as well."

"I suspect that there are many people who will be seeking compensation for their losses," said Nathaniel, "Realistically speaking, it seems unlikely that Congress will be able to satisfy all their just demands, particularly since we are all asked to help relieve the conditions that our poor prisoners in New York are suffering. Did you know that Elias Boudinot has been appointed Commissary General of Prisoners? His job is to procure food, medicines, and money for distribution to the poor wretches languishing in the Sugar House and on the prison ships."

"Annis mentioned that the last time we talked," replied Isabella, "Apparently, Congress has allocated 600 pounds in bills of exchange that Elias is supposed to sell in New York in order to be able to buy supplies. If merchants there are as reluctant to take paper currency as the merchants here, I don't think he will have much success. He will probably wind up paying for the food out of his own pocket hoping that Congress or the Assembly will compensate him at some point. I suspect that he is only doing this to help dispel rumors that Richard Stockton betrayed the cause while he was in captivity."

"Alas, you are probably right," admitted Nathaniel, "And compensation, if it comes at all, will only be possible if we are successful in the field. Fortunately, it looks as though we might be successful in driving the British out of our state. Howe has tried to lure Washington into a pitched battle on several occasions, but Washington has not taken the bait. Between the Continental Army and the militias, I think we are strong enough to discourage Howe from attempting to march to Philadelphia through New Jersey. Although the enemy is extracting a terrible price from us, they are also being forced to absorb vast expense themselves. If we can just endure awhile longer, they might be forced to sue for peace, especially if Benjamin Franklin can convince the French to come into the war on our side."

Over the next few weeks Nathaniel's guarded optimism proved to have some foundation. Washington's cagey strategy combined with the hit-and-run tactics of the militias did, in fact, convince General Howe that marching on Philadelphia through New Jersey would be too risky. By the end of June, it became apparent that he had decided to abandon New Jersey and develop a different strategy. Washington publicly congratulated the New Jersey militias for their dogged determination. No one had any illusions, however, that the British would be giving up any time soon, and the big question on everybody's mind was what the British would do next.

The answer to that question emerged over the summer when rumors reached New Jersey that General "Gentleman Johnny" Burgoyne was planning a two-pronged attack from Quebec to take the Hudson valley, joining up with Howe's forces in New York thus splitting the rebellious states into two pieces. These rumors made it clear that the success in denying the British easy passage through New Jersey would be of limited value if the enemy succeeded in cutting off New Jersey from its allies in New England. There was no use, however, in attacking Howe's vastly superior forces in New York. Every larger encounter typically resulted in more Americans dead or winding up in British prisons. David Forman's vigorously brutal attempts to counterbalance such losses by arresting suspected Tories risked alienating Americans whose loyalties were still undecided.

In August news reached New Jersey that one prong of Burgoyne's army had besieged the American garrison at Fort Stanwix. Another was heading down Lake

Champlain in the direction of Albany. If these two forces joined up at Albany and were met by a force marching north from New York City, things would look very dismal for the Americans. Washington considered marching north to reinforce the militias guarding the Hudson valley. But just as anxiety over the impending disaster reached its climax, something totally unexpected occurred. Howe did indeed load a large portion of his troops onto transport ships but instead of sailing up the Hudson, they sailed out to sea. Washington had no idea where Howe was headed but he thought it might be another feint, so he stayed near New York. Only when word reached him that Howe's fleet had been sighted near the mouth of the Delaware, did Washington realize that Howe was planning to take Philadelphia by sea and rushed southward to defend the capital.

On the one hand the leaders of New Jersey were relieved that the military pressure from New York was reduced dramatically. Burgoyne was now on his own in unfamiliar, wilderness territory where local militias had an advantage. The advantage of the insurgents was clearly demonstrated in Bennington, Vermont where militia forces were able to reduce the size of Burgoyne's army by almost 1,000 men. On the other hand, defending Philadelphia would be a very different kind of war on very different terrain where a highly professional force would be difficult to stop.

As it turned out, Howe's army was indeed not to be stopped. After landing near Elkton, Maryland in northern Chesapeake Bay he easily brushed aside local resistance as he marched north in the direction of Philadelphia. Washington attempted to stop him at Brandywine Creek but was outflanked and had to retreat. Howe marched unopposed into Philadelphia and was welcomed by many enthusiastic Tory sympathizers. Washington attempted to stage a bold surprise counterattack at Germantown modeled on his success at Trenton. This time, however, luck was not with them, and Washington's army suffered heavy losses including Dr. Witherspoon's oldest son, James.

It was, therefore, in an atmosphere of solemnity and foreboding that the New Jersey Privy Council met in October to discuss how to respond to the new situation.

"Dr. Witherspoon, on behalf of the government of New Jersey, I would like to express our heart-felt condolences on the death of your son," began Governor Livingston, "He was a fine young man who was surely destined for great things. It was a loss not only for you but for the nation."

"Thank you, Governor Livingston," replied Witherspoon, "It is moments like this when one most needs to be secure in one's faith. James died for a cause he believed in, and no man can wish for a better end than that. Dulce et decorum est pro patria mori! I am determined that James' death will not have been in vain. We cannot allow temporary setbacks to erode our will to resist."

"Your steadfastness in the face of tragedy is an inspiration to all of us, sir," said Nathaniel, "May God grant us your tenacity in our struggles. I agree completely that just because the meeting place of the Continental Congress has been occupied, that does not mean they have captured our government. It should come as no surprise that our ragged, untrained army is not going to prevail in conventional engagements against the best military professionals in the world. But this country is huge, and there is no way the British army could occupy all of it effectively. We have been very successful with our militia insurgency in New Jersey, but we must avoid pitched battles where we take heavy losses. We need rather to concentrate on solving our problems of training and provision."

"Your strategy is appealing," agreed Witherspoon, "But it could be quite some time until the British have wasted so much money that they give up. If the French were to come to our aid, however, that might shorten the agony."

"It might indeed," announced Governor Livingston, "And I have interesting news that some of our successes on the northern front have reached the French who are negotiating with Benjamin Franklin. Just one more big military success might push the Frenchmen over the brink. But for that to happen, we need to address some of the problems that Colonel Scudder has repeatedly pointed out. I am, therefore, nominating him along with Dr. Witherspoon, Abraham Clark, and Jonathan Elmer to stand for election to represent New Jersey at the next session of the Continental Congress."

Chapter 21

SARATOGA – 1777–1778

"NATHANIEL, I UNDERSTAND THAT it is a great honor that the governor wants you to stand for Congress, but what does that mean for your family?" Isabella could not hide the anxiety she felt over the family's deteriorating finances.

"To be truthful, Isabella, I have not begun to consider that in detail," admitted Nathaniel, "I assume that some compensation will be forthcoming, and the governor has assured me that we will be reimbursed for the expenses we have already incurred. But, in any case, I don't see any alternative but to serve our country in its hour of need."

Isabella nodded her head resignedly. Knowing her idealistic husband as she did, she realized it was hopeless to try to dissuade him from doing what he felt was his duty. "I just hope that the compensation comes in the form of paper that the local merchants will accept."

"It is their patriotic duty to accept the currency of our republic," countered Nathaniel angrily, "And they can get in big trouble as Tory sympathizers if they don't!".

"Even those who consider themselves patriots to our cause and accept the republic's currency do not trade their goods for Continental dollars at face value," explained Isabella, "A Continental buys only about a third of what it did when it was first issued."

"That is true," conceded Nathaniel, "But the value of the Continental as well as that of New Jersey's debt certificates depend in the final analysis on the conduct of the war. We have had setbacks over the summer, but I have just received word of a great victory in New York at Saratoga. I don't have the details yet but apparently Burgoyne has suffered a crushing defeat and our side has taken many prisoners."

"And how will that affect what a local merchant charges me for candles?" asked Isabella.

"Ben Franklin and Silas Deane are in France right now trying to induce the French to give more aid to our side. Up until now the French have been secretly supplying us with some weapons and ammunition but have been reluctant to risk a general war with Britain. But if they believed that the British could lose this war, they might be tempted to invest more in our future by granting us the loans we need to finance our revolution. That would improve our credit standing throughout the world which in turn would bolster the value of our currencies."

"Do you think that the French would actually go so far as to send soldiers and ships to help us?" wondered Isabella marveling at the irony that the sworn enemy of yesterday was now the best hope of today.

"The French have no love for the principles we are fighting for," admitted Nathaniel, "But they would love to pay Britain back for the bitter defeat of 1763. If we can convince them that we are the effective vehicle of their revenge, they might even fight for us. In any case, I will do my best to convince my fellow Congress members that we must forge a united confederation out of the 13 separate states so that the French will take us seriously as a viable ally against the British."

A few weeks later Nathaniel met with David Forman to discuss what implications his new duties might have for the Monmouth militia.

"Congratulations, Nat," David Forman greeted him warmly, "I am glad to hear that the government of New Jersey is finally doing something that makes some sense instead of making a nuisance of itself."

"Thank you, David," replied Nathaniel, "But what is it that displeases you about Governor Livingston's policies? I thought we were all in general agreement about the conduct of the war."

"I think Livingston is sincerely on our side, but I wonder about the influence of certain people in the Assembly who seem to want to block our vigorous prosecution of the war. Some of them have had the gall to accuse me of murdering innocent people without trial. They wanted me to attend a hearing in Princeton to answer false charges, but I resigned my commission as Brigadier General of the Continental Army instead. But, not to worry, I will continue the fight in a different capacity."

"That is outrageous, David, you have risked your life time and again for our cause. If not for you, the Tories would still be in control of Monmouth County."

"That is exactly the point, Nathaniel. Although I have long been disgusted with the indolence and want of attention to military matters in the legislature of this state, I was determined to continue to serve our campaign until victory. But I will not take orders from a set of men who are plotting by the most unfair means to stain my reputation. I will continue the fight but the only man I will take orders from is Washington himself."

"What is exactly is the nature of these trumped-up charges?" asked Nathaniel. "What are you supposed to have done?"

"They claim that I had no right to shoot that Tory bastard from Shrewsbury, Stephen Edwards, without a trial. Everybody knows he was getting rich from the London trade and refusing to help provision our troops. He had it coming. After I shot him, I found proof of his culpability, a small fortune in sterling at his farm which our militia has good use for. It will also set an example for any other Tory sympathizers who might consider opposing us."

Forman's capacity for cold-blooded brutality always had a somewhat chilling effect on Nathaniel although he realized that that capacity was essential if victory in the struggle against a superior foe were ever to be achieved.

"Many in the Assembly have or had business relations with some of the people you suspect to be Tories, so it is not surprising that they might take their sides."

"Many in the Assembly have two strings on their bow," snorted Forman, "They want to ensure that they will come out on top no matter who wins the war."

"Nevertheless, we should endeavor not to make enemies in the Assembly," cautioned Nathaniel, "I have submitted a report of all our losses from Tory depredations last year and hope to convince the Assembly to reimburse us. The last thing we need is to give someone in the Assembly cause to doubt the veracity of our claims. Some have already expressed a keen interest in the disposal of the freight of the *Polly & Anne*."

"As I have said many times, the Tories stole it!" retorted Forman angrily.

"But didn't you tell me that a part had already been sold before the Tory raid?" asked Nathaniel.

"Yes, yes," Forman shifted uneasily in his chair, "But the money and the rest of the cargo were all taken in the raid at New Brunswick."

"That is indeed what I will put in my report. Let's hope they believe it."

"In any case, it is clear that we have to look out for ourselves," continued Forman, "I hope the Assembly reimburses us, but it is very unlikely we will ever get really just compensation. We have to take what we need from the Tories and their allies in the Assembly be damned."

"Many, if not most of the men in the Assembly, are honest Whigs," insisted Nathaniel, "We need to work with them to expose the real Tory sympathizers."

"I know who the real Tory sympathizers are and I will get to all of them in good time," promised Forman grimly, "In the meantime we need to earn money to support our militia since the Assembly never gets the pay out. I have ordered a bunch of my troops to man the saltworks I have set up on the shore. The Continental Army desperately needs salt to store provisions, so this is a patriotic duty. It is going well but I need more workers. If we could offer exemption from militia duty for salt workers, it would be easier to find volunteers."

"That might be a possibility," mused Nathaniel, "You are not the only one to suggest that salt production is a vital part of the war effort. I have heard that one David Knott is also preparing a petition to the Assembly to exempt his salt workers from militia duty. I could submit a similar petition. Perhaps we will be able to convince them."

"Now that is a project worth pursuing, Nathaniel, I can see that your political career is off to a very good start!"

Nathaniel felt pleasantly stimulated by Forman's enthusiasm. After the conversation he became more and more intrigued by the possibility of the good works that high office might afford the Christian man. He convinced himself that by helping David Forman he was helping the cause and, in this way, doing God's work. He resolved to actively solicit additional ideas from his fellow Whigs in the Monmouth County leadership. A few days later he met with his militia colleague, Asher Holmes.

"Asher, you are one our finest young officers and you know that I have the utmost confidence in your judgement," Nathaniel began, "I will now be representing this state in the Continental Congress, and I would appreciate any suggestions you might have as to how we can improve the conduct of the war."

"Success in this war depends on the morale of our militiamen which in turn depends a great deal on the fate of their families," replied Holmes, "Unfortunately many of our men have wound up as prisoners in New York and their families have suffered terribly. If we want our boys to confront the enemy with enthusiasm, they have to believe that their families won't suffer a disaster if they are killed or captured."

"You are certainly correct about that," agreed Nathaniel, "The government understands that as well. That is why Elias Boudinot has been appointed to be Commissary General of Prisoners. We will all do everything we can to help Elias relieve the suffering of our captured colleagues."

"The Brits have no interest in letting anyone relieve the suffering of our men. They refuse to treat them as prisoners of war. Many family members have already tried to visit their relatives on the prison ships and in the Sugar House and bring them food and medicine. They are lucky if they don't get raped and robbed for their efforts."

"I know, Asher, I have read Dr. Witherspoon's report. It is difficult to believe the depths of the wickedness it reveals. But the report could become our greatest recruiting tool."

"It could, indeed, but we must take better care of the families who are affected. Most of the men who wind up there are dead within months. I am told that every morning a boatload of bodies is rowed over to the Brooklyn shore where the rotting corpses are buried in shallow graves in the sand. It is said that you can't walk along the coast for more than a hundred yards without tripping over putrid remains that the waves have washed free. And the families of those poor devils are often left destitute."

"I agree wholeheartedly, Asher, helping those families must become part of our war strategy if we want to maintain morale."

A few days later Nathaniel invited another trusted colleague, his former apprentice, Thomas Henderson, over to his home to discuss the suggestions made by David Forman and Asher Holmes.

"So David wants us to petition for special privileges for his salt workers, does he?" remarked Henderson after listening to Nathaniel's recounting of his conversations with Forman and Holmes, "I would be surprised if the Assembly sees merit in that proposal."

"Why do you say that?" asked Nathaniel, "It seems to me to be a reasonable idea. After all, salt is as strategically important to the cause as gun powder."

"That is not the issue. Of course salt is important, but the question is who profits from this arrangement," explained Henderson, "Many in the Assembly feel that David's exploits have more to do with his personal gain than with the cause of liberty. As you know, both of us have been asked to report to the Assembly details concerning the disposal of the cargo of the *Polly & Anne*. The reason is that some suspect that David has pocketed some of the proceeds. And his refusal to appear before the Assembly to justify his execution of Stephen Edwards without trial only adds to the impression that he considers himself to be above the law."

"David can indeed be rash and impulsive, and I have warned him about the dangers of making too many enemies in the Assembly. But he is also a fearless and energetic defender of our cause and many of his warnings about Tory treachery have turned out to be accurate. As yet, I have no reason to believe that he is not an honest man albeit with certain brutal tendencies. You and I as physicians are naturally repulsed by violence, but we are facing an enemy capable of the most heinous atrocities. In this case we cannot just turn the other cheek, we must pray for the aid of the Lord of Hosts to vanquish the forces of Evil."

"Perhaps," replied Henderson raising his eyebrows, "We can only hope that David's actions always find the approbation of the Lord of Hosts. But we should also never forget that the seeds of corruption are to be found in all of us."

"Of course, we must all pray that we recognize the temptations of the Evil One for what they are and have the strength to resist," agreed Nathaniel piously, "All human projects have the potential for corruption, and I cannot rule that out regarding David's exploits. In the case of Asher Holmes' suggestions, however, I believe we are on safe ground. His description of the sufferings of the families of our militiamen who have been taken prisoner is certainly accurate and implies a clear moral imperative to act on their behalf."

"There I can wholeheartedly agree with you and as physicians we are probably better prepared than most to work out practical solutions."

Just then Isabella came into the room and interrupted their discussion.

"Nathaniel, Thomas, if you want to talk about practical solutions to urgent problems, someone has just arrived who might be able to shed some light on the issues you are talking about. Do you remember Elisabeth Rue?"

"Yes, of course," replied Nathaniel, "She is the wife of poor Matthias Rue who is one of our men captured at Navesink. Please show her in."

Elisabeth Rue, hollow of cheek and clad in tattered clothing, came into the parlor holding an infant in her arms. When she saw Nathaniel, she burst into tears.

"Dr. Scudder, please forgive me for the intrusion but I am so distraught I don't know which way to turn. As you know, Matthias is a prisoner of the enemy in New York, and I fear that he will not survive much longer."

"You do not need to apologize, Elisabeth, your husband is a hero of our cause, and we were just now talking how we might be able to alleviate the plight of people like him and their families."

"We are indeed in dire need of assistance," sobbed Elisabeth, "Since Matthias' capture, we have had no income even though we were promised that we would at least get the back pay due for his militia duty. My children are ill, and we can hardly manage to take in the harvest at our small farm. Without the help of our church, we would have already starved by now. What little money we have come by was given to us by General Forman, but it was really only a pittance."

"That is completely outrageous!" exclaimed Isabella, "Of course we will help you. Nathaniel, why is the Assembly not doing more to support our people and how is it that only David Forman has helped this family so far?"

"The money that David has distributed he probably confiscated from suspected Tories," explained Nathaniel, "With all due respect for David's generosity, that is not really the proper procedure. Any confiscated property is supposed to be turned over to the Assembly which would then use it to support the war effort, including helping the families of our captured militiamen."

"That is obviously not working!" Isabella could not contain her indignation, "I have heard how the Assembly never tires of criticizing David but at least he is doing something for the victims of this terrible war!"

"I know that we are living through dreadful times," continued Elizabeth, "And everyone has sacrifices to make but my reason for coming here today is different. I tried to visit Matthias in New York recently and bring him some fresh vegetables from our farm. When I got there, the guard took the food and tried to ravish me. Only the arrival of an officer saved me just in time. I got to visit Matthias for a few minutes, but he is horribly ill. He said that he and his comrades are packed so closely together that they cannot all lie down at the same time. The place is so filthy and crawling with vermin that the stink makes it almost impossible to breathe. He told me that almost everyone was suffering from camp fever and that everyday dozens of corpses had to be hauled off. Is there any way that a physician could be sent to him? I am afraid that he won't last another week without proper medical care."

Thomas and Nathaniel looked at each other and frowned. As medical men they knew that Matthias' chances of survival were practically nil even if a physician were allowed access, but they did not want to extinguish what little hope Elisabeth still had.

"Elisabeth, unfortunately the British would never allow me to visit our prisoners, or I would go there immediately. However, I will give our new Commissary General of Prisoners, Elias Boudinot, some medicine against camp fever and ask him to try to get it to Matthias as well as to the other suffering comrades," Nathaniel promised, feeling a twinge of conscience knowing full well that without a speedy exchange of prisoners most of the imprisoned militiamen were surely doomed, "In the meantime we must all pray that our men will soon come free. We have taken many prisoners at Saratoga and negotiations for a general exchange are proceeding as we speak."

"God bless you, Dr. Scudder!" exclaimed Elisabeth, "I knew that you would try your best to help. Matthias said that if anyone could help us it would be you. Thank you, thank you!"

"You need not thank me," replied Nathaniel solemnly, "It goes without saying that all of us will continue our humble efforts to do our duty as best we can. But in the final analysis all our fates are in God's hands, He will decide if we are to be successful or not. I firmly believe, however, that we are doing God's work, so my advice to you is to pray for the strength to accept the Lord's judgement whatever suffering that might entail."

"And, of course, in the meantime we will help you and your family as best we can," added Isabella spontaneously, "We have some clothing that we no longer need which you can have for yourself and your children." Isabella summoned one of the female servants and bid her gather together some of the old clothes that her children had outgrown as well as a few frocks that Isabella seldom had occasion to wear.

Elisabeth left the Scudder household, her mood visibly improved by Nathaniel's advice and Isabella's generosity. After her departure Nathaniel, Isabella, and Thomas sat in silence for a long time contemplating the heavy burden of responsibility that Providence had thrust upon them. Finally, Isabella broke the silence.

"Nathaniel, we can no longer wait passively for the politicians to solve these problems," she began, "I think that I will talk to the other ladies in our congregation and see if we cannot organize more help for the poor families of our patriots."

A few days later Nathaniel prepared to attend his first session of the Continental Congress. Having been driven out of Philadelphia by General Howe, the congressmen had fled to York, a small town on the frontier far enough into the wilderness that the British would have difficulty following them there. Nathaniel rode up to Princeton to meet Dr. Witherspoon. Together they made the journey from Princeton in the coach that Witherspoon had used to make his escape to Pequea during the British invasion the year before. As it turned out, Pequea was not far from York where they now had to go to meet the Continental Congress, so Witherspoon knew the way well. He estimated that they would need at least two days to make it there with one or two overnight stops. That gave them many hours to discuss the state of the war and the positions they should be advocating in Congress.

"I think the issue that will be under intense discussion is the rivalries that seem to have surfaced among our generals," began Witherspoon as the coach headed off in the direction of Coryell's Ferry.

"No doubt about that," agreed Nathaniel, "We have to contend with bitter rivalries already within the Monmouth Militia."

"The recent developments in the war have brought new turmoil into the discussions." explained Witherspoon, "Lord Stirling recently told me about a letter he sent to

General Washington informing him about what he considered a budding conspiracy to replace Washington as Commander-in-Chief. Washington's defeats at Brandywine and Germantown as well as the loss of Long Island and New York are alleged to flow from his incompetence while the great success at Saratoga makes Horatio Gates look like the conquering hero."

"How did Lord Stirling find out about this?" Nathaniel asked incredulously, "Who would want to conspire against such an outstanding commander? Have they forgotten the great successes at Trenton and Princeton?"

"The instigator is apparently one Brigadier General Thomas Conway, a scheming, fast-talking, ambitious Irishman, who hopes to profit by a shakeup in the command structure."

"That is a daft plan," reacted Nathaniel angrily, "I have heard from Monmouth militia units returning from the northern front that Gates did not have that much to do with the victory. The real hero they say was Benedict Arnold even though Gates tried to hinder his actions."

"Gates also made a really stupid deal to get Burgoyne to surrender. In return for a promise not to fight against the colonies again he signed a convention to let Burgoyne and 6000 captured troops return to Britain. I think the man has taken leave of his senses! The British will simply deploy those 6000 troops elsewhere and replace them with 6000 others," Witherspoon snorted indignantly, "Anyone in Congress who thinks that that is fine generalship does not understand the most basic principles of warfare."

"I think we must defend Washington vigorously in front of Congress," Nathaniel proposed, "It would be a great blunder to replace Washington with a lesser man."

"Indeed, we must," agreed Witherspoon, "In fact, I have received information that Washington has moved his army to a protected area near the Schuylkill River called Valley Forge where he will make winter quarters. That is not far off our path and is about the distance a coach can travel in one day. I suggest we stop by and acquaint ourselves with the true state of our army. That will give us a firm basis for argument during congressional debates."

Nathaniel agreed immediately, excited at the prospect of meeting the commander-in-chief in person and eager to hear his assessment of the current state of the war. When they arrived at Valley Forge, however, they were subjected to a depressing sight. The army was quite obviously on the brink of collapse and more resembled a ragged mob than a fighting force. Smells of unwashed bodies and fetid wounds mingled with the acrid smoke of campfires as they approached the muddy field where a few hundred exhausted men were constructing rough huts to shelter the troops from the winter cold. An officer was reading aloud charges to an emaciated farm boy tied to wooden post.

"Private Hopkins, for the crime of leaving your unit without leave, we hereby sentence you to fifty lashes," shouted the officer, "And should you attempt to desert again before the agreed-upon end of your term of service, you will be shot on sight!"

As a burly sergeant began to whip the unfortunate lad, the officer turned to the visitors.

"Welcome to our camp, gentlemen," the officer saluted raising his voice in order to be heard over the screams of the writhing would-be deserter, "My apologies that you must bear witness to severe measures, but General Washington has ordered strictest sanctions against desertion."

"I am Dr. John Witherspoon, and this is Dr. Nathaniel Scudder," replied Witherspoon, "We represent the State of New Jersey and are on our way to a meeting of the Continental Congress. We have stopped by to ask General Washington what we can do to ease the lot of our brave soldiers."

"I am certain that General Washington will have many suggestions for inclusion in your deliberations. We are in desperate need of almost everything. We have urgently requested food, blankets and warm clothes from Congress but as yet have received nothing. But I will let the general tell you in his own words what straits we are in."

The officer led the two congressmen to a cabin in which Washington had set up a makeshift headquarters.

"At your pleasure, sir, Dr. John Witherspoon and Dr. Nathaniel Scudder of the Continental Congress requesting an audience," the officer saluted smartly.

"Come in, gentlemen, come in," Washington rose to his feet to greet the two congressmen, "I am always pleased to have the opportunity to hear from Congress. As of late, I hear much too little from them despite my many entreaties."

Standing proudly erect in front of his visitors the Commander-in-Chief was well over six feet tall, broad-shouldered, big-boned and well-muscled. His long face, high cheek bones, large straight nose, determined chin and intense blue-gray eyes reminded Nathaniel of some Homeric warrior prince. His impressive appearance as well as his air of quiet confidence immediately convinced Nathaniel that this was the only man who could lead the rebellion to victory.

"General Washington, we bring no news from Congress. We are on our way there," began Witherspoon, "But we wanted to ascertain the state of our troops first-hand and find out how we can best support you."

"That is a refreshing change!" replied Washington, "All I hear lately are rumors that some members of that august body think they would be better off with a new commander-in-chief. Presumably because I told them that their idea of attacking the British in Philadelphia in the dead of winter with our troops in their current state would be suicidal. I will be very clear on that issue. If Congress decides that someone else can do my job better, I will be delighted to retire back to my beloved Mount Vernon."

"This would be a disaster for our cause!" exclaimed Nathaniel, "We in New Jersey know that without you we would have been defeated already. We want to bring Congress to do that what must be done in order to win this war."

Sensing that this was an opportunity to forge valuable alliances, Washington decided to take the two men into his confidence

"Our problems all center around supply, training, and logistics," explained Washington, "I marched here with 11,000 men who are not wanting for courage and devotion to the cause. Of those about half of them are so sick and undernourished that they could not fight even if the British attacked us tomorrow. Those who are in fighting shape are mostly simple farm boys who have yet to learn the most basic military skills. They also do not understand that healthy camp life requires more strict hygiene than life back on the farm."

"A familiar problem," remarked Nathaniel, "I am a physician and the doctor I trained with used to say that more soldiers die of camp fever than on the battlefield. I encountered the same problem when I visited our Monmouth militia troops in New York before the British invasion."

"In that case, Dr. Scudder, you know what needs to be done," continued Washington, "The problem is that most of our officers do not have the experience to implement those measures effectively. I would like to hire more experienced European officers, but Congress balks at the cost. They tell me I can engage professional officers only if they agree to volunteer and don't expect extravagant remuneration."

"Not a likely prospect, I suspect," mused Witherspoon.

"Indeed," agreed Washington, "I do have some prospects, however. A young French officer named Lafayette has volunteered for purely idealistic reasons. I expect him to arrive in January. A German officer named von Steuben who has served with Emperor Frederick is also willing to help get our troops in shape. I expect him to arrive sometime in February, at which time I will present him to Congress. I hope I can count on your support at that interview."

"I will certainly argue in favor of anything that puts our army on a more professional footing," promised Nathaniel.

"Eventually I will get these boys trained one way or another," continued Washington, "But right now, I would be happy just to keep them fed. As yet, Congress has been unable to provide money for fresh supplies. At present, it looks as though our troops will dine on a meal of rice and vinegar this Christmas. We need blankets and clothing—our barefoot boys are forced to bind their bleeding frost-bitten feet with rags. Tell Congress, please, tell them what suffering these boys are enduring for the sake of our liberty!"

Both Nathaniel and Dr. Witherspoon were deeply impressed by Washington's eloquence, and firmly resolved to do anything in their power to garner as much support in Congress for Washington as possible. Arriving at York the next day they decided that their best strategy to this end would be to volunteer for the committee discussing just how the Convention signed by General Gates at Saratoga would be implemented. In order to blunt the enthusiasm that some members of Congress apparently felt for the idea of Gates as commander-in-chief, Witherspoon immediately expressed a critical view of the way Gates had handled the surrender at Saratoga.

"I am convinced that this event will not equal our expectations," Witherspoon began dourly, "Without great precaution and very delicate management, we shall have all these men—if not the officers—opposed to us in the spring."

"I could not agree with you more, Reverend Witherspoon," said Joseph Jones, a delegate from Virginia, "But there are many such as Thomas Mifflin newly appointed to the Board of War who say that we would sully the honor of Congress if we would renege on the word of one of our top generals."

"Of course, we would never want to imply that Congress would renege on its word once given," replied Witherspoon slyly, "But we do have the right to ensure that the other side is equally faithful to the agreement. I, therefore, propose that we ratify the convention with the following condition: Resolved, that the embarkation of Lieutenant-General Burgoyne, and the troops under his command, be suspended until a distinct and explicit ratification of the Convention of Saratoga shall be properly notified by the Court of Great Britain to Congress."

Nathaniel smiled as he realized what trick the wily theologian had devised. Compliance with this condition would amount to a de facto recognition of the independence of the colonies, something the Royal government could never agree to. Refusal by the British to ratify the Convention, however, would provide a perfect excuse to retain Burgoyne, his troops and the captured Hessian mercenaries. Those 6,000 soldiers would never again be taking up arms against the Americans, but it would be the British and not Congress that had reneged on the Convention.

The rest of the committee members quickly realized how Witherspoon had cleverly freed them from a moral dilemma and voted unanimously to incorporate his condition in the ratification of the Convention.

Nathaniel and Witherspoon spent the next few weeks fervently exhorting their congressional colleagues to organize better provisioning and support for Washington's troops at Valley Forge. Again and again Nathaniel explained the critical importance of keeping the troops as healthy as possible if there was to be any hope of confronting such a formidable foe. Witherspoon, for his part, emphasized the apocalyptic nature of the current struggle casting it as a crusade against the forces of evil and corruption. This was the message, he contended, that could draw in sturdy volunteers from the frontier willing to fight the Beast. After having made good progress promoting their views the two representatives decided it was time to head back to New Jersey and report to the governor. They also wanted to get printed copies of the Articles of Confederation that had been adopted in November to the New Jersey Assembly so that the process of ratification could begin.

Meeting with the governor in Princeton, Witherspoon and Nathaniel briefed him on the logistical chaos that Washington had to contend with. The governor agreed wholeheartedly that more had to be done. Nathaniel was pleased to hear that the Assembly in the meantime had agreed to reimburse him for some of the medical and other supplies that he had made available to the militia. He hoped that this news might assuage some of Isabella's anxieties that his contributions to the war effort might result in their personal insolvency. After the meeting with the governor Nathaniel hurried back to Monmouth to give Isabella the good news.

He arrived at their home just in time to see David Forman ride up accompanied by two Black youths. Hearing galloping horses Isabella opened the door to see who had come, smiling broadly when she realized that Nathaniel was back home at last.

Waving a welcome to David Forman, Nathaniel jumped down from his horse and rushed to embrace Isabella.

"It is so wonderful to have you back in my arms," Nathaniel exclaimed, "And I have encouraging news for all of us. The governor has informed me that the Assembly has voted to compensate us for the expenses we have incurred over the last months."

"I have heard that as well," interjected David Forman, "But what they are proposing is only a small portion of what we have coming. As I have said time and again, we must take matters into our own hands. That is why I have brought you these two young slaves that I confiscated from that Tory bastard, Benjamin van Cleave. Take them as part of what is due you. They are brother and sister and go by the names of Dinah and Jim. You'll have to doctor them up a bit, however. Van Cleave was shagging the girl and beating the boy when he tried to protect his sister."

"That is outrageous!" cried Isabella, "David, you did a Christian service in taking these children away from that animal."

"Have Beth and Pegg make a berth for them in the barn, and I will examine them later to see if they have any injuries that need to be treated," said Nathaniel, "David, I appreciate your generosity, but I think that confiscated property should actually be placed at the disposal of the Assembly."

"Do as you will, Nat," Forman answered, "But there are those in the Assembly who would just give them back to van Cleave. Not all of them are as convinced as I that he is a Tory sympathizer."

Bidding the children to dismount Forman gave one more piece of advice before he rode off, "Make sure, at least, that the Assembly compensates you for the medical care the two will need."

Hearing Forman's remark Isabella took a closer look at the two children. Dinah looked healthy enough physically but exhibited a clearly traumatized demeanor. Jim on the other hand had obviously been severely injured. His ragged shirt was bloodstained, and his face was flushed with fever.

"Compensation indeed," remarked Isabella ruefully, "This looks to me like more unpaid work for the doctor."

Summoning two of her servants, Beth and Pegg, Isabella ordered the sick children to be taken to the slave quarters in the barn. Nathaniel followed with his physician's bag. A careful examination revealed physical evidence of the traumas that Forman had described. The boy had open wounds all over his back caused by several whippings. The wounds had become infected which explained the fever. Nathaniel applied the Indian herbs which were so effective for this kind of injury and was confident that the boy would make a quick recovery. The girl on the other hand had been repeatedly brutally raped. While the physical injuries would heal quickly, the damage that had been done to the girl's psyche could well be long-lasting. She cringed and screamed at the touch of a man and had to be restrained by Beth and Pegg.

After a few days of good care by the Scudders and their servants, however, both children seemed much improved. Jim's fever abated and his wounds seemed to heal well. Dinah still cringed in fear at the approach of any man but quickly developed a strong rapport with Isabella. Whenever the presence of a man caused Dinah to fall into a state of shivering anxiety, Isabella would embrace and reassure her.

"Don't you worry, Dinah," Isabella soothed her, stroking her head "Nobody here is going to hurt you."

"Can't I just stay with you, Miss Isabella?" Dinah asked plaintively.

"We will see what can be done," promised Isabella, "But first we have to get you and Jim back on your feet."

Later alone with Nathaniel Isabella made the case for keeping the two children.

"David Forman is right," argued Isabella, "The Assembly owes us at least as much as those servants are worth in compensation."

"That may well be," answered Nathaniel, "But it is surely improper for me as a member of Congress to appropriate confiscated property under my own authority. The Assembly must at least be consulted. The rules for the expropriation of Tory property are still being debated. Aside from that we already have eight servants, and their quarters will be very cramped with two more."

"In any case, there is no way we can permit those children to be restored to that villain, van Cleave!" exclaimed Isabella, "David said that that might be a real possibility."

"I doubt that very much," Nathaniel reassured her, "But as a member of Congress I must see to it that I am above any suspicion of corruption. I will, however, try to convince the Assembly that the children would be best served by staying under our care for a time."

The children, however, decided to take the question of their future into their own hands. The next morning when Isabella came down to the kitchen, Beth informed her that Dinah and Jim had disappeared during the night.

"Last evening I heard that Jim boy telling Dinah they had to escape to the British cause they don't know where they're going to wind up," Beth explained shrugging her shoulders, "But nobody hear 'em leave."

"Well, maybe that was indeed their best option," Isabella said to herself thoughtfully.

When Nathaniel came down to breakfast and heard of the escape, he was less sanguine.

"I am disappointed but not surprised," he said. "Howe has offered any slaves who escape from supporters of the rebellion their freedom if they come and fight for the Redcoats. That is why I have drummed into Dunmore, Adam, and Frank that the promised freedom is really just the freedom to fight and die for the tyrants. I don't think they will be tempted to follow suit."

"Let's hope not," said Isabella, "But I can't imagine our kitchen family taking up arms against us. Dinah and Jim probably would not have run off if they had been assured that they could stay with us."

A few weeks later Nathaniel received an urgent message from Reverend Witherspoon who had already returned to York. Congress was about to take up important business, he said, and many delegates were missing. It was critical that supporters of Washington be present to block the plans of designing men who were pushing their own selfish agendas. The urgency of Witherspoon's entreaty convinced Nathaniel to depart immediately for Pennsylvania. After a day and a night of hard riding he arrived in the frontier town and rushed to the Presbyterian meeting house where he knew someone would know the whereabouts of Reverend Witherspoon. As it turned out, Witherspoon was there anxiously awaiting Nathaniel's arrival.

"Thank God, you have responded so quickly to my message," exclaimed Witherspoon, "Washington would like to present to Congress that German officer who has volunteered to train our troops at Valley Forge. And, of course, those who would like to see a different commander-in-chief are raising all manner of spurious objections."

"What could they possibly have against Washington's plan?" asked Nathaniel, "My understanding is that this Baron von Steuben has volunteered for duty without insisting on the pay that would be normal for someone with his experience."

"Those who are against Washington claim that the Baron is actually a charlatan who never reached a high position in the Prussian military. Some even hint that he had to leave Europe to escape prosecution for unnatural sexual proclivities."

"The same claims have been made about the Emperor Frederick," countered Nathaniel, "But no one can doubt that his brilliant military leadership has turned Prussia into a major European power. Anyone with experience in Prussia's army is bound to be an asset in Valley Forge."

"Well, all this is probably being orchestrated by Thomas Mifflin and his allies in a bid to replace Washington as commander-in-chief," surmised Witherspoon, "Mifflin resigned a few months ago as Quartermaster General after Washington criticized him for the poor support of our troops. Some think that Mifflin was hoarding goods so that he could get a better price for them. Mifflin was, of course, outraged by this insinuation and has been doing his best to undermine Washington ever since. Now that Congress has appointed him to the Board of War, he probably thinks that he is in a good position to get Washington replaced by Gates. His allies in this project such as Thomas Conway hope that they will also somehow benefit by a shake-up in the command structure."

"God protect us from the schemes of designing men!" exclaimed Nathaniel, "As if our struggle were not difficult enough, we have to put up with these foolish skirmishes which can only weaken us in the face of the enemy!"

"It is to be expected," replied Witherspoon calmly, "As John Calvin has taught, man is fundamentally corrupt so we should not be surprised at such behavior. We can only pray to the Living God that our faith will deliver us from making similar mistakes. In the meantime, we must exhort our congressional colleagues to concentrate on practical measures which will help us defend our freedom. Since Mifflin resigned, they have not been able to find a replacement for the Quartermaster General. That should be one of our first priorities. And, of course, we must see to it that no one blocks Washington's plan to put an experienced officer in charge of the drill in Valley Forge. Today Baron von Steuben is due to be interviewed by Congress so let us be off and lend Washington our support."

As Nathaniel and Witherspoon set off for the York County Courthouse where the Continental Congress was to interview Baron von Steuben, they noticed the approach of a large sleigh pulled by black Percheron draft horses decked out with 24 jingling bells. In it was sitting a large, well-built man wearing a robe of silk trimmed with fur. On his lap was curled up a miniature greyhound which he stroked while conversing in French with two young gentlemen sitting behind him in the sleigh.

Witherspoon quickly realized that this must the man they were waiting for. Having acquired a basic knowledge of French in order to read Calvin's Institutes he addressed the newcomer in that language welcoming him to York and informing him that he and Nathaniel were part of the congressional delegation that would be interviewing him. Von Steuben greeted them warmly, introducing them to his aide-de-camp, Louis de Pontière, and his teenage secretary, Pierre-Étienne du Ponceau. Seeing the delicate, almost beautiful young secretary, Nathaniel could not help but wonder if the rumors about the Baron's unnatural sexual proclivities might not, in fact, be true. He reminded himself, however, that Europe was full of corruption of all kinds and decided not to let the Baron's private life influence his judgement. Washington's troops were in dire need of intense training and an experienced Prussian officer might just fill the bill.

The group proceeded to the courthouse where the other delegates were waiting. Witherspoon introduced the Baron and after everyone was seated, President Laurens opened the floor for questioning. Although the Baron spoke no English at this point, many delegates had a basic knowledge of French. In addition, half of the residents of York were German-speakers, so communication was possible in both of those languages. President Laurens opened the questioning session by asking the Baron how it was that a Prussian aristocrat came to be interested in supporting the American cause. He explained that as Lord Chamberlain of Prince von Hohenzollern-Hechingen he had occasion to visit France frequently where he became acquainted with the French Minister of War, Claude-Louis, comte de Saint-Germain. Saint-Germain was considering French support for the American cause but worried that untrained soldiers might not be able to make efficient use of any military equipment that the French decided to donate to the Americans. When Saint-Germain learned that the Baron had participated in the exclusive special class in the art of war organized by Frederick the Great, he asked if the Baron might consider helping to train the American rebels. Always interested in new adventures, the Baron agreed and was introduced to America's ambassador, Benjamin Franklin, who recommended him to Washington.

"But what exactly do you intend to teach our young men?" asked Samuel Adams archly, making an oblique reference to von Steuben's rumored homosexuality.

"I will teach them how to fight battles and win," responded von Steuben with a smile, refusing to be drawn into any discussion of his personal life, "I have studied the reports of your defeats at Brandywine and Germantown, and it is clear that your troops and officers are brave, but very green and inexperienced, lacking the most basic military skills and discipline. They are essentially just a mob with guns. They are no match for the highly trained and disciplined British forces with their Hessian allies. I have fought battles against such foes since I was a young boy and know exactly what skills are needed to cope with these kinds of challenges. Your command structure is primitive. There are no documented procedures. Your soldiers apparently have no idea, for example, how to maintain a steady volley of musket or cannon fire or deal with a well-organized bayonet charge."

At the mention of a bayonet charge, Nathaniel had to think of the crushing defeat that his militia unit suffered at Navesink. Witherspoon for his part stiffened as he thought of the loss of his beloved son at Germantown. If the Americans had been better trained, perhaps his son would have survived that debacle. He and Nathaniel looked at each other and nodded in solemn, silent agreement.

"Sir, I have a question," said Nathaniel turning toward the Baron, "I am a physician and know that more men die of camp fever than on the battlefield. How do you train farm boys in basic hygiene?"

"A good question, Dr. Scudder," answered von Steuben, "Again it is all a matter of organization. All latrines have to be dug on one side of the camp, preferably on an incline where the run-off cannot pollute the water supply. Cooking facilities must be on the opposite side. Anyone relieving himself in a place other than the latrine must be severely punished."

Deeply impressed by the quality of von Steuben's recommendations, Nathaniel was convinced that he was the man Washington needed. As the questioning went on it became obvious to even the most skeptical delegates that they were dealing with an outstanding professional officer. After all questions had been answered Baron von Steuben concluded his interview with an eloquent summary of his reasons for volunteering.

"My only motivation that has brought me to this part of the world is the desire to serve a people that is engaged in such a noble struggle for its rights and freedom. I demand neither money nor title. I have come here from a far corner of Germany where I have given up high office and position. My only ambition is to volunteer for your cause, to earn the confidence of your commander-in-chief, George Washington, and to accompany him in all campaigns the same way I served the King of Prussia during the Seven Years War. I would like to offer to shed my blood for the honor of being among those who will one day be remembered as defenders of your freedom."

After those words all resistance to the Baron's appointment melted away, and many delegates approached him to shake his hand and thank him for offering his services. Nathaniel and Dr. Witherspoon were ecstatic that some of Washington's most pressing problems were about to be addressed in a professional manner. Over the next few weeks, they threw themselves with great enthusiasm into the task of dealing with the most important remaining problem facing the army: the abysmal state of supply and logistics. As convinced Calvinists both suspected that corruption was the root of the problem.

"I have seen it again and again," muttered Nathaniel angrily, "Farmers who refuse to hand over their best produce to our supply agents because they know they can make a better profit through the London Trade. Washington seems to think that Thomas Mifflin was in league with some of those merchants which was why Valley Forge has been so poorly supplied. When he confronted Mifflin on that account, he resigned in a huff."

"I am sure that some of Mifflin's associates were indeed doing the Devil's work," said Witherspoon, "But the office of Quartermaster General has to be filled again as quickly as possible. It has been vacant now for months. We need a man who can take control and straighten out this mess. That is why I am supporting the nomination of General Nathanael Greene for Quartermaster General."

"An excellent choice," agreed Nathaniel, "I hope he can put the fear of God into some of those greedy merchants. I just received a letter from Governor Livingston about the Assembly elections. Unfortunately, it is not going to get any easier to pursue those scoundrels of questionable loyalty."

"Why is that?" asked Witherspoon, "Hopefully we will not be betrayed on the home front just when things are going so well here."

"Governor Livingston writes that many of those recently elected to the Assembly are disposed toward limiting our prerogatives in the pursuit of Tory sympathizers. He says that the change in both houses is much for the worse, that we have so few members with a turn for business that the machine of government moves slower than ever. He mentioned that James Mott and Joseph Holmes are now representing Monmouth County in the Assembly. I would not consider them traitors, but I know that they are in favor of conciliatory policies toward suspected Loyalists. They will undoubtedly try to limit the pressure that the army can put on hoarders and profiteers. They have often spoken critically of David Forman's vigorous attempts to root out enemies. In addition, they will drag their feet when the Assembly is asked to provide more men and supplies for Washington's army."

"That is, indeed, regrettable, Dr. Scudder, do you have any suggestions how we can limit the effects of your new Monmouth County representatives."

"They have been elected fairly, I am afraid," answered Nathaniel, "They do, in fact, represent a large chunk of the Monmouth County electorate which tends toward Loyalism. In my opinion we cannot wait for the Assembly to take decisive action. The government must have recourse to coercive measures. For if quotas cannot be had by voluntary enlistment and the powers of the government are not adequate to drafting, there is no end to this contest and opposition becomes in vain. For this reason, I have volunteered for the Enlistment Committee which is currently debating how to close the gap between what the army has requested and what the states have provided. I will recommend the implementation of a draft for all states not meeting their enlistment quotas. I hope that this idea meets with your approval."

"Absolutely, Dr. Scudder. It is the only sensible approach. You can count on my support when the proposal comes to the floor, and I am certain that Governor Livingston will be delighted to hear of your initiative."

Nathaniel's initiative was well received in Congress and Henry Laurens asked if the proposal represented the official position of New Jersey. Since only the Assembly could determine that, Nathaniel decided to return home via Princeton so that he could discuss his proposal in more detail with Governor Livingston and find out if and how one could get the Assembly on board. Tethering his horse to Dr. Witherspoon's carriage Nathaniel spent the long journey back to Princeton discussing strategies for opposing the actions of disaffected elements suspected of sabotaging the war effort.

"Those in the Assembly who are secretly opposed to fighting the British will undoubtedly resist implementing a draft, citing the added expense," predicted Nathaniel, "If they would only openly admit that they are on the side of the Crown, we might be able to get them disqualified but they slyly pretend they are loyal to the government while seeking to weaken us at every opportunity."

"Every effort must be made to expose those scoundrels and bring them to justice," agreed Witherspoon.

"A good beginning would be the confiscation of property of anyone found guilty of aiding the enemy," continued Nathaniel, "A man without property cannot run for the Assembly."

"I am sure that Governor Livingston will agree with you on that point," said Witherspoon, "But first we have to deal with the Assembly in its current state."

Arriving in Princeton the two congressmen proceeded directly to the governor's residence to brief him on the actions of Congress in the last few weeks. They were surprised to see a contingent of militiamen in front of the governor's house guarding what appeared to be White men and several Blacks. Near them stood the governor conversing animatedly with the militia captain. When he saw the carriage with Nathaniel and Witherspoon, he hailed them excitedly.

"Dr. Witherspoon, Dr. Scudder, you arrive just in time to witness the booty of one of our most daring exploits," shouted Livingston, "William Marriner raided the enemy at Flatbush a few nights ago and made off with these six men without the loss of a single man. He was trying to kidnap that vicious Tory mayor of New York, Daniel Matthews, who is known as the Tormenter General of our poor prisoners there. Matthews, it turned out was not there, but Marriner and his men made off with these six proving that Tory scoundrels are not safe anywhere, not even behind enemy lines."

Nathaniel had heard of Captain William Marriner, a privateer from New Brunswick who was famous for stealthy nighttime raids using whale boats with a handpicked crew of hardened sailors. On several occasion they had successfully and silently boarded much larger vessels taking the crews by surprise and taking over the vessels.

"One of the men looks like a British major," remarked Nathaniel, "Perhaps he can be traded for one of our more highly ranked prisoners in New York."

"Indeed," agreed Livingston, "That is Major Moncrieffe, and he should be worth a high-level exchange. The other is a Continental Captain captured at the Battle of Fort Washington. He can now return to his unit. For the four Blacks we will certainly find useful work for them. By the way, how did things go in York? In my enthusiasm for Marriner's derring-do, I have not given you a chance to bring me up to date."

"Things are going very well," answered Witherspoon, "General Greene has been confirmed as Quartermaster General and supplies are beginning to flow into Valley Forge. By all accounts the Prussian General von Steuben is working wonders drilling our troops. That scoundrel, Thomas Conway, has offered his resignation. All in all, the threats to General Washington's authority appear to have been beaten back."

"Now our most important task is to see to it that General Washington gets the additional troops that he needs," added Nathaniel, "That is why I will do everything I can to win support for my proposal for a draft for all states not meeting their enlistment quotas."

"That is certainly a laudable project," agreed Livingston, "but after the last elections we will have our work cut out for us to get the Assembly to agree. We not only have clandestine Tory sympathizers but also many Quakers who reject fighting for any cause. The former, of course, are our main problem. The Tory-race has increased in number under our nurture. Our lenient measures have allowed them to triumph on many fronts and, in my opinion, they are now more dangerous that the British troops."

"That is why we must take the battle to that enemy as well," concurred Nathaniel, "David Forman has been warning us for years and now we must heed his advice. I will now hurry back to Monmouth and encourage David to be relentless in his pursuit of traitors. And I will inform Elias Boudinot that we have now hold a prisoner ripe for a high-level exchange."

Nathaniel bid farewell and galloped as fast as he could back to Freehold impatient to bring everyone up to date on all the exciting developments. He felt a sense of mission that was so exhilarating that he could ignore his fatigue. He imagined having Isabella in his arms soon again after so many weeks in York, and that he was flying to her through the air on a winged steed. Approaching his home, he could see her from a distance in the yard talking to the servants, and he urged his horse on to one last sprint.

Thundering into the yard in a cloud of dust Nathaniel swung out of the saddle and rushed to embrace Isabella.

"Oh, my darling, I have missed you terribly," he began, "But I have news of great things that are transpiring, and I can't wait to share my adventures with you!"

"But first you must have refreshment and rest," replied Isabella, "You look as though you have ridden here from the ends of the earth."

"York is not exactly the ends of the earth," laughed Nathaniel, "But I know people who might dispute that. Nevertheless it is a place where a new nation is being born! We will soon be a confederated people and a true nation among the nations of the earth. Being part of this is the most ultimate experience I can imagine."

Whenever Nathaniel exhibited such unbridled exuberance, Isabella always felt a twinge of foreboding knowing too well that her overzealous husband might make commitments that could turn out to be burdensome. Not wanting to dampen his enthusiasm she suppressed the twinge and smiled encouragement. Nathaniel then recounted his adventures in Valley Forge and York, and the successes that he and Witherspoon had in defending Washington, supporting Baron von Steuben and initiating legislation for establishing a military draft. He finished with a report of his visit to Governor Livingston in Princeton.

"Dr. Witherspoon and I had a very good visit with the governor," said Nathaniel, "We agree on practically every point. Governor Livingston will support our efforts to get the Assembly to approve a draft if the state does not meet its enlistment quota. And he also agrees that we must redouble our efforts to suppress disaffected elements who are trying to weaken our cause. This is something that I am sure David Forman will be pleased to hear."

"David Forman does not need any encouragement to pursue Tory sympathizers, real or imagined," replied Isabella skeptically, "Especially since the recent Loyalist raid on the Union Saltworks destroyed much of his investment in that venture, he is out for revenge. But his rash behavior could easily swell the ranks of our enemies. I am not sure that that is such a great idea."

"David is certainly correct that we have dissimulating traitors in our midst who will disrupt our efforts at every opportunity," objected Nathaniel, "And if we want to get some of our poor prisoners in New York freed, we need people we can exchange."

Nathaniel then went on to describe the swashbuckling exploits of William Marriner and the prisoner he had kidnapped who now could be traded for an American prisoner.

"I will write to Elias Boudinot immediately describing our new bargaining chip," continued Nathaniel, "Perhaps this man is worth a number of our lower-level prisoners. Apparently Marriner just missed capturing that cursed Tory mayor of New York, Daniel Matthews, who is the Tormenter in Chief of our poor prisoners. Maybe that will give Matthews pause the next time he considers torturing one of our men."

"More likely it will just lead to more violence," countered Isabella, "Murders and kidnapping will lead to more murders and kidnapping. You don't really think that the British and their Tory friends are going to sit idly by while our privateers make fools of them? They will mount exactly the same kinds of raids right here in Monmouth County because we are the closest to New York. And they will be led by our former neighbors whom David Forman has driven off and who have intimate knowledge of our area."

Nathaniel fell silent, reluctantly considering the wisdom of Isabella's words.

"Well, escalation of the conflict is probably unavoidable in any case," he concluded grimly, "We must pray to the Almighty that we are prepared to deal with whatever trials He sees fit to impose on us."

Nathaniel's stay in Freehold was cut short a few days later by an urgent message from Dr. Witherspoon. An important announcement was about to be discussed in York, and the New Jersey delegation was severely underrepresented. Witherspoon urged Nathaniel to meet him in Princeton as quickly as possible so they could discuss several issues on their way to York. To Isabella's consternation Nathaniel geared up to leave immediately.

"Nathaniel, this is madness, you have hardly had the chance to recover from your journey from York and now you are leaving again!"

"I know this is a terrible burden for you and our family, but I don't see that I really have a choice. This seems to me to be what God wants me to do."

Nathaniel assumed that Witherspoon's urgency had something to do with news on the diplomatic front regarding the proposed alliance with France. After hurrying to Princeton, he discovered that the upcoming announcement in York was only one of the topics that Witherspoon wanted to discuss.

"Dr. Scudder, many thanks for responding so quickly to my request," Witherspoon began, "And I do indeed expect that momentous announcements await us in York. But I had an additional reason for asking you to come to Princeton. As you might know, the board of the college will be meeting in few days, and I would like to suggest that you take the place of Reverend Tennent as a trustee."

Nathaniel was astonished by the unexpected honor.

"Dr. Witherspoon," he stammered, "I am, of course, deeply honored by your suggestion but I can hardly claim to be a worthy replacement for William Tennent. He has been a guiding spiritual light of our college from the very beginning."

"Indeed, he was," continued Witherspoon, "And since he saw fit to make you an elder of his congregation in Manalapan, I am sure he would agree with this suggestion. At the next board meeting I will suggest you as well as Reverend Azel Roe of Woodbridge and John Bayard of Philadelphia. I am confident that we will then have a board capable of dealing with the immense challenges facing our college. We must see to it that we can resume normal operations as quickly as possible, but for that we must find the money to repair the damages done to Nassau Hall by two occupying armies."

"I feel somewhat overwhelmed by the confidence you are placing in me, Dr. Witherspoon," Nathaniel humbly confided, "But I have long believed that our college has a sacred mission to produce men who will defend our freedoms. I cannot, therefore, refuse the call to duty at a time when our college must produce a generation capable of building a nation."

A few days later Witherspoon's suggestions were unanimously approved by the board, and he and Nathaniel were free to leave for York. On their way there they discussed the long list of problems facing both the college and the nation.

"The struggle for our Whig cause is inseparable from the struggle to defend the True Religion," opined Nathaniel, "In Monmouth County most of the disaffected are also opponents of the reformed churches. I can only trust our Presbyterian brethren to be really loyal supporters."

"I suspect that is true in Monmouth," agreed Witherspoon, "In eastern New Jersey and along the coast there are many Anglicans whose clergy pledge allegiance to the king every Sunday."

"There are also many Quakers who oppose violence in any form," added Nathaniel, "They would not be so much of a problem except for the support they give Tory sympathizers. We would like to extract retribution for the depredations that Tory raiding bands inflict on our loyal Whigs. If we cannot get our hands on the Tories themselves, we have to get compensation from their friends and relatives who still reside in Monmouth. All our efforts to this end are being blocked, however, by Tory sympathizers and Quakers."

"I think we need to make clear to Congress just how pernicious the Tory element in Monmouth has become and what must be done to combat it," suggested Witherspoon.

"You are certainly right there, Dr. Witherspoon," agreed Nathaniel "but just as important is to inform Washington about the state of affairs. The intelligence I get from our militia is that all our units are in a deplorable state. Without help from Washington's troops we cannot hope to prevail against the Tory element in Monmouth."

The two men agreed to stop again at Valley Forge on their way to York, not only to brief Washington on the problems in New Jersey but also to see firsthand how the training mission had progressed.

Arriving at Valley Forge they were delighted to see that an immense change had taken place. Gone were the refuse heaps and puddles of human excrement. The dwellings were now clean and well-ordered, the paths between them now swept and well-kept. The soldiers now looked more like professional military than peasants in arms. The guard at the gate saluted sharply and marched with them to General Washington's quarters.

"Ah, Dr. Witherspoon, Dr. Scudder," Washington greeted them warmly, "It is a pleasure to welcome you here again, especially considering the good tidings I have to offer. I now have official word that France is going to enter the war as an ally! The British now have to contend with an additional enemy who can confront them in all corners of the world."

"That is indeed wonderful news!" enthused Witherspoon, "We suspected that this was the reason for the urgent summons to Congress. Our prayers have been answered. With the French on our side, the British will never be able to force our surrender. Sooner or later they will have to negotiate a peaceful solution."

"That is not the only good news I have for you, gentlemen," continued Washington, "With your loyal assistance in Congress I was able to engage Baron von Steuben to train our troops. What he has been able to accomplish in just a few months is truly remarkable. With his assistance we have become worthy allies of our French friends. But see for yourselves, Baron von Steuben is just now drilling a company on the other side of the camp. Let us go and have a look."

The three men walked to the other side of the camp to where about a hundred men were lined up smartly on a parade field. Baron von Steuben would shout an order in French which would then be translated by a young captain into English. The soldiers would then respond immediately shouldering their weapons and marching in perfect formation. At barked orders from von Steuben and the captain the troops would change direction abruptly forming various geometrical designs on the field.

"The young man is Captain Benjamin Walker of New York," whispered Washington, "He has become the Baron's indispensable assistant. Von Steuben calls him his angel from heaven. But together they have worked wonders. Watch the next maneuver."

At a command from von Steuben the troops lined up in two rows, one behind the other. At a further command the row in front knelt down and loaded their muskets while the back row aimed and fired. The kneeling ones then switched places with the standing troops, stood up, aimed, and fired. Although live ammunition was not being used, it was clear from the continuous sound of clicking hammers, that this maneuver would result in a withering fusillade against an enemy.

"This certainly is impressive," remarked Nathaniel, "I wish our militia units could fight like that."

"It is all a matter of good training," explained Washington, "You see how quickly von Steuben has made soldiers out of our farm boys. And he is writing everything down in French which I will have Hamilton translate. It will be the organization manual for our army which all our officers will be required to use for training. I have never been so confident of victory as I am now. And as far as your militia units are concerned, see to it that our draft quotas are met, and we will turn your boys into soldiers as well."

Buoyed up by Washington's upbeat attitude, the two continued on to York where they found their congressional colleagues in a festive mood. The prospect of massive support from the French made anything seem possible. People debated whether it was time to reconsider an attack on the British in Philadelphia. American spies, however, brought news from the city that the British were planning big changes. Due to the debacle at Saratoga William Howe had been replaced as commander-in-chief of the British forces by Henry Clinton, and it was rumored that he wanted to effect some sort of troop consolidation but it was not yet clear what exactly he had in mind. Washington assumed that this was in response to the French entry into the war and considered it to be an admission of vulnerability. His assumption was further strengthened by the news that a commission headed by the Earl of Carlisle sought to present proposals to Congress for a peaceful end to the war. In an effort to find out exactly what the British were up to, Washington sent out a small reconnaissance party under the Marquis de Lafayette to Barren Hill, a village about halfway between Philadelphia and Valley Forge. The British quickly discovered Lafayette's troops, however, and sent out a larger force to destroy it. Lafayette was just able to avoid encirclement and escape with most of his troops down a back road, but could not bring Washington any definitive intelligence except that the British were quite prepared and capable of aggressively engaging American forces.

As Washington delayed taking action waiting to see what Clinton was up to, Nathaniel received an urgent message from Monmouth. A Loyalist raiding party had landed at Middletown Point and captured leading Whigs, including committee chairman John Burrowes and Captain Jacob Covenhoven, as well as many others. In response to this outrage the Monmouth County Court was considering several capital convictions against imprisoned Loyalists. Nathaniel knew that he had to get back home as quickly as possible to help cope with the deteriorating situation. He immediately sought out President Henry Laurens to explain why he had to be excused temporarily from his congressional duties.

"President Laurens, I know that New Jersey has been underrepresented of late in congressional deliberations, but I must nevertheless ask your permission to take leave for a few weeks. I have just received word that Tory elements and their sympathizers are wreaking havoc again in Monmouth, and it is essential that I help organize the resistance. We must avoid a repeat of the Tory Ascendancy."

"Dr. Scudder, you have been one of our most engaged members and represented your state well. If you feel that duty calls you to return home at this time, I certainly respect your judgement. I am well aware of the large population of Tory sympathizers in some parts of New Jersey, and have myself been thinking of ways we could weaken their movement. One way to discourage their activities might be to encourage British and Loyalist soldiers to desert by granting them exemption from military service. I suspect that many would welcome the chance to avoid military duty. Congress has passed a resolution to that effect which I have had printed as a pamphlet. I would ask you to distribute some of them in Monmouth. Perhaps that will contribute to the success of your campaign."

"Any help is welcome, President Laurens, and I will certainly get out the message," replied Nathaniel, "But I fear that words alone will not make a great difference. We will need to put the fear of God into the hearts of those who abet our enemies."

After bidding farewell to Dr. Witherspoon and President Laurens, Nathaniel took off at a brisk pace to get back to Monmouth as soon as possible. Arriving late in the evening, exhausted after a hard ride, he rushed to the bedroom to wake Isabella, and let her know that he had been temporarily excused from congressional duties.

Isabella smiled sweetly at Nathaniel pleased to see that he had returned so soon. As she become wider awake, however, it occurred to her that Nathaniel's unexpectedly quick return might involve ill tidings.

"Is there some emergency that has brought you back so soon?" she asked warily.

"I received news in York of the Tory raid at Middletown Point," explained Nathaniel, "Congress is very concerned that a new Tory Ascendancy might be imminent. I need to meet with Asher Holmes and John Smock as soon as possible to see how we can strengthen our militia to better protect our homes and families."

"Yes, of course," Isabella sighed, "But you will not be meeting anyone at this time of night. You can in good conscience get some rest."

The words were hardly out of her mouth when Nathaniel fell into a deep dreamless sleep without bothering to get undressed.

The next day Nathaniel sent out urgent messages to the leaders of the Monmouth militia to convene at his house so he could brief them on Congress's campaign to encourage deserters and hear what needed to be done to strengthen the militia. As he waited for replies, a messenger arrived with an urgent letter from General Philemon Dickinson, the senior general of the New Jersey militia. Nathaniel seized the letter and began to read it.

"What does it say? What does it say?" Isabella could not contain her excitement and foreboding.

"It says the British are about to invade New Jersey," Nathaniel answered grimly, "Apparently Clinton has decided to abandon Philadelphia by marching his army overland to New York. He probably thinks that is safer than going by sea and risking attack from the navy of our new French allies."

"Oh my God!" cried Isabella, "As if it were not already bad enough with the Tory attacks. Now we will have to contend with a huge part of the British army marching through our country. Whatever are we to do?"

"First of all, you and the children and the servants will move for a few weeks to a safer place out the line of march of the British," replied Nathaniel, "And then the militia will implement what General Dickinson suggests. He writes: 'I beg you will hold your regiment ready to march at a moment's notice. You must pay particular attention to the removal of bridges and felling the trees upon the roads. You will keep your men concealed and act in small parties by a constant and incessant fire upon their front, flanks, and rear as the occasion may require. It is expected that the enemy route will be directed toward South Amboy.' "

"Amboy!" exclaimed Isabella, "That means they will be marching right past us!"

"Indeed, they will," confirmed Nathaniel, "But they will not be able to occupy such a vast territory, and in any case, they probably want to reach New York as quickly as possible with a minimal loss of troops. General Dickinson's strategy is the right way for us to proceed. I will get together with Asher Holmes, John Smock, and some of the other militia leaders, and hear what they need in order to implement Dickinson's strategy effectively."

Meeting with Holmes, Smock, and other militia officers, Nathaniel was forced to the realization that the effective implementation of Dickinson's strategy might be beyond the militia's current capabilities. In response to his queries, he had received a letter from Colonel Samuel Forman of the Upper Freehold militia which he read to the assembled officers:

"There are universal complaints through our militia, their pay being held back. On the late alarm it was supposed the enemy was coming through this state, I received orders for marching with one half of my regiment. I gave orders for that purpose—Stafford, Dover, and Covenhoven's—three companies of stout and poor fellows. From expectations I had of receiving their pay, I had promised I would send it to Major Cook for them. They assembled at Tom's River in full expectations of receiving their pay and marching, but they disbanded and went home, determined to remain there until paid. Five times I had been to our paymaster and with less encouragement the last than the first. Sure I am that there is fault somewhere, where it is I cannot tell you. I am very sorry that at this critical moment we that have borne the heat and burthen of war continue to be neglected. Another matter distresses me, I have express orders for keeping up an important fire on the enemy's flank and rear when they march through this state, this without one single cartridge for my men. I have applied to the governor without success, we are very badly provided."

After reading the contents of the letter, Nathaniel turned to the assembled officers, "Is this depressing state of affairs typical of the militia units under your command?"

As each officer grimly nodded his head, Nathaniel began to understand just how badly mismanagement and corruption had hobbled the Whig mobilization. The world's most effective military machine was about to plow through his beloved home-land, and only the grace of God could avert a catastrophe.

Chapter 22

MONMOUTH – 1778–1779

ON THE 19TH OF June an express rider arrived at Monmouth Courthouse from Pennsylvania confirming that General Clinton had the day before indeed begun to move his 12,000-man army overland through New Jersey in the direction of New York City. Nathaniel met with several senior militia officers at Monmouth Courthouse to debrief the express rider, Jacob McDermott.

"Has Clinton really decided to abandon Philadelphia?" asked David Forman incredulously, "What about all his Loyalist friends?"

"The British have really left completely," confirmed McDermott, "Our forces have begun to re-occupy the city. Clinton apparently sent his heavy supplies and Loyalists to New York by ship, but he doesn't want to risk exposing his main body of troops to the French fleet. He seems to think it is less dangerous for him to march his army through New Jersey. A column of 12,000 troops followed by maybe a few thousand camp followers crossed the Delaware at Cooper's Ferry heading in the direction of Haddonfield."

"Well then, we have to show him that he has made a fatal mistake!" shouted David Forman, "We need to see to it that by the time he gets to New York he will wish he had rather faced the French fleet!"

Recalling his recent meeting with the militia officers and the discussion of Colonel Samuel Forman's letter, Nathaniel sought to inject a sense of realism into the conversation, "David, remember what your cousin Samuel told us about the militia's state of readiness. There is no way our militia could stop a column of 12,000 Regulars marching toward New York. It would only be feasible for us to support an action by Washington's army. In the meantime, those soldiers have been professionally trained and would have a hope of standing their ground against the enemy."

"Nathaniel is certainly correct," agreed Asher Holmes, "It is of the utmost importance that we coordinate our actions with Washington."

"Washington is indeed planning to attack Clinton's column at some point," said McDermott, "Exactly when and where is still to be determined. Washington crossed the Delaware with his army at Coryell's Ferry and will shadow Clinton's troops from the north until an opportunity presents itself to attack."

"How fast is Clinton's column progressing?" asked Nathaniel.

"Well, they have just started," replied McDermott, "But a column of 12,000 men, baggage wagons and camp followers cannot move quickly and is being continuously sabotaged along the way. The baggage train alone stretches for ten miles. But, nevertheless, I would guess you probably don't have more than about ten days before the vanguard arrives. The Hunterdon militia will slow them down as much as possible but a severe lack of ammunition limits what can be accomplished."

"It is clear that the big battle is going to take place near here," asserted David Forman, "This is also the last opportunity to strike them hard before they reach the protection of the guns of the British fleet off Sandy Hook."

"I think you are probably right, David," agreed Nathaniel, "We must ready all of our resources and evacuate our women and children. There is no time to lose. We must also ensure that Washington is provided with the best intelligence possible. Our intimate knowledge of the area could be the decisive factor."

Turning to McDermott he continued, "Please take a message back to Washington. One of our brethren in our church here, David Rhea, is currently serving in the Second New Jersey Regiment. He is a devout supporter of the Whig cause and has intimate knowledge of the terrain here. He can guide Washington to the most advantageous positions for facing the enemy."

Nathaniel, David Forman, Thomas Henderson, and Asher Holmes spent the next days securing what little ammunition was available and evacuating women and children to the north of the suspected path of the British army. David Forman's system of express relay riders kept them well informed of the distance between Monmouth Courthouse and the approaching British column. When the enemy was about a day away, Nathaniel was outside Monmouth Courthouse preparing to lead his militia unit into the fray. A man dashed up on horseback shouting, "Are you Doctor Scudder?"

"Indeed, I am," replied Nathaniel, "But I have urgent business now, and I cannot spare time for patients."

"But, Dr. Scudder, this is a real emergency," pleaded the rider, "When my pregnant neighbor, Mrs. Craig, found out that all women and children were to be evacuated, she became so upset that she went into labor. But it is not going well. She might die if you cannot attend to her!"

Sarah Craig was indeed one of Nathaniel's patients, and he knew that the birth of her child was not yet due. A birth this premature was truly dangerous and could easily end with the death of both mother and child. He also knew that Sarah's husband was called out for militia duty. He could not just let the man's wife and child die for lack of care. He instructed his unit to ride slowly in the direction of the enemy but not to engage until Washington's troops arrived. Promising them that he would catch up with them as soon as possible, he galloped off in the direction of the Craig farm.

Arriving a few minutes later he could hear Sarah's screams already as he approached the house. Rushing inside he found Sarah lying in a pool of water on her bed.

In between screams Sarah wailed, "Dr. Scudder, Dr. Scudder, this is way too early. I am going to lose my baby!"

"No Sarah, you are not," Nathaniel tried to reassure her, knowing that his first duty was to calm the hysterical patient, "If I recall correctly, you are about seven and a half months. That is early, of course, but it is altogether possible that we can still save the baby. The important thing is for you to remain as calm as possible."

Nathaniel rolled up a small towel and instructed Sarah to bite on it.

"The labor pains will come in waves," explained Nathaniel, "Bite on the towel when it feels unbearable and try to press down."

Nathaniel then took a second towel, soaked it in cool water and after rinsing it, laid it across Sarah's head, "Between waves you have to try to relax. Take deep breaths. And pray for your baby."

Sarah nodded gratefully. The doctor's presence and calm confidence made her hopeful that she would survive her tribulations. It helped her endure what turned out to be a long and painful labor.

The waves of pain gradually became more frequent until in the early morning Sarah with one loud shriek was able to expel a tiny but perfectly formed infant into the cold world. Picking up the little girl by her heels and tapping gently on her back, Nathaniel was relieved to hear a weak but clear whimper. He laid the baby on her mother's chest and covered them both with a blanket.

"It is very cold for her outside your body, Sarah," Nathaniel explained, "We are lucky that the weather is so warm lately, but you still have to make sure that she keeps as warm as possible. When she does not have direct contact with your body then she should have a warm water flask next to her."

Nathaniel proceeded to bind the umbilical cord in preparation for severing it. With one flick of his scalpel the little girl became a new individual that now had to survive on its own. The drama of this moment always affected Nathaniel deeply and caused him to ponder the great miracle of the continuity of life. So engrossed in such thoughts was he that he did not notice several dark figures who had quietly entered the house.

"In the name of his majesty, George III, you are now my prisoner, sir!" a large Black man stepped forward with his musket leveled at Nathaniel, "You are wearing a rebel uniform. As commander of this unit of the King's Ethiopian Regiment, I arrest you in the name of the Crown."

Nathaniel was taken aback by the pompous self-confidence of the Loyalist, but his musket had to be taken seriously especially since Nathaniel had come unarmed.

He remembered vaguely hearing about a slave named Titus who had escaped from one John Corlies in Colt's Neck and gone off to join Lord Dunmore's African regiment in Virginia.

"Although I am wearing a militia uniform, I am unarmed," explained Nathaniel, "I am here to try to save the lives of this woman and her newborn child."

The Black leader lowered his musket as a second younger Black man emerged from the shadows. Nathaniel recognized Jim, the brother of Dinah, the two slaves that David Forman had offered him.

"Colonel Tye, sir," the younger man began, "This man is Dr. Scudder. He helped me and my sister when we were running from that pervert, van Cleave. He is a good man, Colonel, and a good physician."

"Good, then, you stay here and guard him," ordered Tye, "Make certain that his activities are confined to doctoring."

Tye left with the rest of his men leaving Jim to guard Nathaniel, mother, and child. Nathaniel hastened to return to his medical duties. In the meantime, the after-birth had come out and Nathaniel had to clean up the mess trying to disturb Sarah and the baby as little as possible. To his great relief both mother and child seemed to have endured the ordeal relatively well and appeared to be resting quietly.

"The baby was born two months too early, because the mother was so stressed by the coming battle," Nathaniel explained the seriousness of the situation to Jim, "The infant might survive but the first hours are critical."

"Battlefield ain't no place for having babies, Dr. Scudder, she's lucky you're around," commented Jim.

The sound of cannon fire interrupted their conversation. It seemed that the British units surrounding the Craig farm were under attack. Nathaniel sincerely hoped that Washington's troops had arrived in force but just as sincerely hoped that the Craig farmhouse would not soon be riddled by cannon fire. He and Jim peered out of an attic window to try to ascertain what was going on. It appeared that an American unit had opened fire on the rear guard of the British column but was now retreating. The British units had formed up smartly and were beginning a counterattack. It was difficult to get an overview from the attic window but the fact that the British troops were pushing steadily in a westerly direction did not bode well for the Americans.

After a while the sound of gunfire died down a bit, and Colonel Tye again appeared at the door of the farmhouse, this time with another prisoner, whom Nathaniel recognized as Captain Elisha Shepard of the state troops.

"Captain Shepard!" exclaimed Nathaniel, "You a prisoner as well? What in the devil is going on out there?"

"Colonel Scudder, the day has not begun well for us," explained Shepard, "General Washington decided to attack the British rear guard at Monmouth Courthouse with 4000 troops led by General Charles Lee. But Lee could not coordinate the units at his disposal and decided to retreat when the going got rough. My unit stayed to fight and that's how I wound up a prisoner. Because of that incompetent bastard, I will probably wind up dying on a prison ship in New York!"

"Or, if you are lucky, get exchanged for some of our men who are currently in rebel custody," Colonel Tye suggested, "So if you remain my obedient prisoners, there may be some hope for you."

Turning to Jim and handing him two pistols he admonished him, "Keep a careful eye on these two. They are worth a good ransom if we can get them back to New York. While you are doing that I will see if I can't capture a few more."

After Colonel Tye went back to the field, Jim and Nathaniel returned to the attic window to see if they could figure out how the battle was proceeding.

"Captain Shepard!" exclaimed Nathaniel suddenly, "Something has changed! The British troops are no longer pushing westward. Perhaps the Americans have stopped retreating. Maybe Washington is mounting a counterattack."

Shepard also rushed to the attic window and peered out. At the same time the sounds of battle began to increase again. The British forces they could see from the window were now firing from their current positions. It seemed that the Craig farmhouse was now right in the midst of the battlefield. Miraculously it had not yet been seriously hit. Seeing billowing clouds of smoke in the distance they had to assume, however, that other houses in the area had not been so lucky. Nathaniel wondered if his house near Monmouth Courthouse was still standing.

The battle noise continued to increase around them seeming to indicate that vast numbers of troops were joining the fray. Suddenly the sound of a large volley of cannon seemed to emanate from the vicinity of Combs Hill.

"Thank God!" exclaimed Nathaniel, "It sounds as though an American battery has had the good sense to set up on Combs Hill. That is the perfect spot to make the British position untenable. One of our Monmouth boys must have been able to get through to Washington!"

The cannon fire continued regularly from Combs Hill wreaking great havoc in its target area throughout the long, hot afternoon. From the attic window they could see exhausted men tending the wounded. Many British Regulars in their heavy uniforms seemed to be dying from thirst in the June heat.

When the sun went down, the dueling cannonades finally came to an end. It seemed that both sides had decided not to continue the battle after dark. Peering from the attic window, they could see, however, that there was much movement in the enemy camp. While Nathaniel was pondering what this could mean, one of Colonel Tye's men appeared at the door.

"Jim, message from the colonel, you are to take your prisoners and join your unit. We are leaving for New York."

"Right now?" asked Jim surprised.

"Right now." confirmed the messenger and left the house.

Holding his pistols on the two prisoners, Jim said, "Captain Shepard, you come with me. Dr. Scudder, you take care of your patients."

Nathaniel could hardly believe his good fortune. After Jim left with the unfortunate Shepard and slammed the door behind him, Nathaniel fell to his knees.

"Almighty God! Thank you for saving me from enemy bondage!" he cried, "I can only believe it is because of more important tasks that await me. I swear I am ready for any sacrifice you might demand of me."

Returning to the task at hand Nathaniel hastened back to Sarah's bedside. He was pleased to see that both Sarah and the little girl were sleeping peacefully. After making certain that bread and water were available next to the bed should Sarah wake up, he sat down in an armchair to wait out the British evacuation. A wave of exhaustion came over him and he fell into a deep sleep. When he awoke, the sun was shining. Sarah was sitting up eating a piece of the bread, he had left for her. The tiny girl was nursing on Sarah's breast. Nathaniel went to the attic window and saw that not British but American soldiers were now filling the fields around the house. Rushing out the door he accosted the first militia officer he saw.

"I am Congressman Nathaniel Scudder, and I am urgently looking for my militia colleagues David Forman and Thomas Henderson. Would you have any idea where they are?"

"Indeed, I do, sir," replied the officer, "All senior officers from the area have been asked to come to Englishtown for a meeting with General Washington. I assume your colleagues are on their way there."

Thanking the officer Nathaniel hurried to the Craig barn to see if by some miracle his horse had not been stolen by the departing British. Entering the barn, he heard the familiar whinny of his beloved Blackjack. Again he praised the Lord for his good fortune and for inspiring an act of decency in the heart of Jim. He jumped on Blackjack and galloped off in the direction of Englishtown.

After about five miles he ran into the main body of Washington's army. Recognizing an officer he had met in Valley Forge, he asked where Washington was holding the conference with the local militia leaders. The soldier obliged by accompanying him to a farmhouse owned by one Moses Laird about a mile away where Washington had set up temporary quarters. Entering the farmhouse Nathaniel was pleased to see his fellow militia leaders, David Forman and Thomas Henderson, sitting together with Washington and several of his senior officers. Nathaniel recognized Colonel Daniel Morgan and Colonel Henry Lee.

"Dr. Scudder, come in, come in," Washington greeted Nathaniel warmly, "I am so glad that you are able to attend this meeting. I have asked you men of Monmouth to come here today to help me determine my next moves. After some initial difficulties we had a very good day on the battlefield. We fought the enemy to a standstill so effectively during the day that he thought he had to abscond under cover of darkness. Now the question is do we follow up on that with another attack before the British column reaches New York. You gentlemen know the terrain intimately between here and New York, and I would like to know your assessment of our tactical chances of success."

"My spies tell me that the main British force right now is in the vicinity of Middletown," began David Forman, "That is on higher ground which will give the enemy a tactical advantage. Our troops would face an uphill battle with enemy cannon fire pouring down on us."

"British ships in Raritan Bay will also be able to assist Clinton's troops," continued Nathaniel, "Once the main body of the enemy gets close to Sandy Hook, there is little we can do to prevent their embarkation."

"I think we will lose at least as many of our own soldiers as we can kill of the enemy," added Thomas Henderson.

"Well, gentlemen, that is clearly a risk not worth taking," concluded Washington, "I thank you for your insights. I will instead put the main body of my troops in motion to New Brunswick. Colonel Lee and Colonel Morgan, you are to put together a force of about a thousand men. Take some from the New Jersey Line but also include local militia units with men who know the terrain. You saw how important that was in the recent battle. Young David Rhea's advice to garrison Comb's Hill is what saved the day. You are not to attack the enemy directly but only harass their flanks, limit their plundering of the local people and gather up deserters and stragglers. In that way we will be able to maximize the damage to the enemy while minimizing our own losses."

Nathaniel was flattered by Washington's immediate acceptance of the advice he and his colleagues had offered and deeply impressed by the swift resoluteness of Washington's leadership. After the meeting he hastened to return to Freehold to see if his house was still standing. Thomas Henderson had told him that his own home had been completely devastated as had many others, and Nathaniel was afraid of what he might find. He thanked God that he had evacuated his family to Hightstown before the British arrived. Riding past Monmouth Courthouse, he did not bother stopping, assuming the British had freed all the arrested Loyalists that David Forman had imprisoned there. When he saw his house standing unharmed at the end of the street, tears of gratitude flowed down his cheeks. He could barely fathom his amazing good fortune amid the chaos and devastation of the last few days. He vowed once again to show himself worthy of the Lord's grace by supporting the Holy Cause with unflinching dedication. He decided to stay at home until the next day before heading for Philadelphia to report on the results of the battle. On the way there he could stop off in Hightstown to give Isabella the good news that she, the children, and the servants could now return safely to an intact home.

Rising early the next morning he galloped the 15 miles to Hightstown at a swift pace, anxious to see his beloved family and give them the exciting details of the last few days. He was confident that he would find them unharmed since they were staying at an inn just a few miles away from where Washington had had his headquarters in

Cranbury. He arrived just as Isabella, Hannah, Kenneth, and Lydia were sitting down to breakfast.

"Good news, my darlings!" he shouted as he entered the inn, "Our brave soldiers have prevailed on the battlefield and, despite vast depredations in our area, the Lord has seen fit to spare our property. You can all return home immediately."

"Praise the Lord!" cried Isabella almost fainting with relief, "I was so distraught I have not slept a wink in days."

In fact Isabella looked as though she herself had endured a battle, and Nathaniel was troubled by her exhausted appearance even though she had suffered no physical harm.

"You are right to praise the Lord, my dear, but you also must have faith in His wisdom," admonished Nathaniel sanctimoniously, "It is only through faith that you can find calm in these tumultuous times."

"I try my best to keep the faith," replied Isabella, "But I cannot be calm when I know that you, John, and Joseph are constantly exposing yourselves to violence. And the violence in our area is not going to stop. We might have been lucky this time, but the next Loyalist raid might well target us and you are gone so much of the time."

"Then I will defend you, mother!" exclaimed young Kenneth jumping to his feet, "I will soon be old enough to join the militia, and I am a better shot than either of my older brothers."

As Isabella rolled her eyes in despair, Nathaniel smiled wryly, "Well, darling with such stout defense, you clearly have nothing to worry about. That is just as well as I must depart for Philadelphia soon to report to Congress. But Kenneth will not be alone in your defense. General Washington has dispatched over a thousand men to harry the enemy and prevent pillaging. You will be safe while I am gone. I will give you a bit of laudanum to help you sleep, and you should try to rest as much as possible in the next few days."

Isabella nodded with a sigh of resignation. She knew that there was no point in trying to dissuade Nathaniel from doing what he thought was his God-given duty.

Nathaniel spent the rest of the day with his family and set out for Philadelphia early the next morning. Arriving in Philadelphia he headed toward Buttonwood Hall at Market and Bank Streets where most of the influential Presbyterians of the city congregated. He hoped that he would find President Witherspoon there or at least someone who knew where he was staying.

When he arrived, he was shocked to see that the formerly lovely building had suffered greatly during the British occupation. It had obviously been turned into a stable with horse manure still littering the aisles. The pews had been ripped out probably for use as firewood. As Nathaniel surveyed the wanton damage, he heard the familiar Scottish burr of John Witherspoon.

Drawing closer he saw Witherspoon inside the building talking to a man Nathaniel recognized as Benjamin Rush, a fellow congressman, physician and graduate of Nassau Hall. He was well known among all the Nassau Hall alumni for his services in convincing John Witherspoon to accept the offer of the presidency.

"Well, Dr. Rush, here we can clearly see how much respect the enemy has for the True Religion," Witherspoon remarked angrily.

"Just so," agreed Rush, "After all, they call our fight for freedom the 'Presbyterian Rebellion'. One can easily imagine what fate awaits us if we lose, and I still worry that Washington's army might not be up to the task. General Sullivan tells me that forces under Washington's direct command are undisciplined and moblike."

"Not anymore," Nathaniel interrupted, "Greetings from Monmouth, gentlemen, I am pleased to be able to report that Washington's army gave an excellent account of itself near Monmouth Courthouse. The training at Valley Forge has made an enormous difference. Our forces fought the enemy to a standstill. After a day of bitter combat, the enemy was obliged to abandon the field under cover of darkness."

"Ah, Dr. Scudder, that is balm to my soul!" exclaimed Dr. Witherspoon, "Dr. Rush, I agree that Washington's army made a very poor impression when they first moved to Valley Forge but what Baron von Steuben was able to accomplish in just a few months is nothing short of miraculous. As I admonished you when I was investigating your charges of misappropriation and mismanagement against Dr. William Shippen, one must be careful in assigning blame for the inevitable weaknesses of our young institutions. The Army Medical Service was certainly in disarray but that was not necessarily the fault of Dr. Shippen. In any case, progress is being made to improve things."

"I can confirm that," added Nathaniel, "The Medical Committee in Congress is aware of the shortcomings of our Medical Service but fixing those problems is easier said than done. We are confronted everywhere with shortages and insufficient funds."

"We are also confronted everywhere by corruption and profiteering!" retorted Rush, "We must be constantly on guard against Satan's wiles. No one is immune to his blandishments!"

Witherspoon smiled indulgently remembering the earnest young man who had come to Scotland ten years ago to convince him that the Calvinist dream of a pious republic could be achieved in the New World, and that Witherspoon could play an important role in that if he would agree to take over Nassau Hall.

"Yes, yes, Dr. Rush," replied Witherspoon, "You are certainly correct in theory, but we must pragmatically adjust our strategies to conform to the corrupt world we live in. For example, instead of fighting with Shippen you might have been more effective in righting wrongs had you stayed on as surgeon-general. And I would advise you to be wary of Conway's gossip. He has already been forced to resign his commission as Inspector General of the Army amid allegations of corruption. General Cadwalader was so outraged over his insinuations about General Washington that he challenged him to a duel. The Conway Cabal is about to collapse, and I would advise you to mend fences with Washington as best you can."

Realizing the accuracy of Witherspoon's criticism Rush sighed deeply, "I know that I am sometimes overly harsh in my assessment of people. I did not mean to cast aspersions on Washington's honor or character. I am as critical of my own shortcomings as I am of those of others, but I understand that a more diplomatic approach would be more effective."

"I think the most important thing right now is to forge a united front against the enemy," opined Nathaniel, "We need to show our allies, particularly the French, that we are a confederated people and stand as one to resist the tyranny of the enemy."

"Of that there can be no doubt," agreed Witherspoon, "Let us all work to convince our respective states to ratify the suggested Articles of Confederation."

"I don't want to seem recalcitrant," objected Rush, "But I am still not convinced that the one-state-one vote rule is appropriate. It is true that the members of the Congress are appointed by the states but represent the people. No state has a right to alienate the privilege of equal representation."

"I know that you and your colleague, James Wilson, from the Pennsylvania delegation have from the beginning expressed the view that Congress represents the entire people of all the states and not just the states themselves," replied Witherspoon, "This idea is theoretically sound perhaps, but again we must proceed more practically. Congress came into existence as a body representing each individual state, and many states would not tolerate the weakening of their powers. The Articles are a compromise perhaps but one that can forge one nation out of thirteen separate colonies."

"It is absolutely urgent that our foreign allies have the impression that we are really one country standing together," added Nathaniel, "As you well know, we are desperately in need of their assistance, and if the Articles are not signed, they will see us as just a chaotic bunch of 13 squabbling rebel colonies. No other country will take us seriously."

"I am not blind to the practical need to appear united," countered Bush, "But the instrument of our unity is flawed and sooner or later, it will cause strife among the individual states."

A few days later Nathaniel met with Dr. Witherspoon to discuss their recommendations to the NJ Assembly.

"I have to report to Speaker John Hart in any case about the success of the engagement near Monmouth Courthouse," began Nathaniel, "He needs to know that it was gained at the cost of great plunder and devastation committed among my friends in that quarter although through the distinguishing goodness of providence, my family and property escaped harm and that almost in a miraculous manner. We can append our thoughts concerning the Articles to that report."

"An excellent idea, Dr. Scudder," agreed Witherspoon, "We must carefully counter the arguments of people like Benjamin Rush. He is a brilliant young man for whom I have the greatest admiration, but he tends to be a bit of purist in political matters.

From a purely practical standpoint, despite any flaws the Articles of Confederation are better than no national compact between the states."

"I agree wholeheartedly," replied Nathaniel, "Unless every one of the thirteen states accedes to it, we remain an unconfederated people. Much wisdom has flowed into its design and perhaps with improvements it has the potential to be a Magna Carta for America."

"At the very least it is the beginning of what will undoubtedly be a long process of forging one nation out of thirteen quite different colonies with very different interests," continued Witherspoon, "Large states like Pennsylvania or Virginia have agendas very different from small states like New Jersey."

"Regarding the protections for smaller states like New Jersey, no plan will ever be adopted that is more equal," affirmed Nathaniel, "And as for the imperial designs of some states I believe that all new territory should belong to the nation as a whole. If states compete for territory, then Dr. Rush's grave predictions could indeed come true."

"After you have sent your report to John Hart, I think we ought to go to Trenton at our first opportunity to personally urge the Assembly to adopt the Articles as quickly as possible," suggested Witherspoon, "I also want to ask their assistance in getting Nassau Hall back into shape. I am firmly resolved to resume commencement ceremonies there in September."

"I agree completely that getting the Articles approved should be our top priority this summer" replied Nathaniel, "I am also delighted to hear that commencement ceremonies will resume in September. My son, Joseph, should be graduating this year if the college deems him worthy."

"At the same Board meeting in April in which you were confirmed as a new trustee the Board decided that Joseph despite the turmoil of the last few years has managed to master the areas of knowledge we require for the first degree," Witherspoon assured Nathaniel, "He will get his degree in September along with the other members of his class as well as several from the Class of 1777 whose commencement had to be cancelled."

The two congressmen spent most of the rest of the summer canvassing support for the Articles among the members of the New Jersey Assembly but also among the population in general. They enlisted the enthusiastic cooperation of their Presbyterian networks by describing a vision of the creation of a new, pious republic which would be cleansed of the corruption of the Old World. They urged parishioners to write to their assemblymen bidding them to give their approval to the Articles. As in many small states some people in New Jersey were apprehensive about being overwhelmed by the power of large states. Such people wanted Congress to control foreign trade and to take possession of any lands that the United States might acquire. While admitting that such concerns were certainly understandable, Nathaniel emphasized the protections that the Articles offered and the possibility that such legitimate concerns could be addressed later. With all the vehemence of a revivalist preacher he stressed the urgency of America's need for foreign support without which the holy cause was surely doomed. He travelled tirelessly throughout the state addressing church groups and town meetings, arguing eloquently in favor of the Articles. His overwhelming confidence in the righteousness of his mission had a contagious effect on many of his listeners. Over the course of the next months the mood in New Jersey began gradually to shift in favor of the Articles and Nathaniel had reason to hope that ratification could happen in the fall.

In September as Nathaniel, Isabella, and Joseph travelled to Princeton to take part in the commencement ceremonies. Nathaniel was particularly anxious to use the opportunity to confer with Dr. Witherspoon about the best strategy for getting final approval for the Articles.

"Well, Dr. Scudder," began Witherspoon, "I have heard that you have made quite an impression on many of our fellow Presbyterians who are now urging their assemblymen to vote for the Articles. Congratulations. If you were a clergyman, I am sure you would save many souls."

"Yes, he can be quite relentless, when he is convinced that he is in the right," added Isabella smiling ruefully.

"In this matter, he is certainly right," confirmed Witherspoon, "And he is right about the urgency as well. I have just learned that Congress has decided to exchange William Franklin for John McKinly. While I am glad for McKinly, I think that this could be a dangerous move. Franklin detests us for forcing him out of power, and I am sure he is out for revenge. I shudder to think what mischief he will be up to as a free man."

"He would probably like to see both of us at the end of a rope. I am sure that he will try to organize all those disaffected elements that were forced by the revolution to abandon their properties in New Jersey," speculated Nathaniel, "After all, those are the people he worked with as governor, and they all share a common interest in turning back the clock. I think we can expect more vicious attacks from the Tory refugees in New York."

"That means that Monmouth County will again bear the brunt of the brutality!" exclaimed Isabella.

"Quite likely," agreed Nathaniel, "Which brings us back to the urgency of getting the Articles approved so that our allies, in particular the French, will commit enough military resources to our cause that we can have a hope of succeeding. Without their help we will never be able to dislodge the British forces from New York which provide a safe haven for murderous Tory bands. Without the Articles we are not a confederated people which makes it highly unlikely that foreigners will take large risks to help us."

Joseph, listening intently to the elders' discourse, became more and more excited until finally he could no longer contain his enthusiasm.

"While preparing on my own for this degree while the college was closed, I spent much time learning French vocabulary," he began excitedly, "I think I could make myself useful in dealings with our new ally."

"Joseph has indeed acquired a good basic knowledge of French," confirmed Dr. Witherspoon, "If he has the opportunity to use the language, he could become quite fluent."

"In fact, there might be something for you at the War Office in Philadelphia," mused Nathaniel, "Now that we have entered into a formal alliance with France, much information is flowing in that is in that language. I suspect there is a need for translators. People there remember your services to Washington's army before the Battles of Trenton and Princeton. You might be able to work your way up into a diplomatic career."

Joseph's breast swelled with pride as his mother breathed a sigh of relief. "At least he won't be risking his life fighting murderous Tory refugees in Monmouth County," she whispered to herself.

"Joseph will have an additional opportunity to use his French in helping to communicate with the European officers who have volunteered to help our cause," added Witherspoon, "French is the lingua franca among Europe's military men."

"Indeed," agreed Nathaniel, "By the way, speaking of French-speaking officers I am told that Casimir Pulaski has been promoted to the rank of a brigadier general with the special title of Commander of the Horse and will soon be returning to New Jersey."

"I have heard the same," confirmed Witherspoon, "Apparently he has organized a cavalry legion that is quite impressive. He has done for our cavalry what von Steuben did for our foot soldiers. We are fortunate to have him but not everyone enjoys serving under him. By all accounts he is demanding, haughty, and arrogant."

"But also highly skilled and fearless in battle," added Nathaniel, "They say he saved Washington's life at the Battle of Brandywine. He rallied fleeing troops and mounted a charge that averted a disastrous defeat of the Continental Army cavalry."

"His mission this time will be to discourage British raids against our privateers along the coast who are doing a fine job of disrupting enemy shipping. Now with William Franklin to guide their hand, it is only a matter of time until they strike back," prophesized Witherspoon.

Just a week later the British indeed decided to move against the Jersey privateers to try to recover confiscated ships and cargo. A fleet of nine ships with 300 regulars and 100 New Jersey Loyalists sailed from New York City under the command of a British Army officer, Captain Patrick Ferguson. The force raided Chestnut Neck, the trading center on the Little Egg Harbor River, which had been the major supply route for Valley Forge and the headquarters of the most successful privateers. General Pulaski was quickly sent there to repel the attack and to block access to the Batso Ironworks. The Batso Forge, only about 20 miles further up the Mullica River, made cannon balls for Washington's army and was thus of great strategic importance for the rebellion. After setting up camp in Little Egg Harbor the Pulaski Legion was betrayed by a deserter who gave Ferguson details of the troop deployment. Ferguson used the information to stage a night attack on an infantry outpost and succeeded in quickly and silently murdering about 50 soldiers with bayonets before an alarm could be raised. By the time Pulaski's mounted troops rallied, Ferguson and his men were off in their boats.

Although Pulaski was successful in limiting much of the damage of Ferguson's campaign, the brutality of the attack sparked widespread outrage.

"It was an unprovoked massacre!" shouted David Forman when Nathaniel brought news of the incident to a meeting of militia officers at Monmouth Courthouse, "Those men were not even given a chance to surrender! That is exactly the way we must act when the shoe is on the other foot. We have a number here under lock and key who deserve a similar fate if only to show the British that their brutality will not go unavenged!"

"We must proceed with caution," warned Nathaniel, "The desire for revenge is, of course, completely natural, but General Washington does not want to give passive Loyalists a reason to become active against us. He would, therefore, like us to avoid escalating the conflicts beyond what is necessary for self-defense."

"If we want to defend ourselves, then escalation cannot be avoided!" ranted Forman, "All those Tory refugees in New York are just waiting for opportunities to attack us. We have to strike first!"

"General Washington has made it very clear that we are to avoid plundering the civilian population, whether Tory or Whig," continued Nathaniel, "I have a cousin from Long Island who operates a sloop on the Sound. He has been issued a privateering license by Governor Clinton, but he is only allowed to intercept British shipping. Although there are many rich Tories on Long Island, he is expressly denied the right to plunder them. I don't know how long he will resist the temptation."

"He should grab whatever he can!" shouted Forman, "The property of those Tory bastards will be used by the enemy against us. It is a perfectly justifiable act in war time to confiscate enemy supplies."

"If it is indeed military supplies that are confiscated, that is entirely justifiable," agreed Nathaniel, "But Washington is certainly correct in wanting to enforce the rule of law in protecting legitimate property rights. Failure to do so would only swell the ranks of our enemies." he added somewhat sanctimoniously.

"I will be happy to thin those ranks at my every opportunity," replied Forman with a cynical smile.

"I agree that we must counter every aggression with great resolve, even as we seek to avoid escalation," continued Nathaniel, "And I will seek the approval of Congress for appropriate retaliation for every Tory transgression."

"An eye for an eye and a tooth for a tooth?" asked Forman.

"An eye for an eye and a tooth for a tooth, as the Scripture enjoins us," agreed Nathaniel.

Later in the day Nathaniel recounted the details of the meeting to Isabella who reacted with surprise, "It seems to me that George Washington and David Forman are in profound disagreement. The General wants to avoid provoking the Loyalist population while David wants to attack it at every opportunity."

Nathaniel squirmed uncomfortably as the extent of this contradiction began to sink in.

"Yes, of course," he stammered, "But … but we cannot let outrages go unpunished."

"Mark my words, Nathaniel, David's bloodthirsty approach will only lead to more escalation and devastation. Every Tory that he hangs here in Monmouth County has a relative or friend who will seek revenge. The gruesome treatment of captured enemies will only give them an excuse to treat our side the same way. That pine robber, Jacob Fagan, for example, was certainly an evil man who deserved to die, but digging up his corpse and hanging it up to be picked at by carrion was disgusting and not worthy of our noble cause. Washington's approach is very wise."

"I know, my dear, it is a delicate balance that we must achieve. We certainly must defend ourselves against scoundrels like the traitor, Gustav Juliat, who betrayed Pulaski, but we also do not want to provoke Tory violence unnecessarily. I have decided to support a resolution in Congress which threatens an eye-for-an-eye, tooth-for-tooth retaliation if the other side continues to perpetrate atrocities. That will hopefully deter refugee gangs from molesting our citizens if they know their friends and relatives will pay the price."

"I will pray that the deterrent effect outweighs the provocative effect," Isabella sighed resignedly, "But I fear that is a recipe for mounting violence."

"Let's hope that that is not the case," Nathaniel quickly changed the subject to something more uplifting, "By the way, I have been selected to serve on a committee of some importance. May I read my appointment notice to you?"

"By all means," Isabella replied smiling, not unwilling to change from an unpleasant subject.

"I quote from the resolution of Congress: "Whereas it hath become necessary not only that speedy and vigorous measures should be taken to regulate the commissary's and quarter master's departments, but also that a constant attention should be paid to those departments: Resolved, That Mr. [Nathaniel] Scudder, Mr. G[ouverneur] Morris, and Mr. [William] Whipple be a committee to superintend the same departments, and that they, or any two of them, be empowered to take such steps relating to the same as they shall think most [advantageous] for the public service."

"Well, that sounds very impressive, it sounds as though you will be imbued with great powers but what exactly do you plan to do with all those powers?"

"Our duty is to see to it that our troops are supported to the absolute best of our abilities. That is clearly not the case at present. Much of the problem has to do with profiteering and corruption. War presents many opportunities for self-enrichment and the temptation is too great for many. We must see to it that we root out such corruption and stay on the path of righteousness. We must prove ourselves worthy of the great destiny that the Lord has offered us."

As Nathaniel spoke these words his voice took on the hortatory urgency of the Presbyterian elder and Isabella shivered at the inevitable implications of such total commitment.

"I am sure profiteering and corruption play a role but those are certainly not the only causes for our difficulties," argued Isabella, "The war causes all manner of shortages, is it not to be expected that merchants will demand higher prices for supplies that are getting scarcer by the day?"

"You are quite correct that better organization of supplies will have to be part of the solution," conceded Nathaniel, "We need to take inventory of what is available in each state and how much is needed to provision the local population. Only then can we determine the fair share that each state must commit to for supplying the army. But the temptation to hoard scarce supplies in the prospect of rising prices will never go away. Intense moral suasion is our only weapon in that struggle."

"Well, good luck with that," replied Isabella drily, "In my experience merchants are unmoved by appeals to morality, pleading always that they are themselves innocent victims of market forces."

In the following weeks Nathaniel came to learn just how intractable such market forces could be. His new committee resolved to take a systematic approach to the organization of logistics. Beginning with North Carolina Governor, William Caswell, they sent secret queries to each state suggesting that commissioners be appointed to create an inventory of available supplies which could be shared with the army. To their chagrin the states contended that they did not maintain the stores of supplies that were required. Such merchandise had to be acquired through tradesmen who dictated the prices, precisely the kind of merchants that Nathaniel suspected were tainted by corruption. What was available depended on how much you could pay and in what currency.

Back in Monmouth Nathaniel vented his frustration in a conversation with Isabella and his father-in-law.

"It is unbelievable," Nathaniel exclaimed, "The more we track down the reasons for supply shortages, the more we run into greedy merchants who hold back on deliveries in order to get a better price."

"That is not really very surprising, is it?" Colonel Anderson replied, "A merchant's success depends on his ability to sell his wares for more than he bought them for. We can be happy that there are still merchants willing to accept payment in proclamation money whereas the British pay in sterling."

"That is why interrupting the illegal London trade is one of our most important priorities," argued Nathaniel, "David Forman plans to use the recent resolution of Congress for retaliation to put more pressure on dissident elements who help the enemy by selling their produce to the British rather than to us."

"David Forman's pressure on dissident elements is already having a backlash," objected Isabella, "It is rumored that some of his prisoners in Monmouth Court jail mysteriously wound up dead without any due process. If we want to be viewed as the guarantors of law and order, we cannot sanction this kind of behavior. People are starting to say that David himself is an unscrupulous profiteer. What about these salt-works he is investing in on the shore for which he has requested government support? Are they mostly to benefit the cause or the fortunes of David Forman?"

Nathaniel squirmed uncomfortably in his seat, having already had misgivings about some of Forman's entrepreneurial projects. Noting his discomfort, Colonel Anderson sought to come to his aid.

"It is altogether possible that Forman's saltworks will benefit both him and the Whig cause," Colonel Anderson offered, "After all, one of the consequences of the recent British attack was the destruction of important saltworks at Little Egg Harbor and the army desperately needs salt."

"Indeed, it is not always easy to determine at what point private gain is inimical to the common weal," admitted Nathaniel, "I have no doubt that David passionately supports the Whig cause but I myself would have qualms of conscience were I to profit in any way from the needs of our troops. This is an issue that we are confronted with frequently. I recently learned, for example, that General Greene who is our Quarter-master General is also a silent partner in the Batso Iron Works that supplies Washington's army with cannon balls. When I discussed this with him, he offered to make me a partner as well but insisted on keeping all such arrangements out of the public eye."

"That sounds like an interesting proposition," replied Colonel Anderson, who as an experienced businessman immediately recognized an outstanding commercial opportunity.

"I don't see how our committee could reliably represent the interests of government buyers if we also have an interest in the seller side of the transaction," countered Nathaniel, "I take our oversight responsibilities very seriously. By the way, apparently our Assembly feels the same way. I just received a note from John Hart informing me that I have been selected for an additional term in Congress."

Isabella was less than enthusiastic, "I am not surprised. You are probably the only member of that august body who is not making money on this war. In fact, you have given away most of your medical supplies and the few patients you still have time to treat pay you in barter."

"I realize that this is a great burden on you and the children," replied Nathaniel, "But it is essential that our cause have unimpeachable moral leadership. Just the corruption that we have uncovered so far proves how important this is. We can just pray that the Lord sees fit to let us prevail soon so we can return to our normal lives."

"Fortunately we are a family who can afford to support a just cause," Colonel Anderson offered, "I am told that your efforts to get the Articles of Confederation ratified are going well."

"They certainly are," replied Nathaniel, "We expect the Assembly to ratify next week, and Reverend Witherspoon and I have been designated to sign the Articles for the State of New Jersey."

"Bravo! Nathaniel, that is a well-deserved honor, you and Witherspoon were tireless in your advocacy," praised Colonel Anderson, "Don't worry about short-term financial concerns. The welfare of our family is secure."

"That is very generous of you, sir," replied Nathaniel, "I am already deep in your debt, but I pledge to honor all my obligations."

"Hopefully, others will honor their obligations to you, Nathaniel," Isabella remarked with a raised eyebrow.

A few days later word arrived that the Assembly had indeed approved the Articles of Confederation, and Nathaniel was summoned to the official signing ceremony in Trenton on the 26th of November. Nathaniel, Isabella, and Colonel Anderson rode in the family carriage to Princeton where they picked up President Witherspoon and proceeded on to Trenton. Arriving at the State House they were met by Governor Livingston and Speaker of the Assembly John Hart.

"A hearty welcome to you!" Livingston greeted them enthusiastically, "Without the amazing campaign conducted by Reverend Witherspoon and Dr. Scudder, we might not be here for this momentous occasion. It is, therefore, my pleasure and honor to invite these gentlemen to sign this document for the State of New Jersey."

For a moment the gravity of the occasion so overwhelmed Nathaniel that he could not reply.

"I think I speak for Dr. Scudder as well when I say that we are deeply honored to represent our state in this matter," began Witherspoon. "When these Articles are ratified by all the states, we will have created a new nation, sovereign and equal among the nations of the earth. May God bless this holy endeavor!"

Amid the polite applause of those present Nathaniel Scudder and John Witherspoon carefully affixed their signatures to the founding document of the United States of America.

"Now we will be taken seriously by the nations of the world," announced Nathaniel, having recovered his voice in the meantime, "Especially by our allies who will now help us drive the tyrant from our shores."

"Hopefully," thought Isabella to herself, "If not, those signatures could turn out to be your death warrants if the British prevail." Isabella was torn by conflicting emotions, pride that her husband was playing such an important role in what was surely a historical event, mixed with anxiety about the escalation of violence that now seemed inevitable.

"It was a close-run thing," commented John Hart, "There are still many in the Assembly who were opposed to ratification but let's hope that they will now line up as loyal patriots of the new nation."

"The fact of the matter is that we must assume that quite a number of our assemblymen secretly hope for a British victory," Nathaniel contended, "They retard every necessary measure for effective conduct of the war. In my eyes they are effectively Tory agents."

"Now, now, Dr. Scudder, I would not want to label all members of the opposition in the Assembly Tory spies." objected Governor Livingston, "I know that you have great problems with disaffected elements in Monmouth, but I am confident that most of our assemblymen are patriots loyal to our state."

"I am sure most are," agreed Nathaniel, "But a few are systematically blocking everything we need to do to win the war."

"That can be proven by careful scrutiny of the legislative records of candidates for re-election," suggested Witherspoon, ever the proponent of scientific investigation, "Take notice of their yeas and nays. A few you will find in every proposed case to be on the nay side. Those are the ones we should suspect of infidelity to America."

"But don't forget, gentlemen," warned Colonel Anderson, "We don't want to increase active resistance to our new country on the part of those dissidents who might otherwise remain passive in this conflict, people such as the Quakers who are simply opposed to any sort of violence. Our great challenge will be to root out the scoundrels who are sabotaging our cause in a way that does not sacrifice the rule of law."

"At the end of the day it comes down to rooting out corruption," declared Nathaniel, "As Calvin has taught us, corruption is an inevitable aspect of fallen man, but it is our Christian duty to be constantly diligent to recognize Satan's wiles and to resist them with all our hearts."

A few weeks later Nathaniel was to experience just how complicated dealing with the subject of corruption could be. The secretary to the Committee of Foreign Affairs, Thomas Paine, suddenly, dramatically, and publicly accused one of America's ambassadors to France, Silas Deane, of war profiteering. Nathaniel immediately sought the council of Reverend Witherspoon.

"This is an outrageous accusation!" began Nathaniel, "No one is more sensitive to the issue of corruption than I, but . . . Silas Deane? . . . Acting as our agent in France he obtained and sent arms valued at more than 6,000,000 livres to America without which we would certainly not have prevailed at Saratoga."

"I know not what temptations Deane might have fallen to," answered Witherspoon, "But, one thing I can tell you, Thomas Paine might have a golden tongue, but he is not to be trusted."

"He enjoys considerable favor among Whigs for his pamphlet *Common Sense*," remarked Nathaniel, "For that reason any allegations he makes will be taken seriously by many."

"He does have a remarkable talent for writing to the temper and feelings of the public," continued Witherspoon, "I met him when he first came to America, and he was against the Whig cause at that time. But then Benjamin Rush managed to convince him that the Whig movement was unstoppable and, being an opportunist, he decided to throw his lot in with us. It was Rush that gave him the outline for *Common Sense*, Rush told me, however, that he is vain, debauched, and intemperate in his private life and stokes his creativity with large draughts of rum and water. When the Committee for Foreign Affairs was formed, John Adams, feeling sorry for the poor and destitute writer, wanted to compensate him for the usefulness of his pamphlet by giving him a job as clerk of the new committee. In that position he could earn a living with his writing abilities and render more service to the cause."

"It seems that he has now just rendered a great disservice to the cause!" responded Nathaniel angrily, "In his exposé he quoted from secret documents that only the Committee of Foreign Affairs is privy to. Whatever the truth is about Deane's alleged corruption, Paine's indiscretions will certainly embarrass us in front of our allies. He revealed things that our French allies most certainly want to be kept confidential. They will be most upset when they find out."

"You are undoubtedly right about that, Dr. Scudder," agreed Witherspoon, "If we are to save face, we must act immediately. The French need to know that the new republic is a reliable ally that can be trusted with secret information."

"It is clear that Paine is only interested in stroking his vanity with sensationalist articles. He cannot be trusted with confidential information. I will introduce a motion at the next meeting of Congress to relieve Paine of his position."

Accordingly, on the 7th of January Nathaniel introduced his motion: "Resolved, That Mr. Thomas Paine for his imprudence ought immediately to be dismissed from his office of secretary to the Committee for Foreign Affairs, and the said Committee are directed to dismiss him accordingly, and to take such further steps relative to his misapplication of public papers as they shall deem necessary". The motion passed by a comfortable margin. Thomas Paine was relieved of his office and never again served in government.

After his success with the motion against Paine Nathaniel resumed his efforts to convince Congress of the strategic importance of the struggle in New Jersey and the urgent necessity to support it better. After much discussion Congress finally approved an allocation of 500 dollars and entrusted the money to Nathaniel to be made available to the New Jersey government.

On his way back to Monmouth Nathaniel stopped in Trenton and delivered the money to John Hart who would apprise the Assembly and discuss the ultimate usage of the funds.

Arriving at home he was shocked to see two dead bodies hanging in chains near Monmouth Court House. Birds and other carrion eaters had already devoured most of the flesh. Even though it was winter the stench of the decaying corpses polluted the air all the way to Nathaniel's home.

When he opened his front door, Isabella called out to him, "Please close the door quickly, Nathaniel, that disgusting smell makes me want to vomit!"

"It is indeed disgusting," agreed Nathaniel, "Since when do we hang up condemned prisoners on public display? Even if they were criminals, they should have a Christian burial."

"This is a new policy supported by our friend, David Forman," replied Isabella, "It is called a degradation ceremony and purports to put the fear of God into anyone considering Tory activities. But it can only provoke more brutality. I warned you that David would go too far one day!"

"I don't know the details of this matter, but I will find out," promised Nathaniel, "I will summon David and ask if we really have to endure putrid bodies on display a few yards from our home."

Nathaniel sent one of the servants to ask David Forman to visit him at his convenience because he wanted to brief him about the disbursements that Congress had approved for New Jersey. An hour or so later Forman knocked on the door.

"Come in, David," welcomed Nathaniel, "I have some good news to share with you. Congress after much debate agreed to send a first installment to support our military operations. But before I go into that, I want to ask you about those corpses hanging over there. Is that really necessary? Rotting bodies are a health hazard, you know."

"Those were two notorious cutthroat members of Jake Fagan's Pine Robber gang," replied Forman, "You remember that Benjamin Dennis killed Fagan last October after Fagan tried to rob him? Well, after that Benjamin got to thinking that the surviving members of the gang were still a danger, so he ambushed and killed three of them. It was Benjamin's idea to set an example by hanging a couple of them near the Courthouse to frighten other Tories, but I will tell him it is time to take them down."

"Many say that the Pine Robbers are not so much Tories as common criminals," said Nathaniel, "They take any opportunity for thievery including against other Tories."

"They are indeed a motley lot," agreed Forman, "The three that Benjamin Dennis killed were formerly members of the New Jersey Volunteers, one of those Tory gangs that William Franklin is now promoting. But military discipline probably got too much for them so they deserted to the Pine Barrens where they could hide out with runaway slaves, moonshiners, bandits and other marauders. They live in caves dug in the sand like the vermin that they are and wait for opportunities to plunder. Dennis managed to get the location of Fagan's hideout out of one of the captured men before he killed him. When they found the place, trap doors hidden under leaves and branches in steep hillsides admitted entrance into 30-foot tunnels. These ended in storerooms that were large enough to hold six men. Buried beneath their floors was thousands of dollars of loot."

"Thousands of dollars!" exclaimed Nathaniel, "The grant of 500 dollars that I just bought back from Congress pales in comparison. What did Dennis' men so with the money?"

"I'm not sure," replied Forman vaguely, "I suppose they will turn it over to the government or maybe reimburse some of Fagan's victims."

"Our militia is not authorized to decide how such contraband is to be disbursed." asserted Nathaniel, "By law they are required to put it at the disposal of the Assembly."

"So the closet-Tories in the Assembly can block its use for effective measures against our enemies!" Forman shot back, "You see what you had to go through to get a paltry 500 dollars from Congress when raids against scoundrels like the Fagan Gang net us ten times as much. I wonder just how much of the 500 dollars you handed over to the Assembly will actually wind up financing our desperate efforts in Monmouth. I say we must provide for ourselves if we want to adequately finance our revolution. There are many fat, rich Tories posing as neutrals who are seriously aiding the enemy. By harvesting that crop we can get the means to strengthen our militia and at the same time eliminate nests of spies who are a present danger to our cause."

"The success of our struggle depends on our moral standing," replied Nathaniel piously, "If we want to ask the Almighty to bless our endeavor, we must not descend to the level of common thieves."

"God helps those who help themselves," countered Forman.

"In any case, I am sure God does not require you to hang any more dead corpses in chains near my home," asserted Isabella acerbically.

Throughout the rest of the winter Nathaniel was occupied by the inability of Congress to provide funds urgently needed to pursue the war. Appeals to state governments were routinely ignored. Instead of searching for practical solutions delegates were more concerned about staking the claims of the large states to new territories in the West.

"Utterly ridiculous," opined Witherspoon discussing the issue with Nathaniel, "States like Virginia think that they will eventually be able to expand westward all the way to the Pacific."

"That would completely shatter our union," Nathaniel predicted, "If some states became many times the size of others, it would be impossible to hold the country together. They would turn into rivals fighting each other like the states in Europe. The only logical solution is for the federal government to assume control of the lands west of the Appalachians. Only in that manner can we create one indivisible nation."

"Right you are, Dr. Scudder," Witherspoon agreed, "If you formulate such a petition for Congress, I will be pleased to support it. If that issue could be settled, perhaps the honored delegates could turn their attention to more practical issues such as the money the government owes us to repair the damage that our army inflicted on Nassau Hall."

"Frankly, given my experience so far I would be surprised if significant help were to be forthcoming," said Nathaniel, "Ever since Robert Morris resigned from Congress there seems to be nobody left who understands financial matters. I can understand that Morris was tired of listening to the insinuations of corruption that gossips like Thomas Paine were bandying about, but it is really a great loss for our cause."

"Indeed, it was," concurred Witherspoon, "Corruption being endemic in all human activity, it is easy to slander successful merchants by recklessly appealing to the envy of the less successful. But if it were not for Robert Morris, the Whig project would long ago have been bankrupt. I heard from Benjamin Rush, however, that Morris will now work with him at the state level to develop a new constitution for Pennsylvania. They envision a strong executive with veto power that can get things done, and an independent judiciary to insure the rule of law."

"Those are interesting ideas," commented Nathaniel, "Let's hope that they are successful with their reforms. I think we should discuss the allegations in a congressional committee and formally absolve Morris of charges of corruption. It is the least we can do for someone who has done so much for our cause."

As winter turned into spring Nathaniel's frustration with Congress continued to grow. Although he was able to convince a congressional committee to clear Morris of all corruption charges, the other items on his agenda stalled. Congress could not agree on a concept for new lands in the West or on a comprehensive plan for financing the war. Witherspoon's efforts to obtain funding for the repair of Nassau Hall resulted in vague promises but no concrete assistance.

Nathaniel had better luck with General Washington. After hearing from Nathaniel about the success that David Forman and the militia had achieved in reestablishing control over formerly Tory areas in eastern New Jersey, Washington agreed to support the effort by establishing an arms magazine in the village of Tinton Falls and stationing a regiment of Continental soldiers there. Colonel Daniel Hendrickson, the senior officer for the northeast part of Monmouth County who had been forced to flee during the period of Tory ascendancy, was able to return home and resume command of the militia. Nathaniel met with David Forman at Monmouth Courthouse to ascertain the new strategic situation.

"Congratulations, David," Nathaniel greeted him warmly, "General Washington is obviously impressed by your successes to date and has decided to support your efforts more vigorously."

"We'll see soon enough how serious he is about that," replied Forman skeptically, "I met his commander of the Continental regiment, Colonel Benjamin Ford. I can't say I was impressed. He told me that Washington had instructed him to avoid a major confrontation with British forces. My spies tell me, however, that many of the Tory bastards we've driven off are now on Sandy Hook plotting revenge. We should have hanged them while we had the chance. I expect an attack any day now and I can only hope that Ford will stand his ground."

"Washington wants, of course, to avoid confronting the British until sufficient numbers of French forces have arrived to make victory feasible," explained Nathaniel.

"That is all very well," countered Forman, "But I am afraid the enemy is not going to wait until it is convenient for Washington to attack. The garrison at Tinton Falls is within easy reach of Sandy Hook where the refugees are organizing to kill us and our families. The wives and families of many of the Tories are still living among us silently awaiting the opportunity to betray us while secretly supplying the enemy with food and other supplies. We need to move against them with much greater vigor!"

"Still," cautioned Nathaniel, "We must respect the rule of law. We do not want to swell the ranks of our enemies by brutalizing innocent people."

"Innocent people will soon be brutalized, but not by us but by Loyalist marauders from Sandy Hook," Forman warned ominously.

"I will return now to Philadelphia and try again to convey the urgency of our situation to Congress," said Nathaniel, "Perhaps I can persuade Washington to strengthen his troop presence here."

"I will see that my relay network keeps you up to date on the movements of the enemy," promised Forman.

Only a few days after Nathaniel returned to Congress in Philadelphia, he was summoned in the middle of the night by his innkeeper who said an express rider had arrived with urgent news for Dr. Scudder. Hurrying down the stairs he saw one of Forman's network couriers obviously exhausted by a hard ride.

"Dr. Scudder, I have urgent news from General Forman!" gasped the courier, "Hundreds of Loyalists and British regulars have marched on Tinton Falls! They have looted the town and burned our munitions and supplies!"

"What about the Continental regiment now stationed in Tinton Falls?" asked Nathaniel, "Were they not able to offer stiff resistance?"

"As soon as they received word that a large enemy force had landed, they immediately withdrew further into the interior," answered the courier, "They left our militia units on their own to fight the enemy as best we could."

Even though Nathaniel understood Washington's strategy of avoiding confrontation with the enemy until French reinforcements were ready, he could not help feeling a sense of betrayal at the government's inability to protect the Whig families of Monmouth. He decided to return immediately and do whatever he could to aid David Forman's courageous efforts to save Monmouth from further depredations.

Riding through the night he arrived in mid-morning at Monmouth Courthouse where he was fortunate to find David Forman inspecting his prisoners.

"David, I just got your news," Nathaniel began, "I was shocked to hear that the Continental regiment did not even offer token resistance against this attack. You were completely correct in your assessment of Colonel Ford."

"Can't really blame him," responded Forman bitterly, "He was just following Washington's orders. In fact, I hear that Washington has decided to pull all Continental forces out of eastern Monmouth country. He says they do rather more harm than good because they are an attractive target for the enemy but not strong enough to prevail against him. Over 700 of the enemy took part in that raid. Washington would have to station a much larger force to deter such an attack."

"If the federal forces can't protect us, then the state has to step in," asserted Nathaniel, "We cannot just stand by and watch the depredations of Whig families. I will talk to Governor Livingston about militia reinforcements to replace the Continentals."

"Best of luck to you with that, Nathaniel," replied Forman, "But that will, at best, take time. I have here a list of over a hundred Loyalists who still have estates in Monmouth although the men have gone off to join the enemy. It's time we expropriated the bastards in order to cut off the supplies that they are funneling to the enemy. Others among the disaffected will then think twice before they take up arms for the British."

"I think that might be justifiable," agreed Nathaniel, "But it needs to be done legally with a public auction. And we need to seek the approval of the Assembly for more vigorous rules for the confiscation of Loyalist estates."

"You work on the legal problems, Nathaniel," suggested Forman grimly, "I will organize the auction and give notice to those who are about to lose their lands."

Washington's withdrawal of the last of the Continental troops from eastern Monmouth County in early May immediately emboldened the enemy. On May 15th two hundred Loyalists tried to launch an attack on Middletown shore but were driven off by the militia. David Forman took this as proof that he needed to pursue his policy of confiscation of Tory properties with relentless brutality. Refusing to wait for approval of the Assembly he served eviction notices to dozens of disaffected families threatening them with arrest and imprisonment if they did not vacate their properties within hours. Any attempts at armed resistance were crushed with shocking violence. Within days Forman was able to put up a hundred properties for auction. In order to demonstrate his solidarity with Forman's aggressive approach, Nathaniel bought a small estate of 21 acres for 147 pounds.

Back at home after the auction Nathaniel discussed with Isabella his reasoning for participating in the auction.

"The auction was a dramatic political gesture of defiance against the machinations of Loyalist sympathizers," explained Nathaniel, "I must show a public display of support for David's bold actions."

"David's bold actions have just created a few hundred more refugees longing for revenge," warned Isabella, "Which family owned the estate you just bought?"

"The owner was Thomas Bills, but he has already gone to serve in the Loyalist New Jersey Volunteers," replied Nathaniel, "His family fled behind enemy lines. The estate is currently abandoned."

"Well, Mr. Bills now has a very personal reason to detest you," said Isabella ruefully, "And similar feelings will be shared by everyone who has been driven off. Not to mention the families with relatives whom David has arrested. Do you know that David's estate is known to some now as the 'Hanging Farm'? Many people who wind up there are never heard from again. Escalation of this dreadful conflict seems more and more inevitable, and David's actions have a lot to do with it."

"Escalation does indeed seem inevitable, but I cannot see how it can be avoided," admitted Nathaniel, "We are being attacked with increasing frequency. We must defend ourselves."

Nathaniel's sense of urgency was furthered heightened a few days later when David Forman informed him that militia captain Benjamin Dennis had been murdered by Pine Robbers near Tinton Falls.

"It was Lewis Fenton, the new leader of Jake Fagan's Pine Robber gang," reported Forman, "It was revenge for Dennis' killing of Jake Fagan at the beginning of the year. But that is not all of what's going on. A bunch of escaped slaves who have gone over to the Brits kidnapped constable Zephaniah Morris a few days after he purchased a confiscated estate. The refugees have allegedly vowed to kidnap or kill anyone who has the audacity to buy one of the confiscated properties. The frequency of attacks has increased dramatically. Several houses have already been plundered and their inhabitants carried off."

"This is an impossible situation," exclaimed Nathaniel, "We must be able to provide security to our families if we claim to be the legitimate government of this state. I will ride to Governor Livingston immediately and describe the urgency of the situation here."

Nathaniel's lurid descriptions of the crimes being perpetrated in eastern Monmouth on an almost daily basis convinced Livingston and the Assembly that dramatic action was urgently needed. Livingston ordered out nine companies of militia to protect vulnerable areas, mostly along the Jersey shore. He petitioned the Assembly to raise the pay for any militiamen required to do extended duty. In the Assembly laws were quickly proposed and passed to create four new battalions of state troops, one of which was to be devoted specifically to the defense of Monmouth County. Encouraged by the progress he was able to make with the governor and the Assembly Nathaniel hurried back home to inform Isabella and David Forman about the help that was in the offing.

Arriving home Nathaniel quickly dispatched a servant with a request to David Forman to come by as soon as possible. He then sought to lessen Isabella's anxiety by recounting his success in soliciting help from the state.

"The governor and the Assembly are aware of the urgency of our situation," he assured her, "And they have quickly approved new battalions of state troops to protect us."

At that moment David Forman appeared at the door.

"I am afraid I have dreadful news," began Forman, "Several gangs of Loyalists have attacked Tinton Falls and razed it to the ground!"

"Oh my God!" cried Isabella, "Those poor people suffered a devastating raid just a few weeks ago and now this!"

"But this time it was different," explained Forman, "The raid on April 15th was a purely military matter. The goal was to capture Washington's regiment which they were not able to do. This time the goal was revenge. Two of the leaders were Loyalists, Okerson and Gillian, who wanted revenge for the confiscation of their estates. They snuck in like thieves just before dawn and took all the leading Whigs in the town prisoner before anyone could raise an alarm: Colonel Daniel Hendrickson, Lieutenant-Colonel Aucke Wikoff, Major Hendrick Van Brunt, Captain Richard McKnight, and Captain Thomas Chadwick."

"But did the militia not turn out to counterattack?" asked Nathaniel incredulously.

"In fact they did, but only a small inadequately armed number," continued Forman, "Chadwick's and Hendrickson's younger brothers led a spirited attack during which young Chadwick paid with his life. He was so outraged to see his brother's estate put to the torch by its former owner, Okerson, that he attacked the Loyalists with reckless abandon. But the Tories were better equipped and scattered Chadwick's militia with a bayonet charge. Then they were able to make it off into their boats with all their hostages and much other booty. What they couldn't take with them, they set on fire. Tinton Falls is a shambles. I don't know if it can ever recover."

"Nathaniel, just before David arrived, you were telling me how much the state is doing to make sure we are protected. I ask you both: will these state forces be able to prevent something like this happening to Freehold?" asked Isabella nervously.

"Whatever forces the state can muster will surely be welcome," answered Forman, "But obviously we cannot rely on outside help alone. What happened to Tinton Falls could not have happened without inside assistance."

"It makes clear that the disaffected among us, as you have always contended, are a dire threat that we must uproot at all costs," added Nathaniel darkly.

Isabella cast an alarmed look at Nathaniel and then at David Forman. She was at a loss for words to express the blindness of the two men to the fact that their plan of action could only result in spiraling violence.

Chapter 23

Retaliators – 1779–1780

A few days later Nathaniel and David Forman travelled together to Tinton Falls to assess the damage in detail. They were shocked by the devastation. Most of the structures had been put to the torch. All the livestock had been stolen or scattered.

"How can people like Okerson be so vindictive as to wantonly destroy the properties they once lived in," asked Nathaniel, "I could not bring myself to burn our home even if it were occupied by Tory enemies."

"Oh, I understand that very well," snarled Forman, "If the enemy occupied my home, I would burn down my house with the Tories in it! Besides, their strategy is clear, they want to undermine our policy of confiscating Loyalist properties by putting the fear of God into whoever dares to bid on such properties at auction. That won't work. There will always be people willing to take the risk if the price is right. We have to concentrate on exposing the network of disaffected who are aiding and abetting the raiders."

"Have your men been able to uncover any evidence of direct collusion?" asked Nathaniel.

"They surely have," replied Forman, "Remember that suspect, James Pew, whom we had in Monmouth Courthouse jail awhile back?"

"You mean the one who died in jail, some say under mysterious circumstances?" asked Nathaniel raising his eyebrows.

"My guard swears he died during an attempt to escape," Forman sought to dispel any insinuations of irregularity, "But be that as it may, we did manage to obtain some useful information about the disaffected in the Tinton Falls area before he died."

Nathaniel shuddered to think of what incentives the wretched prisoner had been given to reveal such information.

"The raiders had several heavy wagons that they used to cart off stolen property and livestock," Forman continued, "But the boats they came in were not large enough to hold such wagons and they abandoned the wagons after they loaded the loot onto their boats. Those wagons were already here when they arrived. Somebody made them available to the raiders. We have found a shed with wagon tracks at the mouth of Conkaskunk Creek where the raiders landed. At the same location there was evidence of burned-out lamps that were placed to guide the raiding party to the landing. If we can find who owns that shed and the wagons, we have our spy."

Nathaniel was impressed by the forensic evidence that Forman had been able to gather in such a short time.

"You certainly seem to be hot on the heels of these dastardly betrayers," remarked Nathaniel admiringly.

"I already have my eyes on two suspects," continued Forman, "I have long suspected Esther and Marcus Headon of illegal trade with Sandy Hook. While most of the people in this area are losing livestock to the raiders, the Headons seem to have doubled theirs."

"Many people in this area are indulging in the London trade," cautioned Nathaniel, "It is illegal and harmful, of course, but it does not necessarily mean that they are spies who are actively abetting the enemy."

"They are not just the normal greedy farmers willing to profit through trade with the enemy. Esther Headon has already been indicted twice by the high court for Loyalist leanings and Marcus Headon three times. I had Esther locked up in the courthouse jail for three days on charges of providing food to Loyalist marauders. She boldly claimed that she was just doing her Christian duty giving hungry travelers sustenance. We only fined her 20 pounds and then let her go. The next time we won't be so lenient." Forman's eyes narrowed as he imagined how he would conduct the next deposition of the Headons.

"I see no reason why the ill-gotten gains of people like the Headons should not be confiscated to reimburse the victims of the raiders." Forman added.

"You are right in principle," agreed Nathaniel, "But there must be due process. I will see to it that a bill is introduced into the Assembly to provide for such just retribution. I will also report this devastation to Congress, so they realize what depredations we are enduring."

After making careful note of the damage done to Tinton Falls, Nathaniel hurried back to Philadelphia determined to give his congressional colleagues a report from the front. He hoped that they would see the necessity of devoting more resources to deal with the destruction wrought by the enemy in those areas adjacent to British occupied territory. Congress was sympathetic but only offered kind words of encouragement, passing a resolution that suggested to the governments of states abutting enemy areas to take particular defensive measures against such depredations. How to accomplish this was to be the concern of the state governments.

Nathaniel's efforts to lobby for more resources were cut short by an urgent message from home. An express rider reported that Isabella had fainted and had had to be put to bed. Nathaniel immediately cursed himself for neglecting to stop at home on his way back from Tinton Falls. After quickly informing the president of Congress that he most urgently needed a leave of absence, he saddled up and galloped off in the direction of Freehold. After a long, sweaty ride with stops only long enough to water his horse Nathaniel arrived at the Scudder residence. He was relieved to find Isabella sitting up in bed with color gradually returning to her cheeks.

Beth, Isabella's favorite servant, was gently wiping Isabella's forehead with a wet cloth.

"Miss Isabell, she fainted dead away!" explained Beth, "Her face was white as a ghost! We thought she was going to die, but after we put her to bed, she started to get better. She don't get enough rest. She don't sleep when the doctor's gone. She just worry, day and night."

Beth's simple explanation caused Nathaniel to feel another pang of guilt as he realized his own culpability for the state of his wife.

"You did the right thing by putting her to bed, Beth," replied Nathaniel, "She is suffering from nervous exhaustion and the best thing for her is rest. I am back now. I am taking a leave of absence from Congress, and I will be staying until Isabella is feeling better."

Nathaniel's promise brought a grateful smile to Isabella's lips.

"Oh Nathaniel, I am so relieved that you are going to stay with me. I feel so weak all the time. I don't know what is wrong with me."

"Most of all you need rest," advised Nathaniel, "These are trying times that are exhausting for all of us. But you must try not to let yourself get too upset. Our best consolation is that we are doing the Lord's will. Whenever you feel overwhelmed, you must try to find solace in prayer."

"I know that is the only hope, but when you are away, I am consumed with fear that something is going to happen to you or one of the boys. How long before you have to leave again for Congress?"

"I should return at least for a short time at the beginning of August. I have been appointed to write the congratulations to the King of France. It is an important duty considering the vital nature of our alliance. But if the truth be told, I am beginning to have doubts that my service in Congress is the most effective way I can support our cause. I don't think I will volunteer for another term."

Isabella's face immediately brightened at the prospect that Nathaniel might be away less frequently.

"Well, it would certainly help our finances if you had more time for your patients," Isabella remarked hopefully.

"Indeed," agreed Nathaniel, "Service in Congress is making a pauper out of me, but I cannot bring myself to take those opportunities for self-enrichment that many of my congressional colleagues seem to be fond of."

"Just what sort of opportunities are you speaking of?" Isabella asked. "I thought that your colleagues were all loyal patriots," she added slyly.

"They are indeed," answered Nathaniel, "But when large procurement transactions are being rushed to approval, there are many ways to personally profit. And as the True Religion teaches us, corruption is endemic in the human condition. In any case, I think I can be more useful here. Monmouth is the front line in this war and Congress seems unwilling to devote additional resources to protect us. I am afraid that David Forman's strategy is the only feasible one for us."

Isabella's face darkened at the mention of David Forman's strategy which she feared could only add to the spiraling violence. Not wanting to start what could only be a tedious discussion Isabella opted to change the subject.

"Speaking of David Forman, I am told that his daughter, Elizabeth, is now at the age when she should continue her training outside the home. She is a fine girl, and I would have no objection to her staying with us."

"I am sure David and Ann will be delighted to hear that," replied Nathaniel, "Perhaps another pair of hands will make life easier for you as well. I will inform David accordingly. I have to meet with him soon in any case to discuss our motion to get the Assembly to sanction retaliation against dissidents."

"I thought David was already confiscating Tory estates and auctioning them off. What further sanctions does he need?" asked Isabella.

"The problem is that many dissidents still reside among us who mask their true allegiances and conspire with the enemy. We must find legal ways of prosecuting such scoundrels so that we can confiscate their properties to finance our own defense."

"As you said, corruption is everywhere," Isabella reminded Nathaniel, "There will be a danger that wealthy farmers who have not actively supported the enemy in any way might become the victims of overzealous retaliators who want to get their hands on the wealth."

"Of course, that is always a possibility," admitted Nathaniel, "That is why it is so important that the Assembly establish clear rules for such procedures. Without the rule of law, we would be no better than common brigands."

For the next few weeks Nathaniel tried to spend most of his time at home limiting his political work to correspondence with members of the New Jersey Assembly exhorting them to support the policy of retaliation. He laid out in detail the damages suffered by defenders of the Whig cause at the hands of Tory marauders. He argued that the only feasible way to finance relief for the victims was to confiscate and redistribute the property of the disaffected. Nathaniel's presence at home helped to calm Isabella's anxieties. After a few weeks of being able to sleep nights, she visibly improved to the point where Nathaniel felt he could return to Congress at the beginning of August. Although he was fairly certain that he did not want another term in Congress, there were several issues he still wanted to influence while he still was serving. The most important item was the issue of restrictions on inland trade between the states. He knew that many of his congressional colleagues wanted to see them abolished and a vote on the subject was expected shortly. He had, however, discussed the matter with David Forman who warned of the dangers of the liberalizing position. Forman pointed out that some of the restrictions gave him the legal right to scrutinize more closely the trade relationships between residents of New Jersey and New York, relationships which often turned out to be fronts for the London Trade. Getting rid of those restrictions could only make his police work more difficult.

In Philadelphia Nathaniel endeavored to present to his fellow congressmen the argument for maintaining restrictions on trade.

"Why Dr. Scudder, I must say I am astounded that you are taking this position," John Witherspoon exclaimed, "Has Adam Smith not proved that restrictions on trade are always counterproductive in the long run? Should our country commit the same mercantile mistakes as England, the very mistakes that led us to rebellion in the first place?"

"I, of course, also agree with Adam Smith in principle," replied Nathaniel, "But right now we are in the midst of a brutal war with many Loyalists now residing in New York. Removing all trade restrictions right now will make it easier for their dissident friends residing in New Jersey to supply the enemy."

"There may be some merit to that argument," conceded Witherspoon. "But one should not abandon important principles lightly," he added sternly, "That is particularly crucial in times of war when the outrages of the enemy can be easily utilized to justify one's own moral failings."

The implicit rebuke stung Nathaniel who considered Witherspoon to be a paragon of ethical wisdom. Nathaniel felt torn between the urgent need to help the victims of Loyalist depredations and the powerful exhortations of a man whom he regarded as the leading religious authority. In the event Nathaniel reluctantly voted against Witherspoon and even called for a written tally of the votes. Despite Nathaniel's plea the majority of Congress followed Witherspoon's lead: "So it was resolved that it be earnestly recommended to the several states to take off every restriction on the inland trade between the said states."

After the session was completed, Dr. Witherspoon exhibited no harsh feelings toward Nathaniel.

"I will not hold it against you, Dr. Scudder, that you voted against the proposal. You are preoccupied with the dreadful situation in Monmouth, and I understand the urgency you feel. But we must not lose sight of the great project of building a new nation, a pious nation that rests on solid moral foundations. In your struggles to defend our compatriots in Monmouth you could wind up violating the rights of neutral parties who do not aid the enemy."

"We must take every precaution that that does not occur," agreed Nathaniel, "That is one of the reasons why I think I can serve our country better by working in Monmouth rather than in Philadelphia."

"If that means you are not planning to run for another term, that would be most unfortunate," cautioned Witherspoon.

"I will continue to serve the cause as effectively as I can," assured Nathaniel, "But Monmouth is the front line and I think that is where I am needed most."

Witherspoon concluded their conversation with an injunction, "Pray that the Lord guide you to do his will."

Back in Monmouth Nathaniel realized that he would be needing a lot of Divine Guidance. Disturbing messages from the New Jersey Assembly were awaiting him. Not only did the Assembly refuse to sanction the practice of retaliation but had also issued subpoenas to several Monmouth leaders to respond to allegations of misconduct by the Monmouth County Commissioners for Forfeited Estates. It was alleged that during the auctioning off of almost a hundred Tory estates in May, the auction criers had colluded with the commissioners to aid favored bidders.

"That is absolute nonsense!" exclaimed David Forman when Nathaniel informed him at Monmouth Courthouse that he and many of his colleagues would be required to answer questions at a session of the Assembly, "These are fake allegations that dissidents are fabricating in order to undermine our efforts to punish Loyalists and aid the victims of their depredations."

"That may very well be," agreed Nathaniel, "But we must respect the authority of the Assembly and testify. I, for one, can truthfully affirm that on the day that I attended the auction, everything seemed to be fair and equitable. I am sure we can find witnesses who will say the same about the other days."

Nathaniel spent the next few days discussing the subpoenas with several of the organizers of the auction and encouraging them to cooperate with the Assembly in order to testify to the legitimacy of the proceedings. The vice president of the New Jersey Council, John Stevens, sent a message suggesting a hearing the following week.

On the appointed day Nathaniel rode to Trenton to testify in front of a committee of the Assembly presided over by John Stevens. To Nathaniel's relief he recognized many familiar Monmouth faces among the people in attendance at the hearing.

Stevens began by reading out the allegations that had resulted in the subpoenas, "It has come to the attention of the Assembly there is reason to suspect misconduct by the Monmouth County Commissioners for Forfeited Estates during the auction held in May of this year. There have been suggestions that there were incidents of collusion to aid favored bidders. I would like to begin by asking our congressman from Monmouth County, Dr. Nathaniel Scudder, if he has any observations on the matter."

"On the day I attended the auction everything seemed to be fair and equitable," replied Nathaniel, "I saw no reason to suspect collusion between the auction criers and any of the prospective buyers."

Joseph Schenck, one of the criers, hastened to affirm his innocence, "As the Lord is my witness, I swear that I favored no one at any auction. The property always went to the highest bidder. And I am certain that my colleagues, Daniel Harbert and Tunis Vanderveer, conducted their auctions exactly the same way."

Harbert and Vanderveer nodded their heads vigorously while glancing beseechingly at their Monmouth compatriots.

"I would offer similar testimony," added Justice John Longstreet.

"The auctions I attended were very fair as far as I know," attested Nicholas Van Brunt.

"We even delayed sales to give people the chance to bid or to appraise the estates," offered Tunis Vanderveer.

"We have received no direct evidence of collusion," admitted Stevens, "But the best estates apparently wound up in the hands of a relatively small number of people, so it is not surprising that some feel disadvantaged. I would like to thank you good citizens of Monmouth for your testimony, but I am sure you will understand that the disposition of confiscated properties will continue to be carefully scrutinized by the Assembly. Our investigation will continue until we are certain that the rule of law has prevailed."

Riding back to Monmouth Nathaniel could not help but feel a slight sense of unease.

Arriving home, he was pleased to find David Forman there who had brought his daughter, Elizabeth, to begin her training in the Scudder household. David, Elizabeth and Isabella were sitting together in the dining room discussing Elizabeth's new tasks when Nathaniel entered the room and interrupted their conversation.

"I am afraid that our testimony was not enough to convince the Assembly of the fairness of our auctions," Nathaniel announced, "John Stevens plans to continue the investigations into the conduct of Monmouth's Commissioners for Forfeited Estates even though he admits having no evidence of collusion. He says it is suspicious that so many of the best estates are winding up in the possession of a small number of people."

"He is just echoing the propaganda of the disaffected who would like to sabotage our strategy of retaliation," Forman argued, "It is completely normal that the best estates always go to the highest bidders and only a small number of people are able to afford the expense. Those that can't afford it or don't know enough about the properties on auction will inevitably grumble that the auctions were unfair."

"Perhaps your testimony was not given the weight it deserves because of your acquisition of the Bills estate," suggested Isabella, "You benefited from the auction so it is not surprising that you would consider the procedure fair. That probably holds true for many of the Monmouth people who testified in Trenton which would explain why Stevens was not convinced."

Nathaniel could not help seeing the logic of Isabella's perceptive analysis.

"You might very well be correct, darling," Nathaniel conceded, "We must use the Assembly's continuing investigation to press the need for the establishment of a firm legal basis for confiscating and auctioning off Tory estates. We must have a procedure which is beyond suspicion."

"No matter what procedures the Assembly approves, there will always be suspicion sowed by the disaffected," countered Forman, "I say we cannot allow that to deter us from doing justice for the victims of depredations."

Isabella was about to voice her reservations about Forman's strategy, when she was suddenly at a loss for words. She stared with open mouth at the doorway where their son, Kenneth, appeared clad in the uniform of a private of the Light Horse Cavalry of the Monmouth County militia.

"Oh, my God!" Isabella gasped.

"Mom, Dad," Kenneth hastened to explain, "I met with Captain Conover and Captain Craig today, and they told me that at 14 I am old enough to volunteer for militia duty."

"Well, son 14 is a bit early, 16 is the normal age to begin militia duty," Nathaniel cautioned although he could not suppress the feeling of pride at the sight of his strapping young son in uniform.

"We are not living in normal times," exclaimed David Forman, "Kenneth, you are honoring a fine family tradition to take up arms in defense of your community. Welcome to our ranks!"

At that remark color drained from Isabella's cheeks, and she looked as though she was about to faint. Nathaniel felt her pulse and had her lie down on the couch. He gently massaged the sides of her head while instructing her to take deep slow breaths. At length color slowly returned to her cheeks as Nathaniel continued to try to calm her.

"Don't worry my dear," he whispered, "I will write to Henry Laurens today and tell him that I can't return to Congress until you are feeling better."

"In your letter to Henry Laurens you might mention that you are needed here more than in Philadelphia," David Forman advised, "We expect the appearance of Admiral D'Estaing and the French fleet at any moment. We need to be in constant readiness to provide him with experienced pilots in case he wants to run the British blockade. They have stationed many men at Sandy Hook erecting a fort and batteries with very heavy cannon in order to prevent the French fleet from entering the bay. With good pilots riding the tide in front of a brisk s'wester, ships may be run by and sustain little damage."

"That is an excellent point, David," agreed Nathaniel, "It is certainly important that Count D'Estaing be greeted by a representative of Congress when he arrives. I can then brief Laurens and Congress on the Count's plans. Perhaps our prayers will be answered, and he will smash the enemy garrison at Sandy Hook. This could be the major turning point in the war. You are absolutely correct that we need to keep excellent pilots on call constantly. If you have suitable candidates, they would be welcome to stay at our house while they are on call."

"I do indeed have two young men that need accommodations," replied Forman, "I will inform them of your generous offer."

Nathaniel wrote his letter to Henry Laurens explaining his situation intimating several reasons why he would probably decline to run for another term in Congress. In response to the letter Laurens suggested that fellow Congressman John Stevenson visit Nathaniel in Freehold and ascertain his political plans. A week later Nathaniel was surprised at the unannounced arrival of his colleague.

"This is a pleasant surprise, Mr. Stevenson," Nathaniel greeted his fellow congressman, "What brings you to Monmouth?"

"Henry Laurens asked me to let you know that you have strong support among us Whigs for another term in Congress," Stevenson came right to the point.

"I am flattered by the trust placed in me," replied Nathaniel, "But the fact is, I can't afford another term in Congress. Serving in Congress has added so much to the reduction of the small remains of my estate, to the distress and uneasiness of my family, to the injury of my children's education, that another year of attendance would be ruinous."

"But the country needs honest and upright citizens like yourself to build the pious republic that we all dream of," objected Stevenson.

"I understand that," agreed Nathaniel, "Our places might be filled by ambitious, designing men, or by others who, being of like fortune with myself, may not perhaps so fully withstand those powerful lucrative temptations which here surround us. I will endeavor to suggest a suitable successor with the requisite moral fortitude. My place, however, is here. Monmouth is the front. The enemy is only a few hours ride away and subjects us to the constant threat of depredation. Besides, when the French fleet arrives, it could be the turning point in our struggle and the Monmouth Militia must be prepared."

"Your motivations are beyond reproach," replied Stevenson, "But I think I speak for many of our fellow Whigs when I say we will miss your wise council in Congress."

"I have no intention of discontinuing my efforts for our crusade," assured Nathaniel, "In fact, I think I can make my biggest contribution here in Monmouth. I plan to visit Governor Livingston in the next few days to discuss several issues including suggestions for my replacement. I have a few people in mind. In any case New Jersey will continue to be well represented by Dr. Witherspoon."

A few days later Nathaniel rode to Trenton for a conference with Governor Livingston.

"I cannot say I was pleased to hear that you no longer want to represent us in Congress," Livingston began, "But I agree with you that Monmouth is indeed the front and that we need you more here in New Jersey than in Philadelphia."

"At this particular point in our struggle I think I can best serve the country by serving New Jersey, but I would like to propose a suitable replacement. I can wholeheartedly vouch for the moral uprightness of Dr. Thomas Henderson, whom I have known since his student days. He is a brave and loyal Whig who would represent New Jersey well."

"I know Dr. Henderson and agree that he would be an excellent candidate," replied Livingston, "Do you think he would accept the candidacy?"

"I will certainly try to convince him to answer the call," promised Nathaniel, "But I cannot be sure since I know what financial strain the office entails. Dr. Henderson's farm suffered great devastation during the battle at Monmouth so he might find himself in straitened circumstances."

"I wish you luck with convincing Dr. Henderson to do his duty, but I have another matter on the agenda. I know that you have served on a committee to oversee the Continental Army Quartermaster, so you have experience in procurement matters. We are currently experiencing increasing difficulties obtaining the supplies we need to feed our state troops."

"Regrettably the Quartermaster agents have the same problem. The truth is farmers will not sell. Some are determined upon this measure through sheer avarice which prompts them to keep what they have as long as there is any prospect of a rising price. And the prices rise continuously. I am afraid that in this case greed clearly trumps patriotism," explained Nathaniel.

"The inflation, of course, makes everything more difficult" agreed Livingston, "but the sheer volume of procurement makes it very hard to combat."

"The volume of procurement also affords endless opportunities for corruption which also no doubt adds to the costs," Nathaniel continued, "In Monmouth we have the additional problem that some greedy farmers refuse to sell for continental currency at all. They prefer to earn sterling through the London Trade. But our militia is scrutinizing these transactions closely. If we can prove that someone is aiding the enemy, that can be a ground for confiscation. David Forman is tirelessly in pursuit of such scoundrels."

"David Forman has acquired a reputation for relentlessness in his suppression of the disaffected. He needs to take care not to provide his enemies with evidence of self-enrichment," warned Livingston.

"David is indeed relentless is his pursuit of compensation for the depredations of Loyalist raids," argued Nathaniel, "But he is an honest and fearless patriot, an avenging angel for the victims of Tory crimes."

"I am sure that with your recommendation the Assembly will chose Dr. Henderson, although all will regret your decision not to run," Livingston quickly changed the subject, "It is true that you have done your share, but there is still much to do, and the number of those who are best qualified is decreasing. Our legislative body suffers more detriment from three or four Tories than it can reap advantages from twenty Whigs."

"I will continue the struggle as before," assured Nathaniel, "Many of the most devious and cunning Tory sympathizers reside in Monmouth County, and those are precisely the ones that David Forman has in his sights."

"I will rely on you, Dr. Scudder, to see that the rule of law is upheld," Livingston replied, "The Assembly has faith in your incorruptibility although many have their doubts about David Forman. It is perhaps indeed fortunate that you will be taking a more active role in the politics of Monmouth. The Assembly might, therefore, see events there in a more positive light."

"We certainly need the Assembly to expand our mandate to punish the disaffected whenever we catch them aiding the enemy," Nathaniel asserted.

"That will not be so easy," Livingston warned, "Did you hear that the law we passed in 1778 that provides legal cover for confiscations is being challenged as unconstitutional?"

"Unconstitutional?" Nathaniel exclaimed, "That is outrageous! That law was passed by a large majority. And, in any case, it does not go nearly far enough."

"It was by virtue of the current law that Major Elisha Walton confiscated an expensive quantity of goods in the possession of John Holmes and Solomon Ketcham, whom he charged with having brought them from within the lines of the enemy," Livingston explained, "Justice John Anderson ruled in favor of Walton last May."

"Yes, I remember that case," replied Nathaniel, "Everyone knew that Holmes and Ketcham were long involved in the London Trade."

"Their guilt was never in question," continued Livingston, "But the bold bastards took the case to the Supreme Court with the argument that they should have been allowed a 12-man jury, not just the six-man jury prescribed by the current law. The New Jersey Constitution guarantees everyone a 12-man jury, so the plaintiff's attorney is arguing that the law is null and void and the conviction has to be reversed."

"That is incredible!" exclaimed Nathaniel, "I can't believe that an honest judge would give any weight to such an argument."

"You might be surprised, Dr. Scudder," replied Livingston, "You never know how a court might decide these issues. Being in court is like being on the high seas—you are in the hands of God."

"Then I will pray that God's justice be done," averred Nathaniel, "But I see your point. There is no guarantee that the judge's ruling will be guided by a divine sense of justice. Legal chicanery could indeed block our efforts to attain retribution for the victims of Tory depredations. The disaffected are particularly fond of using endless lawsuits to frustrate justice. Let us hope that the Assembly will amend the law to avoid such a vulnerability."

"The cause between Walton and Holmes is of the greatest moment and I hope none of the judges have given their opinion. I should be sorry that the supposed event of the controversy should give the Tories any cause of triumph; but the judges, you know, are bound to determine the law in whosoever favor that may appear to be, let the consequences be what they may. In any case I would caution you, David Forman and other Monmouth Whigs to proceed most carefully whenever confiscations are an issue," Livingston advised, "Such actions not only stimulate violent reprisals but also run the risk of being reversed in the courts at some point. The victims you seek to help might wind up losing what compensation you are able to offer them."

"But the victims want revenge for the terrible things they have suffered," countered Nathaniel, "And they also want protection from the kidnappers who drag their loved ones off to the putrid prison ships in New York harbor. Perhaps if the kidnappers realize that their friends and family will have to answer for their heinous deeds, they will think twice about organizing a raiding party."

Livingston emitted a long sigh, "Perhaps . . . perhaps, Dr. Scudder, but it is equally likely that it will only increase the determination, violence, and brutality of the raiders."

"The violence and brutality have already reached a level, that the natural desire for revenge can hardly be suppressed," argued Nathaniel, "Even if retaliatory measures do not solve the problem, it is politically urgent to offer some form of action. It is what our Whig public expects and demands."

"I can well understand that" agreed Livingston, "and I intend to take action so that people there understand that the state government is not abandoning them. I will commission a guard of two hundred men from our state troops to be assigned to the defense of Monmouth. I hope that will prevent the predatory visits of the British and protect patriotic borderers from the freebooting Tories."

After thanking the governor for his willingness to aid Monmouth, Nathaniel hurried home to convey to his Whig colleagues the good news of state reinforcements as well as the admonitions of the governor to adhere carefully to the law. He invited David Forman and Thomas Henderson to his home for a conference.

"I bring good tidings from Governor Livingston," Nathaniel began, "He understands completely the importance of shoring up our defenses in Monmouth and has promised to send 200 state troops to help us."

"Hopefully they put up a better fight than Ford's Continentals did last spring," retorted David Forman cynically, "The only thing the Continental troops did here was to provoke an enemy attack and then retreat without a fight. Those kinds of allies we can do without!"

"These troops are under the governor's orders, and he gave me his word that they will stand by us," replied Nathaniel. "He also accepts the fact that my place is here defending our homes and not in Philadelphia." Turning to Thomas Henderson, he continued, "I proposed, you, Thomas, as my replacement in Congress, and he assured me that you would certainly be approved if you are willing to stand."

"I . . . I . . . am very flattered by your trust in me, Dr. Scudder, but . . . but . . . " Thomas Henderson stammered, "But I am a physician, I am not qualified to be a lawmaker."

"You are a pious and intelligent man, Thomas," replied Nathaniel, "You have the moral fiber to resist the temptations for self-enrichment that congressmen are constantly exposed to. That is the most important qualification."

Henderson, thinking about his straitened financial circumstances since his farm was ravished in the battle of Monmouth, was not at all certain that he deserved to be considered so resistant to temptation, "Your faith humbles me, Dr. Scudder. And I certainly want to do my duty, but the fact is I have to discuss with my family the feasibility of long absences away from my work."

"That is completely understandable," agreed Nathaniel, "No one knows better than I the financial stress associated with public office. Think it over carefully and let me know your decision as soon as you can."

"And if you decide not to take the seat, there will still be plenty of ways for you to serve your country here in Monmouth," interjected David Forman. "And here you will be able to avoid financial sacrifices," he added with a cynical smile.

Nathaniel frowned at Forman's discouragement of Henderson from serving in Congress but since he himself was quitting Congress for financial reasons, he could not in good conscience argue against Forman's point.

The next day Nathaniel set out early once again for Philadelphia to finish up his last week in Congress. He particularly wanted to thank Henry Laurens, the former president of the Continental Congress, for his friendship and support and offer his assurances that he would continue to serve the cause.

Arriving in Philadelphia in the afternoon he immediately sought out Laurens at the house where he usually boarded when in town.

"I am told that you have made the decision not to continue in Congress," Laurens greeted Nathaniel with a concerned expression. "I know you have had to bear unequal sacrifices, but this legislature desperately needs men like you."

"I am now, my dear friend, returning to private life, this being my last week in Congress, but believe me I have no idea of shrinking from any further share in this important contest," Nathaniel assured his friend, "No sir—I will continue to exert myself on all occasions . . . if necessary by again taking up the sword, and even to enlist in the ranks under those over whom I lately held high command. I know you pity me for the unequal sacrifices I have made—I thank you for it, but I know that I have done nothing more than any honest man ought to have done."

"Trouble is there are just not enough honest men around willing to serve," replied Laurens, "And perhaps you have been a bit too reluctant to pursue business opportunities that became available. That might have made your public duties less of a financial burden."

"I could never in good conscience draw personal profit from my public duties," averred Nathaniel solemnly, "But I have proposed a worthy replacement that the New Jersey Assembly will approve. Colonel Thomas Henderson, if he accepts, shall be a very good man. He has the moral fiber to resist lucrative temptations."

"I am sure he is an excellent choice but if he is as strict as you are, he might also not be able to afford to serve for very long," Laurens answered smiling, "Let's hope he finds ways to make his public service feasible. In any case, I have an opportunity which I am sure you can reconcile with your moral principles. I remember your having told me that your son recently completed his studies at Nassau Hall?"

"Yes, indeed, my son, Joseph was awarded his degree at commencement last year," replied Nathaniel proudly.

"I have an opening at the War Office for a bright young man, and I would be happy to have Joseph in my employ," offered Laurens, "You yourself would not be profiting from public office, and I would have an employee I could trust. It could be a great opportunity for Joseph to begin a public service career."

"That is a most generous suggestion," exclaimed Nathaniel, "I am so thankful to you for this. It will give Joseph a chance to serve his country performing important duties, and at the same time get him away from the chaos of Monmouth County. That will be a relief to my wife who has been suffering great anxieties of late."

"I am happy that I am able to show my appreciation for your loyal service in this modest way," replied Laurens, "I add my voice to that of my colleague, Richard Henry Lee, who on several occasions has expressed his gratitude for your support of his diplomatic and economic initiatives."

"Congressman Lee's initiatives were always ultimately rational," explained Nathaniel, "I am in particular agreement with his proposals to bolster the finances of the federal government. That is the only way we are going to be able to maintain the viability of our currency."

"Speaking of currency," continued Laurens, "I have issued this warrant to the treasurer on your behalf for five hundred dollars. Please take this to the New Jersey government and tell them it is to be used for munitions to support our brave compatriots in Monmouth County."

"I am greatly moved by your trust and generosity," replied Nathaniel, "Although our money buys less and less every day, it is an important symbol of commitment to our cause. I will endeavor to get the money to the Assembly quickly while it still buys a decent amount of powder."

Leaving Laurens's boarding house Nathaniel was alarmed to note that the temperature had dropped considerably. Snow propelled by gale-force winds was piling up rapidly threatening to make city streets impassable. Nathaniel galloped in the direction of the Delaware praying that the ferries were still operational. When he reached the river, he discovered that the surface had frozen so hard, that the ferries had been replaced by sleighs. He was able to cross the river quickly and continue on to Trenton to deliver the money that Congress had appropriated for New Jersey's use.

Arriving in the early evening in Trenton Nathaniel was pleased to find Governor Livingston still in his office. He hoped to be able to fulfill his mission quickly and continue to Monmouth.

"Dr. Scudder, thank you for bringing this disbursement," Livingston began, "As usual, it is a pittance compared to our needs, but it is better than nothing. And you have braved dreadful weather to bring it here."

"I am on my way back to Monmouth," explained Nathaniel, "So I had to pass this way in any case. But I must hurry on. This sudden winter onslaught will undoubtedly spur numerous foraging parties to increase their plundering of our yeomen."

"The intensity of the storm increases by the hour," warned Livingston, "This could become the hardest winter we have had in years. You should probably seek an inn to spend the night and continue on in the morning."

Nathaniel reluctantly conceded that a night ride to Monmouth was quite impossible under the circumstances and spent a fitful night at a Trenton inn. Despite his exhaustion from galloping great distances that day, sleep long eluded him as he pondered the additional challenges that a severe winter might entail. Travel by wagon along roads clogged by snow and ice would become nearly impossible. Famine would threaten isolated farmsteads cut off from the markets where they normally traded their goods for the necessities of life. The depredations of Tories and Pine Robbers could only increase in violence as foraging became an increasingly urgent endeavor. Nathaniel prayed to God for the strength to face the challenges awaiting him at home.

Early the next morning Nathaniel awoke to a sunny, clear, and frosty morning. The storm had abated but an arctic cold front remained. The storm had left huge snow drifts partially blocking roads where wagon tracks frozen solid in the mud made the going treacherous for man and beast. Nathaniel proceeded very cautiously, knowing that one slip could mean a broken ankle for his horse and death from exposure for him. For hours on end he saw not a single fellow traveler. The freezing cold, the monotony of the snow-covered landscape, and the slowness of his advance began to make him feel very drowsy. The thought crossed his mind how pleasant it would be just to lie and rest for a few minutes on a soft snowbank. He knew from experience, however, that this was exactly the way winter kills and slapped himself sharply in the face several times. He concentrated his thoughts on his dear wife who at this point was undoubtedly beside herself with concern for his safety. He allowed his anxieties about her safety to escalate to the point where a surge of adrenaline gave him new energy to continue his trek.

Arriving in Freehold in the early evening Nathaniel nearly fell from his horse as servants came to help him dismount. They helped him stumble into the house where an immensely relieved Isabella greeted him with open arms.

"Nathaniel, Nathaniel, I was so worried," Isabella cried, "Why are you travelling in such terrible weather. You might have frozen to death!"

"The thought of you having to deal with this dreadful weather alone gave me no peace," replied Nathaniel, "You have been sickly lately and this cold spell is an additional burden for your health. I will fix an herb decoction for you which will ward off the grippe."

"First you have to rest and warm up or you will be the one who gets the grippe," warned Isabella.

"Indeed," agreed Nathaniel, "Let us all have a cup of warm rum to stoke our inner fires. Then early to bed so I get my strength back quickly. I am sure that from tomorrow on there will be plenty of work for a physician if this cold spell continues. Speaking of physicians, I also have to talk to Thomas Henderson to hear if he is willing to take my seat in Congress. He is probably in the saddle visiting patients. When the temperature drops this precipitously, it always results in health crises for the old and the weak."

It turned out that Thomas Henderson was indeed extremely busy. Many outlying farms were in fact in desperate need of medical assistance and just getting to them in the frozen weather was a time-consuming challenge. It took several days before Nathaniel was able to organize a meeting with Thomas Henderson and David Forman to discuss the issue of a congressional candidacy.

"I have thought long and hard about your nomination of me for Congress," began Henderson, "Your trust in me is very flattering, Dr. Scudder, but I have come to the conclusion that my place is here in Monmouth County."

"Well, Thomas, I can hardly fault you for coming to the same conclusion that I myself came to," replied Nathaniel, "But the question remains who can we trust to represent New Jersey who will be acceptable to the Assembly but also not succumb to the temptations that surround congressmen?"

"I have a suggestion that might surprise you," interrupted David Forman, "Since I noticed that Thomas was less than enthusiastic about your proposal at our last meeting, I asked old Abraham Clark if he might be willing to serve another term. Since he has already served with distinction in Congress, the Assembly can't possibly have any objections."

"An outstanding suggestion," opined Henderson, relieved to see a way out of his dilemma, "And did he agree?"

"He did indeed," answered Forman, "He said that if the Assembly would nominate him again, he would be honored to serve."

"Considering the sacrifices he and his family have made for the Whig cause, I would be surprised if the Assembly did not confirm him, but there are those who have reservations about him," warned Nathaniel.

"What kind of reservations?" asked Forman indignantly, "He and his sons have been ardent and steadfast supporters of the Whig cause from the very beginning. When his son, Andrew, was captured and sent to that notorious prison ship, Jersey, the British offered to release him if his father would renounce the Whig cause. Clark refused and his boy died last year like most of the other poor devils who wind up on that infernal tub. How many of those with reservations have made that kind of sacrifice?"

"Many of the large landowners fear that he is too enamored of government borrowing," explained Nathaniel, "They think he tends to support policies that endanger the value of our money."

"They probably remember how he as a lawyer defended the land rights of our yeomen when the proprietors and their lawyers were trying to cheat them out of their plots," countered Forman, "That is the real reason for their hostility. They are afraid that having people like Clark in the government could endanger their dominance after the war. Many of them are fence-sitters anyway. They hope that, no matter who wins this war, they will still be able to salvage their wealth and influence. I suspect that many of them would welcome an enemy victory."

"I think that many wealthy people who genuinely support our cause are still wary of running up too much debt that someone will have to pay in the end," explained Nathaniel, imagining how his father-in-law would view the issue, "It does not necessarily mean that they are on the side of the enemy. The falling value of our currency is a great burden for all of us. It is not clear that our foreign creditors will lend us enough hard currency to bolster confidence in our money. Merchants are then reluctant to sell us what the army needs or demand higher and higher prices for things in order to hedge their risks."

"Creditors will pay, if they think that our victory is imminent," argued Forman, "This is a hugely rich continent and whoever has control of it has access to vast wealth. That is why I don't worry about Clark's propensity to run up the debt. We must spend whatever it takes to secure victory. And I have no doubt at all that Clark will give his last drop of blood to reach that goal. Meanwhile we can relieve the pressure on our finances by confiscating more of the wealth in the hands of Tory sympathizers and their friends and relatives. Our cause needs hard currency? Our hidden enemies have plenty of it stashed away from the London Trade. You have seen yourself that Congress is totally incapable of financing our war. If we want to win, we have to take matters into our own hands."

Thomas Henderson was impressed by the way Forman's eloquent support of Clark segued directly into a defense of the strategy of retaliation.

"Your argument makes perfect sense, General Forman," Henderson agreed, "Our most important mission is right here on the home front. And I am relieved to hear that such a determined patriot as Abraham Clark has agreed to take the seat in Congress."

"We certainly can all be happy that we have such a devoted Whig to serve New Jersey," added Nathaniel. "And the way this winter is developing Thomas and I will surely have our hands full just coping with medical emergencies here in Monmouth."

"Not only medical emergencies," replied Forman. "If the weather continues to deteriorate, it will force the enemy to dare to stage even more foraging expeditions. What they steal will be at the expense of our loyal yeomen. We must heighten our resolve to see that they are compensated."

The winter did indeed turn out to one of the most severe on record. Nathaniel and Thomas Henderson spent every day making the rounds of farms and dealing with the medical problems they encountered. The prolonged cold combined with frequently inadequate nourishment took a heavy toll, especially on the old and the weak. An elderly person who caught a severe case of the grippe was lucky to last a week. Isolated farms were easy prey to foraging parties of New York Loyalists or Pine Robbers. Once a farm's winter stores had been raided, starvation was imminent even if the raiders had not killed or kidnapped their victims. More than once Nathaniel and Thomas would come upon a farm with no one left alive, the bodies of the deceased lying frozen in their beds. In such cases there was nothing more the physicians could do but to report the deaths to the local church so that a decent funeral could be arranged whenever the ground thawed enough to permit the digging of graves.

Despite working literally day and night throughout the long, harsh winter Nathaniel was unpleasantly surprised to discover that his personal financial situation continued to deteriorate. He was able again to collect more fees for medical services and medications, but the payment was almost always in local currency, the value of which continued to plummet. It turned out to be problematical to adjust the fee schedule of the Medical Association to compensate adequately for the growing weakness of the local money. He began to wonder if the arguments of the large landowners against excessive borrowing might have more merit than David Forman was willing to allow. He asked himself if all the states were similarly affected. Having spent the winter travelling mostly in the rural areas of Monmouth County, he felt cut off from information about the overall situation. For that reason, he was very pleased that, when the winter began to abate in early March, his son, Joseph, was able to get a short furlough to visit home. Nathaniel pumped him for information about his adventures working in Congress's War Office.

"It is exciting work," reported Joseph, "But very demanding. There are not enough hours in the day to translate all the French correspondence into English. I am fortunate that Mr. Laurens treats me very kindly even when I struggle to keep up with the workload."

"Henry Laurens is a dear and loyal friend," replied Nathaniel, "I am grateful that he is affording you such patronage. I really must meet him in Philadelphia to thank him. I would also like to hear how the great struggle is faring from his point of view. Spending all winter in rural New Jersey has shut me off from news of the world."

"Ironically it is news from New Jersey that is currently in high demand in Philadelphia," Joseph informed him, "It has been so difficult to visit Washington's headquarters in Morristown that we are not completely sure of the situation there. The news that does reach us is dire."

"It has indeed been the worst winter in living memory," confirmed Nathaniel, "The road to Morristown has been blocked most of the time with four feet of snow. In February, however, we had a short visit from Dr. James Thacher who is a surgeon in the Continental Army. He sought me out because he was in desperate need of medication for the troops. I gave him what I had available, and he gave me a long account of the conditions in Morristown. It sounded even more disastrous than last winter in Valley Forge."

"I am sure that Henry Laurens would be very interested in hearing the details," said Joseph, "The help of our French allies depends to a great extent on the condition of Washington's army. In the correspondence I have translated, there are often queries about the combat-readiness of the Continental Army."

"Starved as I was for information from the front, I took extensive notes during Dr. Thacher's visit. I shall accompany you on your return trip to Philadelphia," announced Nathaniel, "Then I can personally thank Henry Laurens for kindly mentoring you and also provide him with useful information about Morristown. I had assumed that Philadelphia was informed about the state of our troops, but my account will certainly add urgency to the calls for relief."

Early the next morning Nathaniel and Joseph set out for Philadelphia. Even though it was already March the winter cold lingered, and they maintained as brisk a pace as the snowy, icy roads allowed in order to keep warm. Arriving in the evening at Henry Lauren's boarding house, the weary travelers were pleased to find Laurens sitting next to a blazing fire.

"Welcome, my friends," exclaimed Laurens, "Come in out of the cold and have a warm rum to drive out the chill."

Nathaniel and Joseph gratefully accepted Laurens's offer and sat down near the open fireplace.

"Joseph tells me that communication with Morristown has been difficult due to this dreadful winter," Nathaniel began, "Washington's army is safe from attack there, but it is a remote place and deep snow has made travel there exceedingly difficult. A few weeks ago, the army surgeon from the Continental Army, one Dr. Thacher, managed to make it to Freehold seeking medical supplies for the troops. I gave him what I could and interviewed him extensively. When Joseph mentioned that Philadelphia needs information from there, it occurred to me that what I learned might be useful for you."

"I am sure it will be," replied Laurens enthusiastically, "Please tell me all you know."

"When Dr. Thacher visited in February, the army had apparently already survived the worst part of the ordeal," Nathaniel continued, "When they first arrived near Morristown in December, their baggage had been left behind for want of wagons to transport it. The soldiers had to face freezing cold with two to six feet of snow on the ground without tents or blankets. Many were scarcely clad themselves, sometimes barefoot and almost naked. No forage for the horses and only the bare minimum for the men to eat. They survived by huddling close together around large fires. The baggage wagons finally arrived, but it was still difficult to erect their tents properly on the frozen ground. The soldiers were charged with building log-huts for winter quarters, and they set about that task with grim determination as the only way to escape the ravages of the terrible winter."

"I understand that the winter is a great additional burden for our troops," said Laurens. "But I am surprised to hear that they are so poorly supplied. I thought that Congress had allocated generous sums to feed and clothe the troops."

"That may be," conceded Nathaniel, "But the value of the money they are provided with plummets from day to day. The farmers refuse to sell their produce for currency they fear might be valueless tomorrow. For that reason, Washington despaired of getting the necessary supplies from the commissary-general and applied directly to the magistrates of the state of New Jersey for assistance in procuring provisions. I am pleased to report that our pious Whigs have responded as true Christians and donated enough to sustain the army through the winter. By the time Dr. Thacher visited me, the log-huts had been finished and starvation averted, but the situation remains precarious."

"The situation is worse than I feared," replied Laurens, "I had hoped when the winter finally ended supplying the troops adequately would become more feasible. But if the commissary-general cannot even procure provisions our troubles are far from over."

"Indeed," agreed Nathaniel, "And to add to Washington's travails a small number of the desperate soldiers have taken to robbing chickens, pigs, and other livestock from the farms in the vicinity. Washington punishes wrong doers briskly but the whole matter is dreadful both for the morale of the soldiers as well as for their support in the populace. Many soldiers whose terms of duty are soon expiring will not want to re-enlist."

"Seeing as how it was the generosity of the pious yeomen of New Jersey who saved our army during this winter, Washington is certainly correct to enforce discipline with harsh measures," said Laurens, "But we must see that we overcome our procurement problems; otherwise our army might just disintegrate."

"My experience in the congressional oversight of the quartermaster makes me pessimistic that we can expect the commissary-general to solve our problem," explained Nathaniel, "Our currency weakens by the hour. Only hard currency loans from our allies will suffice to insure adequate procurement. Although there is much talk of money that is on the way from abroad, whatever arrives tends to disappear somewhere in the procurement process before goods are delivered. Trying to track down the roots of this corruption was the most frustrating thing I attempted as a congressman. I must admit that I was not very successful, and that frustration was a big factor in my resigning my seat in Congress."

"But that did not solve the problem, did it?" exclaimed Laurens, "If honest people like yourself abandon the struggle, then we are surely lost."

"As I promised to you last fall, my friend," replied Nathaniel, "I have no intention of abandoning the struggle. I will continue it where I can be most effective, and that is in New Jersey where I will bring the Word to our faithful yeomen who saved the army this winter that they are doing the work of the Lord and that that work in not done yet."

Nathaniel stayed overnight in Laurens' boarding house where Joseph was also boarded. He brooded through the night about the fate of the troops in Morristown. In the early morning he had a vision which he felt was Providence showing him the way. When he met Henry Laurens and his son, Joseph, for breakfast, he exclaimed excitedly,

"I must hurry back to Monmouth, there is much to be done to keep the Continental Army in fighting condition! We must follow the example that the Lord revealed to us this winter. We must appeal to all followers of the True Religion to donate in kind to keep our troops supplied. I spend much of my time now visiting many outlying farms. I will appeal to them to help in any way they can to alleviate the wretched conditions of our brave soldiers. I will also encourage our Presbyterian pastors to spread the Word from the pulpit. It is time to stand up for the Lord of Hosts!"

Taken aback by the vehemence of Nathaniel's morning sermon, Joseph and Henry Laurens simply stared at each other while Nathaniel quickly gathered his gear and readied his horse for the long ride home. As he galloped off into the snowy morning, Laurens turned to Joseph, "If there is anyone who can rally New Jersey for our cause, it's your father."

"It's because he really does not have the slightest doubt that he is but a tool in the hands of the Almighty," explained Joseph, "He truly believes that service to the community is life's only justification."

After a long day's ride over frozen terrain Nathaniel finally arrived back at his home near Monmouth Courthouse. Although totally exhausted from his trip Nathaniel rushed into the house anxious to share with Isabella his vision for rescuing the Whig cause.

"The generosity of our congregations is the best hope for America!" Nathaniel exclaimed to a startled Isabella as he entered the parlor, "And it is that generosity that we must harness to help our patriots in Morristown. I have just returned from Philadelphia where I discussed with Henry Laurens and our son, Joseph, the dreadful conditions that our troops have endured in Morristown this last winter. This is entirely the fault of the corruption in our procurement networks which is so ubiquitous that of the vast sums spent, only a tiny portion finally filters down to our boys in need. I was so upset that I could not sleep that night, but finally in the early morning hours the Lord revealed the solution to me. The troops in Morristown survived this winter because pious yeomen in the neighborhood provided them with the bare minimum they needed to survive. That pious generosity is the key to the survival of our army. We must simply systematically enlist more of the congregations of the True Religion."

"Do you really think our congregations can support an army?" asked Isabella incredulously, "Would it not be easier to punish the corrupt officials who are siphoning off public funds?"

"Corruption is endemic in human nature," replied Nathaniel, "It will not be eliminated until the Final Judgement Day, too late for our troops. But if the Lord so wills, we can feed an army. Think of the parable of the loaves and the fishes. If every pious person in New Jersey can make even the smallest contribution—food, clothing, blankets—our army will be able to survive long enough until help from our French allies makes final victory possible."

Impressed by the eloquence of Nathaniel's reasoning and infected by his missionary zeal Isabella began to rethink her initial skepticism.

"Perhaps it would indeed be possible to organize a network of women who could solicit aid for our troops," mused Isabella thoughtfully, "I know many of us are frustrated sitting at home worrying passively about the fate of our men in this terrible conflict. If we could actively help in some way, it might relieve some of the stress. I will talk to Ann Forman and some of the other Whig ladies and see what they think."

At that moment as if by some portentous coincidence there was a knock on the front door which when opened revealed David and Ann Forman.

"We just wanted to stop over and see how Elizabeth is faring?" Ann Forman began, "I hope she is giving a good account of herself."

"Elizabeth is a lovely, conscientious girl," Isabella assured her friend. "And she learns very quickly. She is already making herself very useful. I am very glad you stopped by, however, because I wanted to discuss some ideas we have been considering for helping our troops in Morristown."

"Indeed," Nathaniel said, "Our procurement services are failing our soldiers due to endemic corruption. I believe our only hope is to mobilize the congregations of the True Religion to share their daily bread with our patriots."

"I wish you the best of luck with that," said David Forman, "But I think a quicker way to accomplish that would be to confiscate the daily bread of the disaffected. By the way, I heard that one John Parker seems to have moved on to the property that you bought last year at auction. He claims that he bought it fair and square from the former owner, Thomas Bills."

"That is outrageous!", exclaimed Nathaniel, "Bills had gone off to fight in the Loyalist New Jersey Volunteers, and his property was legally confiscated. I purchased it in a free and public auction."

"No one knows that better than I," replied Forman, "After all, I was the one who organized that auction. But this is exactly the kind of treachery that is to be expected from Tory scoundrels. Parker is buying up several confiscated parcels from the former owners who have fled to the enemy. He gets them at a huge discount so he figures that if the Brits win, he will make a fortune. I will be happy to visit him with a couple of our lads to show him how we deal with enemy agents."

A stern look of disapproval from Isabella convinced Nathaniel that this was an offer he needed to decline, "Thank you, David, for your willingness to help but I feel obliged as a former congressman to first file a suit in the Monmouth Court of Common Pleas. Politicians must be seen to uphold the rule of law."

"Right you are, Nathaniel," Isabella sought to deflect David Forman's attempt to promote violence as the only feasible solution. "Besides, as you pointed out when you arrived, we have a much more pressing issue to face. Our troops in Morristown are on the verge of starvation, and our best hope right now is to mobilize the pious Whigs of New Jersey to save them. I believe that we women can play a vital role in that."

"It is interesting that you should make such a suggestion," replied Nathaniel, "In Philadelphia I was told that some of the patriotic ladies of Pennsylvania are organizing themselves to exactly that end. They believe that there are many people scattered throughout the state who would be willing to pledge contributions to aid our brave soldiers if they could be sure that the aid gets to the deserving people."

"I am sure that that is also the case in New Jersey," Ann Forman chimed in, eliciting an annoyed glace from her husband, "But we also need to build our own organization. So many of our men including our pastors are now off busy fighting the enemy while we sit at home and worry. We need to take matters into our own hands."

"In Pennsylvania, the ladies apparently are founding committees in each county that will coordinate with each other to organize contributions," said Nathaniel.

"We can do that as well," enthused Isabella, "I can think of a number of ladies here in Monmouth who would be willing to serve on such a committee. I will also talk to Annis Stockton to hear if she thinks such a committee might be possible in Somerset County. She is a good friend of both Lady Stirling and Cornelia Paterson. I would also think that Hannah Caldwell, the wife of Reverend James Caldwell, would be pleased to help."

"I am sure that here in Monmouth the Covenhovens, the Wikoffs, and the Newells would welcome such an initiative," said Nathaniel, "Reverend Caldwell is a convinced Whig and will also exhort his flock to support the cause. I am told he has become very influential since he took over the First Presbyterian church in Elizabethtown. And all of these people have friends and relatives in other counties whom they could encourage to join the network."

The fervor of the conversation impressed even the skeptical David Forman who began to see the movement as a possible vehicle to promote his own agenda.

"Hmm, the more I think about it, the more I come to the conclusion that you may indeed be on to something of significance," he ventured, "I don't know if large contributions will be forthcoming, but it will certainly be an interesting test of loyalty to our cause. I am sure that the Tories hiding among us will not want to participate and that alone would be evidence of a lack of good faith."

It flashed through Nathaniel's mind that framing donations as loyalty tests could easily become a weapon of extortion. He decided not to air his reservations, however, so as not to discourage David Forman's support of a project that was generating such enthusiasm. And, in fact, the enthusiasm did prove to be contagious. Isabella and Ann wrote to their friends from Whig families in other counties describing the project and urging them to solicit participants among their friends and acquaintances. In just a few months a statewide network of Whig ladies from 12 different counties sprang into being and began collecting money and food for the troops.

"You are doing the Lord's work!" Nathaniel praised his wife, "Over a hundred ladies have answered the call. It's an inspiring sight to see."

"It has, indeed, been remarkable," agreed Isabella, "But our work has just begun. The troops need food and clothing but most of our donations are money that declines so quickly in value that it buys less and less."

"I know, it is a terrible problem, but it is not clear how to deal with it. The state needs to borrow to finance the war but the more it borrows the less our currency is worth. Fortunately, the farmers near Morristown continue to be generous. But we need to organize more contributions in kind delivered directly to the troops."

Although the idea was sound, it proved difficult to cope with the logistics in the war-torn countryside where enemy forage parties were always to be feared. Washington's troops continued to suffer great deprivations. Desertions and disease reduced the fighting force to a mere 3,500 men with low morale and many prone to mutiny.

One day in early June as Nathaniel and Isabella were pondering ways that might make the Whig ladies' project more effective, a sharp knock on the door interrupted their deliberations.

"We are calling the militia out!" shouted David Forman, "We have certain intelligence that a British attack on Morristown is imminent. We must gather every available man and repel the attack. We have no time to lose!"

Nathaniel bade a quick farewell to a distraught Isabella, grabbed his sword and musket and rushed to the stable to saddle Blackjack. Within a few minutes he was on the road galloping with David Forman in the direction of Elizabethtown.

"How did you come about this intelligence?" asked Nathaniel, "Is it reliable?"

"Absolutely," replied Forman, "We have suspected for some time that one of Washington's soldiers was a Tory spy. We caught him the other day on his way back from a secret visit to New York City. We took him over to my farm. After being hung upside down in the well for a few minutes he admitted he was a member of the New Jersey Volunteers."

"And you are sure he was not misleading you?" asked Nathaniel.

"I know when prisoners are lying," answered Forman grimly, "And I know how to get them to stop lying. He eventually told us everything he knew, and most of the details corresponded to information my spies have already gathered. My men will also notice when the first troop movements he predicted actually happen, and my couriers will inform Washington within the hour."

"I am delighted to hear that your network is working as efficiently as ever," Nathaniel was genuinely awed by Forman's organizational talents, "How much more were you able to extract from the spy?"

"We were lucky that our spy reported directly to the Hessian commander of the British garrison in New York City, General von Knyphausen. The spy told Knyphausen that Washington's men were weakened by sickness and desertion and could not muster more that 3,500 poorly motivated fighters. Knyphausen thereupon decided that this would be the time to push through to Hobart Gap and finish the rebel army off once and for all. He allegedly has mustered about 6,000 Hessian, British and Loyalist troops and plans to land them at Elizabethtown and march toward Washington's camp in the Watchung mountains."

"God help us!" exclaimed Nathaniel, "If he can get through to Hobart Gap, there is only flat ground between there and Washington's army. Our poorly nourished troops would be outnumbered two to one. Only a miracle can save us."

"We must make that miracle happen," insisted Forman, "We have to see that Knyphausen does not make it to Hobart Gap. I have sent out express riders throughout New Jersey to rouse every militiaman capable of bearing arms. The spy said Knyphausen does not think the people of New Jersey will offer any resistance to the advance of his troops. We will prove to that arrogant bastard that he is badly mistaken."

As they approached Elizabethtown, they encountered more and more militiamen heading in their direction. Foreman's call to arms had apparently been unexpectedly effective. Everyone seemed to realize that if the British succeeded in destroying the remnants of Washington's army before French help arrived, the war for independence would be essentially over. Militia units from as far away as Hopewell rallied to the flag.

"Do we have a plan of action?" asked Nathaniel, "How should we coordinate such a surge of militiamen from all over the state?"

"We cannot, of course, directly confront 6,000 of Europe's most professional soldiers," replied Forman, "But we can make their lives hell while they're here in our territory. They will think they are in a wasp's nest. Our men know every tree and fencepost and will be hiding behind them when the enemy marches through in their bright uniforms. The order of the day is to hide, shoot, kill, and retreat. Whenever the enemy tries to charge us, we disappear into the forest like Indians. We have sharpshooters armed with Pennsylvania rifles stationed on various lookout posts. They can hit a man up to 200 yards away. Ensign Moses Ogden has a few of these men with his regiment of 60 militiamen waiting to greet the Brits when they land at Elizabethtown."

"This sounds indeed like a strategy that could succeed," agreed Nathaniel, "The British and Hessians insist on disciplined drill tactics and coordinated firing. They will make good targets for our backwoodsmen. We cannot stop the advance of the enemy, but we can slow it down and weaken it so that Washington has better odds. We must warn civilians, however, to stay out of the way of the invading forces. I am particularly concerned about Reverend James Caldwell, the Presbyterian pastor in Elizabethtown. Presbyterian pastors who fall into the hands of the Hessians are likely to meet a grim end."

Arriving in Elizabethtown Nathaniel and David Forman together with a small group of local militia hurried to the residence of James Caldwell. They were relieved to find the pastor preparing to retreat in the direction of Springfield with a local militia unit. He and his older children were packed up and ready to go but his wife, Hannah, wanted to remain.

"This is too much excitement for our little ones," she argued, "I will just stay here with the children. I am sure no honorable British officer will harm a mother looking after small children."

"There are a lot of dishonorable enemy officers," growled Forman, "particularly the treacherous Loyalist refugees who seek brutal revenge whenever they can."

Hannah Caldwell was not to be swayed, however, so Nathaniel joined Reverend Caldwell and the other militiamen who set out in the direction of Springfield where they set up a temporary communications base. David Forman sent out dispatches throughout his network to inform everyone that he would coordinate all intelligence from that location. A little after one the next morning a rider arrived informing him that the first enemy boats from Staten Island had arrived at Elizabethtown. The rider hastened to add that one of Ogden's sharpshooters had managed to hit a British general just as he was disembarking causing a great commotion among the enemy.

"Ahhhhh! They have felt the first sting of the wasp!" cackled David Forman, "It won't be the last. Ogden's men are ordered to fight a rearguard action as the enemy column attempts to advance. They will be waiting for them in Governor Livingston's orchard behind every tree."

Early the next morning an express rider arrived to announce that Ogden's militia had engaged the British advance just as Forman predicted and had succeeded in slowing their advance. A few hours later another messenger arrived with the news that the New Jersey Brigade with a force of militia under Brigadier General William Maxwell had received the attack of the British 1st Division and had stopped its advance. It would only be a matter of time until the enemy called up sufficient reserves to overwhelm the rebel defenses, but it was still encouraging that the invincible British war machine could be stopped, even only temporarily. Maxwell's forces yielded ground only grudgingly and slowly. As General Knyphausen later noted, "The Rebels, as they often did, withdrew from house to house and from wood path to wood path, resisting with all means available."

Night arrived and Knyphausen had still not achieved his goal of quickly taking the Hobart Gap. His troops were in an exposed position. The local population had exhibited much more resistance than expected. He needed to return to New York and re-evaluate the situation. He gave the order to withdraw.

As soon as news arrived that the enemy was retreating to New York, Nathaniel, David Forman, and James Caldwell hastened to return with a militia unit to Connecticut Farms to assay the damage caused by the intrusion. They were appalled by what awaited them. The Caldwell home and several homes around it had been burned to the ground. As James Caldwell frantically rushed to inspect the ashes of his home for traces of his wife and children, a neighbor approached to inform him that his wife and children were in a neighboring dwelling. The flash of hope that his wife was still alive was quickly extinguished when he hurried over to the neighboring house only to find Hannah lying lifeless on the ground with two bullet holes in her chest. The little children were standing around her, still alive but shocked by their dreadful experience. Stunned by the sight of his beloved wife's prostrate body the color drained from James Caldwell's face. Regaining his self-control after a few moments he rushed to take the traumatized children into his arms as Nathaniel moved to examine the corpse.

"Has she been . . . ?" Reverend Caldwell could not bring the dreaded word over his lips.

"No, she has not been ravaged, thank God," confirmed Nathaniel, "She was killed immediately by the two bullets, and no further damage was done to her. Her dress was disturbed by someone searching through the pockets."

"She had put the family jewels into her pockets," explained Caldwell, "She could not imagine that the enemy could be so base as to force a lady to empty her pockets."

"You see what swine we are dealing with!" snarled David Forman, "This should make it clear to everyone that retaliation is the only fitting answer. Every one of those Loyalist bastards who perpetrates a crime like this should have to fear that we will soon visit the same calamity on his friends or relatives."

Over the next few days Forman sent out dispatches to militia units all over the state detailing in lurid detail what he termed atrocities committed by Loyalist troops. He warned of the depredations to be expected wherever enemy troops were able to penetrate. He pointed out the selective nature of the destruction focusing on the property of loyal Whigs while other properties were spared. He urged all patriots to be vigilant, to note whose property was vandalized and whose was not. He insinuated that this was the way to identify covert Tory sympathizers.

Forman's dispatches had the desired effect. Over the next few days stories about the brutal murder of Hannah Caldwell spread like wildfire throughout the population and were lavishly amplified with each re-telling. The fact that the innocent wife of a Presbyterian parson was the victim convinced all adherents of the True Religion that the enemy was indeed an emissary of the Beast and to be resisted at all costs. As preachers shouted from the pulpit that now was time to join the Lord of Hosts, more and more militiamen answered the call to arms.

Militiamen from all over the state converged at Newark Mountain ready to guard the routes to Hobart Gap. Nathaniel, David Forman, and other militia leaders met with General Washington to discuss a strategy of deployment.

"Well, gentlemen," Washington began, "I am very impressed by the number of militia you were able to muster. We will need every last man. I have it on good authority that Knyphausen has not given up his plan to push through to Hobart Gap with 6000 troops. He hopes that we will be forced to leave our safe haven in the Watchung

Mountains and head toward the Hudson where we will be attacked by General Leslie with another 6000 men. We cannot fall into this trap and let them destroy what is left of our army. The enemy must not reach Hobart Gap. I have deployed General Greene with 1500 Continentals and 500 New Jersey militia to block the British advance through Elizabethtown and Springfield. We will use the same tactics as last time, fighting from tree to tree and house to house, until the enemy is exhausted."

"We know that the enemy is likely to overwhelm our forces at Elizabethtown. Do we know how they are planning to continue from there?" asked David Forman.

"They will probably make a two-pronged attack after landing at Elizabethtown Point, one column advancing along the Galloping Hill Road via Connecticut Farms and Springfield, the other on the Vauxhall Road north of Springfield. They will try to converge at Hobart Gap. If they get that far, there is only eleven miles of flat ground between them and our main encampment," warned Washington.

"The last time they were here, we gave them a taste of what it's like to be in a hornets nest," said Forman, "We can do even better this time because we have many more militia. Someone will be waiting behind every tree. If we can slow them down until nightfall, I don't think they will dare make camp in the forest after dark. The Galloping Hill Road offers many opportunities for ambushes and the Galloping Hill Bridge over the Rahway is easy to defend."

"The fate of our army and our country could well depend on your militiamen," said Washington.

"Every man who has answered the call is aware of what is at stake," assured Nathaniel, "They are ready to do the Lord's work. They could not be more highly motivated."

A few weeks later it became apparent that the attack Washington had predicted was imminent. Forman's spies reported troops massing again on Staten Island. General Greene organized four successive lines of defense along the Galloping Hill Road, the last defending the Galloping Hill Bridge. The 1st New Jersey regiment was to block the Vauxhall Bridge. Greene himself would stay with troops in reserve at Bryan's Tavern up on the high ground of the Short Hills. David Forman suggested that he, Nathaniel, Reverend Caldwell, and a detachment of the Monmouth militia proceed to the Galloping Hill Bridge to reinforce Colonel Israel Angell's Rhode Island Regiment. In Forman's opinion that position was the key to delaying the enemy's advance to Hobart Gap.

Arriving at Galloping Hill Bridge that evening Nathaniel was disappointed to see that the defenders had only one cannon, although it occupied a well-protected position with good coverage of the approaches to the bridge. Colonel Angell's regiment had been reduced by illness and expiring enlistments to only 160 men. Nathaniel prayed that the militia's guerrilla tactics would work as effectively they had a few weeks ago. If thousands of enemy soldiers made it this far, the defenders would surely be swept away quickly.

News from the front came early the next morning. A rider dispatched from General Greene arrived with information about enemy incursions and new orders for the defenders.

"General Greene has ordered that the planking be removed from all bridges," he exclaimed, "British, Hessian, and Loyalist forces have landed at Elizabethtown Point early this morning and are advancing in two columns just as General Washington had predicted. The enemy is encountering spirited resistance every step of the way. They have been forced to advance more slowly but they will probably be at this bridge in a matter of hours. General Greene orders you to keep the enemy from crossing the Rahway as long as possible but then to fall back in the face of overwhelming force to join his reserves at Bryan's Tavern."

As the express rider hurried off to warn other militia outposts of the approaching enemy, Reverend Caldwell felt called upon to address the defenders of the bridge.

"My brave fellows," he began, "We are facing the imminent attack of a savage enemy, an enemy who wants us reduced to slavery. But the news of the atrocities committed just two weeks ago has kindled the fire of retribution in the hearts of the faithful far and wide. Even as I speak, new militia units continue to arrive at the mountain of the New Ark of the Covenant! Do not fear, the Lord is on the side of the righteous! We will slay the enemy as David slew Goliath!"

The reverend's words were greeted by shouts of acclaim from the soldiers who then proceeded energetically to remove the planks from the bridge and batten down their defenses. After about an hour the approach of the enemy was signaled by sniper shots in the distance. The militia hiding in the wooded heights along the Galloping Hill Road was harassing the enemy column as it headed toward the bridge. The sound of gunfire grew gradually louder until suddenly the van of the enemy column came into the defenders' view.

"That peacock you see over there is Knyphausen himself!" shouted Colonel Angell, "Let's give him a hearty welcome!"

A round of grapeshot from the defenders' only cannon caused the enemy column to halt and assume battle formation. Fortunately for the defenders the width of the enemy's battle line was constrained by the size of Galloping Hill Road preventing the enemy from fully leveraging its overwhelming numerical superiority. Both sides at first exchanged volleys of musket fire with little effect. Then Knyphausen ordered six cannons to bombard the defenders in preparation for an assault on the bridge. At the conclusion of the bombardment enemy soldiers rushed the bridge only to find the planks missing and the defenders' cannon still lethally effective. The attackers quickly withdrew to a safe distance.

A second volley from Knyphausen's cannons signaled that another attempt to storm the bridge was imminent.

"If you boys can just keep that cannon working," Reverend Caldwell sought to encourage the gun crew, "The attackers won't get far."

"We have enough powder for that," answered the Chief Cannoneer, "But we are running low on wadding."

At that Reverend Caldwell rushed to his horse, removed a pile of hymn books by the clergyman Isaac Watts from his saddlebag and threw them on the ground in front of the cannon.

"Give 'em Watts, boys!" he shouted.

After heavy exchanges of cannon and musket fire the attackers were again forced to break off their assault. Just as the defenders were beginning to feel jubilant about their chances of success, however, it became apparent that British and Hessian troops had forded the Rahway downriver and were now driving the Rhode Islanders back toward the bridge. In order to avoid encirclement, it was necessary to retreat to Bryan's Tavern and abandon Springfield to the enemy.

What at first appeared to be an enemy victory, however, soon turned out to be a failure. Night was approaching and Knyphausen had still not cleared the path to Hobart Gap. He feared an attack by Washington's main army and was disheartened by the numbers of New Jersey militia who were gathering on the Short Hills. He ordered the Loyalist New Jersey Volunteers to burn down Springfield and the rest of his force to withdraw back over Galloping Hill Road and Vauxhall Road. Enduring constant harassment by snipers and suffering many casualties Knyphausen led his division at midnight over a bridge of boats from Elizabethtown Point to Staten Island. It would turn out to be Britain's last attempt to impose its will on revolutionary New Jersey.

The next day Nathaniel, David Forman and several other militia leaders returned to Springfield to survey the damage done by the enemy. Except for four houses the entire village had been torched.

"Clearly the work of refugees!" growled David Forman, "It is always the same pattern. They destroy or steal everything except the property of friends and relatives. But that is how we find out who their allies are and those are the ones who must pay."

"You certainly are right that we must excise this cancer from our midst," agreed Nathaniel, "I don't understand why the Assembly does not approve our proposal for retaliation. The victims are clearly in urgent need of compensation and the state government cannot or will not provide adequate protection or support. And how else can we discourage Tory depredations?"

"The Assembly is clearly not doing its patriotic duty," continued Forman, "I have circulated our proposal among the people who are most affected by the marauders, and they overwhelmingly support our ideas. Several hundred people have already signed up for the association. That gives us a legitimacy that the Assembly cannot challenge. I say it is time to call our first public meeting, to elect officers and to get on with it."

"Perhaps you are right, and the existence of an efficient Association for Retaliation might change attitudes in the Assembly," said Nathaniel, "But I believe that we certainly have democratic legitimacy, and I will continue to try to convince doubters that this policy can be carried out within the rule of law."

Chapter 24

AND ALL JERUSALEM AND JUDEA MOURNED FOR JOSIAH – 1780–1781

AND SO IT CAME to pass that on the 1ˢᵗ of July, 1780 the first public meeting of the Association for Retaliation was held in Freehold. Many of those who had signed the Articles for Retaliation answered David Forman's call to meet at Monmouth Courthouse, among them most of the leading Whigs of the county.

"I would like to thank all you patriotic Americans who have answered the cries of distress from our brethren who have endured incredible depredations at the hands of Loyalist traitors," Forman began, "We are all facing relentless attacks on many fronts: refugees who are hungering for their lost estates, Pine Robbers who viciously loot and murder innocent settlers at every opportunity, Colonel Tye and his Black Brigade of escaped slaves who seek vengeance against their former owners, the so-called "cowboy" raiders who steal hundreds of horses and cattle from peaceful yeomen, not to mention, of course, the British Army and their hired Hessian murderers. Neither the state nor the federal government has proved capable of protecting us from this long list of enemies. It is high time we take matters into our own hands for the sake of our women and children!"

Loud cheers erupted from the assembled participants.

"But we have shown them all that we have the spirit to fight back!" Forman continued, encouraged by the approbation of the crowd, "At Connecticut Farms and at Springfield we proved that even the overwhelming numerical superiority of the enemy cannot prevail against a united yeomanry. And it is this unity that will be our salvation. Everyone who joins our Association will be protected by our solemn promise to extract retribution for every wrong suffered by any of the members. Let the enemy be aware! We have already 436 signatures on our Articles of Retaliation, 436 people ready to stand up for mutual protection!"

Again the crowd roared its approval. David Forman was soon elected chairman of the new organization by acclamation. He quickly organized the formation of a nine-man board of directors whose mission it was to select targets for retaliation activities. Forman made clear that potential targets were not limited to people directly involved in depredations but could also include friends and relatives of the disaffected. He also cautioned that all internal deliberations of the board should be kept secret so as not to warn the disaffected that they might be targeted. He announced his intention to apply directly to General Washington for permission to execute captured Loyalists who were proven to be aiding the enemy.

As a member of the Board of Directors Nathaniel promised to initiate petitions again to the Assembly to approve the practice of retaliation in general and to sanction the arrest of those disaffected who were notorious in their rejection of the republic.

Returning home after the meeting Nathaniel sought to convince a skeptical Isabella that the plan of action agreed upon by the Board of Directors of the Association for Retaliation would improve security.

"I am afraid that David's strategy will not discourage the raiders," objected Isabella, "Quite the contrary, these acts of retaliation will probably just provoke more revenge attacks."

"That depends on how well-targeted the retaliations are," countered Nathaniel, "If those who are targeted are really helping the enemy, then prosecuting them can only help our cause."

"I also don't think executing captured Loyalists, as David seems to prefer, will reduce violence," continued Isabella, "You mentioned that he is petitioning General Washington for permission to do just that, but many say he has been doing that already. What about that captured Loyalist who died under mysterious circumstances near Colts Neck? Would it not be better to exchange such prisoners for our men in captivity?"

"He was a Loyalist raider named Joseph Wood," replied Nathaniel, "Apparently he had been involved in many crimes against our people. And as far as exchanges are concerned, David thinks that they only encourage more man-stealing."

"But in any case, Wood should have stood trial and been punished under the law," argued Isabella, "I am sure that Joseph Wood has friends or relatives who are just waiting to repay David in kind."

"You are absolutely right that we must see to it that retaliation happens within the bounds of established law," agreed Nathaniel, "That is why it is so important that the Assembly sanction and regulate our procedures."

"Well, I am off to Trenton tomorrow in the hope of finding more effective and less violent ways of supporting our cause," said Isabella, "I am happy to report that every county in New Jersey is sending delegates for the formation of a Women's Relief Society. Ann Forman and I and several others will represent Monmouth County. Perhaps we will find alternative ways to support our troops and the victims of depredations."

"I think that is a wonderful initiative and I will pray for its success," enthused Nathaniel, "In these grave times we cannot leave a stone unturned."

Upon her return a few days later Isabella was full of excitement and optimism as she reported the proceedings of the meeting to Nathaniel.

"I have never witnessed such determination," exclaimed Isabella, "There must have been over a hundred ladies in attendance from all over the state. It was unanimously decided that Mrs. Dickinson, Mrs. Cox, Mrs. Furman, and Mrs. Cadwallader are to form a committee to open subscriptions and to correspond with all the ladies in the various counties. Miss Mary Dagworthy of Trenton will be our secretary who will receive and answer all letters."

Nathaniel was pleased to hear that the wives of such prominent Whigs as General Philemon Dickinson, the commander of the New Jersey militia, and Colonel John Cox, the owner of Batso Forge, were among the leadership. As he surveyed the list of participants that Isabella showed him, he was amazed to see that it included practically every important Whig family in the state.

"It is truly a remarkable network that you ladies have been able to establish," remarked Nathaniel, "It is a heartening show of solidarity for our soldiers. What next steps do you plan?"

"Before we discuss that, I need to tell you about a visit from our son while I was in Trenton. Joseph heard about our meeting from the ladies from Philadelphia and came over to Trenton in the hopes of seeing me."

"Why that is a surprise," replied Nathaniel, "I know that he is very busy at the War Department, so I am pleased he was able to take the time off."

"I think it was a matter of necessity," explained Isabella, "It seems the poor boy has had to go into debt to support himself in Philadelphia. The meager amount that he is paid for his services is worth less and less every day, and no longer suffices for his basic living expenses. He came to ask me for money. I gave him what I could, but I doubt that it was enough to solve the problem."

"He is facing the same problem I did as a congressman," Nathaniel said, "The government's disbursements cannot keep up with the weakening of our currency. I am still owed much but, by the time I get paid, the amount I receive will buy much less than at the time the debt was incurred."

"That is precisely the dilemma that our Relief Society will be facing," Isabella went on, "What good does it do us to organize subscriptions if the money we collect becomes worthless before it can be delivered?"

"That is another reason why many of us see no alternative to retaliation. Our currency is weak because the disaffected will only accept it, if at all, at huge discounts. They prefer to hoard sterling and Spanish dollars that they earn through the London Trade. When we retaliate, we confiscate things like livestock and real estate that do not deteriorate in value, not to mention the hard currency that are the ill-gotten gains through the London Trade. With retaliation we are able to compensate the victims of depredations with lasting value."

"Unfortunately, we cannot use such funds to compensate Joseph for the declining purchasing power of his government salary even if you can get the Assembly to agree to the practice."

"That is certainly true," agreed Nathaniel, "We need to do more to preserve the value of our money. I will write to Joseph and tell him about recent developments that may alleviate the situation."

"What recent developments did you have in mind?" asked Isabella.

"David Forman reports unusual activity by enemy marines in Sandy Hook Bay." replied Nathaniel.

"Hopefully they are not planning another attack into New Jersey!" exclaimed Isabella.

"No, not this time," assured Nathaniel, "It seems that they have sunk their vessels to obstruct the channel. That can only mean that they fear the imminent arrival of the French fleet. It could be the beginning of the end of the British occupation of New York. That would restore confidence in our struggle and in our currency."

"Even if the fear of the French fleet is only enough to discourage another invasion, that is reason enough to be thankful to God," sighed Isabella with relief.

Over the next few days, the intense desire on the part of the Whigs to greet the French fleet resulted in many accounts of its appearance, all of which turned out to be false. Nathaniel met frequently with David Forman to find out if any of the rumors were substantiated.

"Not so far," informed Forman, "The Brits are certainly very nervous but neither our lookouts on the shore nor our privateers have spotted any French ships. We must assume that for the time being we will have to provide for our own defense. And that means rooting out the traitors who live in our midst. I don't think the British Regulars will attempt another foray into New Jersey, but the refugees remain a constant danger."

"Perhaps the news of the formation of the Association for Retaliation will make them think twice before launching new raids," ventured Nathaniel, "The incursions seemed to have slackened in the last few weeks."

"Let's hope so," replied Forman, "But I have received intelligence from New York that our erstwhile governor has formed a so-called Board of Associated Loyalists and is now negotiating with General Clinton for a broad mandate to organize all disaffected elements against us. Clinton is wary about giving too much power to vengeful refugees whose actions tend to motivate the rebellion. But the British government thinks that an uprising of loyal American subjects can still save the day. And William Franklin is known to believe that the British army is not suppressing the rebellion with sufficient energy. I think we can assume that this new organization will be giving us a lot of trouble."

"All the more reason we must pursue retaliation with extreme vigor," concluded Nathaniel, "I can understand that many worry that this mode of operations risks abuse that could undermine the rule of law but given the injuries our people suffer,

I don't see that we have any other choice. I will write to Henry Laurens and explain our situation here so that members of Congress understand the threats we are facing."

"Many in Congress and the Assembly keep rattling on about the rule of law," Forman continued, "But does anyone think that the Associated Loyalists are going to adhere to the rule of law? Under Franklin's guidance the murders, depredations, and kidnappings by the refugees with help from the disaffected can only increase. Defending ourselves through retaliation is clearly a necessity."

"And necessity has no law," Nathaniel agreed, "Except the lex talionis—an eye for an eye, and a tooth for a tooth."

A few weeks later Nathaniel was confronted with some of the practical difficulties in dealing with Loyalist refugees. A letter arrived from Lieutenant Thomas Cook, a Monmouth militia officer taken prisoner during a Loyalist raid and detained on Long Island. He reported that a Loyalist prisoner, Lewis Thomson, had been sent to effect an exchange for him but had failed. Nathaniel decided to read the letter to Isabella to illustrate some of the problems involved with the issue of exchanges.

"But why did the exchange fail?" asked Isabella after hearing the contents of the letter.

"Probably because Lewis Thomson was not considered by the enemy to be the equivalent of Thomas Cook," explained Nathaniel, "Thomson claimed he was a lieutenant in one of the refugee corps but that was probably an exaggeration. He had been taken prisoner by Major John Cook who is Thomas Cook's brother who was understandably all too anxious to get his brother freed. Now John Cook has a reason to capture a higher-ranking refugee to exchange for his brother. This illustrates how exchanges can encourage further man-stealing on both sides."

"But how should exchanges be conducted?" asked Isabella, "Surely we cannot just let our poor soldiers rot in the hands of the enemy!"

"This is indeed a difficult question," replied Nathaniel, "Exchanges are officially conducted at Elizabethtown via a formal cartel between the armies. The equivalences of the exchangees are carefully investigated with an eye to discouraging private account settling. The problem is that numerous other exchanges are conducted unofficially between Monmouth County leaders and New Jersey Loyalist refugees living behind British lines in New York. These unofficial prisoner exchanges in the opinion of David Forman and many of our board members just encourage additional Loyalist kidnappings."

Isabella nodded thoughtfully considering what was for her a new aspect of the fraught issue.

"I can certainly understand that kidnappings will encourage other kidnappings," mused Isabella, "I can agree with David Forman about that, but I am afraid that his policy of retaliation will do the same."

"There is that danger," conceded Nathaniel, "That is why it is important that retaliation be given a formal legal framework by the Assembly. Retaliation must be a clear and accurate response to crimes that have been perpetrated against us. But the punishment for such crimes will be attenuated if perpetrators can hope to evade justice through exchanges. That is why restricting exchanges is the agreed policy of the Retaliator Board of Directors."

Within days of this conversation the policy was to be severely tested. A small Loyalist raiding party from Sandy Hook managed to slip past the militia defenders and capture Hendrick Smock and his brother, John. Hendrick Smock was not only a prominent Whig militia officer but also a member of the Retaliator Board of Directors. The Loyalists had deliberately targeted Hendrick to create dissension among the Retaliator leadership. The ploy worked as planned: Colonel Asher Holmes, a close associate of the Smocks immediately paroled captured Loyalist John Williams to go to New York to negotiate an exchange. This resulted in tumultuous discussions at the next meeting of the board.

"This is outrageous!" shouted David Forman, "How dare Holmes do this without consulting us?"

"He should have consulted us first," agreed Nathaniel, "But I can understand his concern for the Smocks. Not only Hendrick and John are now in enemy prisons. but also their other brother, Barnes, who was captured some time ago. The Smocks are some of our most important supporters among the Whigs of the shore townships, where, as you well know, many disaffected live."

"But the people in the shore townships are precisely the ones most endangered by kidnappers!" exclaimed Forman, "They must understand that exchanges only increase that danger."

Reverend John Woodhull whose role was that of a chaplain to the board attempted to steer the discussion in a more conciliatory direction, "The logic of your argument is impeccable, David, but we cannot deny the realities of human nature. If a loved one or dear friend winds up in captivity, it is only natural that any possibility to free him will be tempting."

"We all are called upon to make sacrifices for the cause," replied Forman vehemently, "Who, where and when is a matter of chance, but we cannot let sentimentality cloud our reasoning. The fact of the matter is that unofficial exchanges increase the likelihood of man-stealing."

At that moment John Covenhoven, considered to be the elder statesman of the board, proposed a resolution, "Let us send an official communication to Asher Holmes reminding him that our policy is for very good reasons to limit exchanges but that we would like to hear his side of the argument."

"Very well," agreed Forman, "I will send him a note requesting that he attend our next meeting and explain himself."

Weeks passed with no response from Asher Holmes. At the next board meeting David Forman was apoplectic.

"We cannot let him get away with this!" he shouted, "If militia officers can just ignore our decisions at will, we will never get our security situation under control. I say we petition the governor to have Holmes arrested!"

"I cannot imagine that Governor Livingston is likely to entertain such a suggestion," Nathaniel attempted to calm Forman down, "Asher Holmes is a brave and loyal officer who has done much for our struggle. The state is not going to arrest him based on a difference of opinion about how exchanges should be handled."

"The decisions of our board are also not binding law," added John Covenhoven, "If we want to see our decisions respected, we must seek proper authority from the Assembly to practice retaliation."

"I suggest we make another petition to the Assembly explaining our urgent needs," suggested Reverend Woodhull.

"How many more petitions should we make?" snarled Forman, "The Assembly is enthralled by certain wealthy landowners and financiers who have suspicious links to dissident elements. That is why they have blocked us in the past. And those are precisely the people that retaliation should be aimed at."

"I think we have more convincing arguments than the last time we petitioned," replied Nathaniel, "The Associated Loyalists led by William Franklin are a new threat to the well-being of our Whig patriots. We have some reason to believe that the existence of the Association for Retaliation has already provided a disincentive for raiders. The Assembly should not be deceived by the denunciations of us by the disaffected. Of course, they are against us but the Assembly should be representing us and not those traitors."

"I agree that a new petition might be effective," agreed John Covenhoven, "I think it would be possible to get most of the leading citizens of Monmouth to sign it."

"I suggest that Nathaniel Scudder and Thomas Henderson present it to the Assembly. They are both highly regarded as morally upright Christians with no designs for personal gains," added Covenhoven with a sidelong glance at Forman.

"Do what you think you must," growled Forman, "I think it is a waste of time, but I won't diminish your chances by signing the petition myself. What I will do, however, is issue an executive order stating our position on exchanges and inviting Holmes once more to explain himself."

True to his word Forman dispatched Retaliator Committee Order No.16 to all militia leaders stating unequivocally the case against unregulated exchanges and again demanding an explanation from Asher Holmes. At the same time Forman wrote to General Washington explaining how exchanges encourage man-stealing.

As Nathaniel and Thomas Henderson worked diligently to prepare a convincing petition for the Assembly, the controversy over the confiscation of dissident property escalated again as a result of a new court decision. The New Jersey Supreme Court overturned the judgement of Monmouth Judge John Anderson that the confiscation several years ago of contraband owned by John Holmes and Solomon Ketcham by militia Major Elisha Walton had been legal. Although there was little doubt that the contraband had been procured illegally behind enemy lines, the conviction was based on the verdict of a six-man jury. The attorney for the defense argued successfully that the constitution called for a twelve-man jury and that, therefore, the basis for the conviction was unconstitutional.

At the next meeting of the Retaliator Committee David Forman reacted predictably.

"Can there be any doubt that our procedures for dealing with traitors are inadequate?" he shouted, "Under the current statutes legal weasels can always find a way to help their clients slither out of our hands. Everybody knows that Holmes and Ketcham were transporting silk and other expensive merchandise they could only have bought behind enemy lines. Letting them off on such a technicality is a miscarriage of justice!"

"I tend to agree," said Nathaniel, "That is why it is so important that we convince the Assembly that more robust guidelines are necessary to protect our people and reimburse them for the depredations they suffer. Thomas and I have been granted an audience with the Assembly at the end of this month. We will do our best to make them see the light."

"I wish you every success, Nathaniel," replied Forman, "But I am convinced that some with influence in the Assembly are secretly on the side of the enemy. But that will not save them from my avengers!"

Nathaniel silently hoped to himself that Forman's "avengers" did not go to such extremes as to prejudice the Assembly against the whole concept of retaliation.

"Very well, David, but I suggest we hear the concerns of some of those who oppose retaliation and see if we can find common ground. After all, we all share the goal of protecting our loyal citizens from depredations."

A few weeks later Nathaniel and Thomas Henderson were satisfied that they had sufficiently convincing arguments to present in their petition. They took pains to emphasize that retaliation should primarily be seen as a deterrent to would-be raiders and would be constrained by whatever procedures the Assembly should care to impose. No innocent neutrals need fear for their rights. They had managed to formulate their proposal in such reasonable terms as to convince 69 high-ranking Monmouthers to sign the petition as well. To everyone's relief David Forman did not sign it in order not to provoke his many enemies in the Assembly.

The hearing in front of the Assembly went well. After Nathaniel and Thomas Henderson rested their case, a committee was appointed to consider the matter and issue a report. Nathaniel felt fairly confident that an agreement was within reach.

Two days later, however, a petition reached the Assembly from one Joseph Salter, a well-connected creditor and large landholder from Dover Township. Salter alleged that henchmen of David Forman had attacked him and his associate, John Hartshorne, and brutally threatened to confiscate their property to compensate victims of

Loyalist raids. Although Salter's son had come out as a Loyalist, there was no evidence of any illegal activity by either Salter himself or Hartshorne. Since Salter was a close business associate of several important assemblymen, his petition was taken very seriously. Even those who were not in principle opposed to the strategy of retaliation were aggravated to find that Forman's men were not waiting for the Assembly to reach a decision. The result was a stinging defeat for the Monmouth petition.

A few days later the leading proponents of the petition met at Nathaniel's home to discuss the report issued by the Assembly's committee.

"I am afraid the Assembly has not only turned down our petition," Nathaniel announced, "But also denounced the acts of retaliation that we have practiced recently as illegal vigilantism."

"I am not surprised," growled David Forman, "It just goes to show you how many covert Tory sympathizers there are in the Assembly. Everyone knows that Salter's son is an admitted Loyalist, but no one wants to alienate a rich financier."

"I thought we had been successful in convincing the committee of the righteousness of our cause," began Thomas Henderson, "But then Salter brought in his story about how James Green and his men broke into his home like common thieves and seized several items of furniture."

"James Green is a captain in our militia and was acting under my orders!" exclaimed David Forman, "He was quite legitimately extracting compensation for depredations carried out by Salter's son."

"What is legitimate or not is decided by the Assembly," countered Nathaniel waving a copy of the committee's report, "And in this case they denounced us, and I quote, as 'an illegal and dangerous combination, utterly subversive to the law, highly dangerous to the government, immediately tending to create disunion among the inhabitants, directly leading toward anarchy and confusion, and tending to the dissolution of the constitution and government' unquote."

"Oh my Lord," gasped Isabella, "They have essentially branded you as outlaws. Are you in danger of being arrested?"

"As a matter of fact, Assemblyman James Mott tried to get us explicitly outlawed," replied Nathaniel, "Fortunately his motion lost 11 to 14. The report concludes by admonishing us to adhere to existing legislation and requesting the governor to provide us with more militia support."

"That bastard Mott is just the kind of Tory sympathizer I was talking about," exclaimed Forman, "He is typical of those weasels from the shore villages who want to go easy on dissidents so as not to disrupt their London Trade. He should not be representing Monmouth County in the Assembly."

"Well, Thomas Henderson, Thomas Seabrook and I are running for the Assembly in next week's election," Nathaniel continued, "If we are lucky, perhaps Monmouth County will have different representation in the Assembly next year."

"I will certainly do what I can to make sure you are successful," promised Forman, "We desperately need people in the Assembly who understand our plight and do not secretly hope for an enemy victory. The Assembly must also understand that we need a firm policy of discouraging unofficial exchanges. The people from the shore villages do not seem to understand that those practices only encourage more man-stealing. That is another reason why people like James Mott should not represent Monmouth County in the legislature."

"I am sure that Nathaniel, if elected, will represent the interests of all Monmouth County residents fairly," assured Isabella, "including the legitimate concerns of shore residents, many of whom like Hendrick Smock and Asher Holmes have nobly served our cause."

"I will personally organize the polling next week at Monmouth Courthouse," announced David Forman, "We must see to it that dissident elements from the shore villages are not able to disrupt the voting."

Over the next few days Forman sent messages to his network of militia officers instructing them to make certain all militiamen loyal to the strategy of retaliation were able to get to Monmouth Courthouse and vote as early as possible for the Scudder-Henderson-Seabrook ticket. As an elder in the Presbyterian congregation, Nathaniel was able to spread the word quite effectively among adherents of the True Religion. On the Sunday before the election Presbyterian parsons all over Monmouth County admonished their parishioners to be certain to vote for their co-religionists in the upcoming election as the protection of their lives and property depended on it.

On election day Nathaniel hurried to the courthouse early and was delighted to see a long line waiting to vote. He was encouraged by the many familiar faces he recognized including most of the people who had signed his petition to the Assembly in September. Inside the courthouse he was impressed by the efficient operation that David Forman had organized including several clerks and a sergeant-at-arms. Behind the clerks were seats for the candidates where Nathaniel sat down next to Thomas Henderson, Thomas Seabrook, and one of the current incumbents, James Mott. Mott had attempted to get the Retaliators outlawed, and upon taking his seat declared loudly that he intended to see to it that the election was conducted fairly.

"Our appointed officials here will see to that," replied Forman through clenched teeth, "And anyone disrupting our procedures will be dealt with harshly by our sergeant-at-arms."

The voting proceeded rapidly without problems throughout the morning. By the mid-afternoon all the early arrivals had voted, and the arrival of new voters slowed to a trickle.

"At this rate we won't need a second day of voting," announced David Forman, "By this evening everyone who is eligible and willing to vote will have done so."

"We always have kept the polls open for a second day to allow shore residents time to get here and vote!" Mott exclaimed, jumping up from his chair. Rushing across the room to confront Forman face to face he shouted, "You are not running a free and fair election!"

"We are obliged to keep the polls open only as long as voters continue to arrive," countered Forman, "We have already had heavy turnout and can assume that everyone will have had their chance by this evening. Everyone who appeared today was able to cast his vote for any candidate he chose. If so few of your supporters showed up, maybe that has to do with your traitorous attempt to outlaw a patriotic organization!"

"You are calling me a traitor!" screamed Mott in exasperation, "You are the traitor to our constitution and the rule of law!"

At that point Forman backhanded Mott in the face so hard that he fell to the floor. As he tried to scramble to his knees, Forman kicked him in the behind multiple times driving him in the direction of the door. Reaching the door Mott got to his feet, ran out to where his horse was tethered and galloped away.

"David!" exclaimed Nathaniel, "Get a grip on yourself. Mott is our political opponent, but he is still a member of the Assembly. You have just given him an excuse to contest the legitimacy of this election."

"That is the kind of treatment that Tory-sympathizers deserve," snarled Forman, "I will not tolerate anyone calling this election unfair. Everyone who arrived today was able to vote however he wanted. I am responsible for the safety of the poll, and I see no reason to expose our officials for another day to possible Loyalist disruptions."

"That is a fair argument," agreed Nathaniel, "But it should not have come to fisticuffs."

"I know, I know," conceded Forman reluctantly, "But I just can't abide Tory duplicity. People like Mott rile me at their peril."

James Mott had good reason not to be satisfied with the outcome of the election. After the polls closed that evening, it emerged that the Scudder-Henderson-Seabrook team would be the sole representatives of Monmouth County in the Assembly. The Whigs of the shore villages would no longer have any delegates.

Nathaniel decided to begin his term of office with visits to Trenton and Philadelphia to plead the cause of retaliation and to beg for more supplies to strengthen the militia on the front. Before leaving he commissioned David Forman to survey the militia units to determine how much support was still needed and to send this information to him in Philadelphia. Nathaniel asked Thomas Henderson to accompany him in the hope that two pious physicians would be best able to convince both congressmen and assemblymen of the righteousness of their cause.

Just a few days after their arrival in Philadelphia Nathaniel was pleased to greet an express rider sent by David Forman. Nathaniel quickly opened the letter and read it aloud to Thomas Henderson:

"We have this minute an account from a deserter that left Staten Island that 300 Tories under Colonel John Simcoe will land at Amboy. This naturally produced an inquiry into our state's ammunition—Captain Anderson, who commands the company of six-month men at Shrewsbury has six cartridges per man, and that Colonel Holmes has no cartridges to give him—I inquired if there were any cartridges in the magazine at this place—found there was not one—the ammunition that was sent for Colonel Samuel Forman's Regiment I have myself delivered at different times to the troops on duty. Hendrickson's militia has 40 dozen cartridges only. This is our present situation— a frontier county, at all times exposed to incursion, now immediately threatened, with not but a dozen cartridges to be given out."

"That is incredible!" exclaimed Henderson, "It is even worse than we expected."

"Without adequate ammunition even our bravest militia units will be forced to retreat before the enemy," predicted Nathaniel, "We must hurry to Trenton and inform Governor Livingston that we are in dire need of support to fend off an imminent invasion."

In Trenton they found Governor Livingston more than willing to receive them and hear their complaints.

"I am already informed about your predicament," Livingston greeted his visitors, "I have recently received a memorial from Colonel Asher Holmes and was shocked to read that the troops under his command have received no pay since their entering the service."

"Without pay and without ammunition we expect these young farmers to turn back an invasion of the world's most professional army," said Nathaniel bitterly, "The Assembly has denounced our plans for retaliation but how else can we protect ourselves and finance our rebellion?"

"I understand the frustration of the good patriots of Monmouth," replied Livingston, "And the Assembly has acted swiftly to help. I am pleased to tell you that a bill has just been passed authorizing me to provide you with 8,000 cartridges and 1,000 flints for immediate dispatch to Monmouth. A wagon has already been loaded and equipped. One of my servants will accompany you to Freehold and drive the wagon. We will also provide you with several armed guards to make certain that the munitions don't fall into the wrong hands on the way."

"That is very prescient of you, sir," remarked Nathaniel, "David Forman has warned that more Loyalist raids are imminent."

"David Forman sees a Tory sympathizer behind every tree," warned Livingston, "I appreciate his devotion to our cause but his confrontational approach risks splitting our Whig movement. Not everyone who disagrees with his policies is a secret Loyalist. The bill authorizing the munitions, for example, passed 27 to 2. That is a clear indication that an overwhelming number of legislators are truly loyal to our cause. We must see to it that we don't alienate the moderate elements in the electorate who take a more conciliatory approach toward dealing with their neighbors. I have heard, for example, that many moderate Whigs from the shore villages are complaining that the recent election in Monmouth was not free and fair."

"That is an exaggeration," replied Nathaniel, "The balloting was limited to a single day which one person objected to but everyone who appeared was able to cast his ballot as he saw fit. Regarding David Forman, we all know that he can be impulsive at times but there is no more loyal defender of our cause than he. He has his doubts about the motivation of some of our assemblymen, but I think that the impressive swiftness of the Assembly's assistance might help to change his mind."

Nathaniel and Thomas Henderson hurried back to Freehold to deliver the munitions and to inform the Freehold Whigs of the Assembly's demonstration of solidarity. As usual, Forman was not impressed.

"Of course, no one dares to openly oppose supplying us with munitions in the face of imminent invasion," argued Forman, "But there are many in the Assembly who prize their business relationships with the shore villages because that's where the hard currency is. And how do you think that the shore merchants have acquired such currency?"

"There is, of course, the suspicion that some part of it comes from the London Trade," conceded Nathaniel, "But we cannot prosecute people merely based on suspicions. There are also legitimate ways to acquire hard currency and, as Governor Livingston pointed out, we must not swell the ranks of our enemies by alienating Whig allies who favor a less aggressive approach. In those cases where we can find proof that someone is indulging in the London Trade, no one could object to confiscations to benefit the victims of Tory depredations."

"There will always be objections because someone is always profiting directly or indirectly and is reluctant to see the end of the gravy train," asserted Forman, "But my spies keep a close watch on movements of goods in the shore communities and they have noticed that large quantities of provisions are collecting near the front lines in the townships of Shrewsbury and Middletown. Anyone offering to purchase items with continental currency is turned away. As the depots deplete over time, they are periodically restocked. Anyone with half an eye can see that the purpose of these depots is to supply enemies of the United States."

"That is shocking, indeed," agreed Nathaniel, "Even if some are not intentionally supplying the enemy, it is dangerous to store important provisions so close to enemy lines where it could be taken in a raid. Perhaps we could convince a majority of the Assembly that such important stores should be removed inland for their protection. We could issue certificates to the owners of the seized materials to calm fears of unfair confiscations. Those not cooperating with the enemy would then not have to worry about the loss of their property."

"That is a clever plan, Nathaniel," Forman enthused, "It might even make it through the Assembly because nobody is in immediate danger of having their property confiscated, and voting against it would seem like aiding the enemy."

Nathaniel Scudder, Thomas Henderson and Thomas Seabrook presented their case to the Assembly not in terms of punishing London Traders but rather as a security measure to protect private property from the enemy. It passed 18 to 8. Major Elisha Walton was authorized to call up 100 militiamen as speedily as possible and remove every article of provision or supply that can be spared from the necessities of the inhabitants and bring the seized items from the shore. David Forman was delighted to offer some of his militia units to assist the operation.

The leading Whigs of Freehold met at Monmouth Courthouse to congratulate their assemblymen for their achievement and to discuss the next steps.

"Nathaniel, that was a brilliant way to get the Assembly to agree to let us confiscate the property of those Tory bastards," praised David Forman.

"We are not confiscating it," corrected Nathaniel, "We are merely storing it in a place safer from enemy depredations. Rightful owners not trading with the enemy have nothing to fear. They can also sell their goods to our quartermaster general."

"A fat chance they will take payment in our currency," sneered Forman, "They are used to getting paid in sterling. I say refusal to take our currency is proof enough of complicity with the enemy, a charge which justifies confiscation."

"I don't think we would find a majority in the Assembly to agree with that," cautioned Nathaniel, "But I do think there is a case to be made for allowing county contractors to impress forage and wagons to supply the army. After all, the owners will be fairly compensated, the enemy weakened, and our troops strengthened."

"I would go a step further," Thomas Henderson added, "If the Assembly does not want us to practice retaliation, they must at least make it easier for us to seize the goods of suspected contraband traders. If we need a 12-man jury to prosecute notorious contraband merchants, the most blatant crimes will go unpunished. If people are caught in flagrante indulging in the London Trade, one should not need a court order to seize the contraband."

"A very good point," agreed David Forman, "And one that few in the Assembly could dispute. After all no one would want to publicly protect contraband traders even if secretly in league with them. I would also add another item for our legislative team. We need to get the Assembly to officially suspend prisoner exchanges because they only encourage more man-stealing. Asher Holmes continues to defy our recommendations by trying to effect an exchange for Hendrick Smock and others of his political allies."

"I would like to make a suggestion as well." John Covenhoven, a respected elderly stateman known to be on good terms with Asher Holmes and the Smock family but whose loyalty to the Whig cause was acknowledged by all, raised his hand: "I agree we must prosecute contraband traders, but we cannot forget that there are understandable reasons why many merchants are reluctant to accept our currency for their wares. Defending the value of our currency is the best way to counter the London Trade. I, therefore, suggest that our trusted representatives analyze the problems of our currency and suggest solutions."

David Forman rolled his eyes indicating intense frustration with what he considered to be the ultimate naivete. Nathaniel, however, was glad to have the opportunity to reach out to opposing factions within the Whig electorate.

"I think that is an excellent suggestion, John. When I visited Governor Livingston a few weeks ago, he mentioned that Asher Holmes had informed him that his men had not been paid since their enlistment. That pay is not only overdue but needs to be recalculated to account for the weakening of our currency. I know that Reverend James Caldwell has been keeping careful account of the purchasing power of the state's currency for the Assembly. I will discuss this matter with him and produce a report for re-appraising the pay scales of our militia."

The meeting ended in broad agreement about the legislative strategy to be pursued by the Monmouth delegation. Bolstered by the consensus reached, Nathaniel Scudder, Thomas Henderson, and Thomas Seabrook were successful in convincing the Assembly of the urgency of the proposed measures. Although there was some concern that involuntary impressment of forage and wagons for the army could damage private property rights, the bill authorizing it still passed 15 to 14. A bill simplifying the seizure of contraband had a much easier time, passing 26 to 3. As David Forman correctly predicted, no one wanted to publicly stand up for contraband traders.

Energized by the legislative successes of the Monmouth delegation, Nathaniel delved enthusiastically into the problem of currency depreciation. Isabella had long complained that the value of the donations that her Ladies' Association were able to organize melted away before they could be put to use. Here was Nathaniel's opportunity to get to the bottom of the mystery. Together with the punctilious Bible scholar, Reverend Caldwell, Nathaniel analyzed the purchasing records of the state quartermaster corps. What they documented was frightening. Taking 1777 as the base year, they found that a year later a dollar bought only one fourth of what it had a year earlier. In subsequent years the purchasing power continued to decline at an accelerating rate so that the ratio now seemed to be about 1 to 60. It was clear why merchants were so reluctant to accept state currency, but it was less clear about what could be done about it. Perhaps David Forman was correct that the only way to compensate the victims of depredations was with real property confiscated from enemy sympathizers.

That particular strategy continued to provoke energetic political opposition, however. When Nathaniel and Reverend Caldwell appeared before the Assembly to argue for an increase in the wages of the militia, they were confronted with a petition signed by 15 prominent Monmouth residents denouncing the illegal confiscations being carried out by the Committee of Retaliation. Nathaniel was able to use the statistics that he and Reverend Caldwell had developed to argue that retaliation was the only feasible way to compensate the victims of depredations. He regretted that the practice might sometimes be abused but urged the Assembly to alleviate that by making and enforcing fair guidelines. He railed eloquently against the evil practice of man-stealing and argued that retaliation, not exchanges, was the way to deter it.

Nathaniel's arguments achieved at least partial success. Although official approval of the practice of retaliation was not forthcoming, on the 6th of January, 1781 the Assembly ordered the Commissary of Prisoners to suspend prisoner exchanges. The Associated Loyalists had tried to force an exchange by placing three Monmouth prisoners, Hendrick Smock, Hendrick Johnson and John Tanner, in irons. The Assembly defied the move, however, by placing three Loyalist prisoners in irons.

"At last the Assembly seems to begin to understand our plight," Nathaniel was pleased to report back to his Monmouth Whig colleagues, "Perhaps we can now put an end to uncontrolled exchanges and reduce the incentives for man-stealing."

"We will see if they are capable of enforcing their own decrees," replied David Forman skeptically, "I have heard rumors that Asher Holmes continues to seek a possible exchange ignoring the wishes of the Assembly."

"Holmes is a brave patriot, and his militia units are an important part of our defenses. It is unlikely that the Assembly would authorize vigorous measures against him," Nathaniel sought to explain the reluctance of the Assembly to force the issue, "And, besides, many of the more moderate of our Whig brethren are quite sympathetic toward his aims."

"Our moderate Whig brethren include many who would shield Loyalist scum from their just deserts," retorted Forman, "And those are the ones we have to unmask!"

Forman's suspicions of conspiratorial machinations among the moderate Whigs were confirmed a few weeks later when Asher Holmes succeeded in arranging an exchange with Clayton Tilton of the Associated Loyalists to free Hendrick Smock, Hendrick Johnson, and John Tanner. Upon learning that Smock, Johnson, and Tanner had been allowed to return to their homes, Forman, livid with rage, rushed to the Scudder residence to report to Nathaniel what he saw as ultimate treachery.

"You referred to Holmes as a brave patriot!" exclaimed Forman, "What kind of a patriot completely ignores a decree of the Assembly meant to deter man-stealing."

Isabella could not resist the temptation to remind Forman of some of his own differences with the legislature. "Well, David, have you not yourself had occasion to ignore some decrees of the Assembly," she asked archly.

"Never when the safety of our loyal citizens was at stake," retorted Forman, "The freeing of Smock, Johnson, and Tanner will just result in the kidnapping of others. The only way to stop it is to make it no longer worthwhile by refusing exchanges and by confiscating the property of the friends and relatives of the kidnappers."

"I agree in principle," concurred Nathaniel, "But I also understand Asher Holmes' concern for his brothers-in-arms. Hendrick Smock was also a colleague of ours on the Board of the Retaliators. People like him are important if we want to maintain the unity of our movement."

"Don't have any illusions about Whig unity," warned Forman, "People like Asher Holmes and James Mott are our enemies and will stop at nothing to discredit us and our strategy. I have heard, for example, that Holmes has been gathering evidence to fault you personally as a traitor to our cause."

"That is outrageous!" exclaimed Isabella, "Everyone knows that Nathaniel has given his complete support from the very beginning and, unlike many, has rejected every opportunity to profit from the war."

"Of course, he has," agreed Forman, "But Holmes has deposed a suspicious character named Peter Talman who claims that Nathaniel helped to free the Loyalist William Taylor from confinement in Philadelphia in 1776 to win favor with the enemy in case the revolution should fail."

"As a matter of fact, I did recommend back then that William Taylor along with several other Monmouth Loyalists be set free," admitted Nathaniel, "At that time I hoped that parts of the Taylor family might still be won back over to our cause which they once supported. It might have been a naive supposition, but I expected no benefit for myself."

"It is horrible how easily unfounded allegations can result in character defamation," complained Isabella, "I have witnessed how this happened to Richard Stockton who has sacrificed more for our cause than most. By the way, I received a note from Annis today. Richard is in a very bad way. His doctors say he has not much longer to live."

"I am not surprised," replied Nathaniel, "His cancer is incurable, and he is very much weakened by the imprisonment and torture he has endured. I will ride to Princeton and bid him farewell. He is a long-serving trustee of the college, and his death will be a great loss for Reverend Witherspoon just as he is trying to get the college up and running again."

"I will go with you," announced Isabella, "Annis is a dear friend, and I am sure she is very distraught. She has endured so much in the last months."

The next day Nathaniel and Isabella left for Princeton. Isabella was deeply depressed by the impending demise of their old friend. For much of the journey she stared silently out of the carriage window. Turning finally to Nathaniel she murmured, "Such a brilliant man, such a loss to our country and our cause."

"Indeed," agreed Nathaniel, "But his sacrifices were not in vain. Today is the 1st of March and the Articles of Confederation come into effect. The United States of America now officially exists. He suffered greatly for attaching his signature to the Declaration of Independence back in '76 but what that document promised has been achieved. We are now a confederated nation, and we will prevail. Richard leaves an enduring legacy and that is surely a consolation for him in his final days."

Arriving at Morven the Scudders were dismayed to see a casket being carried out by servants to a waiting wagon and Annis Stockton clad in black directing their efforts. Isabella jumped out of the carriage and ran to embrace Annis.

"Oh Annis," cried Isabella, "I am so sorry that we arrive too late to bid farewell to Richard."

"He was in terrible pain," replied Annis stoically, "He passed away yesterday. The Lord in His mercy decided to relieve his suffering. President Witherspoon has suggested that he be taken to Nassau Hall to lie there in state for a time before being buried in the Quaker cemetery in Stony Brook. His parents and grandparents are buried there, and it was his dying wish to be laid to rest beside them. Reverend Smith, President Witherspoon's son-in-law, has kindly offered to deliver the eulogy."

At a nod from Annis the driver of the wagon carrying the casket urged the horses on to move slowly in the direction of Nassau Hall. Isabella and Nathaniel fell in with Annis walking behind the wagon. Grieving town folk lined the half-mile stretch of road leading to the college. Arriving on campus Nathaniel was surprised to see that a relatively large group of mourners had already gathered. President Witherspoon with his students and tutors, Reverend Smith, Reverend Caldwell, and several board members waited solemnly on the front lawn to greet the procession. The wagon pulled up in front of the entrance. Four servants carefully carried the casket inside the building and placed it on a platform in the main auditorium. The mourners filed in and took up positions surrounding the casket. After a moment of silence Reverend Dr. Samuel Smith strode to the casket and turned to face the group.

""The remains of a man who hath been long among the foremost of his country, for power, for wisdom, and for fortune," he began, "and who, if what honors this young country can bestow, if many and great personal talents, could save man from the grave, would not thus have been lamented here by you. Behold here 'the end of all perfection.'"

Annis stifled a sob as Isabella pressed her hand in consolation.

Reverend Smith went on to detail Richard Stockton's many achievements, his integrity and service to the nation. At the conclusion of the eulogy President Witherspoon signaled discreetly to Nathaniel and Reverend Caldwell that he needed to discuss some urgent matters with them.

Isabella took the opportunity to proffer her assistance to Annis.

"Annis, my dear, this has been a terrible day for you. Let me accompany you home. I have brought some of Nathaniel's tonic with me. It will help you relax."

After Annis and Isabella departed, Nathaniel, James Caldwell, and Samuel Smith went with President Witherspoon to what was left of his office. On the way Witherspoon pointed out the damages done to various parts of the building during the occupation.

"There is a lot that needs repair," he explained, "But unfortunately our troubles did not end with the British evacuation. The State continues to quarter troops here in rooms we need for students. We have made a good start in getting the college up and running again. We have six young gentlemen that will be receiving their degrees in September. But we need more space to educate enough students to generate sufficient revenue to pay the staff. And we need contributions to rebuild what has been destroyed."

Arriving in President Witherspoon's office the men could see firsthand one of the major losses: Witherspoon's formerly impressive library was empty of books.

"For the last few years Reverend Caldwell has been generously performing the tasks of Clerk of the Board in addition to soliciting funds for us. He has made a detailed analysis of our situation," Witherspoon began, "And I would like to share some of the details with you in preparation for our next board meeting which I hope will be in May. Reverend, perhaps you could give Dr. Scudder a summary of your findings."

"As you know from the report we recently presented together to the Assembly, the value of our country's currency continues to plummet dramatically," began James Caldwell. "Although President Witherspoon has accepted his salary in local currency over the last two years, it is clearly not feasible to continue on that basis since a growing number of merchants will only accept payment in hard currencies. The salaries necessary to support the president and the professors amount to six hundred pounds a year. It was originally agreed that at least two-thirds of this sum, if not the whole of the six hundred pounds, were to be payable in coin and not in the currency of the time."

"In that case we must specify that the tuition fees also be paid in coin," Nathaniel suggested.

"Indeed," agreed Caldwell, "But even then, the income from that source would not suffice to cover the salary costs, let alone pay for the urgently needed repairs to Nassau Hall. We must find new sources of income, perhaps a surcharge in addition to tuition to finance the renovation."

"The way I see it," opined Witherspoon, "We must be careful not to make the course of study so expensive that the parents of pious students can no longer afford it. We need to cast our net wider. We must convince our religious brethren far and wide of the vital and urgent need for our mission. The United States of America is now a confederated nation, and it needs leaders who understand what we are fighting for in this epic struggle. Guided by people like our noble colleague, Richard Stockton, the college has been at the forefront of the independence movement from the very beginning. We have a sacred duty to produce more men of his caliber."

As Nathaniel listened to Witherspoon's eloquent argumentation, he contemplated the empty shelves which once held an outstanding library. It symbolized for him the vicious and wanton destruction that the enemy had wrought and confirmed once again the mortal danger an enemy victory would pose to religious and intellectual freedom.

"President Witherspoon," he began, "I could not agree with you more. The struggle to rebuild the college is as important as any other battle that we face. When our army was starving in Valley Forge and in Morristown our brethren rose to the occasion. We must convince them that saving the college now is just as important. And regarding the quartering of troops in Nassau Hall, if the Board gives me official authorization, I would be pleased to make a formal request to the Assembly to end that practice."

"And I will notify our Presbyterian brethren that we are again in urgent need of their Christian charity," added James Caldwell.

"Dr. Scudder, Reverend Caldwell I am grateful to both of you for your assistance and support," replied Witherspoon, "I will see that an explicit authorization for our projects is forthcoming at the next meeting of the Board."

"Gentlemen, I shall return to Monmouth and help organize ways to obtain more hard currency for our sacred missions," said Nathaniel, rising from his chair, "May the Lord bless us with success."

The sun was just beginning to set over Morven as Nathaniel hurried back from Nassau Hall. As he approached the estate, he noticed remnants of the depredations caused by the enemy occupation. The elegant statuary that used to adorn the front garden was gone. Entering the main building he was shocked by the empty spaces on the walls where once beautiful portraits had hung. After his release from British captivity, Stockton had tried to restore some of the grandeur of the family estate, but illness and lack of funds had impeded the effort.

A servant appeared and informed Nathaniel that the ladies were resting in the Grotto. She led Nathaniel out through the backyard to a hortus conclusus nestled in a corner of the orchard. Annis and Isabella were sitting on a bench decorated with shells and curiosities that Richard had brought back from a trip to England years before. As Nathaniel espied the two elegant women deep in conversation the thought crossed his mind that this might have been the very place where they had hatched out the plan to invite Nathaniel to Morven so many years ago.

As he approached the Grotto Annis waved to him, "Nathaniel, come join us. It has gotten rather late, and I would be pleased if you and Isabella would stay overnight at Morven."

"That is very generous of you," replied Nathaniel, "But you have had a harrowing day and we don't want to be a burden."

"You are not a burden," assured Annis, "Isabella is a great comfort to me, and your tonic has worked wonders. Besides that, I have a wealth of information to share with you. My brother, Elias, has recently brought me up to date on events in Congress which I am sure will interest you. As Isabella has informed me, the declining value of our currency is a critical issue for Monmouth as well and I am pleased to report that there is some hope that this problem might soon be alleviated."

"That would be a miracle, indeed!" exclaimed Nathaniel, "Together with Reverend James Caldwell I recently analyzed the decline of our local currency for the New Jersey Assembly and found it is worth less than one sixtieth of what it was worth at the beginning. It is no wonder that neither our merchants nor our soldiers want to accept it."

"And no wonder militiamen are considering mutiny if they have to wait for years for their pay and then get paid in worthless currency," added Annis, "Some of the thousands of Continental Army veterans in the Pennsylvania Line who mutinied in January had not been paid for three years! President Reed was able to put down the violence with rigorous measures but that is not a permanent solution."

"The problem is that Congress can only ask the states for funds to feed, clothe, and arm the Continental Army," explained Nathaniel, "During my time in Congress the states never provided enough to finance the nation's operations adequately. Every query was met with the response that the whole point of the rebellion was to avoid taxes."

"You mentioned that Elias had brought you encouraging news from Philadelphia. What has changed that could solve this problem?" asked Isabella.

"As so often in the past, whenever Congress is on the verge of bankruptcy it goes begging to Robert Morris," replied Annis, "He has rescued the country already several times. It was his signature on the Declaration of Independence that allowed Congress to float $ 40 million worth of paper in foreign lands and to borrow more than $ 20 million. General Washington has called Morris' ability to raise money 'magick art.'"

"But surely even Morris cannot solve the nation's financial problems if no one is willing to take our magick money," objected Nathaniel.

"That might change now," answered Annis, "Up until now Morris has had only a limited say in the way the nation's finances are handled. But a few weeks ago, Congress unanimously elected Robert Morris to the post of Superintendent of Finance to head the Department of the Treasury. Morris' personal credit rating abroad is still outstanding, and he controls a huge international network of merchants. If merchants reluctant to accept our currency know that Morris is personally backing it, that will change their attitudes."

"Can one man really have so much influence?" asked Isabella incredulously.

"He can indeed," confirmed Nathaniel, "He was the only person I met in Congress who really seemed to understand the complexities of international finance. He also wields great influence over the merchants he deals with. A price gouger will think twice before refusing an order from him."

"The only problem is that he is reluctant to take the position," continued Annis, "Elias says that he worries about the inevitable insinuations of corruption that could impede the conduct of his own business. He will only accept the position if Congress grants him direct control of the nation's finances without having to seek the collective approval of some committee."

"I think that, under the circumstances, Congress will have no choice but to accede to his demands," concluded Nathaniel, "I remember Morris as a firm supporter of confederation during my time in Congress. He always said that we would only be taken seriously by foreign powers if we stood together as one confederated people. Now that the Articles have come into effect, he is just the right person to convince our creditors that we are united in our struggle and will prevail. When they lend money to us, they are investing in the vast potential of this giant continent."

"I know from correspondence with General Washington that he himself is convinced that Robert Morris is our only hope of financing this struggle," noted Annis, "I am sure he will do everything he can to convince Morris to take the position."

"I, too, hope he is successful," agreed Nathaniel, "I have my doubts, however, that financial machinations alone will suffice. I am sure the good general remembers where much of the food for the troops came from in the last two starving winters. It was donated by our pious brethren who believe we are fighting for a sacred cause. President Witherspoon has suggested we tap into the same resources here and abroad to acquire the urgently needed coin to finance both our army and our college. Both causes are vital. Our army needs the funding to defend the freedom of our young nation and our college to produce its leaders. Tomorrow I shall hasten back to Monmouth and recruit Reverend John Woodhull to help get out the word. He has recently taken over Reverend Tennent's congregation after serving as a chaplain in the militia. He is also a newly appointed member of the Board of the college. He will, therefore, understand the importance of both campaigns. I think I can count on his enthusiastic support."

"You will probably garner less enthusiasm from David Forman," remarked Isabella wryly, "He will undoubtedly say that confiscation by the retaliators of Loyalist property is the only fast and feasible solution, and that you are wasting your time appealing to the parsons."

"He might indeed see it that way," agreed Nathaniel, "But the fact is we need to explore every possible avenue, and the willingness of our pious co-religionists to endure deprivation and hardship to support our cause should never be underestimated. David unfortunately has alienated a number of powerful men in the Assembly which diminishes our ability to get formal approval for our actions. We will continue to try, however."

"I can well imagine that a swashbuckling character like David Forman might frighten some of those staid merchants in the Assembly who fret that their own connections to the disaffected might be exposed," speculated Annis, "I know he can be impulsive, and I have heard frightening reports of his capacity for brutality, but General Washington has said that without people like him we would have probably already had to capitulate."

"He is certainly an energetic and charismatic leader," agreed Isabella, "If only he did not have such a terrible reputation."

"Perhaps I can change that," offered Annis thoughtfully, "The exploits of the great generals of antiquity were memorialized in verse. I shall compose a poem about David Forman and distribute it in our circles. It will present him in a different light and hopefully help improve his image."

"Well, if your poetry succeeds in sanitizing the reputation of the man the Loyalists call Devil Dave," Isabella laughed, "You will have accomplished a major literary achievement."

The next morning the Scudders left early for home. Nathaniel was anxious to inform the Monmouth Whigs about the appointment of Robert Morris and the prospect of relief on the currency front. Arriving at the Scudder residence in the early afternoon they were surprised but pleased to see the horse belonging to their son, John, standing in front of the barn.

Hurrying inside they find John being served a hearty lunch by Beth.

"John, my boy," Nathaniel greeted his son warmly, "I am very glad you can visit us just now. We have some interesting news. Your mother and I have just returned from Princeton where we attended the funeral of Richard Stockton."

"That is very sad news," replied John uncertainly, "Judge Stockton will be sorely missed."

"Indeed," agreed Nathaniel, "But that is not the news I was referring to. While we were there Annis informed us that Robert Morris has been appointed Superintendent of Finance to head the Department of the Treasury. That gives us some hope that we might be able to slow down the depreciation of our money."

Nathaniel went on to explain to John in detail the financial problems facing the struggle with the enemy.

"I am very familiar with these problems," John announced after listening to his father's explanation, "My term in the militia has recently expired and I have also not been paid in many months. That is why I have decided not to re-enlist."

"Perhaps you can now work as a physician with your father instead of as a surgeon's mate in the militia," Isabella proposed hopefully, "You will at least get paid for your work."

"Well actually I don't plan to give up the fight," replied John, "I just want to get paid for my efforts. In Philadelphia I met a man named Captain George Geddes."

"Captain Geddes is well-known as a highly successful privateer," said Nathaniel, "His exploits commanding the brig Holker have been lavishly praised by none other than General Washington himself."

"John, you are not planning to sign on to a privateering vessel, are you?" exclaimed Isabella, her face blanching with fear "That is probably the most dangerous option you could have chosen!"

"But it is also probably the most lucrative," argued John, "Captain Geddes told me that even a common sailor on a privateering vessel can earn as much as a thousand dollars in hard currency from a single cruise in addition to his wages. Father, you just explained to me that our cause is in dire need of specie. What better way is there to get it than to take it from enemy ships?"

"That is certainly a vital part of our war effort," agreed Nathaniel reluctantly, "Our privateers have probably inflicted more damage on the enemy than our land armies and the confiscated goods have been essential for supplying Washington's troops."

"But are not those goods often hoarded by speculators and sold to the army at inflated prices?" countered Isabella, "Rumor has it that Robert Morris has profited greatly from such transactions."

"All merchants make their money by buying cheap and selling dear," conceded Nathaniel, "And Robert Morris is no exception. But I am convinced that he is an ardent patriot who has risked much for the Whig cause. Without his backing most foreign governments would not be willing to lend us the money we need to win the war."

"But what about the moral issue?" objected Isabella, desperately seeking arguments to dissuade John from embarking on this dangerous adventure, "When you quit Congress, you said one cannot serve both God and Mammon, and you refused to be a part of the corrupt activities that some of your colleagues were up to."

"There is a fine line between legitimate business and corruption," explained Nathaniel, "Privateering is legal and essential to our war effort. Commodity speculation is not. Prices rise for many reasons, and it is difficult to determine exactly to what extent the depreciation of our currency is due to speculation, scarcity or lack of confidence in our eventual victory."

"Father, this is all very confusing. Could you give me an example of what would clearly be morally reprehensible corruption?" asked John.

"One very clear example comes to mind," replied Nathaniel, "I learned when I was charged with the oversight of the Quartermaster General's Department that John Neilson of Trenton was buying salt at Tom's River for $15 a bushel and selling it to Washington's forces in Morristown for $35 a bushel. Neilson was more than doubling his money for transporting the salt a relatively short distance, shamelessly exploiting Washington's needs."

"What about this Captain Geddes?" asked Isabella, "Is he just another profiteer seeking to capitalize on the dire straits of our brave soldiers?"

"Captain Geddes is a patriot!" exclaimed John enthusiastically, "From two burnt frigates he has reconstructed a vessel with 92 feet keel, 30 ½ feet beam, mounted 19 twelve-pounders on her main deck and four brass five-pounders on her quarter deck. He plans to hunt down the British ships that have been ravaging plantations in the Chesapeake area. One was even so bold as to attack Washington's estate at Mount Vernon. Geddes' new ship, the *Congress,* will soon put an end to that."

"I know about this project," replied Nathaniel, "It is being organized and partly financed by our Quartermaster General Nathanael Greene and his two assistants, Colonel Charles Pettit and Colonel John Cox. I have no doubt that the venture is in the interests of the Whig cause."

"But will those gentlemen profit personally from the endeavor?" asked Isabella.

"If it is successful, they will undoubtedly profit," replied Nathaniel, "But they will also be taking great risks and could well lose whatever they invest. As General Washington has noted, none of his officers could live on the salary that the government pays them so they can be excused for using whatever opportunities that arise provided that their activities are in the interests of the Whig cause."

"I hope that their losses do not include our son," commented Isabella gloomily, "And I am not surprised that officers cannot live from their salaries, even if they ever get paid. You certainly have not received anywhere near what is due to you both for your services and your medical supplies. How is what Greene and his friends are doing any different from the corruption you quit Congress to avoid?"

"That is a difficult question to answer," admitted Nathaniel, "I think each person must scrutinize his own motivations and answer that for himself. I believe I am doing the Lord's work in supporting this war and expect no remuneration for my efforts. I only wish I could afford to give more to the cause and that others would contribute more out of the goodness of their hearts rather than in the expectation of personal advantage. As regards Greene's privateering projects, there is no doubt that privateer vessels are making a vital contribution to the war effort, and they must be financed somehow. Congress does not supply adequate funding, neither for privateering vessels nor for our army. We have no choice but to rely on private sources of revenue. We can be happy that wealthy men like Charles Pettit are willing to risk their fortunes on our behalf. That is also the reason that I support David Forman despite occasional doubts about his motivations. If the Assembly would sanction and regulate retaliation, we could afford better support for our army."

Isabella realized that she was getting nowhere with her arguments to dissuade both her son and her husband from embarking on the risk-fraught projects that they both seemed stubbornly intent on pursuing. Nathaniel's support of privateering and retaliation she felt was at odds with his own rigid insistence on avoiding any personal benefits from the war effort. She knew, however, that there was no hope of changing Nathaniel's mind on such matters. She could only pray that her loved ones would survive these terrible times. She took some consolation from the hope that at least John might be rewarded adequately for his service.

The next day Nathaniel met with the other leading Whigs at Monmouth Courthouse to convey the news that Robert Morris might soon take over the post of Superintendent of Finance and head the Department of the Treasury and what that could mean for financing the war. He also described President Witherspoon's proposal for again tapping into the Presbyterian network to raise funds for the college.

"Robert Morris will certainly be an improvement over the imbeciles who have been dithering up until now," agreed David Forman, "But if our Presbyterian network is expected to contribute to our finances, they must first be compensated for the depredations they have suffered. If we want them to donate hard currency, we must first confiscate it from the Loyalists."

"It would seem that both efforts have to occur simultaneously," reasoned Thomas Henderson, "But we still have the problem that there is much resistance against the strategy of retaliation amongst many in the Assembly."

"We need to continue our efforts to convince the Assembly that retaliation, if properly regulated, is also morally justified," suggested Nathaniel, "I know that some of the resistance comes from people with ulterior motives, but others could still be won over."

"Many of those who oppose us are Quakers," explained Reverend Woodhull, "They are convinced pacifists and will never see matters our way. They refuse to take up arms against anyone."

"The Quakers are hopelessly naive," replied Forman, "But they are not the only naive ones. Have you heard that our former brothers-in-arms, John Covenhoven and William Wilcocks, are forming the so-called Whig Society of Monmouth County? They oppose retaliation and want instead to concentrate on protecting the value of our currency and boycott the disaffected who refuse to accept it."

"I suppose their goals are laudable enough," ventured Nathaniel, "Even though it seems unlikely that boycotting the disaffected will achieve much. They don't want to take our money anyway."

"Exactly! But that is not the most serious problem," continued Forman, "They are setting themselves up as the moderate alternative to the Association for Retaliation. They will organize to contest our seats in the Assembly and undermine our projects. The disaffected can then just hoard their ill-gotten gains from the London Trade, hard currency that we need to finance the war effort."

"That is the message we need to get out to our parishioners," agreed Reverend Woodhull, "At the same time as we solicit more donations to help the cause, we must also present the issue of retaliation as a just punishment for depredations and confiscation as a welcome source of hard currency to compensate our faithful both for their losses and their contributions."

"We also need to soften your public image, a bit," suggested Nathaniel with a sly smile, "When we were in Princeton to attend the funeral of Richard Stockton, Annis remarked that the exploits of the great generals of antiquity were memorialized in verse. She proposed composing a poem about your exploits casting you in a similar light."

"Well, there are some exploits she should probably leave out," Thomas Henderson added drolly.

Even David Forman could not suppress a chuckle, "Anything that helps our cause is fine with me, but I hope she does not soften my image too much. I am quite keen to put the fear of God into the hearts of Tory sympathizers."

A few days later Isabella reported to Nathaniel that she had received a letter from Annis and that she had indeed composed the promised verse.

"I am not sure she is talking about the same David we know," remarked Isabella with a bemused smile, "But let me read to you *Lines on General Forman*:"

"My muse, to simple objects late confined,
Now strives to scan the General's noble mind,
Whose numerous virtues gracefully arise
With mild effulgence to admiring eyes.
Where e'er I move, his praises meet my ear,
Scandal is hushed, or hesitates thro' fear;
The high distinctions that from virtue flow
On this good man th' Eternal Powers bestow.

Benevolence is pictured on his face
And dignity his manly features grace;
But oh! His mind, rich source of lasting worth,
Replete with charms, calls admiration forth.

With just enthusiasm my bosom swells,
When e'er I hear that he each grief dispels,
That soft humanity with power is joined
In his exalted, generous, virtuous mind.

If, while unknown, his merit gives delight,
If I admire him from a transient sight,
His converse would improve and charm my heart,
But not more admiration could impart.

May the all gracious power protect his life
And guard him from invidious care and strife,
For when such noble characters arise
Their mortal frame, but not their virtue dies!"

Although Nathaniel had to wince during some of the more erotically suggestive verses, at the end he concluded with a nod of his head, "It could indeed be an effective countermeasure against the vicious attacks David suffers in the Tory propaganda. I am sure David will be as embarrassed as I would be if someone were to eulogize me in that manner, but as Aeschylus famously said, 'in war, truth is the first casualty.' But depicting David this way could indeed help us achieve support in the Assembly for our policies."

"If some lady depicted you this way," warned Isabella laughing, "I would ask Reverend Woodhull to remind you of your nuptial vows."

Nathaniel was pleased to experience a moment of light-heartedness on the part of his wife who had become increasingly somber and distraught by the unrelenting stress that they both had had to endure.

"No one need remind me of my nuptial vows," Nathaniel assured her smiling, "You are and always will be the most important person in my life."

The moment of light-heartedness was short-lived, however. The departure of John to board the privateer ship soon forced Isabella back into a state of intense anxiety. The situation on the coast did not help either. Loyalist raiders did not seem to be dissuaded by David Forman's brutal policies. On the contrary every act of retaliation provoked another round of violence. Loyalists continued to attack Whig settlements, steal livestock, and kidnap people with increasing boldness. Isabella could not help but wonder how long it would be before the spiraling violence would affect her personally. She found it impossible to sleep at night and felt fatigued and depressed during the day. Her fears were compounded by the precarious state of their finances. Even though the New Jersey Assembly confirmed in a report that the state owed Nathaniel over 1,100 pounds for wages and other services, there was no point in accepting payment in the rapidly depreciating local currency and Nathaniel stubbornly refused to keep any part of the booty confiscated by the retaliators. He was adamant in his conviction that he had a sacred duty to avoid any semblance of the corruption that sullied the reputation of so many others and insisted that all gains go to the victims of Tory depredations. Because most alarms about raids came to Monmouth Courthouse just down the road from their home, Nathaniel was in a constant state of agitation, and could spend little time pursuing his profession.

Although Nathaniel was acutely anguished by the deterioration of Isabella's health, he remained convinced that he had no choice but to accept the sacrifices that the Lord demanded of him. He felt that the war was going into its final phase and, if he remained true to the cause, Providence would reward the righteous with success. At the urging of Nathaniel and the other representatives of Monmouth County the Assembly finally approved a bill in June to raise another 500 militiamen to guard the shore. More encouraging news arrived in July; the French troops under the Comte de Rochambeau after having spent a year bottled up in Rhode Island were reportedly on their way to join Washington's army. In the same month a heavy cannonade between British and French vessels opposite Frog's Point on the Hudson confirmed that sufficient elements of the French fleet had arrived to limit General Clinton's ability to restrain the French advance. By August Rochambeau's force had crossed the Hudson and joined the Continental Army. It was apparent that decisive action was at hand although Washington was careful to keep his future strategy very secret. Nathaniel prayed that Washington would succeed in some new bold strategy as he had in the Battles of Trenton and Princeton. For the first time in many months, he allowed himself a degree of optimism and tried to comfort Isabella in her depressed state.

"Have faith in the Lord, my darling," he counseled, "It could well be that our suffering will soon be at an end."

"I so hope that you are correct," replied Isabella, "But I am burdened by a terrible feeling of foreboding. If only we would hear from John."

A few weeks later Isabella's prayers were answered as John unexpectedly turned up one morning on their doorstep. As Isabella rushed to embrace their son with tears in her eyes, Nathaniel clasped his hands together and faced the sky.

"Praise be to the Lord for bringing our boy safely home!" he exclaimed.

Noticing that John had lost much weight, Isabella rushed into the house to organize a healthy breakfast for the famished traveler while Nathaniel and John took a seat in the parlor.

"Your mother and I have been so worried," Nathaniel began, "Tell us, son, what has transpired since you left to board the *Congress*."

"It has been a remarkable adventure," replied John, "But, unfortunately not an entirely successful one. The *Congress* was eventually captured by a British ship, and I am very lucky to be alive. Our initial mission was to sail to Cap Francois, Haiti to deliver dispatches from General Washington to the commander of the French fleet there, compte de Grasse. Then, as planned, Captain Geddes set out to capture the sloop, *Savage*, that had been ravishing the Chesapeake coast. We found the enemy cruising off the coast of Georgia apparently looking for more estates to plunder. Captain Geddes immediately gave chaise but the *Savage*, realizing that we were a more powerful ship, sought to escape. The *Congress* was faster and soon overtook the fleeing enemy. As we came abreast of the *Savage*, a fierce broadside duel ensued which resulted in our ship becoming unmanageable. Captain Geddes was obliged to fall back and make repairs."

"Is that when your ship was captured?" asked Nathaniel as Isabella returned with plates of bread and meat.

"No, not yet," answered John, "We managed to repair the ship enough to continue the pursuit. We again closed on the *Savage* and engaged in heavy cannon fire. I have never experienced anything like this. The vessels were so near to each other that the sailors were frequently scorched by the flashes of the opposing cannon. I was treating the wounded under deck and had as many burns to bind as bullet holes."

"Oh, my God!" exclaimed Isabella, "That must have been a nightmare."

"It was how I imagine the entrance to hell to be," agreed John, "In the course of an hour the English ship was reduced to a wreck. Its quarter deck and forecastle were swept clear of men, its mizzenmast had gone by the board and its mainmast was soon to follow. At that point Captain Geddes prepared to board the enemy vessel and take the ship in man-to-man combat. But just then the boatswain of the *Savage* appeared on the forecastle and signaled surrender. It was a Pyrrhic victory, however, with many killed and wounded on both sides. Dozens of horribly wounded sailors were brought to me, and I tried my best to keep them alive. The captain of the *Savage*, Charles Stirling, was among the wounded. Captain Geddes complimented Captain Stirling and his crew for their extraordinary bravery and ordered us to treat them the same as our own men."

"But that sounds as though the *Congress* was indeed successful, although at a dreadful cost," said Isabella.

"We spent the next few days nursing the wounded and trying to repair our ship as best we could," John continued, "But our supplies were nearly exhausted and when a British frigate, the *Solebay*, appeared we had no choice but to surrender. The British then took both the *Congress* and what was left of the *Savage* into Charleston harbor. There the 30 surviving crew members of the *Savage* became prisoners of war."

"And how is it that you are back with us now?" asked Nathaniel, "Did you escape?"

"I did not have to," responded John, "Captain Stirling was so grateful for my medical treatment of him and his men, that he said I was free to go. He even put a horse at my disposal, and I immediately set out for home."

"Thank God that there are honorable men even among the enemy!" exclaimed Isabella.

"Were you able to discover any news about the French fleet on your way?" asked Nathaniel.

"As a matter of fact, when I was debriefed in Philadelphia on my way here, I heard that de Grasse had indeed responded to Washington's dispatches and proceeded quickly to Chesapeake. The British seem to have lost control of the bay."

"Well, that is certainly encouraging!" exclaimed Nathaniel, "The news from the South has been depressing over the last few months. Clinton apparently thinks that he stands a better chance of deciding the war in his favor with the support of the many southern Loyalists. Our spies in New York inform us that he has ordered Cornwallis to build a deep-water port in Virginia where he can land more troops. Perhaps de Grasse's fleet can put a stop to that."

"It seems likely that they will be able to severely disrupt the enemy's plans," agreed John, "When I was in Haiti, I counted 28 ships in de Grasse's fleet. If he has brought his entire force to Chesapeake, the British are in serious trouble. In fact, the British successes in the South are not as devastating as they might seem. On my way through Virginia, I ran into several militiamen who were serving under the Marquis de Lafayette. They told me that Cornwallis has been unsuccessful trying to corner Lafayette who was able to link forces with Baron von Steuben and Anthony Wayne. What is even more interesting from the standpoint of us physicians is that Cornwallis' troops have been severely weakened with the quartan ague. If it comes to a major confrontation, a large portion of the enemy will probably not even be able to fight. Unlike the Virginia militia, most of Cornwallis's troops are newcomers to the area and have no resistance to that particular fever."

"Ah, the Lord of Hosts comes to our aid," remarked Nathaniel with great satisfaction, "As Dr. Clark taught me years ago, more soldiers die of fevers than from enemy bullets. We must inform David Forman and see to it that this vital information gets to General Washington."

"Indeed," agreed John, "Perhaps Washington will have an opportunity to outfox his old nemesis once again as he did in Trenton and Princeton."

Nathaniel hastened to find David Forman and inform him about the encouraging news.

"That is indeed extremely interesting!" exclaimed Forman, "It was rumored that Washington was considering attacking New York City together with the French force, but that the French thought it was too risky. Nevertheless, we were told to let dispatches fall into enemy hands that seemed to portend an assault on New York City. Now it is all beginning to make sense. Those dispatches were probably to mislead Clinton so he would hesitate to reinforce Cornwallis at Yorktown. Clinton is likely unaware that the French have arrived in force in Chesapeake. If Washington and Rochambeau can pull off a lightning strike on Cornwallis at Yorktown, a main part of the British army will be trapped. I will send an express to Washington informing him that the quartan ague is devastating the enemy troops there. Most of those soldiers will probably be too weak to hold up a musket!"

"Praise the Lord!" Nathaniel enthused, "This could very well be the beginning of the end of our struggle!"

"All the more reason for us to increase our operations against the Loyalist bastards," Forman added, "Rats are most dangerous when they are cornered."

"Thomas Henderson and I will make another attempt to convince the Assembly that retaliation is urgently needed."

"That will probably have the same fate as our earlier attempts to get the Assembly to see the light," replied Forman, "I, for one, will pay them no mind. I know what has to be done and I intend to do it!"

Nathaniel and Thomas Henderson nevertheless again petitioned the Assembly to legally authorize the well-affected inhabitants of Monmouth to retaliate upon the property of the disaffected. After considering the request the Assembly again denounced the retaliators as an illegal and dangerous combination, utterly subversive of the law, highly dangerous to government, immediately tending to create disunion among the inhabitants, directly leading to anarchy and confusion and tending to the dissolution of the constitution and government.

Although the Monmouth legislators were deeply disappointed, Thomas Henderson tried one more time to garner support by introducing a somewhat more conciliatory bill entitled "An Act to Procure Reparations to the Loyal Citizens of this State for Damages they may sustain from Nocturnal Plunderers." Although this bill was less provocative than earlier attempts by proposing a tax on the disaffected rather than confiscation, it still failed 10–19 despite all three Monmouth legislators, Thomas Seabrook, Thomas Henderson, and Nathaniel Scudder, voting in favor.

The next election to the Assembly a few days later seemed to indicate that David Forman's policies were increasingly losing support in the Whig community. Although Nathaniel and Thomas Henderson were returned to the legislature, Thomas Seabrook was replaced by one of the leaders of the moderate Whig Society, John Covenhoven.

"Perhaps it is time to rethink your unstinting support for David Forman's radical measures," cautioned Isabella, "John Covenhoven is not only an old friend but also a trusted patriot and elder statesman. He thinks that David's policies are swelling the ranks of the enemy and he could very well be correct."

"I certainly trust John Covenhoven and have no doubts as regards his loyalty," replied Nathaniel, "But I cannot withdraw my support for David now that we are entering what might be the deciding phase of our struggle. Let us pray that a decisive victory on the battlefield will lead to a de-escalation of the bitter struggles with the Loyalists. If Washington is successful, it might convince them to curtail their depredations and accept the new regime."

The depredations unfortunately showed no signs of de-escalation. Early on the morning of the 15th of October just as Nathaniel was embarking on his rounds as a physician, an alarm reached Monmouth Courthouse that a party of Loyalists had landed at Shrewsbury River and attacked Colts Neck kidnapping five people. David Forman quickly rallied the Whigs of Freehold and admonished them to go in pursuit of the raiders.

"Nathaniel don't go!" pleaded Isabella, "You said yourself that we should pray for de-escalation. I have a terrible feeling that this will not end well."

"I will try to avoid bloodshed," promised Nathaniel, "I will go along just to bind the wounds of the poor fellows who might be hurt on this mission."

The Monmouth minutemen galloped off at full speed in the direction of Black Point where the raiding party had landed in the hope of rescuing the kidnapped prisoners. As the Loyalists were preparing to board their vessel David Forman ordered an attack on the rear of the raiding party. At that moment Nathaniel recognized Richard Lippincott, a notorious Loyalist and close friend of the Loyalist raider, Joseph Wood, whom David Forman had dispatched a year before. Lippincott was carefully aiming a fowling piece at David Forman.

"David, beware!" Nathaniel warned, "That scoundrel is taking a bead on you!"

Forman stepped aside just as Lippincott fired his weapon. The ball meant for Forman flew past him and passed through Nathaniel's head instantly killing him.

"Oh my God!" exclaimed Forman falling to his knees beside his friend, "That ball was meant for me, but Nathaniel saved my life!"

The Monmouth men gently laid Nathaniel's body over his horse and rode silently back to Freehold. Arriving at Monmouth Courthouse. Forman, hat in hand, proceeded to the Scudder residence. When Isabella opened the door, she knew immediately from the unfamiliar sight of a David Forman with tears in his eyes, that her greatest fears were realized.

"Isabella," he began almost choking on the words, "I must inform you that our beloved friend and worthy patriot was called upon by the Almighty to make the ultimate sacrifice."

Isabella fainted dead away and had to be carried to her bed where she remained in a semi-catatonic state for several days. When the time came for the funeral, her servants, Beth and Pegg, dressed her and with her sons, John, Joseph, and Kenneth supporting her she managed to struggle into the carriage which took them to the Tennent Meeting House in Manalapan. Her sons helped place her in the front row of the church directly facing the elder's chair where Nathaniel had sat through so many sermons over the years. She simply stared at the empty chair and barely noticed the many prominent guests that had hurried to Manalapan to bid farewell to Nathaniel.

"And all Jerusalem and Judea mourned for Josiah," began Reverend Woodhull, reading from 2 Chronicles 35:24. He recited the story of the Old Testament King Josiah who had done so much to crush idolatry, enshrine the Book of the Law of the Lord, restore the True Religion in Judea and who finally was tragically killed in a battle against a pagan king. Woodhull continued by describing the parallels between that ancient drama and Nathaniel's heroic efforts to establish a pious republic. After he finished Nathaniel's old college friend, Benjamin Prime, rose to deliver his own eulogy. He concluded with an elegy:

> "In med'cine skillful & in warfare brave,
> In council steady, uncorrupt and wise,
> It was thy happy lot, the means to have,
> To no small rank in each of these to rise."

Just as the service was nearing its end David Forman strode up to the front of the church. Choking with emotion he announced that he had just received information that proved that Nathaniel had not died in vain.

"An express rider has just arrived from Virginia," he announced, "The Continental Army has achieved a momentous victory! Cornwallis has surrendered to Washington. He and 9,000 enemy troops are now prisoners of the United States. The war is won!"

Hearing his words Isabella finally understood the meaning of the sacrifice that she had been forced to endure.

Chapter 25

Peace – 1781–1782

David Forman's announcement of the end of the war was, of course, premature. Although the British campaign had indeed been dealt a mortal blow at Yorktown which would eventually result in a peace treaty, hostilities in Monmouth County were far from over. In particular, Article Ten of the capitulation agreement that Cornwallis had signed resulted in frantic attempts by Loyalists to sabotage any prospects of a peace settlement. Cornwallis had attempted to protect American soldiers who had fought beside the regular army during the siege asking in Article Ten that Americans not be punished for their part in the battle. Washington adamantly rejected this proposal arguing that it was a civilian issue to be handled by individual state governments. Cornwallis did not press the issue meaning that American prisoners would not be treated as honorable prisoners of war but could be subjected to charges of treason. When news of this reached the Board of Associated Loyalists in New York City, William Franklin was outraged. He and many of his Loyalists Associators felt betrayed by the country that they had risked so much to support. Rather than passively accept the loss of their country, they felt their only option was to escalate the level of hostilities to make rapprochement impossible. They decided to increase terror and retribution in order to keep the war alive and keep their Loyalist compatriots from losing hope.

Over the next weeks Isabella became increasingly distraught. If peace were really in the offing, there would be some consolation that Nathaniel's sacrifice had not been in vain. Peace, however, seemed even less imminent than before. In addition, she was plagued by anxieties about her financial situation. She had known for a long time that they were in a very precarious position but now even the meager income that Nathaniel had generated as a part-time physician and the pittance afforded by his political office had stopped. She knew that the state owed Nathaniel considerable amounts for past services but had no idea how that money could be collected. Her oldest son John could barely support himself and Joseph, Hannah, Kenneth, and Lydia were all still very young and would not be able to take care of themselves for the foreseeable future. Her eight slaves could keep the farm going so they need not starve but money would still be needed to purchase the bare necessities of life. She decided that she had no choice but to seek out her father and solicit his advice.

Not wanting to alarm the children she waited until they were all out of the house and bid her servant, Adam, to ready the carriage and set off discreetly for Anderson Manor. Arriving there she was greeted affectionately by her father.

"My darling daughter, I am so glad to see you," began Colonel Anderson, "You seemed so distressed and exhausted at Nathaniel's funeral that I hesitated to visit you. I know that in such a state the best thing is rest, and the last thing one needs is to have to cope with visitors."

"In fact, I was bedridden for several weeks," admitted Isabella, "I am feeling somewhat stronger again but my grief over the loss of Nathaniel is now compounded with anxiety concerning our business affairs. As you know, Nathaniel made great sacrifices for the cause and is owed much money for his services. I have no idea how to settle these matters, and I am being hounded by petty merchants who demand money that I don't have. Some have even had the audacity to threaten me with debtors' prison if I cannot pay. You have helped us so much in the past that I am loath to burden you with my troubles, but I am at my wits' end."

Isabella could not stifle a sob as she confessed her plight to her father.

"There, there, my beloved girl," Colonel Anderson tried to sooth his daughter, "This country can hardly repay the debt they owe to Nathaniel but do not fear, I will never allow my only surviving child and my grandchildren to suffer the indignities of debt litigation. Besides, you have the means to raise cash at short notice. You could sell some of your slaves, for example. That strapping young man who drove you over here today would fetch a good price at short notice."

"Oh, but father, the thought of selling anyone from our kitchen family fills me with horror," objected Isabella, shaking her head with dismay. "Beth, Pegg, and Dunmore were the gifts you gave us when we married. Dear old Ellice, Beth's mother, has faithfully served both our families for so many years and would probably not find a buyer anyway. As for the children of Beth and Pegg—Adam, Frank, Matt and Liel—they would surely fetch good prices but breaking up the family would require more cold-bloodedness than I could ever muster. I think I would rather go to debtors' prison than do that."

"Ah, my lovely child," replied Colonel Anderson, "You have always had such a kind heart and I am proud of you for that. You remind me so much of your mother whom I still so painfully miss. I would also be reluctant to part with any of my servants, particularly since none of them were lured into accepting the British offer of emancipation in exchange for betrayal of our cause. No, we will find a different solution. I will talk to Governor Livingston. His family is immensely wealthy and can easily afford to loan you sufficient funds to survive this period of temporary financial embarrassment until the state sees fit to grant you what is due."

"Do you really think the governor would do that?" asked Isabella, her face brightening at the hopeful prospect.

"I am absolutely certain that he will," confirmed Colonel Anderson, "No one knows better than the governor what Nathaniel has done for our cause. There will be formalities involved, of course. You will be required to take inventory of your estate, and I will have to sign as a guarantor of the loan but that will not be a problem. I should think that you can count on a loan of about two thousand pounds very soon. That should keep the greedy merchants out of your hair for the foreseeable future."

"Oh father, I don't know how to thank you!" exclaimed Isabella, greatly relieved that she would be able to solve her financial problems without resort to charity or embarrassing litigation.

The loan was quickly forthcoming as Colonel Anderson had predicted, so Isabella's most pressing problem was solved for the time being. The overall situation in Monmouth County continued to deteriorate, however. Thomas Seabrook, a hardline retaliator, was elected to replace Nathaniel in the Assembly. He and Thomas Henderson continued to try to convince the Assembly of the righteousness of retaliation without success. David Forman after the death of Nathaniel was even more vehement in his desire to exact retribution from any and all suspected Loyalists whether or not the Assembly agreed.

Forman's daughter, Elizabeth, continued to reside in the Scudder household so he had occasion to visit Isabella often and keep her informed about the state of the struggle.

"I will not rest until Nathaniel's murder is avenged," he repeatedly assured Isabella, "If I get my hands on Lippincott, I will give your sons the opportunity to give him the treatment he deserves. They can feed him to the crows, piece by piece."

Isabella was appalled at the thought of her boys indulging in the kind of bloody retribution for which Forman was renowned. She was torn between her desire for justice and closure and her horror at the prospect of spiraling violence and what that could mean for her and her family. She knew that her boys would welcome the opportunity of revenge but feared they would then just become prime targets and meet the same fate as Nathaniel. After all, it was a bullet meant for Forman that had snuffed out Nathaniel's life. What good would revenge be if it resulted in the death of more of her loved ones? Monmouth Courthouse where many Loyalist prisoners were incarcerated was just around the corner. It was rumored that William Franklin had expressly authorized an attack on the jail there to free the prisoners and kill David Forman. Throughout the fall and winter Forman's frequent reports of new skirmishes caused Isabella's anxieties to deepen while at the same time increasing her sons' enthusiasm for joining the fray. She could barely restrain them by arguing that she needed them at home to guard the household.

At the beginning of February her son John, bursting with excitement, came home with news that created yet another crisis for Isabella.

"Mother, I just heard that Captain Jack Huddy has been given command of the blockhouse in Tom's River!" he exclaimed.

"Well, good for him," Isabella scowled, "Let's hope he does not get himself captured again by Tories."

"But he is well-known as a hero to our cause and a very successful privateer," argued John, "Isn't he the one who escaped capture by Colonel Tye, that escaped slave who long wreaked havoc on the good citizens of Monmouth County?"

"He is the one," replied Isabella bleakly, "He was targeted by the Loyalists because he was notorious for executing suspected Tory sympathizers without trial. He likes to brag about having 'greased the rope' that hanged Stephen Edwards. That was the beginning of the escalating violence that eventually resulted in the death of your father."

"But Mother, Tom's River is one of the most important launching points for privateers. If I would volunteer for his garrison, perhaps I would get a chance to earn big profits from raids on the enemy. Then I could help pay off our debts."

"John, please don't start again with these privateering notions!" exclaimed Isabella, "Wasn't being captured by the British once enough for you? You can thank God that you made it through that ordeal alive. Don't tempt fate. Besides, many of those privateers are common thieves, despite their claims to be furthering our cause. They are not the kind of men a pious young man like yourself should be associating with. Furthermore, Huddy is well known as a philanderer who left his lawful wife and was living in sin with some hussy when he was captured. You should not for a moment consider him to be a person worth emulating."

"But mother, the blockhouse at Tom's River is also important for guarding the saltworks there which are of vital importance to our army."

"All the more reason to expect a massive raid there in the near future," answered Isabella, "It is bad enough that we live so close to the jail in Monmouth Courthouse which could also be raided at any time. I need you here to guard our house and family. Your grandfather informed me that peace negotiations are proceeding well, and the British have essentially ceased military actions. There is no point in getting involved in the senseless tit-for-tat violence that the Retaliators and the Loyalists are obsessed with. The only hope I have left is that my children will survive this dreadful war. After that we will have plenty of time to pay off our debts."

A few weeks later just as news was arriving that the British Parliament had voted to concede American independence, a large, irregular force of the Associated Loyalists overwhelmed Huddy's small garrison, took Huddy prisoner and destroyed the blockhouse, saltworks, local mills, and almost all the houses in the village. Huddy was taken to a prison ship in New York in British custody.

The next week David Forman appeared at the Scudder residence with a posse of Retaliators. Isabella happened to be out on an errand to a local tradesman. When Forman banged on the door, he was met by John.

"John, saddle up your mount and come with us," shouted Forman, "The murderer of your father has captured Jack Huddy and we are going to pay him back for that. I have his brother-in-law, Philip White, in my custody, and he is going to have to pay for the sins of his kinsman."

Although John knew that his mother would be very upset about this turn of events, he could not see how he could refuse Forman's challenge without reneging on his filial duty. Somewhat reluctantly he saddled his horse and rode off with Forman's men. He hoped that he might be able to exert a moderating influence on the vigilantes. They proceeded to a glen in the forest where others were holding White bound and gagged.

"Has the man had a trial yet?" asked John tentatively.

"He will get the sort of trial that the Indians give to traitors," answered Forman grimly, "He gets to run the gauntlet, and if he survives that we will send what's left of him to Lippincott."

Forman had brought along another prisoner, Samuel Taylor, also a Loyalist refugee, to witness the spectacle. As John watched with mounting horror, two lines of ten men each lined up armed with clubs and tomahawks. The captive was forced to his feet and pushed into the corridor between the two rows. White ran just a few yards before vicious blows brought him to his knees.

"The man is finished!" shouted John, "Stand down in the name of our merciful Lord Jesus!"

The men paid no heed to John's entreaties but continued to hack away at the wretched creature like wild animals at a feeding frenzy. When at last their fury was spent, John went to examine the bloody remains of the victim to see if there was any life left in him. His body was totally mutilated. His legs had been broken, one of his eyes had been gouged out, and one of his arms were missing. There was absolutely no way he could have survived the ordeal.

"See here, Taylor!" Forman exclaimed, "This is the fate that awaits traitors who dare to attack our allies. Go back and tell your friends in New York that if Jack Huddy is harmed, the same will happen to your friend, Clayton Tilton."

Turning to John he added, "This is how we avenge the death of your father!"

"My father would have been appalled at this barbarity!" exclaimed John, "You have besmirched the honor of our noble cause!"

John mounted his horse and hurried back to the Scudder residence. When he recounted his dreadful experience to Isabella, she turned a ghostly shade of pale.

"John, you must promise me that you will never participate in such atrocities again," Isabella beseeched him.

"I was a witness, not a participant," John assured her, "And now I understand the foolhardiness of all this retaliation. You are absolutely right, violence just begets more violence and now that peace is a real possibility, it makes even less sense than before. Let us pray that all this madness will soon end."

The madness was not destined to end soon, however. As Forman had planned, Samuel Taylor, after his release hurried to New York City, recounted the gory details of White's murder to William Franklin, and encouraged him to appoint Richard Lippincott to organize an appropriate response. Franklin was pleased to oblige for it afforded him a welcome opportunity to further sabotage the peace talks. He summoned Lippincott to the Board of Associated Loyalists to receive his instructions. Under the pretense of arranging an exchange Lippincott managed to effect the release of three captives of the British to his custody, including Joshua Huddy. Instead of exchanging Huddy, however, he brought him to Sandy Hook on a British ship and hanged him. The next day Monmouth militia men found Huddy hanging from a tree with a note pinned to his chest "Up goes Huddy for White."

The news of Huddy's execution spread like wildfire throughout Monmouth County. His body was taken to Freehold to be buried near the Presbyterian Meeting House at Manalapan. A gigantic crowd gathered for the ceremony and were whipped into a rage by reports that the British had allowed the extrajudicial murder of an unarmed prisoner. Over 400 people petitioned Washington to redress this terrible grievance. Washington immediately suspended peace negotiations with the British and demanded that Lippincott be handed over for punishment.

Although General Clinton was furious when he learned what had happened, knowing full well that the Associated Loyalists were trying to sabotage the peace process against his express orders, he could hardly acquiesce to Washington's demands without undermining what little was left of American support for the British cause. In addition, he knew that he was soon to be relieved of his command in North America by General Sir Guy Carleton, and was loath to get involved in an issue that could only create more problems for him at home. Instead, he ordered the court-martial of Richard Lippincott who had acted without his approval in the hopes that this would appease Washington. He knew that by the time the court-martial got under way, Carleton would have taken over command and the whole ugly affair would become his responsibility. Washington, for his part, hoping to avoid another wave of reprisal killings, announced that a captive British officer of the same rank as Huddy would be chosen by lot to be executed if Lippincott were not punished. On May 26, 1782, a young British officer, Captain Charles Asgill, drew the short straw. Washington had Asgill transported to New Jersey for imprisonment to show the outraged populace that the army was determined to see to it that justice would be forthcoming. Stern warnings were issued to Forman and the Retaliators, however, that under no circumstances were they to take matters into their own hands.

Isabella together with a large crowd of onlookers were at hand when the prisoner was bought to Monmouth Courthouse under heavy guard by Continental soldiers.

"He is but a boy," remarked Isabella, as the prisoner was marched past the Scudder residence.

"They say he is just seventeen," added John, standing beside her, "And by all accounts he is an honorable young man, and several of Washington's officers objected to the way he was chosen. They think that there are more deserving candidates for the gallows among our prisoners."

"Seventeen, you say!" exclaimed Isabella, "That is just the age of your brother Kenneth! How can we avenge this crime by executing an innocent boy!"

"Let us pray that Lippincott will be found guilty in his court-martial, and we will not have this sin on our hands," replied John.

In New York City William Franklin tried feverishly to quash the court-martial knowing that any outcome would be a disaster for him. If Lippincott were convicted, the Associators would be outraged over the betrayal of one of their own by their British allies. If he were acquitted, that could only mean that the Board of Associated Loyalists would have to accept responsibility for ordering an extrajudicial murder. Either way the already fraught relationship between the Board and the new commander-in-chief would be strained to the breaking point.

After many delays the court-martial began in earnest, and Lippincott used his only plausible defense that Franklin and the Board had ordered the execution. A fourteen-member jury which included Franklin's old friend Cortlandt Skinner agreed with Lippincott's defense and voted to acquit him. When news of his acquittal became public, Washington was outraged. He insisted that if Lippincott was innocent, then William Franklin was the culprit and should be punished. He demanded that Franklin be arrested. General Carleton, fed up with all the problems the Associators had caused, demanded that they cease all operations and began plans to dissolve the Board of Associated Loyalists. He also made every effort to mollify Washington and get the peace negotiations back on track. Franklin, realizing that his cause was lost, departed for England in August under the pretense of delivering petitions from the Loyalists to King George seeking continued support. He was never to return.

The Asgill affair continued into the fall. In the meantime, Asgill's mother, a lady of considerable influence, had petitioned the French King Louis XVI to intervene on behalf of her son. Citing the opinion of Asgill's fellow officers that the selection of her son was illegal due to the 14th Article of the Capitulation document protecting British officers captured at Yorktown from punishment, she managed to convince the French Court to intervene on her son's behalf. When the French Foreign Minister, the compte de Vergennes, conveyed his desire to Washington that the young life be spared, Washington decided to leave the matter to Congress. Since violation of the Capitulation agreement that was the basis of the Franco-American victory at Yorktown would have reflected very badly on the new republic in the eyes of its most important ally, Congress voted to release Asgill on parole to return to England in December, 1782.

In Monmouth County the news was greeted by consternation by some and relief by others. Predictably David Forman thought that the assassination of Richard Lippincott would be a desirable project. Since the activities of the Associated Loyalists had ceased with the departure of William Franklin and peace negotiations were going well, Forman was no longer able to marshal the broad support for the sort of violence he had always advocated. Isolated acts of violence continued but people were exhausted and only hoped for peace at last. No one was more exhausted than Isabella. The anniversary of Nathaniel's funeral weighed heavily on her and as winter approached, she felt utterly depleted. She spent much of the time in her bed attended faithfully to by Beth and Pegg. Her son, John, as an experienced physician, recognized all the signs of someone ready to give up on life.

"Mother, I am very concerned about your listless demeanor," warned John, "You seem to have a bad case of the grippe, but you can recover if you have the will. I know that you miss Father terribly, but you still have much to live for. Are you depressed that father's murder has not been avenged?"

"Not at all," answered Isabella, smiling, "I am glad that that young man was able to go free. Even Huddy's widow, Catherine Hart, has said that she wanted Asgill's life spared since he is obviously completely innocent. I agree entirely. As you know, I have always been opposed to revenge for the sake of revenge. Did not Jesus advise us to turn the other cheek?"

"Do you think that father was mistaken in his support for the Retaliators?" asked John, "Should he have instead turned the other cheek?"

"That is difficult to know," replied Isabella, "I only know that your father's sincere motivation was to protect the victims of Tory depredations. But man is a cracked vessel and others had different motivations. Still nothing happens but that the Lord wills it, and He works His wonders in ways that are often incomprehensible to us mortals."

"But mother, you have sacrificed so much, it seems so unfair," said John, his voice choked with emotion.

"We must have faith and accept the sacrifices He imposes joyously." answered Isabella, "I have had a very fortunate life in many ways. Your father was a wonderful, generous man and a true Christian. He understood as few do that the greatest evil is our inherent corruption, and that corruption flows from greed which is the source of all suffering. He was more able to free himself from greed than anyone I ever met, and I pray that I will soon be reunited with him."

Isabella closed her eyes and smiled as she recollected that glorious evening in Morven so many years ago. In her mind's eye she saw again the bashful, handsome young man bowing and extending his arm to her, and to her amazement leading her gracefully and self-confidently through all the figures of the minuet.

Epilogue

ISABELLA ANDERSON SCUDDER PASSED away on Christmas Eve, 1782. She was buried next to Nathaniel in the graveyard next to Old Tennent Church in Manalapan where they had met in their youth and married in 1752.

The War of American Independence ended with the signing of the Treaty of Paris by U.S. and British representatives nine months later on September 3, 1783. The British occupation of New York City continued for several more months, because the last British Army and Royal Navy commander, Sir Guy Carleton, had to deal with a surge of Loyalist refugees who fled to the city. Eventually 29,000 Loyalist refugees and over 3,000 Black Loyalists who had been liberated by the British were evacuated from the city. Carleton refused to return the freed slaves to their former owners as the Treaty of Paris had required. Finally, on November 16, 1783, after the last British warship had departed, General George Washington led the Continental Army to the reoccupation of Manhattan exactly seven years after his retreat in 1776.

David Forman devoted his energy thereafter to consolidating the considerable wealth he had acquired during the war and to resisting all claims that former refugees made for compensation. Like most of the Presbyterians in New Jersey he also vigorously opposed the movement initiated by the Quakers to end slavery there. As pressure mounted for gradual emancipation, he eventually bought an estate in Natchez, Mississippi and sent 60 of his slaves to work there. Visiting there in 1796, he suffered a debilitating stroke. When he attempted to return home by ship, he was captured by a British privateer and brought to the Bahamas where he died in September, 1797. According to a recent book by Prof. Samuel Forman, his body was then sent back to New Jersey pickled in a barrel of rum to be interred in the graveyard of Old Tennent Church.

The corruption that Nathaniel was so concerned about continued apace. The high hopes that he had had for reform of the Quartermaster Corps with the appointment of General Nathanael Greene turned out to be misplaced. Over the course of about two years Greene, in collusion with his two assistants, John Cox and Charles Pettit, disbursed over $80 million, some portion of which was diverted to their privateering and other speculations. When Congress insisted on getting a proper accounting of the expenses, Greene angrily resigned his position and returned to soldiering. A

Congressional probe of his activities was blocked by Washington on the grounds that aspersions cast on the conduct of his best general would be disastrous for military morale. The culture of corruption continued unabated even after the war.

Although the privateering business dwindled rapidly after the British defeat at Yorktown as the supply of commodities improved with peace, new avenues of enrichment soon presented themselves. During the war Congress had used certificates of indebtedness to pay soldiers who fought in the war and farmers who supplied the troops. After the war the precarious financial straits of the young government caused the certificates to decline rapidly in value until it became almost impossible to redeem them, even at just fifteen cents on the dollar. In 1790, however, Alexander Hamilton discreetly proposed redeeming the certificates at face value. Armed with this inside information speculators including members of Congress swarmed out to buy up as many certificates as possible before the news got out. A former partner of Nathanael Greene in wartime speculation, Jeremiah Wadsworth, sent out fast ships to southern ports to acquire the certificates at a low price and wound up making $9,000,000. Robert Morris did even better clearing $ 18,000,000. The barefoot soldiers and starving farmers who had sacrificed so much for the cause of independence were cruelly betrayed by the government they had trusted.

John Witherspoon continued to be an influential figure in both government and education. He was a member of Congress from 1777 until 1784 and served on over 10,000 committees. Many of his students played influential roles in the new republic including one president, one vice president, 37 judges (three of whom became justices of the U.S. Supreme Court), 10 Cabinet officers, 12 members of the Continental Congress, 28 U.S. senators and 49 U.S. congressmen. His stern Calvinist views about the ubiquity of corruption are mirrored in the system of checks and balances built into the American system.

Witherspoon opposed the abolition of slavery in New Jersey and was a slave owner himself until his dying day. Several of his successors in Nassau Hall were also slave owners. Despite half-hearted attempts at the gradual abolition of slavery in New Jersey, it continued to exist there until the passage of the 13th Amendment in 1865. A majority of the graduates of Nassau Hall fought on the Confederate side in the Civil War.

The children of Nathaniel and Isabella led successful lives. Their daughters, Hannah and Lydia, grew up to become elegant young ladies and married prominent members of the Whig aristocracy of New Jersey. In addition to practicing medicine, John Anderson Scudder served in the New Jersey State Assembly and the U.S. Congress. He later moved to Kentucky and represented that state in Congress. Kenneth served as a cavalryman in the military and eventually moved to upstate New York. Nathaniel's religious fervor was most evident in his second son, Joseph, who became a prominent lawyer in New Jersey and later helped found the Monmouth Bible Society. He became one of the few non-Quakers in New Jersey to voluntarily emancipate his slaves. Joseph's oldest son, John, after receiving his degree from Nassau Hall in 1811 also became a physician and clergyman and one of the first American medical missionaries to India. His progeny spent collectively 1,000 years attempting to bring the joys of Yankee Calvinism to the 4,000-year-old culture of the Subcontinent. Their conversion efforts were only modestly successful, but did result in the founding of two hospitals which continue to operate to this day. One of them, founded in 1900 by Missionary John's granddaughter, Dr. Ida Scudder, after enduring multiple frustrations at the refusal of Indian men to allow their young wives dying in childbirth to be treated by male doctors, is the largest teaching hospital in southern India and the first to train female physicians—but that is another story.

Dramatis Personae

Last Name * = Historical Person	First Name	Description	Introduced in Chapter
Anderson*	John	Sea Captain of the Unicorn, rescuer of Darien survivors, royal governor of New Jersey, grandfather of Isabella	Prologue
Ferguson	Andrew	First Mate of the Unicorn	Prologue
Paterson*	William	Initiator of the Darien Debacle	Prologue
Leeds*	Daniel	Surveyor of the province of New Jersey	Prologue
Reid*	John	Surveyor-General of the province of New Jersey and representative of the Proprietors	Prologue
Reid Anderson*	Anna	Daughter of John Reid, wife of John Anderson, grandmother of Isabella	Prologue
Scudder*	Jacob	Father of Nathaniel	1
Scudder*	Abia	Mother of Nathaniel	1
Scudder*	Nathaniel	Physician, Congressman, Militia officer	1
Edwards*	Jonathan	New Light Presbyterian evangelist and early president of the College of New Jersey - CNJ (later Princeton University)	1
Burr Sr.*	Aaron	New Light Presbyterian evangelist and early president of the College of New Jersey - CNJ (later Princeton University)	1
Prime*	Benjamin	Classmate of Nathaniel at CNJ, physician, poet	2
Edwards Burr*	Esther	Wife of President Burr and daughter of Jonathan Edwards	2
Anderson Scudder*	Isabella	Granddaughter of John Anderson and later wife of Nathaniel	2

Tennent Jr.*	William	New Light Presbyterian evangelist and early trustee of the College of New Jersey - CNJ (later Princeton University), parson of the Presbyterian Meeting House in Manalapan	2
Dunmore*		Slave belonging to the Anderson family	2
Anderson*	Hannah	Mother of Isabella	2
Clark	William	Physician, mentor of Nathaniel	2
Belcher*	Jonathan	Royal governor who approved the charter of CNJ	2
Boudinot Stockton*	Annis	Poet, friend of Isabella, wife of Richard Stockton	2
Stockton*	Richard	Early graduate of CNJ, lawyer, statesman, signatory of the Declaration of Independence, husband of Annis	2
Brainerd*	David	New Light pastor, evangelist to the Native Americans	3
Brainerd*	John	New Light pastor, evangelist to the Native Americans	3
Okwes		Sachem of Lenape community in Crossweeksung	3
Chinkwe		Son of Okwes	3
Washington*	George	Major of the Virginia militia, later Commander-in-Chief of Continental Army and first president of the United States	3
Braddock*	Edward	Commander of British troops at the Battle of Fort Duquesne	3
Anderson*	Kenneth	Wealthy landowner, son of John Anderson, father of Isabella	3
Stockton*	John	Father of Richard Stockton	4
Stockton*	Abigail	Mother of Richard Stockton	4
Franklin*	William	Son of Benjamin Franklin, later Royal Governor of New Jersey	4
Graeme*	Elizabeth	First fiancee of William Franklin	4
Shippen*	Joseph	Militia officer, son of Judge Edward Shippen	4
Livingston*	William	Scion of the wealthy Livingston clan, later general and governor of New Jersey	4

Boudinot*	Elias	Brother of Annis, later officer in the Continental Army, president of the Continental Congress	4
Alexander*	William	Wealthy landowner, later general in the Continental Army	4
Covenhoven'	John	Whig politician from Monmouth County	4
Loudoun*	John Campbell, Lord Loudoun	Commander of British forces in the beginning of the French and Indian War	5
Scudder*	William	Brother of Nathaniel	5
Scudder*	Lemuel	Brother of Nathaniel	5
Scudder*	Ruth	Sister of Nathaniel	5
Ogden*	David	Lawyer famous for representing the Proprietors against the land claims of Presbyterian yeomen	5
Vaudreuil*	Pierre	Governor of New France	6
Dinwiddie*	Robert	Royal governor of Virginia during the French and Indian War	6
Neolin*		Indian prophet who inspired the Pontiac Uprising	6
Tanaghrisson*		Representative of the Iroquois Confederacy	6
Bigelow*	Sam	Trader and smuggler in Tom's River	6
Forman*	Jonathan	Judge in Monmouth County who married Nathaniel and Isabella	7
Beth*		Slave owned by the Anderson family given along with Dunmore to Nathaniel and Isabella as wedding gifts	8
Pitt*	William	Earl of Chatham, British Prime Minister who engineered the defeat of France in the French and Indian War	8
Hall	Jedediah	Militiaman from Perth Amboy captured by Ottawas at Fort William McHenry, later escaped back to New Jersey	8
Seeker*	Thomas	Archbishop of Canterbury, enemy of the Calvinists	9
Pownall*	Thomas	Royal governor of Massachusetts Bay from 1757 to 1760	9

Abercrombie*	James	British commander-in-chief during French and Indian War after recall of Lord Loudoun	9
Burnes	John and Agatha	Farmer couple from Manalapan, volunteers in the French and Indian War	9
Green*	Jacob	Acting president of the College of New Jersey after the death of Jonathan Edwards	9
Davies*	Samuel	Presbyterian preacher, later president of the College of New Jersey	9
de Montcalm*	Louis Joseph	Commander of French forces during the French and Indian War	9
Covenhoven*	Samuel	New Jersey militiaman who participated in the Battle of Frontenac during the French and Indian War	9
Chew*	Benjamin	Attorney General of Pennsylvania who led successful negotiations with the Indians at Easton during the French and Indian War	9
Forbes*	John	British commander at the Battle of Fort Duquesne	9
Bouquet*	Henry	Swiss mercenary who served for the British in the French and Indian War and the Pontiac Uprising	9
Penn*	Thomas	Son of William Penn, founder of the colony of Pennsylvania and later proprietor	10
Scudder*	John Anderson	First son of Nathaniel and Isabella	10
Halsey*	Jeremiah	Senior tutor at the College of New Jersey	10
Wolfe*	James	British commander at the Battle of Quebec, the decisive battle of the French and Indian War	10
Mayhew*	Jonathan	Reformed preacher very influential during the French and Indian War	10
Henderson*	Thomas	Student at the College of New Jersey, later apprenticed to Nathaniel	10
Henderson'	John	Father of Thomas Henderson, elder at Rev. Tennent's church	10
Rush*	Benjamin	Student at the College of New Jersey, later physician and leader in the Revolution	10
Boudinot Sr.*	Elias	Silver smith in Princeton, father of Annis Boudinot Stockton	10

de Vaudreuil	Pierre Rigaud	French governor of Quebec during French and Indian War	10
Amherst*	Jeffrey	British commander-in-chief who conquered New France during the French and Indian War	11
Johnson*	William	British Superintendent of Indian Affairs	11
Johnson	Caleb	Yeoman refugee whose family was murdered by Indians	11
Finley*	Samuel	Presbyterian preacher, president of the College of New Jersey from 1761 to 1766	11
Franklin*	Elizabeth	Wife of William Franklin	11
Scudder*	Joseph	Second son of Nathaniel and Isabella	11
Elder*	John	Presbyterian minister who advocated Indian genocide	11
Scudder*	Hannah	Third child of Nathaniel and Isabella	11
Gage*	Thomas	British commander-in-chief in North America after recall of Jeffrey Amherst	11
Donnally*	Felix	Workhouse jail keeper in Lancaster, Pennsylvania	12
Tongquas*		Conestoga Indian murdered by White mob	12
Shippen*	Edward	Mayor of Philadelphia, trustee of the College of New Jersey, judge in Lancaster at time of Conestoga massacre	12
McKee*	Thomas	Captain in charge of keeping order in the Lancaster area	12
Tenseedaagua*		Conestoga Indian murdered by Paxton Rangers	12
Sheehays*		Conestoga Indian murdered by Paxton Rangers	12
Kyunqueagoah*		Conestoga Indian murdered by Paxton Rangers	12
Tee-kau-ley*		Conestoga Indian murdered by Paxton Rangers	12
Kanianguas*		Conestoga Indian murdered by Paxton Rangers	12
Smith*	Matthias	Leader of Paxton Rangers	12
Gibson*	James	Leader of Paxton Rangers	12
Hay*	John	County sheriff in Lancaster	12

Slough*	Matthias	County coroner in Lancaster	12
Exundas*		Conestoga Indian murdered by Paxton Rangers	12
Shae-e-koh*		Conestoga Indian murdered by Paxton Rangers	12
Steelman*	Zephaniah	Salvage operator at Tom's River	12
Gallagher	George	Victim of quack medicine in Tom's River	12
Skinner*	Cortlandt	Attorney General of New Jersey under William Franklin and later Loyalist leader	12
Coxe*	William	New Jersey merchant appointed to be royal stamp distributor	12
Scudder*	Kenneth	Fourth child of Nathaniel and Isabella	12
Ogden*	Robert	Speaker of the New Jersey Assembly who attended the Stamp Act Congress	12
Skinner*	Cornelius	New Jersey landowner ally of the Proprietors	13
Burnet*	William	Prominent physician who helped found the New Jersey Medical Society	13
Chetwood	Widow	Owner of the Hogshead Inn in Elizabethtown	13
Blair*	Samuel	Presbyterian minister, interim president of the College of New Jersey	13
Scudder*	Lydia	Fifth child of Nathaniel and Isabella	13
Adams*	Samuel	Prominent member of the Assembly of Massachusetts and advocate of resistance to British taxation	13
Hillsborough*	Wills Hill, Earl of	Secretary of State for the colonies 1768 - 1772	13
Hancock*	John	Wealthy Boston merchant and advocate of resistance to British taxation	13
Skinner*	Stephen	Treasurer of East Jersey whose house was burglarized with a loss of 6000 pounds	13
Morrison	Ebenezer	Perth Amboy merchant	14
McIntyre*	Ben	Perth Amboy merchant murdered for not having adhered to the boycott of British imports	14
LeGrange*	Bernardus	Corrupt lawyer infamous for cheating honest farmers out of their land	14

Whitefield*	George	Famous New Light theologian	15
Ogden*	John Cousins	Student at the College of New Jersey who delivered address at graduation in 1770 in support of the Non-Importation Agreement	15
Baldwin*	Samuel	Student at the College of New Jersey who delivered address at graduation in 1770 in support of the Non-Importation Agreement	15
Freylinghausen*	Frederick	Student at the College of New Jersey who delivered address at graduation in 1770 in support of the Non-Importation Agreement	15
Witherspoon*	James	Son of John Witherspoon who graduated in 1770 and was later killed at the Battle of Germantown	15
Harris*	Robert	Physician from Cape May	15
Hatton*	John	Customs inspector in south New Jersey who met violent resistance	15
Rittenhouse*	David	Philadelphia clockmaker and astronomer who constructed the Rittenhouse Orrery	15
Scudder*	Thomas	First of the Scudder line to migrate to North America in 1632	15
Brackenridge*	Hugh Henry	Graduate of Nassau Hall in the Class of 1771	15
Freneau*	Philip	Graduate of Nassau Hall in the Class of 1771	15
Allen*	Moses	Graduate of Nassau Hall in the Class of 1772 who taught at the Mattisonia Grammar School	15
Croghan*	George	Irish-born fur trader in the Ohio Country, spiritus rector of the Vandalia scheme	16
Murray	William, Earl of Mansfield	British judge who advocated the freeing of any slaves who set foot on English soil	16
Madison*	James	Graduate of Nassau Hall in the Class of 1771, later president of the United States	16
Burnet*	Ichabod	Classmate of John Scudder from the Class of 1775	16
Montgomery*	Jamie	Slave baptized by John Witherspoon in Scotland who later ran away	16
Hyer*	Jacob	Owner of Hudibras Tavern	16
Hutchinson*	Thomas	Royal governor of Massachusetts Bay from 1771 to 1774	16

Oliver*	Andrew	Assistent to Governor Hutchinson	16
Ford*	Samuel	Head of a gang of counterfeiters who allegedly stole the New Jersey treasury	16
Melville*	Thomas	Graduate of Nassau Hall from the Class of 1769 who participated in the Boston Tea Party	17
Beatty*	Charles Clinton	Classmate of John Scudder from the Class of 1775	17
Dunmore*	John Murray, Earl of	Royal governor of Virginia from 1771 until 1776	17
Anderson*	John	Judge, uncle of Isabella, organizer of a public meeting to protest against the Boston Port Bill	17
Covenhoven*	John	Monmouth County Whig, member of Monmouth Committee of Correspondence	17
Holmes*	Asher	Monmouth County Whig, member of Monmouth Committee of Correspondence, later vice president of the Provincial Congress	17
Forman*	Peter	Monmouth County Whig, member of Monmouth Committee of Correspondence	17
Forman*	John	Monmouth County Whig, member of Monmouth Committee of Correspondence	17
Smock*	Hendrick	Monmouth County Whig, member of Monmouth Committee of Correspondence	17
Taylor*	Edward	Whig delegate from Middletown proposed sending aid to Boston, elected chair of Monmouth delegation to the Provincial Congress	17
Galloway*	Joseph	Conservative member of First Continental Congress, advocate of compromise with Britain	17
Henry*	Patrick	Radical member of First Continental Congress, advocate of spirited resistance to Britain	17
Fithian*	Philip	Member of the Class of 1772, organizer of re-enactment of Boston Tea Party at Cohausey Creek	17

Hunter*	Andrew	Member of the Class of 1772, organizer of re-enactment of Boston Tea Party at Cohausey Creek	17
Forman*	David	Monmouth County Whig, leader of radical faction in the Committee of Observation and Inspection, later spiritus rector of the retaliation policy	17
Dartmouth*	William Legge, Lord	Secretary of State for the colonies from 1772 to 1775	17
North*	Frederick, Lord	Prime Minister of Great Britain from 1770 to 1782	17
Waddell*	Henry	Militia captain from Shrewsbury, organizer of grenadier corps to protect British-friendly merchants	18
Taylor*	George	Township Assessor from Middleton, first loyal to Whigs, then siding with Loyalists	18
Winds*	William	Lieutenant Colonel in militia sent to arrest William Franklin	18
Heard*	Nathaniel	Militia colonel who arrested William Franklin	18
Tucker*	Samuel	President of the NJ Provincial Congress at the trial of William Franklin	18
Adam*		Slave stable boy of the Scudder family	18
Mercer*	Hugh	American general killed at the Battle of Princeton	19
Brown*	Oliver	American artillery captain who organized the beheading of the statue of George III in New York City	19
Greene*	Nathanael	Most important American general after Washington	19
Cunningham*	John	Commander of the Monmouth militia units at Ticonderoga	19
Paterson*	William	Graduate of Nassau Hall from the Class of 1763, member of NJ Provincial Congress and State Treasurer	19
Wright*	Samuel	Organizer of Tory militia called the New Jersey Volunteers	19
van Mater*	Daniel	Organizer of Tory militia called the New Jersey Volunteers	19

Scudder*	Amos	Cousin of Nathaniel, active in the Hunterdon militia	19
Scudder*	Jedediah	Cousin of Nathaniel, active in the Hunterdon militia	19
Cornwallis*	Charles	British general	20
von Donop*	Carl	Hessian colonel	20
Howe*	William	British general, commander-in-chief from 1776 to 1778	20
Cadwalader*	John	American commander of Pennsylvania troops	20
Reed*	Joseph	Graduate of Nassau Hall from the Class of 1757, adjutant general under Washington during Princeton campaign, later member of Continental Congress	20
Rosbrugh*	John	Presbyterian chaplain murdered by the Hessians at Trenton	20
Putnam*	Israel	American army general	20
Gurney*	Francis	Officer of the Pennsylvania Continentals who helped end Loyalist uprising in Monmouth County	20
Davis*	John	Cumberland County militia officer who helped end Loyalist uprising in Monmouth County	20
Lawrence*	Elisha	Monmouth County turncoat who tried to organize a Loyalist militia	20
Morris*	John	Monmouth County turncoat who tried to organize a Loyalist militia	20
Hartshorn*	Richard	Quartermaster of the Monmouth militia	20
McClees*	Peter	Tory traitor who betrayed the Monmouth militia at Navesink	20
Crawford	Jim	Monmouth militiaman killed at the Battle of Navesink	20
Rue	Matty	Monmouth militiaman captured at the Battle of Navesink	20
Burgoyne*	John	British general who lost at the Battle of Saratoga	20
Clark*	Abraham	Representative of New Jersey in the Continental Congress	20

Elmer*	Jonathan	Representative of New Jersey in the Continental Congress	20
Deane*	Silas	Delegate to Continental Congress and first American diplomat to negotiate with France	21
Edwards*	Stephen	Tory sympathizer from Shrewsbury executed by David Forman	21
Rue	Elisabeth	Wife of Matty Rue who was captured by the British at the Battle of the Navesink	21
Gates*	Horatio	American general at the Battle of Saratoga	21
Conway*	Thomas	American general who hatched a conspiracy to replace Washington	21
Arnold*	Benedict	American general at the Battle of Saratoga who later defected to the British	21
Lafayette*	Marie-Joseph Marquis de	French military officer who volunteered to fight for the Americans	21
von Steuben*	Friedrich Wilhelm	Prussian baron who trained American troops	21
Jones*	Joseph	Delegate from Virginia to the Continental Congress	21
Mifflin*	Thomas	Delegate from Pennsylvania to the Continental Congress	21
van Cleave*	Benjamin	New Jersey slave owner	21
Pegg*		Slave owned by the Scudders	21
Dinah*		Slave confiscated from Benjamin van Cleave	21
Jim		Slave confiscated from Benjamin van Cleave	21
Frank*		Slave owned by the Scudders	21
von Hohenzollern*	Frederick	German emperor	21
de Pontière*	Louis	Aide-de-camp of Baron von Steuben	21
du Ponceau*	Pierre-Étienne	Secretary of Baron von Steuben	21
Laurens*	Henry	President of the Continental Congress from 1777 to 1778	21
de Sainte-Germain*	Claude-Louis, comte	French Minister of War	21
Mott*	James	Representative of Monmouth County in the NJ Assembly suspected of Loyalist sympathies	21

Holmes*	Joseph	Representative of Monmouth County in the NJ Assembly suspected of Loyalist sympathies	21
Marriner*	William	American privateer from New Brunswick famous for his daring raids	21
Matthews*	Daniel	Tory mayor of New York City during the British occupation	21
Walker*	Benjamin	Captain in the Continental Army, assistant of Baron von Steuben	21
Hamilton*	Alexander	Senior aide to George Washington	21
Clinton*	Henry	British commander-in-chief in North America after recall of William Howe	21
Burrowes*	John	Monmouth County Whig kidnapped by Loyalists	21
Covenhoven*	Jacob	Monmouth County Whig kidnapped by Loyalists	21
Smock*	John	Leading Whig in the Monmouth Militia	21
Dickinson*	Philemon	Senior general of the New Jersey militia	21
Forman*	Samuel	Colonel in the Upper Freehold militia	21
McDermott*	Jacob	Express rider who brought news to Monmouth of Clinton's march into New Jersey	22
Rhea*	David	Monmouth County Whig serving in the Second NJ Regiment	22
Craig*	Sarah	Patient of Nathaniel who gave birth during the Battle of Monmouth	22
Tye*	Colonel	Titus, an escaped slave formerly belonging to John Corlies from Colt's Neck who led the King's Ethiopian Regiment	22
Shepard*	Elisha	Captain of the state troops captured by Colonel Tye at Monmouth	22
Lee*	Charles	General in the Continental Army who disobeyed Washington during the Battle of Monmouth	22
Morgan*	Daniel	Colonel in the Continental Army at the Battle of Monmouth	22
Lee*	Henry	Colonel in the Continental Army at the Battle of Monmouth	22

Shippen Jr.*	William	Surgeon General of the United States Army, graduate of Nassau Hall from the Class of 1754, co-founder of America's first medical school	22
Hart*	John	Speaker of the NJ Assembly	22
Pulaski*	Casimir	Polish aristocrat who volunteered to help the Americans in the Revolution	22
Ferguson*	Patrick	British captain who attacked the Pulaski Legion at Little Egg Harbor	22
Fagan*	Jacob	Pine Robber leader killed by Benjamin Dennis	22
Juliat*	Gustav	Turncoat who betrayed Pulaski's Legion	22
Morris*	Gouverneur	Representative of New York in the Continental Congress	22
Whipple*	William	Representative of New Hampshire in the Continental Congress	22
Paine*	Thomas	Secretary to the Committee of Foreign Affairs	22
Dennis*	Benjamin	Monmouth County Whig who murdered Jacob Fagan	22
Morris*	Robert	Wealthy merchant who financed the Revolution	22
Hendrickson*	Daniel	Colonel who commanded regiment of Continental soldiers at Tinton Falls, kidnapped by Loyalists	22
Ford*	Benjamin	Colonel in the Continental regiment assigned to defend Tinton Falls	22
Bills*	Thomas	Loyalist whose estate Nathaniel acquired at auction	22
Fenton*	Lewis	Successor of Jacob Fagan as leader of Pine Robber gang	22
Morris*	Zephaniah	Monmouth Whig kidnapped after buying a confiscated estate at auction	22
Okerson*	Thomas	Loyalist who organized the razing of Tinton Falls	22
Gillian*	Will	Loyalist who organized the razing of Tinton Falls	22
Wikoff*	Aucke	Militia officer kidnapped during the razing of Tinton Falls	22

Van Brunt*	Hendrick	Militia officer kidnapped during the razing of Tinton Falls	22
McKnight*	Richard	Militia officer kidnapped during the razing of Tinton Falls	22
Chadwick*	Thomas	Militia officer kidnapped during the razing of Tinton Falls	22
Pew*	James	Loyalist prisoner who died in Monmouth County Courthouse jail	23
Headon*	Marcus	Loyalist from Tinton Falls	23
Headon*	Esther	Wife of Loyalist Marcus Headon	23
Forman*	Elizabeth	Daughter of David Forman who trained at the Scudders	23
Forman*	Ann	Wife of David Forman	23
Stevens*	John	Vice president of the New Jersey Council	23
Schenck*	Joseph	Auction crier at the auction of confiscated estates	23
Harbert*	Danniel	Auction crier at the auction of confiscated estates	23
Vanderveer*	Tunis	Auction crier at the auction of confiscated estates	23
Longstreet*	John	Justice from Monmouth County	23
Van Brunt*	Nicholas	Monmouth County Whig	23
D'Estaing*	Charles Henri	French admiral who aided the Americans	23
Stevenson*	John	Member of the Continental Congress who tried to discourage Nathaniel from leaving congress	23
Holmes*	John	Merchant engaged in the London Trade	23
Ketcham*	Solomon	Merchant engaged in the London Trade	23
Walton*	Elisha	Militia major who confiscated goods of Holmes and Walton	23
Thacher*	James	Surgeon in the Continental Army in Morristown	23
Parker*	John	Loyalist sympathizer who laid claim to the Bills estate bought at auction by Nathaniel	23
Caldwell*	Hannah	Wife of Reverend James Caldwell	23

Caldwell*	James	Presbyterian minister from the Class of 1759, ardent supporter of the Whig cause	23
von Knyphausen*	Wilhelm	Hessian general who commanded enemy forces in New York in 1780	23
Ogden*	Moses	Ensign in the Monmouth militia who commanded a regiment of sharpshooters at Elizabethtown	23
Angell*	Israel	Colonel in the Rhode Island Regiment	23
Wood*	Joseph	Loyalist raider executed by David Forman	24
Dickinson*	Mary	Wife of Philemon Dickinson active in the formation of the Women's Relief Society	24
Cox*	Esther	Wife of Colonel John Cox, active in the formation of the Women's Relief Society	24
Dagworthy*	Mary	Trenton schoolteacher who served as secretary of the Women's Relief Society	24
Cox*	John	Colonel in the Continental Army, Assistant Quartermaster General and owner of Batso Forge	24
Cook*	Thomas	Monmouth militia officer taken prisoner in a Loyalist raid	24
Thomson*	Lewis	Loyalist prisoner sent to be exchanged for Cook	24
Cook*	John	Militia major who tried to effect exchange for his brother Thomas	24
Woodhull*	John	Pastor of the Meeting House in Manalapan	24
Salter*	Joseph	Merchant from Dover Township suspected of dealing with the enemy	24
Hartshorne*	John	Merchant from Dover Township suspected of dealing with the enemy	24
Green*	James	Militiaman working for David Forman	24
Seabrook*	Thomas	Whig ally of the Retaliators	24
Smith*	Samuel	Presbyterian minister who delivered the eulogy for Richard Stockton	24
Geddes*	George	Captain of the privateering vessel *Congress*	24
Neilson*	John	Wartime speculator from Trenton	24
Pettit*	Charles	Colonel in the Continental Army, Deputy Quartermaster General 1778-1781	24

Wilcocks*	William	Founder along with John Covenhoven of the moderate Whig Society of Monmouth County	24
de Rochambeau*	Jean-Baptiste, Comte	French general whose army played the decisive role in helping the Americans defeat the British at Yorktown	24
Stirling*	Charles	Captain of the British vessel *Savage* which battled with the *Congress*	24
de Grasse*	Francois	French admiral who helped the Americans to defeat the British at Yorktown	24
Lippincott*	Richard	Loyalist raider, suspected to have fired the shot that killed Nathaniel	24
Huddy*	Joshua	Militia commander and privateer executed by Richard Lippincott	25
White*	Philip	Brother-in-law of Richard Lippincott	25
Taylor*	Samuel	Loyalist refugee who witnessed the murder of Philip White	25
Carleton*	Guy	British commander-in-chief who took over from General Clinton	25
Asgill*	Charles	British officer chosen by lot to be executed as reprisal for the murder of Joshua Huddy	25

www.ingramcontent.com/pod-product-compliance
Lightning Source LLC
Chambersburg PA
CBHW080242030426
42334CB00023BA/2667